Principles of Modern Physical Education, Health, and Recreation

Wynn F. Updyke
THE UNIVERSITY OF TOLEDO

Perry B. Johnson
THE UNIVERSITY OF TOLEDO

Holt, Rinehart and Winston, Inc.

NEW YORK / CHICAGO / SAN FRANCISCO
ATLANTA / DALLAS / MONTREAL
TORONTO / LONDON / SYDNEY

Lew Alcindor photograph and story, page 4, copyright AP; photo,
World Wide Photos. "Pollice Verso," page 4, courtesy Phoenix Art
Museum, Phoenix, Arizona. Miss Peach cartoon, page 62, by Mell
Lazarus © Field Enterprises, Inc. "Doryphorus," page 148,
Alinari–Art Reference Bureau.

1 2 3 4 5 6 7 8 9

Preface

Our purpose in writing this book has been to provide for students planning careers in health, physical education, or recreation an introduction both to the scientific core of information about human physical activity and health-related behavior and to the philosophy, procedures, and purposes that we consider relevant for professional experience in the disciplines these students have elected to follow. We have wanted our book to serve the needs of teachers and students who are seriously involved with the very foundations of health, physical education, and recreation.

In preparing the text and assembling its supporting data and demonstrations we have been mindful of the changes occurring in education as the result of world-wide social and political turmoil, changes that have affected the professions of physical education, health education, and recreation just as profoundly as they have all other aspects of modern life.

Like all of today's college students, majors in physical education, health, and recreation reflect the strengthening of academic standards throughout the school system. They also exhibit the increased sophistication characteristic of earlier physical and social maturity. Although the complexities of modern life have multiplied the pressures placed upon them, there is little doubt that young people are better prepared than ever before to cope with the problems left to them by preceeding generations.

Today's students come to college not only academically well grounded, but also philosophically committed to idealistic goals. It is now up to the colleges and universities to give these eager young recruits the modern weapons and training they will need if they are to be successful in attacking the crucial problems they will have to face. It is increasingly clear that their success (and the survival of their professions) depends upon their ability to establish themselves in the minds of the public as *knowledgeable experts* in matters of human physical activity and health-related information and behavior.

We believe that if students are to develop an adequate expertise in their profession, they must first develop a healthy self-respect based upon pride in their *potential* professional contribution. The fostering of this desirable self-image can best be facilitated through early exposure to the true *substance* of the profession. In expressing this philosophy, we have wanted:

1. To introduce the student to his chosen profession by indicating not only what his profession is, but also what it can become.
2. To provide a practical handbook of important principles and a useful source of documented information for the use of the student throughout his preparatory training as well as for the graduate on the job.
3. To establish an integrating element that could function to help the student perceive the relationships among the many courses he will encounter during his professional training.

As a means of organizing some of the ideas contained in this book we have utilized two terms borrowed from the field of neurology. The expression EFFERENT CONCEPTS has been used to identify those ideas dealing with the effects that physical activity and health-related behavior have upon man's biological function, his social conduct, his philosophy, his art, and his culture in general. Conversely, AFFERENT CONCEPTS refer to those ideas that are concerned with how man's physical makeup, his environment, his philosophy, and his culture act to influence, modify, or direct human physical activity and health-related behavior.

As a further attempt to aid students in understanding the material presented, an extensive glossary is included. As each technical term is introduced it appears in boldface, indicating that a definition can be found in the glossary.

So as to distinguish the present effort from the earlier book entitled *Physical Education: A Problem-Solving Approach to Health and Fitness* (Holt, Rinehart and Winston, Inc., 1966), which resulted from a collaboration with our colleagues Donald Stolberg and Maryellen Schaefer, we should like to emphasize that the 1966 work was written as a text for a new type of combined health and physical education course, one directed more specifically to students not concentrating professionally in health, physical education, and recreation. It was inspired by the idea that today's more mature, intelligent college student deserves to be given the opportunity to study and evaluate for himself the available evidence concerning human physical activity and behavior related to health and fitness.

Many people agreed that this kind of information is valuable for the general student but pointed out that it is of even greater importance for the student preparing to work professionally in health, physical education, and recreation. The obvious objection to the use of the first book for majors has been, however, that it is addressed to a different audience and fails to consider several topics of particular importance to professional students.

Thus, in this book, which is designed for majors, we have deliberately retained significant portions of the scientific content from the 1966 volume and even expanded them considerably into the fabric of the preponderance of new material making up the present text.

We would like to express our appreciation to the many fine people on our own faculty and to those at other institutions who have contributed so much to the genesis of the ideas expressed in this book. Dr. Donald Stolberg has been a particularly stimulating co-worker, and many of his ideas have found their way into this text. We are grateful to several other dedicated professionals whose imaginative work with the introductory majors' course at the University of Toledo has contributed in many ways to our writing of this book. Dr. Harriett Williams, Dr. John Drowatzky, Dr. Jack Schendel, Dr. John Burt, Dr. Jan Broekhoff, and George Gilmore have all made valuable contributions to the philosophy and content of our program at this level.

Our thanks are also extended to Dr. Marguerite Clifton of Purdue University, Dr. Marvin Eyler of the University of Maryland, and Dr. John Cooper of Indiana University, whose many sound criticisms and suggestions for changes in our manuscript have contributed to its substantial improvement.

To Dan Wheeler, of Holt, Rinehart and Winston, we express our appreciation for his enthusiastic encouragement and knowledgeable advice. We would also like to thank Jeanette Ninas Johnson for her advice, patience, and very real assistance in putting this book together.

Finally, we are grateful to our wives, June Updyke and Ann Johnson, for their loyal support, encouragement, and frequent unselfish assistance in this undertaking.

W. F. U.
P. B. J.

Toledo, Ohio
October 1969

Contents

Introduction

Times are changing rapidly. The ever increasing complexity of society demands that we expand our understanding of man and his world if we hope to survive as individuals and as civilized nations. At the same time that pleas for increased breadth of knowledge are being raised, there arises an insistence upon increased professional and technical specialization. The beleaguered student is caught in the middle.

Today's college student, whatever his major field of interest, is expected to master facts and concepts that will give him far greater expertise upon graduation than has been possessed by preceding generations. In becoming an expert, however, the student has found it impossible to pursue as wide a variety of interests as once was possible.

Few people would deny that physical education, health education, and recreational leadership have become distinct and separate professional specialties. There is simply too much of a specialized nature within each field to expect one individual to become adequately prepared in more than one of them in four years. Recognition of this fact has led to the establishment of separate curricula for the preparation of professional workers in each of these areas.

It is not surprising to discover that these curricula contain certain very important common elements, since the three professions share several of the same important objectives. All three professions, for example, are directly concerned with helping man to understand himself and his biological and psychosocial needs. All three are devoted to fostering habits and techniques that will serve not only to help preserve man's health but also to enable him to achieve a full, satisfying life.

The purpose of this book is to provide students with a summary of concepts and principles important to health educators, physical educators, and recreation leaders alike. This is not meant to imply, however, that every concept and principle discussed in the text is considered equally important to each of the professions. Neither is it assumed that all important concepts and principles have been covered, or that judgments made concerning the placement of emphasis are infallible.

We do believe that each chapter in some way provides a substantial portion of the general foundation that must undergird the more specific knowledge and skills of persons embarking on a career in health, physical education, or recreation, and that there is no concept or principle presented that does not hold significance for at least one (if not all) of these professions.

Chapter 17 (Concepts Underlying Special Programs) provides an example of material that is not of equal concern to recreation specialists, to health educators, and to physical educators. While only members of the latter group would be expected to become actively involved in physical activity programs for the atypical child in school, health educators must certainly be aware of the need for such programs and should be intimately concerned with fostering sound philosophies of physical education and recreation for atypical persons as an integral part of the total health education program. Recreation leaders will be increasingly called upon by communities to provide facilities and programs for handicapped youngsters and adults; knowledge of appropriate opportunities, as well as understanding of the limitations imposed by various conditions is essential to the provision of meaningful programs.

Other examples of mutual concern are provided in the brief sections dealing with diseases and disorders of the various systems, and those related to exercise concepts. In the case of diseases and disorders, awareness of these matters may be of pratical significance to the practicing physical educator and recreation specialist even though knowledge of such disorders may be of more direct concern to the health educator. In the second instance (exercise concepts), physical educators will regard concepts pertaining to physical activity as being of paramount importance. The potential health benefits and dangers of various kinds of exercise and physical activity will also be of more than passing interest to the health educator. The recreation leader will make considerable use of such information in planning sound, effective programs to meet the leisure needs of the community.

As a summary of principles and a review of important concepts, it is apparent that this book is intended to go beyond serving as an introduction to the professions involved. It is hoped that as you progress through your academic programs, its pages will provide practical assistance in the development of projects and that its many references will serve to give initial direction in the search for further information for papers and presentations. When you near completion of your training, we hope this book will assist you in integrating the detailed and widely divergent aspects of your preparation. And as you begin your professional career, you will find it useful as a review of pertinent ideas and important professional responsibilities and objectives.

Because it is meant to be more than an introductory text, we have included brief sections dealing with procedures and programs. The chapters in Part IV (for example, Essential Emergency Procedures, and Selected Issues) are intended to provide some exposure to these less conceptual but nonetheless basic concerns of the true professional.

It is hoped that this book and the philosophy out of which it has developed will help to identify and strengthen the common goals of physical education, health education, and recreation leadership in order that through their separate, unique contributions these professions may fully achieve their potential for the improvement of man and society.

THE BLADE: TOLEDO, OHIO,

Rewarding Experience

★ ★ ★ Alcindor Working With Underprivileged Youngsters

NEW YORK ⒨—Lew Alcindor, who could now be getting ready to lead the U.S. basketball team in the Olympics, is working instead with the underprivileged youngsters of New York.

"I don't know of anything I've done yet that's been more rewarding," he says. "We know what we've done has worked. It's been that good. It's wonderful."

This is the same man who long ago said of the ... out for the ...

sidered one of the greatest of modern basketball players, was a cinch to make the Olympic team.

He is now part of Operation Sports Rescue along with other famous athletes. Teams each headed by an athlete talk to youngsters in small groups.

"Young people ...

able skills, and to encourage youngsters to take an active part in community affairs.

Among the athletes working on the project in addition to Alcindor are Emmette Bryant of the Boston Celtics, Tom ... Mayor ... Carlos ... the ... York ...

PART I

Essential
Backgrounds

The Prospective Professional

Chapter 1

VITAL QUESTIONS

"Why am I here?" "Why have I chosen a career in physical education—or health—or recreation?" These are questions that each person should ask himself early in his educational career.

There are, of course, any number of possible answers to such questions. However, the nature of these answers may be of vital importance to you and to your profession as well.

Some categories into which typical answers fall are:

1. The desire to pursue personal interests and aspirations; to do something one enjoys.
2. The desire to influence the behavior of others; to achieve acclaim or status.
3. The desire to be of service to others who need assistance.

It is obvious that one's motives might involve all of these desires. It is equally possible, however, that a given individual might enter a profession primarily motivated by one of them. It is conceivable, for example, that one might choose to become

LEW ALCINDOR
Finds youth stimulating

Rewarding Experience

★ ★ ★ ★ ★ ★ ★ ★ ★

Alcindor Working With Underprivileged Youngsters

NEW YORK (AP)—Lew Alcindor, who could now be getting ready to lead the U.S. basketball team in the Olympics, is working instead with the underprivileged youngsters of New York.

"I don't know of anything I've done yet that's been more rewarding," he says. "We know what we've done has worked. It's been that good. It's wonderful."

This is the same man who not long ago said of his decision not to try out for the Olympic basketball team:

"We have a racist nation and my decision not to go for the Olympics is my way of getting the message across."

Alcindor, the 7-foot plus center of UCLA's collegiate champions and already con-

sidered one of the greatest of modern basketball players, was a cinch to make the Olympic team.

He is now part of Operation Sports Rescue along with other famous athletes. Teams each headed by an athlete talk to youngsters in small groups.

"Young people idolize athletes," says LeRoy Wilkins, director of the project. "If you can get athletes to say the same thing that religious leaders and educators are saying, they'll listen."

The objectives of Operation Sports Rescue are to instill self-pride in youngsters of the street, to impress on them the value of remaining in school, to underscore the value of independence by acquiring market-

able skills, and to encourage youngsters to take an active part in community affairs.

Among the athletes working on the project in addition to Alcindor are Emmette Bryant of the Boston Celtics, Ron Blye of the New York Giants, Tom Hoover of the Houston Mavericks, Bobby Hunter of the Harlem Globetrotters, Carlos Ortiz and Jose Torres, the boxers, Oscar Robertson of the Cincinnati Royals, and Walt Bellamy of the New York Knicks.

"Alcindor has worked almost as much as all the rest put together," said one of the project officials.

Operation Sports Rescue is sponsored by the Mayor's Urban Task Force and financed by the Bristol-Myers Co.

FIGURE 1.1 As they become mature, most great athletes become interested in identifying with a "cause" that is greater than self. (Copyright AP; photo, World Wide Photos.)

a health educator because he loves biology or immunology. A love of history might lead another to become a history teacher. A successful high school athlete might choose to enter physical education because he loves sports competition.

The question is, have we chosen this profession because we wish to prolong pleasant experiences in our own lives, or is it that we wish to extend to others the benefits of enjoying for themselves the kinds of experiences we have found meaningful and pleasurable?

Maturity brings changes in philosophy and objectives. It has been said of the typical athlete that when he is young, he wants to be *good*; as he grows

older, he wants to be good for *something*. This increasing awareness of the influence that he can have on others through his athletic achievements can lead him in many different directions. Figure 1.1 illustrates the fact that many people who have achieved athletic fame find even greater rewards in forgoing the pursuit of further public acclaim in favor of giving of themselves to others who really need help.

It is doubtful that maturity can be gained by any means other than personal experience. Therefore, the only real justification for pointing out the matters discussed in this chapter is that responsible decisions (if and when they are made) depend upon the availability of accurate information. On the other hand, if one is to really profit from his educational experiences, he must approach them with a sense of perspective that makes the various courses take on meaning.

At the very beginning of a career it is important to have a serious talk with oneself. It is important to make some definite decisions now (painful though the process may be) about what your real goals in life are. In making these decisions you are really spelling out your philosophy of life. Do you wish to serve others or to be served? Are you anxious to become a coach or teacher or recreation leader in order to be in a strong position to exert an influence in the lives of youngsters, or does this kind of life appeal to you because of the opportunity it gives you to stay in the environment you love? Steinhaus has said that the person who is interested

in getting the most dollars does not have the instincts of a teacher (543, p. 256). This does not mean the teacher should not expect fair remuneration for his expensive training and important work. It does mean that if his goal is the gathering of material goods, he does not really have the capacity for putting other people's welfare ahead of his own.

At this point it should be pointed out that no good coach or teacher is entirely unselfish in his motivation. Of course he is fond of the subject he is teaching. Of course he loves the excitement of hard fought contests. But he recognizes that these experiences must be directed toward meeting the needs of the youngsters rather than meeting his own needs. In other words, the truly *professional* person recognizes that his primary responsibility is the improvement and nurture of the student; the

FIGURE 1.2 "Maybe I ought to become a surgeon. . . I've always enjoyed cutting and stitching."

professional's own enjoyment and even his professional advancement must be secondary considerations. And certainly neither his enjoyment nor his advancement are ever to be attained at the expense of his students.

In learning to subjugate one's own selfish interests to the best interests of others, many people have found unexpected rewards. No one would deny the thrill to be gained from putting a team of talented performers together and guiding them step by step to victory. Even more gratifying, however, can be the experience of developing the capacity to analyze the subtleties in complex performance and then to creatively utilize this knowledge in producing performers when there were apparently no performers. Anyone can slavishly initiate the systems of others, but what could be more soul satisfying than being the originator of a concept, system, or idea? Anyone should be able to win with good material, but what can be said of the man who can win with players who began as only mediocre performers? And what of the person who uses his influence to expand the creative imagination of an "ordinary" child? That man has the qualities of a *teacher*!

As soon as one begins to direct his thinking in terms of his profession as a service to others, it becomes obvious that the number of youngsters he can help is much larger than he may have realized. Although interscholastic athletics can directly involve a few elite performers, all of the students in a school system profit from a well-conceived program of physical education. Because the life of a normal child is intimately bound up with physical activity, physical educators, recreation leaders, and health educators take advantage of every opportunity to utilize natural urges and desires in achieving a variety of worthwhile educational objectives. However, this must not be understood to mean that such objectives will automatically be achieved. We will have a great deal to say later on about the necessity for careful planning and preparation, if *any* of the potentially valuable outcomes of physical education, health, and recreation are to be realized.

INTERRELATIONSHIPS OF THE PROFESSIONS

To someone who has thought of physical education only in terms of the opportunities it provides for the teaching of motor skills and coaching, it may not be clear what physical education has in common with health education or recreation education. On the other hand, if it is recognized that regular physical activity of appropriate kinds has a profound effect on the physical welfare of all people in terms of growth and development and on the prevention of certain degenerative diseases, it becomes obvious that the positive health of people ("preventive medicine") is a common objective of both physical education and health education. Furthermore, the kinds of activities we engage in during our leisure hours, the types of diversions we pursue as a means of maintaining our sanity in times of stress, are mutual concerns of all three professional areas. Certainly all three are ultimately concerned with the well-being (physical, mental, and spiritual) of the individual. The means utilized in the attainment of these lofty objectives may vary considerably, and the place within the community where these objectives are sought may also be different. But to the extent that all three are concerned with frequent use and knowledge of physical activity in meeting the physical, mental, and spiritual needs of human beings, they are related.

It is also important to recognize that because of the fact that physical education, health education, and recreation are all concerned with the effects of their programs on man's welfare, they all require training and background in the physical and psychological makeup of man.

Certainly it would be foolish to presume that there are no major differences in the three programs under discussion. Although there may be even greater differences developing as changes occur in our society, there are still sufficient similarities to justify a common core of early training experiences. For this reason it is assumed that the readers of this book will represent all three professional areas, and it is hoped that even though illustrations and examples may be taken from one or another particular field, it will be realized that the principles involved are intended for physical educators, health educators, and recreation specialists alike.

THE QUESTION OF "MEANING"

After Hillary first conquered the terrifying heights of Mount Everest, he was asked why he would take such terrible risks and subject himself and others to such hardships in order to reach the top of a mountain peak. His famous response of "Because it is there!" seems, somehow, unsatisfactory. To most of us, sports, games, and other vigorous activities are *means* to the achievement of some goal rather than *ends* in themselves. Sometimes our actual purposes or goals may not be clear even to ourselves, but generally we can identify some motive for our actions such as the physical challenge involved, love of competition, desire to excel, better health, fitness needs, or, simply, the pleasure derived from success.

Because it is possible to derive different kinds of outcomes from a given activity, it becomes necessary for the educator to decide what specific outcomes he wishes to produce. How does one go about deciding what his specific aims are? Or should one simply provide instruction in the desired skills and give people the opportunity to participate and let *them* worry about the outcomes of this kind of behavior?

In physical education, for example, there are teachers who have no desire to get involved in the questions of "meaning" in physical activity. Their only concern is to teach people *how* to perform certain activities. The development of skill is their ultimate and only objective. Whether or not the learner continues to utilize the skills, whether he derives any social, psychological, or physiological benefits, or whether he understands that there may be some such benefits are of no concern to this individual.

On the other hand, there are teachers who are deeply concerned about the values that students may be developing through participation. These teachers spend considerable time and effort in organizing their instruction so that skill development is accompanied by the acquisition of physical fitness. They strive to be certain that students understand the benefits and limitations of specific activities in terms of fitness and other factors. These teachers are concerned with the function of physical education in the total educational picture. These two types of teachers (those concerned with "meaning" and those not) are representative of two divergent philosophical viewpoints that characterize not only physical education but also health education and recreation.

TECHNICIAN OR PROFESSIONAL?

To view the physical educator, health educator, or recreation leader as a technician means that he deals primarily with techniques. There is no implication that the *quality* of his work is inferior. There are excellent technicians and there are poor technicians; their distinguishing characteristic is that the *scope* of their activity is comparatively narrow. The technician's responsibilities are limited to the actual implementation of a program. He *administers* the activities that are set up by someone

else. In some cases he may actually select the activities in his program, but this selection is based on the fact that they are being used by someone else. In short, the technician is concerned only with the practical matters of getting the program across to the students. He is not really concerned with *why* particular activities are presented at a certain level in the curriculum. The *theoretical* aspects of the function of his profession are neither his concern nor his responsibility. Someone else makes the decisions about what is "good."

The philosophical considerations and analytical processes that go into determining *why* the technician is teaching what he is teaching are the hallmarks of the professional. He must have the depth and breadth of knowledge to understand the needs of people and the means by which these needs can best be satisfied. He must be able to critically evaluate the effects of his program and make appropriate revisions. His *number one* characteristic is capacity for critical thought and analysis. He must be able to answer the question "Why?"

It is probably true that some people are more suited to the role of the technician than to that of the professional, and vice versa. It is apparent, for example, that most athletic coaches are technicians. How many different offensive formations or systems are in use in football today? Presently, the I formation (in which three backfield men line up directly behind the center and in which the fourth splits out to one side or the other as a potential pass receiver) is coming to the peak of its popularity. A few years ago nearly every team in the country was using something called the split **T**. Prior to that we had the **T** formation that "revolutionized football." The old single wing is now nearly forgotten, and many players today have no idea how it would operate. Yet there was a time when it was considered the ultimate weapon of the game. (Similar "band wagon" phenomena could be identified in health education and recreation.)

Why do these changes occur? Do they just happen by coincidence? Is it a kind of spontaneous combustion? Or is there someone, somewhere, who has carefully studied the structure of the game and has analyzed, on a theoretical basis, the effects of certain kinds of action?

Why is there such widespread adoption of certain systems, to the exclusion of almost all others? Is it because the newest is the best? Could it be that when a famous college or professional coach is successful with a particular system, others rush to its adoption simply because he is successful with it? Are such innovations studied carefully with respect to the ability, size, or maturity of the players who are expected to execute them?

The coach who is a true professional fully understands the capabilities and limitations of his players and *creates* or *adopts* a system to fit these criteria. In order to create something new he must, of course, have some understanding of mechanisms, psychology, and even human anatomy and physiology. (Effective blocking technique, for example, is dependent upon factors in each of these categories.) Of course, the mere *possession* of a storehouse of knowledge

is not enough. The ability to *use* this knowledge in unique ways is essential if one is to be a true professional in any career. Creativity and the ability to think critically are indispensable assets.

The question now becomes, should physical educators, health educators, and recreation leaders be expected to function primarily as technicians or primarily as professionals? Is there room for both? If so, how does one decide which to become? And if one decides to become an excellent technician (as a teacher of skills, for example) what assurance does he have that after a few years he will not wish to move into a position requiring the background and training of the professional?

Some schools have attempted to solve this problem by training at least all majors as potential professionals. Other schools have been content to concentrate on techniques and skills, assuming that most teachers and leaders will be functioning at the technical level.

Other professions have recognized a need to provide separate training programs for technicians and professionals. Medicine, for example, has the curriculum for the M.D. as well as the medical technician. Each is thoroughly trained in his field, but there is no expectation that the technician will ever be interested in assuming the responsibilities of the "professional." At the same time it is also assumed that the technician will be highly proficient through excellent training and diligent practice of his particular specialty. In other words, the assumption is that the jobs of the physician and the medical technician are *different*, requiring dif-

FIGURE 1.3   Examples of the "bandwagon" effect of certain attributes that often seem to gain un-critical approval because "everybody's doing it": (A) health movies, (B) jogging, (C) isometric exercise, (D) steam bathing.

ferent kinds of people. Neither job can be adequately performed without the conscientious dedication of the person involved. Although the physician's training requires greater depth and diversity of study (and therefore more time), that of the medical technician requires mastery of intricate procedures and techniques, many of which require constant practice for the maintenance of proficiency. In many cases these are techniques that physicians are never taught. They must rely on the skill and know-how of the technician to supply them with reliable information on the patient. It is obvious that an incorrect diagnosis due to either faulty judgment or unreliable information could be disastrous to the patient.

Thus, medicine has learned to handle many of its rapidly growing problems by a division of labor. A relatively few people are educated in the theoretical "whys and wherefores" requiring ex-

(C)

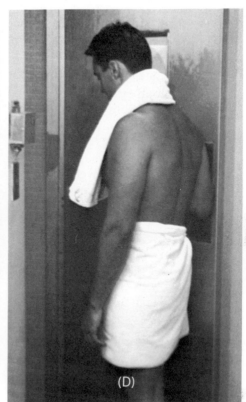
(D)

tensive background upon which under-standing and judgment can be built. A great many people are recruited for training in the important, time-con-suming laboratory tasks required in today's medical practice. The physician, with his theoretical knowledge, can then decide what procedures are neces-sary and can direct certain treatments that are then carried out by those who are primarily trained in the intricacies of the techniques involved.

There are signs that public education is following the lead of medicine. The preparation of the subject-matter *spe-cialist* is being advocated; such special-ists would act as "master teachers" and would determine what is to be taught and the sequence in which educational experiences would appear. The re-sponsibility for determining what the "patient" needs and in what doses the prescription is to be administered would belong to the master teacher.

He would be the planner and coordinator. Teachers with less background but with very specialized training would complete the team. These team teachers would then be responsible for implementing the courses; that is, they would do the actual teaching.

This pattern, or modifications based on the team teaching principle, has been proposed for physical education and health education as well. The problem of what training the master teachers should have as compared with that required of the other team members has not been solved.

It is at this point that the medical analogy breaks down. In medicine the professional, with his mastery of physiological and pathological considerations, has been carrying the load for years. It is only recently that the technician has come onto the scene to aid him in doing a better job for society.

In physical education the *reverse* is true. For many years the vast majority of physical educators have been trained as technicians. They have been trained in the physical performance of skills and in techniques of teaching others how to perform the skills. But where is the professional who can provide the "diagnosis" of what skills students need and at what age and in what sequence? Where is the professional who can state, with authority based upon unimpeachable fact or logic, which of the benefits claimed for physical education are fact and which are myths or old wives' tales?

Only very recently have our universities turned their attention to the preparation of experts in study of human movement in all of its specialized ramifications. Only recently have programs sprung up for the education of specialists in the fields of exercise physiology, community health problems, consumer health, recreation and aging, psychology of motor learning, sociology of physical activity, recreation for the handicapped, philosophy of physical education, and other related subjects.

The rapid development of the attitude that we need to have experts to study and understand the "whys" of physical activity has caused considerable controversy within the profession. There has not been universal agreement as to exactly what the major objectives of physical education should be.

SUMMARY

It is important for the student in health or physical education or recreation to closely analyze his motives for choosing his prospective profession. While curiosity about or *personal* interest in a subject may be sufficient reason for embarking upon some careers (astronomy, engineering, computer programming, automobile racing, and so on), success as an *educator* must be based upon an interest in people, not as objects to be studied or used, but as human beings to be helped. Such a focus of interest demands no less scholarship, however, than a more selfish approach. But it does modify the uses to which scholarly knowledge is applied.

While the three fields of physical education, health education, and recreation are distinct entities, they do have significant areas of overlap. Many of their objectives are held in common, particularly those that relate directly to improving man's physical and mental well-being. The settings in which these objectives are pursued, however, differ in many ways.

Because health, physical education, and recreation can all profoundly affect the human organism, they have a common need to understand in some detail how that organism functions. For these reasons it is deemed entirely practical for beginners in these three areas to take many of the same basic courses.

The matter of whether the training an educator receives should concentrate on techniques and skills (as opposed to emphasis on theory and basic knowledge) is one that is important to all three fields. Is it more important to produce technicians or professionals? How much emphasis should be placed upon understanding *why* we do certain things in comparison to *how* they should be done? How much time should be devoted to preparing teachers and recreational leaders to cope with the questions of "why?" While it may be difficult for one who is trained as a professional to find time to develop all the technical skills he may someday have use for, it is nearly impossible for the technician, no matter how well trained, to assume professional responsibilities without additional formal education. Because most people entering our three fields have been trained as technicians, there is a serious lack of authoritative leadership at all levels of the educational and recreational structure. In light of the obvious need for improved programs,

it is believed that all qualified physical educators, health educators, and recreation leaders should receive training designed to prepare them as professionals rather than technicians.

PRINCIPLES

1. A person's motives in selection of a career are factors in shaping his perception of what is important in his preparation for that career.
2. Almost unanimously man has discovered that greatest personal satisfaction and happiness ultimately results from activities involving service to others.
3. In order to become a productive professional person it is important to develop inquisitive attitudes and creative thought patterns.
4. Greater satisfactions result from creative work than from well-performed duties of an imitative nature.
5. The fields of health, physical education, and recreation are distinguished from one another more by the setting in which their objectives are pursued than by differences in those objectives.
6. The distinction between the professional and the technician is not based upon the degree of excellence with which his job is performed, but rather upon the *nature* of the job which is his and his *objectives* in performing his responsibilities.

EXPERIMENTS AND EXPERIENCES

Construct a brief questionnaire to obtain responses to the following questions: What is your major? List the factors that prompted you to pursue this career—enjoyable work; creative work; chance for rapid advancement; opportunity to take responsibility; chance to help others; good financial possibilities; security; parents wanted me to choose it; and so on.

Contact majors in five different areas. Select both men and women. Tabulate results in such a manner that reasons for going into a given profession can be compared.

Observe whether reasons given by prospective teachers differ from those given by other candidates.

SUGGESTED READINGS

Grissom, Deward K., "Man Living Healthfully Our Common Goal," *JOHPER,* 39:33-35, 1968.

Steinhaus, Arthur A., "A New Image for Physical Education," "More and Better Teachers," in *Toward an Understanding of Health and Physical Education.* Dubuque, Iowa: William C. Brown Company, Publishers, 1963.

Nature
of the Professions

Chapter 2

THE NATURE OF PHYSICAL EDUCATION

If someone were to ask you to define the word *force,* what would you tell him? Chances are you would need to resort to examples of how force acts and to describe it in terms of what it *does* rather than what it *is.* In attempting to define *physical education,* similar difficulties are encountered, but for different reasons. Force means pretty much the same thing to most people; it is difficult to describe only because it is a complex natural phenomenon. The problem in defining physical education is not only that the term is broad and complex, including so many kinds of phenomena, but also that it means so many different things to different people. Someone has suggested, in exasperation perhaps, that physical education is whatever physical educators do!

Although defining a discipline in terms of what its practitioners do may be an effective way of ending an argument on a humorous note, it does not clarify anything for the person who is sincerely interested in discovering the actual content and limitations of that discipline. The fact remains, however, that no one has been able to put forth a definition of physical education that is satisfactory to all physical educators.

DEFINITIONS

Throughout the history of physical education in this country, as well as other countries, health has been one of the values claimed. Many of the early American physical educators were physicians, and their aims were to improve and maintain the health of students within their institutions. Edward Hitchcock of Amherst, who was the first college "professor" of physical education stated:

Physical education, as the term is understood in Amherst College, is such a cultivation of the powers and capabilities of the student as will enable him to maintain his bodily conditions in the best working order, while providing at the same time for the greater efficiency of his intellectual and spiritual life (176, p. 110).

Harvard University was another of the early institutions to provide students with a physical education program. In 1879 Dudley Sargent described his aims:

. . . to improve the mass of our students, and to give them as much health, strength, and stamina as possible, to enable them to perform the duties that await them after leaving college (176, p. 110).

Although health continued to be a prominent objective of physical education, as time passed more and more emphasis was placed on other values to be derived from participation in such programs. The extent to which such broadening has occurred over the relatively few years that physical education has been a part of our school curricula can be seen by examining statements of writers who have had great influence in the profession during the last twenty-five years. Brownell and Hagman defined physical education as . . .

. . . the accumulation of wholesome experiences through participation in large-muscle activities that promote optimum growth and development. . . . It relates also to a variety of knowledges and understandings about physical experiences that enable the individual to formulate social and aesthetic judgments of inestimable value in a democratic society (76, p. 17).

In 1949 Voltmer and Esslinger suggested this definition:

Physical education is that part of education which proceeds by means of, or predominantly through, physical activity; it is not some separate, partially related field (591, p. 14).

It is interesting to note that the latest edition of this text (1967) has modified the definition to meet changing perspectives:

Physical education is the process by which changes in the individual are brought about through his movement experiences . . . (592, p. 17).

In 1960 Bucher stated:

Physical education, an integral part of the total education process, is a field of endeavor which has as its aim the development of physically, mentally, emotion-

ally and socially fit citizens through the medium of physical activities which have been selected with a view to realizing these outcomes (79, p. 40).

Eight years later Bucher's definition had not changed substantially, but several pages were devoted to the development of an appropriate understanding of education in general.

. . . when you add the word physical *to* education *you are referring to the process of education that goes on when activities that develop and maintain the human body are concerned (80, p. 17).*

Such views differ little from that presented by Hetherington over fifty years ago. He defined *education* as a lifelong process in which the individual's powers were developed "and adjusted to a social order for complete living." He equated physical education with fundamental education and suggested that it provided the basis for all the rest of education (176, p. 115).

In 1910 T. D. Wood and Clark Hetherington began writing about "the new physical education" as a broadening experience in the lives of students. Wood concluded that "physical education should occupy itself with a program of activities which would foster physical health, but they should be considered as by-products while the pupil was being guided toward the acquisition of mental, moral, or social benefits" (176, p. 115).

Despite some widespread insistence upon narrowing the objectives of physical education to those of "preparedness" during and following World War I, the focus of physical education during the first half of the twentieth century was on the broad contributions that could be made to the development of good citizenship. As wartime emergencies and cold-war pressures persisted, the fitness objective periodically waxed and waned in prominence, but "there is little doubt that the idea of physical education as a contribution to 'education for complete living' has been the dominant theme of the field since the early years of the twentieth century" (176, p. 122). Physical education proclaimed its value in terms of the contributions it could make to the "total education" of the individual "through the physical." As a specific medium of education, it could (and did) claim widely diversified objectives accumulated from the procession of educational theories that have influenced education since 1900.

One of the great difficulties encountered in trying to state the nature of the profession lies in the nature of the term *physical education* itself. One of the great early spokesmen for physical education, Jay B. Nash, has said that the word *physical* is a misnomer because it implies that there is some sort of inherent conflict between physical and mental activity (418). The idea of "educating the physical" has long been dismissed because it is self-contradictory. Still persisting, however, is much of the original confusion that has always accompanied the use of this term. Nearly thirty-five years after Nash's time, despite suggestions by many leaders that the name of the profession be changed to reduce confusion, the old problem is still with us. In 1967 Janet Felshin wrote: "The name itself is unfortunate, of course, because it explains nothing. We know—unless we wish to deny overwhelming evidence to the contrary and claim a dualism of mind and body—that the 'physical' cannot be educated, and even if it could be, as programs of physical education have long seemed to suppose, what would such an education mean?" Felshin goes on to point out that a true discipline must be defined in terms of its unique subject matter.

Physical education has been explained not as the "study of . . ." but as the "teaching of . . . ," which has resulted in the paradox of an academic discipline in colleges that is defined by curriculum in schools (176, p. 140).

No one would seriously suggest that by merely changing the name of our profession could any of these problems be solved. On the contrary, the changing of the name would merely be a reflection of the changes in the concepts of physical education that are presently occurring.

If we are to survive as an effective, contributing, educational agency, we must accept the obligation to become experts in the unique subject matter of our profession: *human physical activity* in all of its ramifications and implications. The current emphasis is on determining logical boundaries for the discipline. Although agreement has not yet been reached on details, it seems evident that our profession is moving rapidly toward defining its overall concern in terms of "man in motion." Thus, the study of man as a *moving* being becomes the focus of the profession, and all aspects of human movement become the unique domain of its members. The physiological effects of physical activity (or lack of it), the sociologicial implications of sports and games, the mechanical efficiency of motor skills, the psychological effects of participation, as well as the esthetic aspects of movement as represented by the dance (but not limited to dance) would all be legitimate parts of the discipline. Study would be devoted not only to the effects of movement (or exercise) on the life and welfare of the individual but also to the effects that the various forms of movement activity have on his surroundings and his culture.

It should be evident that in this system the educational aspects of human movement (including the preparation of teachers, skill instruction, and coaching) would be only a part of the profession's concern. Study of the movement-related phenomena for their own sake, regardless of any practical applications, would be a legitimate pursuit of scholars. Conceivably, some people would find positions in industry, the arts, government, and other environments on the basis of their expertise in exercise or movement.

NATURE OF HEALTH EDUCATION

The term *health education,* in contrast to *physical education,* enjoys much greater universality of definition. The term *health* is itself more broadly conceived now than formerly. Instead of the old negative concept of "freedom from disease and infirmity," it now carries a positive connotation: good health is a "state of complete physical, mental and social well-being" (500). Thus *health education* is defined as "the process of providing learning experiences which favorably influence understandings, attitudes and conduct in regard to individual and community health" (410, p. 7).

Health education is typically viewed as part of a more diverse school health program that also includes health services to pupils and a program of healthful school living. In small schools, especially elementary schools, there is usually no health education specialist, and all three phases of school health are distributed among the teachers and administrators. There is usually no school nurse, and health appraisal is limited to yearly hearing and vision testing by a visiting school nurse or some other trained person. Larger schools, especially high schools, are more likely to provide a resident school nurse who is responsible for most of the services such as referral, caring for sickness and injury while at school, appraisal, and so on. Such a specialist is also usually responsible for evaluating and upgrading healthful school living, often in cooperation with the health educator. Apparently, more large secondary schools are providing full-time health education teachers, even though a recent survey shows that there are still few health teachers who are strictly full-time; only about 7 percent of all health teachers for grades 9 through 12 are full-time in health education (500).

Although, in one recent study, over 50 percent of all "large" schools sampled in grades 9 through 12 offered a separate health education class, only 25 percent required health education for all grades 9 through 12. These percentages are slightly different for medium-sized and small schools. Interestingly enough, more medium-sized school systems required health instruction (37.5 percent) than did large schools, and small schools were very similar to large ones in this respect (24.9 percent) (500). All too often the health educator's "other" responsibility is coaching. Experience has shown that this is often not the best combination of responsibilities, and it is usually the health education that has suffered. The professional health associations are concertedly attempting to change this situation. There is little question that well-trained, full-time health educators are needed to carry out most effectively the objectives of the new health education.

Health education cannot be handled by a technician. It is multidisciplinary in nature. Its content is "derived from medicine, public health, and the physical, biological and social sciences" (500). It covers diverse areas from the nature of disease to marriage and parenthood. Modern health education methodology draws from the behavioral sciences. The nature of today's health education is such that programs must be implemented and conducted by well-trained professionals, not part-time or, for that matter, full-time teachers who are trained only as technicians (see pages 12–16).

In summary, health education is:

1. Multidisciplinary in nature
2. Dynamic (growing and improving) in nature

THE NATURE OF RECREATION

"The most dangerous threat hanging over American society is the threat of leisure . . . " (161, p. 390). "The darkest threat to the well-being of the working man and the subject of increasing concern on the part of organized labor" is the burden of leisure (161, p. 390).

These grim statements from responsible leaders leave little doubt about the urgency of preparing Americans to cope with leisure. The problem of leisure in American life is intimately bound up with our consideration of recreation. This is not to imply that leisure and recreation are the same thing but to imply that it is difficult to consider recreation in any setting that does not involve leisure.

DEFINITIONS

There is no universal agreement about the definition of leisure. It has been claimed that no real definition can be given. One of the problems is that the term is used to describe a block of available time, a feeling about obligations or lack of them, a tool for social control, an opportunity for self-improvement, or as a part of a work-rest dichotomy. It has been stated that the term should really be a verb, "to leisure," implying that some kind of a conscious process is going on (4).

The traditional definitions of leisure regard it as a block of time. This time is distinct from that spent in work or preparing for work. Even this concept, however, has its problems.

Work is something to fulfill yourself with. Work is something you love to do, not something you do with your eye on the timeclock. . . . A job is different. We have replaced the concept of work with the concept of the job. A job is something we give as little of ourselves to as possible and try to get as much for as we can, and try to get away from as soon as we can. . . . I don't use the term "leisure." I use the term "work" as I'm going to use the correlative term "play." It is work in the old sense which we need to recapture, work that gives us buoyancy and a feeling of expressiveness, work which we may do while we're making a living, but also that we may do off the job while we're making a life . . . .

I suggest that there is something very different from fun. There is play . . . Play is something which is totally expressive but doesn't end in a product. It doesn't have to end in a product. It is a thing in itself, worthwhile in itself" (335).

Another has made the distinction between work and play in other terms:

Work is the main course, the meat and the substance of our lives. Recreation is the dessert; we like it best in modest proportions at the end of a good meal. When we try to substitute the dessert for the meal itself, we lose our taste for it (72, p. 23).

Kelso and Adler stated the relationships among work, leisure, and play this way:

*Play, like sleep, washes away the fa-
tigues and tensions that result from the
service occupations of life, all the forms
of labor which produce the goods of sub-
sistence and all the leisure activities which
produce the goods of civilization. Play
and sleep, as Aristotle pointed out, are
for the sake of these services and socially
useful occupations. Since the activities
of leisure can be as exacting and tiring as
the activities of toil, some form of relaxation, whether sleep or play or both, is required by those who work productively
(300, p. 17).*

Brightbill has defined "play" as "the
free, happy, and natural expression
of animals—especially the human
animal . . . When we refer to adult
activity," he continues, "play might
more fittingly be called *recreation*"
(72, p. 30).

It is clear that when we refer to recreation we are not indicating any particular activity or class of activities.
That which is work for one can easily
be regarded as recreation by another.
There is another important distinction
to be made with regard to this term.
Whereas recreation up to this point has
been discussed in its general connota-
tions, we are particularly interested in
it as an organized service profession.
Perhaps the term Recreation Education,
or Recreation Leadership would be
more appropriate in this context. In
any event, we will need to look at both
the general nature of recreation, its
history and cultural implications, as
well as at the systematized structure
that has been created to deal with the
leisure time activities of human beings.

PROFESSIONAL OBJECTIVES

OBJECTIVES OF PHYSICAL EDUCATION

It has been mentioned that regardless
of the philosophical winds that have
blown through physical education over
the years, certain objectives have consistently retained a prominent place in
the overall aims of the profession. Two
of these are, of course, health and physical fitness. Because these particular
objectives have persisted, it must not
be assumed that they are universally
accepted as being the most important
objectives. Because disagreement about
the relative importance of particular
objectives is inevitable, it is impossible to make any list of primary and
secondary objectives that will be satisfactory to the entire profession.

On the other hand, it is possible to
group most of the commonly held objectives into a few descriptive categories. This has been done in a great
variety of ways, some more detailed
than others.

Organic development is generally considered to be of importance. This would
include, among other things, the maintenance of health through good health
practices and the development of physical fitness including sufficient strength,
circulo-respiratory and muscular endurance to avoid excessive fatigue and
to insure adequate energy levels. Although the development of sports and
recreational skills is usually covered
under a separate heading of *neuromuscular development*, it too could
be considered one of the organic objectives.

Social development is another objective that is universally listed. The ability to function effectively with others and in groups is usually considered an important outcome to be sought through physical education. The emotional control that may be learned as a part of participation in games and contests is considered important. The acquisition of the qualities of cooperation, leadership, and related factors is also valued.

Closely related to social development is the objective of *psychological development*. Subsumed under this heading would be such things as improved personality characteristics, self-confidence, self-respect, and opportunity for self-fulfillment and self-realization. Frequently included in this category are claims that physical education contributes to the generalized learning abilities of the child. A few schools have deliberately designed their curricula with this objective uppermost in their thinking.

The *cognitive objective* (sometimes called *intellectual development*) is that traditionally stressed by teachers of "academic" subjects. Although health educators have long been concerned with helping students gain understanding of certain facts and principles, physical educators have generally limited their cognitive emphasis to knowledge of rules and strategy of sports and games. It is apparent, however, that the cognitive objective has assumed a role of major importance in recent years. Much of this book is devoted to the subject matter of physical education in the belief that the knowledge of such

information is important to the welfare of professional and layman alike.

An objective that is seldom discussed is that of *philosophical development*. The great difficulty in dealing effectively with the teaching and evaluation of ethics and values is apparent. It has become increasingly apparent, however, that society is in urgent need of coming to grips with the problem of values in today's world. The question of whether sports and physical education effectively shape desirable value systems is one that must come under increasingly close scrutiny. The quality of the professional leadership available is obviously crucial to the attainment of any objective; it is of particular importance in the case of realizing philosophical objectives.

CURRENT PRACTICE IN PHYSICAL EDUCATION

Which objectives are being stressed in physical education today? Of course, if one looks hard enough almost anything can be found somewhere. On the other hand, it is frequently possible to identify trends or patterns as they emerge in response to changing circumstances over a period of time.

After World War II, and especially since the late 1950s, the physical fitness status of American youngsters has certainly received a great deal of attention. Similarly, it is apparent that interscholastic athletics (beginning even at the elementary school level in some cases) are enjoying unprecedented popularity. On the basis of these informal

FIGURE 2.1 Physical education has taken many different forms. Widely differing emphases can be found, as illustrated: (A) modern dance, (B) sports skills, (C) physiological effects of exercise, (D) gymnastics.

observations it can be concluded that physical fitness and skill development are currently valued objectives.

Basis of Current Emphasis

If it is true that the organic objectives of physical education are particularly stressed today, what are the reasons? It will be recalled that before World War II the primary emphasis was on the social objectives. As has always been true, wartime resulted in a national emphasis on increased fitness. The unusual thing about this particular "fitness for fighting" emphasis was that it did not die the usual lingering death as soon as the national crisis ended. Actually there *was* a slump in the insistence upon strong fitness programs. Physical educators were apparently ready to return to their broadly conceived objectives of preparing youngsters for responsible citizenship in a democracy. It quickly became evident, however, that this was not to be. As international unrest persisted, the posture of preparedness could not be abandoned by the United States. The Korean conflict, followed by other threatening "brush fires" around the world, maintained the necessity for fitness of fighting age youth.

During this same period (1952) another occurrence outside of the professional education community created reactions that were to have far-reaching consequences for physical education. The reference here is to the Kraus-Weber tests (325). The report that 58 percent of a large sample of American children were unable to pass a simple test of strength and flexibility that only 2 percent of European children had failed was reported to have "shocked the President." One result was the appointment by President Eisenhower of the President's Council on Youth Fitness. A national fitness test was conducted under the auspices of the American Association for Health, Physical Education, and Recreation (AAHPER), and subsequent comparisons were made with the children of other nations (see page 101). Governmental and private agencies contributed large amounts of money and publicity to fitness programs at local, regional, and national levels. The AAHPER launched an educational campaign entitled "Operation Fitness, USA." The new, dynamic, young President Kennedy gave further impetus to the fitness effort. His publication of an article entitled "The Soft American" in *Sports Illustrated* in December 1960 brought smiles of approval from fitness buffs around the country. The Youth Fitness Council was renamed the President's Council on Physical Fitness as it became apparent that the fitness of adults was just as great a national concern as was that of the school children. (It is also significant that "Physical" was inserted to clarify the objectives of the Council.) Charles "Bud" Wilkinson was appointed as Special Consultant on Fitness of Youth. As leader of the council, Wilkinson utilized news media and personal appearances to push the Council's recommendation of a fifteen-minute daily minimum of vigorous physical activity in every school.

Despite the great upsurge in interest in the physical fitness of school children (or perhaps because of it) the voices of few professional physical educators were heard concerning these programs. There were many who believed that the evidence on which the conclusions of inferior fitness were based was not valid. There were others who believed that there was a grave mistake being made in allowing physical fitness to appear to be equated with physical education.

In a speech before the American College of Sports Medicine, Arthur Steinhaus, former Dean of George Williams College, made the following statements:

Even as every pagoda needs a strong foundation to carry its beautiful superstructure, so every person must be possessed of physical fitness to support the burdens that life will place on him. But as we look upward we find that every pagoda culminates in a point that is directed to the heavens. It is as though the entire structure is for the purpose of permitting this upward thrust that transforms a mere wooden structure into a pagoda. So also man's entire being must support an upward thrust which in giving purpose to his life, transforms man the animal, into man the human being . . . (541, p. 196).

Does this mean that all objectives—social, physiological, psychological, intellectual—are equally important and equally worthy of pursuit? How does one go about determining where to place the priorities in professional emphasis?

Determining Objectives

There are two separate ways of attacking these problems. One is to try to determine the most important needs of school age children and then to decide how physical education can contribute to the fulfillment of those needs. Thus, if it is believed that the most important objective of the school is to develop a taste for and a healthy attitude toward competition as a way of life, games and contests that pit individual against individual and team against team would be stressed. The necessity of "paying the price" for success, frequently at the expense of another who is unwilling or unable to do so, would be stressed as a worthy and desirable creed.

If, on the other hand, it is determined that students need to be more aware of their social responsibilities toward one another, to be more sensitive to the principle of the brotherhood of man and to develop a greater compassion for the downtrodden, different approaches are indicated. Under these circumstances physical education might stress the necessity for team efforts as a prerequisite for success. The star's willingness to sacrifice himself for the team is regarded as the ultimate in desirable behavior. No person is expected to perform his assigned task entirely unaided; "we all help out" becomes first a coaching cliché and finally a deeply ingrained attitude.

The other way of determining what professional aims should be adopted is to identify the unique effects that physical education can have on human living and well-being and to concentrate on the most valuable of these. This would mean that even though society may value very highly the ability of its citizens to get along with one another peaceably, physical education would not make these its major aims because many other aspects of the school program (drama, music, school government, and classroom and committee assignments) contribute to the social objectives. It would, of course, cooperate in making efforts wherever it could to reinforce desirable behavior in this regard.

Illustrations of the things that might be seen as being unique to physical education would be concerns such as physical fitness, sports skills, exercise techniques, and intellectual awareness of the physiological and psychological effects of exercise and sports participation. It should be noted that these are only examples and should not be interpreted as being an exhaustive list of the unique concerns of physical education. The only criterion required for determining whether a given objective should be placed on the list would be that of unique and ultimate responsibility. That is, if a given individual appears to have failed in the attainment of certain objectives, *to whom can he be referred for remedial action?* If, for example, a student seems continually depressed and uncommunicative despite all efforts of the instructor, he should be referred to the school psychologist. On the other hand, where does the instructor send the youngster who is chronically low on the physical fitness scale? The fact is that there is no one

(including physicians, physiologists, and therapists) who have the training and background in this area that the physical educator is expected to have. Therefore, physical fitness is classified as one of the unique objectives. The only question remaining is whether it is a sufficiently important objective to be given priority. This decision must be made on the basis of philosophical considerations.

From the preceding discussion it should be clear that if one views physical education primarily as a tool to be used in achieving overall educational goals, then its primary objectives will change whenever changes in society's educational emphasis occur. Under such conditions physical education is a process or procedure, not a discipline, and cannot logically have any objectives of its own. If, however, physical educational emphasis occur. Under such conditions physical education is ber of legitimate objectives can be established *independent* of the goals of general education. Because such goals would be oriented to the preservation of the efficiency of movement (that is, the prevention of degenerative disease, the acquisition of desirable body image, the development of certain kinesthetic appreciations, and so on), they would generally be in harmony with the aims of general education. In many cases the realization of the goals of physical education (particularly those related to physical and mental health) would be prerequisite to the pursuit of many of the socially and/or politically determined goals of general education.

Up until the present, however, it is evident that physical education has been viewed pretty much as a tool of general education in the achievement of broad, cultural goals. As a result there have been a great many changes in the emphasis of physical education both in this country and abroad.

Opportunities in Physical Education

Physical education is an extremely broad profession frequently merging into health education programs or recreation programs. Because the programs he is equipped to direct and the objectives he is dedicated to pursuing are utilized by different organizations in a variety of settings, the competent, *well prepared* physical educator will discover that he has a choice of many professional opportunities.

The various divisions of the school structure offer a great many opportunities to the prospective professional. Physical education teachers are needed at elementary, junior high, senior high, junior college, and college levels. Elementary specialists are in increasing demand, including both men and women. Some of the most challenging and exciting work in physical education is now being conducted at the elementary school level.

The junior and senior high schools continue to provide the bulk of positions. With burgeoning populations and new construction everywhere, positions are more numerous than ever before. It should be carefully noted, however, that in some areas of the country there are more male physical educators graduated than there are positions, particularly at the secondary level. Keep in mind, however, that there is always a demand for the *good*, well prepared physical educator. This concept, involving a clearcut distinction between positions in coaching and physical education, will be amplified later. Of course positions for women at the secondary level are always available, many of them remaining unfilled for lack of applicants.

At the college level there are several kinds of professional opportunity. One of these involves teachers of skills and games. Traditional college programs usually provide opportunities for students to enroll in classes in which they can improve or maintain physical fitness levels and learn skills that will be useful to them in their post-college years. Most colleges require at least a master's degree of all teachers, and many require higher degrees.

In recent years there has been considerable interest in revising college required physical education programs to place more emphasis on the *understanding* of how physical activity, sport, and play contribute to the health and well-being of the individual. Such programs are designed to add a dimension to traditional skill and fitness-oriented programs and should not be interpreted as a substitution of intellectual activity for physical activity. Teachers in this kind of program require greater depth of training than is usually available in the master's degree curriculum. Most schools employ team teaching techniques in conducting the various aspects of such programs.

Of course the training of future teachers of physical education requires large numbers of competent professors. Such positions almost always require a doctoral degree as well as teaching experience at other levels. In addition to professional teaching opportunities, many universities now have research specialists who have only limited teaching responsibilities and spend most of their time in research endeavors.

Other positions for which graduate work is required include administrative or supervisory positions at all levels of physical education. While coaching responsibilities are not generally regarded as requiring advanced graduate study, many colleges do not hire people for coaching responsibilities alone, and in such cases advanced degrees are mandatory.

Opportunities existing outside the schools cannot all be listed. Some of those most commonly pursued by physical educators are found in organizations such as the YMCA, YWCA, YMHA, community centers, and municipal or private clubs. Boys' clubs, hospitals, churches, industrial concerns and other agencies also frequently employ physical education specialists.

It is becoming clear that this is an age of specialization. While a broad background is always necessary for effective professional accomplishment, today's problems require an expertise that cannot be attained without specialized study. This means not only better undergraduate theoretical and technical preparation but also advanced study. Specialists are commonly employed for positions in dance, acquatics, elemen-

tary physical education and gymnastics in the public schools. At the college level specialization is even more narrow. The person who plans to make the most of his potential must strive to secure the best possible undergraduate preparation upon which to select and build a future specialty.

OBJECTIVES OF HEALTH EDUCATION

In terms of the establishment of general objectives, health educators have (at least in recent years) achieved greater unanimity than have physical educators. Since "health" has been defined in rather specific terms, it has been relatively simple to devise objectives for the educator to pursue.

It must be emphasized, however, that the field of health education is so broad (encompassing everything from sex education to the problem of metabolic disturbance resulting from rapid time zone change in east-west air travel) that it is essential that priorities be established on the basis of importance. Since there is always basis for disagreement on relative importance of specific objectives, there is still considerable disparity among health education programs throughout the country.

Many problems have been encountered in dealing with controversial topics such as sex education, birth control, drug abuse, alcoholism, fluoridation, and smoking. It is virtually impossible to separate social issues and value judgments from such issues, yet health educators are frequently forbidden to utilize any methods other than an objective approach (if indeed, they are permitted to deal with the particular problem at all). Barriers such as these have been disappearing rapidly in recent years, however, probably because of the widely perceived need for changes of attitude and behavior with respect to many of those problems.

Despite this development, other frustrations remain. One of these is the problem of getting people to *act* on the basis of their own health knowledge. Controversy still abounds over what kinds of programs should be instituted in order to eradicate diseases such as syphilis or rheumatic fever, or to prevent smoking-related lung cancer; and in such cases we know how to prevent or cure the disease, yet they not only persist but (as in the case of syphilis) are actually on the increase. It is clear that simply *informing* people about health matters is not generally sufficient to alter specific behavior patterns, particularly if problems of psychological dependency or social approval are involved.

In general, however, it appears that there is widespread agreement on the broad objectives of health education, even though the means of reaching these may vary. An NEA-AMA committee listed these objectives for health education (410):

1. To instruct children and young people so that they may conserve and improve their own health and thus be more able to secure the abundant vigor and vitality that are a foundation for the greatest possible happiness and service in personal, family, and community life.

2. To promote satisfactory understandings, attitudes, and ways of behaving among parents and other adults so that they may maintain and improve the health of the home and community.
3. To improve the individual and community life of the future; to work toward a better second generation and a still better third generation: to build a healthier and fitter nation and world.

These objectives are directed to the end that each educated person shall understand the basic facts concerning health and disease, protect his own health and that of his dependents, and work to improve the health of the community (410). It is our feeling that the concept of "dependents" as used here should be expanded to include *all* persons for whom one has any responsibility. In order to fulfill its obligations to society as expressed by its objectives, health education must seek to facilitate for its students the development of:

1. Health *knowledge*
2. Positive *attitudes* toward good health
3. Positive *health practices*
4. Effective and appropriate *health skills*

Though we have not mentioned public health education, it is obvious that its objectives and the desired outcomes of its programs are the same as those of school health education.

Opportunities in School and Public Health

There is a vast array of opportunities to serve mankind in the health and health-related professions. The medical profession comes immediately to mind, but many of the other possibilities for service in this important area are not so apparent to the student beginning his college studies. Medical sociology, physical therapy, sanitation engineering, public health nursing, hospital administration, medical technology, biostatistics, and dental hygiene are just a few examples of many health-related career opportunities. These, of course, require preparation of varying kinds and amounts not usually a part of the programs in university departments of health, physical education, and recreation. The careers for which you can prepare in such departments are more likely to directly involve education. There is a need for more well prepared health educators, public and school. The school health educator is concerned primarily with planning and conducting educational programs within the public school organization, though he certainly can promote public health education as well. Most persons trained in health education have naturally gravitated in the direction of public school teaching positions. But public health departments and agencies are more and more becoming interested in utilizing the full-time services of public health educators. They also recognize the need for more in-depth preparation of such persons, especially with regard to the scientific bases of health.

The health educator with a baccalaureate degree may also continue his professional preparation by studying for a master's degree. Those with the interest, background, and intellectual capacity can achieve a doctorate, spe-cializing either in health-related research or in health education or both. Such professionals most often choose to affiliate themselves with colleges or universities, but there are other agencies and institutions in need of these professionals as well.

The need is apparent and the opportunities for service in the health-related professions are both great and varied.

OBJECTIVES OF RECREATION

Like the objectives of physical education and health education, the objectives of recreation have undergone change over the years. The goals sought by each teacher will, of course, vary depending upon the people and problems with which he works.

The Commission on Goals for American Recreation has produced a statement encompassing six objectives (119).

1. Personal fulfillment. In emphasizing the importance of the individual in our society, recreation is viewed as having one outstanding purpose: to enrich the lives of people. "One approaches personal fulfillment as he narrows the gap between his potentialities and his accomplishments." The recreation leader's challenge is to provide experiences "through which the individual may enjoy success in his search for adequacy or self-esteem."

2. Democratic human relations. Since exclusive concentration on personal goals may lead to the development of

selfish, noncooperative individuals, other goals relating to ethical behavior and social responsibility are important. Leaders are urged to be alert for opportunities to cultivate "respect for human beings and concern for their welfare."

3. Leisure skills and interests. People engage in activities that they perform well. Development of a high degree of skill is regarded as the best means of insuring interest and participation in a given activity. Enlarging the scope of people's interests is regarded as contributing to a more rewarding life.

4. Health and fitness. Vigorous muscular exercise is regarded as an essential factor in the maintenance of the healthy, vigorous organism. Because contemporary society has so drastically reduced man's opportunities for vigorous activity, it is regarded as essential that recreation programs include and encourage involvement in vigorous physical activity.

5. Creative expression and esthetic appreciation. Emphasis on opportunities for personal expression and creative experiences is important as an antidote for some of the negative effects of an increasingly materialistic society. With increased leisure for all people creative participation in life is seen as assuming unprecedented importance.

6. Environment for living in a leisure society. Recreation seeks to counteract some of the effects of the destruction of our natural resources by providing facilities and experiences that will bring people into contact with nature. Participation in and enjoyment of music and drama as well as other artistic and esthetic endeavors is another goal which is sought by recreation leaders as they work to add meaning and enrichment to the lives of people.

It is apparent that to select any one objective as being more important than others is difficult because they are closely interrelated. There are certain aspects of each, however, that are of common interest to health and physical educators as well as recreation people. Because of these common objectives it is possible for training in certain professional subjects to benefit individuals preparing for each of these professions.

If the recreation person is to be interested in the fitness of those with whom he works, he must have a basic understanding of fitness, what it is, how it is maintained, and what its limitations are. The same is true for motor development and the teaching of motor skills.

Psychological principles are particularly important. Because there is no real coercive element in recreation programs, programs will be engaged in solely on the basis of their appeal or the appeal of the recreation personnel. An understanding of human behavior can spell the difference between success and failure.

Although the public does not really understand what a university recreation course consists of, the prospective recreational specialist should. Obviously, it is not necessary to have four years of college training in order to teach a class in crafts or square dance. Nor is such training necessary for success in leading sports programs and running tournaments. If recreation programs are to achieve more than simply "keeping the kids off the street," however, preparation of leaders who understand the problems and know the principles involved in developing solutions requires *at least* four years of college level preparation.

Opportunities in Recreation

Recreational opportunities, as one would expect, have expanded enormously in the past twenty years. Because so many kinds of programs are provided in communities, people with widely divergent interests may find employment in one of them.

Some of the institutions and agencies with organized recreation programs and recreation personnel are:

1. Federal, state, city, and local governmental divisions. This includes parks, schools, conservation departments, military establishments, forestry service, and welfare agencies. Federal grants are currently providing a number of extensive recreation programs.
2. Private agencies. Well-known agencies such as the YMCA, YWCA, YMHA, church-sponsored community centers, Boy Scouts, Girl Scouts, and Campfire Girls continue to require large numbers of qualified leaders. Other organizations such as private clubs, camps, and charitable organizations require leaders with training to operate camps and organize community projects.
3. Commercial agencies. Many commercial enterprises hire specialists in the organization and teaching of recreational activities. Summer resorts, bowling alleys, theaters, food specialty chains, and manufacturers of sporting goods are some of the kinds of agencies interested in recreation.
4. Industrial plants. Industrial plants have moved into the area of recreation with large programs. Frequently programs are sponsored throughout the year for the entire family of the employee. With the recognition of the fact that private industry must take a large share of responsibility for the provision of things that will assist less affluent members of our society to achieve their potential, more emphasis is likely to be placed on programs such as these.
5. School programs. It has long been evident that schools in city and suburban areas needed to become centers for more kinds of community activity. Taxpayers are beginning to insist that the vast funds expended in school construction return greater dividends in terms of more use. This means that recreation programs, not just for children but for all segments of the community, are being established in school facilities. Although school personnel may occasionally be involved in such endeavors, the programs themselves are frequently separate from the school operation, and personnel are not school teachers putting in extra hours. Such "lighted schoolhouse" programs can aid in solving the fundamental problems of providing the necessary funds to meet the needs of the community.

Effectiveness of Recreation Programs

The evaluation of the effectiveness of recreation programs in terms of the established objectives is exceedingly difficult. Because other factors also bear on those that the recreation professional is interested in, it is difficult to conclude just which factors produce what effects.

The new governmental programs mentioned previously, for example, utilize a great many techniques in attempting to get potentially capable youngsters prepared for college. Recreation is only one of these techniques. It is difficult to evaluate reports claiming success in teaching Spanish or geometry in Head Start programs by the incorporation of recreation techniques. Another problem is that when we begin talking about the use of recreational techniques in teaching or in obtaining some desired behavior, are we still talking about recreation? Some people feel that we are not.

It is easier to assess the effects of leadership on the kinds of programs produced and the number who participate. These kinds of research have considerable usefulness in establishing the need for capable recreation leaders. For example, a report by Chandler and Hyde (98) indicated that in an institution for elderly people, the social interaction and participation of socializing activities were dependent upon the presence of a recreation leader. His absence resulted in a 50 percent reduction in socializing behavior.

Other studies relating to health, physical fitness, social, and psychological characteristics have been reported in other sections of this book. Many of these could be regarded as being pertinent to recreation because of the kinds of activities involved.

There remains a great deal to be learned about the overall effects that recreation programs can have on our complex, confusing culture. Can the depersonalizing effects of the computer age be forstalled? Can concern and compassion be a part of a mechanized, sophisticated (sometimes cynical) society? These are only examples of the important questions that need answers.

Play is more than a pastime, it is a fundamental tool for the discovery and rediscovery of the meaning of living. An understanding of the relationship between play and the development and fulfillment of the self is a prerequisite for effective programing. The creation of recreation theory rests upon this cornerstone (506, p. 50).

SUMMARY

Definitions of physical education vary significantly and are usually phrased in terms of what physical educators *do* rather than what they study. Part of the difficulty in coming to substantial agreement on primary objectives for physical education may stem from lack of agreement about what physical education really is. It has been suggested that the study of human physical activity, with all its implications, should define the limits of physical education.

Health education has had few problems of definition, but "health" as a concept has undergone considerable expansion in recent years. While separate classes in health education are found in most of the larger schools, full-time health educators are still the exception rather than the rule.

Recreation, as a career, defies precise definition, much as physical education does. Its operation is closely associated with man's leisure but is certainly not synonymous with it. The concepts of work, play, and recreation are complexly intertwined making the tasks of recreation leaders exceedingly important, as well as difficult.

Although it is not currently possible to get physical educators to agree on the *primary* objectives of physical education, the major objectives most often articulated can be placed into general categories such as: (1) organic development, (2) social development, (3) psychological development, (4) development of cognition, (5) philosophical development. The objectives most commonly stressed have fluctuated with social conditions and shifts in educational philosophy. It is suggested that the objectives most commonly pursued with greatest vigor are not necessarily the objectives of greatest importance to the welfare of the student.

Criteria for the establishment of objectives are based on philosophical considerations. The wide variety of objectives is understandable in the light of differences in philosophy within the profession. One way to simplify the problem of selection of primary objectives would be to make selections on the basis of the *uniqueness* of contributions of physical education to individuals. One problem is that this procedure ignores the establishment of priorities in terms of the relative *importance* of all possible objectives. That is, if uniqueness *alone* were used

as a criterion, the matter of whether a given objective has any relevance to the needs of individuals would not even be considered. Selection of only the unique, *important* objectives again involves philosophical considerations and may narrow the scope of professional concern excessively.

The broad, basic objectives of health education have been well articulated and are widely accepted. Other problems have been encountered, however, in the matter of controversial subject matter (such as drugs, sex education, and smoking) and in the matters of exactly which techniques should be used in the pursuit of desired objectives.

Objectives of professional recreation leaders have changed considerably in recent years as social problems have multiplied. Although *primary* objectives of recreation may differ substantially from those of health education or physical education, the tools and activities used in their achievment are nearly identical with those used in the other professions. Opportunities for employment in each of the three fields are greater today than ever before. The serious nature of the problems now being faced has, however, made the quality of professional preparation an extremely important factor in securing desirable positions.

PRINCIPLES

1. If man is viewed as an entity (as opposed to the old dualistic concept of a mind and a body), the term "physical education" becomes entirely unwieldy as a name for a discipline.

2. The boundaries of a discipline cannot be adequately defined in terms of what its professional members do. Generally, it must be described in terms of "the study of . . . " rather than "the teaching of. . . . "

3. If an overall discipline can be defined as the study of human physical activity, physical education (the teaching of concepts, skills, and techniques), would logically become the educational arm of the discipline.

4. Health, as a concept, is more than mere absence of disease; it is a state of complete physical, mental, and social well-being.

5. Political and economic conditions have resulted in the possibility of mass leisure that looms simultaneously as a potential threat and a potential blessing.

6. The fact that a given professional objective has widespread approval and practical support does *not* necessarily mean that it is more important than other less popular objectives.

7. Two distinct approaches to the problem of determining objectives to be given priority can be identified. One is to determine the needs of the student and shape objectives to fit these needs; the other is to identify the potential *unique* contributions of the discipline and structure objectives around them.

EXPERIMENTS AND EXPERIENCES

1. Create a check sheet listing as many "possible objectives" of physical education as the class can formulate. Each class member should then rank these objectives in the order that he *believes* most accurately reflects the objectives of high school physical education programs.

2. Survey the class and determine the percentage of students who have experienced formal, classroom instruction in health (apart from that incorporated into science courses).

3. Contact all available community recreation agencies and determine the number of events sponsored that have as their objective the improved health of their members.

4. Obtain a list of facilities available for recreation in your city. Estimate the maximum number of people that could be accommodated at any one time. What implications does this have for future programs of recreation?

SUGGESTED READINGS

Brightbill, Charles K., *Man and Leisure.* Englewood Cliffs, N.J.: Prentice-Hall, Inc., 1961.

Plato, "Physical Education," in *Background Readings for Physical Education* (Ann Paterson and Edmond G. Hallberg, Eds.). New York: Holt, Rinehart and Winston, Inc., 1965, pp. 99–109.

Steinhaus, Arthur H., "The Challenge of Health Education to the YMCA," in *Toward An Understanding of Health and Physical Education.* Dubuque, Iowa: William C. Brown Company, Publishers, 1963.

Williams, Jesse F., "Education Through the Physical," in *Background Readings for Physical Education* (Ann Paterson and Edmond C. Hallberg, Eds.). New York: Holt, Rinehart and Winston, Inc., 1965, pp. 191–196.

Development and Current Status of the Professions

Chapter 3

STATUS OF PHYSICAL EDUCATION

In looking at the picture in the public schools today, it is easy to identify the major patterns followed by physical educators. Sports skills and physical fitness are obviously the two factors most commonly stressed. Furthermore, in many instances the fitness objective is applied to the great mass of students while the skills objective is vigorously pursued with only a relatively few talented performers, who are usually members of interscholastic teams. Although it is true that the skills of team and individual sports are used as the basis of the curriculum in most schools today, inadequate facilities, large classes, and other factors have resulted in programs providing very little individual evaluation and instruction for most students. On the other hand, great attention has been given to this type of instruction at the varsity level.

In very blunt terms this means that in too many schools physical education classes consist of large groups of students being turned loose in small gymnasiums to play some form of team game. Instruction is usually minimal or entirely absent.

Evaluation of student needs and progress is usually a matter of guesswork rather than objective measurement. On the other hand, varsity sports are given a great deal of attention, time, and money. The coach-player ratio is very low, and several assistants are usually available to aid the head coach.

FIGURE 3.1 Even in the finest American school systems, the best conditions for skills instruction (as illustrated by student-teacher ratio and adequacy of facilities) are provided for those who have the greatest ability. Pictured are: (A) varsity basketball players and coaches and (B) girls' physical education class and teacher.

DEVELOPMENT OF PHYSICAL EDUCATION

As has already been pointed out, several factors in our recent history have combined to shape our present philosophies and practices in physical education, as well as health education and recreation. If you are typical of the student who is just entering one of these professions, you are more interested in considering the future than the past. For that reason a detailed discussion of the history of physical education will not be presented. But because it is helpful in many ways to understand some of the events that have led up to our present circumstances, a brief backward glance will be taken here.

Physical education as a part of the public school curriculum may well owe its existence to war. The physical survival of individuals, as well as societies, has historically depended upon the ability of men to defeat other men in physical combat. It is not surprising to find, in looking back over the years, that nations have always demanded increased fitness for their citizens whenever wars have threatened.

PREHISTORY

If one is willing to interpret *physical education* in a very liberal way, it is possible to say that the instructions given by cave-dwelling fathers to their sons in techniques of stalking and killing game (as well as human enemies) constituted a kind of physical education. Indeed, survival depended upon

swiftness of foot and strength of arm; survival of the fittest was the most fundamental of laws. Under such circumstances of daily crisis (or "war") there is no doubt that physical fitness was a state to be highly valued. Observations of this kind have only limited value, of course, because no one would suggest that there existed any kind of formalized program of education during this period.

The earliest known records of systemized instruction in exercise for purposes other than combat are those from early Egypt and surrounding regions. It is apparent that, for certain classes of people at least, skill was developed in activities such as swimming, wrestling, dancing, and gymnastics as early as 2000 B.C. Instruction in activities more directly related to combat, such as archery, riding, and boxing, was also common.

EARLY CIVILIZATION

Although it is generally agreed that civilization developed earliest in the southern Mediterranean countries, it is also apparent that the Chinese produced a remarkable early culture. As the mystical religions of the east developed, less and less emphasis was placed on the care of the body. Because war was viewed more as a necessary evil than as a worthy pursuit of life, educational systems for the training of soldiers did not become as highly developed as in other countries. Ancient China did, however, produce a system of light exercises designed to prevent disease. This form of medical gymnastics called *Cong Fu* combined stretching and breathing exercises and was usually performed in a sitting or kneeling position.

Examination of historical accounts of other ancient civilizations indicates that most activities that could conceivably be labeled "physical education" were generally connected either with religious rites (as with the dance) or with preparation for combat. From a recreational standpoint there have been games and pursuits such as hunting, fishing, and other activities practiced since antiquity. Some of the most ancient artifacts are toys that were used by children in their play. Ancient references to ball games of one kind or another can be found in both written accounts and art of the various periods.

EARLY JEWISH INFLUENCE

One of the ancient cultures having most influence in the development of Western civilization was that of the Hebrew people. Whereas the great emphasis on education generally excluded anything that could really be called physical education, it is of great interest to note the fact that the religious laws provided for health practices that were far advanced over other civilizations of the time. Cleanliness in the preparation of foods, the cleansing of eating utensils, and the washing of wounds under running water anticipated many modern disease-prevention practices.

Although the ancient Hebrew people apparently had great respect for human strength and although they certainly recognized the need for training for warfare, their culture made little provision for sport or games. Whereas the influence of conquerors had, from time to time, caused Jewish communities to build stadiums or other sporting facilities, such influences were usually rejected when the domination of the conquerors ended. So, although we have derived many of our precepts about education and the responsibility of parents for the education of their children from the Hebrew tradition, little else that directly applies to physical education or modern recreational practices can be attributed to the ancient Jewish influence.

THE GOLDEN AGE

On the other hand, one of the cultures having the greatest influence on modern practices in our profession was that of the early Greek civilization. One of the most obvious signs of this influence is that of the Olympic Games; this sporting festival originated in Greece about 776 B.C. as one of several such festivals held periodically. They achieved such importance that wars among various city-states came to a halt temporarily in order that the Olympics might be held every fourth year.

The idea of periodic international athletic competition is only one of many concepts that have been borrowed from the remarkable culture of the early Greeks. This period has been called the Golden Age because of the almost unbelievable contributions it made to the culture of man. Art, science, music, drama, philosophy, education, commerce, agriculture, and practically every other endeavor of man received a tremendous acceleration during this period. In short, this was the birth of Western civilization.

Most of the information we have about the ancient Greeks has come to us through such accounts of life as were recorded by Homer in the *Iliad* and the *Odyssey*. Through the accounts of such heroes as Achilles and Odysseus we learn not only of the ideals valued by society but also of the educational aims and goals. The detailed accounts of the funeral games and the religious ceremonies give us a picture of a vigorous people who, even though they were in a position to make choices, apparently had no desire to lead a life of ease. We are also led to see the development of a society that placed the highest possible value on the harmonious development of all aspects of an individual's capabilities; action and wisdom were highly prized as characteristics to be equally developed. It is interesting to note that as the Greek culture evolved, it became taken for granted that every citizen had a responsibility to exercise daily in addition to other duties, including strenuous military training. The state provided gymnasiums for the use of all male citizens, and it was expected that even older men would make use of the facilities for their physical well-being. Of course, it must be remembered that cultural activities of other kinds also took place at the gymnasium, especially during the later period of that age.

It must not be assumed that aims and practices were uniform throughout ancient Greece or that these remained constant across the years. You will remember that Greece was composed of a group of city-states, each independent from the other. Athens and Sparta were two of the largest and most influential and are representative of differing attitudes toward the citizen's preparation to meet these responsibilities. Although a more detailed discussion of the philosophies involved will be found in Chapter 7, you will remember that, in general, Sparta stressed military preparedness and discipline whereas Athens was noted for its more democratic emphasis in securing the services of the individual for the state. There were other differences as well, but there were also some significant similarities.

One of the most interesting characteristics of the city-states was their belief in the involvement of citizens in the affairs of the state. This is exemplified not only in the training for fighting that was expected of every citizen but also in the fact that the citizens themselves were the participants in the games of the various festivals. Apparently nothing was more highly prized than to be the well-rounded man, a perfect balance between the man of action and the man of wisdom.

It has been said that one of the significant reasons for the great cultural accomplishments of this period was that unusual individual freedom of thought and action was coupled with individual responsibility for civic affairs. Similarly, it has been observed that this society passed its pinnacle when freedom led to individualism without a civic concern. When prestige

 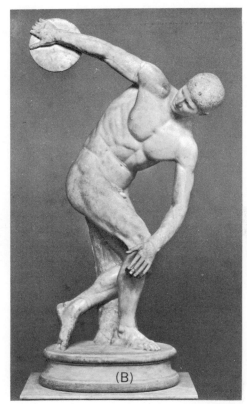

(A) (B)

FIGURE 3.2 Ancient Greece was remarkable for its equal emphasis on the perfection of physical and mental attributes. (A) Demosthenes, antique sculpture (Vatican Musuem, Rome, Alinari—Art Reference Bureau); (B) Myron's Discobolus, Roman copy after bronze original (National Museum, Rome).

became more easily obtainable through wealth and political power than through individual cultural and physical accomplishments, the strength of the city-states began to crumble. The vulnerability of Greece was further increased by the shift in concept from idealizing the man of balanced action and wisdom to idealizing the man of wisdom only.

If the story of physical education in Greece were nothing more than another example of how a young, vigorous nation rose to a position of prominence and then, through neglect of physical vitality, fell prey to another more vigorous culture, there would be little that is unique to study. In this case, however, physical activity, athletic performance, and the maintenance of physical fitness were regarded, for the first time, as something more than mere preparation for war or individual combat. There was a period at the height of the Greek civilization when education was thought to be complete only when a man could perform as well as think. For a young man to exhibit a flabby body was to admit a deficiency in his education (see Chapter 7).

Furthermore, the esthetics of performance were highly valued. The appearance of the body was ideally to suggest a fine balance and harmony of development. The classical Greek statuary indicates the esteem in which grace and harmony were held, as opposed to muscular bulk for its own sake. It is also true that during this period the quality or appearance of the performance was regarded as highly as was the final outcome in terms of winning and losing.

With the decline in participation in games by the citizenry and the concommitant increase in professionalism, less and less emphasis was placed upon the *experience* of performing; the *outcome*, as well as the entertainment provided by the spectacle, became the important factors.

ROMAN INFLUENCE

After the Greek civilization fell to the Macedonians, and later to the Roman Empire, much of the unique character of the Greek attitude toward physical education was lost. The Roman had no taste for the Greek tendency to involve himself in the games and contests of the many festivals. The Roman preferred to observe the giant free spectacles from the comfort of the grandstand. Furthermore, the Roman had become accustomed to the emotionally charged spectacles of bloody gladiatorial combat and brutal contests between animals as well as between men and animals. The relatively tame contests involving the throwing of the javelin or the discus had little attraction for him. And whereas he found some entertainment in observing the time honored wrestling and boxing contests of the Greeks, he found it necessary to brutalize even these. The wearing of nailed gloves and riveted fist wrappings became so popular that blows produced gory wounds and hideous permanent injury, if not death. It is little wonder that after years of observing "athletic" contests of this nature, founders of the early Christian church turned away from any consideration of physical activity or exercise as a worthwhile pursuit. The fact that many of the early Christians were slaves who might themselves be subjected to deadly mock wars or animal combat in the arena for the pleasure of the masses might well have encouraged them to emphasize the spiritual, otherworldly aspects of their religion.

Whatever the reasons, it is a fact that as the influence of Christianity grew, the legitimacy of sport and physical training declined. The glorification of the body came to be regarded as a sinful tendency to be resisted at all costs. It was during this period that the body and spirit were pictured as two separate entities constantly warring against each other. In order to elevate the spirit, and thereby come closer to God, people subjected themselves to all kinds of physical discomforts and tortures. Any suggestion during this period that man was a single organism and that the well-being of the body could be a positive contribution to his spiritual condition would have been vigorously rejected.

As more and more attention was given to the staging of splendid entertainment and as vast sums of money were devoted to luxurious living, the economy of the Roman Empire began to collapse. Those who were wealthy tried to outdo each other in extravagance, while the peasants became progressively poorer and almost without influence in a land that had once prospered with the proud peasant-soldier as its backbone. The paid professional soldiers felt little civic pride or responsibility. Oratory, always prized by the Roman as being almost more desirable than wisdom itself, became a tool merely to sway the voters. Statesmanship disappeared into a welter of selfish, individual aims.

As the training of soldiers became a matter of preparing professionals, the military education of the general male citizenry became less and less necessary. Whereas the war-related activities such as riding, swimming, archery, and so on remained popular activities among the rich for some time, gradually a love of luxurious living replaced these things. The famous Roman Baths were extremely popular among both men and women. Here one could while away countless hours in the warmth and steam of these luxurious facilities. Strenuous activity held little attraction for people under these conditions.

With the decay of civic pride and economic responsibility came political vulnerability. Invaders from the north were successful in raids upon Roman communities. As the barbarian attacks increased, the beautiful cities were plundered and the population was scattered and killed. People were forced to seek shelter in castles or similar fortified communities, each an independent unit. Peasants worked the fields around the walled sanctuaries in exchange for the protection of the owner in times of danger.

THE DARK AGES

The destruction of the Empire left centuries of progress lying in the dust. Cultural and economic interchange ceased almost entirely. Society took a backward step into an almost tribal existence. The one remaining factor giving some semblance of order and continuity to society was the Church. Remote monasteries had become the repositories of the accumulated knowledge derived from the Greek and Roman civilizations. Throughout the nearly 500-year period of the Dark Ages, during which little or no cultural progress was possible, the Church served as the only unifying factor in human existence. If there was anything that could be rightly called *formal education,* it consisted of the limited scholarly activity pursued in the scattered monasteries. Physical education, of course, reverted to its primitive tribal status, consisting merely of the skills that were passed on for their value in fighting and hunting wild game.

It is difficult for us today, with all our problems of coping with the explosion of knowledge, to comprehend the period of nearly a thousand years of retrogression and stagnation as far as learning was concerned. Only a worldwide nuclear holocaust could approximate today the conditions prevailing at the depths of the terror-ridden Dark Ages. Under such circumstances survival is the only objective of any personal importance; cultural considerations are nonexistent.

THE RENAISSANCE

About the tenth century, however, there were stirrings of interest in matters beyond the local level. The causes and implications of this beginning of the period known as the Renaissance cannot be discussed here, except to indicate that religion and the Church played an important part in this revival of culture. The simple fact that representatives of European areas began to venture once again into unknown lands created the conditions for exchange of knowledge, an aroused curiosity concerning other peoples, and a basis for at least a limited commerce among peoples. The crusades into the holy lands, as destructive and as poorly conceived as they often were, did contribute substantially to the rekindling of interest in learning and culture.

It was during this time that knighthood provided the only arena in which any physical education was practiced. The familiar stories of jousting and tournaments provide descriptions of the kinds of activities that young men

of noble birth, at least, might hope to pursue. But it is clear that these activities were really no different than those practiced over a thousand years earlier. One significant difference, however, was the creed of chivalry that served over the years as a prominent factor in raising barbarianism to the level of civilization.

Despite the fact that the new enlightenment brought the development of universities and the congregation of young men who frequently engaged in games and sports of one kind or another, there was no official sanction or encouragement of such amusements. Gradually some of the private schools of southern Europe began to include some provision for exercise and recreation. In most others, however, such activities were either ignored or frowned upon by educators of the day.

This is not to say that there was not considerable interest in sporting activities during the Renaissance. Fencing masters were in great demand among the wealthier segments of society. Bowling on the green, tennis, and dancing, as well as other spectator amusements, were very popular. In an era when courtliness and good manners were stressed, many of these activities were considered indispensable means of promoting proper carriage and grace. All this was in addition to the time-honored practices of riding, wrestling, swimming, shooting, and other combat-related activities.

As the renewed interest in learning progressed, it was accompanied by a great social and political upheaval. Dissatisfaction with punitive economic practices spelled the collapse of feudalism, just as revolt against religious despotism resulted in far-reaching political and religious reforms. And although the Protestant reformation led to the creation of many denominations and sects, it did not produce greater religious tolerance. Conflict and persecution were responsible in a large measure for the establishment of colonies in the lands newly discovered by those who were seeking new trade routes. The hard work and privation required for survival in frontier settlements combined with religious doctrines (that tended to brand as sinful any form of recreation) to effectively prevent acceptance of physical education as a part of the school curriculum in the New World, as well as throughout much of the Old World. Social events were generally built around one of two legitimate activities: worship or work. Any activities that might be termed recreational needed to have some productive purpose such as that provided by quilting bees, house raising, or harvest contests. Even the natural playfulness of children was considered frivolous activity that must be curbed as early as possible.

THE ENLIGHTENMENT

In the seventeenth century it was the rule rather than the exception to regard children as being little adults. In this kind of atmosphere it is not surprising that little thought was given to needs for physical education in the school programs of the day. There were those, however, who were strongly opposed to this philosophy. One of the best known of the so-called naturalists, who led the philosophical revolt against the practices in the eighteenth century, was Jean Jacques Rousseau. This noted French philosopher meticulously outlined an educational program that gave great emphasis to the development of physical stamina, strength, and coordination. The concept that it was a *human being* that was to be educated rather than a *mind* (as distinct from a body) was in direct opposition to the then current beliefs and practices.

Although Rousseau's ideas were tried in only a few private schools of his day, the ideas did not die. As cultural climates became more amenable to ideas of individualism, his concepts and others of similar direction came to be included in the design of curricula in various countries.

However, it was only through a long, complex series of social changes, including wars, political upheavals, philosophical and scientific advancement that physical education became an integral part of any educational system. As always, preparation for war continued to be one of the strong motivating forces for the inclusion of physical education in the school programs. This factor alone, however, seldom seemed sufficient for the justification of its inclusion. In most nations the increased awareness of the necessity for adequate exercise in the optimum development of children was an important consideration.

EUROPEAN SYSTEMS

Germany and Sweden are the two countries that come to mind most readily whenever early programs of physical education in the schools are discussed. Out of Germany evolved gymnastics oriented to the use of so-called heavy apparatus such as parallel bars and vaulting horses. Friedrich Ludwig Jahn and, later, Adolph Speiss were responsible for development of much of the German System. Swedish gymnastics, largely attributed to Per Henrik Ling, were performed in conjunction with balance beams, stall bars, and other equipment of a "lighter" nature. Elaborate progressions and stipulations of proper form for the performance of exercises in both systems were painstakingly developed by their respective proponents.

At about this same period of the nineteenth century, the "public" schools of England were developing their own approach to physical education. These schools (which, despite their name, were maintained for the benefit of the aristocratic families only) stressed classical studies of language and literature as well as some science. In addition to these studies, the boys participated in a growing number of individual and team sports and games. Tennis, swimming, boxing, soccer, cricket, boating, and other activities became extremely popular at these institutions. Administrators of these schools encouraged this kind of participation not only for the physical fitness values they provided but also for the qualities of leadership, perseverence, and sportsmanship that

they were believed to promote. It is noteworthy that despite efforts to popularize the formal European gymnastics programs in England, the populace never accepted them with the enthusiasm that they retained for their sports and games.

Today, as we look around the globe at the various systems of physical education as they are currently practiced, we can see clearly the influence of the three systems just discussed. The intensely competitive colonization not only expanded empires but also carried cultural influences, such as these favored systems of physical education, to many parts of the world.

Of course, the cultures into which systems were introduced determined whether they would be successful in meeting the needs and desires of the people of the culture involved. In America, for example, both the Swedish and German systems were introduced into the school systems at approximately the same time; both enjoyed some success. It is apparent today, however, that the predominant influence in American schools is that derived from the British society. It is clear that the nature of a people combines with prevailing economic and political conditions to produce educational practices. The United States has adopted a blend of the European systems to which it has added its own unique modifications. This is not to say that there is any such thing as a *national* curriculum in physical education. Surely many regional and local variations persist, both in regard to type of activity and quality of program. Generally speaking,

Courtesy Adidas

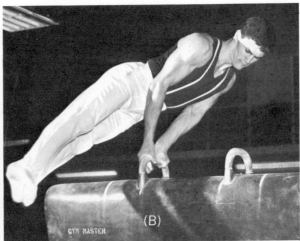

FIGURE 3.3 Modern programs of physical education still reflect the influence of three early systems: (A) English, (B) German, and (C) Swedish, picturing the Sofia Girls, 1968, courtesy Swedish Information Service.

however, programs of physical education in this country are built around the sports-and-games concept. Criticisms regarding the alleged inadequacy of such programs for the building of adequate fitness levels have been met by the addition of more formal types of activity to existing programs, in most cases, rather than a change in emphasis and replacement by activities designed strictly for the development of physical fitness.

TODAY'S PHYSICAL EDUCATION

If we discount the remarkable culture of the early Greeks, we can see that physical education is really a very recent development in man's history. When we stop to consider that the earliest systems of physical education were introduced into the schools only about 150 years ago (and less than 100 years ago in the United States), it is apparent that we are dealing with a very young aspect of education. When we then look at the changes that have occurred in the world within the last 100 years as compared with all that have gone before, it is not surprising that there are differences of opinion about what the main purpose of physical education should be in America and the world.

THE FUTURE

There is little doubt that the next ten years will be critical ones for physical education in the United States. We will be facing problems that man has never before encountered. The role that physical education is to play in the lives of people will be determined by a great many factors, including social preferences, educational aims, economic goals and conditions, and political pressures. If our profession is to survive and emerge as a truly positive contributor to the welfare of mankind, physical educators themselves must become aware of:

1. The ways in which physical activity affects man and his environment

2. The ways in which man and his environment limit, encourage, and generally affect human physical activity

CURRENT STATUS OF HEALTH EDUCATION

When we address ourselves to the question, "Where is health education today?" we naturally turn our thoughts to the questions: "Where were we?" and "How long has it been since we were there?" Investigation leads to two somewhat striking answers to the latter questions: "It was awfully dark and bleak where we were and it has been less than a hundred years since we were there." To put it another way, health education is "young," and it has grown and developed tremendously since its earliest beginnings about 1870, when it was nothing more than a temperance and antivice program with some anatomy, physiology, and hygiene thrown in for good measure.

EARLY PRACTICES

Ancient societies, including the Chinese, Egyptians, Hebrews, Greeks, and Romans, including a period from about 3000 B.C. to A.D. 1700, were concerned to some extent about physical well-being and stressed certain rules for hygienic living. Emphasis was placed most commonly upon "physical" health and well-being and the absence of disease. Horace Mann, in 1840, stressed the importance of physical well-being and "educating for health," (188, p. 14) but was largely ignored. The public health movement in the United States began in 1850. At that time city governments began to establish and upgrade health departments as a direct result of Lemuel Shattuck's *Report of the Sanitary Commission of Massachusetts* (188, 223). In this report, Shattuck described a modern program of public health—especially preventive programs—and gave impetus to the idea that health was more than absence of disease. Perhaps of even greater importance were his suggestions for *health education*.

Ohio instituted a state program in 1872; it was typical of those instituted from that time until about 1918 in that it was "anti-vice and function-of-the-body" oriented as a result of the powerful temperance-sponsored propaganda movement. Health as it is now conceived was not emphasized until sometime after World War II.

We can approximate the progress of health education from the early 1930s to the present by perusal of several typical health texts for college students. Williams' (609) fourth edition of *Personal Hygiene Applied*, for example, was published in 1931 and included several chapters on the meaning of health, the health problem, man in society, the approach to health knowledge, and science and attitudes, all apparently directed at setting the mood for effective learning. The remainder of the text was devoted to "the hygiene of" each of the major systems of the body and to nutrition, the mouth, eye and ear, and "sexual aspects of life." One chapter was devoted to "prevention of specific diseases." Hygiene and the study of body function was still in vogue in 1931, but *eleven* small-size pages were devoted to some sex education!

By the mid 1950s there was less emphasis on the systems of the body per se. See, for example, Kilander's *Health for Modern Living* (310). Personality and mental health, dating, courtship and marriage, growth and development, nutrition and weight control, relaxation and recreation, study of stimulants and depressants, alcohol and tobacco, more extensive treatment of disease, planning medical protection, and national health resources were now typical of health education content.

TODAY'S HEALTH EDUCATION

In the mid 1960s we apparently had returned to some emphasis on the function of the body's system per se and some effort at defining the importance of health education. In Miller and Burt's *Good Health* (390) we see that physical fitness was added and that there was more extensive treatment of sexuality and reproduction. Family planning appeared, and strong emphasis on problems related to tobacco, alcohol, and narcotics was continued. Consumer health appeared on the scene, as did greater emphasis on *community* health and personal appearance. Some coverage of emergency first-aid procedures and a discussion of radiation dangers were also included.

Another development has been health education's recent trend in the direction of the conceptual or "big ideas" approach to learning. Perhaps it is too early to call this a trend, but considerable time and money was spent on the development of a conceptual model for school health education, and it appears most likely that the approach will be more and more utilized. The approach is based on the precept that the "big ideas" or basic concepts are better retained and assimilated than are facts. There are three key concepts: growing and developing, decision making, and interactions. The new terminology may be somewhat misleading, but when we turn to the ten concepts subsumed by the three key concepts, the picture becomes clearer. These ten concepts are listed in Table 3.1. Categorized under each of the ten concepts there are from two to four **substantive elements,** a total of thirty-one of these in all. The curriculum then is organized around these substantive elements in terms of goals for the learner and be-

havioral outcomes at a particular developmental or grade level.

There is yet another bit of evidence that leads one to believe some health educators have awakened. The *ideal* approach is no longer viewed as the textbook and lecture method; there are problem solving and experiments (as well as the older movie-film, posters, pictures and television methods). Although the idealistic new programs are not yet widely being used, the fact that they are being utilized at all is encouraging.

THE FUTURE

As a final note and fitting close to the discussion of the question, "Where is health education?", let us say "not where it *has* been (fortunately!) but not yet where it can be." To be sure, there are encouraging signs as we have pointed out. But every school does not yet teach health as it should be taught (too many still do not teach it at all); and the

TABLE 3.1 Ten Concepts for Health Education

Growth and development influences and is influenced by the structure and functioning of the individual.

Growing and developing follows a predictable sequence, yet is unique for each individual.

Protection and promotion of health is an individual, community, and international responsibility.

The potential for hazards and accidents exists, whatever the environment.

There are reciprocal relationships involving man, disease, and environment.

The family serves to perpetuate man and to fulfill certain health needs.

Personal health practices are affected by a complexity of forces, often conflicting.

Utilization of health information, products, and services is guided by values and perceptions.

Uses of substances that modify mood and behavior arise from a variety of motivations.

Food selection and eating patterns are determined by physical, social, mental, economic, and cultural factors.

SOURCE: Health Education: A Conceptual Approach to Curriculum Design. Washington, D.C.: School Health Study, 1967, p. 20.

conceptual model is still just that—a *model*; the test is yet to come—can and *will* these dynamic new ideas in health education be utilized effectively?

THE DEVELOPMENT OF RECREATION

EARLY BEGINNINGS

The concern over the problem of learning to deal with leisure has sprung from several sources. Americans tend to believe that the phenomenon of free time is unique to the modern, industrialized societies. You may recall that the ancient Greeks (and the Egyptians before them) had a great many festival days during the year and that the Romans are reputed to have had nearly as many holidays as workdays. It is generally conceded that the failure to wisely utilize this time was a contributing factor to the downfall of the Roman empire.

Of course, festivals and religious holidays are only one means of assessing the degree of recreation engaged in by ancient societies. There is no doubt that man has always been compelled to play. "Abolish religion and recreation from the face of the earth and within two moons they would return again" (72, p. 106). Both of these activities involving man's attempts at self-fulfillment and search for meaning have played significant roles in the development of civilization. Recreation is a means of dealing with boredom, and it is clear that much of the leisure of man has been spent in imagi-

native ways of meeting challenges presented to him by his culture.

Although recreational pursuits must have persisted among common people during the Dark Ages, the available records concerning such activity deal only with royalty and Church figures. The Renaissance produced another kind of activity to be utilized during leisure, that of learning. It was during and after the Reformation, however, that the roots of the "evils of idleness" idea took hold.

The period of colonialization carried cultures of established societies throughout the world. Religious differences provided the impetus for many of the early settlers to leave Europe, and some of the persecuted groups colonizing the inhospitable new lands developed attitudes that have had profound effects on succeeding generations.

ATTITUDES TOWARD PLAY

One of the most enduring of these attitudes was that developed concerning work. Any unproductive activity was deemed sinful. Because play and other recreational activities were obviously unproductive, they were equated with the sins of idleness and sloth and were firmly discouraged. Many of the recreational activities of that time were "disguised" by the addition of a work element. Husking bees, barn raisings, and similar events became events to look forward to with great anticipation. Even though the harsh environmental conditions were gradually controlled, the Puritan "work ethic" persisted, and its influence spread throughout the early United States.

It is of considerable interest to note the relationship between recreation and the Church during this time. Although "play" was not permitted (or was frowned upon, at least) the religious activities became extremely popular. Lonely settlers came great distances to attend evangelistic meetings in tents or cleared areas. Accounts of these services give an indication of the extent to which religion, in a sense, became a substitute for recreation (161, p. 80).

It was not until the Industrial Revolution, however, that the American citizen (as well as the European) began to learn what leisure meant. Less time was required to meet the requirements of life, and more money became available for recreational use. The expansion of business opportunities, however, became almost a "game" in itself. Because work had always been a legitimate outlet for one's energies, the excitement of commercial competition, getting and spending, attracted the attention of many.

The money produced by this rush of business activity, associated with the growth of cities around industrial complexes, made possible the development of "spectating." Horse racing, professional foot racing, boat racing, and other types of competition attracted large throngs of spectators, frequently taxing the capacities of transportation and housing facilities. "Phineas T. Barnum of circus fame stands out as the leading figure of this period in amusing the populace. No struggle be-

tween dramatic standards and popular taste ever troubled the master showman of them all. He was not one whit interested in art; he was interested in entertainment" (161, p. 122). Barnum's ability to provide a vast variety of entertainment for the people of the 1850s may have had a significant effect on their readiness to pay for the opportunity of viewing athletic teams compete.

The first recorded football game between colleges was played in 1869 between Princeton and Rutgers. Three games were played, and there were twenty-five players on each side. It took a few years for the game to catch on (it was banned because of increasing roughness), but after some rules changes and after further exposure, the groundwork was laid for the establishment of rivalries that have since attracted millions of spectators.

The growth of sports not only provided people a chance to observe and to be entertained but also gave them new outlets for involvement and participation. In addition to these, activities such as bicycling and then "joy riding" in automobiles provided opportunities for fun and excitement that are still enjoyed today.

MODERN LEISURE

The changes of the first half of the twentieth century are of little interest to the youngster who has never known anything but television, supersonic aircraft, and computer technology. He will be interested, however, in the effect that the changes produced in

FIGURE 3.4 Modern man is little different from his predecessors in his love for the diversion and entertainment provided by colorful and violent spectacles. (Top, half-time entertainment at college football game; center, "Pollice Verso," 1874, by Jean Leon Gérôme, now in Phoenix Art Museum, Phoenix, Arizona; bottom, Ringling Bros. and Barnum & Bailey Circus photograph.)

society by automation will cause in his personal life. It is precisely this kind of problem that the professional recreation worker will be trying to help solve.

THE FUTURE

In justifying the need for recreational leaders and recreational programs, authorities point to a number of factors of which we are all basically aware. The forty-hour work week may be reduced to thirty within the next ten years. Increased wages and the guaranteed annual wage (which has become a reality for more and more people) coupled with an unprecedented production have increased the spending power of millions. Unemployment rates have seasonal fluctuations, but unemployment insurance helps to reduce the difficulties encountered during such times. The population explosion has created a housing and a school crisis in the cities. The burgeoning social expectations of minority groups have produced a restlessness and a social mobility that is unprecedented in the history of the world. The combination of increased leisure, more money, and unfulfilled expectations is expected to produce social and economic problems whose solutions will require the dedicated efforts of a great many people. We can expect increased concern on the part of government and industry as well, and not always on the basis of objective humanitarianism. Concerning the relationships of recreation to the economy, *Fortune Magazine* reported: "The leisure market may be-

come the dynamic component of the whole economy" (161, p. 393). In reviewing publications of the amounts spent by Americans for equipment and services related to recreation (such as the *Life* article, "A $40 Billion Bill Just for Fun"), Dulles came to the conclusion that "Play had to be considered a virtue for the sake of the nation's prosperity" (161, p. 392).

Work and Play Today

As a consequence of the factors that have been mentioned (as well as others), the concepts of "work" and "play" in our society have undergone curious changes. This change is pointed out in Chapter 17 in terms of the implications it has for physical education in the schools. It has just as serious implications for nearly all other professions.

After reviewing the research in this area, Sessoms notes:

Traditionally, Western man has viewed work as the major determinator of social status, but with advanced technology and mechanization, work is losing its social importance. Increasingly . . . leisure has replaced work as life's central interest.

For many, it is not an easy transition. There are feelings of guilt and shame; leisure has been for too long synonymous with idleness, and the prestige ascribed to adult play is woefully low. Work may not be meaninfgul but neither may be leisure (506, p. 44).

" . . . neither may be leisure"—this is the problem that faces the prospective recreation professional. The task of helping to create a new value system in which meaningful leisure pursuits are possible is a tremendously important one. It is apparent that jobs can no longer provide meaning for the vast majority of people, and it is certain that this situation will not improve.

SUMMARY

Examination of the current status of physical education reveals a strong emphasis on physical fitness for the masses of students while a concern for the teaching of physical skills is limited to a relative few. Highly talented individuals, especially those engaging in varsity sports, appear to receive the bulk of attention given to intensive skills training.

A brief historical survey indicates that the fitness objective has long been likened to the objective for preparedness for war. While fighting and hunting skills were prized in past ancient cultures, the early Greeks stand out for their remarkable contributions to physical education as well as to all other aspects of civilization. Few if any cultures have had as profound an effect upon the modern philosophies of physical education as that of the Greeks.

Other cultures, including that of the once-proud Roman Empire and some of those rising out of the dismal years called the Dark Ages following Rome's fall, have made contributions to physical education. With the Renaissance and the Protestant reformation, great strides were taken toward regaining the levels of civilization once enjoyed.

With the advent of improved education, ideas about the role of physical activity in man's life again stirred some interest. "Systems" of physical education gradually developed around individuals and came to be identified with specific countries.

With expansion of colonial territories in the new world, these systems became incorporated, adapted, and modified to blend into the new cultural setting. The phenomenal growth of population centers, educational systems, and economic opportunity provided by our civilization has created a culture that has affected American physical education in many ways. The rapidity of growth and the absence of clear-cut goals has placed physical education in the position of being forced to justify its very existence at a time in history when it should, theoretically, be making its greatest contribution. The challenge is clear and the opportunities will be great in the years immediately ahead. Realization of the potential contribution of physical education will be dependent upon the dedication and preparation of tomorrow's physical educators.

Health education, as distinct from interests in medicine itself, is really much younger than physical education. Practices of early people, including taboos and rituals designed to preserve health, were often specified by decree or custom. Aside from scattered records, little is known about efforts to educate people concerning personal health practices.

The origins of health education in the United States as well as its evolution can be conveniently traced by examination of the content of popular health texts from the early 1930s up to the present time. Recent years have seen a great expansion in breadth of health topics as well as intensified interest in new and more effective ways of making health knowledge a meaningful factor in human behavior.

The history of recreation is as old as play itself. From a formal standpoint, however, the festivals of ancient peoples give us our first glimpse of organized recreation. Physical education and recreation suffered common fates during the Dark Ages and the succeeding years. Religion played a large part in formulating attitudes toward work and play, with the latter being, for a time, practically equated with sin.

The Industrial Revolution, accompanied by economic development and increased leisure, gave birth to an upsurge in recreational interest and activity. In the United States, these conditions contributed to a tremendously increased interest in spectator sports. Modern automation has only accelerated the trend to greater economic growth accompanied by increased leisure. The concepts of work, play, fun, job have become less and less clear as profound cultural changes have occurred with increasing rapidity.

Heavy responsibility for helping to create new value systems for an age of leisure rests with today's recreation personnel. The significance of recreation in American life within the next few years can scarcely be overemphasized.

PRINCIPLES

1. Attitudes of a populace toward the concepts of work, play, leisure, and recreation have profound effects upon the vitality and direction of the society.
2. Failure to utilize free time in a meaningful, satisfying way can contribute substantially to the decay of an otherwise sophisticated society.
3. Historically, concern for the physical fitness of any population has been linked to the objective of military preparedness.
4. Physical education takes on profoundly different values when viewed from the standpoint of dualism (mind versus body) as opposed to monism (a single, unitary being).

SUGGESTED READING

Dulles, Foster R., *A History of Recreation.* New York: Appleton-Century-Crofts, 1965.

Means, Richard K., *A History of Health Education in the United States.* Philadelphia: Lea & Febiger, 1962.

Weston, Arthur, *The Making of American Physical Education,* New York: Appleton-Century-Crofts, 1962.

Van Dalen, D. B., E. D. Mitchell, and B. L. Bennett, *World History of Physical Education.* Englewood Cliffs, N.J.: Prentice-Hall, Inc., 1953.

PART II

Essential Understandings

Critical,
Systematic Thinking

Chapter 4

The "Miss Peach" cartoon (Figure 4.1) says it. Our experience with college students says it. Students say it, and some have started to rebel against its repression. Some educators are enough concerned about it to try to do something about it. We have attempted to do something about it in our own classes. This book is an attempt to do something about it. What is "it"? "It" is the need for developing an atmosphere for creativity and critical, systematic thinking. Unfortunately, our educational system has for years promoted just the opposite: conformism and regimented, "Polly-parrot learning." Fortunately, formal education has never been 100 percent successful in converting all of its products to conformist automatons incapable of critical and creative thinking. But, in our opinion, it has been far too successful. We see an effort in many schools to get away from this kind of "education," which is really more like indoctrination. You are fortunate if you have come up through a system of schools where the problem-solving approach to education is in vogue or at least present to some degree. If you are not so fortunate, you will have to go through some kind of a conversion process. It can be a painless con-

MISS PEACH   By Mell Lazarus

FIGURE 4.1   Miss Peach by Mell Lazarus © Field Enterprises Inc.

version because it would seem to us to be more in keeping with the nature of man to wish to be his own master, so to speak, and not to be an automaton. Perhaps not. Perhaps all persons are not built of such stuff. But it can be said with certainty that only the ones who can think creatively and objectively and who can use the problem-solving scientific process will be the true professionals in our fields (see page 12). The rest will be technicians; for the ability to think systematically, critically, and creatively is the earmark of the professional. The professional *can think effectively for himself. He can make decisions.*

PROBLEM SOLVING AND DECISION MAKING

You have already learned something about making decisions. Although technically there may be little difference between making a simple "choice" and making a "decision," the difference is essentially one of the stakes involved. Thus, it may be relatively simple to choose which shoes one will wear with a particular suit but quite another matter to decide on whether to pursue a career in engineering, medicine, or education. Choice is often based on whim or fancy; wise decisions are based on facts.

As society becomes more and more complex, the range of decisions one is called upon to make increases. Thus, it has become necessary to develop ways of insuring that wise decisions are made. In business and government, when the stakes are high, complex and technical systems have been developed to aid in the process of decision making. The laws of probability have been utilized by the statistician and a whole field of study called "decision theory" has been born. Although the ordinary citizen does not have at his disposal the resources of industry, he can adapt the basic ideas successfully employed there to make appropriate decisions in his own life. It is important that we understand the scientific principles that can be applied to the problem of making sensible decisions.

There is nothing particularly complex about the application of these principles. A review of the steps that should be utilized in problem solving and decision making may be helpful.

LOGICAL STEPS

The first step is to recognize the problem. One may be aware that things are not right but have difficulty in identifying what is wrong. In this case, some careful observation of the circumstances is indicated. A scientist might call this "preliminary data collection." This careful and more purposeful kind of observation should help in formulating a theory about what steps might be useful in identifying and overcoming the problem.

Next, armed with this knowledge of what conditions actually exist, a theory or hypothesis about the kind of action that appears to be desirable can be formulated. This hypothesis may be worded in predictive terms: "If situation A exists (as it appears might be the case), then action B should result in outcome C." The careful statement of the problem in the form of a hypothesis is a major step in the direction of solution of the problem.

Once the hypothesis has been set up, it should be a relatively simple matter to test it in order to see whether the predicted results actually occur. If they do, then the appropriate course of action is clear. If the expected result does not come about, the original theory should be adjusted in the light of the new facts available and a new hypothesis set up for testing. In this manner it is often possible to determine not only "better" decisions for important problem-solving action but often "best" decisions.

Let's take a look at an example of how an individual might go about applying some of these principles to a personal problem. Suppose Mr. X has recently graduated from college. As a typical student he has always been fairly active in extracurricular activities that have kept him relatively trim and fit. As fall rolls around, he discovers that all last year's winter clothes are too tight. About the same time he notices that he seems to be a little soft and bulgy around the middle. Taking his cue from these simple observations, he makes certain other preliminary observations. He consults the most recent height-weight tables provided by his insurance man and discovers that he is about fifteen pounds above the weight recommended for one of his height and general stature. His physician also tells him that he is indeed overweight and should reduce. In studying his diet in order to determine whether his caloric intake is excessive, he discovers that it is about the same as it was all the time he was attending college.

Like all of us, he has been the target of a great deal of advertising concerning the benefits of vibrators, diet foods, drugs, exercise fads, and other "packages" designed to get rid of unwanted pounds and to restore a youthful appearance. Unlike many of us, however, he has taken the time to check into some of the claims made for the various reducing systems and has concluded that weight gain or loss in the normal healthy person is the result of the balance between caloric intake and energy expenditure.

One obvious course of action in this case is simply to reduce caloric intake to an appropriate level and to attempt to maintain weight by diet control. This, of course, implies the necessity of enduring moderate levels of chronic hunger, possibly for the balance of his lifetime. On the other hand, an increase in energy expenditure should aid in the reduction of excess weight. Mr. X reasons that because he has not changed his dietary habits since college days his weight problem must be the result of the reduced level of physical activity inherent in his occupation. He hypothesizes, therefore, that if he compromises by increasing his level of activity by playing handball or tennis three times a week and by reducing his caloric intake moderately, he should be able to regain and maintain a more desirable weight and still enjoy a sense of fulfillment at the dinner table.

(It should be noted that there are other possible courses of action open to Mr. X, all dependent, of course, on the approval of his physician. One possibility might be to change the composition of his diet from predominately carbohydrates to proteins. Another might involve the use of appetite-inhibiting drugs or the institution of a series of starvation diets. In this case, however, he has selected the elements that seem to be most advantageous to him and has manipulated them into a pattern he plans to test.)

Once under way, Mr. X keeps a regular weight chart in order to assess his progress. At the end of six months he discovers that he has lost eight pounds and has suffered no discomfort. In addition, the bulge around the middle has nearly disappeared. At the end of a year he finds that he has slightly exceeded his goal and that his weight-loss pattern has leveled off. His hypothesis has been proved to be true and his problem has been solved.

Other examples of the scientific problem-solving approach could be given, but they are all based upon the same general considerations. The single, most important step in the whole process is the formulation of an appropriate hypothesis. When knowledge of underlying conditions is limited, it is, of course, difficult to visualize other courses of action. It has been observed that "a proper construction of the question is often half of its solution." But in order to "phrase the question," or sometimes even before one can recognize that he *has* a specific problem, it is necessary to have some understanding of the basic facts. In terms of individual health and physical fitness it is important to know, for example, what the relationships are between physical activity and caloric balance. One needs to understand how the human machinery utilizes its fuel and how it responds to various changes in grade and amount of fuel.

For the solution of other kinds of problems relating to individual welfare it is necessary to be acquainted with certain other basic facts about how the body works, not only as a biological machine but also as a *person,* an integrated human being with needs, desires, aspirations, hopes, and fears. This is not to say that one must become a physician or a psychiatrist, but only that it is important that we all become acquainted with certain basic things about how we work and think and learn.

Merely possessing this knowledge is, of course, not enough. It takes a little creativity, a willingness to manipulate and examine the facts in order to be able to come up with a properly phrased question—a productive hypothesis.

ACQUIRING DECISION-MAKING ABILITY

In order to develop this ability to make intelligent decisions based on facts and knowledge of the process, practice is necessary. No one is born with the knowledge of how to solve his own (or anyone else's) problems. This is a task that takes practice just as any skill requires practice if improvement is to take place. For this reason you should take the opportunity to experiment with some particular problem as it relates to your own health and fitness. You will need to give attention to the techniques of observing the available information, formulating your hypothesis and collecting and analyzing your data. You will also need to learn how to avoid certain errors in drawing conclusions, and, finally, you should use your imagination in the general application of your findings.

It should be apparent that the decision-making process just described in no way rules out individual human judgment. On the contrary, it simply harnesses it and provides it with much more favorable operating conditions.

The steps used in this "do it yourself" approach are simple. First, be aware of the general problem to be studied. Next, hypothesize about the outcome of the experiment: What do you think the results will be? You will then engage in the actual collection of data, which you will then need to organize in a meaningful manner. This usually involves drawing a picture of the results in the form of a graph, as well as organizing the data into chart form. When more than one person is involved you will also want to convert the performances of individuals into a single mean or average performance. Following this you should be able to look back at your original hypothesis or theory and decide whether or not it has been supported. Finally, you should make some judgments about whether your findings have any practical or general application.

There is an infinite number of examples of situations in physical education, health education, and recreation that require "decision making in the face of facts." Some problems are obvious and *require* some kind of decision before any appropriate action can be taken. Others result from the professional's dissatisfaction with the status quo or his curiosity about a better way to do something or concern about whether his students are really learning. Listed below are some hypothetical examples of each kind of problem the professional may face.

OBVIOUS PROBLEMS

There are too many serious injuries in our intramural touch football program.

An alarming percentage of our sophomores are contracting venereal disease.

Attendance in our recreation program has dropped off 42 percent in the last month.

A certain ninth-grade student has suddenly stopped dressing for physical education class without apparent reason.

Students have asked for a program in sex education but parents have a negative attitude.

Our community has a heart disease death rate and a mental illness frequency that are well above even the national averages.

SILENT PROBLEMS

Are my students really assimilating the important health concepts? If not, how can I improve my program to that end?

Is each of my students as physically fit as he or she can be? If not, why not? Then, what can I do to motivate them to improve within their individual capacities?

Is there a better method than my current one of teaching swimming skills?

Is my recreation program really meeting community needs?

Are my basketball players properly conditioned, or is there a better way than I am currently using?

Does regular exercise cause changes in the heart muscle that make it more resistant to coronary artery disease?

These are but a few examples. How would you go about solving these problems or answering these questions? You can certainly add many, many more.

The general pattern for decision making can be applied in every case, but creativity will be required to select the specific approach that best fits the particular problem. Some will involve experimental research, others will require only an appraisal of the *existing* situation. But each involves the basic pattern: recognition and identification of the problem (which may involve preliminary observations and/or data collection); a formulation of an hypothesis; testing of the hypothesis by appropriate means (collection of data, experimentation); drawing conclusions and making a decision.

REPORTING EXPERIMENTAL DATA

As an illustration of how experimental research data are commonly reported, a simple experiment, performed during a class period, is presented. A simplified version of the format used by many scientific journals is used as the model.

AN EXPERIMENT IN HUMAN STRENGTH

I. Purpose: The purpose of this experiment was to observe the relationship between **isotonic strength** and **isometric strength**.

II. Hypothesis: The original hypothesis was that isometric strength should be found to be greater than isotonic strength.

III. Procedure: Six student volunteers

were selected from a class. Students were tested singly and were not permitted to observe each other's performance.

A. Isometric test. Each student, in turn, was required to stand with his back against the wall and his feet on a low platform about eight inches from the wall. A five-foot bar was placed in his hands (palms up) after the elbows were flexed to a measured angle of 90°. A chain and cable arrangement extended from the center of the bar to a spot on the platform directly between the ankles of the subject.

Each subject was asked to make a maximal attempt at further flexing the elbows. The tension produced in the cable under these circumstances was measured by means of a **cable tensiometer**. Results were recorded to the nearest pound.

B. Isotonic test. The subject assumed a position similar to that described above; the maximum amount of weight (to the nearest five pounds) that each subject could "curl" from thighs to chest was determined. A series of trials with approximately five minutes of rest between each trial was instituted to determine maximal isotonic strength (the greatest load that could be curled *one time*). The first attempt was made with 60 percent of the maximal isometric performance placed on the bar. For subsequent trials, adjust-

ments were made in increments of five pounds. All subjects' maximums were determined within four trials.

IV. Limitations: The small number of subjects was a limiting factor in this study. The order of presentation of the exercise tasks may have produced a fatigue effect which may have distorted the results.

V. Results and Discussion:

A. Results. The raw scores of each individual are shown in the table below.

| | STRENGTH | |
SUBJECT	ISOMETRIC	ISOTONIC
1	72	45
2	90	60
3	103	75
4	85	60
5	60	35
6	70	45
Total	480	320
Average	80	53

The graph in Figure 4.1 shows a comparison of isometric and isotonic strength. The mean isometric strength was found to be eighty pounds, whereas the mean isotonic strength was fifty-three pounds.

B. Discussion. The apparent difference may be due to the fact that the angle of attachment of the biceps muscle to the bone is very efficient at 90° but progressively less efficient in either direction from this position. Thus, moving the bar bell through the full range, which begins at about 180°, where the angle of attachment is less efficient, is more difficult than exerting force at the single point of the relatively ideal 90° of elbow flexion.

VI. Conclusions and Implications: On the basis of the data *collected in this experiment* the following conclusions are drawn:

1. It appears that isometric strength is greater than isotonic strength, at least at 90° elbow flexion. It is possible that at other angles, isometric strength could be less than isotonic.

2. Under these conditions the isotonic strength would appear to be approximately 68 percent of the isometric strength.

It might be implied from this experiment that it is possible to exert more force through muscle contraction in slow movements than in more rapid ones.

CONSTRUCTING AND INTERPRETING GRAPHS

In the sample experiment above, a simple graph was used to illustrate the experimental findings. In this book, one of the techniques for facilitating your understanding of health and fitness information will be simply to present a table or graph that is self-explanatory and is not discussed at length. Despite the fact that graphs are widely used in popular magazines, newspapers, and books, many of us are

not really graph-oriented. In order to assist those who have difficulty in interpreting graphic materials, several examples are presented below.

THE BAR GRAPH

One of the simplest and most effective graphs for showing comparisons between groups or individuals is the bar graph. As shown in Figure 4.2, the message conveyed by such graphs is easily grasped. Here the average isometric strength of six men (eight pounds) is

FIGURE 4.2   A comparison of the means of the maximal isotonic and maximal isometric strength of six men.

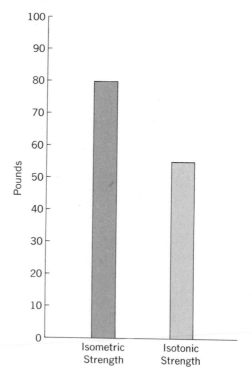

represented by the bar labeled "Isometric Strength." The other bar represents maximal "Isotonic Strength," and extends upward until a value of fifty-three pounds is reached on the vertical scale.

In order to make the discussion of all graphs more simple, certain terms have been adopted to make communication easier. For example, the vertical scale on all graphs is called the *ordinate*. The horizontal scale is called the *abscissa*. Traditionally, the lowest or poorest scores of values begin at the bottom of the ordinate. When such a scale is used on the abscissa, the low values are placed at the extreme left and the high values at the right.

THE LINE GRAPH

The line graph is another device commonly used to show changes in status.

Here changes taking place over a period of time can be conveniently illustrated, as shown by the acceleration of the heart rates of the two groups shown in Figure 4.3. As can be seen, the average heart rate of the twelve men in Group E was 82 before the exercise began. As soon as they started walking on the treadmill, the heart rate began to increase. As the exercise progressed, the heart rate rose to a maximum of 160 beats a minute, where it leveled off and remained until the exercise was terminated. It can be seen that as soon as the exercise stopped the heart rates of both groups began to drop back toward normal. It should also be noted that the average heart rates of the men in Group E did not rise as high as shown for those in Group C, and also that Group E returned to normal more quickly than did Group C. In observing a plot like this we might conclude

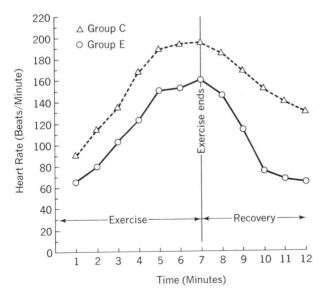

FIGURE 4.3 Mean heart rate responses to exercise of two groups of twelve men.

that the men in Group E were in better condition than those in Group C because they performed the standard task with less effort (as indicated by lower heart rates) and recovered from the exertion more quickly.

THE CORRELATION PLOT

A device frequently used to illustrate the degree to which separate qualities are related is the correlation plot or scattergram. If we were interested in the relationship between IQ and academic success, for example, each individual in our study would need to have two scores: an IQ score and a cumulative grade point average. By arranging the possible IQ scores from low to high on the ordinate of the graph, and the academic achievement scores in the same manner on the abscissa,

each individual can be represented by a single point on the scattergram. As shown in Figure 4.4, an individual with an IQ of 122 and a grade point average of 3.2 would be placed as indicated by the open dot. The solid dots all represent other individuals.

These questions now arise: Are IQ scores and grade point averages related, and if so, how closely? And is this relationship positive or negative?

It should be evident that if grade point averages went up one unit for every increased IQ unit, we would have a perfect positive relationship. All points would lie along one line and this line would form a 45° angle with either the ordinate (vertical scale) or the abscissa (horizontal scale). This would be a perfect positive correlation represented by a correlation coefficient of 1.0. Figure 4.5 illustrates such a correlation, indicating that academic achieve-

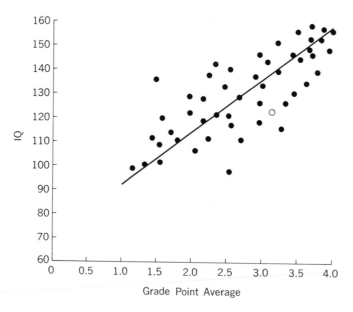

FIGURE 4.4 A scattergram comparison (correlation plot) of IQ and grade point average indicating the line of best fit. Open dot represents a student with IQ of 122 and grade point average of 3.2.

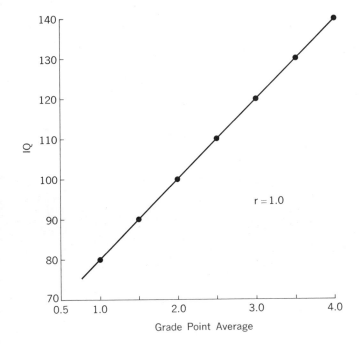

FIGURE 4.5 Hypothetical plot that might be obtained if IQ and grade point averages were perfectly correlated.

$r = 1.0$

ment (as measured by grade point averages) is directly proportional to IQ.

Of course, two given factors are almost never perfectly correlated. A more realistic picture of the relationship between our two variables is shown in Figure 4.4. Here it will be seen that the scores, while forming a definite "directional" trend, do not all fall on the same line. A "line of best fit"[1] has been superimposed on this pattern to show the actual slope of the scattergram pattern. Because all points do not fall exactly on this line, and because the line does not slope at a 45° angle, the correlation is *less than* 1.0, and actually

would be about .76. This is still a fairly strong correlation, indicating that there is a strong relationship between the two variables. That is to say, there is a strong tendency for those with high IQ's to attain better grade point averages.

Sometimes two items are related to each other, but in a *negative* direction. There is such an inverse, or negative, relationship between amounts of alcohol consumed and a test of balance (Figure 4.6). In this case a correlation of −.84 indicates strongly that the more alcohol one consumes the more poorly he is apt to score on the balance test.

If there is no correlation between two variables, the correlation coefficient approaches zero as shown in Figure 4.7.

There are other kinds of graphs, but these are the ones most commonly en-

---

[1]This can be calculated mathematically. There is only one line of best fit for a given set of points.

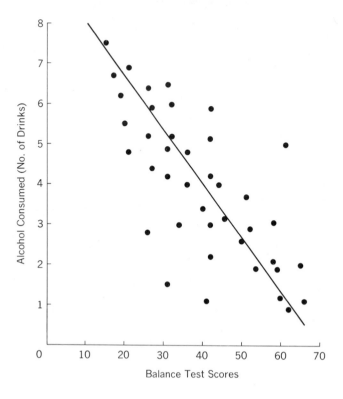

FIGURE 4.6 Hypothetical plot of scores on a balance test and amount of alcohol consumed. Line of best fit indicates a negative correlation.

countered. Sometimes a great many variables are all recorded on the same graph, so that considerable patience is required to determine exactly what is shown by the various curves. Interpretation of these more complex graphs is basically no different, however, from the interpretation of the simple ones just discussed; they merely require a little more study.

It should be pointed out that a high positive or negative correlation is not necessarily indicative of a cause-and-effect relationship. A correlation coefficient can be calculated or portrayed in a plot where two kinds of numerical scores are available, whether or not a real and practical relationship exists between the two measures. The clas-sic example goes something like this: There is a high correlation between the number of storks per month flying over a large city and the number of births per month; this obviously is coincidence, not cause and effect, and does not prove that storks do, after all, bring babies! It may also be that two factors *are* related, not just coincidentally, but from the experimental data we cannot establish which is "cause" and which "effect." Be careful to use some common sense in interpreting correlations.

CREATIVITY

It is our hope that you will have ample opportunity in your formal college

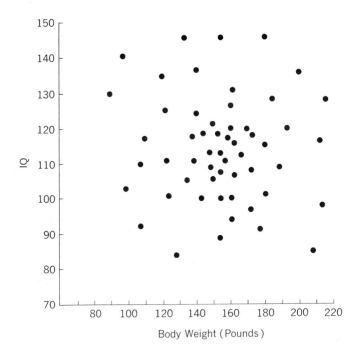

FIGURE 4.7 Hypothetical plot of IQ and body weight. No single line of best fit can be established; no relationship exists between the variables.

education to develop a creative, critical, and systematic approach to your profession. Given that opportunity, some will respond, some will not; some will become professionals, some will not. Of course it takes more than a knowledge of *how* to solve a problem *or how* to conduct an experiment or research project to be the complete professional. One must be alert to the subtle personal needs of the persons with whom one is dealing and to the program needs that *all too often are not very obvious.* One cannot assume that "no news is good news," that "no complaints from administration and no complaints from students" means that a program is sound and effective. This is where it takes a professional,

a dedicated person who can and *will* think critically, creatively, and systematically. In other words, one cannot sit back and wait to solve problems that are brought to him. He must, as often as possible, seek them out and initiate solutions before they become any more detrimental to the welfare of the people involved and to the ultimate success of the program. This is part of the "creativity" aspect of the professional's job and is, of course, *directly dependent upon his interest in his program and its participants.*

The concepts presented in this chapter lead logically to a discussion of health and well-being of the individual because the creative and systematic thinking is ultimately directed at im-

FIGURE 4.8 © 1968 United Feature Syndicate.

proving programs so as to promote and improve man's well-being. In the next chapter, we will discuss health and physical fitness concepts as one of the specific and common concerns of health education and recreation.

SUMMARY

The ability to think systematically, critically, and creatively distinguishes the professional from the technician. He can and should make intelligent decisions.

The professional must be alert to "silent" problems as well as those which have become obvious.

Use of appropriate bar and line graphs provides for better understanding of the data and their interpretation.

PRINCIPLES

1. The problem-solving or scientific method involves recognition and identification of the problem or question, formulation of a working hypothesis, testing the hypothesis, drawing conclusions and making some kind of decision.

2. There is a basic format for reporting research results which insures that the essential elements are covered and which also facilitates follow-up research by other investigators.

3. A positive or negative correlation or relationship which exists between two variables may mean one of three things:

a. Nothing—the numerical manipulation provides a high correlation but the basic assumption is in error and thus the correlation is meaningless (example: high correlation between physical fitness and height when sample included ages 6 through 17).

b. Relationship is meaningful but "cause and effect" is not established (example: high negative correlation between daily activity and degree of obesity in rats; which causes which?)

c. Relationship is meaningful and "cause and effect" has been established (example: follow-up study to one in (b.) alone indicates that rats forced to exercise daily do not become as obese as those forced to remain sedentary; thus inactivity apparently precedes obesity and not vice versa).

EXPERIMENTS AND EXPERIENCES

1. List some examples of variables which might be correlated but in a meaningless way.

2. Write up two research reports (one a survey, one an experiment) as follows:

    a. Identify a problem or question which interests you.

    b. State your working hypothesis.

    c. Describe the procedure in careful detail (as though you have carried out the study).

    d. Describe and graph three possible alternative results (two extremes and "nothing").

    e. Draw conclusions based on each of the three alternative results.

    f. Make a decision based on each alternative result.

3. Describe how you might apply the problem-solving method to a theoretical nonexperimental problem in physical education, health education, or recreation.

4. See how many examples of inappropriate use of statistics you can find.

5. Many of the experiments and experiences listed at the end of other chapters will also provide opportunity to develop the scientific, problem-solving techniques of inquiry.

SUGGESTED READING

Hanson, D. L., "Influence of Hawthorne Effect Upon Physical Education Research," *Research Quarterly*, 38:723, 1967.

Huff, D., *How To Lie With Statistics.* New York: W. W. Norton & Company, Inc., 1954.

Teraslinna, P., "On Publishable Research Articles," *Research Quarterly*, 38:154, 1967.

VanDalen, D. B., "Hypotheses and Deduced Consequences," *Research Quarterly*, 33:316, 1962.

Health
and Physical Fitness
Concepts

Chapter 5

In order to discuss *health* and *physical fitness,* the status of both, and the means of improving these qualities, we must come to some understanding of what these terms mean. We will operate on the basis of the following definitions, treating these qualities for the moment as though they were separate, distinct, and unrelated qualities (which, in reality, they are not). **Health** is generally taken to mean "freedom from defect and disease" or, in a more positive sense, "mental and physical well-being" or "soundness of body and mind." **Physical fitness**, although there are many and varied definitions, each with its own peculiar tangent, is generally taken to mean "the capacity to carry out physical tasks" (especially those tasks requiring considerable muscular effort, which tasks in turn require a well-conditioned neuro-skeleto-muscular system and/or circulo-respiratory system).

We will first take a look at our current health status, then discuss some misconceptions about physical fitness before analyzing current fitness status. We will then direct attention toward the theoretical relationship between health and physical fitness, the effects of regular exercise on health (longevity,

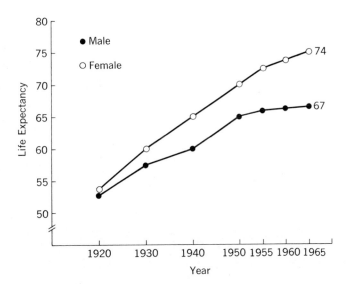

FIGURE 5.1 Life expectancy for men and women in the United States, 1920-1965. Adapted from *Statistical Abstract of the United States* (578).

CURRENT HEALTH STATUS

It is difficult to find incontrovertible evidence regarding the actual causes of gross population changes in health status. We can, however, identify relevant facts and figures. These data, coupled with discrete observations and new statistics presented from time to time, can aid in the process of deduction. You can then reach some logical conclusions of your own. These conclusions, in turn, can be interpreted in the light of health needs. Again, we have employed the problem-solving technique: the data are presented in simplified form, thus challenging you and allowing you to reach your own conclusion

resistance to infection, and so on), and, finally, will discuss health appraisal.

as to the meaning of each particular table or graph. Study each table and illustration carefully and ask yourself, "What does this imply?" You should be looking for answers to many questions: What are some of the most likely causes of our national health problems? Are automation and overmechanization involved? Do not expect simple answers; in some cases the evidence is conflicting. There are not enough pieces to complete most of these puzzles, but each piece of evidence presented does somehow fit into the larger puzzle; ultimately all conflicts will be explained on the basis of new and better studies. At present, these conflicts are actually good and essential: they promote further and more careful work that will lead to better answers. In some cases, you may be able to resolve and explain an apparent paradox. In any case, you will be armed with more information

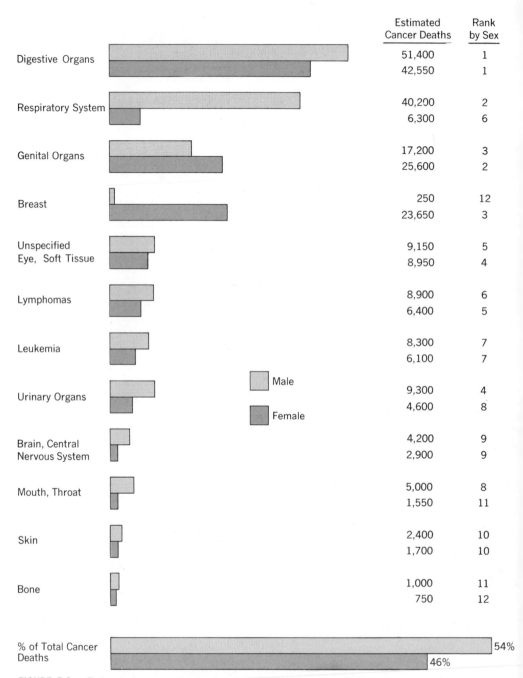

FIGURE 5.2 Estimated cancer deaths by site and sex, 1964, United States. Data from *Facts on the Major Killing and Crippling Diseases in the United States Today* (172).

with which you can better interpret current and future scientific developments as they are reported, and you should come to a better understanding of our current health status and how it can be improved.

TABLE 5.1   Selected Causes of Death in the United States, 1900-1965 (Deaths per 100, 000 Population)

CAUSE OF DEATH	1900	1910	1920	1930	1940	1950	1960	1965
Major cv—rª diseases	345	372	365	414	486	511	522	516
Heart	132	159	159	206	295	357	369	367
Arteriosclerotic heart disease	—	—	—	—	—	213	276	287
Cancer	63	76	83	97	120	140	149	154
Influenza and pneumonia	203	162	208	103	80	33	37	32
Diabetes	10	15	16	19	27	16	17	17
Cirrhosis of the liver	13	14	7	7	8	9	11	13
Ulcer	3	4	4	6	7	6	6	5
Tuberculosis	194	154	113	71	46	23	6	4
Bronchitis	46	23	13	4	3	2	2	3

ªCardiovascular-renal.
SOURCE: U.S. Bureau of the Census (578).

TABLE 5.2   Days of Disability Due to Chronic Disorders, per Year per 100,000 population, United States Average for 1958 and 1959

CAUSE	RESTRICTED ACTIVITY	RESTRICTED TO BED	WORK LOSS	SCHOOL LOSS
C-v	269	93	100	6
Digestive	115	42	75	3
Arth.-rheumatoid	141	36	46	0
Other	738	236	327	81

SOURCE: U.S. Bureau of the Census (578).

TABLE 5.3   Average Prevalence of Selected Chronic Conditions, Number per 1000 Population

CONDITION	1957-1959	1959-1961
Heart disease	29.5	30.2
High blood pressure	30.8	32.3
Ulcer	14.4	15.9
Arth.-rheumatoid	63.9	65.6

SOURCE: U.S. Bureau of the Census (578).

TABLE 5.4 Selective Service Statistics, Percent Rejected, World War I through 1965

	WW I	WW II	1950-56	1958	1960	1962	1963	1965
Rejected	21.3	35.8	33.5	41.9	44.8	49.8	50.0	44.0
Medical only	—	—	15.7	19.0	22.1	22.7	24.0	21.8
Mental only	—	—	13.6	18.0	18.8	21.5	21.6	18.6
Both	—	—	3.I	3.3	2.9	3.0	3.1	2.3

SOURCE: U.S. Bureau of the Census (578).

HEALTH KNOWLEDGE

No discussion of current health status would be complete without some consideration of what kind of knowledge our population has about matters of health. This leads us to consider the question of medical quackery and old wives' tales. To further acquaint you with the problems associated with the public's lack of health knowledge and wisdom, two excellent articles are reproduced here.

Health Education vs. Medical Quackery*

JAMES L. TRAWICK
DIRECTOR, DIVISION OF CONSUMER EDUCATION
BUREAU OF EDUCATION AND VOLUNTARY COMPLIANCE
FOOD AND DRUG ADMINISTRATION

Children learn at an early age that there is a certain amount of dishonesty and fraud in the business world. My 9-year-old son suffered a disappointment bordering on shock when he received a toy he had seen

*From the *Journal of Health, Physical Education and Recreation,* 36:28, 1965, by permission of the American Association for Health, Physical Education, and Recreation.

ballyhooed on television. The difference in what he had expected and what he actually got was remarkable indeed. That same youngster has now learned to be wary of the cereal box-top come-ons, after similar disappointments. Come to think of it, he is pretty sophisticated in his small world as a consumer.

Likewise, my teenage son has learned some lessons about gasoline additives to double your mileage and so-called high-powered spark plugs advertised to the high school set. When I was his age, I had no car, but I had freckles. Freckles were not as socially acceptable then as they are now, and I learned a few things about cosmetic advertising after spending several dollars on freckle cream.

If there is any bright side to this kind of experience, perhaps it is simply in the "once burned, twice shy" adage, since such experiences may help to immunize young people against the bigger—and more dangerous—types of fraud they will meet up with as they grow older.

In the health field, we call this kind of fraud and cheating "quackery." The definition is important because by today's usage, quackery refers not only to the quack practitioner but also to the worthless product and the fraudulent promotion.

It is not a life-or-death matter if the teenage debutante does not get the results she expects from a bust developer or an acne lotion, or if the tanning preparation used before the high school prom leaves her face covered with orange-red splotches a few days later. But it may be a life-or-death matter if a few years later that same young woman discovers a lump in her breast and decides to try out some quack remedy because she is afraid to tell her doctor about it.

The knowledge of how to seek competent medical advice in such a situation, how to evaluate labeling claims and advertising, books used in promotions, articles in magazines, claims of so-called health lecturers and of house-to-house peddlers, and radio and television promotions—such knowledge may in fact be the most important health education message that youngsters can be taught today. I am not going to presume to tell you as professional teachers how to do your job of teaching. But I think you will be interested in some of our material on the subject of health education as it relates to medical quackery.

These are true-life cases from FDA files. For example, consider the outer carton from a package of Nutri-Bio—a vitamin-mineral preparation containing a number of miscellaneous ingredients such as unsaturated fatty acids, bioflavonoid complex, alfalfa juice, and various minerals and trace elements. Back in 1961 and 1962 Nutri-Bio was promoted with labeling statements that "the American people are the most undernourished people in the world even though overfed" and that Nutri-Bio was of special dietary value because the ingredients were of natural or organic origin.

I mention this type of product first because nutritional quackery is an important subject for teachers, and yet a difficult one because of the well-known atrocious dietary habits of teenagers. This is complicated by the fact that children nowadays have been brought up on vitamins (it used to be cod liver oil) and many of us are conditioned to believe that supplementary vitamins and

minerals are an absolute must for everyone if he is to enjoy good health. This is not so!

The fact is that food faddism and nutritional quackery rank as the biggest racket in the health field today. This quackery thrives on the major themes of the food faddists—and the willingness of people to believe them. These are:

1. That all diseases are due to faulty diet;
2. That soil depletion and the use of chemical fertilizers cause malnutrition and poison our crops;
3. That modern methods of food processing and cooking have robbed our foods of their nutritional value; and
4. That anyone who has the "tired feeling" or an ache or a pain is probably suffering from a "sub-clinical deficiency" and needs to supplement his diet with some special concoction.

Nothing could be further from the truth. While there are, of course, special circumstances in which dietary supplementation is necessary, advice of a competent physician is needed to identify vitamin or mineral deficiencies and to prescribe their proper treatment.

The promotion of Nutri-Bio a few years ago provided a classic example of food faddism gone wild. More than 75,000 full and part-time sales agents were selling Nutri-Bio at $24.00 per packet for a six-months' supply for one person. The promotion involved one of the largest collections of pseudo-scientific literature and books ever assembled. Nutri-Bio was being recommended as the answer to practically all health problems—anemia, arthritis, cancer, diabetes, heart troubles, nervousness, and so on. It promised health, beauty, athletic ability, radiant living, and the capacity to stay young and vital. It was even recommended as a cure for juvenile delinquency. The sales distribution plan was based on a chain-letter type scheme and many people invested their life savings in it, lured by the prospect of quick riches.

When FDA moved in with a court action challenging the promotional claims being made for Nutri-Bio, about fifty tons of the false and misleading literature were turned in by agents at Chicago alone.

The point for those of us interested in consumer education is that foods from the supermarket or the corner grocery are the best source of our nutritional requirements, and there is much, much false information being spread about the alleged values of so-called natural or organic foods, trace elements and other mysterious ingredients. This information comes at us in books, magazines, syndicated medical columns in newspapers, radio and TV advertising and program content, and on labels and in various promotional literature. We must prepare our young people to defend themselves against such nutrition nonsense.

Illustrating another area of medical chicanery is one of the many forms of vibrating devices that have been popular in recent years, the Slenderoll device. This might have appealed to the over-weight teenage girl worried about her figure, because it was claimed to help reduce weight by a combination of massage and vibration. It has rather attractive and suggestive illustrations on its package, and states "Roll away ugly fat," "Ideal as a spot reducer," "Achieve a slimmer figure," and so on.

This device is worthless for these purposes. There is no device that will "spot reduce." The most one could hope to get from vibration and massage of this kind would be a pleasant sensation, perhaps with temporary relief of minor muscular aches and pains. But vibrator devices using this same principle have been sold in the form of hand units, pillows, chairs, and even mattresses —and sometimes with claims for the prevention and cure of serious ailments, including migraine headaches, heart and circulatory conditions, and defects of the bony structures.

The Abunda Beauty device is one that might have appealed to the self-conscious, flat-chested teenage girl worried because she did not fill out a sweater in the same proportions as some of her companions. The plastic cup was to be placed over the breast and the hose connected to the household water supply. Water swirling through a perforated disc in the base of the cup provided a massaging action that was supposed to help enlarge the breasts.

FDA charged in court that claims for this device were false, and the court ordered the company to stop the violation. The promoter was sentenced to serve 30 days, given a $500.00 fine and a one-year suspended jail sentence, and placed on five years' probation.

Some of the devices of this general type are quite capable of causing serious injury.

One of the problems that teachers—and all of us in the consumer education profession—are up against is that people nowadays are conditioned to believe in medical miracles. Some modern medical machines are truly miraculous and life-saving. The quack and the charlatan know this and take advantage of our interest and of the little bit of knowledge we do have. Electricity, magnetism, radiation—all are mysteries to most of us and we are setups for the glib-tongued promoters of even the most worthless gadgets claiming one or more of these properties, especially if they look impressive.

The devices I have demonstrated so far have been do-it-yourself types, but some are also designed for the quack practitioner. They are frequently put up in handsome console cabinets with knobs and dials and lights and electrodes for the patient to hold. Sometimes there is a wall chart to be consulted for diagnosis, using readings from the fake meters. They frequently are supposed to perform both diagnosis and treatment. The practitioner wears a white coat, has some impressive looking framed documents on the wall, and speaks about new scientific discoveries as if he knew what he was talking about.

I have brought one of these professional looking diagnostic-treatment devices with me to show you what they look like. This one is called the Ellis Micro-Dynameter. More than 5,000 of them were sold to practitioners throughout the country for as much as $875.00 each. It is basically a simple device for measuring minute electric currents. The patient was supposed to hold these electrodes and the machine was supposed to detect differences in electrical potential caused by disease. It was supposed to enable the practitioner to diagnose practically every kind of disease, as well as the general health of the patient.

The Federal Courts have ruled the Micro-Dynameter not only worthless but also unsafe for use even by a licensed practitioner, since it does not do what it claimed. FDA caused over a thousand of these machines to be recovered and destroyed.

So—what can we tell our students that will be helpful? Here are a few general guidelines. As for products, first learn the authoritative sources of information, as for example your family doctor, or the American Medical Association, or your state or county medical society; the national (or your city) Better Business Bureau; the voluntary health agencies in the field, such as the American Cancer Society and the Arthritis and Rheumatism Foundation; your city or state health department or food and drug law enforcement agency; and the Food and Drug Administration. Remember, too, that licenses and diplomas can be checked through your county or state medical society.

While these sources can be most helpful, one can determine for oneself simply by asking these questions:

1. Is the product claimed to involve a secret principle or formula or device that no one else has?
2. Does it promise a quick cure?
3. Is it advertised by case histories or testimonials?
4. Does the sponsor clamor for medical investigation or recognition?
5. Does the sponsor claim medical men are persecuting him or fear his competition?
6. Are the recognized treatments belittled?
7. Is it sold by "specialists"—or door-to-door peddlers?

If the answer to any of these questions is "yes"—be skeptical—investigate before you invest!

The Food and Drug Administration's experience in the investigation of medical quackery underlines some important points:

First, that medical problems can be extremely complex, and the layman can easily be mistaken about the value of a drug even when he is convinced by his own experience.

Second, that the annals of medicine are full of the unusual and the unexpected. Statistically the quack is bound to pick up a few cases now and then that make his treatment look miraculous. It takes the most expert medical knowledge to evaluate these properly.

Third, that the layman often aids and abets quackery by giving his testimonial for use in persuading others. He may lead his neighbor to disaster.

And, lastly, tomorrow's breadwinners, homemakers, and heads of families should be given as much knowledge as possible to help them make intelligent decisions in health matters.

Fortunately, today we have a new and stronger law to deal with worthless and falsely promoted drugs. But law enforcement alone cannot deal adequately with quackery. Quackery, of whatever kind, thrives on the combination of ignorance and fear. It uses misinformation to arouse false hope. Education is the greatest of all weapons against this evil.

Herein lies a golden opportunity, and a moral responsibility, for health education.

In summary, the following list of the ten most common types of quackery is presented. The list is not meant to imply that none of these diseases and problems can be improved or cured, but one should be cautious in accepting this kind of "help" from nonprofessional sources. Investigate carefully!

1. Magic weight reducing schemes (formulas, exercises, food supplements and pills, etc.)
2. Arthritis and rheumatism "easy" cures (from machines to so-called radioactive minerals)
3. Miracle cancer cures (from machines to drugs)
4. Beauty aids (especially for skin, hair removal, hair coloring, and mole removers)
5. Food fads and special supplements ("all ill health is related to diet")
6. Special cures for baldness
7. Alcoholism and smoking cures
8. Wanton use of hormones for various ills and deficiencies
9. Breast development drugs and schemes
10. Cures for tuberculosis, diabetes, influenza, kidney disease, and ulcers.

Too Much Health*
ARTHUR H. STEINHAUS, Ph.D.

FORMER DEAN, GEORGE WILLIAMS COLLEGE
CURRENTLY DISTINGUISHED RESEARCH PROFESSOR,
MICHIGAN STATE UNIVERSITY

---

*"Too Much Health," in *Toward an Understanding of Health and Physical Education.* Dubuque, Iowa: William C. Brown Company, 1963, pp. 336–339. By permission of the author.

Many a man both young and old,
Has gone to an early sarcophagus,
For pouring water icy cold
Down a hot esophagus.

Can you hear it sizzle? This one rhymes also: "Early to bed and early to rise, makes a man healthy, wealthy, and wise." Every family has its pet stock of health rules. Some are in blank verse: "Stuff a cold and starve a fever." Incidentally, this one suffered abbreviation with time. Originally it was: "If you stuff a cold, you will have to starve a fever." The shorter form, tho opposite in meaning, had the advantage of brevity. In fact, it makes little difference which one you follow. Both are false.

Too often health rules merely forced the prejudices of one generation on the next. About a generation ago such dogmatic rules began to lose their grip on us; so we turned to science for health facts. Now in place of one health rule, we have a score of statements claiming to be health facts. In a certain midwestern university (name withheld for ethical reasons) product "A" was experimentally proven to be superior for the relief of so-and-so. Conclusive scientific tests have shown that cigaret "Y" is less irritating to rabbits' eyes than all others. Are you bothered with skin blemishes? Take what Peter did and find yourself again successful on the dance floor. Deception in every breath, yet all so factual sounding that the average person is misled.

The era of health facts has brought us a confusion of claims made by manufacturers and advertising experts, all purporting to bring us health in return for a consideration. We are, therefore, being forced into the third era of health education. This is the era of "health reasons." We must learn to ask for the evidence back of a statement. We must develop a mental nose for distinguishing clean facts from moldy tradition and both from foul falsehood. What are some of the areas of greatest confusion?

Why must everybody eat spinach? Why, except to bring profits to some growers' association, is any one food worthy of universal consumption? The calcium in spinach is useless to man because with the oxalic acid also found in spinach it forms insoluble and, therefore, useless calcium oxalate. The phosphorus content is not important enough to warrant its listing with high phosphorus-bearing foods such as beans, lentils, brazil nuts, cheese, crabs, eggs, fish, liver, meat, and milk. As a source of iron it is no better than apricots, beans, beets, broccoli, eggs, heart, kidney, molasses, wheat, oysters, and many others. Yet how many protesting children have been stuffed with this unnecessary weed! Why must everybody drink orange juice when tomato juice and all fresh, green vegetables are good sources of vitamin C?

Is white bread harmful? Advocates of brown breads who answer yes are placed in a ridiculous position by the facts. In the milling of white flour much of the mineral and vitamin content of the wheat kernel is removed; but that does not convert what is left into a poison. The simultaneous consumption of vegetables and meats compensates for such shortages where laws ensuring the use of *reinforced* flour do not operate. Doubly swindled are those who decline white bread for the more righteous-appearing rye bread. Ordinary rye bread has had just as much of the mineral and vitamin values removed. There is no virtue in the dark hue of the rye kernel in spite of such ignorant jingles as, "the whiter the bread, the sooner you're dead."

Some decry eating proteins and carbohydrates at the same meal. To follow this most irrational edict literally would mean starvation. Milk, meat, potato, wheat, and almost every food found in nature is composed of varying amounts of proteins, carbohydrates, and fats. Separation is artificial.

Then there is the mother who returns from the lectures of some self-appointed apostle of natural living to run her home on a new dietary order that revels in celery, orange, carrot and prune juice, plus plenty of nuts and cooked vegetables — but no meat. A purely vegetarian diet if carefully selected will not harm, in fact it can sustain perfect health. Hinhede of Denmark reported keeping his gardener healthy for six months on a diet of potatoes, margarine, and water. Later it was found that the six months were not consecutive; but even if this had not been misleading reporting we could say it proved very little.

The meat interests of this country kept two ex-arctic explorers in perfect condition on a pure meat diet for an entire year. Among 158 outstanding Swiss athletes there was not a single vegetarian. In the midst of such conflict, what is the course of sanity? If we look into a man's mouth, we find sharp teeth for tearing, side by side with flat molars for grinding. The former belong to flesh eaters, the latter like those of the horse spell readiness for vegetables and other grasses. If we look to the digestive tract for advice, the answer is the same. In herbivores the digestive tube is almost endless (about 100 feet in sheep). In carnivores it is short (about 15 feet in the dog). Man's tract-length is intermediate (about 30 feet). Vegetables require a long time for digestion, hence a long tube, whereas meats are digested adequately in a much shorter tube. Our entire insides bear witness to the reasonableness of meat *and* potatoes.

From the senseless notions of diet quacks it is just one fool's length to the more dangerous pronouncements of the shysters who have made America bowel-conscious. One need but tune his radio to be persuaded during those critical after-breakfast moments of surer acting laxatives, of sweeter tasting ones, or of ones that are especially suited for persons, who already past 35 years, cannot be expected to withstand the more highly explosive charges contained in the ordinary kind. Some have names which sound more natural in reverse. Perhaps therein lies also a suggestion for their method of administration.

At the other end of the line are those who advocate the internal bath. Why not? How vivid the need of passing a quart and a half of cleansing water, with or without salt or soap, in thru the back door of the digestive tract. Such large quantities of water distend the bowels to proportions that make them insensitive subsequently to the pressure effect of the normal bowel content. There is also danger of driving the putrid fecal mass from the large intestine where its presence is harmless back into the small intestines where its absorption may injure health. These many "aids to nature" are, in fact, no kindness. A wiser course would be to lay off a day or two from incessant artificial stimulation to give nature a chance to catch up and strike her own pace under the influence of a sensible diet.

But to wait a day or two without a bowel movement seems criminal to the millions who, trembling under the threat of the poisons of auto-intoxication, nervously clock themselves to daily regularity. It may allay their ungrounded fears to know that the medical literature contains many instances of persons who live happily with weekly or semiweekly movements, while more rarely weeks transpire between bowel action.

What is the nature of this monster "auto-intoxication" who stalks the peace of mind of millions? In the first place, he is virtually nonexistent. There is no absorption of putrid poisons from constipated large intestines. What then is the cause of the headaches, the irritability, and the bleary eyes that in some people accompany constipa-

tion? When a balloon is inflated in a man's rectum or when a wad of cotton is inserted, he experiences all of the symptoms above described. It is all a reflex effect initiated by a distention of the rectum. Whether this distention is due to food residues or to a rubber balloon makes no difference in the symptoms. Their instantaneous disappearance when this pressure is reduced is further evidence of a reflex effect rather than a chemical poisoning, for how could poisons leave the body so promptly?

More or less regular bowel movements are still desirable; but it is no more necessary to worry about poisons. It is entirely safe in most instances to wait for water, applesauce, sauerkraut, and other bulky foods plus exercise to exert their effects in the way intended by nature long before the advent of lax-lax.

Strenuous exercise injures the heart. This is another absolutely groundless statement. From a study of hundreds of autopsy records, it is now possible to say that never has a *healthy* heart been damaged by exercise, no matter how strenuous. Even the rare cases of acute cardiac dilatation recover perfectly. Far different, of course, may be the fate of a previously diseased heart when it is subjected to the strain of exercise. The *athlete's heart* is superior in every way. With each beat it may expel twice as much blood as can the untrained heart. Consequently, it need not beat as frequently. The heart of Lash while running pumped so much blood that he was able to absorb over five quarts of oxygen per minute; the untrained individual does well to absorb about half this amount. That is why Lash was world's champion in the two-mile. Sudden cessation of training has never been shown to be harmful in spite of the scores of so-called authorities who claim the contrary. The enlarged heart of a highly trained athlete becomes smaller after the training season. Fatty degeneration of the heart has nothing to do with exercise or the lack of exercise. But when a man breaks training, he may suddenly return to his tobacco and other dissipations which do injure his health. This plus of deleterious habits is only fortuitously connected with the breaking of training and must not be confused with it. Many animals have been put in and out of training abruptly. Never has it harmed them to stop suddenly.

Is it O.K. to drink water with meals? Earlier views held that it was harmful because the stomach juices were thereby seriously diluted. Experimentation has proven that water is one of the best stimulators to stomach secretion. Digestion is improved. Shall athletes avoid candy and other sweets while in training? The answer is *no!* A diet rich in all kinds of carbohydrates is favorable to the economic operation of muscles. It does make sense to eat sweets in their natural form, such as honey, maple syrup and raisins, and this for two reasons. In their natural form sugars are accompanied by vitamins and minerals that assist their metabolism in the body. Also, the *by* taste in these natural forms tires one's taster so that there is less danger of overeating.

Is there any danger in eating at irregular times? The traditional three square meals a day is purely a matter of convenience. Much more sensible would it be to eat whenever we become hungry. For young children and certain adults five, six, or seven light meals per day would be more effective.

Never eat shrimp with strawberries, milk with fish, or starchy foods with acids. All such statements are groundless. Any foods that are enjoyed singly may also be taken in combination. Try it.

Another favorite among health barkers is *acid stomach,* to be cured by various expensive forms of baking soda, with or without bubbles. A stomach ulcer or even a tumor may be the cause, but more commonly it's excessive drinking, smoking or worry. Anger, anxiety and love all paralyze the stomach. The "nervous stomach" is also a by-product of every national crisis, a big football game, or a family quarrel.

But it has nothing to do with *acidosis,* which is a much rarer condition of the blood caused by faulty body chemistry, as in diabetes.

Don't try to correct your "acid stomach" by avoiding foods which taste sour. In fact, acid fruits actually contain so much sodium that their end effect in the body is to alkalinize it. Starches and fats also cannot contribute to acidosis. Proteins, whether of plant or animal origin, may; but this is entirely harmless. It would be better if you never thought about acidosis—you probably don't have it and worrying about it may give you *heart burn.*

Have we too much health? We certainly have too much talk about it. I dare say many Americans really have no idea how they themselves, alone and unassisted, really feel. How can they know? They barge into the new day under the stimulation of caffeine-laden java. Soon they deaden their jangled nerves with nicotine. From half past afternoon until late at night their irritated minds find solace in alcohol. At headache time an aspirin gives them escape. Bubbling alkalizers remove yesterday's brown taste to make room for today's.

If foodless and matchless, John Doe would some day walk thru the woods, upon tiring sit by a stream to straighten out his cockeyed thinking, then when hungry pass up hamburger stands and taverns and turn homeward to a plain wholesome dinner, and after helping with the dishes, play with the kids or otherwise occupy himself with socially constructive work, he might be surprised with himself. It might take several days, but eventually he would find that it feels good to be John Doe with a clean mouth and lungs, to be John Doe without war news of stomach versus in-testines, to be John Doe with mind and emotions at peace with the world. To be John Doe, alive and healthy, uncramped by artificial aids, would give him a feeling as priceless as it is costless.

SUMMARY: CURRENT HEALTH STATUS

Study the tables and articles carefully. Are the facts and statistics worthy of national concern? Are there technical explanations that eliminate any real health implications? For example, what factors complicate the statistics on in-crease in heart disease deaths, or cancer deaths from 1900 to 1965? It should be obvious that the facts and statistics we have cited cannot, alone, give us ab-solute answers, but with the proper analysis they can indicate certain trends in health status. Important questions can be asked. For example, with im-proved diagnostic and therapeutic methods, why has heart disease stead-ily increased since 1900? Unless there has been a radical change in autopsy technique and the mechanics of report-ing the cause of death such that simply *more* deaths formerly attributed to other causes have progressively been reported as due to heart disease, then this increase in coronary deaths must be carefully and methodically studied and researched. Thus, one can see that the constant analysis of health sta-tistics and surveys is an important and vital step in man's battle with and pre-vention of the degenerative diseases.

More important, such statistics help us to see that, in spite of improved medical techniques and medicines, the health status of our citizens is not improving. The picture is certainly not as rosy as we would like it to be, and because much of our poor health is preventable, it is a legitimate cause for concern; the statistics certainly have important implications for the need for better health education. Physical educators and recreation personnel must also stand ready to prepare them-selves to more effectively play their roles in the drive to improve our na-tional health status. To many of you it may not be clear what these roles are or how important they are; you must have an adequate foundation upon which your understanding of these roles may be built (and that is one of the major purposes of this book). Make no mis-take about it; once you *have* this foun-dation, if you are a professional, your role and its importance will become clear!

PHYSICAL FITNESS

MISCONCEPTIONS AND THE DISTINCTION BETWEEN PHYSICAL FITNESS AND MOTOR ABILITY

The term *physical fitness* is included in many familiar test batteries commonly used in the schools. In many cases, the inclusion of *fitness* in such titles is a most unfortunate error and one that logically could account, at least in part, for the current apathy of some people toward total personal physical fitness. This is not an indictment of "physical fitness" test batteries. Most of the bat-teries are excellent and include tests that do have some definite value, but it is our feeling that many of the tests in these batteries are *not* actually tests of physical fitness. Misconceptions, then, can result from inappropriate names of the test batteries or from failure to educate those tested as to the *meaning* of each individual test in the battery. It has not usually been made clear to those tested which individual tests are truly measures of physical fitness and which are more appropriately measures of ability and skill.

To clarify the point, we shall point out how this kind of misconception might grow, especially at the elementary school ages. Imagine two youngsters, a boy and a girl, who are both a little taller, heavier, and less active than the other children and who do not score well on a sixth-grade "physical fitness" test battery that includes push-ups, pull-ups, sit-ups, and agility run, and the sixty-yard dash. They are especially "low" in agility and speed. At this age, they certainly are not capable of understanding the meaning of such tests without help from their teacher. They do understand, however, that they are below the class and national average on the total score for the battery. They are told to work hard to improve! In each subsequent year, they fail to reach "average" for their particular sex and age group, primarily because they are still "slow of foot" and poor in agility. By the time they graduate from high school, both may be firmly convinced that, because they have never "measured up" on "physical fitness" tests, they are not really capable of being "physically fit." A different name for the battery of tests

and perhaps a careful lesson or two on the actual meaning of each of the tests might prevent such an attitude.

Below-par performance on standardized tests, especially on such items as speed and agility, is not necessarily indicative of poor physical fitness. If total fitness is an individual matter, then physical fitness tests are more relative than absolute, and *there is no such thing as a reasonably healthy person who cannot improve his physical fitness level.* Is it necessary that someone be able to run fast or that he be very agile to be physically fit? Even if one successfully argues that speed and agility are essential for some professional athletes, how can we set these same standards for everyone if fitness is indeed personal and based, at least to some extent, on an individual's capacity?

Part of this misconception about physical fitness may stem from the lack of agreement among experts as to exactly what elements constitute physical fitness. We propose that it is realistic to place the common test parameters or measures into two basic categories: (1) physical fitness parameters (those that are actually essential for health and physical fitness as defined on page 99 and (2) motor performance parameters (see Figure 5.3). Although this categorization admittedly applies only to the man or woman in the more *typical* vocations, it certainly applies to the great *majority* of children and early teenagers. The line separating these categories is often very fine, and for a given person in a particular job some of the motor performance parameters may of necessity have to be placed

HEALTH AND FITNESS
PARAMETERS

MOTOR PERFORMANCE
PARAMETERS

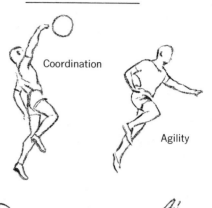

Coordination

Agility

Circulo-respiratory
Capacity

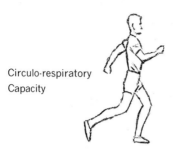

Flexibility

Power

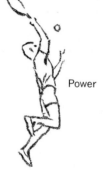

Balance

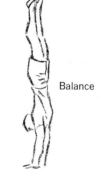

Muscular Endurance

Strength

Reaction
Time

Speed

in the physical fitness category because they relate to his health and well-being.

One should also consider the point of view supported by Yost (623) and others: many accidents "can be prevented through possession of the qualities which describe the totally fit individual." One of these qualities is physical fitness, and since better agility, speed, reaction time, and coordination might better prepare a person to avoid certain kinds of accidents, some would include these qualities as physical fitness elements rather than separate them out and label them primarily motor ability elements as we have done. This is a theoretical issue but is of considerable importance. Our position is that we should certainly strive to promote attainment of higher levels of general motor ability for better skill performance and for the sake of safety, but that, since it is highly questionable whether these general traits can be significantly improved, they should not be labeled physical fitness elements. This is in keeping with our contention that any reasonably healthy person can make dramatic and significant gains in physical fitness level if the effort is made. At any rate, it is certainly *imperative that each person understand exactly what each of these qualities is*. This understanding might very well be the basis for acceptance of a sound personal health and fitness concept. It is also important that a fully educated person know whether

and why each parameter is necessary for optimal physical fitness. Some of the subsequent chapters of this book are devoted to this end.

PHYSICAL FITNESS PARAMETERS

Circulo-Respiratory Capacity

This parameter, **circulo-respiratory (CR) capacity,** is more commonly called circulatory or circulo-respiratory fitness, which allows the individual to persist in strenuous tasks for periods of some length. The limit of persistence in such tasks is determined primarily by the functional capacity of the CR systems, and is specific to the various kinds of tasks and the work intensities. It is difficult to measure CR capacity with great precision because of the obvious importance of motivational factors involved in "quitting" a strenuous task. There are, however, objective ways of measuring this quality, methods that minimize the individual's subjective decision as to when to "quit." Standardized bench-stepping tests are often used as a measure of CR capacity (see page 210).

The important point in this particular discussion is that CR capacity is important in health and fitness. Nearly all people with a normal systemic health base, and even many without, can dramatically improve CR capacity with a reasonable amount of energy expenditure. As surprising as it may seem, even cardiac patients can make dramatic gains in CR capacity through appropriate exercise programs. The degree of

FIGURE 5.3   Distinction between health and fitness parameters and motor ability parameters.

desired attainment should be based on the individual's needs and his systemic health base. As discussed in Chapter 8, improved CR capacity may also be an important factor in the *maintenance* of the systemic health base by means of helping to prevent degenerative changes in the heart and circulatory system.

Muscular Endurance

Muscular endurance is sometimes erroneously referred to as "strength." This quality, hereafter called ME, involves the capacity to persist in localized muscular effort. The physiological limit for this functional quality is apparently localized in the muscle group itself and is not determined primarily by the failure of the CR systems to supply oxygen. Again, the need for this quality is specific to the individual. It is not possible to measure ME with great precision because of the same problem associated with measures of CR capacity: the motivational factors involved in "quitting."

It is not difficult to evaluate muscular endurance grossly, however. This quality is commonly measured by such standard tests as pull-ups, sit-ups, and push-ups. It is obvious that there are other muscle groups of importance and that a high degree of attainment in these typical tests is not necessary for every person. It is apparent that certain levels of muscular endurance are needed, and that this is another quality that must be included if *optimal* physical fitness is to be achieved. Important and specific relationships of ME

to health and fitness are discussed elsewhere in this chapter.

Flexibility

Flexibility is a component of physical fitness that pertains to the functional capacity of the joints to move through a normal range of motion. It involves the muscular system as well as the bones and joints; lack of adequate flexibility has often been linked with low back pain as well as with muscle and joint injuries. It is commonly measured by such tests as toe touching and back curls, but these typical tests assess the range of motion in certain specific joints only. As with CR capacity and ME, this quality can be strikingly improved in the person with an adequate systemic health base. There have been some claims that lack of range of motion is causally related to subsequent development of rheumatoid arthritis. Although the two are obviously related once the disease has set in, there appears to be no scientific foundation to support the contention that lack of flexibility actually causes this arthritic condition.

Muscular Strength

In discussing **strength,** it is important that we recognize two current misconceptions about this common term. First, strength is not necessarily synonymous with the size or the so-called definition of the muscles, although there is little question that people with large and well-defined muscles are usually physically strong. The emphasis in health and fitness is not on "looks," but functional capacity and individual needs. Second, strength is quite often confused with muscular endurance (see Chapter 9). The measure of true strength is the maximal amount of force that a muscle or muscle group can exert. It is not properly measured by determining the maximum number of repetitions of a certain activity, such as push-ups or sit-ups; for example, the strength of a beam in a house is not measured by how long it stands but rather by how much weight it can support, although we might expect these two characteristics to be related.

Maximal strength is evaluated by determining the maximal one-effort force. "If" and "why" we need strength will be discussed subsequently. It will suffice now to say that a minimal level of strength is obviously necessary; without it, one cannot function or even move about normally. Strength gains, for most persons with a normal systemic health base, can be dramatic.

MOTOR PERFORMANCE PARAMETERS

Coordination

Coordination is probably the common denominator of all motor performance parameters. It involves the nervous system and the skeletal-muscular system and may be defined as the "smooth flow of movement in the execution of a motor task." We would be hard pressed to argue that minimal, general coordination is not required by everyone. But beyond a minimal, "normal" level of

coordination—and this argument holds for all the remaining motor performance parameters—we maintain that, for most people, *a gain in this quality is not essential for improving health.* There are exceptions to this. A football player's health, for example, depends partly on his coordination: he may be physically injured unless he has *better*-than-average motor coordination. But most people, provided they have just minimal coordination, can *improve* their physical fitness level tremendously without improvement in coordination. It should be noted that we are speaking here of the gross motor coordination involved in large-muscle skills, such as walking, and not of the fine, "microscopic" coordination that may well account for gains in strength and muscular endurance. Certainly an improvement in the coordination of shoveling dirt or snow would improve the efficiency of that task and make the weekend yard job easier, but our argument is that improved levels of coordination are not *required* for physical fitness gains.

Balance

The complex quality called **balance** is actually a specific kind of coordination involving reflexes, vision, the "inner ear," the cerebellum, and the skeletal-muscular system. Static balance involves equilibrium in one fixed position, whereas dynamic balance refers to the maintenance of equilibrium while moving. Common tests involve the use of the balance beam, various ways of standing on one foot with eyes open or closed, the use of electronic devices for measuring "sway," and so on. We maintain that for the average person little or no improvement beyond "normal" balance is needed for gains in physical fitness.

Power

Power involves one of the basic fitness parameters—strength—but adds another factor—speed of contraction (see page 263). It is measured and exemplified by activities or movements of an "explosive" nature, such as the vertical jump, the shot-put, the ball-throw for distance, and the "leap" of the dancer. Power is certainly a necessity for most athletic activities if the performer is to "survive" and excel in his particular sport. To enjoy successful participation in recreational games, such as badminton, tennis, handball, softball and golf, it is normally desirable to have some of this "power." Except for some sports skills and possibly some home-centered work activities, it is conceivable that a person *can* improve his physical fitness level without increasing his power. Obviously, many occupations require "power" of some sort; for the people in these jobs, this item should be placed in the list of health and physical fitness parameters.

Agility

Agility is generally defined as "the ability to change directions quickly and effectively while moving as nearly as possible at full speed." In ballet, modern dancing, and some folk danc-

ing, agility also means a quick and efficient upward or downward move. This quality may be essential to success in certain sports but hardly needs to be developed to a *high* degree by most persons, who do not participate in contemporary dance or in high-agility sports, or by one who participates only for "recreation." Such an individual can develop a high level of physical fitness—based on individual needs and interests—assuming only minimal agility. The common tests of this parameter involve such tasks as the zigzag run for time through a maze of obstacles (see page 306).

Speed

Speed of specific and localized movement, more properly called movement time, has been discussed under "Power." What we commonly refer to as **speed** is the kind measured by *total* body movement from one place to another, usually at least for a distance of fifty yards. The relative need for this quality is rather obvious: some need it, but most people do not. For them it is not a requisite for the optimal level of physical fitness.

Reaction Time

Reaction time is the length of time required to *initiate* a response to a specific stimulus. It is essential for the good shortstop in baseball, the football lineman, the wrestler, the fencer, and so on. It is also critical to the girl who suddenly looks up to find herself under a falling brick! Normal levels are certainly important, but beyond this, one need not develop extremely fast reaction times to become healthier and more physically fit.

SUMMARY: THE DISTINCTION BETWEEN PHYSICAL FITNESS AND MOTOR ABILITY

In order to clarify our viewpoint concerning the difference between physical fitness and motor ability, the following points are offered in summary:

1. Only qualities essential to health and/or work capacity should be classified as components of physical fitness.
2. Qualities primarily essential to skill and motor performance, and not to health, should not be classified as physical fitness components but, rather, as motor performance or motor ability qualities.
3. Physical fitness components, then, are CR capacity, muscular endurance, flexibility, and strength.
4. Motor performance components are coordination (their common denominator), agility, speed, power, balance, and reaction time.
5. For a given *individual,* the above categorization may not hold true.

CURRENT LEVEL OF PHYSICAL FITNESS IN THE UNITED STATES

RESEARCH EVIDENCE

Limited data are available on physical fitness levels of children and adults in the United States. Tabular data of these kinds are meaningful only to the extent they make one aware of conditions that call for attention. Is physical fitness a national concern today? It is our belief that physical fitness is most properly a personal matter; however, population averages and statistics, along with experimental data, may help you as a professional to reach a decision about general physical fitness status. A sampling of the applicable evidence is presented here. No attempt has been made to slant the evidence or its implications; evidence is presented in a straightforward and simplified manner, much of it in the form of simple tables or graphs. In short, this is a problem-solving chapter. You can draw your own conclusions for each exhibit and, if you wish, read further by going to the references cited.

Obviously an exhaustive presentation of all pertinent data is impossible. Additional current information is readily available to the interested student and should be secured in order to substantiate or contradict conclusions based on the evidence presented here.

The alert reader will find newspapers and news magazines as well as professional journals valuable sources of recent scientific information.

The results of any *single* study, no matter how impressive, should seldom if ever be accepted as conclusive. One should also exercise caution in the evaluation of studies of large populations over which there was no effective control. The results of such "population studies" may or may not apply to other populations at another time or in another place.

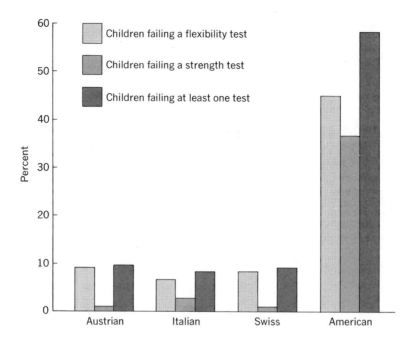

FIGURE 5.4   Comparison of European and American children on the Kraus-Weber Minimum Muscular Fitness Test (measures of minimal strength and flexibility). Adapted from Kraus and Hirschland (325).

Figures 5.4 and 5.5 portray the results of studies comparing the fitness of youth in the United States with other countries. In addition, Knuttgen (316) reported in 1961 that 70 percent of the Danish school boys' scores and 86 percent of the girls' scores exceeded the American mean scores on the AAHPER Youth Fitness Test. Ikeda (263) reported in 1962 that Tokyo children scored better than Iowan (U.S.A.) children in pull-ups (boys), bent-arm hang (girls) and the grasshopper (a test of endurance) while the Iowan children scored better in sit-ups. Sloan (524) tested a limited number of college students (sample size ranging from fourteen to twenty-eight per group and not randomly selected) and found that the English men and women physical education majors he tested had significantly higher mean fitness indexes than their counterparts in a North Carolina university (as did the English sophomore nonmajor men and women when compared with their North Carolina counterparts). South African male physical education majors were also significantly superior to their counterparts at the North Carolina university.

A comparison of the muscular and CR endurance tests of the AAHPER battery in 1958 and 1965 is presented in Figure 5.6.

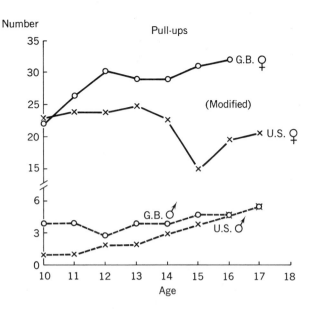

FIGURE 5.5 Comparison of boys and girls in Great Britain (GB) and the United States (US) on the AAHPER Fitness Test items that measure muscular and circulo-respiratory endurance. By permission from Campbell and Pohndorf (93).

Isolated bits of information also provide some insight. Cooper (124) recently reported that of 3544 men between the ages of 17 and 35 (mean age was 24.3 years), only 27 percent could cover 1.5 miles within twelve minutes. This figure was increased to 70 percent after six to thirteen weeks of a regular, progressive exercise program. In a 1953 study at a large Eastern university only 53 percent of 132 male college students tested could climb to the top of a twenty-foot rope, and 11 percent could not even get off the floor. In another study in 1962 (549) only 28 percent of 28 tested could make it to the top (14 percent could not get off the floor).

PERSONAL OPINION AND OPINION BASED ON FACT

In order to objectively survey the fitness status of our country, we should also like to expose you to information other than the graphs and statistics just presented. We are presenting several articles that seem appropriate. Some are not favorable to physical fitness in that they question the importance of the *stress* placed on physical fitness; all include pertinent facts and ideas that are worthy of your consideration in the process of taking a thorough look at the status of physical fitness in this country.

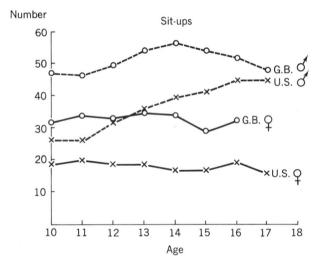

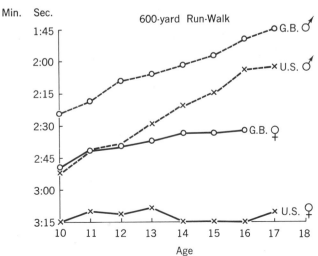

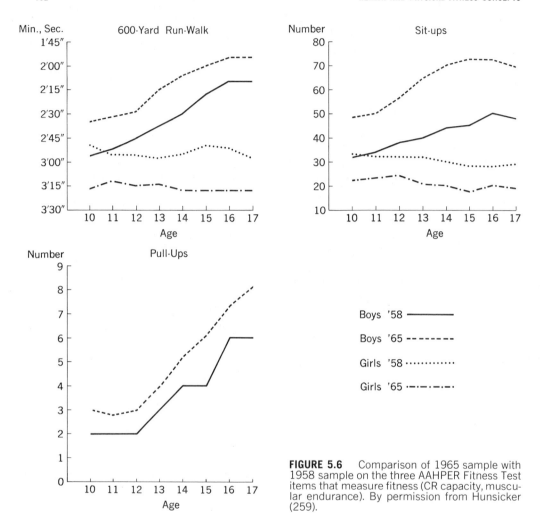

FIGURE 5.6 Comparison of 1965 sample with 1958 sample on the three AAHPER Fitness Test items that measure fitness (CR capacity, muscular endurance). By permission from Hunsicker (259).

In reading these articles, you should be alert to:

1. Confusion of terms basic to the issue; for example, *athletics* and *physical fitness* used as synonyms
2. Tongue-in-cheek expressions of opinion that may actually be attempts at "reverse psychology"

3. The use of satire, humor, dramatic appeals, isolated cases, and so on, to distract from and gloss over the facts

4. False statements, statements out of context, omission of facts, half-truths, and "stretching" and misinterpreting facts, and the clever and deliberate confusion of fact with opinion

FIGURE 5.7   "There's nothing wrong with our fitness, Gramps. We're just tired."

Fits Over Fitness*

GEORGE A. SILVER, M.D.
CHIEF OF THE DIVISION OF SOCIAL MEDICINE
MONTEFIORE HOSPITAL, NEW YORK

There is a wild and rather high-pitched call for more muscle as the prime need of Americans. Sandwiched between dire warnings of the Communist menace, democracy's difficulties in Africa and Asia and the need for protection against nuclear holocausts, are constant pleas for developing the American biceps. To this end, the American Association for Health, Physical Education and Recreation has been set up as a department of the National Education Association; the American Medical Association has appointed a consultant body on physical fitness; there is the President's Council on Youth Fitness, which runs frequent advertisements in the daily press (complete with flags) with the help of the Advertising Council and the Newspaper Advertising Executive Association.

The advertisements urge parents to invade the next P.T.A. meeting to press for the adoption of vigorous school programs to improve physical development. Our children are weak and helpless, it is said; we are falling behind the Europeans, the Japanese, even the aboriginal Australians, in physical condition. Get off your backsides, spectators! Exercise! Get into active sports! Build up your body! Prepare yourself!

For what?

This cogent question is never answered. Implicit is the assumption that physical fitness (which we apparently lack) is a vital link in the defense of America. For want of

*"Fits Over Fitness," *The Nation,* June 9, 1962, p. 515. (Reprinted by permission of the publisher).

it, Democracy will crumble and our lives will be shortened, sickly, depressed.

What is physical fitness? What is its relation to health? What is health? Is participation in athletics an aspect of physical fitness? Does one have to perform physical activity of a regular kind in order to be physically fit? Are athletes healthier than non-athletes? Are we really below par physically, as a nation?

The National Education Association reported that the physical condition of American youth is a "real cause for national alarm." The statement derives from a number of findings. For example, Hans Kraus, who invented the term "hypokinetic disease," gave European and American children a group of tests for muscular fitness. Only about 10 percent of the European kids failed to pass all these tests, whereas 100 percent of American kids failed. In one test, fewer than 2 percent of European children failed, while over 35 percent of American children failed. (For the benefit of those seeking black marks against their public-school system, it should be pointed out that the American private-school children approximated the European school children in their performance.) In another instance, tests showed that arm strength for Japanese girls was 18–47 percent greater than that of our girls.

To the viewers with alarm, this is incontrovertible evidence of muscular incompetence.

There are gloomy correlates. Jerry Morris, an English epidemiologist, has shown that heavy workers have a lower death rate than light workers, and that coronary disease is twice as frequent among sedentary as among active workers. Everyone knows how sedentary we are today. Some psychiatrically-oriented muscular apologists have concluded that the combination of neurosis and muscular deficiency produces painful tension symptoms like low-back

pain, lumbago and even tension headaches. At West Point, Appleton showed that of the cadets discharged for psychiatric causes, an undue number had scored low in their entrance physical-aptitude tests.

And, of course, the gloomiest statistics of all are from Selective Service. Of 3.7 million men under twenty-six who were examined for the draft, 1.7 million were rejected as physically unfit for fighting.

Most often named as the causative element of declining physical efficiency of the American people is the "civilization" package: automobiles, television, progressive education. It is noteworthy that when Brig. Gen. S. L. A. Marshall testified before a Congressional committee, defending our youth against attack as weaker than their soldier ancestors at Gettysburg or the Alamo, he was forced to admit that "We're a nation that has become flabby in the legs. The automobile has done this to us. As the legs grow weaker," he added ominously, "we lose a certain amount of our 'moxie.'"

The power package that is supposed to put us back in the running as healthy muscular models for the world includes daily exercise and lots of competitive sports.

The emphasis on active sports has no real relevance. Men with very seriously impaired health have been known to be excellent athletes: I give you the number of diabetic tennis stars in the American Davis Cup Team as an example. And a study of Air Force cadets revealed that those who had recently been discharged from hospital for various upper-respiratory diseases did better in physical-fitness tests than enlisted men in good health who had not been in hospital. Jokl, another writer in this field, noted: "Few erroneous ideas are so deeply rooted among the public as that of physical training promoting health. Physical training is a procedure capable of improving efficiency, but incapable of improving health." The case of a champion sprinter who developed tuberculosis two months after winning the championship, and died less than a year later, is good evidence that ability to perform outstandingly in athletics is no indication of health.

A well-developed body does not mean health. An appalling number of psychoneurotic and psychotic individuals have sound bodies. One might ponder the mental health of some of the characters who decorate the books and magazines on muscular development, or some of those you see sunning themselves and developing their muscles in the various beaches and gymnasiums of the American scene.

Physical fitness does not provide immunity to disease. In epidemic times, the physically fit are stricken as often as those who aren't. (Physical fitness certainly does not seem to protect against venereal disease.) It is argued that children who are physically fit, and take regular gym exercise, show a better attendance record in school. I doubt if it means that they are healthier. It may simply mean that children who compete in school athletics may be a little more reluctant to absent themselves or to report sickness. In any case, the relevant statistics are contradictory. In some states where data are available, the incidence of illness among school athletes is exactly the same as among non-athletes.

Last winter the papers reported the death of a fifty-year-old man after taking a swim in the icy waters of the Charles River in Boston. As a member of the local Polar Bears Club, he had been chopping into the ice and jumping into the water every year along with his fellows. Presumably, his fellows will now be discouraged from these activities, but I doubt it. Newspapers constantly report the coronaries that follow upon snow shoveling, tennis matches and quick games of touch football in which some of our older citizens seem to feel that

it is necessary to engage in order to demonstrate their physical fitness. Health departments have taken to publishing warnings to the citizenry in winter *not* to shovel snow. (Hire those weak high school kids!)

And as a final note, before we go on to a consideration of what this all may mean, it should be pointed out that although a third or more of the young people who came up for Selective Service were rejected as physically unfit for military duty; this doesn't necessarily mean that they were physically unfit in the generally accepted sense. It means that they had visual defects, or defects of hearing, or hernias (and I am not sure that exercise is a modern treatment for hernia) or some defect due to poliomyelitis or congenital absence of a muscle, or shortness of a leg or arm—none of which is curable by exercise and none of which unsuits them for normal life.

It is difficult to take issue with the laudable objective of most of the physical-fitness proponents, but some sense needs to be put into their data. Peter Karpovich, one of the saner advocates of physical fitness and currently president of the American College of Sports Medicine, has written, "There are two main stumbling blocks to the definition of physical fitness: one, the relation of physical fitness to health; and the other, the consideration of what constitutes a physical-fitness test." Karpovich goes on to say that physical fitness is a "fitness to perform some specified task requiring muscular effort."

This definition gets us somewhere. Karpovich very sensibly notes, "The ideal goal is to be sufficiently fit to accomplish each day's work with a minimum of fatigue and to remain active to a good old age." If you need soldiers, then they should be able to crawl under barbed wire and climb mountains and do all the various things that soldiers have to do under difficult field conditions. Certainly a much greater degree of muscular competence is required of them than of the writer of this article, who needs a degree of muscular activity sufficient only to hold down the button on the dictating machine.

What do we learn from all this? I would say that a great deal of the energy that is being spent on physical-fitness programs is really designed to improve the condition of the experts and the specialists in the field rather than of the citizenry. I have no doubt that after an individual takes moderate exercise of one kind or another, he feels better and possibly sleeps better. This feeling of well-being should be encouraged. Given the fact that different individuals have a different inheritance of muscular ability and different degrees of muscular coordination, different kinds or amounts of exercise are desirable. There is no such thing as a physical-fitness program applicable to everyone. For many individuals, their normal daily activities may be quite adequate.

There is no evidence that without some type of organized athletic activity or physical-education program, people will be unhealthy or die young or be unprepared to carry on their life work satisfactorily. Equally, there is no evidence that a physical-fitness program will protect against illness or against sudden death. This kind of reckless propagandizing and pamphleteering should be discouraged.

A great deal of scientific investigation remains to be done on the effect that muscular exercise—including athletics—has on the human body. Some of this is now being carried on, particularly in England, and *The Journal of Applied Physiology* makes information on the subject available. The best measures of physical fitness today relate to capacity to do work. Oxygen utilization as a measure of physiologic efficiency is widely accepted as significant, and there seems to be some evidence that short periods of training, with not too severe physical

activity over a period of time, will improve the rate of oxygen consumption.

The British investigators tend to be critical of the classical tests of physical fitness because the training is not comparable to what is done in life. There is no relationship between various muscular tests used and the actual physical-fitness training programs. Furthermore, most of the statistics now in vogue have been derived without control groups, from small numbers, and under such conditions that the numbers themselves must be seriously questioned. Among the research programs that should be carried out are those that would help to define "training" and "exercise." Do these mean a season of athletics each year for every individual, and if so until what age? Do they mean playing tennis or handball or some comparable sport daily? Further research is needed to determine what is meant by *keeping* physically fit. How long do you have to take exercise, over what period of time, and what happens after you quit, in this business of staying fit?

I suspect that in addition to this research, there ought to be some exposure of the quacks in the field who are milking Americans of huge sums of money for exercise courses, posture and exercise classes and devices supposed to improve muscular efficiency.

We might also debunk the theoretical substructure relating to the inactivity of the mass of Americans—these car-riding, television-viewing, inactive blobs of fat and jelly. It should be pointed out that more sports equipment is being sold today than ever before: there are more swimming pools, more basketball courts, more gymnasiums and swimming pools in the public schools, and more people participating in sports than ever before in our history. If anything, it is not cars and TV, but the social conditioning separating the rich from the poor, the minorities from the majority, that tends to hold down the number of sports participants.

If there is such a thing as physical fitness, it isn't related directly to muscular competence, but rather to the ability to carry on one's life work competently and with personal satisfaction. Sports should be engaged in for the pleasure they give—not as strenuous competitive efforts to "keep fit"—and with a judicious eye toward reducing the strenuousness as we grow older. Moderation, please! And paradoxically, perhaps the more sedentary one's occupation, the *less energetic* should be the exercise one takes. As the playgrounds and swimming pools are opened to all, including the slum children and the Negroes, the natural activity available may be all any of us need—except for an occasional Peace Walk or Freedom Ride.

Rx for Health: Exercise*

PAUL DUDLEY WHITE, M.D.
BOSTON CARDIOLOGIST AND
PHYSICIAN TO FORMER PRESIDENT EISENHOWER

By many physicians, especially by those of us who are interested in physiology and health as well as in disease, physical exercise is considered to be just as essential for the best health as are rest and sleep, food, one's job, recreation and peace of mind. Sometimes, however, one hears remarks, usually made by those habituated to a very sedentary life and to more or less obesity, that one can live quite happily and healthily to a ripe old age without taking any exercise at all. It is true that adequate statistics on this point about exercise seem to be lacking, although life insurance and other figures clearly indicate the harmful

---

*"Rx for Health: Exercise," *New York Times Magazine,* June 23, 1957, p. 9. © 1957 by The New York Times Company. Reprinted by permission.

effect of obesity both on health and longevity. Some fat people do exercise a lot but most do not, and it is unusual for an athlete who continues to exercise vigorously to become very fat.

Despite our unsatisfactory knowledge about the possible beneficial effects of exercise on longevity and on health, we do know of certain advantages of exercise which are not always adequately appreciated, and it is on these that I would like to comment briefly.

It may be said, however, at the outset that several follow-up studies have shown that vigorous exercise in youth, and later in life, too, in healthy individuals does not cause harm, barring accidents, or shorten life. A book entitled "University Oars" written by John Morgan, a physician, himself an oarsman, and published in 1873, showed slightly better than average longevity and health for members of the Oxford and Cambridge crews who took part in the annual races from 1829 to 1869. I myself made the same observations in a long follow-up study of Harvard College football players of the teams from 1900 to 1930.

It may be true that the mesomorphic (broad muscular) athlete is an earlier candidate for coronary heart disease than his ectomorphic (skinny), or endomorphic (rotund) contemporary, but it is also possible that the maintenance of vigorous physical exercise throughout life with the avoidance of obesity may protect such a mesomorph from a serious degree of coronary atherosclerosis (patchy degenerative changes in the walls of the arteries) early in life or in middle age. We have as yet inadequate knowledge about that very important possibility.

Now let me present what we do know. First, there are the immediate physical effects of exercise on the circulation of blood. Good muscle tone in the arms and *particularly in the legs,* resulting from regular exercise, maintains an improved circulation of blood in the veins. Actually, since the veins have valves, which when in good condition prevent the blood from going the wrong way, the compression of the veins by the skeletal muscles helps to pump the blood back to the heart, thus decreasing stasis (a slackening of the blood flow).

Soft, unused muscles do not accomplish as good a job, and make clotting (thrombosis) in the veins more likely also, as when one sits for a long time in an airplane, or after an operation or any illness which keeps a person in bed or inactive for a long time. It is best on long trips by plane or train or automobile to get up or out and walk a bit at intervals to combat this tendency. Thrombosis in the leg veins can on occasion have serious consequences when some of the clot (embolus) breaks off and blocks an important blood vessel in the lung (pulmonary embolism).

An interesting experience suffered by an aged friend and patient of mine, then 103 years old, illustrates the value of the exercise of simple walking in controlling a stasis in the leg circulation. He had had the grippe in midwinter and was housed for two or three months. While he sat about waiting for spring, both legs began to swell with no symptoms of pain anywhere or of breathlessness. When I saw him in the early spring he was discouraged, bored and apprehensive about the dropsy. Examination, however, showed that his heart was not responsible, nor any actual thrombosis, but simply a very sluggish circulation and the effect of gravity in an aged person. Instead of medicine, the resumption of his regular exercise of walking, up to a mile or two a day, was prescribed and within a week or ten days the leg swelling disappeared. Now, three years later, he continues to be in excellent health.

In addition to its beneficial effect on skeletal muscle tone, exercise also improves the tone of the diaphragm, which results in its better function as the piston of a pump, not only for bringing a full supply of oxygen to the lungs with removal of carbon dioxide but also for the suction of blood into the heart via both inferior and superior *venae cavae* (great veins). Vigorous exercise is best for this, but if an individual is unable to undertake such activity, deep breathing exercises several times a day are of definite value. Of course, it is always wise also to avoid restriction of the motion of the diaphragm by excessive abdominal fat.

Another part of the circulatory apparatus helped by exercise is that of the smallest blood vessels, arterioles, capillaries and venules, which are rendered more active in their function by their response to regular exercise. The peripheral vessels of the hands, the feet and the ears react beneficially with less likelihood of sluggishness and stasis.

Thus it is evident that although the heart is, of course, the main agent in maintaining the circulation of blood, the aid it receives from these other structures is considerable and may indeed on occasion mean the difference between good health and physical unfitness.

Let us turn now to other beneficial effects of exercise which are often overlooked. In the first place, the course of human existence does not always run smoothly. Not infrequently in the lives of all of us emergencies arise which demand a fully efficient circulation with reserves, not just a sluggish one that is adequate for a sedentary life only. An accident or an illness or operation may test to the full the resources of the body, and it is probable that the difference between a state of positive health and a state of mere existence—although not diseased—may mean the difference between life and death.

Digestion, when meals follow exercise and do not just precede it, and bowel function are improved by exercise. Not infrequently vigorous sport renders laxative medicine quite unnecessary. Sleep is favored, too; in fact, a brisk long walk in the evening may be more helpful as a hypnotic than any medicine, highball or even television show.

Finally, and I believe most important of all, there is the beneficial effect of exercise on the nervous system and the psyche. Here is the reverse of the effect of mind over matter or psyche over soma. The importance of somatopsychic physiology and medicine has not been adequately appreciated. It has been said that a five-mile walk will do more good to an unhappy but otherwise healthy adult than all the medicine and psychology in the world. Certainly it is true that in my own case nervous stress and strain can be counteracted and even prevented by regular vigorous exercise; it is the best antidote that I know.

It matters little, if at all, what kind of exercise it is, provided it suits the strength and liking of the individual concerned. It is well to establish a regular habit and to maintain it through thick and thin. One should regard it as just as essential to good health as eating, sleeping and working.

An intense mental worker needs exercise to keep his mind clear, and it is well if mental concentration can be alternated frequently with exercise or even accompanied thereby, as was the common custom of the peripatetic philosophers in Athens in the days of its prime.

A few hours before I wrote these lines in a plane while returning home from Greece, I had the privilege of exploring the Agora in Athens with Prof. Homer A. Thompson, director of the American excavations there. We promenaded along the reconstructed stoa where once the great statesmen and philosophers had walked while teaching and discussing problems in many fields. They had doubtless themselves discovered that their minds were clearer when they kept moving to bring more blood to the head and more oxygen to the blood. It would be well for the present generation to return to some of the good habits of our ancestors for the restoration of better physical and mental fitness and for their maintenance.

Now a word as to specific forms of exercise. It is my strong belief that all healthy persons, both male and female, should exercise regularly, no matter what their ages. Of course, in advanced age—that is, past 70—it is doubtless wise to exercise less strenuously than earlier in life, but no strict rules can be set. Every person must be considered individually according to his condition, habits, preferences as to the kind of exercise and the circumstances of his life. Some healthy, vigorous persons in "good training" can play tennis, even singles, in their seventies and golf in their eighties. John D. Rockefeller and Adelbert Ames were golfers together when both were in their nineties.

Other types of exercise that can be recommended for healthy older persons are long walks, swimming, fishing, skiing, moderate hunting, bicycling, snow-shoveling, gardening, woodcutting, horse-shoe pitching, less strenuous gymnastics and curling. Milder games may suit some individuals, such as croquet, shuffleboard, bowling on the green and archery. Stairclimbing, though a dull exercise, and calisthenics are not infrequently of some use, too. Doubtless, persons with much muscle, especially men, can and should exercise more vigorously than those with less; in fact, to maintain the best of health this may be necessary.

In the case of persons who have an important but not crippling disease, cardiac or otherwise, mild exercise may still be advisable for the sake of the maintenance of health, but each one must be carefully considered individually by his or her physician and so advised. Instead of forbidding exercise like golf in the case of a person who has had coronary thrombosis—whether or not it has left a scar—but who is free of symptoms, the establishment of a habit of regular exercise is usually an important part of the treatment. Of course, in the presence of symptoms of importance the exercise should be limited, but even in such cases some sort of exercise is usually advisable, even if only short walks or light gardening, or deep breathing.

And, of course, it is not sensible for a person, even if very muscular, suddenly to take on some unusually strenuous exercise without working up to it gradually. It is always wise to get into a conditon of so-called training gradually. But it is time for us at all ages to be more than spectators of the sports of the day. We should expand our physical activity beyond that of getting into and out of automobiles and riding in elevators, buses, trains and planes. A return to the use of our legs is to be highly recommended.

There may be more truth than poetry after all in a letter in verse which the poet John Dryden wrote to a kinsman in 1680. One of the stanzas in that letter went as follows:

By chase our fathers earned their food,

Toil strung [improved] the nerves and purified the blood,

But we their sons, a pampered race of men,

Are dwindled down to three score years and ten.

Better to hunt in fields for health unbought

Than fee the doctor for a nauseous draught.

The wise for cure on exercise depend,

God never made his work for man to mend.

No Thanks, I'll Just Sit This Out*

LOIS MARK STALVEY

I'm about as physically unfit as I can manage and I intend, happily, to stay that way. For a while, I felt guilty about it, but reading between the lines of recent research has convinced me that I'm on the right track and I plan to go on, through the years, as sedentary as life allows.

As I carefully combed through an article by a famous doctor, certain phrases popped out . . . "We have no statistics to prove this, but it *seems. . . .* " and "A survey of the 1912 varsity hockey team's present health was *not conclusive.*"

See! They *think* exercise *ought* to be good for you.

Well, I've developed my theory, too . . . while others are tramping around golf courses, I've used all that extra time thinking.

As far as longevity is concerned, they admit there are no measurable facts to prove athletic types live longer. On the other hand, we sloths might. You sure can't drown, ski into a tree or get kicked by a horse if you're sitting home reading *The Group.*

There are other ways of departing this life besides hardening of the arteries and, although hiking in the mountains is supposed to keep your arteries loose, it looks to me as if you'd run a good risk of getting bitten by a snake or falling off that darned mountain, flexible arteries and all!

From the viewpoint of the female, I can see many advantages in simply sitting, with your legs crossed gracefully, while some

*"No Thanks, I'll Just Sit This Out," *The Sunday Bulletin Magazine,* October 27, 1963. Reprinted with permission from the author and *The Sunday Bulletin Magazine.* Copyright 1963 Bulletin Co.

other girl gets her face all red chasing a tennis ball. First of all, the athletic girl is likely to develop strange bulges and bumps called muscles. Now, this may be great if you're a Soviet woman, assigned to hoisting cases of caviar onto government trucks . . . and I won't stoop so low as to accuse physical culturists of subversive sympathies . . . but, as for me, I'm the capitalistic type and aspire only to look as weakly decadent as a fashion model.

And if you develop muscles, you're liable to be tempted to *use* them. As it is, everyone knows I couldn't possibly tote that couch or lift that chair, so I just give advice and suggestions.

If I were capable of opening windows on trains, I might just go ahead and do it, thereby depriving some men of a feeling of superiority and, Heaven knows, they're complaining enough about *that* already!

My exercise is provided by a sievelike mind that keeps me running up and down stairs after things I forgot on the first trip. This is enough to use up my daily caloric intake and keep my dress size down.

My husband suggests I could occasionally violate my pro-lethargy policy by walking when we're going to a neighbor's party three or four blocks away. "Good exercise," he says. Standing solidly on his flat-soled oxfords, he has never really been able to understand my attitude . . . that walking four blocks in party heels is not exercise, it's the kind of unproductive self-torture practiced by those Indians who sit on nails.

Instead, I have a loyalty to the American economy and the persistence of Henry Ford that makes me cling stoutly to the automobile. If everyone walked when they could drive, what would happen to the annual earnings of gas and tire companies? Mr. Ford didn't spend all that time tinkering in his drafty Dearborn garage just so we could buy English bikes and go puffing up hills to the grocery store.

As long as no one has proof that exercise is the key to an unused health insurance policy, I'll continue to lump it in with the other superstitions such as walking under ladders and not petting black cats on Friday the 13th.

I will also ignore those who view-with-alarm the unfitness of American youth. My kids are fit enough to climb trees to fall out of. Anyway, dedicated inventors have been busily creating a modern life where our children will need even less physical prowess to exist than we do. As to muscles for national defense, it would almost be a cheering thought to believe our country would be defended by physical combat rather than the monstrous weapons unleashed by a finger or a button.

I have no desire to picket the country's gymnasiums, plow up tennis courts or drive water-ski sales into the hands of bootleggers. Let those who want muscles grunt away. I'm usually far enough away from any sports event so I'd never hear them.

I'm just declaring myself and warning those who'd lure me onto a golf course with appeals to my esthetic side. "But you'd enjoy the scenery," they say. Nonsense! You've got to tramp around, getting all scratched up by some of that scenery, hunting for the golf ball you're committed to keeping your eye on. If it's all the same to you, I'll sit on a park bench, enjoying the same kind of scenery without the burden of sock-and-seek!

Until the advantages of perspiring heavily in bowling alleys are established as irrefutable health requirements, apathy will continue to appeal to me. I needn't even query our family doctor . . . he's a nice chubby type whose spare time exercise is bridge!

So far, the only positive effect they've established is that increased physical activity steps up the circulation of the blood. Who knows if wildly circulating blood is necessarily good for you! For my taste, I prefer the serenely flowing type. It certainly *sounds* much healthier than catapulting corpuscles taking artery corners on two wheels.

However, if all those experts who would have me touching my toes and slipping my disc with push-ups will promise to sit down and think this whole fad over, I'll try to buy one of their precepts . . . that deep breathing caused by exercise increases the oxygen in our blood. I won't even ask them to prove that air in your blood is desirable. If they'll leave me alone I promise, faithfully to *breathe* . . . in *and* out . . . for as long as I live.

And while I'm breathing, I'll just sit comfortably, if you don't mind, giving loads of sympathy to my sunburnt, ski-injured, muscle-strained friends.

You supply the vigor, please, and I'll supply the Band-aids!

Exercise and Fitness*

Fitness for effective living has many interdependent components involving intellectual and emotional, as well as physical, factors. These differ in relative importance from one period of life to another, depending on varying individual roles and responsibilities. But in every part of life, each of these factors is significant.

Fitness rests first of all upon a solid foundation of good health. Be it in the home, on the farm, at the office, in the factory, or in military service—fitness for effective living

---

*A statement on the role of exercise in fitness by a joint committee of the American Medical Association and the American Association for Health, Physical Education, and Recreation. Reprinted from *The Journal of the American Medical Association,* May 4, 1964, Vol. 188, pp. 433–436. Copyright © 1964 by American Medical Association.

implies freedom from disease; enough strength, agility, endurance, and skill to meet the demands of daily living; sufficient reserves to withstand ordinary stresses without causing harmful strain; and mental development and emotional adjustment appropriate to the maturity of the individual.

Fitness does not come in a "have" or "not have" package. The level of fitness attained is a resultant of ability to cope with the varied and interacting stresses of life. *Optimal* fitness permits a person to enjoy life to the fullest. In addition to the day's ordinary work requirements, one should still have enough vitality to enjoy avocational interests, and to meet special challenges that may interrupt the daily routine. In emergencies of various types, sudden and unusual physical demands may be laid upon individuals and groups. The possession of physical strength, agility, and endurance may enable the individual or group to survive, whereas the lack of fitness may spell catastrophe.

The upper limits one can achieve in fitness are determined largely by inheritance. However, the extent to which the individual develops his own potential for fitness depends on his daily living practices and exercise habits. Adequate nutrition, sufficient rest and relaxation, suitable work, appropriate medical and dental care, and the practice of moderation are also important in maintaining fitness.

This report, however, is intentionally limited to the contribution of exercise in the total program of fitness. Points of special emphasis are, *first,* that the body is responsive to training and, *second,* that the body operates under wide margins of safety and is remarkably resistant to strain.

Increased availability of labor-saving machinery and easy modes of transportation have changed modern living. As a result, more and more persons tend to lead sedentary lives. The increased leisure time that accompanied these changes can be merely a continuation of this sedentary existence, or it can be the opportunity for regular, enjoyable exercise. The active nature of young children has not changed, but unless they continue this inclination later in life they will not maintain their level of fitness.

PHYSIOLOGICAL FACTORS

In essence, the greatest effect of an exercise program is the improved organization of the body functions which support activity. This improved physiological efficiency is reflected in increased endurance, strength, and agility.

The oftener the normal heart and circulatory system are required to move blood to active regions of the body, the more efficient they become. This is accomplished chiefly by improved muscular tone of the heart, an increase in its output of blood per minute, and an increase in the number of active capillaries in the lungs. Protracted exercise improves the work of the lungs by increasing their ability to expand more fully, take in more air, and utilize a greater proportion of the oxygen in the inspired air. Games and sports involving extended running, vigorous swimming and dancing, and other sorts of forceful effort serve this purpose. Activities of this type involving leg muscles also help to maintain good circulation against gravity through a "milking" or "squeezing" action of the muscles on the veins. This benefit cannot be achieved by any other means.

Prolonged inactivity, on the other hand, results in a decline in circulatory and pulmonary efficiency.

The ability of the body to function according to purposeful patterns is vested in the central nervous system. With practice and training, many complex movement patterns become second nature and almost automatic. The nervous system can adapt itself to permit proficiency in an almost unlimited variety of physical activities.

An individual's ultimate performance is limited by the physiological capacity of the body systems involved. Subjective factors such as a feeling of breathlessness, general weakness, or muscular discomfort evoke reduction or cessation of activity. These are part of the body's mechanism for protection and survival, although they can also reflect inhibitions of a psychological nature. Usually the untrained individual reduces or discontinues his performance long before physiological limits are reached —when he feels slight fatigue or fears overexertion.

The untrained person can increase his tolerance for exercise by following a regular regimen, but under ordinary circumstances he still will not approach his physiological limit of activity. Repeated periods of *intensive* exercise, however, alternating with light exercise or rest, enable the well-trained person to overcome these inhibitions and experience the phenomenon known as "second wind." This represents an adjustment of the physiological reserves of the body which temporarily banishes fatigue and enables the individual to continue his activity with renewed vigor.

A distinction should be made here between healthful fatigue and harmful exhaustion. Exercise which regularly approaches physiological limits—coupled with adequate rest—results in the development of increased strength and endurance. The term "fatigue" usually connotes this principle. By contrast, exercise carried to the state of *exhaustion* may do harm, particularly to the unconditioned individual. This is especially likely to happen if there is insufficient time for recovery after fatigue.

The voluntary muscles become stronger when they work against gradually increasing loads. Activities requiring relatively short bursts of intense effort such as lifting, pulling, pushing, climbing, jumping, and speed running tend to increase muscular strength.

In a sedentary existence, or where physical activity is not diversified, certain body muscles may not develop sufficiently. These underdeveloped muscles may be needed for unanticipated work activities, sports activities, or, as in the case of the muscles along the spine, for the continual support of the body. Various forms of prescribed activities can be used in training programs to overcome muscular weakness. These activities usually take the form of selected conditioning exercises, including calisthenics, which employ the weaker muscles as well as those which are used more frequently.

Much attention has been given recently to *isometric* exercises, to which some persons attribute gain in strength in shorter periods of effort than are needed for the traditional *isotonic* exercises, and for which no special apparatus is required. In isometrics, a vigorous muscular contraction is sustained for a brief period without producing movement; in isotonics, muscular contraction produces a range of movement of body parts. Since isometric exercises have no beneficial effect on range of motion, and present difficulties in motivation, they should be considered as only part of an exercise regimen. Neither isometric nor isotonic exercises improve circulatory endurance unless involved in a total activity that taxes the cardiovascular and pulmonary system.

The potential for muscular strength increases throughout childhood and adolescence, usually reaching a maximum in early adulthood. In the 30's or 40's most individuals experience the onset of a gradual decline of strength, endurance, and agility. The heart and circulatory system also tends to exhibit lessening of functional capacity for exercise and resilience in recovery after exercise. The extent and rapidity of this decline is partly dependent on exercise habits in adult life. The beneficial effects of exercise are transient; persons who continue to train retain their capacities longer than those who neglect training. Individual differences, dependent on constitutional disposition and basic organic health, affect the rate of decline of strength and endurance.

INDIVIDUAL AND ENVIRONMENTAL FACTORS

There is a considerable range of individual variation in need and capacity for exercise. A physically active person may need little, if any, additional exercise to maintain fitness, whereas an inactive, relaxed person must add exercise to prevent becoming less fit. Some individuals, even at an early age, recover poorly from breathlessness and general fatigue after exercise. In some, unfavorable emotional reactions are also noted. Attempts to modify these responses through planned exercise should proceed carefully under medical supervision. Such persons frequently cannot reach the levels of fitness achieved by those to whom exercise is an exhilarant and a stimulant.

Advanced age, in itself, is not a contraindication to exercise, but is actually an indication for it. Precluding accidents, a healthy person of any age will do himself no permanent harm by suitable physical activity. Moreover, exercise that has been specifically selected and prescribed is needed for convalescing and disabled persons.

Evidence as to the effect of exercise on digestion indicates that physical exertion does not necessarily interfere with the digestive process. Strong emotion may do so even unaccompanied by exercise. Laborers and farmers customarily work hard immediately after meals. On the other hand, it has been found advisable for athletes to eat their pre-game meals three or four hours prior to competition. Otherwise, the time of day for exercise may well be in accord with personal inclination, hours of leisure, and other determining circumstances.

Vigorous outdoor exercise under conditions of high temperature (over 80°F [>26.7° C]) and high humidity (80%–100%) should be limited to short periods of about one hour, with rest intervals and planned intake of small amounts of fluids. If such conditions of climate can be anticipated, extra salt may be added to food at mealtimes. Acclimation is also involved in significant changes in altitudes. Participation in activities requiring endurance often produces feelings of discomfort at high altitudes. Until adaptation is achieved, the intensity and duration of activity must be reduced.

When averages are considered, there are measurable differences between the sexes in heart capacity, muscular strength, and skeletal proportions. In planning exercise programs for groups, these differences should be taken into consideration, and activities planned for girls and women may well be less strenuous than those for boys and men. However, the range of physical capacities in individuals of each sex is much greater than the average differences between sexes. In the case of individuals, therefore, sex is less significant than constitutional capacity, personal inclination, and physical condition in determining the suitability of any strenuous activity. To a very great extent, social custom may determine the appropriateness of specific activities for either sex.

No harm to normal menstrual function has been shown to result from vigorous exercise. In fact, exercise can be beneficial in relieving certain types of menstrual pain which are common in young women. Whether exercise is continued as usual should depend on the individual's menstrual experience and reaction to physical activity.

EXERCISE AND HEALTH

Belief in the healthfulness of regular, suitable exercise, previously based on tradition and logic, is constantly being bolstered by evidence from research. As far as can be determined at the present time, the study of the life histories of those who maintain a relatively higher degree of fitness through the nature of their work or through other activities seems to indicate that they suffer less degenerative disease and probably live longer than those who follow a sedentary life.

Obesity, muscle atrophy, cardiovascular inefficiency, joint stiffness, and impairment of various metabolic functions are possible effects of prolonged inactivity. Sudden cessation of work activity in older individuals, as sometimes happens on retirement, often seems to lead to rapid physical degeneration if no substitute activity is provided. The successful use of physical activity in the medical management of patients indicates the beneficial effects of exercise in preventing or delaying organic disease and degeneration.

Exercise, regardless of its nature or extent, cannot provide immunization against infectious illness nor cure communicable disease. The benefits of physical activity are more clearly observable in their relation to certain organic diseases. Regular exercise is now considered to help retard the onset or further progress of diabetes, for example, and man's most common threat to health — atherosclerosis.

There is no longer any doubt but that the level of physical activity does play a major role in weight control. Maintaining a good caloric balance between dietary intake and energy output requires a sound approach to both food consumption and exercise. There is some evidence to suggest that exercise has a beneficial effect on metabolic functions that combat obesity, in addition to burning calories. The high mortality rate associated with being overweight suggests that obesity contributes to organic degeneration.

The relation of physical activity to mental health should not be overlooked; from this standpoint, the ability to be engrossed in play is basic. Pleasurable exercise relieves tension and encourages habits of continued activity. In fact, muscular effort is probably one of the best antidotes for emotional stress. Fortunately, such a variety of activities is available that everyone should be able to find some from which he gains pleasure as well as exercise.

EXERCISE SUGGESTIONS

The following suggestions will be useful in deriving the maximum enjoyment and benefit from exercise:

1. A program of exercise should be started at an early age and be continued throughout life with certain adjustments from time to time as life advances and needs, interests, and capabilities change.

2. The amount of vigorous exercise that is desirable each day is largely an individual matter. Recommendations range from 30 minutes to an hour daily as a minimum.

3. Something of interest for every individual can be found to make exercise satisfying and enjoyable. In addition to numerous sports, the variety of choices includes daily habits such as walking, bicycling, and gardening.

4. Hard, fast, sustained, or highly competitive games and sports should not be played by persons of any age unless these persons have attained an appropriate state of fitness through systematic training.

5. All persons should be shown by medical examination to be organically sound before training for competition or other strenuous exercise. The examination should be repeated periodically and whenever special indications appear.

6. An individual in good physical condition may appropriately participate in an activity that might be harmful to another person of the same age who is not in a comparable state of fitness.

7. Persons who are out of training should not attempt to keep pace in any vigorous sport with persons who are properly conditioned and accustomed to regular participation in that sport. Being in condition for one sport does not always mean that a person will be in condition for another.

8. Persons long out of training, or "soft" (who have not practiced strenuous exercise regularly), will need an extended period of conditioning to facilitate gradual return to full activity.

9. A person's ability to recover quickly after physical activity is a good indication as to whether or not the exercise is too strenuous. If breathlessness and pounding of the heart are still noticeable ten minutes after exercise, if marked weakness or fatigue persists after a two-hour period, if a broken night's sleep is attributable to exercise, or if there is a sense of definite and undue fatigue the following day, then the exercise has been too severe or too prolonged for that person in his present stage of training and physical strength.

10. Medical supervision of the amount, type, and effect of exercise during convalescence is essential.

11. Persons should not compete in body-contact sports or activities requiring great endurance with others of disproportionate size, strength, or skill. If risk or injury can

be controlled, carefully supervised practice periods against such odds may occasionally be warranted as a learning device for gaining experience or improving performance.

12. Sports involving body contact or traumatic hazards necessitate the provision of protective equipment. Such protection is especially important for the head, neck, eyes, and teeth. Other activities should be substituted when adequate protection cannot be provided.

13. Careful preparation and maintenance of playing fields and other arenas of sports are essential to reduction of injuries and full enjoyment of the activity. Competent supervision and proper equipment are necessary for the same reasons.

SUMMARY

1. Exercise is one of the most important factors contributing to total fitness.

2. The contributions of exercise to fitness include a sense of well-being, and development and maintenance of strength, agility, endurance, and skill in persons who are organically sound. Active games, sports, swimming, rhythmic activities, prescribed exercises, and vigorous hobbies all can make distinctive general contributions to fitness.

3. Each individual differs in his capacity to enjoy and benefit from participation in exercise because of constitutional variations in body size, strength, and structure as well as differences in genetic mold, previous experience, and present condition.

4. One must continue to exercise in order to maintain fitness. The nature and severity of the exercise should be graded according to age, individual reaction to activity, and the state of the person's fitness. After age 30, more frequent medical evaluation of the individual's capacity for exercise is imperative.

5. Activities for girls and women should be selected with regard for their psychological as well as physiological characteristics. Those which involve grace and rhythm, and which have a minimum of body contact, should be favored. Regularity of exercise should be stressed, with activity continued, if it is well tolerated, during the menstrual period.

6. Systematic training for any activity contributes effectively to fitness. The conditioning program involved in preparation for athletic competition contributes as much or more to fitness as does participation in the sport itself.

7. Time and care taken to condition the body for sports and athletics through appropriate activities will improve enjoyment, up-grade performance, help prevent injury, and increase the ability to continue participation over a period of years.

8. Consideration must be given to unfavorable environmental conditions of weather and climate. Modification of one's exercise regimen may be necessary, or, in other instances, sufficient compensation can be achieved by modification of dress and diet.

9. The proper use of protective equipment is essential to safe and effective participation in certain sports. Competent supervision, careful maintenance, and proper control of facilities also will help to prevent accidents and reduce injuries.

10. The rules of the game or specifications for play in an activity are made to protect participants and to enhance enjoyment. They should be properly interpreted, scrupulously observed, and vigorously enforced.

11. The vigor and regularity with which an individual participates in an activity will modify his fitness more than the particular activities or events in which he elects to participate.

Fitness and Creativity*

There can be little doubt that, in most respects, our educational system is one of the finest in the world. Yet there are two very serious deficiencies which all too often result from this system. In dealing with college students, I find these two deficiencies most alarming because they are both qualities which are found almost without exception in normal pre-school children. I refer, of course, to *creativity* and *physical vitality*.

These two qualities either are lost naturally as part of the aging process, or our formal education process stunts their growth. If we assume the former to be the case, then we no longer need concern ourselves with the problem. If, however, we consider the latter to be true (and the evidence strongly points in this direction) then we had best put considerable effort into correcting this detrimental and unfair outgrowth of our educational system.

The primary purpose of this paper is to present critical points leading to a logical expansion of the basic concepts of creativity and physical vitality. These points will be presented as briefly and as clearly as possible. It is *not* the purpose of this paper to review all of the research pertinent to creative vs. conditioned learning, early vs. late learning and the benefits of regular activity. However, where there is evidence pertinent to the major points, reference will be made to representative research and where there is little or no evidence, this too will be pointed out. It should be made clear that I am not implying that creativity will automatically spring from physical fitness; neither will creativity lead to fitness. But handled properly, the two may complement each other and become a part

*An original article by Perry B. Johnson, first published in *Educational Comment*, 1962.

of the total school effort to effect a gradual improvement in these two qualities in our society.

1. *Two qualities essential for optimal human existence and growth, ability to think for one's self and physical vitality, are too often lost between birth and early adulthood.* High school and college students are conditioned to "regurgitate" that which has been given to them. This is the format which carries over even to many of our graduate schools. Many high school and college instructors even take pains to teach and emphasize that which has been done traditionally, and they actually frown upon new ideas and approaches.

There is concrete evidence regarding the lack of physical vitality. To cite one classic example of the many studies which reveal this lack, British boys and girls 10–18 years old were far superior to their U.S. counterparts in all but one test of fitness. They showed greater shoulder girdle strength, superior agility, greater abdominal endurance, leg power and circulatory endurance. (2)

2. *In certain developmental tasks, creative learning (problem-solving) is superior to conditioned learning.* Animal experimentation indicates that conditioned responses are not always the most efficient. For example, a group of rats were taught a specific, rather complicated route through a maze to a food compartment. Another group of rats, left to their own devices, found a way to make the trip in *less* time and also showed more ingenuity in opening the door latch, using either their paws or their noses while the conditioned group invariably opened the door latch with the same paw. (6) There can be little doubt that things in which we participate ourselves are more meaningful and are more apt to remain "with" us.

Caution: We must be careful not to attempt to swing the pendulum too far in the direction of creative learning. There must remain certain basic principles which are more effectively learned by non-creative experiences.

3. *The "mind" and the "body" are not two separate entities.* The mind is not a magic, mystic, non-physiological "thing." It is composed of cells just as our muscles are. It requires glucose and oxygen to function and hardly qualifies as a thing apart from our body. True, it is complex and difficult to understand, but it is a part of us, not at all physiologically dissimilar to other important organs.

From a less basic point of view, one must feel well in order to think well. The most brilliant mind must be housed in a reasonably healthy, efficient body in order to function optimally. As Schopenhauer has so aptly stated it: "The greatest fallacy is to sacrifice health for any other advantage." (3)

Further evidence of the unity of mind and body is presented by the alarming increase in psychosomatic disorders. Emotional stress can cause actual physical disorders such as hypertension (high blood pressure with no apparent cause), ulcers, chronic diarrhea, and colitis as well as certain skin diseases. (11) It is rather obvious, then, that we cannot separate mind and body.

4. *The schools can best contribute to the realistic objectives for fitness and vitality by:*

A. *Teaching the skills of attaining and maintaining fitness.* All students should be exposed to methods of attaining this physical vitality which is so necessary to health and happiness. They should learn these methods based on their individual needs and not be merely taught to play softball, basketball, etc.

B. *Facilitating the development of concepts of fitness.* It is even more important that students should be guided toward a thorough understanding of *why* this physical vitality is important. This means a rather thorough understanding of principles of mechanics (as applied to the human body) and the physiology of exercise and techniques and principles of relaxation as related to mental, emotional, and physiological fatigue.

C. *Teaching recreational "emotional-release" skills.* On the basis of the need for recreational skills for emotional release, we must teach and teach well the carry-over skills which can meet future needs in this respect. There is evidence that well adjusted people have more hobbies and participate more intensively than do the less well adjusted.(9)

5. *Logical thinking and research support the concept that "early learning" is superior to late learning.* Educators have observed that children can learn languages more effectively than can adults. There is the old saying: "You can't teach an old dog new tricks." Much work needs to be done in this area, but there is evidence to support that position of the superiority of early learning over late learning. Both co-twin control studies and animal studies have indicated the importance of early learning. (1, 4, 5, 7, 10)

Attitudes toward fitness and personal ability have been developed long before we reach children as teenagers in junior and senior high schools. But these attitudes most often result from "hit or miss" experiences in primary grades, entirely non-directed. Poor experiences and unsuccessful competition have led many youngsters to the firm conviction that they are physically inept and cannot participate in anything "physical." Physical activity, then, is actually unpleasant to them as teenagers and this compulsion to avoid public exposure in a physical activity often lasts throughout life.

Caution: We cannot assume that early learning is an irrefutable "law" of learning. We must keep in mind that for a given developmental level there is a level of difficulty which cannot be effectively surpassed. (8)

6. The strong interrelationships among the foregoing bases strongly indicate the feasibility of programs of *creativity through physical education* or vice versa—*vitality through creativity.*

It is extremely difficult, if not actually impossible, to deny the value of a sound body for a sound mind. In a biological sense exercise is secondary in importance only to eating and sleeping, yet the techniques and concepts of proper exercise and fitness are seldom offered in our present educational system. What little physical education that *is* offered is reserved until the formative years are long past—in high schools and colleges we must then actually conduct "deficiency" or "rehabilitation" programs. If exercise is second in importance only to eating and sleeping, why do we fail to begin scientific foundational instruction in its techniques at the primary level? Is this not the proper time to develop important life-long concepts? Do we wait until junior high school to teach mathematics or English? Yet, which would most adults be willing to trade off, their ability to solve trigonometry problems or their physical health?

The answer is rather obvious. The primary grades are the grades where such concepts can be most effectively nurtured; and effective concept development means for the most part problem-solving—not conditioned learning!

Students can be taught to set up their own activity programs on the basis of sound physiological and mechanical principles. For an example of how creative expression can be developed in physical education, the reader is referred to an excellent article by Professor Hope M. Smith. (12)

7. *Every elementary school in this country must meet these needs by allotting the instructional time and providing the personnel trained in this "new" physical education program.*

Obviously this article or talk about this problem will not solve it. We must act in two directions. First of all, time must be allotted for this work, preferably beginning in kindergarten. When the job has been properly done, we can then eliminate required physical education from the colleges and offer only advanced skill classes at the high school level.

The trained staff person is quite another matter. Either an elementary teacher will need to attend summer workshops in elementary physiology of exercise and body mechanics or qualified physical education graduates with this kind of training and this kind of philosophy will need to be hired.

The Department of Physical, Health and Recreation Education at the University of Toledo has made definite changes in its program in an attempt to instill this philosophy and to teach the techniques of instruction in elementary body mechanics and physiology of exercise. There are courses in elementary physical education and techniques of fitness instruction required of all physical education majors and minors. Similar material on a more advanced level is presented in a graduate level course. We must get people into the field who are aware of the acute needs and who can implement these programs.

The need for *creativity and vitality* has been pointed out on the basis of certain principles of learning (early learning, creative learning, unity of mind and body, realistic objectives for school physical education). On the basis of this need for physical fitness and the ability to think for one's self, the following is strongly recommended: All elementary schools should have at least one full-time person, trained in health and fitness, who will incorporate the problem-solving approach as much as possible into the following three-point physical education program:

1. Teach the techniques and skills for attaining and maintaining fitness.

2. Facilitate the development of concepts of health and fitness through instruction, geared to the particular grade level, in applied physiology, principles of exercise and fitness, and body mechanics and movement fundamentals.

3. Teach carry-over recreation skills at the level of difficulty which the particular developmental level permits.

This must be done, even if it means removing one physical education teacher from each high school! In this case, some re-training in terms of this rather "new" approach to physical education might be necessary.

REFERENCES

1. Beach, Frank A., and Julian Jaynes, "Effects of Early Experience upon the Behavior of Animals," *Psychol. Bull.,* 51:239–263, 1954.
2. Campbell, W. R., and R. H. Pohndorf, "Physical Fitness of British and United States Children," in *Health and Fitness in the Modern World.* Chicago: The Athletic Institute, 1961.
3. Fraley, L. M., W. R. Johnson, and B. H. Massey, *Physical Education and Healthful Living.* Englewood Cliffs, N.J.: Prentice-Hall, Inc., 1954.
4. Gesell, Arnold, and Helen Thompson, "Learning and Growth in Identical Infant Twins: An Experimental Study of the Method of Co-Twin Control," *Genet. Psychol. Monogr.,* 6:1–124, 1929.
5. Hebb, Donald O., *A Textbook of Psychology.* Philadelphia: W. B. Saunders Company, 1958.
6. Johnson, Warren R., "Physical Education and the Learning Process," *Progr. Physical Educator,* 33:14–17, 1950.
7. King, J. A., "Parameters Relevant to Determining the Effects of Early Experience upon the Adult Behavior of Animals," *Psychol. Bull.,* 55:46–58, 1958.
8. McGraw, Myrtle B., "Maturation of Behavior," in *Manual of Child Psychology,* L. Carmichael (Ed.). New York: John Wiley & Sons, Inc., 1946.
9. Menninger, W. C., "Recreation and Mental Health," *Recreation,* 42:340–346, 1948.
10. Nissen, H. W., K. L. Chow, and J. Semmes, "Effects of Restricted Opportunity for Tactual, Kinesthetic and Manipulation Experience on the Behavior of a Chimpanzee," *Amer. J. Psychol.,* 64:485–507, 1951.
11. Selye, Hans, *The Stress of Life.* New York: McGraw-Hill, Inc., 1957.
12. Smith, Hope M., "Creative Expression in Physical Education," *JOHPER* 33:38–39, 1962.

SUMMARY: PHYSICAL FITNESS STATUS

The decision is really yours to make. What is our physical fitness status? What is a sensible approach to physical fitness? The decisions on these two related questions might best be deferred until you have given some thought to the concepts presented in the next section, and even then, you should keep clearly in focus the concepts presented in the previous section. In other words, the answers to questions must be tempered with other decisions relating to "What is physical fitness?" and "How does it relate to health and to the individual's ultimate concern?" The answers to these questions about physical fitness have obvious implications for health education, physical education, and recreation programs.

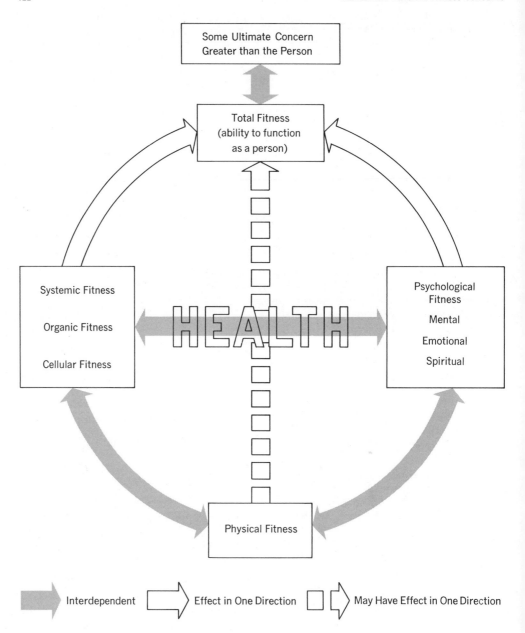

FIGURE 5.8   Circle illustrating the relationships among physical fitness, health (systemic and psychological fitness), and total fitness.

THE RELATIONSHIP BETWEEN PHYSICAL FITNESS AND HEALTH

Does physical fitness really contribute to health? This is an often asked question and is indeed an important one that has implications for physical education, health education, and recreation. One might also ask, "Does physical education contribute to health?" Because there are as many kinds of physical education as there are physical educators, this could never be answered with any degree of certainty. At any rate, there is a larger and more important consideration: If physical fitness is related to health, is health in and of itself the ultimate end; that is to say, is health the ultimate purpose for which physical and health education and recreation exist? Our answer is simple and, to us, unequivocal: No, health is not an end in itself; it in turn contributes to what is often called something like *total fitness,* that is, *the ability to function effectively as a person.* To us, even this is not the end; total fitness must contribute to *some ultimate concern greater than the person.* We have presented the theoretical relationship between physical fitness and health as a part of this greater relationship in Figure 5.8.

It is simple enough to establish adequate grounds for the claim that physical fitness and health are related. Both logic and scientific evidence (see Chapters 8, 9, and 10) support such a position. Let us accept this position without delay and proceed to the more important concepts that can grow out of this position. Whenever a theoretical, schematic representation of an "idea" is presented, there are misunderstandings and invariably there are those who can find loopholes in the schematic. Some of the loopholes can be closed by eliminating misunderstandings, but we know that all of the holes cannot be thus repaired. We shall, however, at-

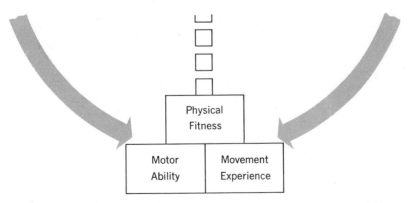

FIGURE 5.9 An illustration of the relationships among physical fitness, motor ability, and movement experience as part of the total health picture.

tempt to eliminate as much misunderstanding as possible by presenting as clearly and concisely as we can the basic concepts related to this schematic illustration (Figure 5.8).

1. It is not claimed that all (or *any*) of the concepts represented are completely original. Perhaps the *totality* of the relationships, as represented, provides a different and more easily interpreted view.

2. Physical fitness and physical education, health education, and recreation are not the only factors contributing to health and total fitness. It is recognized that *many* other factors play a vital role in this relationship and thus contribute directly to "health" and/or "total fitness" (for example, religion, all forms of education, proper nutrition, and medicine).

3. The mid-third of the circle (which is blocked out and enclosed) is to us what is typically referred to as "health."

4. The upper third is perhaps the aspect of life that relates more closely to what is called philosophy or man's religion.

5. The lower third is *a* primary concern of physical education (note the emphasis on *a*; we did not say *the*).

   a. Physical Fitness is one of three qualities that seem to us to be related aspects and responsibilities of physical education; the others (as shown in Figure 5.9) are movement experience and motor ability. We are talking about these as *qualities,* not the process of attaining these qualities, the qualities of *being* physically

fit, of *having* movement experience, of *possessing* motor ability. These are interrelated but not uniformly so in all persons. One may have very little motor ability, very little and limited movement experience, but may be very physically fit. On the other hand, one may have a high level of motor ability, have had very narrow and limited movement experiences, and be very physically unfit. But each quality exerts an influence on the others, and, in physical education, it seems to us the aim is to do as much as we can for the qualities of physical fitness and movement experience within the limitations imposed by the individual's quality of motor ability. (Needless to say, such limitations, although very real, impose serious limitations upon the attainment of physical fitness and movement experience *only when and where there is an obsession with the importance of superior performance of sports skills.*)

   b. Formal physical education, then, might be conceived as the process through which:

    (1) The three qualities of physical fitness, movement experience, and motor ability are evaluated for the individual.

    (2) Opportunity is provided for the individual to attain and/or improve any or all of these qualities.

    (3) The concepts and methods for evaluating, attaining, and improving these qualities are taught.

    (4) The concepts relating the lower third to the upper two thirds of

the circle are taught (that is, the concepts of physical fitness, movement experience, and motor ability, relating the qualities to health, total fitness, and an ultimate concern).

6. Formal health education is the process through which concepts relating the two basic qualities depicted (systemic fitness and psychological fitness) to each other and to all other aspects of life are developed.

7. Recreation provides *one* means through which the individual can attain the qualities included around the circle.

In summary, we suggest that there is little question that physical fitness and health are related but that this relationship becomes more meaningful only when (1) health is viewed as contributing to a greater end and (2) *physical fitness is viewed in proper perspective* in its relationship to total physical education and recreation. The theoretical relationship among physical fitness, health, total fitness, and man's ultimate concern, as we have schematically proposed it, in turn gives rise to a clear and workable concept of the relationship among physical education, health education, and recreation.

If physical fitness and health are related as we suggest, what does this mean? The relationship we have presented means, for one thing, that physical fitness is one quality that can contribute to man's living better, to his total fitness.

DESCRIPTION OF THE THREE LEVELS OF TOTAL FITNESS

Subminimal Total Fitness

If one's total fitness (TF) is subminimal, it may well be because he has expended little energy and time to attempt to reach his physical fitness potential. It is a state characterized by physical inefficiency and quite often by some degree of emotional instability as well. He is easily "fatigued," often "edgy," and unable to meet physical or emotional challenges head-on with confidence, determination, and a reasonable share of success.

Minimal Total Fitness

When someone reaches the level of minimal TF he is characterized as a person who has the ability to respond physiologically and emotionally to typical daily patterns and problems in such a way as to maintain health and to carry out his function in society effectively. There is obviously a "gray" area here, and one will not always know and be able to evaluate objectively the criterion we have described for this level of TF. For example, there may be some hidden progressive degenerative change in health that is clinically silent for many years. Because of the limitations of current medical knowledge and diagnostic techniques, such a change may not be noticeable and thus may be beyond personal control until some symptom occurs. But one can take stock and determine whether he is responding to the challenge of life in such a way that he is not constantly "fatigued." He should know if he is happy and generally "relaxed" when he should be, and whether he has the capacity to enjoy life. On the other hand, if he is constantly "fatigued," often gloomy, prone to temper tantrums, unable to relax, and can see no ultimate purpose in life, it takes only a little self-analysis to become conscious of these conditions. If this is the case, then it is quite likely that he has *not* attained the minimal total fitness level. In such a case, one should be able to see that he is not capable of the total response to daily stimuli that is necessary for the maintenance of health. He could develop an ulcer or high blood pressure or any one of several psychosomatic disorders and may move slowly but steadily back toward the subminimal TF level. It is possible that TF *capacity* may even be reduced as a result of poor health.

One can readily see that this minimal level of total fitness is more than the traditional "physical" fitness, for it also includes spiritual and sociopsychological components. It is obvious that this type of fitness *is* an *individual* concern. Because people are engaged in such widely divergent kinds of work, and because any given situation may produce very different responses in different people, plans for the maintenance of fitness (broadly conceived) must be extremely flexible and highly individual. Whereas someone engaged in a physically demanding occupation may require a nonvigorous recreational activity, a more sedentary individual may well need activity that involves a

relatively high energy expenditure. Some people may find fulfillment and emotional release in hobbies or sports. Others may find the satisfaction of these particular needs, as well as others, in their religious faith. In the event that the psychosociological equilibrium should become disrupted, there are a number of avenues available through which the informed individual can seek revitalization. Through knowledge of the body and an understanding of health and fitness, he can put the problem-solving and decision-making processes into action. His ultimate decision *can* be based on his intelligence and training; it may or may not involve vigorous exercise, relaxation techniques, a change of job, and so on. He must and can make an intelligent decision if he first admits the problem exists and then puts to work all of his own knowledge and training plus any necessary professional help. He can at least make a decision that enhances the probability that he will stop the downward fall on the TF scale and, in fact, remain at or move up to the minimal TF level; he may eventually even rise to the optimal level.

Optimal Total Fitness

We progress now to what we consider to be the ideal or optimal TF level. At this level a person has the capacity to respond to near maximal, short-term effort or submaximal (but long-term) work without physiological or emotional debilitation. He is emotionally quite stable and has a tremendous capacity to "enjoy life." Such a person is capable, because of a high *physical fitness* level, of carrying out a number of common tasks (even though he may be unaccustomed to them) without undue discomfort or injury. For example, it is doubtful whether the housewife and her businessman husband ever spend an entire eight-hour day moving heavy furniture or digging up shrubs and replanting them. Yet they may well want to (or have to!) do these things on a given Saturday. Some interesting and very appropriate questions immediately arise: Will they make it through the day? Will they be injured? Will they be so sore and stiff that they will hardly be able to move their aching and supersensitive masses of tissue from the bed next morning? Will this condition annoy them for several days and impair their work at the office and in the home? One must admit that chances are good that, for the typical American couple, at least, one (if not *all*) of these questions will be answered in the affirmative. People who speak from experience say that, for those eking out an effortless existence at a poor physical fitness and minimal total fitness level, the phenomena of sore and aching muscles and general irritation that result from unaccustomed work increase in severity and intensity with age.

How can one avoid such "weekend pathology"? Is there a magic panacea? You are probably thinking, "Aha, now they will tell me that exercise is *the* answer." It is obviously not that simple. The lack of adequate evidence precludes any definite, simple prescription. But we do know that in order to arrive at this optimal TF level, a person must ex-

pend *more* energy, and in *different* ways, if he is to avoid the more serious consequences of unaccustomed, occasional, near maximal work or play efforts. "Play" is included because the same symptoms (and probably more severe ones) commonly occur as a result of the weekend picnic softball game or the *annual* handball match. These consequences are not as likely to result from noncompetitive activity because one can stop whenever he wants to. At any rate, the best "prevention" appears to be some personally designed, *never-ceasing* plan for attaining physical fitness. This almost invariably means extra energy expenditure! There are two important suggestions for those who would like to attain an optimal physical fitness level: (1) "prevention" through slow and comfortable attainment of optimal physical fitness, in an ongoing, relatively simple maintenance program, is the safest and the most reliable prescription; (2) a high level of proficiency in games and skills is not only relatively unimportant but unnecessary—athletic ability is *not* a prerequisite to success in attaining optimal physical fitness (this has been discussed in greater detail on page 92).

In discussing the health base for total fitness, we should mention the need for knowledge on the part of the individual himself—it is not possible to make the best of the available medical knowledge without some *personal* understanding to supplement it. First, one must be familiar with the common communicable diseases, their symptoms and preventive programs (**immunization**) designed to eliminate them. Second, he must understand and appreciate the current evidence with respect to the chronic degenerative diseases; furthermore, he should be able to interpret such evidence on the basis of some knowledge about the organs or systems involved. Third, he should be well informed about the availability and purposes of the public health agencies (see page 145). Fourth, he should be aware of the current community health problems, such as air pollution and water pollution, and their health implications (see page 145). Because the emphasis in this chapter is on concepts, these knowledges are discussed elsewhere. The diseases are discussed in appropriate chapters, depending upon the system(s) involved.

THE RELATIONSHIP BETWEEN PHYSICAL FITNESS AND LONGEVITY

We have just addressed ourselves to "physical fitness and living better." Now we turn to the question "Does physical fitness contribute to a longer life?" or, to put it another way, "Does regular physical activity increase longevity?" Discussion of this question has provided a great deal more "heat" than "light." In short, there is no direct and unequivocal answer. Logic and some indirect statistical and experimental evidence lend support to the position that there is a positive relationship between physical fitness or regular physical activity and longevity. Logic would lead us to hypothesize that if physical fitness (which can only

be attained via physical activity) is positively related to health, then it must be positively related to longevity because health is logically related to length of life (excluding accidental death and suicide). It is also logical that because psychological fitness is a positive aspect of health, living "better" should also have a positive effect on longevity.

Scientists have attempted to get at this question by studying the longevity of former college athletes as compared to the total population or to their former nonathlete classmates. Montoye (397) correctly points out the inappropriateness of the comparison with the total population. The other studies[1] in general find no significant longevity differences between former letter-winners and other college graduates; in other words, former college athletes, on the average, die no sooner, nor do they live longer, than their classmates. But the limitation in these studies is serious: what a man *did* or did *not* do with respect to college athletics has little to do with the amount of physical activity in his life after college. Furthermore, stress, diet, and genetic factors are not usually accounted for.

There is, on the other hand, considerable indirect evidence, especially that which deals with occupation and ischemic heart disease, which supports the position that regular physical activity promotes longevity. It might be helpful to refer to the material on pages 196 through 200 in this connection.

---

[1]Dr. Henry Montoye and his coworkers have published two excellent reviews of the sports participation-longevity studies (395, 397).

Hammond's (226) study reveals startling and dramatic longevity differences between no-exercise and heavy-exercise subjects as well as the two degrees of activity in between. For example, reading from Figure 5.10 we see that even in the 45–49 age group, there were 4.6 times as many deaths in the no-exercise group. As Hammond is careful to point out, "ill health may reduce the ability or the desire to exercise." This could account for some of the differences in this study, but it appears to be another fragment of evidence which supports regular exercise as a valuable adjustment to good health.

PHYSICAL FITNESS AND RESISTANCE TO INFECTION

Physical fitness enthusiasts have been known to claim somewhat positively that fitness will prevent everything from the common cold to cancer!

There is no evidence to support this contention. In fact, in her excellent review, Baetjer (29) presents evidence that, in animals innoculated with bacteria, infection is more likely to occur if exercise-induced fatigue follows the innoculation; fatigue occurring before innoculation also increases the likelihood of infection. Steinhaus, in sum-

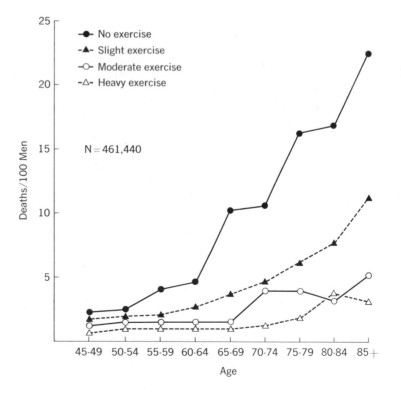

FIGURE 5.10 Death rate by degree of exercise and age group during a period of approximately one year after first survey. For example, in the age group 60–64, 1 percent (1/100) of the men in the heavy exercise category died, whereas 5 percent of those in the no-exercise group died during the follow-up year. Adapted from Hammond (226).

marizing experimentation in this area, says, "It is fair to conclude that physical training probably does not augment the body's specific disease fighting agencies" (543, p. 128). Logic indicates that, in line with the fatigue-bacteria evidence, the ability to postpone fatigue which usually results from regular training may indirectly reduce chances for infection.

Merrill and Howe (387) in 1928 presented evidence that supports Baetjer's work but also reported that training greatly increased the resistance of rats even when severe exercise-induced fatigue followed the infection.

HEALTH APPRAISAL

The various tests of physical fitness are described in Chapters 8 and 9. With respect to health appraisal it seems logical to classify health examinations according to these arbitrary boundaries:

Routine (regular checkups)
  Physical (becoming more common)
  Mental (not yet accepted as necessary)
Suspect (when disease or disorder becomes apparent)
  Physical (common)
  Mental (less common than physical, but becoming more so)

It is the health educator's job to educate people with respect to the importance of both the routine and the suspect health examinations and the responsibility of the physical educator (and under certain circumstances, the recreation worker) to require a routine physical examination prior to participation in vigorous activity programs. All these people should be expected to make referrals when a suspect examination appears to be necessary.

ROUTINE EXAMINATIONS

In order to establish his health status, one should regularly visit his physician for a health examination. Once a year is recommended for adults, but this will vary for some individuals (see Table 5.5). One should expect and demand certain tests. An excellent discussion, written in lay terms, is reproduced here to familiarize you with the criteria for a thorough physical examination.

TABLE 5.5   Recommended Frequency for Physical Examinations

AGE (YEARS)	FREQUENCY FOR NORMAL PEOPLE, NO CHRONIC ILLNESS
0–1	Every six weeks
1–2	Every three months
2–6	Twice yearly
6–45	Yearly
45+	Some recommended once every nine months

SOURCE: Adapted from *Consumer Reports*, 21:31, 1956.

Just What Is a Complete Physical?

It's a physical examination that doctors say you should undergo regularly, the frequency depending on your age and general health. The completeness of a "complete" medical checkup often varies with what the doctor already knows or suspects about you. In most cases, such a checkup is merely routine, takes probably no more than an hour, and is performed in the doctor's office. A typical examination might be something like the following, although, depending on the circumstances, your own doctor may do less or more.

HISTORY If he hasn't already, the doctor will take your complete personal-health history. This is generally considered the most important part of the examination. It supplies the doctor with specific things to watch for during the checkup.

For instance, there are questions on how well you eat and sleep and about any symptomatic aches and pains. You are asked to describe the exact nature of your job, in case there are occupational hazards that could cause physical or emotional illness. The medical history (past illnesses and causes of death of relatives) of you and your family is noted. And questions about how you get along with your family, friends, and co-workers, whether you worry, and whether you like your job may be asked as leads to any psychological problems.

OBSERVATION The doctor examines you primarily through observation, feel, and use of instruments such as the stethoscope, his listening device. He makes you sit, lie, and stand in various positions according to what he may be looking for. Much of the checkup is by simple observation, and you may not realize that you're being examined. For example, the doctor takes note of the color and quality of skin, the luster and dryness of hair, the condition of nails, and so on. If abnormal, these things may be significant clues to specific ailments. He checks for scars, rashes, scabs, skin tumors, moles, swellings, discolorations, or similar visible conditions, which occasionally indicate the possibility of a serious disease. He notes your general posture, especially looking for any abnormal curvature of the spine.

MEASUREMENTS He records temperature, pulse, and weight and, when possible, compares them with those noted in any previous examination. If the doctor suspects any heart disease (or even if he doesn't), he may have you do some simple exercise to find out how quickly your pulse rate returns to normal. It should do so in about a minute; if it doesn't, the doctor then has at least an indication of your tolerance for exercise.

EYES, EARS, ETC. The doctor works from head to feet, first checking your scalp, eyes, ears, mouth, teeth, throat, and nasal passages for infections, inflammations, and growths. He or his office assistant records your blood pressure. He gives vision and hearing tests in various ways—for example, he uses a lenslike instrument to look for eye defects. Hardening of the arteries, hypertension, and kidney trouble are sometimes indicated by changes in blood vessels within the eyes.

LYMPH GLANDS When a doctor touches you in the neck, armpits, and crooks of the arms, he is determining that lymph glands at those points are normal. Glands such as these generally cannot be felt. If the doctor does feel them, the swelling tells him there may be infection or malignancies somewhere else in the body. Enlargement of the thyroid gland (in the neck, in front) may indicate abnormalities of function that could be serious.

CHEST, LUNGS These are examined by touch, by tapping, and with a stethoscope. Inhaling deeply and then exhaling shows the amount of chest expansion—useful in checking for lung ailments, notably asthma, where the chest wall is fixed and there is little, if any, expansion. The doctor listens for normal breathing signs. For example, abnormal sounds can indicate such things as pneumonia, collapsed lungs, heart disease, and pleurisy. Women's breasts are examined for any lumps which could be indications of cancer.

HEART Examining your heart, the doctor listens (with the stethoscope) for variations from normal sounds and rhythms. Slight variations may merely mean that you smoke too much, drink too much coffee, etc. But they may mean more serious trouble, and the doctor may then use more thorough heart tests.

ABDOMEN The doctor tests for hernia by having you cough as he looks for reactions —in the abdominal wall or the groin for men or in the thighs for women. He may have you lie on your back as he presses and feels various parts of your abdomen. He is probing, among other things, for the kidneys, liver, and spleen. If any appear to be too enlarged, the doctor may order further tests. For instance, if he feels the edge of your liver and it's hard or knotty, he checks for possible cancer or cirrhosis (a condition that usually causes a deterioration of liver function). While poking and feeling, the doctor watches for any lumps or masses that may be tumors.

Lymph glands in the groin are examined for enlargement that might indicate infections elsewhere in the body. Thighs and legs are checked for varicose (swollen and knotted) veins, and feet are inspected for swelling or signs of strain, caused possibly by overweight. Reflexes, such as the knee jerk, are also tested for signs of possible brain or spinal-cord damage.

RECTUM, PELVIS A rectal examination is to detect any tumors which can be early signs of cancer. Women undergo a pelvic examination (which includes the uterus and ovaries) also primarily to detect cancer.

LABORATORY TESTS Those given depend on what the rest of the examination turns up. Assuming nothing out of the ordinary is suspected, they usually include only a urinalysis, a chest X ray for tuberculosis, and various blood tests.

Usually, after the age of forty, vaginal smears (to detect cancer early) are part of all routine checkups for women, and an electrocardiogram becomes a regular test for men. An electrocardiogram—which registers heart activity by tracing a curve on graphlike paper—is also given women in many routine checkups after the menopause. Another routine test for men and women over forty is a sigmoidoscopy. This involves examination of the rectum and colon for cancer through the use of a special instrument.

Laboratory tests occasionally turn up something the doctor has not spotted in other phases of his checkup. And the tests often serve as confirmation for the doctor's preliminary diagnosis.[2]

As a person ages, he should request additional tests if they are not automatically included by the physician. We highly recommend, in addition to the routine procedures, that an exercise ECG should become a part of the physical examination after age 35. There is evidence that such a test, in the hands of the skilled physician, can be a valuable diagnostic and predictive tool in the case of otherwise silent heart disease (73, 369).

A routine but thorough health examination will establish, to the best of

---

[2]The foregoing discussion of a physical examination is reprinted by permission from the August, 1960, issue of *Good Housekeeping Magazine*. © 1960 by The Hearst Corporation.

medical science's knowledge, one's systemic health base, at least from the physical standpoint.

SUMMARY

Health is "mental and physical well-being," and physical fitness is "the capacity to carry out physical tasks involving considerable muscular effort and, thus, requiring well conditioned neuromuscular and circulo-respiratory systems."

We have proposed a distinction between physical fitness and motor ability in keeping with the above definitions wherein only the qualities related to good health and to total fitness are classified as physical fitness components (strength, flexibility, muscular endurance, and circulo-respiratory capacity). These are qualities that nearly all normal persons can improve with some effort.

Although there may be some disagreement as to exactly how our nation's health status and physical fitness status should be rated, there is little argument that improvement in both is desirable.

Health (systemic and psychological fitness) and physical fitness are most assuredly related but both contribute to a more important fitness—total fitness (the ability to function as a person) and, hopefully, to a still more important end—man's service to some ultimate concern greater than himself. We have defined and interrelated the roles of the health educator, physical educator, and recreation specialist in keeping with these relationships.

Although there is logic and some strong indirect evidence in support of the contention that physical fitness (regular physical exercise) increases longevity, there is as yet no direct, irrefutable evidence to support such a statement. There is little support for the claim that regular exercise will prevent viral and bacterial infections.

The three levels of total fitness (ability to function as an individual) are characterized as follows:

1. Subminimal—physically inefficient and inadequate; unable to meet emotional challenges successfully.
2. Minimal—physically and emotionally capable of meeting the demands of the normal day.
3. Optimal—physically and emotionally capable of meeting the demands imposed by extreme physical work loads and/or mental tasks (see principle 5 below).

PRINCIPLES

1. Optimal levels of health and physical fitness are not ends in themselves. They are, however, prerequisites to the achievement of one's fullest human potential.
2. Health and physical fitness are separate and distinct characteristics, but each can serve to place limitations on the other.
3. *Any* reasonably healthy person can achieve vast improvement in his physical fitness status.
4. Exceptional motor ability is *not* a prerequisite for the attainment of high levels of physical fitness.

5. Minimal, optimal, and maximal levels of physical fitness can be defined only in terms of a given individual and his unique requirements—*not* in terms of a group or a population.

6. Physical fitness is not a single factor or quality of being; it is made up of several components, each of which requires specific means of improvement.

7. The attainment of optimal levels of physical fitness is directly dependent upon a progressive expenditure of energy over an extended period of time in a variety of appropriate activities.

8. There appears to be a widespread willingness among people of almost all cultures to accept and perpetuate *misinformation* pertaining to health related behavior.

9. In order to effect desirable changes in matters of health or fitness, the educator must become aware of the following:

a. The perceptions, attitudes, and knowledge of the population with which he is dealing;

b. The sources from which people have obtained the information on which their perceptions and attitudes are based;

c. The basic physiological, psychological, and social phenomena underlying human function and behavior;

d. The principles of effective interpersonal communication.

10. Despite the efforts of the medical professions it is impossible for medical knowledge to be fully effective in the lives of individuals unless they have some understanding of the basic health-related problems of modern living.

11. Because many serious diseases do not produce obvious symptoms in their early stages, routine medical checkups are essential for the early detection of many serious health problems.

12. For the protection of the participant (and the supervising individual or agency, as well), medical examinations must be obtained before participation in vigorous sports or exercise programs.

EXPERIMENTS AND EXPERIENCES

1. Survey current magazines for articles concerned with fitness. Analyze each article for expressed or implied definitions of physical fitness. Compare these definitions with the concepts outlined in this chapter.

a. How many articles include motor ability items in discussions or descriptions of fitness?

b. How many articles describe exercises such as push-ups or pull-ups as being designed for strength development?

c. How many articles include flexibility as a fitness element?

d. How many of the articles include body fatness as part of physical fitness?

e. How many of the articles appear to equate sports programs with fitness programs?

f. How many of the articles appear to equate fitness programs with calisthenics; with weight lifting; with running?

2. Contact a sample of people including representatives (both male and female)

of different generations. Survey them concerning their attitudes on the importance and meaning of physical fitness. Some questions might be:

    a. What does physical fitness mean?

    b. What does health mean?

    c. Does physical fitness contribute to better health?

    d. Does physical fitness help to prevent infectious diseases?

    e. Does physical fitness contribute to longer life?

    f. Does physical fitness improve the *quality* of one's life?

    g. Is it possible for someone who is completely unskilled in athletics to be physically fit?

    h. Can a person who has a paralyzed leg be physically fit?

3. Design a downtown, street-corner observation survey. Using hand counters or tally sheets, determine what percentage of the people passing have the following characteristics:

    a. Are obviously overweight

    b. Appear to be self-assured and confident

    c. Appear to be unsure, insecure, depressed

    d. Are obviously physically impaired in some way

Compare the results of your observations with published figures on the percentage of our population suffering from obesity, physical impairment (of the kinds observed) and mental illness.

How can the discrepancies between your observations and published figures be explained?

SUGGESTED READINGS

Clarke, H. Harrison, "Contributions of Physical Education to Physical Fitness," in *Anthology of Contemporary Readings* (H. S. Slusher and A. S. Lockhart, Eds.). Dubuque, Iowa: William C. Brown Company, Publishers, 1966.

Kennedy, John F., "The Soft American," *Sports Illustrated,* December 26, 1960, pp. 15–17.

Sanborn, M. A., and B. G. Hartman, Chapter 10: "Issues Dealing with Fitness," in *Issues in Physical Education.* Philadelphia: Lea & Febiger, 1964.

Steinhaus, Arthur H. "Health and Physical Fitness," "Fitness — A Definition and a Guide to its Attainment," "Fitness and How We May Obtain It," "Fitness for Modern Living," all in *Toward an Understanding of Health and Physical Education.* Dubuque, Iowa: William C. Brown Company, Publishers, 1963.

"Who Needs Physical Fitness?" *Science Digest,* July 1964, p. 80.

Yost, C. P., "Total Fitness and Prevention of Accidents," *JOPHER,* 38(3):32, 1967.

The Concept of
Health and Fitness
Education

Chapter 6

INDOCTRINATION OR EDUCATION?

For your students to answer the question "Are you well informed or 'educated' on matters of health and physical fitness?" with the response "I have taken courses in health and physical education" is no more justifiable than for you to claim that you have a sound general education simply because you have a high school diploma. The term *educated,* when applied to a particular discipline, implies a reasonable degree of *mastery* of the content of the field. It means that a person has sufficient knowledge and understanding of the field to identify its problems and propose reasonable solutions, that he is able to discuss intelligently ideas and concepts germane to the field. This ability does not come from exposure to isolated facts or from limited contact with situations that are not intellectually challenging to the individual.

For example, a girl who has had a bout with pneumonia will have acquired certain information about the disease, but it is doubtful whether anyone would be likely to assume that she really knows much about pneumonia. No doubt she has

Figure 6.1

developed certain attitudes as a result of her experience, but what has she really learned about her illness?

On the other hand, the physician who treated her would be expected to have considerable knowledge concerning pneumonia. He was armed with more than simple firsthand experience with the disease, however. His professional training provided him with the necessary understanding of the cause and usual course of the illness, as well as a knowledge of appropriate methods of treatment, enabling him to see the girl safely through her unpleasant ordeal.

It is evident that mere exposure to selected situations can provide an individual with experiences that may result in the formation of certain *attitudes*. This, however, does not enable him to take successful steps for the preservation of his own well-being through purposeful changes in behavior and intelligent manipulation of his environment. Ability to do so comes only after he has also developed a substantial *understanding* of (1) the nature of the human organism and (2) how it is affected by various behavioral and environmental alternatives.

Each of us has his own personal interests, goals, and aspirations as well as differing likes and dislikes, unique talents, and limitations. It is therefore absurd to think that any one person or group of persons can design a health and fitness program that will meet *all* the needs of *every* individual. Furthermore, if such a procedure were possible, it would not be classified as education. Unfortunately, many of the traditional programs in the areas of health and physical education have bordered on indoctrination and regimentation instead of providing the individual with factual information that will give him a basis for determining an intelligent course of action.

At the high school and college levels it seems particularly important to emphasize that *each person must take the responsibility for what he does with his own life.* If, however, such a goal is to be successfully realized, the colleges and high schools must provide each individual with an *education* in the true sense of the word. From the standpoint of physical education and health education this means that every person must be acquainted with pertinent information relating to health and personal well-being as it is affected by exercise, social practices, occupation, personal habits, and diet. In addition, the methods whereby personal health and fitness can be achieved and maintained must be presented and scientifically evaluated. Provision for the development of a personally satisfying level of skill in one or more of these physical activities is a responsibility of high schools and colleges if these institutions subscribe to the belief that the attainment of a reasonable level of skill is a factor of consequence in the decisions that students make about their activity regimens.

Finally, as in all phases of education, presentation of information must be as complete and as unbiased as possible. Fact must be clearly distinguished from opinion. Such an undertaking, although enriching and rewarding, is never easy. Teachers find the task of collecting and organizing great masses of data time consuming and tedious. The student, in meeting his responsibilities, similarly discovers that indoctrination is a much simpler process than education! The learning of basic facts and evaluating and examining the relationships between them are processes that are conveniently circumvented in many programs where indoctrination rather than education is the ultimate goal.

So it is in answering the question "Are your students well informed or 'educated' on matters of health and physical fitness?" that the answers to three subordinate questions are important:

1. Do they have a comprehensive understanding of the physiological and psychological effects of physical activity and other health-related behavior?

2. Do they possess sufficient information to enable them to decide what kinds of behavior are best for them as individuals?

3. Have they a knowledge of a sufficiently wide variety of activities and techniques so that they could select and practice behaviors suitable to their interests, needs, and abilities?

The individual who can intelligently answer these questions is well on his way to being educated in matters of health and fitness.

SELF-ANALYSIS

"Know thyself" is a phrase that is familiar to all of us. It is stressed as a goal particularly in the disciplines of philosophy and psychology. From a practical standpoint, it is essential that we all learn to evaluate realistically our talents as well as our limitations. It is important for our own welfare that we neither grossly underestimate nor overestimate our own capacities and capabilities!

In order to do this adequately, however, we need some means of getting information about ourselves. Psychology provides intelligence tests and aptitude tests for our guidance. A simple mirror or perhaps some candid photographs frequently tell us how we look to others. A visit to the physician's office helps us to get a good idea of our status with respect to disease and physical degeneration.

There is, however, the need for a little more information about ourselves if we are going to be able to do an adequate job of problem solving and decision making in terms of our personal health and fitness.

It seems to be characteristic of people to harbor certain unrealistic ideas about their own capacities and even their physical appearance. For some reason a man in his forties may stoutly maintain, "I'm as good a man as I ever was!" and frequently, with disastrous results, he attempts to demonstrate his point. Women who steadfastly refuse to acknowledge their requirement for a larger size in a dress or a shoe are by no means unusual.

It is quite obvious to the intelligent individual that simply denying the existence of an undesirable situation affecting a person is not an effective way of correcting it. If real progress is to be made, it seems only sensible to analyze the prevailing situation as objectively as possible. This, of course, implies securing an accurate appraisal of one's condition at the time. As soon as such an appraisal is obtained, the necessary steps to improve the situation can be undertaken with relative ease.

For this reason when one is given the opportunity to participate in a series of tests that will provide him with a realistic profile of himself, he should take advantage of it, for he will be in a position to correct or adapt to his physical inadequacies and to maintain his present assets effectively.

If it has not already occurred to you to ask a leading question or two about *why* this whole approach to health and fitness is necessary, it probably will soon. This is a question that should be asked and one that deserves a satisfactory answer.

It is probably true that many high school and college students, particularly men, do not have to be convinced of the desirability of participating in sports, games, and other forms of strenuous physical activity. They participate because they are young and vigorous and because they *enjoy* the challenge and the excitement involved. Some forms of physical activity contribute to social standing and are, to some people, highly desirable for that reason alone. In any case, such people do not have to be urged and cajoled into participating in physical activity.

It may also be true, however, that as the pressures of responsibility mount, the level of participation, which is motivated by the desire for pleasure and social standing, tends to diminish. "I just don't have the time," is a typical complaint, and as the individual grows older and his responsibilities increase and pressures multiply, such participation drops proportionately. The active team games in which one learns to compete and pit his own prowess against that of others are no longer a practical or appropriate vehicle for the expression of such urges. The logical alternative is to turn to less strenuous, more convenient activities that retain the element of skill, challenge, and competition, such as bridge and bowling.

If the social and psychological fulfillment that can be gained from such activities is all that is being sought by the individual, then his switch from the active to the inactive pastimes must be considered a wise move. This implies, however, a fundamental lack of knowledge concerning the total picture. One major consideration—that of the physiological effects—has obviously been overlooked. As will be discussed later, there is a great deal of evidence to indicate that physical inactivity, coupled with our stressful pattern of living, has much to do with our present high incidence of degenerative disease affecting virtually all the systems of the body.

In the past, most programs of physical education have stressed the need for people to remain physically active throughout life. It has been reasoned that if a person is proficient in a skill and enjoys it he will continue his activity. For certain sports this logic holds, but many of the skills in which young people become interested and proficient are the team games and other sports that may be impossible for them to engage in after leaving school. Theoretically, the problem could be resolved by providing instruction in the so-called carry-over sports, such as swimming, tennis, badminton, skiing, archery, golf, and others.

In practical terms an individual sports program is difficult to institute under present conditions because of the lack of proper facilities and equipment in most schools. It is possible, however, and is being accomplished in some communities. In such cases the question now becomes, "Does this step alone ensure continued participation of the individual on a regular basis?" Unfortunately, the answer appears to be in the negative.

We believe that one of the reasons for this failure is that the matter of people's *knowledge* or lack of knowledge concerning the physiological consequences of physical inactivity is almost entirely ignored in traditional health and physical education programs. People who gain tremendous satisfaction from sports competition may, as they grow older, discover other equally satisfying outlets for their competitive urges in less strenuous pursuits. Those who have gained social recognition and approval through athletics are able to move on to other less vigorous activities in which they can continue to experience the same sort of psychological benefits. Although these people may never lose their love for sports and games, they find that this need can be at least partially met through watching others compete.

At this point we could well sketch a picture of a successful college athlete who takes on the responsibility of a job and a family. Because of pressures, changing social patterns, and other circumstances he finds that he transfers his love for competition in basketball or football to bowling or perhaps even to his business. He still enjoys attending sporting events or watching them on television and he may even become active in some sort of organization that sponsors boys' leagues of one kind or another. In short, he has been able to satisfy many of the needs formerly met by sports activity by means other than that of active participation—all his needs, in fact, except one kind: the biological.

The irony of this situation is that he is unaware of any deficiency. If he is typical, he thinks that he is getting adequate exercise through his bowling and through coaching a little league team. His lack of knowledge and understanding of how to assess and adequately meet his own health needs may well have robbed him of benefits that he might easily and enjoyably have derived from suitable exercise.

If the former athlete may find himself divorced from physically active pursuits, what can be expected for the average nonathlete? In this category we may have people with all sorts of attitudes toward physical activity, ranging from moderately frustrated fascination to complete disinterest and dislike. Such individuals would certainly be no better off than the athlete, if not considerably worse. Whereas the former athlete may be ignoring certain physiological needs, the nonparticipant may well have unmet social or psychological needs superimposed upon these as well. This is not to presume, however, that vigorous physical activity is a panacea for all of man's ills. It is merely an affirmation of the position that regular exercise is *one* of the important requirements for long-term well-being in the times in which we live.

This book places the emphasis on the personal program approach to health and to exercise. In direct contrast to some systems of physical education, it recognizes that although all people need and can profit from exercise, everyone does not want or need the *same kinds* of activities. Some people are "games players." They love competition and are adept at skills involving throwing and catching. Other people derive great satisfaction from pitting their strength and stamina against another human being. Still others prefer to engage in activities in which the only standard is their own previous performance. And, finally, there are those who, for one reason or another, do not enjoy *any* activity that remotely resembles exercise. All these groups, however, regardless of their own particular likes and dislikes, have one thing in common: a biological need for regular, vigorous, physical activity. (Documentation of this point of view will appear in subsequent chapters.) It also points out the need for "active" and dynamic learning experiences in health education. The time-honored "textbook, poster, and movies" approach is archaic and is not likely to promote learning.

How then can any program possibly hope to cope successfully with diversity of interests? The obvious answer, we believe, is to provide all these individuals with the facts about health and the interrelationships with physical activity, acquaint them with a wide variety of basic techniques that can be used to attain adequate levels of physical fitness; next assist them in acquiring experience and reasonable proficiency in some practical or individual activity, and then encourage them to make their own decisions about the importance of good health and physical activity in their lives. Under such a plan, those who elect to supplement their occupational duties with some type of regular exercise program will be able to select —or design—the type of activity that appeals to them and that will, at the same time, meet their personal physiological, social, and psychological needs.

PROMOTING HEALTH AND FITNESS

Any plans to attack the fortress of "Mr. and Mrs. Modern," unaware and sedentary, must take into account the fact that they are surrounded by a moat of *misunderstanding* and, possibly even more resistant to attack, a wall of *indif-*

FIGURE 6.2   Mr. and Mrs. Modern Sedentary U.S.A.

ference. Misunderstanding and indifference will be difficult to penetrate in the adult population — perhaps even difficult to push aside in the present school-age youngsters and college students. Community leaders and parents should be aware of the problems, needs, and possible solutions. The following suggested approaches are advanced in full knowledge that, although each is important, probably the critical and most hopeful approaches involve the preschool program and a new and revitalized program of *integrated* health and physical education in the schools.

FOR THE ADULT, NONSCHOOL POPULATION

The best hope for the adult population is that, through the popular communi-

cation media and through contact with children in the program recommended below, they will become aware of and interested in moving up the health and fitness ladder. Specifically, we recommend that leaders in health, physical education, and recreation recommend and *publicize* personal programs based on the suggestions outlined on page 624.

FOR SCHOOL-AGE CHILDREN AND YOUTH

It is our firm belief that the most promising, long-range solution to this total problem lies in an integrated school health and physical education problem for grades K to 12. It is the purpose of this kind of program, some form of which is practiced at a few colleges and high schools, to supplement the

FIGURE 6.3 Physical and mental takeiteasyism.

traditional skills approach with opportunities to experience and evaluate objectively the need for and the values of being healthy and fit. These opportunities come through *personal* experiences in life—meeting *personal* needs based on capacities. In addition—and these are the missing ingredients in traditional health and physical education curricula—our schools must teach the research-substantiated benefits *and limitations* of health practices and exercise and fitness programs; and they must emphasize the importance of a body of scientific knowledge for making intelligent decisions relative to exercise, health, and fitness. In such a program students can truly become "health- and fitness-educated." This book is dedicated to supplying these two missing ingredients.

It is our contention that misconceptions, frustrations, and fears often result from health education and physical education programs limited to memorization, skills instruction, and participation in games. We often forget that memorization of health principles is boring, that some youngsters do *not* enjoy sports, especially when skill level is poor and there is little or no success. Indifference often results over a period of years from the misconception that skills, health, and fitness are all one and the same. This indifference and frustration can best be prevented by a well-planned, early, and dynamic exposure to a sound personal health and fitness program. There is evidence that **early learning** is superior to late learning (see page 119. Does it not seem logical that health and fitness education should capitalize on this "law of nature"? It is possible that the much-discussed lack of creativity and vitality in our people can be at least partially minimized through such an effective and creative approach to health and fitness. *Making decisions relative to health and fitness certainly involves creativity and, hopefully, will also lead to improved "vitality" and fitness.*

FOR PRESCHOOL CHILDREN

The importance of early training in the home has obvious application to the development of the total health and fitness concept. If health and fitness, including all controllable factors, is established firmly as a "way of life" in the home, we will have the best start possible in the push to develop some semblance of a respectable health and fitness level in our population. If a baby sees from his crib a vigorous way of life going on about him, will he not be likely to *join* in that way of life on his own level at his own time and accept this as his way of life? Steinhaus (543, p. 28) may have been very close to the truth of the matter when he maintained that mothers are our first physical education teachers! (A recent study 482) presents evidence that high school students who are active are given significantly better examples to follow concerning physical activity than are inactive students. Their fathers are physically more active and their parents give them more encouragement to participate in vigorous activities than is true of inactive students.) The quality of the early parental "instruction" and the example of planned, regular, and vigorous activity by mother and father may well be the key that opens the door to a creative and healthful life.

COMMUNITY HEALTH AGENCIES

It is imperative that health educators, physical educators, and recreation leaders have some knowledge about typical community health services and some of the specific health organizations available for assistance of various kinds. A listing of these services and health agencies is outlined.

A. General functions: Each state has a health department (a city or a county may also have a health department). The services usually include:

1. Recording births, deaths, sickness
2. Sanitation (water, milk, food, air, inspection of swimming pools, garbage and sewage disposal, inspection of restaurants)
3. Laboratories for supervision of sanitation and for communicable disease control
4. Control and prevention of communicable disease
5. Public health education
6. Hygiene during maternity, infancy, and childhood for those who cannot afford proper care
7. Occasionally: crippled children's services, dental health, mental health clinics, school health screening programs

B. Some specific health organizations (national, state, community, and voluntary), which provide some patient

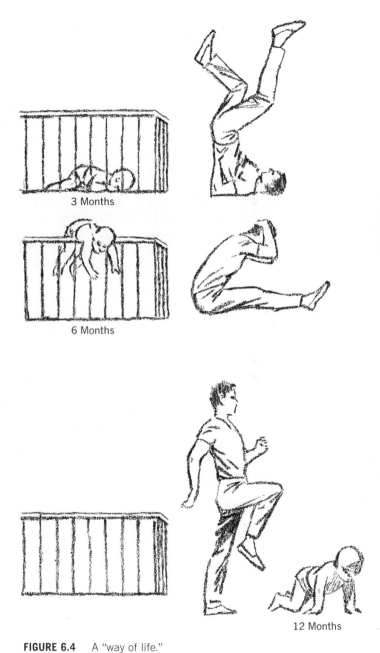

3 Months

6 Months

12 Months

FIGURE 6.4 A "way of life."

services, are listed. Offices are not necessarily located in every area, but one can determine what services are available by checking with the city, county, or state health department.

1. U.S. Public Health Service
2. Local or State Health Department
3. Community Chest
4. U.S. Veterans' Administration
5. Council of Social Agencies
6. State Board for Crippled Children
7. State Commission for the Blind
8. American Cancer Society
9. The American Red Cross
10. The American Hearing Society
11. The American Heart Association
12. The National Multiple Sclerosis Society
13. The National Foundation for Neuromuscular Diseases, Inc.
14. National Society for the Aid of Retarded Children
15. National Tuberculosis Association
16. The National Society for Crippled Children and Adults
17. United Cerebral Palsy Associations

SUMMARY

Neither mere exposure to facts and experiences nor indoctrination techniques lead to true education.

Each person must be helped to realize that he must take responsibility for what he does with his own life.

The health- and fitness-educated person: (1) understands the physio-logical and psychological effects of physical activity and inactivity; (2) knows how to decide how much and what kind of activity is best for him; (3) can select skills or techniques suitable to his interests, needs, and abilities.

The personalized approach to health and fitness holds the most promise for promoting sound health and fitness education at all levels of instruction.

The public's misunderstanding of and indifference toward the real nature of health and fitness must be overcome by an intelligent and dynamic approach to teaching about health and fitness.

Misconceptions, frustrations, and fears often result for health and physical education programs based on memorization and over-emphasis on games participation.

PRINCIPLES

1. In order for people to be in a position to take successful steps for preservation of their own well-being, they must have an understanding of the nature of the human organism and how it is affected by behavioral and environmental factors.
2. The best way to reduce the misconceptions and frustrations associated with health and fitness concepts is to *prevent* such unfortunate blemishes through purposeful *education* provided early enough in the child's life to capitalize on the principle of early learning.

EXPERIMENTS AND EXPERIENCES

1. Systematically survey your own classmates. How many claim to have

had a good "health" education? A good "physical" education? What do they mean by good? When did such programs begin? Have they known persons who had misconceptions and ungrounded frustrations about health and fitness? What seemed to have caused these attitudes or feelings?

2. Identify recent examples of health and/or fitness education for the adult population. Evaluate them in terms of accuracy and effectiveness. What improvements could you suggest?

3. Did you graduate from high school well educated in matters of health and fitness? Why so or why not?

4. Select some health and fitness concepts which you feel are essential and also realistically attainable for a given age child. Talk with some children in that age group to determine: (1) do they have the concept in hand? (2) if not, can they assimilate it with your help? Discuss your results with your contemporaries. Try the same survey on the same concepts with high school youth, college students, young adults, and older adults. What meaning do you attach to your results and how do they relate to the concepts and two key principles of this chapter?

SUGGESTED READINGS

Fodor, J. T., and G. T. Dalis, *Health Instruction Theory and Application.* Philadelphia: Lea & Febiger, 1966.

Johnson, P. B., "An Academic Approach to College Health and Physical Education," *JOHPER,* 37:3, 23, 1967.

Pleasants, F., "Fitness Education," *Physical Educator,* 25:77, 1968.

School Health Education Study. Washington, D.C., 1964.

Steinhaus, A. H., "What Is Fitness Education?" "Health Education in the United States," "The Story of Susie," all in *Toward an Understanding of Health and Physical Education.* Dubuque, Iowa: William C. Brown Company, Publishers, 1963.

PART III

Philosophic and Scientific Foundations

Basic
Philosophic
Considerations

by Jan Broekhoff[1]

Chapter 7

What is mind?/No matter!
What is matter?/Never mind! (100, p. 51)

Earlier in this book you may have come across the word *philosophy* and read about the desirability of developing a philosophy of life. We must now ask ourselves the question of what philosophy is and what possible significance it has for physical education. Perhaps no word in the English language has lost so much of its original significance in its daily usage as the word philosophy. Nowadays, when a person refers to his "philosophy" with respect to certain problems, he usually does not pretend to offer more than a personal opinion. But it is precisely personal opinion that is furthest removed from true philosophy.

In the famous "Allegory of the Cave," the great philosopher Plato compares men of opinion with prisoners in an underground den who mistake shadows cast on a wall for realities because they have been chained in the dark from childhood. The only way for the prisoners to gain real knowledge would

---

[1]This chapter was written especially for this book by Dr. Jan Broekhoff of the University of Toledo. Dr. Broekhoff is a specialist in the philosophical and historical aspects of physical education.

be to break their chains and turn to the light at the risk of being blinded by its intensity (456, p. 773). Plato alludes of course to the fact that most of us are prisoners in a world of bias, partly of our own making. By this allegory he also shows a deep distrust for the world of the senses, a position not universally shared by philosophers after him. Regardless of this, however, the philosopher emerges as the man of knowledge distinguished from the man of opinion. *Philosophy*, as the word itself indicates (*philein*—" to love," and *sophos*—" wisdom"), is the search for wisdom.

At this point you may ask yourself what distinguishes the philosopher from the scientist, because the latter, too, has a stake in knowledge. And science was indeed in its early stages of development nothing but an offshoot of an all-encompassing philosophy. Science gained its independence, however, primarily through the type of questions scientists posed and through the method by which they sought to answer these questions. In studying and observing the physical world, the scientist formulates problems that ultimately must be answered and verified by empirical evidence. One of the most important scientific tools is the controlled experiment in which only selected aspects of reality are allowed to vary. In contrast, few if any answers to philosophical questions can be subjected to empirical verification and experimentation. The meaning of this difference between science and philosophy will become clearer to you when we discuss specific issues later in this chapter. For the moment it is important to realize that, as a rule, science cannot provide answers to philosophical questions.

In several periods of its history, notably during the Middle Ages, philosophy had a close connection with religion. Even today, many speculative philosophical inquiries into the nature of man and the universe border on questions asked in religion. Whereas the answers to such questions in philosophy are reached through the power of human reason, they are guided in religion by faith. Part of the philosophic enterprise has been and still is to determine the rules of reasoning in what is called the study of logic. In the search for knowledge, logical analysis has always been the hallmark of the philosophical method, but this is not to say that philosophers have always closed their minds to knowledge of a more intuitive order.

Although the history of philosophical thought shows a wide variety of concerns, certain themes have recurred with great consistency. The eighteenth-century German philosopher Immanuel Kant summarized the main speculative and practical philosophical problems in the following three questions: (1) What can I know? (2) What ought I to do? and (3) What may I hope? For Kant these three questions were focused and synthesized in the one basic problem: What is man? (117, p. 315) In a more formal way, but very much related to Kant's fundamental questions, one can distinguish several branches of philosophy according to the emphasis on particular problems. Thus, the study of knowledge is called *epistemology*, the

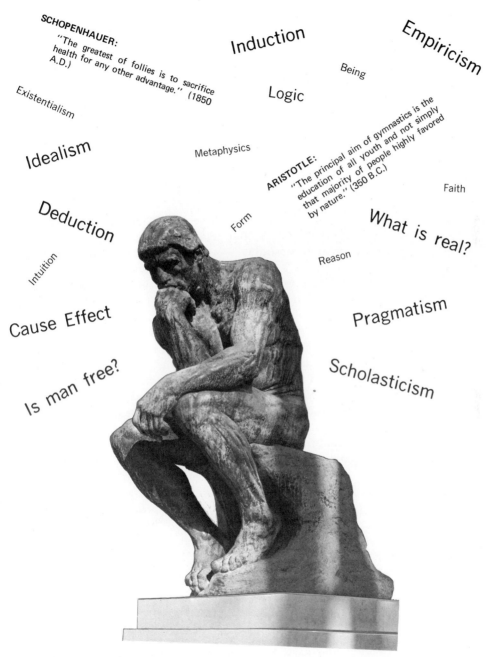

SCHOPENHAUER: "The greatest of follies is to sacrifice health for any other advantage." (1850 A.D.)

Induction

Empiricism

Being

Existentialism

Logic

Idealism

Metaphysics

ARISTOTLE: "The principal aim of gymnastics is the education of all youth and not simply that majority of people highly favored by nature." (350 B.C.)

Faith

Deduction

Form

What is real?

Intuition

Reason

Cause Effect

Pragmatism

Is man free?

Scholasticism

FIGURE 7.1   The philosopher attempts to reach the answers to questions concerning the nature of man and the universe through the power of human reason. (Auguste Rodin, "The Thinker," Rodin Museum, Philadelphia. Courtesy Philadelphia Museum of Art.)

study of reality, *ontology* or *metaphysics,* and the study of values, *axiology.* The third can be subdivided further into *ethics,* the study and evaluation of human conduct, and *aesthetics,* the concern with criteria of artistic judgment.

Just as it is possible to discern recurrent problems in the history of philosophy, it is also possible to recognize basic positions with regard to these problems. Frequently one refers to these basic positions as "philosophical systems" or "schools of philosophy." The "schools of philosophy" have often been founded by a great philosopher who defined the premises of a philosophical point of view and attracted a large following. The *Neoplatonic School,* for example, was developed by Plotinus in the third century A.D., although it derived many of its tenets from the earlier teachings of Plato. Some of the important philosophical positions such as idealism and realism developed into frameworks of philosophical thinking through the contributions of many philosophers over a long period of time and cannot be linked to the name of one particular man.

Physical educators have usually indicated the importance of philosophy for their profession by explaining the traditional philosophical systems and inferring the relevance of these positions for the practice of physical education. In the following sections we shall take a different approach. First we shall examine the influence of philosophy on physical education by considering the problem of monism-dualism in a historical perspective. In a second section we show how physical education

can "goad one into philosophizing" by looking at some current problems in physical education with definite philosophical implications.

AFFERENT CONCEPTS: EFFECTS OF PHILOSOPHY ON PHYSICAL ACTIVITY

CLASSICAL GREECE

Physical education and athletics in classical Greece certainly occupy a place of honor in the long history of physical education. And when we think of Greece we think especially of the city state of Athens at the height of its development during the middle of the fifth century B.C. It is hard to find another period in history when physical education played such a vital and integrating role in the lives of children as well as adults. The ideal of the upper classes to be "good as well as beautiful" (the *kalokagathia*), had been extended to the common people in a democracy where the educational goals were no longer determined by military objectives. Artists portrayed bodily perfection and harmony on the vases and in the sculptures of an era that historians called the "Golden Age of Pericles" after the great statesman who led the Athenians to uncommon achievements in politics, literature, art, philosophy, and education. Pericles himself presented Athens as an example to the rest of the world, calling it the "School of Hellas" (562, p. 106).

The importance of physical education for the Athenians is best illustrated in

FIGURE 7.2 Greek ideals of bodily perfection and harmony have been preserved in the remarkable sculpture that is characteristic of an era called the "Golden Age of Pericles." (Polyclitus' "Doryphorus" [spearbearer]. Roman copy of original of c. 450-440 B.C. Marble, 6'6" high. National Museum, Naples. Photo, Alinari–Art Reference Bureau.)

Plato's dialogue the *Meno*, in which Socrates and Anytos discuss the education of the sons of some of the most illustrious citizens. Plato gives the following account of their conversation:

Socrates: . . . *I suppose you have heard that Themistocles had his son Cleophantes taught to be a good horseman. At least, he could remain standing upright on horseback, and cast a javelin upright on horseback, and do many other wonderful*

feats *which the great man had him taught, and he made him clever in all that could be got from good teachers.*

(. . .) *Or Pericles, if you like, a man magnificently wise — you know he brought up two sons, Paralos and Xanthippos?*
Anytos: *Oh yes.*
Socrates: *Well, he taught them (you know that, as I do) to be horsemen as good as any in Athens; he educated them in the fine arts and gymnastics and all the rest, to be as good as any as far as education goes.*

(. . .) *remember Thucydides again — he brought up two sons, Melesias and Stephanos, and gave them a proper education; in particular they were the best wrestlers in Athens . . . (455, p. 100).*

It is not surprising that in the Athens of those days an uneducated person would be described as someone who "knows neither how to read nor how to swim" (454, p. 464). Yet, at the time of the dialogue between Socrates and Anytos, presumably toward the end of the fifth century B.C., a profound educational revolution had taken place. In drawing his examples, Socrates had no intention of glorifying the traditional educational system, but he wanted to point out to Anytos that in spite of the best that the old education could offer, the famous fathers had not succeeded in teaching their sons virtue. Socrates is speaking out for an education that places more emphasis on intellectual development.

The change toward a more intellectual education took place during the latter third of the fifth century B.C., while Athens was engaged in a struggle of

life and death with Sparta. Besides
Socrates, there was a group of professional educators called the *Sophists*
that was particularly effective in spreading educational innovation. The Sophists lectured about their new ideas to
large groups of students who paid a
fee to attend the lectures. Aristophanes,
the great comic poet of that time, gives
a biting comment on educational change
when he describes a youth with a traditional education as modest, broad-shouldered, and well-built, spending
his time in the gymnasiums, and Aristophanes adds: "But if your mode of life
is up-do-date, you will have a weak
body, a colour sickly pale, narrow shoulders, an immense tongue . . . " (18,
p. 1002).

The traditional ideal of the *kalokagathia* expressed the harmony of the
physical, moral, and intellectual qualities of man. If initially traditional education put undue emphasis on physical training, later it balanced physical
education with music and literature.
Underlying the educational innovations of the Sophists is a philosophy
that regards man in the first place as
an intellectual being. The next step is
the total separation of physical and intellectual qualities, a **dualism** of body
and mind that finds its ablest expression in the philosophy of Plato. In his
political philosophy, especially in *The
Republic,* Plato still seems to advocate
the traditional education. The citizens
of his ideal state must have "gymnastics for the body, and music for the
soul" (456, p. 640). There is no doubt,
however, that the soul or mind is the
leading principle and more honorable

than the body. In his speculative philosophy, Plato describes the body frequently as the contamination of the
soul, even as a prison from which the
soul can only escape through death
(453, p. 62). It is not surprising then,
that Plato distrusts the bodily senses
and that, in his view, only the mind
can have access to real knowledge.

The teachings of Socrates and the
Sophists, and later the philosophic dualism of Plato, did not result in the disappearance of physical education. Long
after Athens had ceased to be the leader of the Hellenic world, physical education continued to be taught in the
schools and adults kept visiting the
gymnasiums. The place of physical
education as the integrative and powerful force of the total educational system
had been increasingly taken over by
intellectual pursuits. The gymnasiums
(*gymnadzein*—"to exercise," and *gymnos*
—"naked") became the meeting places
for orators and their audiences and for
philosophers and their students.[2] At
the root of this transition from an education that emphasized physical development to an intellectually oriented
education we can find an important
change in the philosophical concept
of man.

RATIONALISM AND SYSTEMS OF PHYSICAL EDUCATION

The dualism of mind and body that
Plato implanted in the history of West-

---

[2]It is interesting to note that the highly intellectual classical high schools of some Western
European countries are called "gymnasiums."

ern thought was freshly stated in the seventeenth century by the French philosopher and scientist Rene Descartes. His famous phrase, "I think, therefore I am," is the philosophical expression of the superiority of the rational over the physical powers. According to Descartes, the body belongs to the realm of material substance (*res extensae*), it occupies space, and it is divisible. The mind or soul, on the other hand, is a thinking, spiritual substance (*res cogitans*); it is indivisible, and it does not occupy space. Descartes can describe the body, therefore, as a complicated, vital machine that needs to be joined to the soul to become a spiritual human being. He actually locates the spot where the soul affects and acts upon the body, at the pineal gland, a pea-sized structure at the back of the midbrain (586). It is this rigid separation of body and mind that prompted the English philosopher Gilbert Ryle to refer to Descartes' dualism as "the ghost in the machine" (490).

The philosophy of Descartes made a big impact on the Western society of the next centuries. His dualistic conception of man placed a great premium on the power of reason and led to an increasing reliance on the rational solution to problems. In a practical sense this brand of **rationalism** resulted in a strong faith in progress through the expansion of the powers of the mind, and a belief that most, if not all, problems could be solved by reason. Descartes' writings, in conjunction with the work of the English empiricists, also proved a great impetus for the de-

velopment of the sciences. One of the contributions to science in Descartes' thinking was the recognition that complex material substance can be broken down into component parts that can then be studied in their simpler forms.

The influence of rationalism and the dualistic conception of man upon physical education is clearly evident in the emergence of the European systems of physical education during the nineteenth century. The German system started out as a patriotic *Turn* movement (somewhat comparable to gymnastics) under the leadership of Friedrich Ludwig Jahn, but it reached its characteristic form when Adolf Spiesz introduced the exercises into the German schools around the middle of the century. To adapt the gymnastics of the *Turners* to the highly intellectual school system, Spiesz first considered the movement possibilities of the body. In typically rational fashion he viewed the body as an object, a marionette, in which the joints form the natural dividing points. Ideally, the movements of arms and legs take place in straight lines along the geometrical axes of the body joints, and end positions are preferably held at ninety-degree angles to the body. In this way, Spiesz constructed his famous free exercises and group exercises from basic body positions such as lying, kneeling, squatting, and standing. The possibilities for variation appeared unlimited, and Spiesz carefully maintained a progression from simple to complex and from easy to difficult movement forms. His formal system of exercises fitted perfectly into the educational climate of the nineteenth century. The **pedagogical** purpose of the exercises was to bring the body under control of the mind, so discipline was foremost in the mind of the physical education teacher.

Although the Swedish system of physical education differed in many respects from the German system, the Swedish exercises clearly bore evidence of a rationalistic approach. For Per Henrik Ling, founder of Swedish gymnastics, and his followers the guiding principle was not movement possibility but rather movement utility. The Swedish educators were interested in the anatomical and physiological effects of exercise on the body. Because anatomical effects could best be studied and controlled in simple, isolated movements, functional human movements were dissected and reduced to component parts. The Swedish exercises had, therefore, many of the same mechanical and geometrical qualities as the German exercise. Through the dichotomy of

FIGURE 7.3 Dualistic concepts of mind and body shaped the stilted, unnatural systems of physical education of the 19th century.

body and mind, the body could be viewed as any other material object, a complicated machine that needed to be kept in good shape. This dualistic tendency that is so evident in the stilted and unnatural movements of the systems of physical education pervades the nineteenth century and even shapes the formal movements of the classic ballet.

RETURN TO THE UNITY OF MIND AND BODY

Even during the time in which rationalistic philosophy enjoyed its greatest influence, divergent philosophical positions were appearing, notably from philosophers and educators of the naturalistic tradition. The reactions against the dualistic conception of man and the unlimited faith in progress through reason culminated in our own twentieth century, especially after the shock of the two world wars. After World War I, the German philosopher and psychologist Ludwig Klages presented a theory of particular interest to physical education because it directly influenced the development of rhythmic gymnastics in western Europe. Klages' philosophy lay still within the dualistic tradition, but it marked a radical reversal of the prevalent conception when he opposed to the unity of body and soul the mind as a hostile element. For Klages the soul is the meaning of the body, and the body the appearance of the soul. Through this unity of body and soul, the human being partakes of the unity of the cosmos, the movements of wind and waves, and the rhythm of day and night. The mind, however, disturbs the unity and harmony of body and soul. According to Klages, the mind strives for the eternal, that which is strange to life, and degrades the body into a machine (586, p. 106).

Klages' conception of man finds its expression in the rhythmical gymnastics of Rudolf Bode. In contrast to the geometrical, angular movements of the Swedish and German systems, the rhythmical movement is initiated at the center of gravity of the body and from there flows smoothly to the body's periphery. Bode points to the importance of eliminating the will (mind) from the flow of movement. Motion is evoked and sustained by music; the important thing is the emotional experience of realizing the unity of body and soul, not the mastery of mind over body (59).

After centuries of predominantly dualistic conceptions of man, our modern time has signaled the return to a monistic position that emphasizes the unity of mind and body. No longer is the mind considered as an immaterial substance that does the thinking, but rather as the thinking activity itself (116, p. 42). The mind finds its expression in the body but cannot be separated from it nor located in a particular part of its structure. This shift in the philosophical conception of man is not only evident in the **pragmatic** philosophy of the United States but also in the **existential** and **phenomenological** movements of the European continent. Progress in the sciences also has contributed to the image of man as a psychosomatic unity. The sciences have

often presented empirical evidence leading to the re-evaluation of speculative theory. It would be hard, for example, in the light of the recent heart transplantations, to maintain the medieval image of the heart as the animated center of the human being.

The change to a **monistic** conception of man has not missed its effect on the theory and practice of physical education. The formal European systems of physical education no longer advocate the stilted, angular movements of the past but recognize the desirability of natural, functional movements related to concrete tasks. Children no longer lift arms and legs on command but explore possibilities and limitations in movement situations that involve them entirely in the solution of a problem. In the wake of the philosophical writings of William James and John Dewey, American physical educators earlier in this century rejected the formal European exercises and turned to functional movements in games and play. Although an increasing emphasis on physical fitness has overshadowed the play-and-games theory, physical educators today are keenly aware of the advantage of exercise forms that involve the "total" child. In contrast, the concern for physical fitness has resulted in the continuation of some of the old, "rationalistic" exercises, such as pull-ups, push-ups, sit-ups, and jumping jacks.

The changes in attitude toward the body are reflected in many aspects of everyday life. We can, for example, draw many inferences from a comparison of women's clothing in the Victori-

FIGURE 7.4 Clothing of the Victorian period contrasted with that of the present day reflects changes in philosophical concepts pertaining to the relationships between mind and body.

an period with that of the present day. The dualistic position was and still is often linked to the religious belief in the transient quality of the body and the immortality of the soul. The body or the "flesh" was frequently considered sinful, and it is not surprising that people attempted to cover it up as much as possible. The monistic view of the human being has nearly always allowed a freer expression of the body, because it does not reject it as an inferior part of the human being.

There is a danger that the monistic position leads to a naive conception of the unity of mind and body. Several existential philosophers have pointed out the differences between "the body I *am*" and "the body I *have*." When we are totally involved in a familiar game situation, we seldom consciously think about our own body. In a sense we "forget" our body in the immediate action of the game. A difficult move or a missed chance, however, may make us suddenly aware of the body we *have,* and we may even experience our body as a thing or an obstacle. These modes of experience can be of great value for the teaching of physical education. The distinction, which need not lead to classical or rational dualism, certainly merits the attention of the philosophizing physical educator.

EFFERENT CONCEPTS: HOW PROBLEMS OF PHYSICAL ACTIVITY AFFECT PHILOSOPHY

In the introduction to this chapter we made the statement that, as a rule, science cannot provide the answers to questions of a philosophic nature. In this section we shall attempt to illustrate this point by discussing the problems surrounding physical fitness and the differences between the physical educator and the coach. Hopefully, such discussions may also contribute to an understanding of the term *physical education.*

PHYSICAL FITNESS FOR WHAT PURPOSE?

Hardly any physical educator will disagree with the claim that physical fitness is one of the legitimate objectives of physical education. Elsewhere in this book physical fitness is defined as "the capacity to carry out tasks involving considerable muscular effort and thus requiring well-conditioned neuromuscular and circulo-respiratory systems." In its objective formulation, this definition is a good example of the scientific approach. The capacity for muscular work is subject to scientific measurement, and there is the possibility to isolate the factors that determine such a physical performance. At present, the components of physical fitness most frequently mentioned are muscular strength, muscular endurance, circulo-respiratory capacity, and flexibility. Although the definition of physical fitness needs further refinement, our knowledge of anatomy and physiology, together with modern techniques of measurement, enable us to assess physical fitness with a reasonable degree of accuracy.

Because children and adults in our society live under similar conditions, physical fitness norms can be established through statistical sampling procedures. It is also conceivable that absolute as well as relative norms could be constructed through different scientific techniques that could allow for individual differences and the need for an emergency surplus of physical fitness. The applied sciences also help to evaluate the effectiveness of exercise programs in meeting physical fitness norms. The task of the physical educator with respect to physical fitness objectives would, therefore, seem relatively simple. To meet the physical fitness needs of his students, all that he would have to do would be to establish the desired norms and select the proper exercises. And, to be sure, many physical educators would agree that such is the correct way to go about it. But

is the problem of physical fitness really that simple?

In 1933 Adolf Hitler emphasized in his notorious book *Mein Kampf* that physical fitness is more important for the welfare of a nation than the development of intellectual capacities:

The people's republic must presuppose that a physically fit individual with a good, strong character, full of determination and will power, is of more value to society than an intellectual weakling, even if the former has had little education. . . .

The total education and instruction [of a young citizen] must be directed to give him the conviction that he is definitely superior to others. Through his strength and agility he must regain the belief in the invincibility of the entire nation (249, pp. 21–23).

Physical fitness has here become a means toward an end with far-reaching implications for the individual and society. Hitler in effect gave his answer to the question: "Physical fitness for what purpose?" It is precisely this question that cannot be answered by science, because it deals with human values. By his demand that physical fitness lead to individual and collective feelings of superiority and invincibility, Hitler indirectly shaped the norms of conduct that became characteristic of Nazi Germany.

The physical education literature during the Nazi period gives ample evidence that the majority of German physical educators accepted Hitler's aims. With the Nazi ideology in mind, physical fitness was taught with great emphasis on discipline as the collective enterprise of a superior race. The physical fitness programs were indeed geared to Hitler's wish that the army would not have to bother with fundamentals, would have nothing to do but "change already perfectly fit young men into soldiers" (249, p. 24).

Nazi Germany was by no means the only country where physical education, with the main objective of physical fit-

FIGURE 7.5 The heroic art forms of Nazi Germany reflect the great emphasis that was placed upon the ideals of physical fitness and strict discipline by the leaders of that totalitarian society. ("Faustkämter," by Thorak. Photo, Bruckmann–Art Reference Bureau.)

ness, served the nationalistic tendencies of that time. The history of physical education abounds with examples of similar servitude. Some people, observing the connection between physical fitness and military preparation, have claimed that physical fitness is morally bad. Such an argument has no validity, because fitness could very well be the decisive factor in a rescue operation to save the lives of people in distress. Physical fitness in itself is neither good nor bad. It is rather the ends, toward which physical fitness is used, that are good or bad. One could hardly say that a man's eyes are morally bad because he got himself into trouble by looking at an immoral act.

If physical fitness is neither good nor bad, would it not be safer to remain uncommitted and provide one's students with scientifically adequate levels of fitness, without posing the question of purpose? After all, a physician does not ask questions about his patient's behavior once he has cured him. But perhaps the relationship between teacher and student is fundamentally different from the relationship between physician and patient.

Nearly ten years ago some schools in the United States introduced a colored trunk system to motivate the development of physical fitness. The color of a pair of trunks represented a certain fitness level, and the ideal was to reach the highest fitness level: a golden pair of trunks. On first impression this system may seem to be just another motivational device to enhance the physical fitness of the students, without any commitment to normative values. A closer inspection, however, reveals the system as a microcosm of values with a strong emphasis on competition and the survival of the fittest. In such a system the physically gifted rise rapidly to the top, whereas their less fortunate peers are doomed to wear trunks that will forever remind them and others of their inadequacy. The ideal result would be, of course, "a perfect zoo of nearly perfect monkeys" (459, p. 317).

In physical education it is extremely hard if not impossible to develop physical fitness in students, while maintaining the detachment of a surgeon. The contact between teacher and student is a pedagogical encounter that does not take place in a neutral atmosphere. Consciously or subconsciously, physical educators express values and establish rules of conduct by the way they approach a problem such as physical fitness. For the physical educator as an individual as well as for the profession as a whole, the question of the purpose of physical fitness or any objective of physical education is a vital ethical issue. Do we follow the aims of society, regardless of the consequences, as the physical educators in Nazi Germany did, or do we actively participate in shaping these aims? In this book the authors have expressed their ideas about these problems, and it is up to you to evaluate these ideas and start philosophizing about them.

PHYSICAL EDUCATOR AND COACH

In the United States the tasks of the physical educator and the coach are often confused by the average citizen. When an outsider asks a physical educator how his football team is doing and hears that he does not coach at all, there is often the question "But what *do* you do?" Because in the United States physical educators often coach athletic teams and because coaches teach physical education classes, the confusion is not surprising. In most European countries, on the contrary, the differences between a physical educator and a coach are clearly recognized. One of the important distinctions is that, as a rule, the European coach does not teach physical education classes. In The Netherlands, for example, the Minister of Education has repeatedly refused to employ coaches in the schools, although in many respects the coaches have a better understanding of physical exercise than does the classroom teacher.

To understand the distinctions the Europeans draw between the physical educator and the coach, we must first look at the professional world of the former. In the preceding section we indicated that the physical educator, in emphasizing physical fitness, expresses values and establishes rules of conduct that point beyond the immediate concern of fitness to normative behavior in our society. The world of the physical educator is in touch with the values of society, and he tries to prepare his students for those values. Besides the social world in which normative behavior is important, the physical educator is also and above all concerned with the individual well-being of *every* person under his care.

He must pay attention to the growth and development of retarded as well as advanced children in all physical, psychological, and social dimensions. The means through which the physical educator attempts to achieve his task are physical exercises of all kinds. His students, the goals, and the tools of his trade constitute the pedagogical world of the physical educator.

To understand better the world of the physical educator we must follow him in a specific pedagogical situation. Let us assume that he has selected a competitive sport to achieve certain educational objectives. It is very important to recognize that the physical educator uses the sport as a means toward certain goals. This means that he must have the freedom to manipulate the pedagogical situation, if he is to derive any benefit from it. There are many ways in which a physical educator can adapt a pedagogical situation to his objectives. He may change the rules of a game so that the weaker players get a better chance to participate; he may form teams so that he gets an evenly matched game; and he may stop the game at any moment to point out lack of cooperation or poor sportsmanship. This freedom to create the pedagogical situation is the physical educator's only guarantee of reaching his aims with respect to the individual well-being of all students and the social norms operating among them.

From this description it must be obvious how the world of the coach differs from that of the physical educator. The coach works only with a select group of students who are highly talented physically. The weak and the retarded are spectators on the fringe of the coach's world. Whereas the physical educator has many forms of physical activity available as tools, the coach must remain a specialist in only one or two sports. He can neither manipulate the rules of these sports nor choose sides to make the contest even. Whereas the aims of the physical educator are the individual well-being of his students and their social adjustment, the coach is often forced to work toward the single goal of winning the game. If we are honest, we must admit that in highly competitive athletics the coach must look at his players as the means to an end.

Many people may object to these distinctions, as they remember their days of interscholastic competition as rewarding "educational experiences." A summer job at the factory, however, may also have been such an "educational experience," but this does not imply that the factory foreman was an educator. There are, of course, many shades of gray between black and white, and it is possible that a coach places the individual and social well-being of his players above the winning of a game. Such a coach may even occasionally be successful; he may manage to combine the tasks of coach and physical educator. Such occasional success does not, however, disprove the fact that the worlds of the physical educator and the coach are only marginally related.

In the United States many coaches have graduated with a diploma in physical education and are therefore entitled to teach physical education classes. Sometimes the combination works, but all too often one interest pushes the other into the background. Each individual must decide in his own conscience what he really wants to do and then try to do well what he has chosen. It is important to understand, moreover, that the distinction between physical educator and coach does not result in labeling the one as good and the other as bad. They are simply different, and it is high time that both physical educators and coaches come to recognize the differences.

In spite of all their differences, however, the worlds of the physical educator and the coach obviously have their meeting points. European interscholastic sports still have a very strong educational character, due to mass participation in which one school will often field as many as ten or fifteen teams in a particular sport. The preparation and selection of the teams are mostly organized by the students themselves with the help of the physical educator. Here he steps partly into the role of a coach. When he discovers talented players in his school teams, he will most likely encourage them to join a sports club, and that is where the real coach makes fine athletes out of them.

The distinctions between physical educator and coach may help us to gain a better understanding of physical education. In conclusion, we could state: "Whatever physical education is, it is not athletics." This is a negative statement but therefore no less important. To arrive at this conclusion, moreover, we had to define the world of the physical educator which forced us to clarify our thinking about physical education

itself. How can we be sure that our reasoning and observations were true? The answer to that question is that we can never be absolutely certain. Somebody else may very well present an analysis that would compel us to revise our thinking. This would never be an arbitrary revision, however, but one based upon comparison, reason, and insight; in short, upon the search for wisdom we call philosophy.

SUMMARY

Philosophy, as the search for wisdom, is concerned with real knowledge, not mere opinion. Philosophical knowledge, in contrast to scientific knowledge, cannot always be verified through experimentation. Philosophy differs from religion in that the philosopher relies on the power of human reason rather than on faith in his search for knowledge. One of the perennial problems in the history of philosophy has been the question: "What is man?"

Afferent: Philosophical conceptions about the nature of man have had a great influence on physical education. In the Greek society of the fifth century B.C., physical education formed an integrative part in a well balanced educational program until philosophers and sophists proclaimed a dualism of mind and body. The dualistic conception of man as a combination of separate entities led to the affirmation of the superiority of the mind and its intellectual qualities over the body. Physical education remained part of the Hellenistic school curriculum, but it had lost its vital role, as more and more emphasis was given to intellectual pursuits.

The formal exercises of the German and Swedish systems of physical education of the nineteenth century form a true reflection of the rationalistic spirit of the times, long after Rene Descartes had laid the foundations for this rational dualism. Descartes' philosophy led once again to a deep faith in the mind and its rational powers. The exercise systems were true products of their time. The formal movements were constructed to fit geometrical designs and were executed at straight angles, moving along straight lines. The German system aimed especially at the educational goal of bringing the body under control of the mind.

Reactions against the dualistic conception of man have culminated in our own century. The human being is no longer regarded as a combination of separate entities but as a unity of body and mind. In this monistic view, the mind is often seen as an expression of the body rather than a separate, superior entity. In physical education this new concept has resulted in freer movement forms through which the human being expresses himself in his totality. Movement exploration, games, and the dance have taken the place of many of the formal exercises of the past, although some of the latter still linger on.

Efferent: Physical education presents us with many problems that can "goad" one into philosophizing. One such problem is physical fitness, when, for example, the question is asked: "Physical fitness for what purpose?" In Nazi Germany physical fitness became a means to reinforce the feelings of superiority and invincibility of a nation.

Physical educators directly contributed to Adolf Hitler's political ambitions by the way in which they emphasized physical fitness. In physical education the philosophical question of ends and means cannot be avoided.

Another problem deals with the difference between the physical educator and the coach. The aims of the coach are often limited to the winning of the game. The coach works only with the selected few and "uses" his athletes in a situation he cannot manipulate. The physical educator, on the contrary, can change the pedagogical situation to suit his aim of the optimum development of every student under his care, retarded as well as advanced. Can one man step from one world into the other and do justice to both?

SUGGESTED READINGS

Brauner, C. J., and H. W. Burns, *Problems in Educational Philosophy*. Englewood Cliffs, N.J.: Prentice-Hall, Inc., 1965.

Davis, E. C., *Philosophies Fashion Physical Education*. Dubuque, Iowa: William C. Brown Company, Publishers, 1963.

Frankena, W. K., *Philosophy of Education*. New York: Crowell-Collier and Macmillan, Inc., 1965.

Plato, "Physical Education," in *Background Readings for Physical Education.*, Ann Paterson and E. C. Hallberg (Eds.). New York: Holt, Rinehart and Winston, Inc., 1965.

Zeigler, E. F., *Philosophic Foundations for Physical, Health, and Recreation Education*. Englewood Cliffs, N.J.: Prentice-Hall, Inc., 1964.

Circulation
and Respiration

Chapter 8

The events represented by the headlines in Figure 8.1 are but dramatic examples of events that occur every day, events about which you should be vitally concerned. Preventable deaths are always a concern, and there is ample evidence that those attributed to degenerative diseases of the heart and circulatory system occur all too often in the United States (Figures 8.2 and 8.3). Lest one have the impression that the degenerative diseases are associated only with "old age," it should be reported that in an autopsy study of 300 American soldiers killed in action in Korea, 77 percent had significant coronary artery disease. Their average age was but 22.1 years, and their average body weight was 146 pounds (164). We now draw your attention to Figure 8.4. Does this shock you? Can you explain the jury's decision? If not, perhaps by the time you have read and studied this section of the book you will be able to understand the important point that this illustration is intended to make.

If you are to visualize your role in the prevention of such tragedies as those represented by the headlines, you must first come to some understanding of the systems of the body involved. If you hope to be a professional rather than a technician,

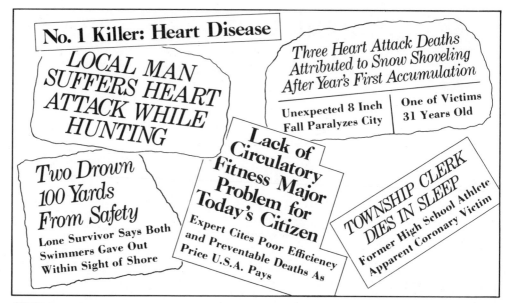

FIGURE 8.1   Typical headlines in American newspapers.

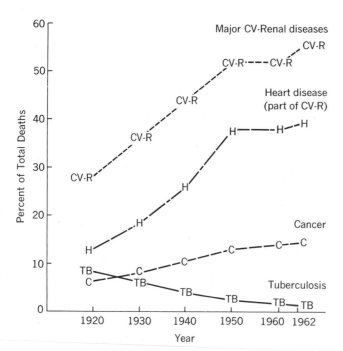

FIGURE 8.2   Changes in major CV-r, heart, cancer, and tuberculosis death rates, 1920–1960. Adapted from *Statistical Abstract of the United States* (578).

you will also want to know the *facts* about the role you can play. First, let's look at this frightening thing commonly called a "heart attack." Just what is a "coronary"? Is it truly a "nice, painless way to go"? What are the facts? Mr. B.'s story, as presented in an American Heart Association pamphlet, will answer these questions and others.

Coronary Atherosclerosis

Mr. B., a business executive in his early fifties, had eaten an unusually hearty dinner after a long hard day at the office, and had retired early. He felt weary but otherwise well. Shortly after midnight he was awakened by a sense of heavy pressure under the breastbone (sternum). It persisted and grew steadily more severe, although he took soda in hot water. He felt faint and perspired profusely. As the pain became more and more severe he agreed to let his wife call the doctor, who arrived soon after one o'clock. He immediately gave Mr. B. an injection of morphine to ease the pain and had him transferred by ambulance to the hospital. In the hospital, he was placed in the coronary care unit where the electrical activity of his heart could be constantly monitored.

Mr. B. was quite tired upon arrival at the hospital, and the discomfort in the chest was troublesome enough to require morphine or similar drugs several times during the next twenty-four hours. On his second day in the hospital he had a slight fever, and this persisted for four days. The pain in the chest was only slight on the second day, and ceased by the evening of that day.

Within a week he felt perfectly well, but his doctor wisely insisted that he remain at almost complete rest for another two or three weeks in order to ensure more com-

plete healing of the injury that had occurred in his heart.

For almost three weeks after his attack, Mr. B. remained in bed. Mr. B. was given small portions of food during his stay in the hospital, to lessen the demands made upon the heart by digesting heavy meals.

FIGURE 8.3   Average annual mortality due to arteriosclerotic heart disease in men age 55–64. Figures represent either 1956–1958 or 1957–1959. Adapted from Yudkin (626).

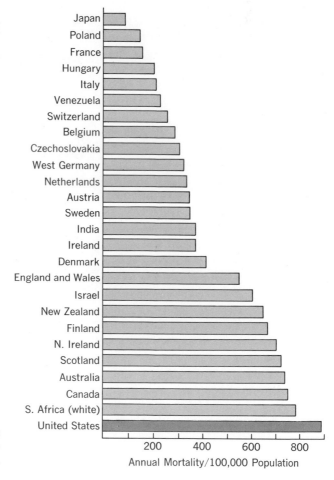

FIGURE 8.4 Since you failed to educate people properly with respect to the possible preventive measures they could take to at least minimize their chances of developing coronary artery disease, the jury finds you, Health Education and Physical Education, guilty of duplicity in the many preventable heart disease deaths which occur annually in the U.S.A. Recreation, you have been found guilty of the same crime for your failure to provide and promote adequate exercise opportunities for the strengthening of the heart and circulatory system.

The number of calories was also limited, to help bring his weight down.

Mr. B. was discharged from the hospital a little more than one month after his admission, feeling perfectly well except for slight physical weakness. His doctor encouraged him to increase his stair-climbing and walking slowly but steadily. Within several weeks he was able to go for rides in his car. Two months after his attack Mr. B. felt as well as ever, and was eager to resume his regular business life. His physician persuaded him to postpone his return to work for another two weeks, when he was allowed to go to his office for half of each day. By the end of two weeks he was working on his regular schedule again, but was careful to avoid unnecessary physical fatigue as well as those business matters that caused emotional stress. He had lost twelve pounds of excess weight and had not smoked cigarettes since the day of his attack. He declared that he felt better than he had in many years.

This is a very brief account of the experience of Mr. B., one of the many thousands of persons who have recovered admirably from a "heart attack," known medically as coronary thrombosis (or coronary closure) with myocardial infarction (see Figure 8.5). Most doctors use the terms "heart attack," "coronary closure," "coronary occlusion," and "myocardial infarction" as having exactly the same meaning, although they are not in fact always synonymous. "Myocardium" is the Latin name of the heart muscle. The word "infarction" means death of tissue caused by loss of its normal supply of oxygenated blood. So the term "myocardial infarction" indicates that a small portion of the heart muscle has died because the artery which formerly supplied it with blood has been closed.

Heart attacks do not always cause the same symptoms that Mr. B. experienced. Sometimes the pain in the chest is extremely severe and may extend into the throat, shoul-

ders, arms, and even into the back. It may be accompanied by profuse sweating, weakness, shortness of breath, nausea, and vomiting. On the other hand, attacks may occur with very slight pain or without any pain whatever. In such cases the symptoms may consist of unexplained weakness, sweating, or breathlessness. A great many people have closure of a coronary artery with little or no injury to the heart muscle.

The physician thus explained it to Mr. B.: "Actually, the heart attack that you had is not primarily a disease of the heart muscle. It is really the result of a condition in the arteries — the coronary arteries — that supply the heart muscle with blood.

"The heart muscle, or myocardium as it is called, is so thick and strong and constantly active day and night that it needs its own rich blood supply. The blood that simply flows through the chambers of the heart does not supply blood to the heart muscle.

"Therefore in the development of the human heart an extensive network of arteries has grown out from two main trunks, the right and the left coronary arteries. These main coronary arteries branch in somewhat the same manner as a tree. Every branch is smaller than the main trunk, and

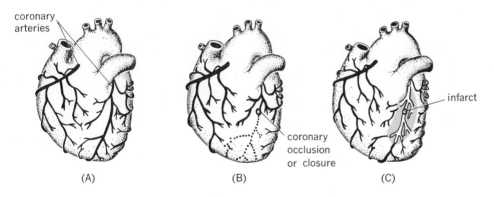

coronary arteries

coronary occlusion or closure

infarct

(A)   (B)   (C)

FIGURE 8.5   The heart: (A) coronary arteries, (B) coronary closure (occlusion or thrombosis), (C) myocardial infarct (death of cardiac muscle caused by reduction in blood supply). Source: *Heart Terms*. Public Health Service Publication No. 1073.

each one soon subdivides into smaller branches. These in turn divide into still smaller ones which are like very tiny twigs. Every portion of the heart, no matter how small, is supplied with blood and oxygen through this system of coronary arteries.

"Over a period of years these coronary arteries were setting the stage for your heart attack through the gradual development of atherosclerosis. This is a form of arteriosclerosis, which is usually known to laymen as hardening of the arteries. Atherosclerosis leads to a thickening as well as a hardening of the walls of arteries. The process usually begins with the deposit of fatty material on the inner lining of the arterial wall; each individual deposit is known as an atheroma.

"As more and more of these deposits are formed and increase in size, they gradually narrow the channel through which the blood flows. This happens in much the same way as deposits of rust clog a water pipe. This process leads to roughening of the lining of the artery, which is normally smooth and glistening. Some sections of the arteries may remain largely unaffected, while other sections nearby may be altered greatly.

"There are many people with advanced and widespread changes in their coronary arteries who give no evidence of artery disease throughout a long and active life. Many such people die at 75 or 80 years of age from some condition not related to the heart: malignant tumors, infections, accidents. The reason why these people continue living without symptoms of heart disease is that enough blood still flows through the coronary arteries to provide nourishment and energy for the heart muscle.

"In your case, Mr. B., a blood clot formed in the narrowest part of one of the branches of a coronary artery. This clot blocked the blood supply to one part of your heart muscle, a section perhaps the size of an almond. This part of the muscle began to ache; that

was the pain you felt. You had just had a heart attack, or coronary thrombosis. Thrombosis means the formation of a blood clot (thrombus). So coronary thrombosis simply means the formation of a blood clot in a coronary artery.

"The ache or pain in your heart muscle continued for some hours. During this time the portion of the heart muscle that was cut off from its supply of oxygen-carrying blood continued to struggle along in its work with the rest of the heart.

"Gradually, the fibers of this small portion of muscle stopped contracting. They became swollen and died, and the pain slowly went away. This portion of heart muscle actually suffered an acute injury. Like acute injuries in other tissues of the body, it requires time for its healing.

"Your body began the healing process by sending 'wrecking cells' (leukocytes) to clear away the muscle fibers that were no longer able to contract. This has to be done before the tissue can heal and form a strong scar. The clearing-away process takes about a week or a little longer. During this time there may be slight fever.

"At the end of the first week you may feel perfectly well; but actually that injured portion of your heart forms a weak area in the muscle wall. Until a scar forms and toughens, you must remain at complete rest.

"Meanwhile other repair work goes on. It started, in fact, the moment the clot closed off a branch of your artery. Other arterial branches enlarged and new branches began to form to bring a supply of blood to the area around the injury. These new branches are known as the collateral circulation; they often play an important part in the healing process.

"We will be watching the mending process by making certain blood tests, by examining your electrocardiograms, by taking your pulse and blood pressure frequently, and by noting any symptoms that you may report to us. Later, when you are strong enough, we may want to take x-ray pictures of your heart and lungs.

"If the healing progresses in you as it does in the great majority, you will probably be allowed to sit up in bed after about two weeks, and you may be sitting in a chair and walking about the room soon after that. Most people who have mild or only moderately severe attacks are well enough to be discharged from the hospital after about four weeks if there have been no complications.

"You might want to think of your injury as similar in some respects to the fracture of a bone in your leg. Even if a large bone were fractured, you would be comfortable within several days, but the bone could not support your weight until the injury had healed solidly. For much the same reasons we ask you to let the injury in your heart heal solidly before you call upon it to resume its full activity.

"If the injury is going to leave a small scar in the heart, this will probably be formed within the first two or three weeks. During the second month it should become firm and the new blood channels should become wider and carry ample blood to nourish the heart muscle that is dependent upon them.

"Both bone fractures and injuries in the heart vary in their severity and in the length of time required for healing, and, as with any kind of healing process, some people mend faster than others. That is why doctors would rather not estimate in advance exactly when you will leave the hospital and exactly when you will be at work again. But just as a bone fracture heals with care and time, so, if all goes well, several months should be enough to get you fully back into normal activity again—and that means back to your job.

"We have every reason to believe that you will resume your regular life although we may have to ask that you reduce some of your more strenuous physical activities."

The doctor explained to Mr. B. and his wife that a perfectly firm, well-healed scar may cause no trouble for the remainder of a long life. But he added that optimism can be overdone and lead to overconfidence and carelessness. In a few cases, complications may delay the healing process.

The doctor had the assurance of knowing that only in the minority of cases is a heart attack fatal, usually within the first few hours or days. The majority survive their first heart attack and most of them recover fully enough to enjoy many years of productive activity.[1]

This chapter is designed for the potential professionals who are concerned with the important scientific concepts relating your professions to the circulatory and respiratory systems of the body (with some attention directed to auxiliary systems). It is specifically meant for the professional who is not satisfied with a superficial, conditioned "knowledge," which leads him to promote strenuous exercise for what purpose he knows not, and which does not even motivate him to exercise himself.

AFFERENT CONCEPTS

GENERAL FUNCTION AND ANATOMY OF THE CIRCULO-RESPIRATORY SYSTEM AND RELATED SYSTEMS

The primary function of the circulatory system may be stated in one simple

---

[1]This information has been reproduced by permission of the American Heart Association from the pamphlet "Heart Disease Caused by Coronary Atherosclerosis."

word—"transport." It transports essentials like **glucose** and oxygen to the cells, and by-products of metabolism, such as carbon dioxide, from the cells.

There are four basic components of respiration: lung **ventilation** or breathing; external respiration or the exchange of oxygen and carbon dioxide between the air sacs of the lungs and the blood; internal respiration or the exchange of oxygen and carbon dioxide at the cell membrane; true respiration or the actual oxidative process within the cells.

In discussing the functional parts of the circulatory system, it is most logical to include the blood, the heart, and the vascular bed. The **plasma** portion of the blood is primarily water, which acts mainly as the solvent. The remainder of the plasma, about 10 percent, is composed of dissolved solids and the gases, oxygen and carbon dioxide. Among the more important solids are nutrients for the cells such as glucose, lipids (fats and fatlike substances), and **amino acids.** Important ions, such as sodium, potassium, calcium, magnesium, chlorides, bicarbonates, and phosphates, are also present in amounts controlled within very precise limits. The plasma also contains the important blood proteins **fibrinogen, albumin,** and the **globulins,** all of which contribute to blood viscosity and the **osmotic pressure** of blood. Fibrinogen is essential to blood clotting; the gamma globulin fraction is concerned with immunity against certain foreign substances. The plasma also carries all-important **enzymes, antibodies,** and **hormones,** as well as certain waste

products to be removed by the kidneys.

The formed elements or cells constitute about 40 to 45 percent of whole blood. The cellular portion is made up almost entirely of **erythrocytes,** or red blood cells; this percentage is known as the **hematocrit.** The red coloring matter, or **hemoglobin,** in these cells carries nearly all the oxygen and about half of the carbon dioxide transported by the blood. The **leukocytes,** or white cells, are less numerous than the red cells and are primarily concerned with fighting off infections. By making a "differential" white-cell count the physician can gain further insight into infections and better determine the cause of infection; the different kinds of white cells appear to increase as a result of different kinds of infection (acute, chronic, parasitic, and so on). The last of the formed elements, the **platelets,** are involved in the vital blood-clotting process.

The heart, composed of specialized tissue known as cardiac muscle, is innately rhythmic. It has its own rich blood supply (the coronary arteries are illustrated in Figure 8.5) and needs nutrients and oxygen in order to function, just as any skeletal or smooth muscle does. Consisting of four chambers and a series of valves (Figure 8.6A), it serves as the pump that circulates and recirculates the fluid medium (blood) throughout the closed vascular system. The right atrium receives the deoxygenated or "spent" blood from the body; the left atrium receives the freshly oxygenated blood from the lungs. The right ventricle pumps the deoxygenated blood to the lungs; the left ven-

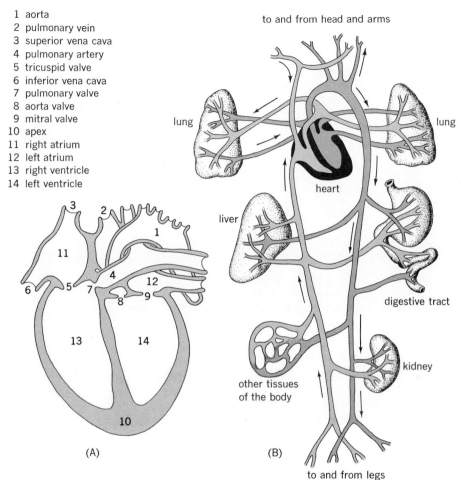

1 aorta
2 pulmonary vein
3 superior vena cava
4 pulmonary artery
5 tricuspid valve
6 inferior vena cava
7 pulmonary valve
8 aorta valve
9 mitral valve
10 apex
11 right atrium
12 left atrium
13 right ventricle
14 left ventricle

to and from head and arms

lung

lung

heart

liver

digestive tract

kidney

other tissues
of the body

(A)

(B)

to and from legs

FIGURE 8.6   The heart and the circulatory system.

tricle pumps the oxygenated blood out through the body.

The vascular bed (Figure 8.6B) consists of the large arteries, the small arteries, the arterioles leading to the tissues, and the capillaries, where oxygen, CO_2, nutrients, and waste products are exchanged with the tissues. Also included are the venules, small veins, and large veins, which return the blood to the heart and lungs for reoxygenation. Some of the blood vessels, primarily the arterioles, contain smooth muscle fibers in their walls (under the control of the **autonomic nervous system**) that enable them to constrict or dilate. This change in diameter serves to alter general systemic blood pressure and blood flow to particular areas of the body. Very slight changes in the arteriolar diameter cause dramatic changes in blood flow because

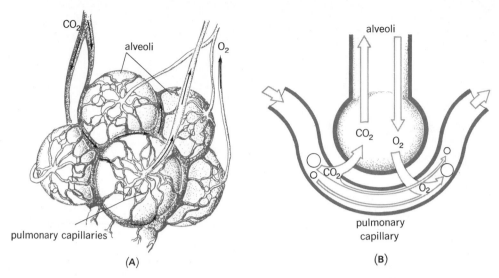

(A)

(B)

FIGURE 8.7 Oxygen and carbon dioxide exchange between alveoli of the lungs and pulmonary capillaries.

flow varies directly as the fourth power of the diameter. In other words, doubling the diameter would increase flow sixteen times.

The actual macroscopic parts of the respiratory system are illustrated in Plate 1, which also depicts the basic elements of oxygen and CO_2 movement at the **alveolar-pulmonary** capillary exchange area in the lungs (see Figure 8.7). The opposite, of course, occurs at the tissue level where O_2 is diffused *to* the tissues and CO_2 *from* the tissues to the blood.

The excretory system and the liver are closely related functionally to the CR system. The excretory system, composed of the kidneys, skin, respiratory system, and digestive tract, is concerned with the removal of waste products. The kidneys (Figure 8.8) filter the blood (about one fourth of the blood volume is filtered per minute) and excrete water, excess materials, and waste products, such as urea, uric acid, and creatinine. In addition to water, some CO_2 is eliminated through

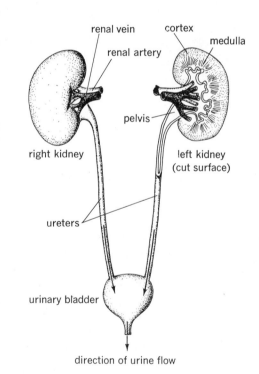

FIGURE 8.8 The urinary system and the kidneys. By permission from A. C. Guyton. *Function of the Human Body*. Philadelphia: W. B. Saunders Company, 1964, p. 9.

the skin, although most of the CO_2 is blown off by the lungs. Some water vapor is also lost in ventilation. The waste products eliminated by the digestive tract in the form of feces are primarily the end products of digestion, although small and variable amounts of water are also lost in the feces.

Much of the detoxification of blood is accomplished by the liver. It is especially well situated for this function (see Figure 10.1) because the blood leaving the intestinal absorption areas flows first through the liver. Much of the absorbed bacteria is destroyed in the liver. It also removes ammonia that results from protein metabolism and converts it to urea. In short, the liver removes (or converts) many waste, foreign, and toxic substances found in the blood stream. The liver also acts as a storehouse for blood in that its sinuses or cavities are capable of storing several hundred milliliters of blood.

FUNCTIONS OF THESE SYSTEMS IN EXERCISE

As one would expect, the circulatory system is called upon to increase its transport of essentials to the cells and of waste products from the cells during muscular exertion. This need, of course, is directly related to the intensity and duration of exertion. The limitation in certain kinds of activity is partly imposed by the eventual failure of this system to meet the demands of the tissues, although the ability of the tissues to *get* the essentials provided by the CR system is perhaps an even greater limiting factor.

Total body blood flow, or **cardiac output,** is increased in even the mildest activity. It may increase to as much as 35 liters per minute in a highly conditioned male, which may represent as much as a sevenfold increase over resting cardiac output. This increase (up to a certain point) is the result of somewhat proportional increases in **heart rate** and **stroke volume.** Some researchers have presented evidence that exercise causes the stroke volume of sedentary individuals to increase very little, and that the increase in cardiac output is due almost entirely to an increased heart rate (483). Whatever the mechanism, the increased cardiac output speeds delivery of essentials to and waste materials from the working muscles during exercise.

Because of increased blood flow and the constriction of arterioles in nonparticipating areas of the body (such as the stomach and kidneys), **systolic blood pressure** rises during exertion. This increased working pressure, along with a simultaneous arteriolar dilatation in the muscles, means increased blood flow through the working muscles. Flow to the brain remains relatively constant and blood flow to the heart muscle is increased (Figure 8.9). Thus the blood not only is circulated faster; it is selectively circulated to the areas where it is most needed at the expense of portions of the body that are relatively nonessential during exertion.

There is a possibility that the **spleen,** which is especially rich in red blood cells, ejects some of these "reserve" cells into circulation during exercise. This would increase the blood's oxygen and carbon dioxide–carrying capacity.

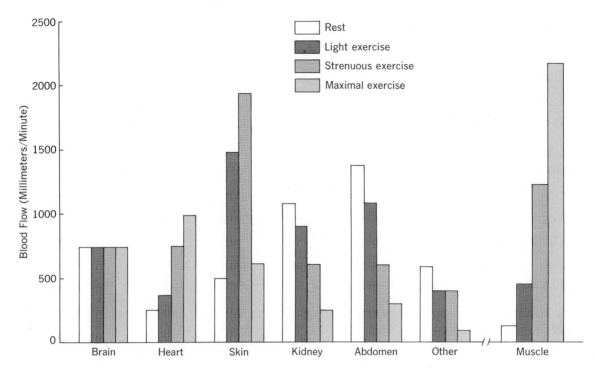

FIGURE 8.9   Effects of increasing exercise intensity on blood flow through various parts of the body. Adapted from Chapman and Mitchell (99).

During even the mildest exertion there is an increased demand for oxygen by the cells. In response to this increased O_2 **requirement,** the entire respiratory system steps up its activity. The actual degree of increase in respiratory functions depends upon the intensity and duration of the exertion. Both the depth (**tidal volume**) and the rate of breathing increase so that, in a trained man, the ventilation rate may increase from a resting level of 6–10 liters per minute to as high as 120–150 liters per minute (Figure 8.10). At the same time, decreased venous O_2 and increased venous CO_2 improve the exchange of these gases at the lungs be-

cause of the greater concentration differences across the gas exchange membrane. The stepped-up ventilation and the increased diffusability of O_2 and CO_2 lead to a greater external respiration (gas exchange between alveoli and pulmonary capillaries). There is also a greater difference in the oxygen content of the arterial and venous blood: more O_2 is actually taken from the blood by the tissues. This larger arterial-venous O_2 difference is primarily due to the greater blood pressure and to decreased O_2 and increased CO_2 within the body tissues. There are at least two other possible explanations: (1) it is possible that chemical changes

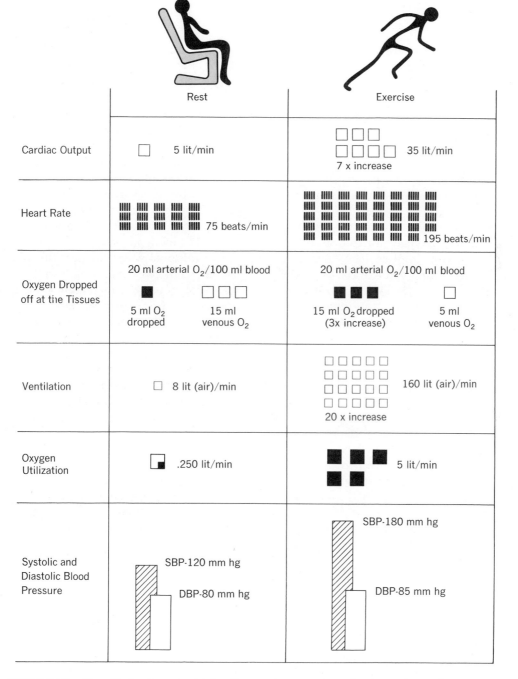

	Rest	Exercise
Cardiac Output	☐ 5 lit/min	☐☐☐ ☐☐☐☐ 35 lit/min 7 x increase
Heart Rate	▦▦▦▦ ▦▦▦▦ ▦▦ 75 beats/min	▦▦▦▦▦▦▦▦ ▦▦▦▦▦▦▦▦ ▦▦▦▦▦▦▦▦ ▦▦▦▦▦▦ 195 beats/min
Oxygen Dropped off at the Tissues	20 ml arterial O₂/100 ml blood ■ ☐☐☐ 5 ml O₂ dropped 15 ml venous O₂	20 ml arterial O₂/100 ml blood ■■■ ☐ 15 ml O₂ dropped (3x increase) 5 ml venous O₂
Ventilation	☐ 8 lit (air)/min	☐☐☐☐☐ ☐☐☐☐☐ ☐☐☐☐☐ ☐☐☐☐☐ 160 lit (air)/min 20 x increase
Oxygen Utilization	▣ .250 lit/min	■■■ ■■ 5 lit/min
Systolic and Diastolic Blood Pressure	SBP-120 mm hg DBP-80 mm hg	SBP-180 mm hg DBP-85 mm hg

FIGURE 8.10 The effects of maximal intensity exercise on various circulo-respiratory "contributors." The increases represented for cardiac output, ventilation, and O₂ utilization are not likely to be so great in the untrained person.

in the cell membrane allow for easier passage of blood gases (increased cell permeability); (2) changes in osmotic pressure may also aid gas exchange at the cellular level. During strenuous exercise the O_2 drop-off may increase threefold—from about 5 ml/100 ml blood at rest to 15 ml/100 ml blood (Figure 8.10). This means that the rate of internal respiration is also increased considerably.

As a result of the just mentioned changes, oxygen utilization may increase to as high as 4000–6000 ml/min from a resting value of 200–350 ml/min (Figure 8.10). If the O_2 utilization does not equal the O_2 requirement, a person can still continue activity until he reaches his maximal O_2 debt tolerance. This ability of the muscles to function anaerobically (without O_2) allows us to perform tasks that we otherwise could not perform. Generally speaking, sprints are considered O_2 debt-producing or anaerobic events, whereas distance events are aerobic or steady-state events. When the respiratory and circulatory systems are able to keep up with the O_2 requirement, then O_2 utilization and heart rate level off and one can continue this effort for a longer period of time. This leveling off, referred to as "steady state," can only be observed in submaximal work tasks, not in all-out exertion. For example, one would not reach steady state while sprinting at full speed to catch a bus, but steady state might easily be reached in a less than all-out effort, such as walking to catch the bus or even in cross-country hiking.

Blood volume is affected to a large extent by the kidneys' excretion of water. During exercise blood flow to the kidneys is reduced and therefore less blood is filtered. As a result, less urine is formed and blood volume is reduced less severely. It is probable that the antidiuretic hormone of the posterior pituitary, which increases renal water reabsorption, comes into play to further conserve plasma water. These renal functions help to maintain systemic blood pressure and also provide additional water for heat dissipation through sweating.

It is obvious that increased ventilation results from exercise. One of the most powerful stimuli for this increase is excess CO_2 in the blood. By increasing CO_2 removal during exercise, the respiratory system plays a very important role in the maintenance of a nearly normal blood pH value (the measure of acidity). This is important because the blood pH must be maintained within very narrow limits: about 7.1–7.5.

As one would expect for an organ with some five hundred functions, the liver contributes to exercise indirectly in many ways; attention here is focused on three of the more direct roles played by the liver in exercise.

Adequate glucose levels in the blood and tissues are maintained to a large extent by the liver's release of stored glycogen (glycogenolysis) and even by the conversion of nonglucose nutrients, such as fats, to glucose. In this fashion the liver helps control blood glucose levels during exercise.

Exercise can continue anaerobically (without sufficient oxygen) for a limited period of time (see oxygen debt, page 182). Scientists formerly believed that the liver's conversion of lactic acid to glycogen or glucose, in the presence of O_2, was essential to the payment of the O_2 debt and, of course, to maintaining a steady state performance. There has recently been some doubt cast upon this theory, however, so that is not certain whether the fact that the liver *is* capable of this lactic acid conversion is a major factor in endurance activities.

By converting lactic acid, however, the liver plays a role in maintaing blood pH within normal limits and it is possible that this conversion of lactic acid also increases the CO_2 carrying capacity of the blood.

EFFERENT CONCEPTS

EFFECTS OF EXERCISE ON CIRCULO-RESPIRATORY AND RELATED SYSTEMS

Because any effects that physical education and/or formal recreation programs may have on the actual integrity of the circulo-respiratory system would, naturally, be exerted only by the consequences of exercise, the efferent concepts have almost exclusively to do with the effects of regular physical exercise rather than formal physical education per se. That is, the effects involved here do not depend on a "physical education class," but rather on what the individual *does,* whether it is in a formal class situation or not. This does not imply that there are not "psychological" factors involved. As you will see, this is far from the case. The importance of the CR system in health and fitness cannot be overemphasized. The healthy and fit circulo-respiratory system has been associated by most physicians and physiologists with high levels of general health. The primary benefits to be derived from a functionally efficient cardio-respiratory system are threefold: improved work capacity, increased efficiency in daily living, and prevention or delay in the onset of certain chronic degenerative circulatory diseases. It is fitting, then, that the concepts concerning the circulo-respiratory system should be discussed under these specific headings.

Work Capacity

Although physiologists have not identified the exact mechanisms involved in determining the working capacity of human beings, much has been learned about the adjustments that are made to the demands of activity. There is no question that certain critical factors determine an individual's work capacity for a given task. It matters not whether the task is "work" or "play" —the same factors are involved. At this point it would be well to review briefly the distinction between circulo-respiratory fitness and muscular endurance. You will recall that circulo-respiratory fitness involves the capacity to persist in rather generalized, total body tasks. On the other hand, muscular endurance involves a more localized part of the body, the limit for which seems to be established in the muscles or muscle groups involved and not by the inability to supply adequate oxygen to the tissues. The work capacity we refer to as associated with circulo-respiratory health and fitness, then, is generalized and involves a major proportion of the total body. If this picture of the CR capacity is kept clearly in focus, we realize that the critical factors determining the working capacity of the individual are the oxygen requirement of the task, the oxygen debt tolerance, and the **maximal oxygen intake.**

OXYGEN REQUIREMENT OF THE TASK   The energy for contraction of the muscles involves the use of oxygen. Obviously, the greater the metabolic demands of the muscles, the greater the O_2 requirement. In other words, the more intense the exercise or the work task becomes, the greater is the demand for oxygen. This demand of the tissues for oxygen is referred to as the oxygen requirement of the task. It follows logically that the greater the O_2 demand per minute, the less likely it is that the circulo-respiratory system can meet these demands, a factor that is an important determinant of the length of time one can perform a given task.

OXYGEN DEBT TOLERANCE   When the demand of the task exceeds the capacity of the CR system to meet the oxygen requirements of the tissues, a deficit exists. Because oxygen is not actually required for the muscle contraction itself but apparently is involved only in the removal and conversion of waste products resulting from contraction, a considerable amount of work can be done in spite of this apparent deficit.

Although the exact mechanism of oxygen debt and, in fact, the role that oxygen plays in the energy cycle has not been clearly established, it is known that the organism is capable of functioning with an apparent oxygen deficit. The level to which this deficit can be built before one must cease working is called **oxygen debt tolerance.** The term *debt* refers to the fact that following the completion of the task, oxygen continues to be delivered to the tissues in amounts above resting levels (breathing continues to be "heavy") until the deficit is eliminated. It is obvious that, for a given task, an individual with a larger oxygen debt tolerance has a greater work capacity.

MAXIMAL OXYGEN INTAKE FOR A GIVEN TASK   The third factor involved in determining work capacity—maximal oxygen intake for a given task—completes the equation:

$$\text{Work Capacity (minutes)} = \frac{O_2 \text{ Debt Tolerance (in liters)}}{O_2 \text{ Requirement (in lit/min)} - O_2 \text{ intake (in lit/min)}}$$

The higher the O_2 intake during the task (given a constant O_2 requirement) the slower will be the accumulation of an oxygen debt. The relationship between these factors and work capacity for a given task is illustrated in Figure 8.11. An increase in work capacity can be brought about by one or a combination of the following factors: (1) increased maximal O_2 intake, that is, increased aerobic capacity; (2) increased oxygen debt tolerance; (3) decreased oxygen requirement of a task. There is

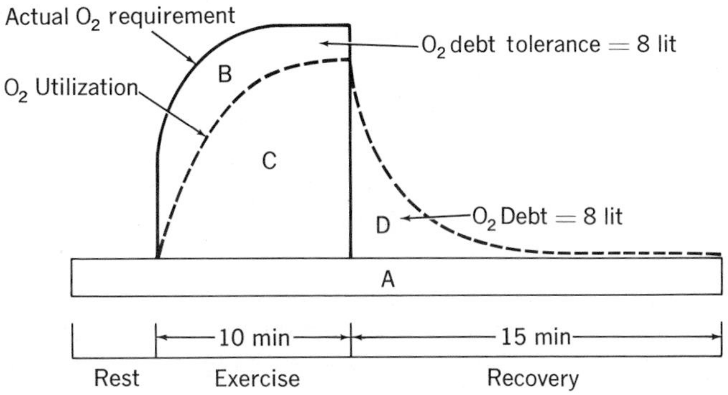

FIGURE 8.11 The role of O_2 requirement, O_2 utilization, and O_2 debt tolerance in determining work capacity. $A = O_2$ utilization at rest and what it would have been had the exercise not "intervened." B = the O_2 deficit due to difference between requirement and actual utilization. $C = O_2$ actually utilized during the exercise. $D = O_2$ debt: the amount of O_2 utilized, over and above what the man *would* have used (at rest) had he *not* exercised. Notice that O_2 debt = O_2 deficit $(D = B)$, as it should.

evidence that all of these can result from training. Figure 8.10 depicts how these factors, singly or combined, can increase work capacity. The exact mechanisms involved in these training changes are not well established, but they do occur.

It is fortunate that the heart rate is a reasonably valid indication of the physical intensity of an activity and, as such, really serves as a crude index of the value of an activity for development of circulo-respiratory capacity. In this manner a person can roughly determine whether the sport, exercise, or work task is effective in improving his circulo-respiratory fitness. Of course, the length of time involved in the activity is an important factor and must be considered along with the intensity of the activity. But it is reasonably certain that such an activity as bowling, which increases the heart rate little if at all, is not an activity conducive to promoting circulo-respiratory fitness in the healthy individual.

You should be aware of the basic concepts related to three special as-

pects of work capacity: effects of smoking, effects of sleeplessness, and effects of anemia.

SMOKING AND PHYSICAL PERFORMANCE
Statistical research has linked smoking to certain kinds of respiratory and circulatory diseases, although the mechanisms have not been precisely established. In addition, carefully controlled laboratory experiments have all yielded the following physiological results of smoking: (1) heart rate is increased; (2) blood pressure is increased; (3) peripheral circulation is reduced with accompanying skin temperature decreases as great as 15°F (27, 444, 498). A recent investigation by Westfall and Watts (604) indicates that significantly larger amounts of epinephrine are secreted in smokers. This would tend to explain the cardiovascular changes associated with smoking.

On the basis of the time segments obtained in the electrocardiogram we have calculated the relative work and rest phases of the cardiac cycle. Smoking caused a decrease in the rest phase (from 45 percent of control to 29 percent during smoking) while heart rate increased eighteen beats per minute. By way of contrast, a moderate work load for three minutes on the bicycle ergometer caused a heart rate increase of twenty nine beats per minute (thirty seconds after exercise) and little change in percentage of rest.

There has been very little experimental work concerning the immediate effects of smoking on physical performance. Little, if any, effort has been made to establish the longitudinal effects of smoking on performance, but it has been shown that, as a result of cigarette smoke, the inclination for spontaneous activity in male rats is reduced from one third to one half (543, p. 317). Hand steadiness may be reduced as much as 330 percent after smoking a cigarette (543, p. 348). The majority of performance studies indicate that there is no apparent immediate effect of smoking on hand grip, speed of tapping, Harvard Step Test score, oxygen intake or debt, or net oxygen cost of exercise (242).

These studies all involved the acute effects of cigarette smoking in young smokers or nonsmokers and were *not* concerned with the longitudinal effects. At the present time one can only speculate as to the true effect of chronic smoking on athletic performance and work performance. There is a complete dearth of direct evidence. Unfortunately, it is still not known whether the well-documented effects of smoking on ventilatory function, heart rate, blood pressure, and so on, lead to reduced work efficiency.

Although there is no direct evidence with regard to the "wind-cutting"

effect of smoking, there are several interesting possibilities that could explain the labored breathing often experienced by smokers during exertion. Cigarette smoking causes (1) a twofold increase in airway resistance; (2) a decreased pulmonary circulation; (3) an increase in blood carbon monoxide that cuts the oxygen-carrying capacity of the blood by as much as 5 percent; and (4) hyperlipemia, which reduces oxygen content of the blood (121). A recent study by Oring (440) indicates that smokers may well have significantly lower maximal breathing capacities than nonsmokers (see Figure 8.12). Although these smoking effects *individually* may not cause shortness of breath, and even *added together* may cause no problem during rest, under conditions of exertion they may

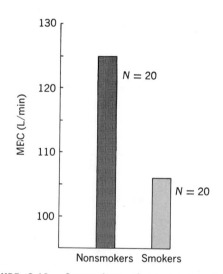

FIGURE 8.12 Comparison of smokers' and nonsmokers' Maximal Breathing Capacity. Average height and weight of two groups nearly identical. Data from Oring (440).

combine to exert a considerable handicap on ventilation.

INSUFFICIENT SLEEP AND WORK CAPACITY

There is a widespread belief that lack of sleep is a serious deterrent to physical and mental efficiency; yet few experiments indicate significant curtailment of physiological function even when subjects have gone without sleep for as long as eight days (280, 481). Reaction time, body steadiness, and alertness are often impaired (163, 481), but these changes appear to be more psychological than physiological in nature. Holland (254) reported that one night's sleeplessness resulted in no impairment in discrete, short-term motor tasks but did result in impaired long-term performance. In a study conducted in our own laboratory (280), only the reaction time and movement time were significantly impaired after one night's sleeplessness, while the heart rate response to exercise was actually improved (Figure 8.13). Both reaction time and movement time returned to normal within twelve hours, even without sleep. It would seem that short bouts of sleeplessness, such as one night, are not as serious as we formerly believed. This is not meant as a recommendation of sleep deprivation, but that one need not allow his whole day to be ruined because he has had a sleepless night under trying circumstances.

ANEMIA If the blood has too few red cells or too little hemoglobin, the condition is called **anemia.** Typical symptoms are fatigue, lack of pep, a

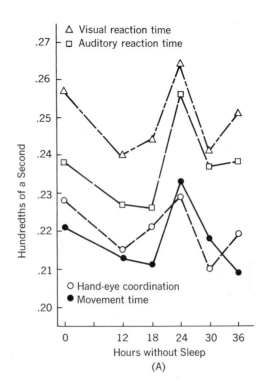

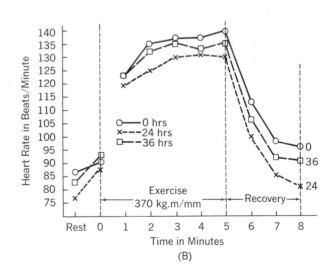

FIGURE 8.13 (A) Effects of up to 36 hours of sleep deprivation on coordination and movement time. (B) Effects of 24 and 36 hours of sleep deprivation on resting, exercise, and recovery heart rate. Source: Physiology of Exercise Laboratory, University of Toledo, Toledo, Ohio.

washed-out feeling, shortness of breath. If you believe you may be anemic, consult your doctor. It is not safe to treat this illness yourself.

Anemia can be brought about by improper diet, faulty absorption of food, loss of blood, injury to the marrow of the bones, and certain infections and parasites. Only a competent physician can diagnose the cause and prescribe proper treatment for specific types of anemia.

The body cannot function without oxygen. When anemia reduces the number of cells and the amount of hemoglobin, the blood can no longer carry enough oxygen for your body's needs.

The common causes of anemia follow:

1. Insufficient iron, protein, vitamins, or minerals.
2. Faulty intestinal absorption of iron.
3. Excessive loss of blood due to hemorrhage, ulcers, **hemorrhoids,** and so on.
4. Bone marrow damage.
5. Certain **bacterial** infections.
6. The exact cause of pernicious anemia is not known, but if diagnosed correctly it can be treated successfully.

Although there are some contradictory studies, there is some evidence in support of the claim that regular exercise does increase red-blood count, hemoglobin, and total blood volume (144, 312). In instances where such changes do occur, one of the obvious benefits is the increased oxygen-carrying capacity of the blood. It has been reported that there is an almost perfect positive correlation between total hemoglobin and maximal oxygen intake (21), but such a correlation may be spurious in view of the fact that there is also a high correlation between body weight and maximal O_2 intake and between body weight and hemoglobin (21).

It should be obvious that any person suffering from anemia will have an impaired work capacity because there is a reduction in the capacity of the blood to pick up and carry oxygen. If one gram of hemoglobin is capable of carrying 1.34 ml of oxygen during maximal exercise, what would the reduction in ml of available O_2 per minute be if a person's hemoglobin concentration fell from 15 grams/100 ml of blood to 10 grams, assuming he had in both instances a maximum cardiac output of 25 liters per minute?

Of course, such an anemia (10 g%) would likely result in reduced work capacity at far less than maximal efforts, and less severe anemias would likewise cut into work capacity at high intensity and/or long duration physical activity. The physical educator, health educator, and recreation worker should certainly be aware of this and should not be insensitive to the individual who is apparently not able or willing to "push himself" in an effort to develop stamina. Can we expect the Spartan attitude and hard work to improve endurance and work capacity when the cause is anemia?

EFFICIENCY IN DAILY LIVING

The relationship between circulo-respiratory fitness and efficiency of daily living is somewhat closely related to improved work capacity. By definition, efficiency is the ratio of work done to energy expended. For example, we can convert work and energy to thermal units (calories) and then:

$$\text{Efficiency of Work} = \frac{\text{Work Accomplished in Calories}}{\text{Energy Expended in Calories}}$$

From such an equation, we can see that if the task or "work accomplished" remains the same, a reduction in oxygen requirement and "energy expended" would mean increased efficiency. It has been difficult to determine whether this increased efficiency associated with regular exercise is in fact responsible for the feeling of well-being that is almost unanimously reported by people as one of the subjective benefits of regular activity. There is considerable evidence that this reduction in energy expenditure for a given task does occur as a result of regular CR exercise so that efficiency of specific tasks *is* increased. Not only is energy cost reduced and mechanical efficiency increased; other changes that might tend to increase the feeling of well-being throughout the normal day have been associated with regular exercise programs. Heart rate and ventilation, both resting and exercise, are commonly decreased as a result of training (241, 281, 314).

In our laboratories we have experimented with a new concept in efficiency of daily living and the feeling of well-being. It appears possible that the trained or physically active person is able to maintain his efficiency in given work tasks throughout the workday so that his efficiency at 5:00 P.M. is

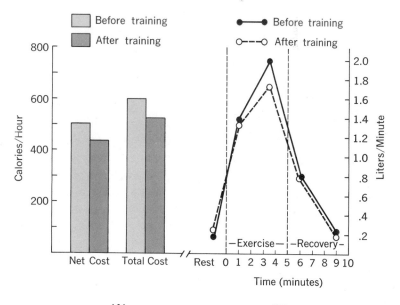

FIGURE 8.14 Effect of a four-week moderate and regular exercise program (20 minutes per day, 3 days per week) on nine college professors: (A) rate of net and total energy cost during standard treadmill walk, (B) O_2 utilization during treadmill exercise and recovery. Data from Johnson, Updyke, and Henry (281).

(A) (B)

as high as it was at 9:00 A.M. Conversely, it appears that the sedentary or unfit individual quite often has a *higher* energy cost for a given task in the late afternoon when compared with the cost for the same task at the beginning of the work day. For these individuals it is quite plausible that this unfavorable **diurnal variation** in work efficiency might well account for much of the undue "fatigue" that occurs in the late afternoon and evening. The subjects in our experiment (male college professors) demonstrated definite beneficial changes in work efficiency as a result of a minimal four-week exercise program in which they exercised twenty minutes a day, three days a week (see Figure 8.14). After training, those who

had previously exhibited the greatest decrease in work efficiency from early morning to late afternoon, experienced the most dramatic improvements in minimizing or reversing this unfavorable decrease in efficiency (281).

Although there is some objective evidence for the increase in efficiency of daily living associated with regular exercise, the evidence is certainly by no means sufficient to explain the mechanism in its entirety. But the evidence that we do have, coupled with the almost unanimous agreement that "when I am exercising regularly I feel better," leads to the conclusion that something must be said for circulo-respiratory fitness as a benefit for efficiency of daily living and for the feeling of well-being.

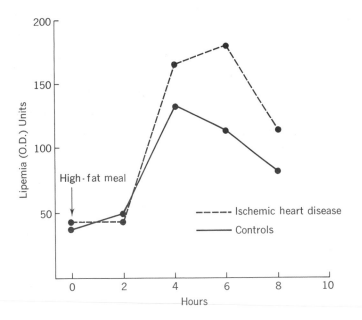

FIGURE 8.15 Increase in level of circulating fats (lipemia), following a high-fat meal, in controls and ischemic heart patients. Adapted from Bouchier and Bronte-Stewart (63).

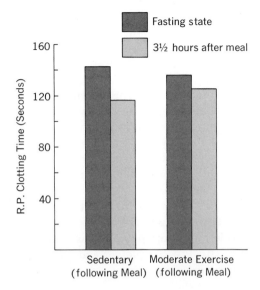

FIGURE 8.16   The effects of a high-fat meal and subsequent inactivity or activity on blood clotting time. Data from McDonald and Fullerton (354).

PREVENTION OR DELAY OF CHRONIC DEGENERATIVE CIRCULATORY DISEASE

There is considerable evidence, and such evidence continues to accumulate, that lack of adequate physical activity is a causative factor in the development of chronic, degenerative diseases of the heart and circulatory system. The following experimental and population studies provide the basis for some insight into the possible relationships between physical activity and the mechanisms involved in the chronic, degenerative circulatory diseases. It may be helpful to point out that there are two currently popular theories on the etiology of atherosclerosis and AHD. The lipid deposit theory holds that

some fatty substance is deposited in the arterial walls, thus reducing the effective diameter of the blood vessel, whereas the fibrin deposit theory suggests that **fibrin** is deposited in the arterial wall, forming a **thrombus** and thus decreasing the effective diameter of the vessel. One should also remember that since both heart attacks and strokes can be caused by blood clots blocking important vessels, it is obvious that blood clotting (**coagulation**) and the dissovling of blood clots (clot **lysis**) are also important factors in cardiovascular disease and CV accidents.

Heart Disease, Postprandial Lipemia, Blood Clotting, and Exercise

There is considerable evidence that in coronary and atherosclerotic patients there is a higher and more persistent **postprandial lipemia** or elevation in the level of fats circulating in the blood after a high-fat meal (63, 399, 415, 503). This "oral fat tolerance" test appears to be useful as a predictor of AHD, especially in older persons (244, 616). The typical results of the oral fat tolerance tests in coronary and normal subjects are illustrated in Figure 8.15. It appears that lipemia interferes with blood supply and oxygen delivery to the heart muscle (468), and there is evidence that postprandial lipemia shortens blood coagulation time (354) (see Figure 8.16).

Recent studies have demonstrated that exercise following a high-fat meal significantly reduces postprandial lipemia, hastens lipid clearance (94, 428), and nearly abolishes the postprandial acceleration of the blood clotting time

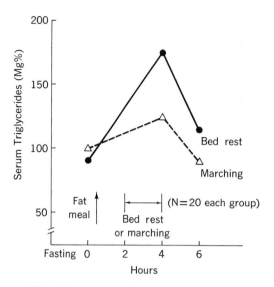

FIGURE 8.17 Effects of postprandial exercise (following a high-fat meal) on postprandial lipemia. Adapted from Nikkila and Konttinen (428).

(354) (Figures 8.16, 8.17, and 8.18). The faster lipid clearance occurs even when exercise begins after lipemia has reached its maximum (354), as illustrated in Figure 8.19. This indicates that the mechanism for reducing postprandial lipemia is not altogether a matter of reduced intestinal absorption of fats as has been suggested (63). Whereas exercise *after* the meal is beneficial in this respect, Zauner and Burt (630) originally found no beneficial antilipemic effect of vigorous exercise *prior* to the high fat meal. Subsequent work by Zauner and Mapes (631) indicates that *mild* preprandial exercise resulted in significantly faster clearance after the meal. A more recent study by Zauner, Burt, and Mapes (632) indicated that vigorous premeal exercise hastened lipid clearance after the meal but did not reduce the maximum lipemic level reached. Mild exercise, on the other hand, not only hastened clearance but also reduced the maximum postprandial level attained. It remains to be seen whether improvement in fitness per se has any beneficial effect on postprandial lipid clearance, although recent work by Melling and Burt (379) indicates that five weeks of regular exercise significantly improved clearance. Another study comparing noncoronary convalescent patients with healthy medical students shows significantly greater acceleration of postprandial clotting times in the completely sedentary patients (354).

Heart Disease, Blood Cholesterol Levels, and the Interrelationship of Diet and Exercise

The relationship between blood cholesterol levels and heart disease is discussed on page 218.

Mann (366) found that increased food intake in men did not cause obesity or high blood lipid levels if the excess caloric intake was expended in the form of exercise. Brown and co-workers (75) used rabbits to determine the effects of exercise in preventing coronary atherosclerosis, admitting that there was probably little application to human beings because of the differences in cholesterol **metabolism.** In rabbits on diets of 0.1 percent and 0.5 percent cholesterol, there was a lowering of total serum cholesterol after just four weeks of exercise. At the end of the comparatively short experiments (six, eight, and twelve weeks), exercise

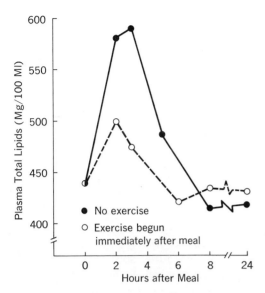

FIGURE 8.18 Effect of exercise (begun immediately after high-fat meal) on postprandial lipemia. Adapted from Cantone (94).

tions of cockerels fed cholesterol and exercised daily for seven weeks as compared to a cholesterol-fed, no-exercise group. The author also noted a significant reduction in the formation of atheromatous plaques in the abdominal aortas of the exercised birds.

The effects of daily treadmill walking on nine university students were studied by Taylor, Anderson, and Keys (557). The exercise consisted of two hours at 3.5 miles per hour, 10 percent grade, and equaled 1280 calories' work. The diet was increased by 900 calories and the proportion of fat held constant. There was no change in mean body weight and no significant change in blood serum cholesterol concentrations. The authors conclude that this supports their hypothesis that serum cholesterol is related to the proportion

had no effect on the development of atheromata in the aorta and the coronary arteries. Exercise was also ineffective in speeding disappearance from the vessels once the atheromata were developed. It should be pointed out, however, that these rabbits were exercised only twenty minutes daily, which seems to be far less than a rabbit would normally exercise.

Rabbits were also used in an experiment by Myasnikov (416). These rabbits, however, were exercised to the point of exhaustion daily for six months. There was a marked decrease in the serum cholesterol concentration of the twenty-five exercise rabbits and also some reduction in the development of atherosclerotic changes.

Wong (620) reported a significant reduction in serum cholesterol concentra-

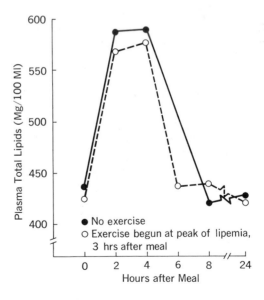

FIGURE 8.19 Effect of exercise (begun at peak of postprandial lipemia) on lipid clearance. Adapted from Cantone (94).

of total calories derived from fat, not to exercise. In a similar study of nine university students on a 1300-calorie daily treadmill walking program, the same authors again reported no serum cholesterol changes and no weight changes. They concluded that in calorie balance, serum cholesterol concentration is independent of caloric intake, absolute fat intake, and physical activity level when the kind of fat and the percentage of fat calories are constant.

Campbell (91) reports a cholesterol lowering effect of regular exercise in obese subjects independent of weight loss and diet but did not find the same for lean and muscular subjects whose cholesterol levels were lower to start with. Mann, Nicol, and Stare (365a) reported differences in cholesterol concentrations among Nigerian subjects in three separate areas of the country. Since total caloric and total fat content of the diet was similar and since there was a difference in muscular exercise, they believed that the physical work patterns may have had an effect in controlling serum cholesterol concentrations. Mann (366), reporting the results of a study of three subjects, states that young men consuming high-fat diets were able to double their caloric intake without increasing the level of their serum lipids or cholesterol so long as the surplus of energy was expended as heat and muscular energy. On the other hand, restricting exercise and allowing fat deposition doubled serum cholesterol concentration. The serum concentrations were returned to normal by food restriction and weight reduction.

Other studies, too numerous to cite, have reported a decrease in blood cholesterol levels as a result of some kind of regular exercise. There are also studies that report no significant change in blood cholesterol levels due to regular exercise (77, 255). It should be kept in mind that the kind, amount, and intensity of exercise involved in the training are important factors, that is to say, one program may cause blood cholesterol reductions whereas another may not. For example, it appears that isometric training does not cause blood cholesterol reductions, whereas vigorous CR training does (92). Also, the initial cholesterol level, unless it is high, is not likely to be affected. With respect to diet per se and cholesterol levels, it is interesting to note that caloric restriction alone does not necessarily reduce cholesterol level. Even weight losses of forty pounds in obese subjects did not significantly reduce cholesterol levels in one study (158).

Blood Clotting and Clot Lysis as Related to Exercise and Training

The results of studies on exercise and blood clotting time are not in complete agreement. Some report a shortening of coagulation time (499), that is, quicker clot formation, whereas others report no effect of exercise (297). Studies by Ogston and Fullerton (435) and by Burt and co-workers (85) shed further light on the effects of exercise on clotting and clot lysis and the effects of training on these measures (Figures 8.20 and 8.21).

Keys and his co-workers reported faster clotting times in business and

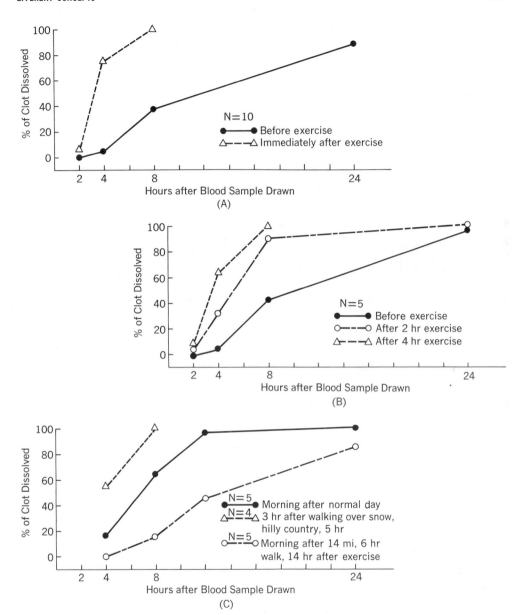

FIGURE 8.20 Effect of exercise on time of clot lysis (dissolving of blood clot). For example, one can see that a clot dissolves faster after exercise (A) when the blood sample is taken immediately after exercise (completely dissolved in 8 hours). Lysis is faster after four hours of exercise than after two hours of exercise (B). Lysis is slower the morning after strenuous, long-term exercise (C). Data from Ogston and Fullerton (435).

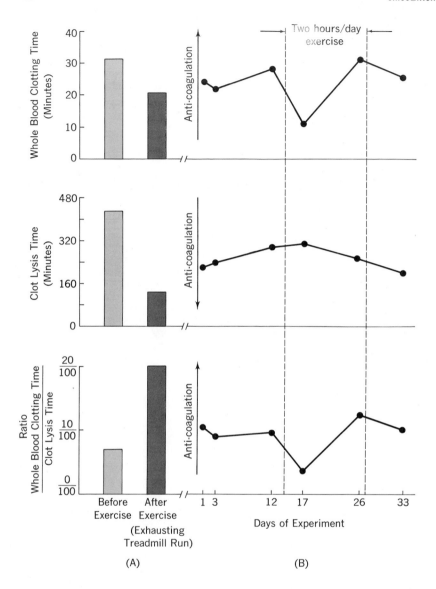

FIGURE 8.21 Effects of vigorous exercise (A) and regular daily exercise (B) on clotting time, clot lysis time (dissolving of a clot), and ratio of clotting to lysis times (coagulation-fibrinolysis equilibrium). Notice that longer clotting time, faster lysis time, and a higher clot-lysis ratio are relatively beneficial ("anticoagulant" in nature). Data from Burt, Blythe, and Rierson (85), and Burt and others, "Changes in the Blood Coagulation Complex in Sedentary Middle-Aged Males during Two Weeks of Strenuous Exercise," presented at American College of Sports Medicine Meetings, 1963.

professional men than in active rail-road workers (307), and an animal study demonstrated a significant prolonging effect of seven weeks of regular exercise in clotting time (596).

Regular Exercise and the Efficiency of the Heart

There is little doubt that regular and at least moderate exercise will reduce the resting heart rate (Figure 8.22); and up to a point, the more vigorous the regular exercise, the greater the reduction.

Although mathematically this does not necessarily mean more total rest for the heart (length of each total contraction is also a factor), it obviously means that the heart rests more *often* and there is evidence that the total work is decreased and that both efficiency and coronary reserve are increased. Mallerowicz presents data indicating that there is less heart work and lower O_2 consumption of the heart in trained persons. He claims that this increases the coronary reserve, that is, allows a greater safety margin between normal, resting de-

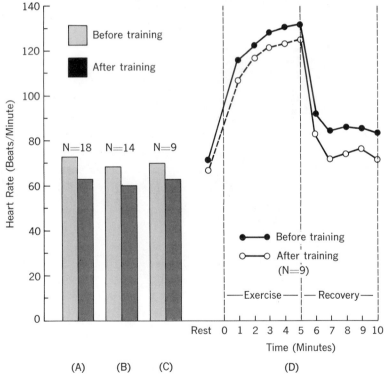

FIGURE 8.22 Effect of training on resting heart rate (A, B, C) and on exercise and recovery heart rates (D). (A) data from F. Henry (241); (B) data from Knehr (314); (C) and (D) data from Johnson, Updyke, and W. Henry (281).

mands and the demands of increased heart work.

Regular Exercise and the Development of Ischemic Heart Disease

There are scores of studies indicating that people in the more "active" occupations suffer less ischemic heart disease than those in sedentary occupations (see Figure 8.23). The limitations in using "occupation" or "last-known

occupation" as a measure of the degree of activity are obvious. How long has a person been "at" this job? What are his other activities? The presence of other factors, for example, diet, emotional stress, and genetics, may affect the findings. The degree of regularity of exercise since birth has obviously not been available to the statisticians. The theories and the evidence pertaining to the many aspects of heart disease (postprandial lipemia, coagulation-

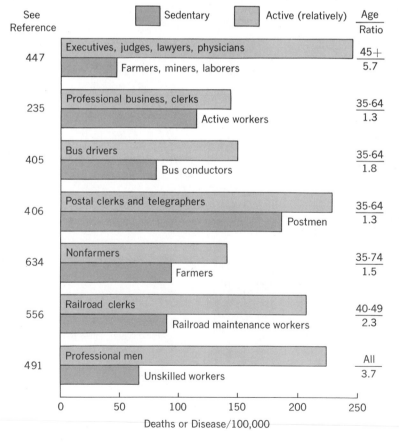

FIGURE 8.23 Coronary heart disease and CHD deaths related to occupation —sedentary versus active. A summary of studies. "Age" refers to the age range of subjects; "ratio" is the ratio of sedentary to active. Data from references as cited on the ordinate.

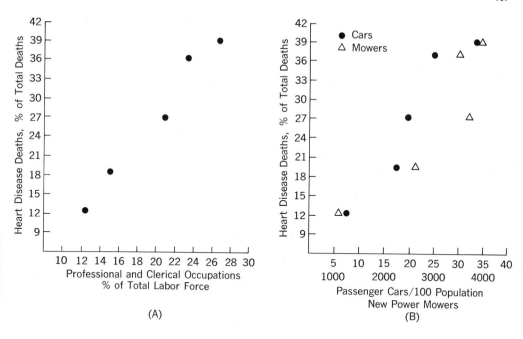

FIGURE 8.24 Relationship between heart disease deaths, professional and clerical occupations (A), passenger cars (B), and new power mowers (B). Each plotted point represents a given year, 1920–1960. Data from *Statistical Abstract of the United States* (578).

fibrinolysis equilibrium, blood lipids, and so on) have been presented (pages 189–195). At this point, for the purpose of this discussion of claims for the benefits of exercise, it is enough to say that the evidence, both statistical and experimental, is strong enough to support the claim that the sedentary individual is more likely to develop ischemic heart disease. Some of this evidence is presented in Figures 8.23 through 8.27 and in Table 8.1. You will note that the results presented in Table 8.1 are somewhat contrary to those depicted in Figure 8.23. The explanation is not apparent. The other figures all provide indirect evidence concerning changes in society that tend to promote more sedentary living and, in some cases, the relationship to heart disease deaths.

TABLE 8.1. Death Rates from Arteriosclerotic Heart Disease in the City of Chicago during 1951, Distributed according to Occupation

OCCUPATION	DEATH RATE NUMBER PER 100,000 White	Negro
Professionals, managers	365	437
Clerical and sales	559	256
Craftsmen, foremen	370	279
Service workers	440	351
Laborers	813	826

SOURCE: Stamler, Kjelsberg, and Hall (537).

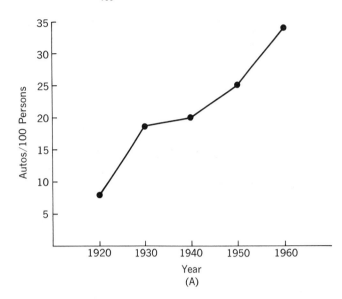

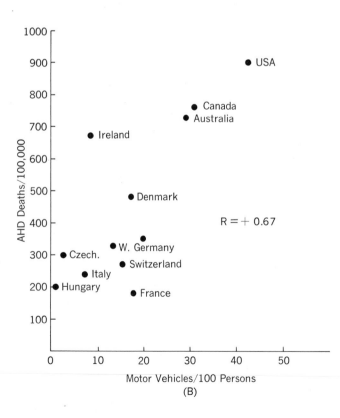

FIGURE 8.25 Motor vehicles and arteriosclerotic heart disease deaths. (A) Increase in passenger vehicle registrations in the United States, 1920–1960. (B) Motor vehicles and AHD deaths (males 55–64) during the period 1957–1959 in the United States and eleven similar countries.

Careful and exhaustive work by Brunner and Manelis (78) has shed more light on the question of the relationship of physical activity to heart disease. In the communal settlements of Israel, uniform living conditions and diet exist for all, irrespective of their work or profession. Over a fifteen-year period, 10,514 men and women in the 41–65 age range have been studied. In spite of equivalent diet, and so on, **angina pectoris** and fatal **myocardial infarction** were from 2.5 to 4 times higher for the sedentary workers than for nonsedentary workers. It was also noted that the mortality rate of those who had suffered heart attacks and survived was three times as great for the sedentary workers. The six-year follow-up mortality rates were similarly higher for the inactive workers. In addition to the data from heart disease deaths, several investigators have also reported more nonfatal *coronary heart disease* among sedentary workers than among those doing heavy work.

Summary of Evidence Concerning Exercise and Heart Disease

In summarizing the evidence, we might add that medical researchers and physiologists generally agree that there is no single factor standing alone as the causative agent in the chronic degenerative circulatory disorders (see Table 8.8). Most authorities agree that there are very likely at least five major offenders:

genetic factors, improper diet, stress, lack of physical activity, and obesity. To this list smoking probably should be added. It is very probable that the process is a slow one and that at least several of the above-mentioned factors, if not all, interact with one another in the given individual and thus determine whether or not he will develop significant degenerative circulatory pathology. There has been no evidence that physical activity is detrimental in any way to the normal person, and there is a wealth of evidence to support the thesis that regular physical activity aids in preventing and postponing the onset of cardiovascular degenerative changes. Therefore, it appears that if a person is concerned about doing those things he can do in order to decrease the probability of suffering from these degenerative changes, he must logically include in his prevention program some regular activity that will lead to optimal circulo-respiratory fitness. A person cannot change the existing genetic factors, but he should consider the obesity, stress, diet, and smoking factors in designing an AHD prevention program. He should request that the important predictive items listed on page 224 be included in his physical examination when he reaches 35 or 40 and even sooner if he has a family history of heart disease, or has high blood pressure or a tendency toward obesity.

MISCELLANEOUS CLAIMS FOR CR BENEFITS OF EXERCISE

Does training result in slower, deeper breathing at rest and, if so, does this mean greater respiratory efficiency? The evi-

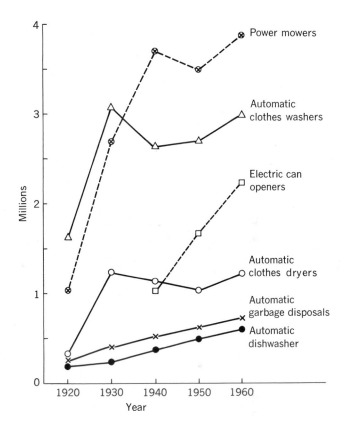

FIGURE 8.26 Increase in automation in the United States, 1920–1960. Data from *Statistical Abstract of the United States* (578).

dence supports the claim for slower, deeper ventilation (314). It is questionable whether this necessarily means greater respiratory efficiency, because respiratory efficiency can mean many things. If we define respiratory efficiency as the energy requirement of the ventilatory muscles, then we must say that there is no evidence that resting respiratory efficiency is increased with training. However, a decreased rate of breathing would logically be expected to result in less work per minute for the inspiratory muscles.

Does training result in a greater vital capacity associated with better pulmonary gas exchange and increased oxygen utilization? There is some evidence that regular exercise which actually involves very deep breathing can increase one's vital capacity (28, 138, 502). It is, however, conjectural whether this means better gas exchange at the alveoli-capillary exchange surface. There would have to be a concomitant increase in pulmonary capillarization in order to make any increased lung area effective as a gas exchange area. If increased vital capacity results only from the development of inspiratory muscles, then a greater exchange area would not automatically exist. The latter statement concerning increased oxygen utilization is not supportable because oxygen utilization, as we have already learned, is proportional to the *need* of the tissues and not to the amount of oxygen *supplied.* It is interesting to note that one team of investigators (147) reports a possible relationship between vital

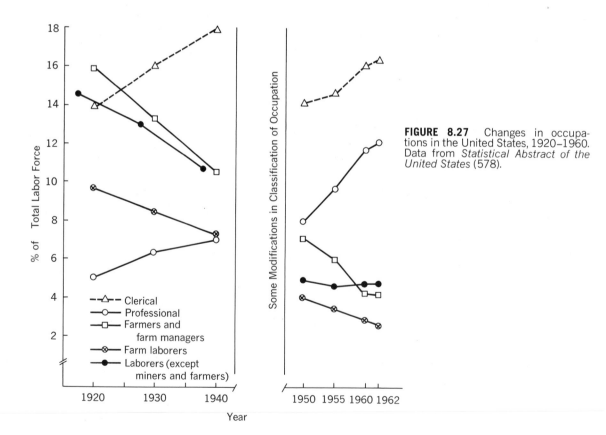

FIGURE 8.27 Changes in occupations in the United States, 1920–1960. Data from *Statistical Abstract of the United States* (578).

capacity (as an index of physical activity level) and coronary heart disease, those with higher initial vital capacity have lower coronary heart disease risk.

Does the increased blood pressure associated with exercise mean a healthier vascular system? First, although it is obvious that exercise per se increases blood pressure, there is no evidence that training affects *resting* blood pressure at all. Second, there is no evidence that regularly increasing one's blood pressure is beneficial to the integrity of the vascular system. Based on the law of use and disuse (see page 611), one would suspect that this increased pressure might exert some beneficial influence on the elasticity of the vessel walls. It is possible that "disuse" hastens hardening of the arteries because the walls of the arteries are seldom subjected to stretch by increased pressure, but this is slim justification and certainly not adequate support for this claim.

Does training result in cardiac hypertrophy and increased coronary circulation? Steinhaus (543, pp. 90, 93, 181) cites considerable evidence that regular vigorous exercise can cause cardiac muscle hypertrophy; this should mean a stronger heart (see page 90). The claim that regular exercise causes increased coronary circulation is probably based on Eckstein's (162) classic work, which indicates that after blockage or **occlusion** of one of the main coronary arteries, regular exercise promotes the development or opening up of collateral or additional pathways that bypass the occlusion. However, it appears that the blockage or oxygen-lack stimulus must occur *before* this collateral circulation

can develop (84). With respect to an increase in cardiac muscle **capillarization** due to training, there is some evidence that this occurs (543).

ACHIEVEMENT AND MAINTENANCE OF ADEQUATE CIRCULO-RESPIRATORY CAPACITY

The exact type of circulo-respiratory training program that you recommend to a group of adults, prescribe for an individual, or utilize in a formal class situation is, of course, dependent upon certain very important factors. This is the first and most important principle of circulo-respiratory training. When you recognize the importance of this principle and put it into practice in your profession, you will have taken a vital step along the road to crossing the barrier that separates the professional from the technician. With a little effort, you should be able to list the factors that determine the kind and amount of exercise a given person should have if he or she wishes to achieve a higher circulo-respiratory capacity (see Table 8.2).

TABLE 8.2   Factors Affecting Selection of CR Conditioning Program

1. Health Status
2. Age
3. Sex
4. Current CR capacity
5. Desired general CR capacity or specific CR capacity

Science has not and probably never will establish strict and definite guidelines for any of these factors. Concerning health status, it is reasonable to say that you should never prescribe, recommend, or require (depending upon your relationship to the person) *any* kind of program unless you are certain that there is no health deficiency or condition that makes exercise hazardous. This means a recent and complete physical examination, and this can be handled in numerous ways, depending upon your operational situation (schools usually require such certification). With respect to three of the remaining factors, age, sex, and current circulo-respiratory capacity, a sound principle is *"underexert* at first, until a reasonable acclimatization occurs."

This will allow a more normal and less "painful" adjustment period for the exerciser and will need to be based on common sense, yours and the exerciser's. The fifth factor, desired circulo-respiratory capacity, obviously determines the eventual kind and intensity of the program and is in turn related to the actual method of circulatory-respiratory training.

General Principles of Circulo-Respiratory Training

OVERLOAD PRINCIPLE The **overload principle** simply means that stress must be placed on the system or systems whose capacity you wish to increase. In this case, you are dealing with the heart, circulatory system, and respiratory system, or, to look at it another way, you wish to improve the delivery and waste-removal mechanisms of the body. Certainly the neuro-skeletal-muscular system and the endocrine system are involved, but they do not bear the "overload" in the same sense if the pro-

gram is properly designed to develop primarily circulo-respiratory capacity. That is, if the muscles are overloaded and become impaired *before* the capacity of the circulo-respiratory system has been taxed, then the objective has not been met. Use of the muscles is, in this case, primarily the *means* to an end, that end being circulo-respiratory overload. (Let us pause here to point out that the term *overload* is actually a misnomer in that once the circulo-respiratory system is truly overloaded it cannot function.) In a true circulo-respiratory "overload" activity the individual should be forced to discontinue only because of the inability of his circulo-respiratory system to meet the demands of the task. This is, admittedly, difficult to achieve in a pure form, but the closer you come to such a condition (that is, where local muscle fatigue is not a factor) the closer you have come to circulo-respiratory overload.

If any appreciable improvement in circulo-respiratory capacity is to occur, this overload must take place, and it must take place *regularly*. Because such an overload invariably causes an increase in heart rate, one might reduce this principle to a simpler form. The heart rate must be increased significantly and regularly for improvement in circulo-respiratory capacity to occur. What is "significant" and what is "regular"? Answers to these questions, while not as absolute as they should and hopefully will be, are dealt with later in this chapter, and obviously depend upon other factors such as age, current status, and desired circulo-respiratory capacity.

SPECIFICITY PRINCIPLE   The principle of specificity is an important one and implies that training is highly specific. It is perhaps less applicable to circulo-respiratory capacity because the heart and lungs are "*general* servants" of the entire body. Because they are the primary organs involved in true and pure circulo-respiratory capacity, it is conceivable that they could become highly conditioned to handling delivery and waste removal at a very efficient and intensive rate so that they could handle any work requirement that does not exceed that rate. Assuming that the most demanding form of training is utilized, such a theory should hold. But the vascular system in the muscles per se may adapt to training and become more efficient in delivery and waste removal, and thus contribute to the total improvement in circulo-respiratory capacity. Therefore it is not quite so simple to separate the pure circulo-respiratory from the pure muscular efficiency changes.

At any rate, an efficient and highly trained circulo-respiratory system does render the person better able to persist in any activity where the *capacity of the circulo-respiratory system is a primary limiting factor,* even though more specific training in that activity will undoubtedly improve the capacity for that activity even further. Of course, where localized muscles are significantly involved in limiting work capacity, this is a different matter. For example, a swimmer may well develop stamina and a strong circulo-respiratory system, but for such a person to try to compete in the mile run, even if his circulo-

respiratory capacity exceeded the demands of running a four-minute mile, he would not be immediately successful because of the different load placed on the muscles of the body, particularly the added load to be handled by the legs. But to work at any task where the local muscle demand was less than in swimming, he would be well equipped to demonstrate excellent circulo-respiratory capacity, no matter what the task might be.

In short, one kind of circulo-respiratory conditioning does not necessarily prepare a person for another activity, because localized muscle effort usually is involved. But as far as the circulo-respiratory system per se is concerned, there can be considerable beneficial carry-over.

Specific Principles of Circulo-Respiratory Training

Specific principles of circulo-respiratory training, of course, are applied in the light of the general principles just discussed, and, as you will see, all have to do with the principles of overload and specificity in some way.

1. *The greater the proportion of the total body musculature involved, the greater the circulo-respiratory load.* That is, if the muscles of both the legs and arms are vigorously contracting, there is greater circulo-respiratory load than if either muscle group is working alone.
2. *The intensity of the circulo-respiratory load is partially determined by the proportion of maximal force exerted by the muscles and/or the frequency of exertions.* That is, if a given set of muscle groups

is working at 80 percent of maximal force, the circulo-respiratory load is greater than if they were working at 40 percent of maximal. Likewise, for a given percent of maximal force, more frequent contractions, say thirty per minute as compared with ten per minute, will result in a greater circulo-respiratory load.

3. *The greater the intensity of the exertion, the more rapidly the circulo-respiratory overload will be achieved.* That is, the greater the intensity of the circulo-respiratory load, according to Principle 2, the sooner the person's circulo-respiratory system will be working at overload.

4. *In a given person, the greater the intensity of the activity, the shorter the period during which overload can be maintained.* That is, the closer one comes to all-out effort, the shorter period of time that effort can be maintained.

These principles are straightforward enough. But how do we take advantage of them to formulate a training program to achieve optimal circulo-respiratory capacity? This is, of course, where the principle of specificity crops up again; it depends upon what one wants! Does the person want to be able to run a four-minute mile or a twenty-five minute four mile race or to swim for distance or just to develop good, general circulo-respiratory capacity? Obviously the miler does not train by running four miles every day at the four-miler's rate, the four-miler doesn't run a mile each day at the miler's speed, and so on. Though the program can be varied, one basically trains for what he wants to do.

The man wishing general circulo-respiratory capacity can combine intensity and duration. Although exercise physiologists do not have any definite answers, it appears safe to assume that the greater the *total* work of the heart (contractions) accomplished over as short a time span as possible, the greater will be the gain in circulo-respiratory capacity. Assuming they both started at the same circulo-respiratory capacity, a man whose heart contracts 6000 times during a daily one-hour walk (an average of 100 a minute) would not expect as much circulo-respiratory gain as a man whose heart beats 6000 times during a daily forty minute jog (an average of 150 a minute). A third man whose heart beats an average of 150 times a minute for sixty minutes would most likely exhibit a greater gain than the second man. This principle only takes us so far, unfortunately, and then drops us right in the middle of an abyss of ignorance! How long would the first man have to walk at 100 beats a minute to achieve what the second man would achieve? This is one of the very pressing needs for our profession; to be able to quantify the work output necessary to achieve *optimal* circulo-respiratory capacity. The picture is not all that bleak, however. The need is only to determine the *best* way. We know that circulo-respiratory capacity gains *can* be achieved by using the principles listed here.

Actually, a happy medium between intensity and duration is best. If more bouts a day can be added, this will help, and once a week is not going to accomplish the same gains as three, four or five times a week.

In summary, the following may be concluded concerning the principles of circulo-respiratory training:

1. Overload is absolutely necessary. In the normal person, it is doubtful whether any gain can be expected from programs in which heart rates of less than 120 per minute are attained. Sharkey (510) presents evidence that 180 is superior to 150, which is in turn superior to 120.

2. Specificity is important for specific "events." The person should train basically at the distance and rate at which he intends to compete. Overload in terms of both distance and rate can also be very valuable.

3. Although the exact combination of intensity, duration, number of bouts, and days a week has not been determined for general circulo-respiratory conditioning, we are led to conclude that at least three times a week is necessary. Furthermore, when the other three factors are held constant, greater intensity or greater duration or more bouts a day should lead to greater gains in circulo-respiratory capacity.

4. All of these principles must become subservient to the first principle discussed in this chapter. *Intensity, duration, and so on must be based upon the individual's current status, and you should err on the side of underexertion initially.*

Specific Approaches to Circulo-Respiratory Training

CIRCUIT TRAINING Circuit training was originated at the University of Leeds in Great Britain. Its purpose was to give students a vigorous, all-around workout in a short time. Combining the elements of calisthenics, running, weight lifting, and the "competing-against-time" appeal of the obstacle course, circuit training aims at the progressive development of muscular and circulo-respiratory capacity. A general conditioning technique, it can be loaded to concentrate on specific weaknesses when it is set up on an individual basis. Although it is not a complete gymnastic system nor a recreational activity, many who cannot enjoy other fitness activities are enthusiastic about this system. The "near maximal" concept and the principle of progressive loading are integral parts of the "circuit," which includes items for all parts of the body as well as some sort of CR activity, such as running or rope jumping. Generally speaking, the individual is competing against himself, trying to increase the "dosage" or number of repetitions of each item while also trying to lower his time for the total circuit.

Following is an example of a beginning general circuit, involving very little equipment. It is obvious that this illustration includes exercises other than those that benefit CR fitness, but it has the advantage of diversity. An individual program can vary considerably and stress CR fitness a great deal more than this example. Incidentally, rope jumping (Item 6 in the example) has been shown to be an excellent CR fitness activity (33, 287).

After familiarization with the circuit, you can increase the items where endurance is not "near maximal"; when you reach the point where no more

SAMPLE OF A BEGINNING CIRCUIT FOR COLLEGE WOMEN

1. Jumping jacks—12
2. Bent-arm hang on high bar—20 seconds
3. Bent-knee sit-ups—10
4. Push-ups from knees—12
5. Toe-touches—10
6. Rope jumping—30 turns
7. Back extendors—12
8. Wrist curls—6
9. Jogging and walking—.5 mile.[a]
10. Maximal vertical jumps—6

[a]Bench stepping may be substituted for an indoor program when space is limited.

time can be shaved off, you should increase the intensity or duration of the various items.

An excellent little book, *Circuit Training,* by Morgan and Adamson (401) of the University of Leeds, is available for those interested in more detailed information for setting up circuits.

INTERVAL TRAINING Interval training was developed for endurance training, primarily in running and swimming, but the general principles are applicable to any kind of conditioning or training where staying power of *any* kind is essential. At least four elements are involved: (1) speed or rate, (2) distance or length of time, (3) rest interval, and (4) number of bouts or sets. Any of the four elements can be varied in order to increase the work load, or as a means of adding variety to the program. An example of how these elements can be set up follows.

Interval training has been used successfully in rehabilitation of cardiac patients. An excellent paper on the

theory and specificity of interval training has been prepared by William Heusner (245).

CONTEMPORARY DANCE (MODERN DANCE) In such a program the emphasis is on movement and grace, although flexibility, muscular endurance, and CR capacity can be improved if they are specifically involved in the movements selected. In our culture, generally speaking, men have trouble with rhythmic exercises, but this appears to be more social than functional ineptitude. Although modern or contemporary dance is considered as an esthetic art, and is not a "strength" builder, it may well be unsurpassed for improving the combined qualities of grace, body control, balance, flexibility, and agility. (see Figure 21.3). In the more vigorous forms, dance also contributes to muscular endurance and CR fitness.

SPORTS ACTIVITIES If time and facilities are available, many will choose some competitive sport for exercise.

ELEMENT	RUNNING
Rate:	1 mi/5 min (440 yd/75 sec)
Distance or time:	440 yd
Rest int.:	5 min
Bouts:	4
Variations:	When 4th bout does not produce excessive discomfort, shorten interval to 3 min.

Swimming and distance running, although competitive sports, can be engaged in without an opponent and are excellent CR conditioners. Singles handball, badminton, tennis, squash, and paddle ball are enjoyable games and can be excellent conditioners, but appear to do little for flexibility and overall muscular endurance, and essentially nothing for strength. Some strength is certainly necessary to compete and have fun in these games and we would agree that some specific and localized muscular endurance is improved.

Golf, if it involves more walking and less waiting at the tee and on the fairway, can be a valuable fitness activity to a completely sedentary or older person, but soon reaches a point of no return, at least as far as physical fitness is concerned.

Bowling is obviously ineffective as a fitness activity except perhaps to improve the very specific endurance involved in the arm swing and ball release. One gets a fairly accurate picture of the CR value of the various activities by comparing average heart rates attained during actual competition and recovery heart rates following various exercises or activities (see Figures 8.28, 8.29, and 8.30). Based on heart rate and time involved, how would you rate the activities in Figure 8.30 as to their relative value for CR fitness?

One can also get a reasonably clear picture of the CR value of various activities by referring to the caloric expenditure table on page 338.

"AEROBICS" Major Kenneth Cooper's book entitled *Aerobics* (123) has provided a planned and rather specific prescription for CR conditioning. Based on one's fitness category (see page 214), Cooper prescribes specific weekly

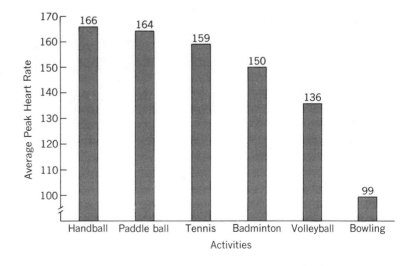

FIGURE 8.28 Peak heart rates in college male attained during various intramural contests. Data from Kozar and Hunsicker (321).

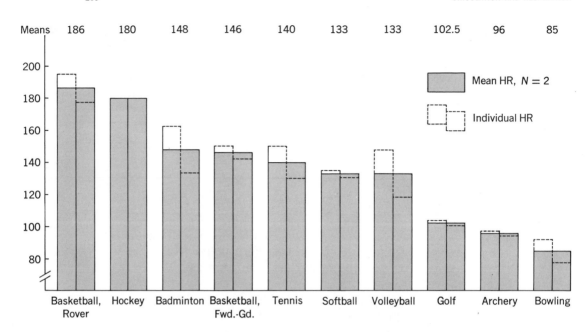

FIGURE 8.29 Mean heart rate during women's competition (mean for entire contest). Only two subjects utilized, but application is index of *relative* strenuousness of activities for a given person. Data from a study by Skubic and Hodgkins (523).

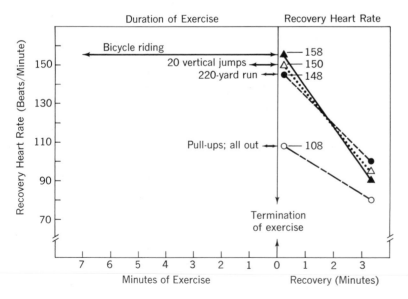

FIGURE 8.30 Effects of various activities on recovery heart rates. Arrows represent length of time for exercise on time scale to left of zero. Data from Physiology of Exercise Laboratory, University of Toledo.

amounts of exercise from any one or a combination of several activities including running, walking, cycling, swimming, stationary running, and squash, handball, or basketball; his program is based upon the accumulation of weekly points. It seems to us that every physical educator and recreation worker should have a copy of this little book at his disposal for purposes of suggesting specific exercise programs for the development and maintenance of CR fitness.

EVALUATION TECHNIQUES; HEART DISEASE AND OTHER DISORDERS

APPRAISAL OF CIRCULO-RESPIRATORY CAPACITY

Several laboratory tests are recognized as sound CR tests. For example, there are several good tests of maximal O_2 intake or aerobic capacity, one of which is Balke's (34) Standardized Treadmill Test. He has tested some 700 males, ages 18–65, and has classified men from very poor to superior on a scale of oxygen intake in milliliters O_2 per minute per kilogram of body weight. Balke classifies 35–40 ml/min/kg as "fair" and 40–45 as "good" (Figure 8.31).

Wahlund (593) has devised a test based on exercise heart rate that appears to be very successful for classifying degrees of CR capacity. His PWC 170 test (physical working capacity heart rate 170) utilizes increasing work levels on the bicycle ergometer until a heart rate of 170 is reached. He has even classified subjects according to disease states. The average healthy man is expected to attain a work level of 900 kg-m/min before reaching the 170 level.

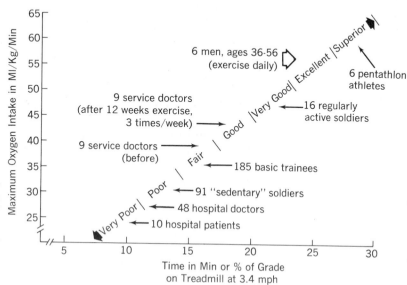

FIGURE 8.31 Balke's classification of CR capacity in terms of maximum oxygen intake per kilogram of body weight. For example, a 70 kg man should be able to attain a maximum O_2 intake of 2450–2800 ml per minute to be classified as "fair." Adapted from Balke (34).

Two somewhat common and easily administered laboratory tests of pulmonary or respiratory function are apparently related to fitness and are almost certainly related to the functional capacity of the lungs. Serious lung disorders almost always cause a noticeable decrease in vital capacity.

Vital capacity is determined by having the subject take as deep a breath as possible and then, with his nostrils pinched closed, having him exhale maximally into an instrument called a *spirometer,* which records the volume of air expired. It is related to body size and should be divided by body weight or body surface to get standards, but an average figure for young men is about 4.6 liters and for young women about 3.1 liters. In **emphysema,** left heart disease, chronic asthma and bronchitis, carcinoma, tuberculosis, and fibrotic pleurisy, vital capacity (VC) can fall (as much as 70 percent); a decrease of even 20 percent should lead one to suspect some kind of pulmonary dysfunction.

The maximal breathing capacity test, which involves more elaborate equipment, is essentially a measure of the volume of air that can be "moved" or ventilated in a given time, usually 15 seconds. It is apparently more closely related to fitness than the less dynamic VC test. An average value for men is about 100–150 l/min but this rate cannot usually be maintained for more than 15 seconds because dizziness caused by a temporary **alkalosis** often occurs.

You have seen evidence that heart rate taken at rest and during a standardized exercise is reduced with training. It follows, then, that these measures of heart rate should in some way serve as an index of CR capacity. The "step test" is based on this principle, as are many other exercise and recovery heart rate tests. Of the simple tests that require little equipment, the heart rate recovery tests are apparently accepted as the best and most reliable means for evaluating CR capacity. Any means of standardizing work load will do, but stepping up and down appears to be the simplest and certainly involves the least expensive equipment. Although there *are* established tests and norms, such as for the Harvard Step Test and its modified forms (see Tables 8.3–8.5), it is well to teach each person to select his own specific "test procedure" so that he can use it at home if necessary. The following procedure is recommended for home testing.

1. Select a surface for alternately stepping up and down. The usual recommended height is 16–17 inches, but the exact height is not critical and could be lower, even down to 8 inches, for older persons or persons with conditions that limit their ability to step up. (Care should be taken that the surface is stable and will not easily tip over.)

2. Secure a metronome or a recording that will establish a rhythm of about 100–120 beats per minute (march tempo is satisfactory). This will allow you to standardize your *rate* of stepping. This is extremely important as you can see in Figure 8.33.

3. Secure a watch or clock with which you can easily begin and stop your

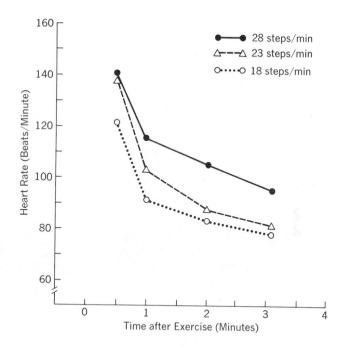

FIGURE 8.32 Effect of varying rate of stepping on heart rate recovery. A 21 in. bench was used; the test was 2 minutes in length. Source: Physiology of Exercise Laboratory, University of Toledo.

stepping time and count your pulse rate during recovery after exercise.

4. If at all possible, take the test after thirty minutes of complete relaxation, preferably in the lying position. Mid-morning is best. Wide deviation in temperature and humidity from test to test can easily render your results unreliable.

5. Familiarize yourself with the rhythm and order of stepping. Use a rate of 120 beats per minute (100–120 acceptable), which means 30 complete up-down cycles per minute. That is, you step up on the bench (and down) thirty times each minute if you step with each beat —"left foot up, right foot up; left foot down, right foot down." You should rise to full leg extension each time (Figure 8.33).

6. Time yourself precisely and step for three minutes, or according to the following table.

AGE	TIME[a]
Under 30	3 min
30–45	2 min, if currently sedentary
45 and over	1 min, if currently sedentary and then only after physical examination

[a]The time will, of course, be affected by the height of the bench. The lower the bench, the longer you can step without CR or leg muscle impairment.

7. Stop precisely when you are supposed to, sit down and quietly wait for fifteen seconds. During this time, locate your "pulse" at the carotid artery (see Figure 8.34). Do not press hard

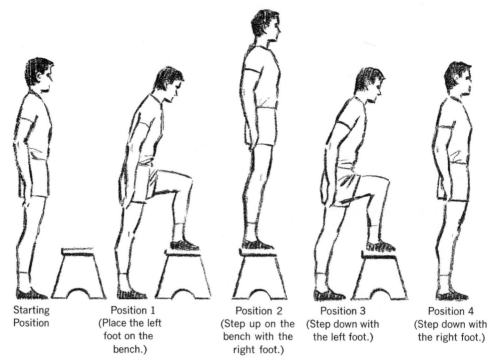

| Starting Position | Position 1 (Place the left foot on the bench.) | Position 2 (Step up on the bench with the right foot.) | Position 3 (Step down with the left foot.) | Position 4 (Step down with the right foot.) |

FIGURE 8.33   Proper order of stepping for "step-test." You can begin with either foot, but the alternating pattern should be maintained as illustrated.

at this point, as pressure could cause a slowing of the heart rate.

8. Count your pulse for fifteen seconds and record the count.

9. Count pulse again 1 minute to 1:15 after exercise.

10. Count pulse again 2 minutes to 2:15 after exercise.

11. To check for reliability repeat this test again after several days, under exactly the same conditions.

12. Repeat at least twice a year under conditions that are as nearly the same as possible: Time of day, time and composition of last meal, temperature and humidity, emotional state, no immediately preceding exercise, and so on.

Compare your test results through the years as an index of your CR capacity. *Report these comparisons to your physician if there has been a drastic change that you cannot logically explain.*

Of course, as the professional, you will want to use a standardized test for purposes of evaluating and recording circulo-respiratory capacity. The same principles outlined for "home testing" apply. Standardization is *most* important. What you intend to do with the results should affect the procedures. For example, if you simply wish to have students evaluate their own circulo-respiratory capacity, mass testing in

TABLE 8.3

TEST:	Modified Step Test		
BENCH:	17"		
RATE:	30 steps per minute (metronome = 120)		
TIME:	Men: 3 min		
	Women: 2 min		
PULSE COUNT:	From 1:00 to 1:30 post exercise		
SCORING:	Multiply count by 2.		
NORMS:		MALE	FEMALE
	Poor	Above 125	Above 135
	Avg.	111–124	121–134
	Above Avg.	100–110	110–120
	Excellent	Below 100	Below 110
AGE GROUP:	High school students, college students		

pairs is acceptable, with each student having his partner count his pulse. However, if you wish to use the results to study the effectiveness of some particular training program, mass paired testing is out of the question; you need highly standardized and reliable procedures with as few pulse counters as possible.

Three modifications of the original Harvard Step Test are presented in Tables 8.3, 8.4, and 8.5 as practical, valid, and reliable procedures for your professional use. The following precautions, if they can be observed, will serve to render your results more valid and reliable:

1. Standardize time of day test is given.
2. Do not use test after heavy meal.
3. Do not use test after physical activity.
4. Use only trained pulse rate counters if you wish results to be most reliable, valid, and objective.

Major Kenneth Cooper (M.D.) has developed what he calls the "12 Minute Field Test" (123) as a measure of CR capacity. It can be used for almost any

TABLE 8.4

TEST:	Michael-Adams One-Minute Step Test
BENCH:	17"
RATE:	Men: 36 steps per minute
	Women: 30 steps per minute
TIME:	One minute
PULSE COUNT:	From 1:00 to 1:15 post exercise
	2:00 to 2:15 post exercise
	3:00 to 3:15 post exercise
SCORING:	Total of three counts multiplied by 4
NORM:	Average score for men and women is 300
AGE GROUP:	High school students, college students and young adults in good physical condition

SOURCE: E. D. Michael and A. Adams, "The Use of the One-Minute Step Test to Estimate Exercise Fitness," *Ergonomics*, 7:211, 1964.

TABLE 8.5

TEST:	Tecumseh Submaximal Exercise Test[a]
BENCH:	8″
RATE:	24 steps per minute
TIME:	Three minutes
PULSE COUNT:	Method A: Time 10 heart beats beginning at 1 minute post exercise
	Method B: Count heart beats for 15 seconds beginning at 1 minute post exercise
SCORING:	Method A: $\dfrac{600}{X}$, where x = time (to nearest tenth of a second) for 10 heart beats
	Method B: Multiply count by 4

NORMS:[a]	PERCENTILE	MALE	FEMALE
	95th (Exc.)	67	75
	75th (Ab.Avg.)	79	85
	50th (Avg.)	90	95
	25th (Poor)	100	110

AGE GROUP:	10–69 unless in poor health

[a]Approximation based on average of age groups 10–11, 12–13, 14–15, 16–17, 18–19, 20–29, 30–39, 40–49, 50–59, 60–69. Actual figures were no more different than 0–4 beats per minute except one case (Female 25th percentile) where difference was 8 beats per minute between 10–11 and 60–69 age groups.
SOURCE: H. J. Montoye, P. W. Willis III, and D. A. Cunningham, "Heart Rate Response to Submaximal Exercise: Relation to Age and Sex," *J. of Gerontology*, 23:127, 1968.

person who has his physician's approval and certainly for youngsters in good health from ages 12 through college age. Table 8.6 gives the rating scale; the test is based on the distance one can cover in exactly twelve minutes.

TABLE 8.6 Rating Scale for 12-Minute Field Test

IF YOU COVER:	FITNESS CATEGORY
less than 1.0 mile	I Very Poor
1.0–1.24 miles	II Poor
1.25–1.49 miles	III Fair
1.50–1.74 miles	IV Good
1.75 or more	V Excellent

FACTORS OTHER THAN PHYSICAL ACTIVITY ASSOCIATED WITH HEART DISEASE

In addition to the facts and data concerning the relationship between circulo-respiratory integrity and exercise and training per se, there are conditions not at all or only indirectly related to exercise with which you should be acquainted. Many of these relationships have great meaning for programs in physical education, health education, and recreation, and any good professional in these fields should have at least a basic familiarity with them if he is to operate effective programs based on the best foundation possible.

As you study the following pages, you will at once recognize most of the tie-ins with your profession. In most cases you will see how this information is an important part of your profession's foundational body of knowledge. Some facts are obviously more directly germane to one of the professions than to the others, but all are in some way a part of this important foundational framework.

Obesity and Body Type

High blood pressure was 2.5 times more prevalent in Army officers who were overweight as in those not overweight (343). In the Framingham study, overweight individuals showed twice as many new cases of **arteriosclerotic heart disease** as those weighing less than average (146). However, Spain and co-workers (535) concluded that there is no association between weight and arteriosclerotic heart disease (AHD) when **hypertension** and diabetes are excluded. Nevertheless, those in the distinctly "below average" weight range have a significantly lower prevalence of arteriosclerotic heart disease. They found that **endomesomorphic** men (somewhat obese but mostly muscular builds) had a greater prevalence of arteriosclerotic heart disease than **ectomorphs** (thin build).

The Nervous System and Emotions

In addition to the **epidemiological** data presented earlier there is some experimental evidence that lends credence to the theories that emphasize the role of emotional stress in the cardiac atherogenic process.

In experimental animals, cardiac ischemia and damage (381), as well as hemorrhages in the cardiac muscle itself (313), have been triggered by stimulation of discrete areas of the brain and sympathetic cardiac nerves. In both hyman beings and animals (32, 101, 193, 339, 472) stress, excess secretion of **adrenalin** and **noradrenalin**, and incidence of **myocardial infarction** have been linked together. Furthermore, there has been a report of a small but significant increase in the incidence of **coronary occlusion** in persons with **duodenal** ulcer (74).

Dr. S. G. Wolf (618) surveyed a small town in Pennsylvania in which the population is relatively obese. These native Americans of Italian descent eat at least as much fat as does the average American. Furthermore, serum cholesterol values are almost identical with those reported in other studies. Compared with neighboring communities, these people are gay, unpretentious, and even boisterous; there is no crime nor real poverty. The death rate from coronary heart disease is less than half that of neighboring towns and the rest of the United States. Dr. Wolf adds that it does not appear that genetic or ethnic factors are responsible for this lower rate, but that the "social pattern may be the relevant factor." Figures 8.35

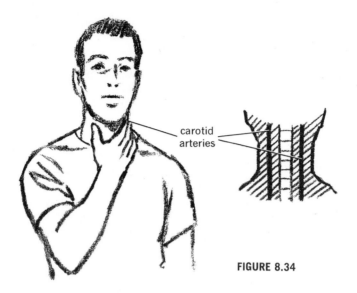

FIGURE 8.34

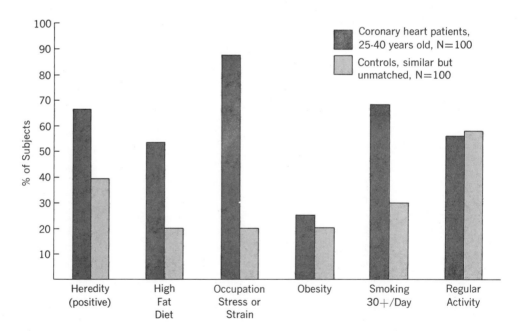

FIGURE 8.35   Prevalence of various factors, supposedly related to coronary heart disease, in young CHD patients compared with non-CHD controls. Data from Russek and Zohman (484). Twenty-five percent had an extra job; 60 percent put in 60+ hours per week; 20 percent had unusual fear, discontent, frustration, and so on, associated with job.

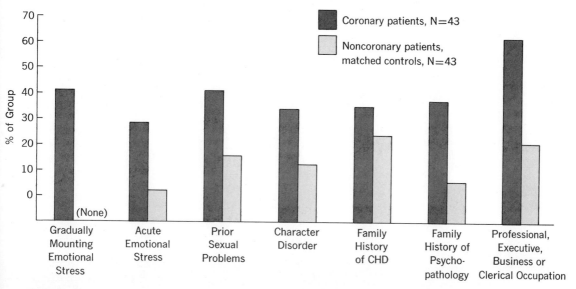

FIGURE 8.36 Occupation, family history of CHD and psychopathology, and emotional factors. Coronary patients compared with matched controls. Data from Weiss and others (600).

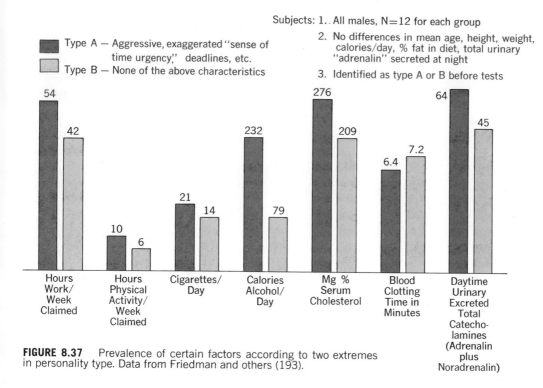

FIGURE 8.37 Prevalence of certain factors according to two extremes in personality type. Data from Friedman and others (193).

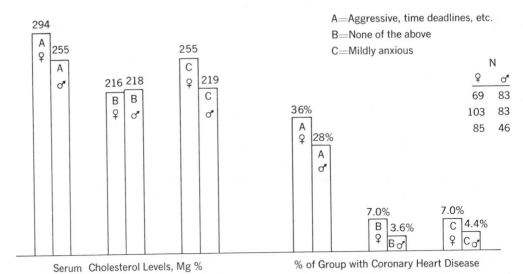

A=Aggressive, time deadlines, etc.
B=None of the above
C=Mildly anxious

Serum Cholesterol Levels, Mg %   % of Group with Coronary Heart Disease

FIGURE 8.38   Personality type, serum cholesterol level, and incidence of coronary artery disease in men and women (age 30–60, all identified according to type before tests and diagnosis). Data from Friedman and Rosenman (194) and Rosenman and Friedman (477).

through 8.39 provide additional information regarding stress or anxiety and heart disease.

Cigarette Smoking

Spain and Nathan (534), after an autopsy study of 3000 males, found 11.7 percent of the heavy smokers had arteriosclerotic heart disease whereas only 6.5 percent of the others had this disease. Your attention is also directed to Figures 8.35, 8.37, and 8.40.

Blood Cholesterol and AHD

Gofman and others (213) and Gertler and others (208) report not only that high blood cholesterol is found in coronary patients but also that it and certain other lipid fractions of the blood

are reasonably good predictors of AHD. Figures 8.38 and 8.41 are representative of many studies that show high serum cholesterol levels related to coronary artery disease.

Genetics

A thorough discussion of heredity and a detailed presentation of evidence regarding inherited predisposition to **atherosclerosis** are beyond the scope of this text. We trust it will suffice to say that there is considerable evidence that genetic factors do play a role in **atherogenesis.** Two common and major clinical problems have been recognized: essential familial hyperlipidemia (elevation of fasting **triglycerides**) and essential familial hypercholesterolemia (elevation of total **serum cholesterol**).

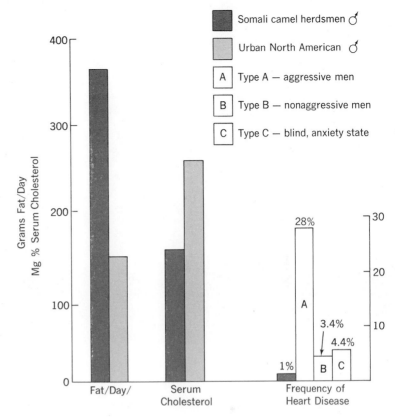

FIGURE 8.39 Daily fat intake and serum cholesterol in Somali camel herdsmen and North American urban men. The herdsmen are said to be very physically active but lead a tranquil life; their urinary adrenalin secretion was uniformly low, indicating a less stressful life. Frequency of coronary heart disease in the Somali herdsmen as compared with three personality types of American men. Adapted from Lapiccirella (329) and Friedman and Rosenman (194).

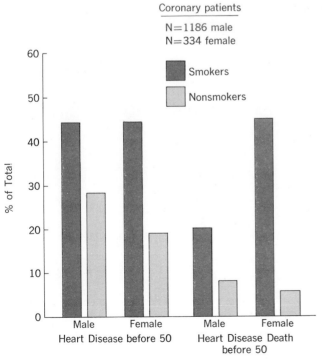

FIGURE 8.40 Percentage of coronary patients developing heart disease before age 50 and percentage of those dying before age 50, smokers versus nonsmokers. Data from Sigler (517).

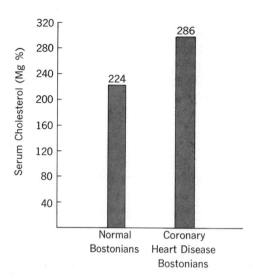

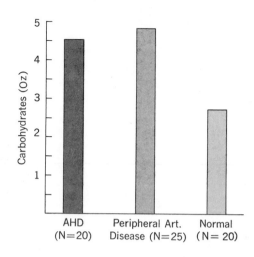

FIGURE 8.41 Serum cholesterol levels in coronary heart disease patients. Data from Gertler and White (209).

FIGURE 8.42 Past sugar intake per day by normals, arteriosclerotic heart disease patients, and peripheral artery disease patients. Data from Yudkin (625).

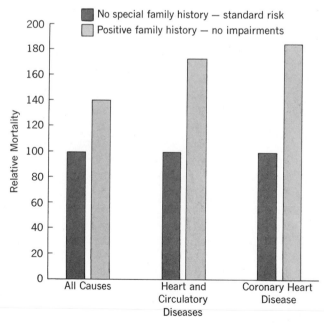

FIGURE 8.43 Relative mortality among insured persons with family history of early CV-renal disease. Adapted from Katz, Stamler, and Pick (294) after Lew (344).

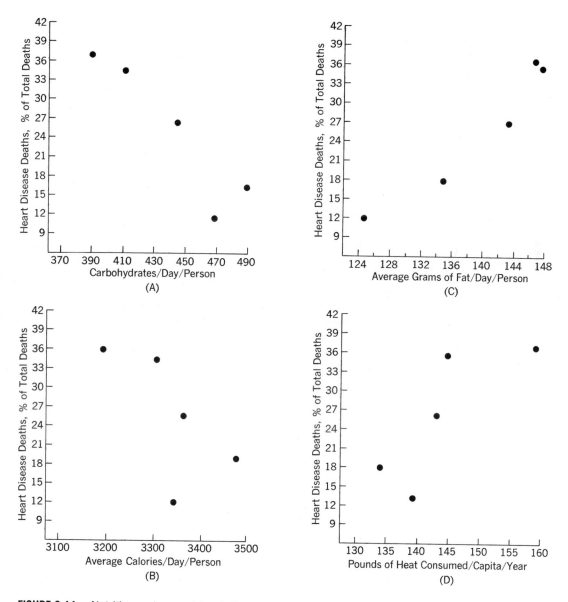

FIGURE 8.44 Nutrition and percent heart disease deaths in the United States. Each plotted point represents a given year 1920–1960. Adapted from *Statistical Abstract of the United States* (578).

Readers interested in a more thorough discussion of these factors are referred to Moses' text, *Atherosclerosis* (409).

Three representative and typical studies are depicted in Figures 8.35, 8.36, and 8.43.

TABLE 8.7   Rank Correlation Coefficients[a] between Various Dietary Components and Death Rates for 22 Countries — Males, Ages 55–59

DIETARY COMPONENT	CORRELATED WITH DEATH RATE FOR ARTERIOSCLEROTIC AND DEGNERATIVE HEART DISEASE
Total calories	0.723[c]
Calories from fat	0.659[c]
Calories from animal fat[b]	0.684[c]
Calories from vegetable fat[b]	−0.236
Calories from protein	0.709[b]
Calories from animal protein	0.756[b]
Calories from vegetable protein	−0.430
Calories from carbohydrate	0.305
Percent calories from fat	0.587[c]
Percent calories from animal fat[b]	0.677[c]
Percent calories from vegetable fat[b]	−0.468
Percent calories from protein	0.172
Percent calories from animal protein	0.643[c]
Percent calories from vegetable protein	−0.651[c]
Percent calories from carbohydrate	−0.562[c]

[a]See pages 74–76.
[b]Number of countries = 21.
[c]Statistically significant (.02 level).
SOURCE: Yerushalmy and Hilleboe (622) after Katz, Stamler, and Pick (294).

Nutrition

Certain aspects of food intake have been linked with AHD by many investigators. A representative sampling of the most prominent correlations are presented in Figures 8.42 and 8.44 and in Table 8.7.

Age, Sex, and Race

Figures 8.45 and 8.46 provide some insight into the age, sex, and race factors as related to AHD and stroke deaths.

Summary of Factors Relating to AHD

Table 8.8 summarizes the various factors that have been experimentally or statistically linked with AHD.

OTHER DISORDERS AND DISEASES OF CIRCULATION AND RESPIRATION

Infectious Diseases

The following infectious diseases of the blood, heart, blood vessels, and

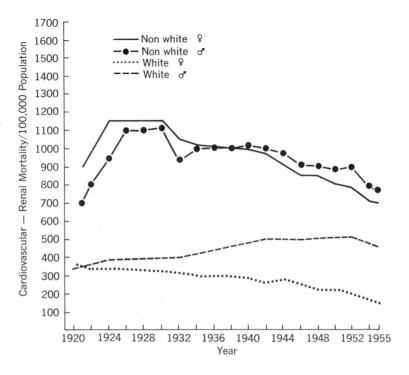

FIGURE 8.45 Changes in CV-renal mortality rate in middle-aged Americans, by sex and race, 1920–1955. Adapted from Katz, Stamler, and Pick (294) after Moriyama and Stamler (403).

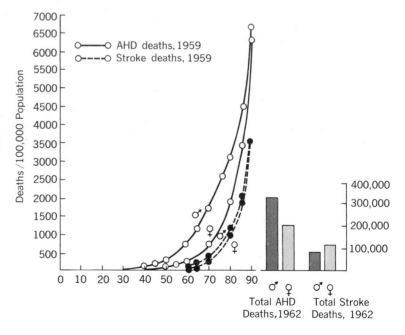

FIGURE 8.46 Arteriosclerotic heart disease deaths and "stroke" deaths, related to age and sex. Data from *Facts on the Major Killing and Crippling Diseases in the United States Today* (172).

respiratory system are described in   heart valve in-   malaria
Appendix D.   fection   measles
bronchitis   common cold   influenza   measles, German
chickenpox   diphtheria   laryngitis   paratyphoid fever

TABLE 8.8 Factors That Appear To Predispose or Predict AHD

FACTOR	EFFECT	REFERENCE
NOT CONTROLLABLE:		
Heredity	Genes may predispose. Family history valuable in prediction.	(344) (484)
Age	Susceptibility increases with age.	(419) (172)
Sex	American white males more susceptible and earlier. Not true in all countries or all races; American Negro, no sex difference.	(419) (172)
Race	Negroes appear to be more susceptible.	(208) (403) (537)
Body type	Endomesomorph more susceptible.	(535)
POSSIBLY NOT CONTROLLABLE:		
Cholesterol and triglyceride levels	Higher levels, especially above 275 mg% cholesterol, good predictors of AHD. Can be genetic.	(146) (209) (208) (213)
Hypertension	High blood pressure, especially diastolic score above 95, good predictor of AHD. Can be genetic.	(208)
Uric acid level	High, fair prediction of AHD (8 mg% and above).	(208)
Exercise ECG	Ischemic ECG response to exercise good predictor of AHD.	(369)
USUALLY CONTROLLABLE:		
Diet	High fat diets and high percentage of fats in diet and high **saturated fats** may predispose, especially in the coronary-prone. Simple overeating may also be important factor. Sugar excess has also been implicated.	(228) (407) (308) (625) (484)
Stress and tension	May predispose, even predict AHD.	(484) (194) (329) (618) (600) (193) (477)
Physical activity	Lack of adequate physical activity may indirectly hasten onset of AHD.	(477) (235) (405) (406) (634)
Obesity	As degree of obesity increases, AHD risk increases in both men and women. Can be genetic.	(556) (491) (329) (146) (513)

parrot fever   "strep throat"
pneumonia   trench mouth
rheumatic fever   tuberculosis
Rocky Mountain   typhoid fever
  spotted fever   typhus fever
scarlet fever   undulant fever
smallpox   whooping cough

Sinusitis is an infection of the lining of the sinuses, the air spaces in the bones of the head and face. Infection may come from blowing the nose violently, from diving, or from swimming with the nose under water, which may force infectious material from the nose and throat into the sinuses. **Allergies,** enlarged adenoids, or other nasal obstructions may also cause sinusitis. Usually there is headache or pain in the cheek or the upper teeth or pain over the infected sinus in the morning, easing in late afternoon. The forehead may be tender to pressure. Often there is drainage of pus from the nose or a dripping from the back of the nose into the throat. The nasal passages may be dry and clogged because of the swollen membrane and lack of drainage. The sense of smell is sometimes partially lost and there may be fever, cough, swelling of the cheeks, eyelids, or forehead with general fatigue and aching.

Glandular fever, with enlarged **lymph glands** and spleen but no throat symptoms, is common in children. A similar infection in young adults is **mononucleosis,** with typical symptoms of fever, headache, fatigue, sore throat, and lymph gland swelling. There is an unusual "mononuclear" type of white blood cell present in the blood. During the acute fever, bed rest is prescribed

and, unless there are complications, recovery with no apparent aftereffects occurs in several weeks.

Endocarditis is a bacterial infection of the inner layer of the heart muscle, and **pericarditis** is an inflammation of the thin sac surrounding the heart.

THE IMPORTANT NONINFECTIOUS DISEASES

Heart Disorders

MYOCARDIAL FAILURE (CONGESTIVE HEART FAILURE) When, for any reason, the heart is unable to pump out all the blood that returns to it, there is a backing up of blood in the veins that lead to the heart. The heart's failure to maintain good circulation may result in an accumulation of fluid in various parts of the body such as the abdomen, lungs, legs, and so on.

CONGENITAL HEART ABNORMALITIES There are now thirty-five known kinds of inborn heart defects, nearly twenty of which can be cured or improved by surgery. One signal that a newborn baby may have a heart defect is a blue tinge to the baby's skin called **cyanosis.** "Blue babies" have heart defects that prevent enough blood from getting to their lungs to pick up oxygen. An inborn defect may prevent a child from growing and gaining weight normally. He may tire easily or feel weak. There may be spells of breathing difficulty, with the child having to stop often to catch his breath. **Heart murmur** refers to abnormal or unusual sounds resulting from vibrations produced by the motion of the blood within the heart. It is usually associated with valvular disorders.

Arrhythmia is a change in the rhythm of the heart that may be caused by physiological or psychological disturbances. The patient may not be aware of its existence for it can be detected only by careful physical examination. Some changes can be identified by observing the pulse rate or rhythm, whereas others require an ECG to be discovered and identified. Some "arrhythmia" is normal, especially during exertion, and a change in rhythm is not necessarily indicative of disorder.

Mr. S.'s story, as presented in an American Heart Association pamphlet, describes the course of a not uncommon heart disorder.

ANGINA PECTORIS   It was a clear crisp morning late in the fall. The first white frost was on the ground. Mr. S. was a little late in finishing his breakfast and had to hurry to the station to catch the eight-fifteen train for town, where he had an important appointment in his law office. It was his fifty-second birthday and he had taken this half-mile walk nearly every weekday morning for the past ten years, in fact, ever since he had moved his family to their suburban home. He had never felt better than on this fine day, and the cold air was good to breathe as he hurried along.

Gradually he became aware of a slight sensation of tightness in the center of his chest, behind the breastbone. Later he described it as a sense of pressure, rather than actual pain. He wondered if he had gulped his breakfast too hurriedly, and was having indigestion. He was tempted to stop for a moment, but heard the train coming, so he continued walking. By the time he reached

the station platform the pressure had increased, but it disappeared completely several minutes after he sat down. Then he felt as well as ever.

As he sat in the train, Mr. S. remembered that he had had the same kind of sensation in his chest a few times before. Each time it happened, he recalled, he had been exercising right after eating. He was sure that it was simple indigestion in each case. However, this morning's episode was the most uncomfortable one so far, and he decided to report it to his doctor if it happened again.

Several days later he was returning to his office after luncheon, feeling very well. As he walked up a slight incline leading to his office building, he felt the same sensation of pressure and tightness in his chest. This time there was also a very slight tingling along the inner side of his left upper arm. He was not particularly alarmed, but decided to stand still for a moment. A minute or two later the discomfort had vanished completely.

During the afternoon he mentioned casually to a business associate that he was "having a little indigestion after meals." This associate had several relatives and golfing partners who had angina pectoris, and he immediately suspected that Mr. S's "indigestion" might be angina. He persuaded him to consult his doctor that same evening.

Mr. S.'s physician examined him carefully and found nothing significantly wrong. His heart seemed to be normal and his blood pressure was perfect. The physician saw through the fluoroscope (a kind of x-ray machine) that Mr. S's heart had not changed in size or shape since the last examination. Even the elctrocardiogram showed no significant changes.

But the doctor's careful questioning convinced him that the pressure in Mr. S.'s chest was actually a symptom known as angina. (Other names for it are angina pectoris, anginal pain, heart pain, or coronary pain, but the great majority of doctors and patients simply call it angina.)

Angina is not a disease. It is a symptom that results when some portion of the heart muscle is not furnished with enough blood and oxygen for the work being performed at that instant. Angina is an indication of diminished blood supply, not absence of blood supply as in a heart attack, and there is no actual muscle injury.

In most cases the anginal pain does not appear while the person is at rest, but only when the heart is asked to perform extra work—during physical exertion or emotional excitement, for example. Even slight exertion shortly after a meal may provoke the symptom, which usually appears more quickly in cold weather than in warm if the exercise is out of doors.

The doctor explained all this to Mr. S. He gave him a prescription for some tiny pills that would stretch, or dilate, the coronary arteries whenever the heart muscle needed a more abundant supply of blood and oxygen. These pills—nitroglycerine or some other form of nitrite—are effective within a few minutes. The doctor emphasized that the pill was to be taken before any activity which might cause the tightness in the chest. In other words, Mr. S. was instructed firmly to prevent the discomfort as completely as possible. He was warned especially about exercise soon after a meal.

He was urged to learn by careful trial whether any of his usual physical activities caused discomfort. If, for example, he found that climbing steep hills on the golf course caused pressure in his chest, he was told he would have to avoid such hills by playing around them; walk up the hills slowly or with several pauses for rest, so that discomfort would not occur; or take a pill several minutes before reaching the hill,

to give the heart a greater supply of blood and oxygen.

The doctor made it clear that these pills could be used as often as desired over many years without any harmful effects and without any loss of their effectiveness.

In addition to this simple and very effective medicine, Mr. S. was strongly advised to lose twenty pounds of fat that had accumulated over a period of several years. He was told of the present evidence which suggests that there may be a cause-and-effect relationship between cigarette smoking and coronary atherosclerosis. The doctor advised him to reduce the animal and dairy fats in his diet, and substitute for them the vegetable fats such as corn oil, soybean oil, cottonseed oil, and fish oils. He was careful to explain that some doctors believe such changes in the diet to be without value, while others think that they might possibly prevent or retard further development of atherosclerosis in the coronary arteries.

The heart, like all other muscles, must receive an extra amount of fuel—blood and oxygen—when it performs extra work. If some part of the heart does not receive enough extra blood because its supply lines (the coronary arteries) are narrowed by atherosclerosis, the result may be an attack of angina. It is thought that the uncomfortable sensation in the chest comes from the heart muscle itself.

Many men in their fifties and sixties develop aching pain in their leg and thigh muscles when they walk, because the arteries which supply these muscles have been narrowed in the same manner as the coronary arteries of people who have angina. In fact, many men have both angina and the pain in the legs (known as claudication); often they comment upon the similarity of the two.

Luckily the coronary artery system has a lifesaving method of growth and repair. When some of the coronary arteries become narrowed by gradual development of atherosclerosis so that they cannot carry enough blood to the heart muscle, nearby arteries get wider and even open up tiny new branches to deliver blood to the area of muscle that needs it. This is called **collateral circulation.** (Other names for it are *compensatory circulation* and *substitute circulation.*)

Collateral circulation often develops while the main coronary arteries are becoming narrowed. This explains why many people who have narrowed arteries are not troubled with angina pectoris or with heart attacks. When for any reason this compensatory circulation does not develop properly or the atherosclerosis develops too fast, there is trouble in the form of heart disease.

Once a heart attack occurs, the development of collateral circulation may help the heart to mend itself. It is this collateral circulation that we hope for and which so often takes place in the course of some weeks or months after the first attack of angina pectoris.

The term *angina pectoris,* a name introduced by William Heberden of London in 1768, literally means "strangling in the chest." It remained for Edward Jenner (famous for his connection with smallpox vaccination) to point out several years later that angina pectoris and coronary artery disease were related.

It is important to understand that in almost all cases the diagnosis of angina rests entirely upon the history given by the patient — not upon changes that can be discovered by the doctor. Angina is a subjective symptom without objective changes to identify it. In this respect it is like a headache, which is usually not accompanied by any signs that would enable a doctor to recognize its presence. Although angina has so many characteristic features that the diagnosis can almost always be made easily, the patient may be asked to make more

careful observations before the doctor can be absolutely certain.

Angina may be very mild or quite severe. It is almost always located in the very center of the chest, behind the breastbone, but it may extend from this area to either shoulder and into either arm. It may occur many times a day with slight effort, or only rarely in association with vigorous exercise. Sometimes it appears for the first time after recovery from a heart attack, and sometimes the first known heart attack occurs after many years of angina.

As a rule, the patient with angina lives a good many years after the first attack of angina, and he may die of some other disease or accident in old age. If the patient understands his condition, uses his medication intelligently, and is able to prevent situations that provoke anginal discomfort, he is usually able to lead an active life without discomfort. The development of an adequate collateral circulation may very likely improve his condition and permit a gradual increase in physical activities.

The cardinal rule for the patient is to prevent anginal discomfort. It is almost always possible to do this by avoiding certain kinds of effort and emotional excitement or by using the proper medicine before exposure to exercise or excitement. Sometimes it is wise or necessary for the patient to modify certain aspects of his life, but only occasionally is it necessary to eliminate normal activities.

It is very important for a person to consult his doctor as soon as possible after the appearance of any discomfort in the center of the chest. If it is angina, correct diagnosis and treatment at this stage may be very important to the patient's future health.[2]

---

[2]This information has been reproduced by permission of the American Heart Association from the pamphlet "Heart Disease Caused by Coronary Atherosclerosis."

Extracts from a pamphlet published by The Public Affairs Committee, Inc., describe disorders of the blood and blood vessels.

Disorders of the Blood and Blood Vessels

HYPERTENSION (HIGH BLOOD PRESSURE) Strictly speaking, hypertension is not a disease but a sign. It is like the headache or fever that may accompany a cold. High blood pressure is characterized by narrowing of the arterioles, through which the blood passes to feed the body tissues. The smaller the channel, the greater the pressure required to force the normal amount of blood through. So the heart works harder (not faster) and blood pressure rises. If the blood vessels are sturdy enough to withstand the extra pressure, their owner may be unaware of the trouble for years.

When high blood pressure cannot be attributed to any specific disorder of the body or mind, it is called *essential hypertension*. *Malignant hypertension* is a complication with more abrupt characteristics and with greater damage to the kidneys. It need not be considered hopeless, for treatment may bring improvement. Nor is it very common. Only 5 percent of 2147 patients studied at Columbia Presbyterian Medical Center had the malignant form.

Many people think that the higher the pressure, the greater the risk of damage. Science disagrees. The only important question is whether pressure is above normal, and what is normal depends on the person. Anyone who tries to forecast his future by comparing blood pressure readings at different times is wasting emotional energy —and probably boosting his pressure.

The danger in hypertension has been described by Dr. Page: "Persistent high blood pressure sets off a chain of events which cause hardening or scarring of the artery walls. These scars finally lead to closing of some of the vessels. As they close, the tissues become weak and are themselves changed to scar tissues which tend to check the blood flow."

Atherosclerosis, a form of hardening of the arteries, is a main cause of death among hypertensive patients. Cutting off the blood supply to vital tissues is as serious as depriving a plant of water. But not all sufferers from high blood pressure develop atherosclerosis, and among those who do there is variation in degree and intensity. Some patients are not affected for decades.

The three areas where the process is most serious are the heart, the brain, and the kidneys.

The heart will be temporarily or permanently damaged if one of its arteries is narrowed or closed. Clotting of blood within an artery of the heart is **coronary thrombosis,** commonly called a "heart attack." If the heart muscle is injured when blood flow is abruptly cut off, as in the case of a blocked artery, the result is **myocardial infarction.**

If brain vessels rupture or are blocked by a clot, the result is a stroke. Only a minority of patients succumb to strokes.

Reduction of the blood supply to the kidneys through hardening and narrowing of their arteries will scar the tissues and lower the kidneys' efficiency as a waste remover. If the damage is severe, poisons may pile up in the blood stream and produce **uremia.**

Some persons with high blood pressure have no symptoms whatever. Even when symptoms do exist, they are often not enough for diagnosis. You cannot determine, without consulting a physician, that your blood pressure is high.

A common symptom is headache. The headache may darken your outlook on life, further increasing your blood pressure. Usually the physician can put an end to this symptom.

Dizziness and light-headedness may persuade you that you are about to faint. (You probably won't.) Again the physician can help. **Vertigo,** a feeling that the world is revovling around you, is of more consequence than plain dizziness.

It must be emphasized again that you should not jump to any conclusions on the basis of symptoms. Most people who have headaches or feelings of dizziness do not have high blood pressure, and most people with high blood pressure do not have headaches or feelings of dizziness. A medical examination is necessary for diagnosis.

In making an examination the physician will, of course, take your blood pressure. Getting a reliable reading is not so easy as it would seem. The machine he uses is a simple one, found in every doctor's office. But human emotions are anything but simple. If you think any kind of heart trouble means death or disability, you are apt to record your fear with an abnormally high blood pressure. You may have to come back for additional readings before the physician is satisfied that the high pressure was not produced by nervous tension.

An important fact for patients to remember is that high blood pressure is not necessarily a serious ailment. The average arterial wall is strong enough for pressures twice as high as any that have been recorded.

One part of the body gives the physician a chance to see the condition of the blood vessels. By dilating the pupil of the eye, the doctor can examine small blood vessels in the retina and note changes in their appearance.

Another part of the examination is testing the urine to determine whether the kidneys are affected. Cut-rate tests using material bought at the drugstore will not answer all the questions that the physician considers important. The patient should not be frightened if traces of albumin are found, since practically normal kidneys may yield some.

A more informative procedure is the urine concentration test. This requires the patient to go without water and watery foods for 24 hours and to collect the urine voided in the final 12 hours. The average person's kidneys handle up to 185 quarts of water a day, reabsorbing all but three pints. The kidneys of a person with high blood pressure will not reabsorb water efficiently if they are damaged. The damage, if any, will show up in the concentration test.

There is no specific treatment for high blood pressure and there is not even general agreement on the best treatment. More than many other disorders, hypertension varies with the patient, and the treatment should fit him. Drugs, surgery, psychotherapy, and special diets have been used in recent years with encouraging results.[3]

A publication of The Heart Information Center describes cerebral vascular disease and strokes as follows.

Cerebral Vascular Disease and Strokes

The cells of the brain require a good blood supply in order to work properly—more so than most other cells in the body. Blood flow to and from the brain is by way of a complex network of blood vessels—arteries and veins.

The main arteries of the brain branch off into smaller and smaller branches which carry blood to every part of the brain.

If anything happens to significantly reduce or stop the flow of blood to any part

---

[3]This information has been reproduced by permission of the Public Affairs Committee, Inc., from the pamphlet, *Your Blood Pressure and Your Arteries,* by Alexander L. Crosby. Copies may be obtained from Public Affairs Committee, Inc., 381 Park Avenue South, New York, N.Y. 10016.

of the brain, that part will not function properly; this may cause weakness or numbness or loss of sensation or of movement in some part of the body. The decrease or loss of function depends on the extent of damage; the part of the body affected depends on the area of the brain involved, and is usually on the side of the body opposite to the affected side of the brain.

DISEASES OF BLOOD VESSELS OF THE BRAIN
From birth to old age there are several things that can happen in the blood vessels of the brain to impair the working of the brain itself. A blood vessel may rupture or may become blocked, causing blood flow to the brain to be reduced or even stop. In all, there are four important ways in which this may occur. [See Figure 8.47]

There are a number of causes for the four different ways in which the circulation of blood to the brain may be disturbed.

These include defects of the vessels which may develop before birth, as well as physical injury, infections of the blood vessels, general infections, blood diseases, heart disease, hardening of the arteries, and high blood pressure.

Headaches, difficulties of vision, dizziness, fainting spells, numbness of hand or face, weakness, paralysis, difficulty in speaking, poor memory, difficulty in thinking, personality changes, and mental disturbances are among the common results of cerebral vascular disease. Nearly one sixth of all patients admitted to some mental

hospitals have cerebral vascular disease. (On the other hand, most people with cerebral vascular disease may have no mental disorders.)

Any of the above symptoms, of course, may be caused by conditions other than cerebral vascular disease, and not all of them are always present in any one patient with cerebral vascular disease. The symptoms present depend upon the severity of

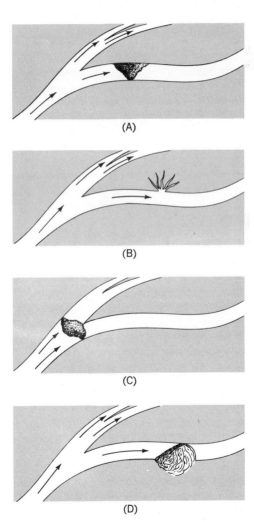

(A)

(B)

(C)

(D)

FIGURE 8.47 Ways in which blood flow to a portion of the brain can be blocked. (A) Blood clot forming in vessel (thrombosis); (B) rupture of vessel (hemorrhage); (C) a piece of a clot or other material from another part of circulatory system which circulates to the vessel (embolism); (D) pressure on a vessel caused by a tumor or swelling. (A), (B), and (C) occurring in a coronary vessel can also cause "heart attack." Source: *Heart Terms*. Public Health Service Publication No. 1073.

the cerebral vascular disease, the areas of the brain affected, and other variable factors.

STROKES (CEREBRAL VASCULAR ACCIDENTS) One of the most alarming results of cerebral vascular disease is a "stroke" — referred to by physicians as a "cerebral vascular accident." (Strokes, especially those caused by hemorrhage, are sometimes called "apoplexy.") A stroke occurs — usually suddenly — when an artery to a portion of the brain ruptures or is closed by thrombosis, **embolism,** or any of the other causes already mentioned. A patient who has had a stroke may have paralysis of an arm and leg and, often, difficulty in speaking. Occasionally these symptoms clear up rather quickly. Frequently, however, some physical disability remains.

With present knowledge it is not possible to prevent the majority of strokes and other causes of cerebral vascular disease. However, some of the conditions causing cerebral vascular disease can be treated. Such treatment may help prevent strokes. High blood pressure is one of the major diseases associated with strokes, although the exact relationship is not yet fully understood. Most patients with high blood pressure can be helped by modern treatment. Such treatment often reduces some of the effects of cerebral vascular disease and may help prevent strokes.

Strokes among young people are caused most frequently by rupture of a congenital defect in a blood vessel, known as an *aneurysm;* under favorable circumstances surgical treatment of such aneurysms may prevent further strokes. Also, strokes among young persons may be caused by small blood clots (emboli) formed in the heart and pumped into a blood vessel in the brain. These emboli usually form as a result of rheumatic heart disease or a bacterial infection of the lining of the heart. Both of these conditions usually can be prevented or treated successfully and strokes thus prevented.

Several conditions associated with blood clot formation, which often results in strokes, may be effectively controlled in some patients by the use of anti-clotting drugs. In some cases warnings in the form of brief attacks of numbness or weakness or visual difficulty precede the onset of a stroke, and treatment in time may prevent the stroke.

A great deal of research is under way to learn more about hardening of the arteries (arteriosclerosis), the largest single cause of cerebral vascular disease. More research must also be done regarding many other problems to make possible better prevention of cerebral vascular disease.

But even today, with existing knowledge much can be done to prevent some cerebral vascular disease and some strokes.

A stroke can occur while a person is awake or asleep. If it happens while he is awake he may fall suddenly to the floor because of paralysis of one of his legs, or he may suddenly become unconscious. If the stroke occurs while the patient is asleep he may be found unconscious, or he may fall as he attempts to get out of bed. In about half the instances he will have some difficulty with his speech, and people may mistakenly think he has "lost his mind." The person and his family at first may be greatly alarmed, but a stroke is not necessarily as disastrous as it may first appear.

In most cases the patient does not die, and if he survives the initial attack and has no recurrences, his life expectancy is often as great as that of persons of the same age who have not had strokes. In only a minority of cases is the stroke caused by a severe hemorrhage from which the patient may die.

Some patients recover from a stroke within a few weeks or months; in others varying degrees of paralysis of an arm and leg and some difficulty in speech may persist. This paralysis of the arm and leg and lower part of the face on one side is known as *hemiplegia* (half stroke, or paralysis of one side of the body). The hemiplegic patient need not be doomed to a life of helplessness — 90 percent can be taught to talk again, to care for their own bladder and bowel needs, and 30 percent can be taught to do gainful work.

When a person has had a stroke, a physician should be called immediately. The doctor will advise whether the patient should be treated at home or taken to a hospital. In years past there was very little that doctors could do for patients who had had strokes. Today, however, there is a much more hopeful attitude even though present knowledge does not ensure the recovery of every stroke patient. Physicians have several methods of treatment which often help patients immediately after a stroke has occurred.

Very soon after the stroke has occurred — often within 24 hours — treatment should be started to help restore use of the affected arm and leg. This begins with assisted movements of the arm and leg. Within a few days the patient is encouraged to move his arm and leg himself. He is gradually encouraged to sit up, then to stand, and finally to walk. The physician may instruct the family how it can help in these procedures, or he may suggest someone with specialized training in this work, a physical therapist. The physician may also prescribe a brace or support to assist the patient to function better, for example, in walking.

Ideally the patient who has had a stroke should be started promptly on the road to rehabilitation. Unfortunately, however, there are thousands of persons who have been disabled for years by strokes which occurred long ago. Many of these people are lying in beds or sitting helplessly in chairs, unable to get about, unable to care for their own simplest needs.

Even among those patients who have been disabled for months or years as a result of strokes, the majority can be at least partially rehabilitated — can be trained to get about, to care for their own bladder and bowel needs, and to perform activities of daily living. Some can even be taught to do gainful work.[4]

Disorders of Respiration

CANCER OF THE LUNG **Cancer** is a disease of the cells in which the cell division is not orderly and abnormal growth takes place. In lung cancer the first symptoms are a cough, a wheeze, a vague chest pain, which are so commonplace that they rarely cause a physician to suspect lung cancer. The symptom most likely to send the patient to the doctor is blood-streaked sputum, but this occurs in only about 5 percent of the cases.

The causes of lung cancer are not fully understood but the Public Health Service believes that the best way to avoid it is not to smoke (see Figure 8.48). As a public health measure, every effort should be made to reduce air pollution from all sources, another cause of lung cancer.

ASTHMA **Asthma** is a disease marked by recurrent, intensified difficulty in breathing, with wheezing, coughing, and a sense of constriction due to spasmodic contraction of the bronchi. It may be caused by allergy, bacterial in-

---

[4]Selections from *Cerebral Vascular Disease and Strokes,* prepared by the Heart Information Center, National Heart Institute, Bethesda, Md.

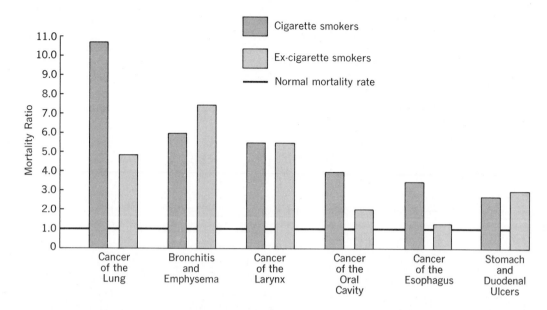

FIGURE 8.48   The mortality ratio for various respiratory diseases and ulcer in smokers and non-smokers (comparison: normal mortality rate). Data from *Smoking and Health,* Report of the Advisory Committee to the Surgeon General of the Public Health Service. Public Health Service Publication No. 1103, pp. 102, 105.

fection, upward pressure on the diaphragm, dilatation of the alveoli of the lungs, disease of the tonsils, irritation of the skin, dyspeptic disorder, or nervous impulses.

The results of treatment are usually better in children than in adults, but it *is* a chronic disease and only a small percentage of asthmatic people outgrow asthma spontaneously. Unless treated, most of them will become worse. Prolonged treatment and proper supervision are usually necessary for severe, chronic asthma.

EMPHYSEMA **Emphysema,** which literally means "blown-up" or "overfilled" lungs, is most often a chronic disease and represents a state of distention of the alveoli of the lungs. Although overdistension might appear to be harmless, it results from disruption of the integrity of the alveoli, making them large and destroying their capillaries. Whereas the *total* lung volume is increased, the *effective* lung volume and vital capacity are decreased and the loss of pulmonary capillaries means a reduction in aeration of the blood. The person may even become **cyanotic** upon exertion, will almost always suffer from **dyspnea,** and heart action may be impaired.

This chronic disease is increasing and appears to be highly related to cigarette smoking (see Figure 8.48).

Brief Summary of Other Noninfectious Circulo-Respiratory Disorders

ARTERIOSCLEROSIS Commonly called "hardening of the arteries," arteriosclerosis includes a variety of conditions that cause the artery walls to become thick and hard and to lose elasticity. It is a common cause of high blood pressure and "heart attack."

ATHEROSCLEROSIS Yellowish accumulation of fatty plaques or deposits along the walls of the arteries leads to atherosclerosis (see Figure 8.49). Cells are destroyed by the fatty substances and a fibrous covering is formed. Eventually, the plaque calcifies and the artery

hardens. The cells have lost their ability to dispose of fats in the diet, leading to a build-up in the artery lining. Other contributing factors apparently include high blood pressure, physical inactivity, cigarette smoking, obesity, diabetes, and heredity.

BUERGER'S DISEASE In Buerger's disease a thickening, chronic inflammation (possibly blood clots) in the vessels interfere with the blood supply of the region, usually the legs. This may result in swelling, ulceration, and **gangrene**. Allergy is suspected but it has been suggested that a major factor in its causation is the constriction of the blood vessels of the extremities due to

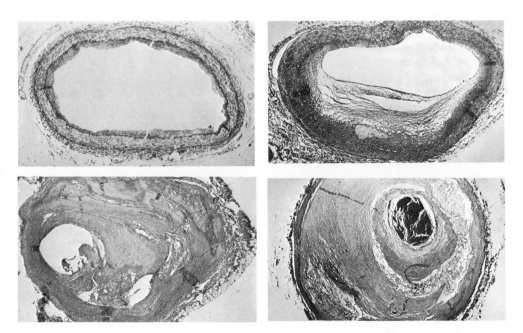

FIGURE 8.49 Illustration of the four stages of atherosclerosis, from a normal vessel to one so narrow that blood flow becomes so slow that coagulation occurs. This blockage, depending upon the site, can cause "heart attack," "stroke," and so on. By permission, American Heart Association.

the use of tobacco. Eighty percent of all cases are smokers.

CANCER The mouth, the esophagus, and the larynx are common sites for cancer in men and women (see Figure 8.48). It is highly associated with smoking. Symptoms are a sore in the mouth that does not heal, hoarseness or a persistent cough, and difficulty in swallowing. Cure rate is good if detected early and followed by prompt treatment.

EDEMA Abnormally large amounts of fluid are present in the intercellular tissue spaces of the body and give a bloated and swollen appearance. **Edema** may be localized or generalized, depending upon the cause.

HEMOPHILIA An inherited deficiency characterized by delayed clotting of the blood makes it difficult to check hemorrhage. **Hemophilia** is a sex-linked characteristic inherited by males through the mother.

HODGKIN'S DISEASE In Hodgkin's disease there is a painless and progressive enlargement of the lymph nodes and frequently of the spleen and liver. Fever, anemia, and general ill health are prominent in the later stages. The causes of the disease are unknown and the progression is fatal.

LEUKEMIA Sometimes called "cancer of the blood," **leukemia** is usually a fatal disease that affects the organs which make blood (lymph glands and bone marrow). In leukemia, the blood "composition gets out of control" and there is a tremendous overproduction of white cells that do not mature and are not able to fight infection. The number of red cells is reduced and the patient becomes anemic. The blood does not clot properly. Symptoms resemble those in anemia, with enlarged lymph glands and spleen. Recurring fever is likely to be present also.

PHLEBITIS The formation of a blood clot causes inflammation of a vein or phlebitis. It is often present in the leg. The abnormally large amounts of fluid in the intercellular spaces of the affected part are accompanied by stiffness and pain.

VARICOSE VEINS The cause of **varicose veins** is not definitely known, but any factor or combination of factors that brings about increased pressure within the vessels in the legs will most likely lead to a thinning and weakening of the walls of the veins and finally result in varicosities. These are veins that bulge and cause irregularity in the contour of the skin and are common in adults of all ages, sexes, and races. Persons with varicose veins usually complain that their legs feel tired and heavy. There may be a burning, stinging sensation with aches and cramps in the calves of the legs.

SUMMARY

Degenerative disorders of the circulatory and respiratory systems are alarmingly prevalent in the U.S.A. today and are increasing.

Some of the degenerative disorders are to some extent preventable; in other words, we can reduce the risk by controlling certain factors.

Physical education, health education, and recreation have very definite responsibilities in the drive to educate people about these disorders and to develop programs to provide preventive measures.

In order to fulfill the responsibilities mentioned above, professionals in these fields must understand the systems involved and the evidence upon which educational and activity programs should be based.

The function of the circulatory system is transport of materials to and from cells.

The respiratory system is responsible for gas exchange (CO_2 and O_2), with the help of the circulatory system.

The excretory system (waste removal) is intimately and functionally related to both the circulatory and respiratory systems since circulation is required for removal of most waste products and the respiratory system is needed for CO_2 removal.

A healthy and fit CR system is generally associated with good general health.

It is important for professionals in health, physical education, and recreation to be aware of and alert to the common circulatory and respiratory diseases and disorders discussed in this chapter.

There is much physiological evidence that, taken collectively, provides a theoretical basis for the poor pulmonary function of smokers.

It is still conjectural whether training can increase blood hemoglobin concentration but it is certain that low hemoglobin (anemia) interferes with work capacity by reducing the oxygen carrying capacity of the blood.

Concepts involving indirect but positive effects of regular exercise, health education, or recreation on the degenerative circulatory and respiratory disorders:

Obese persons have more hypertension and more arteriosclerotic heart disease. (Regular exercise aids in weight maintenance; see pages 345–352.)

Emotional stress and tension has been statistically linked with heart disease. (Recreation and physical activity can provide an outlet.)

Cigarette smokers suffer twice as many heart attacks, six to seven times as much emphysema, and eleven times as much lung cancer. (Health education must become more effective.)

High blood cholesterol levels are associated statistically with heart disease and atherosclerosis. (Regular exercise can lower cholesterol level as can a significant decrease in saturated fat intake.)

Excessive saturated fat intake and excess simple sugar intake have been linked statistically with heart disease and atherosclerosis. (Health education must become more effective.)

Males suffer more coronaries in the United States than females. (Health education must point out extra preventive care for males.)

Prolonged postprandial lipemia has been associated with coronary artery disease and heart attacks. (Exercise following a high fatty meal hastens lipid clearance, and lipid clearance is faster in the physically fit.)

PRINCIPLES

1. The process of degeneration of the heart and arteries is a slow one and begins in many persons in the United States as early as the late teens.
2. To improve circulo-respiratory capacity, the heart and lungs must be taxed ("overload" principle).
3. To improve a specific circulo-respiratory capacity for a given task, that task or one very similar in demands must be involved in the training task (principle of "specificity").
4. All other factors being constant:
   a. The greater the proportion of total body musculature used, the greater the CR load.
   b. The greater the proportion of maximal force exerted by the muscles, the greater the CR load.
   c. The greater the frequency of contraction, the greater the CR load.
   d. The greater the intensity, the shorter is the time the load can be maintained and vice versa.
   e. Intensity and duration can be combined; thus there is an optimal load for a given duration.
   f. Optimal intensity and duration must be based on an individual's current health and physical fitness status and is best underestimated when in doubt.

g. Exercise and/or recovery heart rates provide a simple and reliable index of exercise intensity.
h. The threshold heart rate for CR improvement is apparently about 140 beats per minute or .60 (Maximum Exercise HR − Resting HR) + Resting HR; on the average this will be .60 (180 − 70) + 70 = .60 (110) + 70 = 136 .
i. The total length of time the threshold heart rate is maintained or exceeded will roughly determine the improvement in CR capacity up to a given point beyond which additional improvement will not occur unless the intensity is increased.
5. In keeping with the principles outlined above, there are many methods and combinations of methods which can, by application of these principles, produce CR capacity gains (for example, circuit training, interval training, certain sports, modern dance, any kind of "aerobic" activity).
6. When testing CR capacity, careful standardization of the work task, counting or measuring techniques, time of day, and so on, are of critical importance.
7. All other factors being constant, improved CR capacity is associated with improved work capacity and work efficiency, at least for the specific task involved, and possibly for other tasks which place similar demands on the CR system.
8. There is strong statistical evidence that, all other factors being equal, regular exercise prevents or postpones the onset of coronary artery disease or reduces the severity of such disease.

9. There is experimental evidence that regular CR loading can physiologically enlarge and strengthen the heart and provide for the opening up of pathways of collateral circulation in the heart muscle which has a restricted blood flow.

EXPERIMENTS AND EXPERIENCES

1. Determine the extent to which the normal heart rate fluctuates during a twenty-four–hour period. At appropriate intervals, a thirty-second pulse count should be made and recorded. Hourly rates are best, and the activity engaged in at that time should be carefully noted. A plot of the data for the entire period will provide a comprehensive picture of the observed variation. What is the trend, if any, and how can it be accounted for?

2. Determine the relative circulo-respiratory value of various activities. Using an appropriate logbook or other recording system, a series of exercises, games, and so on, can be engaged in with pulse rates taken during special time-out periods. Needed will be a resting rate, a pre-exercise rate taken immediately before participation, a rate taken at the peak of activity, and a count at termination. Plotting such rates for each of the activities will provide a picture of the relative strenuousness of each of the activities. Compare with other individuals for the exact same activities, if possible. Are there differences? Does the relative strenuousness of the different activities vary from one individual to another? If so, how do you explain such a difference?

3. Determine the effects of "aerobic" training on CR capacity as measured by one of the tests described in this chapter, using yourself as a subject. Pretest, enter into the training program, retest every other week, and note the changes. Be sure to standardize all aspects of the testing.

4. Determine the heart rate after standing at attention for five minutes (remain in this position while the count is taken). Then begin walking slowly about; after several minutes of this slow walking, count the heart rate while continuing to walk. Compare your results and contrast with others' results. Which HR is lower? How do you explain the difference? Has the result any implications for the value of exercise?

5. Survey adults and high school students concerning their knowledge about the heart, what helps keep it healthy, what kinds of infections and disorders it can develop and the causes, relationship of heart disease to smoking, obesity, and so on. Develop a plan to correct the misconceptions you uncover and carry it out with the assistance of your instructor.

6. Survey the adults at a nearby YMCA, YWCA, or comparable recreation agency, and determine what knowledge they have of the relationships between physical activity and CR health, what constitutes "nonfitness" recreation as opposed to recreation which also provides CR benefits, and so on.

7. Determine the number of nearby recreation facilities which provide CR fitness activities, convenience of location, cost to users, and so on. Make a decision based on the facts as to the

adequacy of such community and private facilities. (It may be interesting to analyze summer and winter facilities separately.) Compare with opportunities for *non*active recreation such as listening to music, viewing films, and playing cards.

8. Study the heart rate increase caused by activities so as to isolate the effects of varying the percent of total body musculature, percent of maximal force exerted, rate of contraction, and length of exercise.

SUGGESTED READINGS

The following references, which appear in the list beginning on page 689, are highly recommended: Bruner and Manelis (78); Burt and Jackson (84); Cantone (94); Chapman and Mitchell (99); Cooper (123); Eckstein (162); Heusner (245); McDonald and Fullerton (354); Morgan and Adamson (401); Morris and others (406); Nikkila and Konttinen (428); Sharkey (510); Zauner, Mapes, and Burt (629).

•

Neuromuscular Function

Chapter 9

AFFERENT CONCEPTS

For years comic book advertisements have not only provided amateur and professional humorists with joke material but they have sold millions of dollars worth of "courses" on strength and muscle building. Could such a childishly simple appeal to the underdeveloped male's ego meet with this kind of success if the claims for these courses were entirely fraudulent? Considering the demonstrated gullibility of the American public this is, perhaps, a moot question. But in this particular case the promoters do not have to depend on claims that are completely false. There is enough truth apparent to the prospective customer to encourage him to give it a try. After all, who has not at least heard of someone in his circle of friends who has tremendously (even "fantastically") increased muscle girth and strength through some sort of "body-building" program? "If it can happen to him, why not to me?" is the logical query.

The fact is that, *under the proper circumstances,* practically anyone can substantially increase his strength and muscular endurance. He can almost certainly also increase muscle girth and bulk. The only questions remaining are: by how much, under what conditions, and at what physical expense? These are all questions that any good physical educator should be able to answer with authoritative certainty. This is information he should be giving his students in a well-planned, systematic manner. And, more important, it is information that he himself should thoroughly *understand* from a scientific standpoint, based upon his knowledge of how the human being functions. Although this book is not intended to provide you with the extensive knowledge you will need about the function of human beings, a few basic concepts are presented as a means of introduction to some information you will need to acquire.

The human being would be utterly unable to function without the intimate interaction of three distinct systems: (1) the skeletal system, (2) the muscular system, and (3) the nervous system. Obviously these systems can be separated by dissection for minute study, but in terms of their actual function in human movement it is essential to realize that there is no simple way to separate their activities. Although the primary function of the nervous system is commonly defined as "communication" and that of the muscular system as "contraction," it should be readily apparent that one function without the other is essentially impossible. The interrelationship becomes evident when one recognizes that even quiet thinking cannot occur without certain minimal activity of muscles in-

volved in the speech apparatus. And although we can readily identify two of the functions of the bones as protection and support, it must be recognized that muscles cannot produce tension unless they have something to pull against, and that movement in space cannot occur without the leverage provided by the long bones. Most of the discussion in this chapter centers about the function of the neuromuscular system with only minimal discussion of the role played by the bones in movement.

What can the human organism do? It is important to recognize that even the most noble thoughts of man cannot be recorded or expressed without movement of some kind. In other words, everything that man can do is dependent upon his ability to move in complex, purposeful ways. Painting a portrait, guiding a pencil, wielding a sledge hammer, walking a tightrope, playing the piano, transplanting a heart, striking a tennis ball, guiding a rocket, programming a computer, shoveling snow, and countless other tasks we generally take for granted are all dependent upon the effectively integrated action of the neuromuscular system. Furthermore, the remarkable efficiency we have come to expect of this dual system is due, in large measure, to the great adaptability inherent within it. Fostering understanding of the conditions under which such adaptation occurs most readily in desired directions is a primary task of physical educators and health educators.

The jobs of communication and decision-making within the human organism are the responsibility of the nervous system. Decisions concerning whether to kick or kiss, to smile or smite are made after proper evaluation of all incoming stimuli. Instructions are then transmitted to the muscles for appropriate action. In order to understand adequately how important the proper functioning of this system is in our lives it is necessary to understand certain basic facts about it.

THE NERVOUS SYSTEM

Anatomy and General Function

The nervous system includes the brain, the spinal cord, and a network of thread-like nerves that spread out from these structures to every part of the body. Because of the great complexity of this system it has been necessary to consider it as being composed of separate segments, in order to make the discussion of its structure and function somewhat easier. Therefore, when we speak of the **central nervous system** (CNS) we are referring to the brain and the spinal cord, both of which are enclosed within bony structures (the skull and vertebral column). All the nerves and the ganglia (clusters of nerve cell bodies) outside these structures are grouped under the heading of the **peripheral nervous system.** Obviously these are not two separate systems, but rather two parts of the same system (see Color Plate 8 and Figure 9.1).

Certain functions of the body, such as walking or speaking, are under the conscious control of the will. Con-versely, there are certain body functions over which we have little or no control at all. The portion of the nervous system responsible for the activity of the **skeletal muscles,** which enable us to move and speak, is called the **somatic system.** The **autonomic system,** on the other hand, controls the functions of the heart, intestines, urogenital tract, blood vessels, endocrine glands, and certain other portions of the body that are not under our conscious control.

Because the functions of these organs may need to fluctuate in either of two directions (either *increased* or *decreased* activity), it is not surprising to learn that there are two separate portions of the autonomic system that make this possible (see Figure 9.2). In general, the activity of one of these portions is antagonistic—or opposite—to the activity of the other. The **sympathetic** portion of the autonomic nervous system, for example, increases the rate and force with which the heart beats. The effect of the **parasympathetic** portion is to slow down the heart rate. Although the sympathetic system does not cause *every* organ or gland it serves to *increase* its activity (intestinal activity, for example, is *decreased* by increased sympathetic stimulation), it consistently opposes the activity of the parasympathetic system. It is the balance between the effects of these two systems that determines the actual level of activity of a particular organ of the body at any given time (see Chapter 12).

In general the sympathetic nervous system acts to prepare the body for responding to emergency situations. Thus, in times of danger the heart sud-

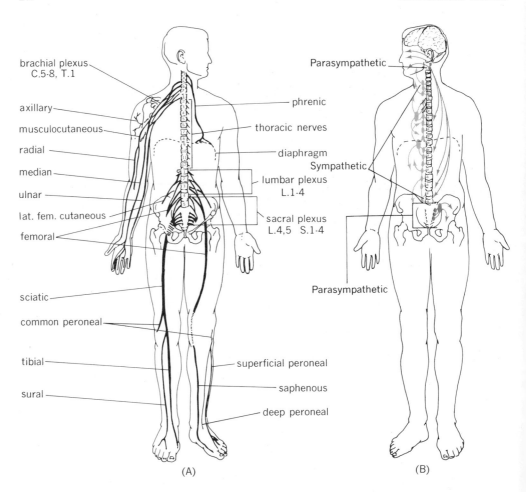

brachial plexus
C.5-8, T.1

axillary

musculocutaneous

radial

median

ulnar

lat. fem. cutaneous

femoral

sciatic

common peroneal

tibial

sural

phrenic

thoracic nerves

diaphragm

lumbar plexus
L.1-4

sacral plexus
L.4,5 S.1-4

superficial peroneal

saphenous

deep peroneal

Parasympathetic

Sympathetic

Parasympathetic

(A)

(B)

FIGURE 9.1   (A) Distribution of the major nerves of the voluntary (somatic) nervous system. (B) Schematic diagram of the autonomic nervous system. Note the two divisions: sympathetic (or thoracolumbar) and parasympathetic (craniosacral). The sympathetic system passes through the ganglionic chain before going to its destination (shown here on only one side of the spine). Adapted by permission from B. G. King and M. J. Showers, *Human Anatomy and Physiology*. Philadelphia: W. B. Saunders Company, 1964, p. 68.

denly accelerates, the muscles become tense and infused with blood, digestive activities cease, and the individual is automatically prepared for a primitive reaction to the situation: fight or flight! Of course in our civilized state we sel-

dom follow either of these courses of action, but the body efficiently prepares us for them anyway.

In cases where movement of any kind is engaged in by the body, it becomes the function of the somatic nervous system to initiate and coordinate such activity. Such activation may be the result of a conscious wish of the individual or entirely of a reflex nature, or perhaps a combination of the two. Because little muscular activity can be accomplished without an increased blood supply to the muscles involved, it is important that the autonomic nervous system function properly to produce an increase in heart rate and in stroke volume, and alterations in the caliber of the blood vessels. Intelligent direction of the activities of the muscles is provided by the higher centers of the brain, usually the subcortical areas.

All the various functions mentioned above depend upon the ability of nerve cells, called **neurons,** to transmit im-

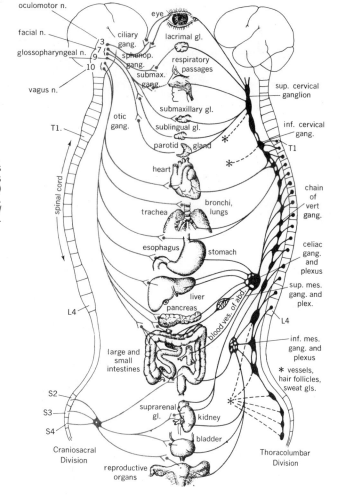

FIGURE 9.2 Diagram of the autonomic nervous system. The parasympathetic (craniosacral) is on the left and the sympathetic (thoracolumbar) on the right. Adapted by permission from B. G. King and M. J. Showers, *Human Anatomy and Physiology.* Philadelphia: W. B. Saunders Company, 1964, p. 125.

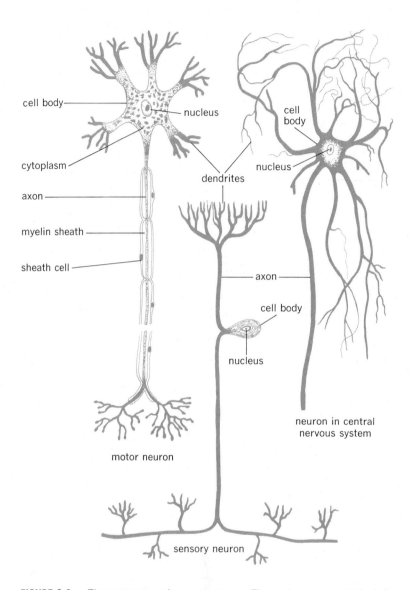

FIGURE 9.3   Three neurons of common types. The motor neuron at the left shows the myelin sheath formed from sheath cell membranes several layers thick around the axon. Many neurons are much longer, relative to the diameter of axon and cell body, and many have much thinner myelin sheaths. By permission from D. R. Griffin, *Animal Structure and Function*. New York: Holt, Rinehart and Winston, Inc., 1962, p. 100.

pulses rapidly and in complex patterns from one part of the body to another. At this point it is important to recognize that the terms "nerve" and "neuron" are not synonymous. A **nerve** is made up of many neurons, whereas a neuron is a single nerve cell or fiber. Neurons may vary in length from just a fraction of an inch to nearly six feet (see Figure 9.3). Some of them carry impulses from sensory receptors (pain, heat, pressure, sight, smell, sound, and so on) to the central nervous system. Such nerve cells would be called **sensory neurons.** Because such fibers conduct impulses toward the CNS, they are also called **afferent neurons.** Those that carry impulses *from* the CNS to the muscles of the body are called **motor neurons** because they are responsible for producing movement. Since these carry impulses *away* from the CNS, they are often referred to as **efferent neurons.** The major "nerves" of the body include both sensory and motor neurons. A third major classification of neurons is collectively labeled **internuncial neurons** or, sometimes, central neurons. These fibers serve to make all the millions of connections necessary for coordination of the various levels of activity within the CNS. Such neurons are involved in integrating all the complex processes of thought, memory, learning, balance, sight, speech, movement, and other functions of the human organism. (Cells that serve to support the shape and structure of the nervous system but have no neural function are called **glial cells**.)

Although neurons vary considerably in length and diameter, as well as in the speed with which they conduct impulses, they are all essentially similar in basic structure and function. Neurons conduct impulses in much the same way that a fuse carries a spark; that is, the neuron itself supplies the energy for the propagation of the impulse. Because of this fact, each neuron conducts in an **all-or-none** manner. That is, either the neuron fires in a given situation or it does not. If a given stimulus is of sufficient strength to cause the neuron to fire, the application of a stronger stimulus would have no greater effect in so far as the intensity of the discharge is concerned.

If, on the other hand, a given stimulus is not strong enough to cause the neuron to fire, such a stimulus is said to be below the **threshold** of the neuron. When we refer to the threshold of a given neuron or sensory receptor, we are talking about the minimal level of stimulation that is sufficient to activate that neuron or sense organ.

The simplest example of how structures of the nervous system work together is demonstrated by the **spinal reflex arc.** When the physician taps your knee (the patellar tendon) with his small rubber hammer, you have observed the response that is elicited: the foot swings forward in a kicking motion. Figure 9.4 illustrates how the muscle spindles are stretched by this stimulus causing an impulse to be sent from the quadriceps muscle group to the spinal cord. When the impulse arrives at the spinal cord, it must cross the small gap that exists between the sensory (afferent) neuron and the motor (efferent) neuron. This junction be-

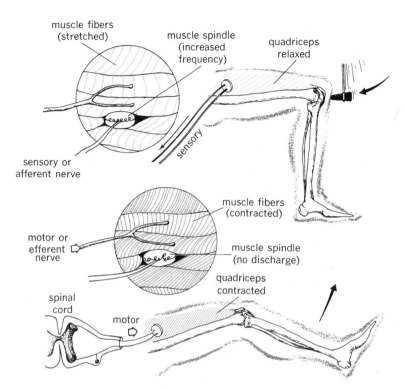

muscle fibers
(stretched)

muscle spindle
(increased
frequency)

quadriceps
relaxed

sensory

sensory or
afferent nerve

motor or
efferent
nerve

muscle fibers
(contracted)

muscle spindle
(no discharge)

quadriceps
contracted

spinal
cord

motor

FIGURE 9.4   Action of muscle spindles. Tapping of patellar tendon stretches relaxed quadriceps muscles. Spindles within the quadriceps respond to stretch by sending impulses to spinal cord. Reflex is completed when motor impulse is returned to the quadriceps, causing them to contract, thus removing stretch from spindles.

tween the two neurons is called the **synapse.** Here at the synapse impulses are permitted to cross in one direction only: from afferent neurons to efferent neurons. In our example the sensory neuron synapses directly with the motor neuron. (In most instances, whether they are reflex or higher order functions, there are one or more internuncial neurons interspersed between the sensory neuron and the motor neuron.) As soon as the motor neuron is

stimulated by the impulse from the sensory neuron, it carries an impulse rapidly back to the quadriceps muscles causing them to contract suddenly. The result is the kicking motion which you observe.

The total time required for this reflex action (from the time the hammer strikes the knee until the leg begins its forward swing) is called reflex time. Reflex time is composed of the time it takes for the stimulus to travel over the sensory neuron, cross the synapse in the spinal cord, and return to the muscle causing it to contract. It is known that the time for an impulse to traverse a *single* synapse between neurons is from .5 to 1.0 **millisecond.** This period of time constitutes the **synaptic delay.** By determining the actual synaptic delay in various reflexes it has been possible to estimate the number of synapses that are involved. Of course, the more neurons and synapses there are involved in a neural pathway the longer it will take for an impulse to pass over it.

A term that is very much like reflex time is **reaction time** (Figure 9.47). This can be defined as the time elapsed between the presentation of a stimulus and the initiation of the response. The important difference to be noted here is that the response called for may not be a simple reflex activity. One might be asked, for example, to push a certain button when a particular combination of lights flashes on, but *not* to push it whenever some other combination is lighted. Such a response requires a certain amount of judgment and as such would naturally be slower than a simple reflex.

In both of the previous cases it should be noted that time is measured only to the *beginning* of the movement. The time for the movement (from its instant of starting to its specified conclusion) is called movement time. If we are interested in the total time it takes for an individual to complete his response to a stimulus (called **response time**) we would simply add reaction time and movement time together.

THE MUSCULAR SYSTEM

Anatomy and General Function

If you are to teach about the muscular system and how it can be understood and efficiently used, there are certain basic characteristics of this type of tissue that must be recognized.

You are probably aware of the fact that skeletal muscle is only one of three kinds of muscle tissue in the body. This type of muscle, which is responsible for movement of the limbs and support of the body, is also called *striated* muscle because of its striped appearance when viewed under the microscope. Another term for this muscle is *voluntary* muscle, because it can be controlled by the will of the individual. This is not true for cardiac or smooth muscle, at least under ordinary circumstances (see Figure 9.5). A second kind of muscle is that found in the heart. It is similar in many ways to skeletal muscle, but does not bear the same kind of distinct striations. In addition, the small muscle fibers of skeletal muscle are more completely insulated from each other than are those of cardiac muscle.

The third kind of muscle tissue is called *smooth* muscle and is found in the walls of the digestive tract, the blood vessels, and certain other organs. Smooth muscle is much slower acting than striated muscle and is easily distinguished from the two other kinds of muscle.

Although the fibers of all three types of muscle tissue share the property of

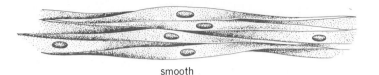

smooth

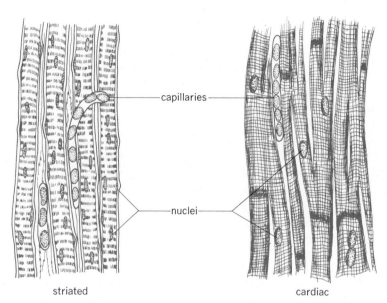

capillaries

nuclei

striated   cardiac

FIGURE 9.5 The three types of muscle cells. Note capillary containing red blood cells located close to the muscle cells. By permission from D. R. Griffin, *Animal Structure and Function.* New York: Holt, Rinehart and Winston, Inc., 1962, p. 60.

being able to shorten when stimulated, we are most interested here in how this is accomplished in skeletal (voluntary) muscle.

The exact mechanism by which muscle is able to contract is not yet understood. We do know, however, that the fibers of muscle tissue are made up of long chainlike molecules of protein. The two predominant proteins in these molecules are called *actin* and *myosin.* The research of several physiologists

(notably A. F. Huxley and H. E. Huxley) has shown that these molecules of actin and myosin are arranged alternately in a pattern such as is shown in Figure 9.6. If you will look carefully at the diagram, you will see that the alternating light and dark bands of the fiber are made up of rodlike filaments that slide between one another. Where these filaments or rods overlap with one another, the bands appear dark. Where they do not overlap, there are light

FIGURE 9.6 Striated muscle shown diagrammatically at successively higher magnification. The A-band contains most of the myosin, while the long filaments of actin are believed to slide past the thicker myosin filaments as the muscle contracts and relaxes. By permission from D. R. Griffin, *Animal Structure and Function.* New York: Holt, Rinehart and Winston, Inc., 1962, p. 61.

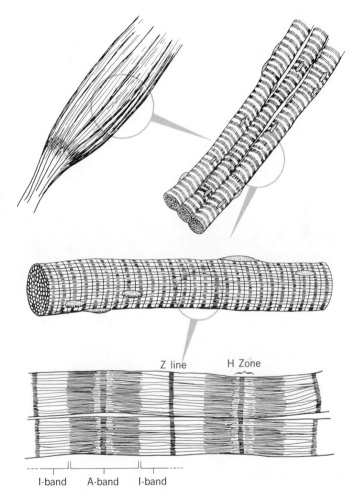

Z line   H Zone

I-band   A-band   I-band

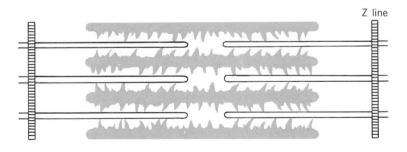

Z line

bands. The dark areas are called A-bands while the light areas are known as I-bands. The dark line in the center of the I-band is called a Z-line (and sometimes a Z-membrane). You will notice that the smaller filaments (composed of actin) are attached to the Z-line.

As the actin filaments are caused to slide between the larger myosin filaments in the A-band, the Z-lines are drawn closer together. Although it is not yet clear how the interaction between the actin and myosin filaments occurs, A. F. Huxley has presented interesting evidence (261) of a ratchet-like action involving minute cross-bridges between the filaments. By successively attaching, pulling, releasing, and reattaching themselves to receptor sites on the adjacent filament, these tiny cross-bridges are believed to cause the sliding movement that is ultimately responsible for all muscular contraction.

As Figure 9.6 shows, the tiny muscle filaments are grouped together to form single muscle fibers. These fibers, in turn, make up little bundles (called fasiculae) that, in turn, combine to form the familiar muscle bundle. These mus-

cle bundles are combined in a number of different patterns and ultimately compose the 600 muscles of the human body. These muscles, together with the skeleton, provide a basic framework and determine the actual shape of the body and its various parts.

The various ways in which muscle fibers are combined in order to provide joint movement under a variety of conditions is interesting in itself. Figure 9.7 shows how some muscles are made up of fibers running parallel to one another, whereas others are made up of various combinations of diagonally pulling fibers that utilize a central tendon to deliver their force to the bones involved.

The functional organization of the muscles is of great importance. Whenever one of the tiny muscle fibers is stimulated by the neuron (nerve fiber) that innervates it, it shortens to its maximum capacity. This is true of all muscle fibers. That is, when they are stimulated they either contract maximally or not at all because the stimulus delivered by the neurons is always of the same magnitude or intensity in the normal individual. The term used to describe the phenomenon is the *all-*

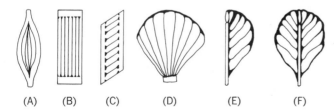

(A)   (B)   (C)   (D)   (E)   (F)

FIGURE 9.7 Example of different arrangements of fibers within muscles: (A) fusiform or spindle; (B) rectangular or parallel; (C) rhomboidal; (D) triangular; (E) penniform; (F) bipenniform. Adapted from D. F. Wells, *Kinesiology*. Philadelphia: W. B. Saunders Company, 1961.

or-none law. You must keep in mind at this point that we are discussing individual muscle fibers only, not the entire muscle.

If you were somehow able to examine the organizational structure of the muscles of the body, you would discover that the fibers are arranged in "squads" or scattered groups, with each squad of fibers served by a single nerve fiber (Figure 9.8). Whenever an individual nerve fiber "fires," all of the muscle fibers to which it is connected will contract in an all-or-none manner. One such neuron or nerve fiber may serve as few as 3 muscle fibers or as many as 2000 (177), depending on the size and function of the muscle in which it is located. Muscles engaged in movements requiring extremely fine adjustments, such as those that control the movements of the eye, have a much lower ratio of neurons to muscle fibers than do muscles involved in more gross movements, such as jumping and running. This would mean, of course, that the calf muscle might have one motor neuron for every 800 muscle fibers, whereas the muscles controlling the fingers might have only one neuron for every 50 fibers. The term commonly used in discussing neuromuscular organization of this type is **motor unit,** defined as a single motor neuron together with all the muscle fibers it innervates.

Each muscle, then, is composed of a number of motor units, all of which act as independent elements in the sense that they "fire" in a random, "unsynchronized" way whenever they

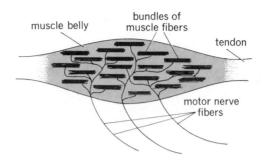

FIGURE 9.8 A schematic diagram of the arrangement of the muscle fibers into "squads" or motor units. By permission from A. C. Guyton, *Function of the Human Body.* Philadelphia: W. B. Saunders Company, 1969, p. 69.

are activated. (Perhaps it would be more accurate to say that the separate units operate in harmony with one another, much like the separate instruments of a symphony orchestra. They operate independently, but the overall result is a smooth, harmonious "orchestration.") It should be easy to see that if only a few motor units were firing at any given time, the force being exerted by the muscle would be relatively slight. In order to increase this force it is a simple matter to bring in or "recruit" more motor units to participate in the task.

It should be made clear here that there is a very distinct hierarchy among the motor units. That is, some motor units "fire" in performance of the most simple movements, whereas others are never utilized until the task attempted requires maximal exertion. The former group of units would be referred to as having a *low threshold,* whereas the latter would be called *high-threshold* motor units. Thus the low-threshold units would be involved constantly throughout virtually *all* movements, but the units of very high threshold would become activated only on the rare occasions when maximal force is required. Between these two extremes there are, of course, motor units that range in threshold from low through moderate to high. The significant factor is that these units always come into play at about the same tension level each time they fire. As this tension is maintained or increased in the muscle, they would continue to fire, and then, as tension is decreased, they would drop out of activity at about the same level at which they had entered (see Figure 9.9).

One theoretical way of increasing strength would be to involve somehow the normally inactive motor units of very high threshold in lower-level activities in which they would ordinarily not be involved.

INCREASED FREQUENCY OF MOTOR UNIT FIRING   It has been pointed out that in addition to muscle hypertrophy, maximal strength can be increased by means of "permanent" recruitment of motor units of very high threshold. Another change that can produce an increase in the force muscles are able to exert is the increase in the *frequency* of motor unit firing. It has already been mentioned that motor units fire asynchronously, that is, out of phase with one another. This asynchrony of motor unit activity ensures smoothness of movement. It is easy to see that if all

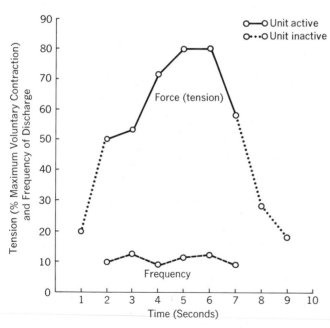

FIGURE 9.9   Plot of a single motor unit coming into action at 50% tension and continuing to fire (at 13 cycles/second) until tension again drops to about 58%. Adapted from B. Bigland and O. C. J. Lippold, "Motor Unit Activity in the Voluntary Contraction of Human Muscle," *Journal of Physiology*, 125:322, 1954.

motor units fired simultaneously, the result would be a sudden, jerky movement of great force. For most purposes this would be an inappropriate action. Picture what would happen every time you tried to lift a pencil or a glass of water if muscles responded in this fashion!

The **synchrony** of motor unit function is directly related to the frequency with which the individual motor units fire. It should be realized that motor units are capable of altering the rate at which they fire, and that this change in frequency is directly related to the amount of force exerted at any given time. Consider, for example, a group of motor units, with each unit firing in an unsynchronized manner with respect to the other units, at a rate of 5 cycles per second. This means that the separate fibers of each unit are all contracting 5 times each second, but that very few of the fibers of the total muscle are contracting simultaneously. Now, if the rate of firing of the motor units is suddenly increased to 50 cycles per second, it should be clear that it is much more probable that some of these muscle fibers will be contracting simultaneously with others. Since more muscle fibers are contracting at any given instant when the frequency rate is high than when it is low, it is obvious that more force is being exerted by the muscle involved when frequency of firing is high.

CHANGE IN AMOUNT OF CENTRAL INHIBITION AND FACILITATION One of the most fascinating aspects of the study of human strength deals with the many

reports of "superhuman" performances of people who are involved in emergencies. An example of such reports appeared in the press a few years ago. As the story was reported, a young man was working under his car, which he raised by means of an automobile jack. Suddenly the jack slipped and the man was pinned beneath the car. The father, who was nearby, rushed to his aid and feverishly began attempting to reposition the jack. The victim's mother (who suffered from arthritis) ran to the car, grasped the bumper, and lifted the car off her son. The effort caused a compression fracture of one of her vertebrae, but she *had* mustered enough strength to lift the car from her son!

How is it possible to explain such extraordinary feats? Obviously there is no long-term training effect involved; yet there is undeniably an increase in the measurable strength levels. Perhaps you are now in a position to attempt a partial explanation, at least, on the basis of your knowledge of motor unit recruitment and frequency of firing. In this connection it is interesting to note that it has been estimated that if all the muscle fibers of the body could be induced to contract at one time a force in excess of six tons would be exerted. This would certainly be more than the human frame could withstand and would result in the total ruin of the organism. Apparently there are built-in mechanisms that prevent such massive simultaneous contractions.

These same mechanisms are continually active in preventing damage in more ordinary circumstances. Although some are of a reflexive nature and are activated by the tension within a muscle or a tendon, others originate in the higher brain centers. Such stimuli have been called **inhibitors;** the process, **central inhibition.** These terms imply that people are capable of much greater performance than they are ordinarily able to demonstrate, simply because their activity is inhibited by impulses from the brain. If it were somehow possible to reduce or release these inhibitors, remarkably greater performance in terms of strength or muscular endurance would be expected. In extremely stressful situations where great excitement or anxiety prevails it is believed that such a release takes place. This, in turn, could lead to greater synchrony or to decreased motor unit thresholds or to both, which could explain unusual displays of strength or muscular endurance.

Another neurological process that affects the degree to which muscular contraction can occur is **facilitation,** a positive process by which impulses that cause contraction are sent from the central nervous system (chiefly the brain) to the motor neurons. In such situations, more activity than normal may result because many "protective" inhibitory impulses are overridden. Although it is difficult, if not impossible, to determine whether unusual strength is due to facilitation or to decreased inhibition, it seems safe to assume that *both* processes are involved.

It has been demonstrated a number of times that "cortical inhibition," or inhibition originating in the cerebral cortex, can serve to hinder performance drastically. If a person as a child has always been cautioned not to overdo, or has been continually warned about the dangers of injury involved in physical performance, he may well develop serious limitations in his physical capacities. Fear of social criticism, especially true of women, has very real consequences in terms of ability to excel in activities requiring strength. Hypnotism has been used in a number of interesting ways to attempt to "disinhibit" people. Dr. Arthur Steinhaus has reported the case of a girl who was able to increase her strength by more than 50 percent while in a hypnotic trance (543, p. 142). Once this breakthrough was achieved, she was able to continue to perform at this level even in the waking state. It was later discovered that the girl had always been cautioned not to overdo because of a childhood asthmatic condition. In addition, earlier teasing about being unusually athletic (despite her genuine femininity) had created a socially induced inhibitory state.

Other studies concerning the effects of hypnotism have attempted to determine the psychological limits on performance. Although reports are somewhat contradictory, it appears that the strength and endurance of highly trained athletes cannot be greatly increased by hypnotism. (Hypnotic **suggestion** can dramatically *decrease* performance, however.) Among nonathletes, on the other hand, it appears that hypnotism can produce an increase in muscular performance, particularly in respect to strength (110, p. 53). See Chapter 13 for further discussion of this topic and results of some studies.

Identifying Muscles

In learning to identify specific muscles it is helpful to know how muscles have been named. Basically there are four ways in which names have been applied: shape or appearance (the trapezius is shaped like a trapezoid), location (subclavius is located below the clavicle), bones connected (the intercostals are attached between the ribs), and their action (the supinator supinates the hand, that is, turns it palm upward). Some muscles, of course, do not appear to fall into any of these classifications.

Identifying Movements

In any discussion of human movement it is necessary to be acquainted with the names of the muscles involved but also to know the terms used to identify the specific movements involved. In Table 9.1 is a list of common terms with their definitions. Figure 9.10 identifies some of the frequently discussed movements.

CONTRIBUTIONS TO PHYSICAL ACTIVITY

The Nervous System

From the preceding discussion it can be seen that the nervous system is the key to all body movement, including exercise. It is involved not only in initiating, coordinating, and directing activity but also is largely responsible for producing the necessary adjustments in body functions to make the exercise possible. Plate 2 and Figure 9.1 show

TABLE 9.1   Definition of Terms Commonly Used in Describing Movement

TERM	DEFINITION
Agonist	Any given muscle that is responsible for the action under consideration. Example: Biceps brachii, causing elbow flexion.
Antagonist	Muscles so located that they can oppose the action of the agonist. Example: Triceps brachii, causing elbow extension.
Fixator	Any muscle that performs the act of "locking" a part firmly in place, thereby giving other muscles a firm base from which to work.
Prime mover	A muscle or group that is primarily responsible for a given joint action. It may be responsible for more than one action, and two or more muscles may be prime movers for a single action.
Synergist	A muscle, other than the prime mover, that acts to aid, support, and guide the action caused by the prime mover.

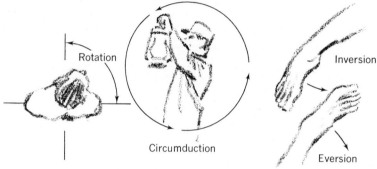

FIGURE 9.10 Types of joint movements. Adapted from Franz Frohse, *Atlas of Human Anatomy*. New York: Barnes & Noble, Inc., 1961.

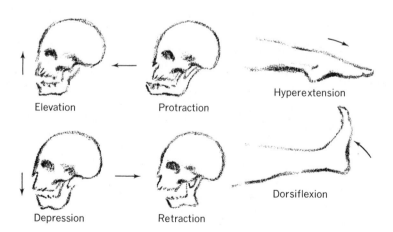

some of the major divisions of the central nervous system that are intimately associated with activities essential to physical activity. The **cerebrum** is the part of the brain concerned with all conscious functions. Sensations, voluntary movements, memory of skills, judgment of distances, appropriate force of movements, and many other of the "highest" levels of activity are centered here.

The **thalamus** appears to be an important relay center for almost all complex reflex movements and the perception of sensations. The **hypothalamus** is responsible for the coordination of such autonomic functions as the control of body temperature by sweating, **vasoconstriction** (narrowing of the blood vessels), **vasodilation** (dilation of blood vessels), shivering, and so on.

The coordination of skilled movements, making them smooth and effective, is a function of the **cerebellum.** Through its action on the skeletal muscles, this part of the brain makes it possible for us to maintain equilibrium.

The increase in the rate and depth of breathing as well as the elevation of the heart rate and blood pressure during exercise are brought about through the activation of reflex centers contained in the portion of the brain called the **medulla oblongata.**

Extending upward through the brainstem, the medulla and the pons is a complex network of nerve cells, called the *reticular activating system*. This area serves the extremely important function of sending alerting messages throughout the brain whenever stimuli from the sensory system are received.

The Muscular System

The contribution of the muscular system to exercise is obvious. Without muscle function there would be no exercise because movement of any kind would be impossible. Of course, the muscular system has important functions in addition to the primary one of providing movement. It is also responsible for producing most of the body heat and for maintaining upright posture. The last function is technically one of stabilizing body position rather than causing movement.

SETTING LIMITS   It is apparent that the functional ability of the muscular system is not an "either/or" proposition. That is, we do not think in terms of either having strength or of not having strength. The same is true of endurance, power, and flexibility. Instead, we usually think in terms of *how much* (or how little) of these factors we possess. Indeed, the *degree* to which neuromuscular function has been developed is frequently the deciding factor in whether one succeeds or fails in a given activity. In other words, each of us is *limited* in what he can accomplish by the degree to which the neuromuscular system has become developed. It is for this reason that the great adaptability of the neuromuscular system is of such importance. Unlike certain other limitations imposed upon us, the neuromuscular limits are, to a large extent, under our own control. Once this is understood, decisions concerning one's optimal level of neuromuscular development can be made and activity programs designed to achieve the desired goals.

In discussing the limitations imposed upon us by the neuromuscular system we will need to consider not only strength but also muscular endurance, power, coordination, and flexibility. In addition, we will give consideration to some of the basic mechanics of human movement.

The Skeletal System

Although this chapter is basically devoted to the ways in which the nervous and muscular systems work together to produce movement, it is impossible to discuss human motion without an occasional reference to the skeleton.

In everyday activity the skeletal system can be said to have at least five important functions. First of all, it provides protection to vital organs of the body, the brain, the heart, the lungs, the spinal cord, and so on. In addition, it supports the body in much the same way that steel girders give support to modern buildings. It provides a system of levers upon which the muscles can act to produce locomotion and other movements. A fourth service performed by the skeleton is to store calcium needed by other body systems for proper function. And finally, the long and flat bones of the body provide the important manufacturing process of blood cells, both red and white, as well as the blood platelets that are essential for clotting.

Color Plates 5 and 6 show most of the major bones of the body. From time to time you may wish to refer to these illustrations as various movements are discussed. In addition, it is suggested that you familiarize yourself with the terms and definitions at the end of this chapter. You will find this information helpful in the discussion to follow. Although more detailed explanation of how these systems do their jobs will be presented later, we are presently interested in discussing some of the observable outcomes of neuromuscular teamwork.

EFFERENT CONCEPTS

STRENGTH

The ability of the muscles to exert force is called *strength*. It is obvious that some people are stronger than others. If we wish to find out how much stronger one person is than another, we must then measure *maximal strength*. This can be determined by measuring the greatest amount of force each person can exert for a brief instant. Under this definition it is apparent that the measurement of total body strength is very difficult, if not impossible. Because it is possible for someone to have a very strong grip despite having weak legs, it is obvious that strength is a factor specific to individual muscles, and that the strength of one muscle group is not necessarily related to the strength of another group.

Another interesting fact about strength is that there are different "kinds" of strength. The ability to lift a heavy suitcase to an overhead rack would be an example of dynamic strength. In this illustration, several muscles are involved in a series of smooth, continuous contractions. These contractions are called **isotonic** because even though the length of the muscle changes, the tension within the muscles remains essentially the same (*iso = same; tonic = tension*).

As an example of **static strength** consider what happens when you attempt to pull a croquet stake out of the ground after it has been securely pounded into hard soil. In this case, your muscles attempt to shorten, but the resistance is so unyielding that no movement actually occurs. This expression of static strength results from **isometric** contraction of the muscles involved (*iso = same; metric = length*).

Up to this point we have discussed two types of muscle contraction: isotonic and isometric. Although most muscular activity can be described fairly adequately by these two terms, it should be recognized that there needs to be some elaboration of the term "isotonic." As you have learned, "isotonic" means a change in length of the muscle. Ordinarily we think of this change only in terms of a *shortening* of the fibers. That is, if you were to take a drink of coffee you could pick up a cup from the table and, by shortening the biceps muscle, bend your elbow in raising the cup to your lips. This would certainly fall into the category of isotonic contraction. But what about putting the cup back down on the table? Obviously you cannot simply let go and allow it to fall. Normally, you would carefully, and somewhat slowly, lower the cup and set it down gently.

FIGURE 9.11   Lowering a cup gently illustrates eccentric contraction of the elbow flexors (biceps) whereas swatting a fly illustrates vigorous elbow extension utilizing concentric contraction of the triceps.

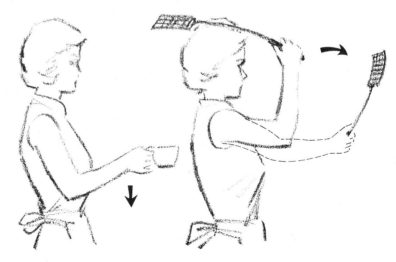

Because the event has involved movement it must be isotonic,[1] but does it involve a shortening of the musculature involved? Obviously it does not. As a matter of fact, quite the opposite is the case. The biceps muscle is actually involved in a process exactly opposite to its activity in raising the cup. Now, instead of bending the elbow against the force of gravity, it *gradually allows* the elbow to be extended by the force of gravity. Note that in this situation, as shown in Figure 9.11, the triceps is not needed to extend the elbow, because, if the biceps were not contracting, gravity alone would be sufficient to extend the elbow. The muscle, instead of shortening to perform the task, actually *lengthens* slowly until the cup rests firmly on the table. This lengthening of muscle fibers to do work is called **eccentric contraction.**

It should be easy to see that approximately half of the work done in most lifting movements involves eccentric contraction of muscles.

On this basis, then, we could talk about static strength as being the greatest force a given muscle group could exert with no movement involved. By **dynamic strength** we would mean the force required to move the greatest

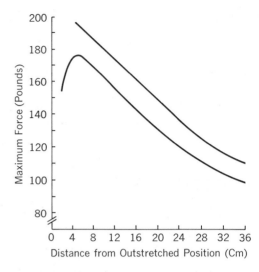

FIGURE 9.12   Maximum isometric force (top) compared with maximum isotonic force (bottom). In this test of elbow flexion strength, position is indicated in units of distance from the completely outstretched position. Adapted from E. Asmussen, O. Hansen, and O. Lammert, "The Relation between Isometric and Dynamic Muscle Strength in Man," *Communications*, Danish National Association for Infantile Paralysis, Hellerup, Denmark, 196 , p. 8.

resistance possible through the complete range of strength. We would discover that for any given muscle group (the biceps, for example) static strength is somewhat greater than dynamic strength (see Figure 9.12). This can be seen in the fact that a light object can be lifted quite rapidly, but if one attempts to lift heavier and heavier objects, his movements become slower and slower. Finally, the object may not be moved at all, despite the efforts of the lifter. At this point, however, he is exerting greater force than at any previous time, assuming, of course, that all other factors, such as motivation, effort, and fatigue level, remain constant.

---

[1]Dr. Alfred Hubbard (257) has suggested that the terms **"miometric," "pliometric,"** and "isometric" be used to indicate shortening contraction, lengthening contraction, and no change in muscle length during contraction, respectively. Although these terms appear to cover the possibilities much more simply than does the traditional terminology, they have not yet achieved widespread acceptance.

MUSCULAR ENDURANCE

In addition to those already mentioned there is another factor closely related to strength, and, as a matter of fact, often confused with strength. The term used to describe this phenomenon is **muscular endurance.** Essentially, muscular endurance is the ability to persist in any given muscular activity in which *local* fatigue rather than general exhaustion becomes the limiting factor. The number of push-ups or chin-ups you can perform is a measure of muscular endurance (assuming, of course, that you are able to do more than one of these). In these exercises it is obvious that you do not stop because of a general breathlessness or respiratory distress. The musculature in a certain area becomes uncomfortable and seemingly is unable to contract further, so activity ceases. In this respect, muscular endurance should not be confused with circulo-respiratory endurance, which will be discussed later.

The fact that tests such as chin-ups or push-ups have frequently been used as tests of *strength* rather than *muscular endurance* has introduced some confusion into this topic. It should be remembered, however, that if more than one repetition of movement such as a push-up or a chin-up can be performed, this is a test of muscular endurance, *not* maximal dynamic strength.

Just as there are two types of strength, there are also two types of muscular endurance. These should be fairly obvious to you now that you have studied the section on strength. Dynamic (or isotonic) endurance involves the number of repetitions of a given isotonic contraction that can be performed. Static (or isometric) endurance involves the amount of *time* a contraction of a given magnitude can be held. It will not surprise you to learn that generally the greater the force exerted initially by an individual, the less will be his "holding time."

The body seems to compensate automatically when we become aware that a maximal exertion over a period of time is required. As Figure 9.13 shows, four strong young men were asked to exert maximal force against a strain gauge. After establishing that such a measurement was repeatable, they were asked to pull *just as hard* but to hold the pull for as long as possible. In every case the greatest force exerted under these conditions was considerably less than was observed under the original conditions.

MUSCULAR POWER

Another term sometimes confused with strength is "power." With respect to human performance, power refers to the degree of "explosiveness" with which force is applied. It is quite possible for a man to have very strong legs, strong enough, in fact, to enable him to life great weights on his shoulders. This same man, however, may not be able to jump straight into the air for more than five or six inches. On the other hand, another person of similar weight and build but with less strength may be able to jump vertically more than thirty inches. The difference lies in the ability

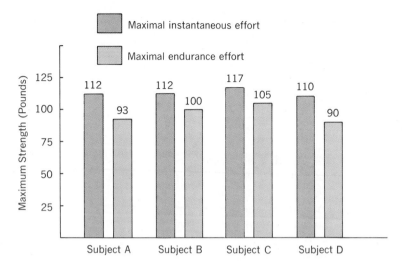

FIGURE 9.13 Comparison of performance when subjects were asked to exert the greatest force possible (maximal instantaneous force) with the same condition except that they were told to *hold* their maximum as long as possible (maximal endurance effort). Unpublished data, Physiology of Exercise Laboratory, University of Toledo, 1963.

to exert the available force (supplied by the muscles and called strength) over as short a period of *time* as possible. Thus, power is made up of three factors: force, time, and the distance over which the force is applied. Mathematically this can be expressed as a formula:

$$Power = \frac{Force \times Distance}{Time}$$

Assuming the distance through which the force acts remains constant, it should be possible to increase power by either increasing the ability to exert force or *decreasing* the time period over which the force is acting. Both are reasonable approaches and both can be used to improve performance requiring power.

The importance of power in most athletic activities should be obvious. The quick jump-turns required in skiing, the "firing out" of the blocker in football, the rapid leg movement required in the hundred-yard dash, the swing of the golf club, the snap of the badminton racket, the upward thrust of the leaping dancer are only a few illustrations of how power is a requisite for even mediocre performance in many activities.

IMPORTANCE OF ADEQUATE NEUROMUSCULAR CAPACITY

The question of how much strength, muscular endurance, and power are needed by any given individual can be answered only on a personal basis. It is obvious that the professional football player needs more of these attributes than the office secretary does. On the other hand, to assume that some people need only small amounts of each of these qualities may be a mistake. The number of low back injuries that occur annually as the result of household accidents certainly point up the need for more strength in certain muscle groups. Most adults have experienced the discomfort associated with unaccustomed weekend work or sports activity. Much of this problem can be traced to a lack of sufficient strength or muscular endurance to raise the individual above a minimal level of fitness.

For a number of years Dr. Hans Kraus has studied the increasing incidence of chronic low back pain in the United States. His research has led him to the conclusion that 80 percent of the low back pain is muscular in origin. Kraus states:

The large posture muscle groups of the trunk and back are frequently involved in the vicious circle: inactivity — deficiency — tension — pain — more enforced inactivity, etc. . . . This muscular — postural — back pain accounts for a majority (over 80 percent) of back sufferers. Reconditioning by exercise and proper supportive treatment can fully rehabilitate most of these patients (326, p. 24).

Strength is much like many of the other things we ordinarily take for granted; we are not concerned about it until, for some reason, we are deprived of it. People who have suffered accidents or a severe illness that has made it necessary to them to have arms or legs immobilized for certain lengths of time know that inactive muscles **atrophy,** or shrink in size and strength,

very rapidly. Accidents that result in the severing of nerves also result in extreme atrophy, and even though nerves will regenerate in cases where the break is outside the central nervous system, it takes considerable effort to regain the lost strength and ability to manipulate the affected limb.

As you have already learned from Chapter 5, everyone needs sufficient levels of fitness (including strength, muscular endurance, and flexibility) to handle his daily responsibilities *and to meet any emergency situations that might arise from time to time.* (See Figure 9.14.) But above and beyond these general requirements for optimal fitness, there are specific benefits to be derived from having and maintaining adequate levels in these three areas.

Low Back Pain

In 1945, Kraus and Weber published a report that vividly demonstrated the extremely high incidence of serious low back pain that is due to muscular deficiency. In this publication it was reported that approximately 80 percent of all the patients examined for low back pain were unable to pass at least one item in the Kraus-Weber battery. As a means of screening people to determine who the likely candidates for this disability are, Dr. Kraus recommends, in addition to a thorough medical examination, a series of six tests that have become well known as the Kraus-Weber Test of Minimal Fitness. If you have not already performed the items in this test you may wish to do so soon. They are not designed to test all areas of the body but only to evaluate grossly those factors Dr. Kraus has found to be associated with low back pain.

FLEXIBILITY

Any consideration of the factors that limit human physical performance must include some discussion of flexibility. In simple terms, flexibility is the de-

FIGURE 9.14 An example of emergency conditions requiring fitness. This woman and six others escaped from a burning building by means of a rope suspended more than 100 feet above the street. Twelve others perished in the fire that swept a six-story building in Kawasaki near Tokyo. (Wide World Photos)

gree to which a joint is free to move throughout its "normal" range of motion. Consistent with this definition is the fact that flexibility is a highly specific quality; full range of motion in one joint is no indication of the status of other joints of the body (338).

It is obvious that a significant lack of flexibility could impair physical performance, whether of an athletic nature or simply that involved in routine daily activity. Complaints of chronic or acute lack of flexibility are more often brought to the attention of the physical educator than almost any other. Regardless of whether such conditions are because of a lack of physical activity or created (directly or indirectly) by trauma or injury, it is essential that the physical educator have a thorough understanding of joint structure and function. He must also be intimately acquainted with approved remedial and preventive exercises and techniques because he will be called upon frequently to work closely with medical personnel in cases involving flexibility problems.

The seven types of joints found in the body are illustrated in Figure 9.15. Although it is beyond the scope of this discussion to outline all of the common abnormalities associated with these joints, some of the factors contributing to the limitations of joint flexibility will be discussed.

Injured or Diseased Joint Surfaces

Many kinds of crippling arthritis may lead eventually to actual fusing of the joints so that there is no longer a possibility of any movement in the afflicted

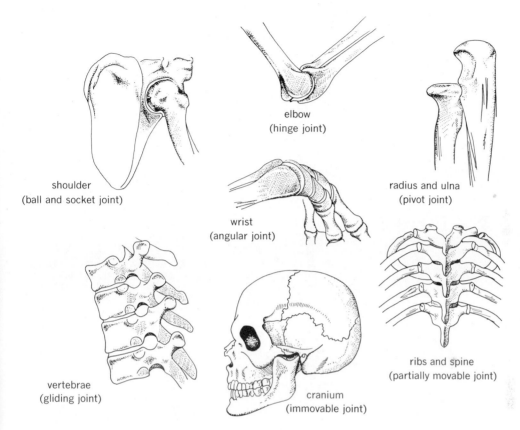

shoulder
(ball and socket joint)

elbow
(hinge joint)

radius and ulna
(pivot joint)

wrist
(angular joint)

vertebrae
(gliding joint)

cranium
(immovable joint)

ribs and spine
(partially movable joint)

FIGURE 9.15   The seven types of joints found in the body. Source: J. H. Otto, C. J. Julian, and J. E. Tether, *Modern Health*. New York: Holt, Rinehart and Winston, Inc., 1963, p. 254.

areas. Of course, there are many less severe forms of joint disease, but all are painful and all restrict movement to some extent.

Calcification

Closely related to arthritic problems is the calcification of joints, which can result from a number of causes. It is quite common for individuals involved in activities that place great strain on joints to develop calcium deposits within joints that seriously restrict movement.

Pain

One of the biggest problems in dealing with joint diseases or injuries is how to eliminate or relieve the pain invariably associated with them. In many cases joint movement is actually possible but the pain of movement is so great that the afflicted individual refuses to make

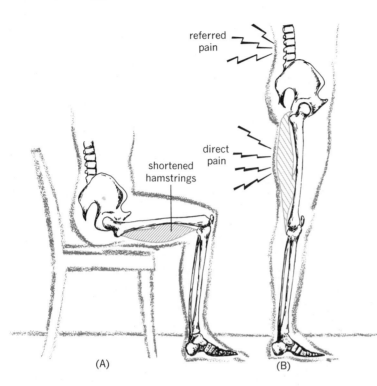

referred
pain

direct
pain

shortened
hamstrings

(A)   (B)

FIGURE 9.16 Contracture ("permanent" shortening) of the hamstring
muscles as a result of sedentary
occupation.

the attempt. The result of this perpetual disuse is, of course, a gradual worsening of the condition until there is no longer any possibility of movement.

Shortened Muscles and Tendons

Many of us may be fortunate enough to avoid the debilitating effects of arthritis or joint injuries, but we may develop a shortening of certain muscle groups because of faulty postures that are habitually assumed. One of the most familiar illustrations of muscle contracture resulting from faulty day-to-day postures and stances is the shortening of the hamstrings group (see Figure 9.16). These muscles, which are located on the back of the thigh, are responsible for bending the knee and extending the hip. These are the ones that complain whenever you attempt to place the palms of your hands on the floor without bending your knees. In most instances this difficulty arises because of the muscle-tendon adjustments that result from long periods of sitting. The knees are flexed at a 90° angle much of the day, allowing the muscles attached to the back of the knee joint to become permanently shorter than they should be. Then, when you attempt to bend over with the knees straight, or when you attempt to kick one foot high into the air you suddenly, and sometimes painfully, discover that you have lost a certain amount of flexibility.

Damaged Ligaments

Another cause of decreased flexibility is torn or damaged **ligaments,** which are tough bands of connective tissue that hold the joints together. These bands connect bone to bone (tendons connect muscle to bone) and are non-elastic. Very frequently, because of trauma of some kind, these ligaments may become stretched, torn, or pulled from their attachments. When this happens the joint becomes painful, of course, and perhaps cannot be used at all. As healing takes place the pain will subside, but frequently permanent injury results unless proper medical care has been given. Permanent joint loose-

ness and even a tendency to chronic dislocation may result from such an injury. Frequently a piece of cartilage may "float around" in the joint, occasionally lodging between the articulating surfaces and causing the joint to lock. In almost all such cases surgery can prevent or correct serious problems, but the sooner such corrective surgery is performed the better are the chances for complete return to normal function (see Chapter 17).

Muscle-Boundness

All of us have heard the term "muscle-bound" and most of us have a pretty good idea of what is meant by it. The assumption is that if an individual has bulging muscles he must have sacrificed some degree of flexibility. The truth of the matter is that, with intelligent training methods, normal flexibility will not only be unaffected but may even be increased (see Figure 9.17). The principle

FIGURE 9.17 Extreme muscular development and flexibility are not mutually exclusive, as demonstrated by a professional football linebacker and former "Mr. Toledo."

involved here is that both the agonist and the antagonist must receive equal attention in any overload training program.

It should now be clear that if one wishes to strengthen a particular muscle group, but also wishes to avoid a loss in flexibility he should give just as much attention to the development of the antagonists as to that of the agonists. This type of "balanced" training has produced a number of outstanding performers in many different sports, such as gymnastics, swimming, and other activities that require high levels of flexibility as well as great strength.

BODY MECHANICS

In addition to the factors already mentioned, there are several others that affect the efficiency of the human organism. One such factor is that of body mechanics. In one sense, an individual's body mechanics are dependent on his levels of strength, endurance, and flexibility. It is equally true, however, that adequate development of these characteristics, to say nothing of their proper application in effective performance, is greatly dependent on how these factors are "strung together" and utilized.

It is very clear, for example, that a man who lifts incorrectly may seriously injure his back even though he may be an extremely well-conditioned person. It is also possible (although not nearly so clear-cut) that habitually poor postural habits may produce permanent structural damage, regardless of the relative strength of muscles.

Posture

There is considerably less emphasis on the study of human posture today than at times in the past. Perhaps part of the reason for this is that experts in this field have been unable to agree on the importance of posture to the health of the individual. Arguments can be advanced supporting both sides of this issue and research studies have also been somewhat contradictory (42, 460).

It has become apparent to most people that because we are all individuals with different characteristics, there can be no such thing as an ideal posture for all. As a matter of fact, we are less interested in the somewhat artificial positions assumed by people who are being examined for postural deviations than we are in their normal, spontaneous ways of carrying themselves as they go about their daily routines.

Whether or not a slouching sort of stance can be said to predispose an individual to organic disorders that may seriously impair his health is questionable. There are certainly cases on record of individuals who have developed extensive structural abnormalities because of faulty habits of sitting and standing, but these are extremes. Many other people are apparently able to slouch through a lifetime with no organic difficulties. These puzzling discrepancies can be at least partially explained on the basis of the mechanical principles involved in human movement.

Basically, the human body is a group of levers suspended from a central post. These levers are operated by the muscles through a wonderfully complex system of communication, all of which must operate according to certain precise physical laws. In this sense, the human body is indeed a machine, very little different from other complex machines. (One fundamental difference here is that whereas the manmade machine tends to wear out with hard use, the human machine becomes more efficient with use.) It should be evident that any activity of a machine, human or otherwise, that violates fundamental mechanical principles is bound to suffer in terms of efficient function. It is with this idea in mind that human movement and stance are studied today.

Static Stance

The position in which you find your body as you read these words is an example of **static stance**. It is one of the positions normally assumed by most of us in pursuing our daily activities. Other examples of static stance can be easily observed in any one who is quietly sitting or standing, regardless of the circumstances involved. From a standpoint of mechanics it is possible to evaluate whether or not any laws are being violated and thereby to predict, to a limited extent, some of the difficulties that might be expected to occur.

If, for example, you are in the habit of reading with your book lying flat on the table and your head bent over the desk, the laws of equilibrium and stability would indicate that since the center of gravity of that heavy object (your head) is not directly over the supporting spinal column, an excessive strain must be placed on the muscles at the back of the neck in order to prevent the head from dropping all the way forward to the chest. Ordinarily, a static muscular strain of this kind persisting for any length of time would be expected to generate within the musculature involved a distinctly painful sensation. Such pain would certainly cause the reader to discontinue his activity in order to stretch and massage the neck in an attempt to alleviate the distress of these muscles. Under such conditions it is doubtful that any one would be able to continue long with study or reading of any kind.

Of course, the solution to this problem is relatively simple. Probably the best approach would be to purchase a book stand that would hold the book in a more nearly vertical position, thereby allowing the head to be held erect as the eyes focus on the printing. Some people may prefer simply to prop their heads on their hands in order to take the strain off the neck muscles, and this is certainly mechanically sound. It does, however, have the disadvantage of permitting only very shallow breathing and may position the eyes at an inefficient distance from the page. Both conditions, as well as certain others that could be considered, may interfere with the efficiency of the student in this very important activity.

A great many other illustrations could be cited, but they would all have essentially the same characteristics. The basic principle involved in an analysis of static stance is that of keeping the body segments balanced as well as possible over the bony supporting

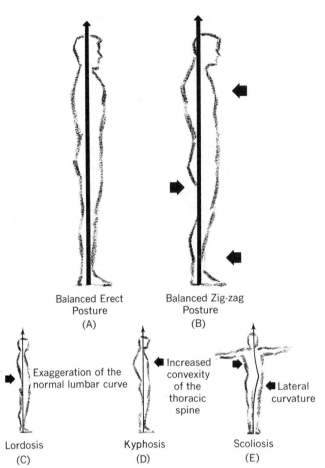

Balanced Erect
Posture
(A)

Balanced Zig-zag
Posture
(B)

Exaggeration of the
normal lumbar curve

Increased
convexity
of the
thoracic
spine

Lateral
curvature

Lordosis
(C)

Kyphosis
(D)

Scoliosis
(E)

FIGURE 9.18 Balanced posture is not necessarily erect posture: (A) no observable faults; (B) slouch with forward head; (C) lordosis; (D) kyphosis; (E) scoliosis.

structures of the body so that no undue "guy-wire" efforts are required of the muscles. It should be recognized that whenever one body segment deviates from a position directly over its point of support, compensation must occur elsewhere in the body in order to prevent the whole body from becoming unbalanced in that direction. In other words, for every "zig" there must be a "zag." As indicated in Figure 9.18, an individual may be able to maintain

perfectly adequate balance among body parts even though one or more of them may initially be out of alignment, but in doing so a certain price must be paid—usually in terms of loss of an esthetically pleasing upright carriage.

Dynamic Stance

So far we have restricted our discussion to static stance. **Dynamic stance** is certainly of equal or even greater importance in terms of body efficiency because most people spend the majority of their waking hours in tasks that require such movements as bending, reaching, walking, sitting down, and getting up. The balance of body parts over their respective bases of support is just as important during movement as it is in static situations. Frequently the stance of individuals reflects things other than merely muscle weakness or other **orthopedic** difficulties. As a matter of fact, these more basic considerations — poor vision, lack of confidence, extreme shyness, and so on — may actually lead to permanent orthopedic problems. Any of these characteristics might result in a habitual stance, such as walking with the head down and the eyes looking at the ground.

Deviations

Some of the common deviations from normal body structure that result from muscle weakness and/or faulty habits of sitting, standing, reading, viewing TV, and studying involve, among other things, exaggerated spinal curvatures.

Of course the normal spinal column has certain curvatures that are *supposed* to be there. These normal curves serve a number of practical functions, one of which is to cushion the brain from the shocks generated by walking, running, and jumping. If the spinal column were constructed without any curvatures, the head would be sitting on top of a rather rigid pillar of bones very much as a building sits on top of its solid foundation blocks. Because, however, the spine does curve, and since, in addition,

there is a compressible cushion between each of its "blocks," the head actually rests on top of a very efficient shock absorber. In this fashion the delicate brain is protected from jarring forces that would otherwise be disastrous.

As shown in Figure 9.18, all the normal curvatures are in a single plane: that is, they run forward and backward only and not from side to side. Between the head and shoulders is the cervical curve. In the shoulder area is the thoracic or dorsal curve; below that, in the hollow of the back, is the lumbar curve. The sacral curvature is formed by the fused bones, on the back part of the pelvis, which are collectively called the sacrum.

An exaggerated humping of the thoracic curve, usually accompanied by round shoulders and a head carried forward of the central axis of the body, is called **kyphosis** (Figure 9.18D). Another condition, sometimes associated with kyphosis because of the "zig-zag" principle just discussed is **lordosis** (Figure 9.18C). In this condition, there is an excessive hollowness of the lumbar area resulting in a swaybacked appearance. This is one of the most frequently observed spinal deviations and one that is often implicated in the cause of low back pain, as has been pointed out previously.

A third spinal deviation frequently observed is one called **scoliosis** (Figure 9.18E). This lateral curvature of the spinal column from left to right, or vice versa, may be present in a single direction in the form of a **C** curve or it may appear as an **S** curvature.

The important thing to realize is that spinal curvatures and other orthopedic abnormalities may start out as merely **functional deviations**. This means that with a change in position the deviation can be corrected or removed. If, however, such deviations are not recognized and the habitual stances responsible for them are not removed, they may become **structural**. This means that the bony structure has actually become permanently modified to accommodate to the habitual position.

Although pride in appearance is sufficient to induce most of us to attempt to stand tall and to walk with a semblance of erect carriage, many of us become careless in the stances we assume while absorbed in our daily tasks. If these unconscious habits become bad enough they may result in our developing conditions unattractive to others and debilitating to ourselves.

Principles Governing Body Mechanics

The efficiency of any activity or performance (including maintenance of static or dynamic posture) depends upon adherence to certain principles (physical laws) of mechanics. Although understanding such principles is obviously not necessary for efficient performance, it is nevertheless true that performance will never reach its maximal effectiveness unless it is actually in harmony with such principles. At the same time, any teacher or coach who has a sound knowledge of such basic principles also has a distinct advantage in correcting errors in performance or in devising new techniques.

Considerable study and experience are needed before one can expect to

FIGURE 9.19 Two factors affecting stability of an object: area of supporting base and height of center of gravity.

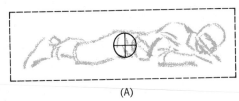
(A)

(B)

(C)

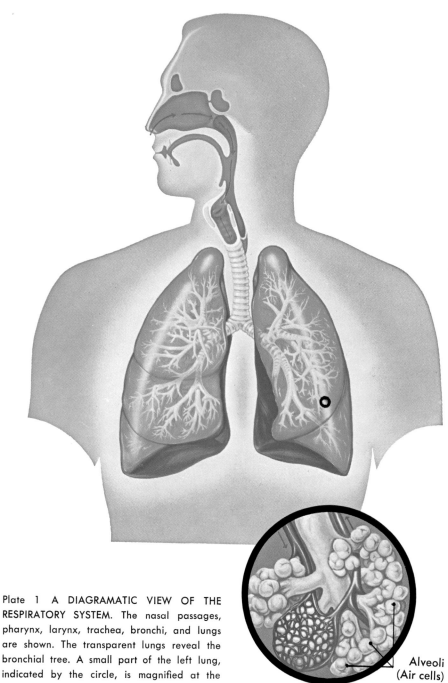

Plate 1 A DIAGRAMATIC VIEW OF THE
RESPIRATORY SYSTEM. The nasal passages,
pharynx, larynx, trachea, bronchi, and lungs
are shown. The transparent lungs reveal the
bronchial tree. A small part of the left lung,
indicated by the circle, is magnified at the
right to show a small bronchus and bronchioles
ending in alveoli, surrounded by a capillary
net between a pulmonary artery and vein.

Alveoli
(Air cells)

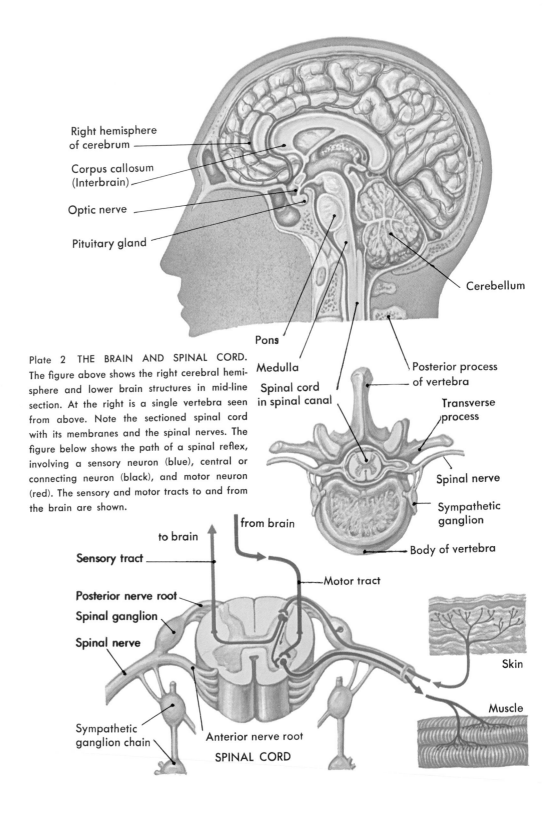

Right hemisphere of cerebrum

Corpus callosum (Interbrain)

Optic nerve

Pituitary gland

Cerebellum

Pons

Plate 2 THE BRAIN AND SPINAL CORD. The figure above shows the right cerebral hemisphere and lower brain structures in mid-line section. At the right is a single vertebra seen from above. Note the sectioned spinal cord with its membranes and the spinal nerves. The figure below shows the path of a spinal reflex, involving a sensory neuron (blue), central or connecting neuron (black), and motor neuron (red). The sensory and motor tracts to and from the brain are shown.

Medulla

Spinal cord in spinal canal

Posterior process of vertebra

Transverse process

Spinal nerve

Sympathetic ganglion

Body of vertebra

from brain

to brain

Sensory tract

Motor tract

Posterior nerve root

Spinal ganglion

Spinal nerve

Skin

Muscle

Sympathetic ganglion chain

Anterior nerve root

SPINAL CORD

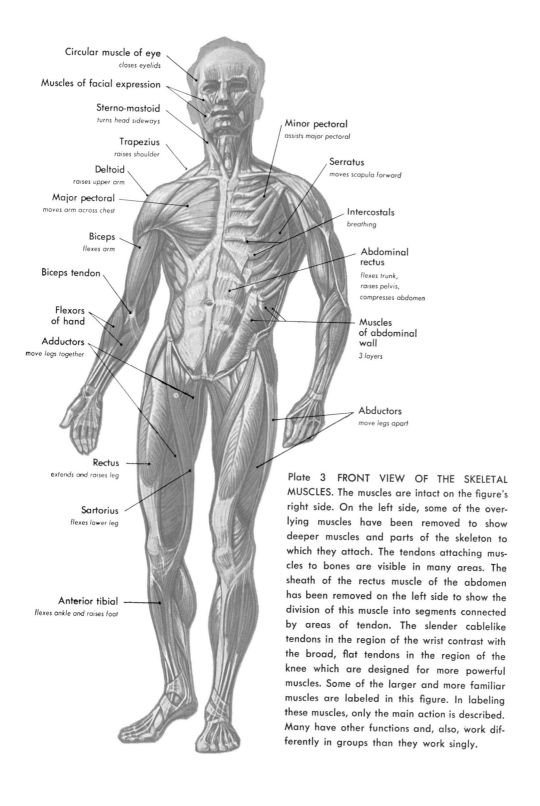

Circular muscle of eye
closes eyelids

Muscles of facial expression

Sterno-mastoid
turns head sideways

Trapezius
raises shoulder

Deltoid
raises upper arm

Major pectoral
moves arm across chest

Biceps
flexes arm

Biceps tendon

Flexors of hand

Adductors
move legs together

Rectus
extends and raises leg

Sartorius
flexes lower leg

Anterior tibial
flexes ankle and raises foot

Minor pectoral
assists major pectoral

Serratus
moves scapula forward

Intercostals
breathing

Abdominal rectus
*flexes trunk,
raises pelvis,
compresses abdomen*

Muscles of abdominal wall
3 layers

Abductors
move legs apart

Plate 3 FRONT VIEW OF THE SKELETAL MUSCLES. The muscles are intact on the figure's right side. On the left side, some of the overlying muscles have been removed to show deeper muscles and parts of the skeleton to which they attach. The tendons attaching muscles to bones are visible in many areas. The sheath of the rectus muscle of the abdomen has been removed on the left side to show the division of this muscle into segments connected by areas of tendon. The slender cablelike tendons in the region of the wrist contrast with the broad, flat tendons in the region of the knee which are designed for more powerful muscles. Some of the larger and more familiar muscles are labeled in this figure. In labeling these muscles, only the main action is described. Many have other functions and, also, work differently in groups than they work singly.

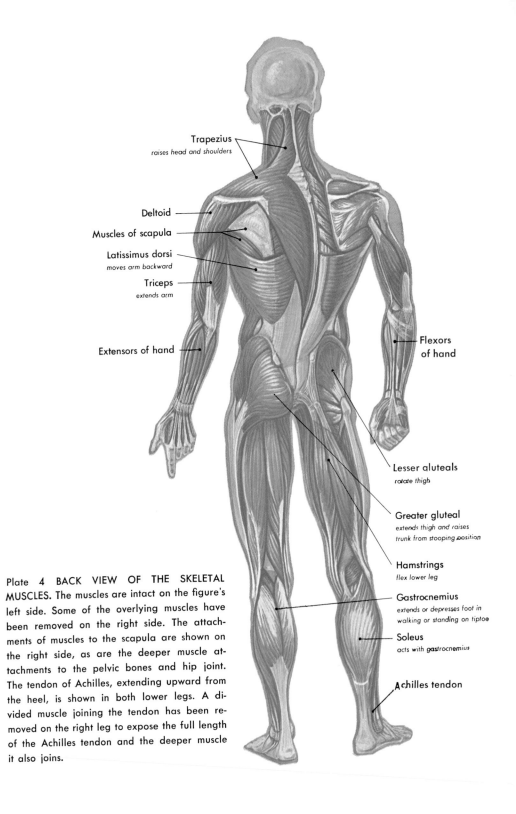

Trapezius
raises head and shoulders

Deltoid

Muscles of scapula

Latissimus dorsi
moves arm backward

Triceps
extends arm

Extensors of hand

Flexors
of hand

Lesser gluteals
rotate thigh

Greater gluteal
*extends thigh and raises
trunk from stooping position*

Hamstrings
flex lower leg

Gastrocnemius
*extends or depresses foot in
walking or standing on tiptoe*

Soleus
acts with gastrocnemius

Achilles tendon

Plate 4 BACK VIEW OF THE SKELETAL
MUSCLES. The muscles are intact on the figure's
left side. Some of the overlying muscles have
been removed on the right side. The attachments of muscles to the scapula are shown on
the right side, as are the deeper muscle attachments to the pelvic bones and hip joint.
The tendon of Achilles, extending upward from
the heel, is shown in both lower legs. A divided muscle joining the tendon has been removed on the right leg to expose the full length
of the Achilles tendon and the deeper muscle
it also joins.

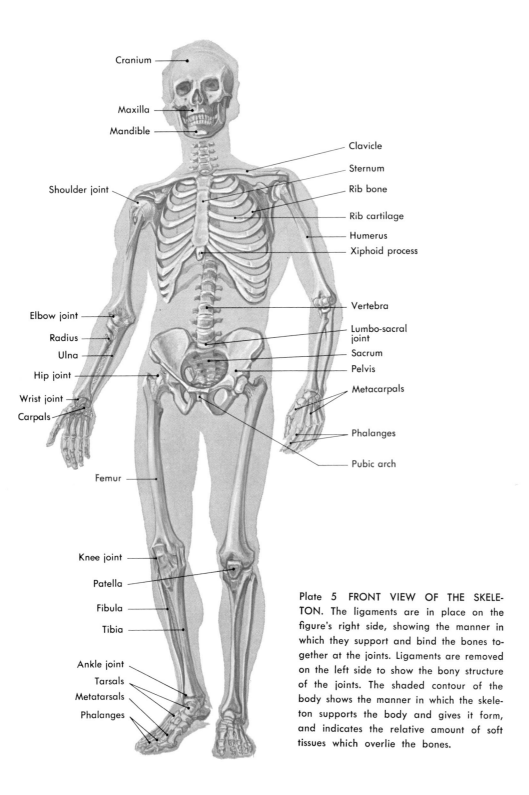

Cranium

Maxilla

Mandible

Clavicle

Sternum

Shoulder joint

Rib bone

Rib cartilage

Humerus

Xiphoid process

Elbow joint

Radius

Ulna

Wrist joint

Carpals

Hip joint

Vertebra

Lumbo-sacral joint

Sacrum

Pelvis

Metacarpals

Phalanges

Pubic arch

Femur

Knee joint

Patella

Fibula

Tibia

Ankle joint

Tarsals

Metatarsals

Phalanges

Plate 5 FRONT VIEW OF THE SKELE-TON. The ligaments are in place on the figure's right side, showing the manner in which they support and bind the bones to-gether at the joints. Ligaments are removed on the left side to show the bony structure of the joints. The shaded contour of the body shows the manner in which the skele-ton supports the body and gives it form, and indicates the relative amount of soft tissues which overlie the bones.

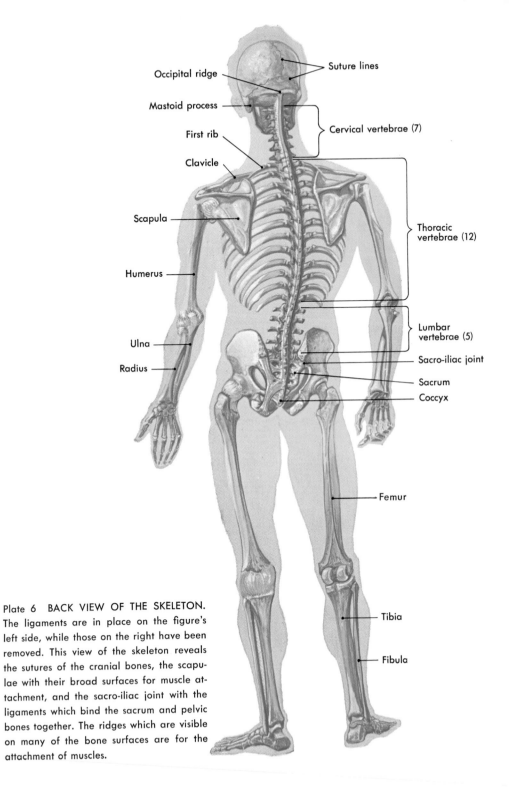

Occipital ridge

Mastoid process

First rib

Clavicle

Scapula

Humerus

Ulna

Radius

Suture lines

Cervical vertebrae (7)

Thoracic vertebrae (12)

Lumbar vertebrae (5)

Sacro-iliac joint

Sacrum

Coccyx

Femur

Tibia

Fibula

Plate 6   BACK VIEW OF THE SKELETON.
The ligaments are in place on the figure's
left side, while those on the right have been
removed. This view of the skeleton reveals
the sutures of the cranial bones, the scapulae with their broad surfaces for muscle attachment, and the sacro-iliac joint with the
ligaments which bind the sacrum and pelvic
bones together. The ridges which are visible
on many of the bone surfaces are for the
attachment of muscles.

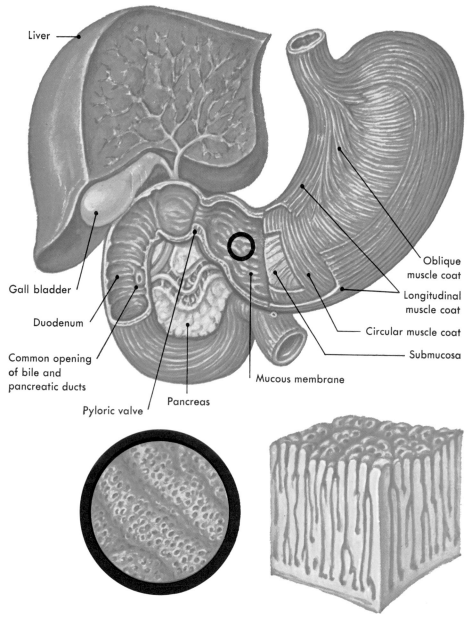

Liver

Gall bladder

Duodenum

Common opening
of bile and
pancreatic ducts

Pyloric valve

Pancreas

Mucous membrane

Oblique
muscle coat

Longitudinal
muscle coat

Circular muscle coat

Submucosa

Plate 7 THE STOMACH AND RELATED ORGANS. The upper view shows the muscle layers and mucous membrane lining the stomach. The sectioned pyloric valve and upper duodenum show internal structure. The sectioned liver shows small bile ducts joining to form the hepatic duct. The cystic duct from the gall bladder joins this and becomes the common bile duct, which enters the duodenum with the pancreatic duct. The black circled area at the lower left is a portion of the mucous membrane of the stomach highly magnified. Note the folds and the many tiny pits, which are openings of the gastric glands. Lower right, a block of mucous membrane shows these glands and their ducts in longitudinal view.

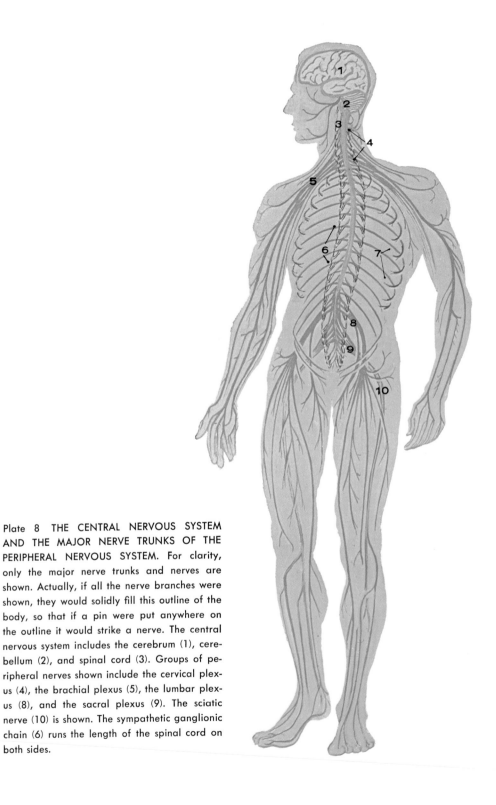

Plate 8 THE CENTRAL NERVOUS SYSTEM
AND THE MAJOR NERVE TRUNKS OF THE
PERIPHERAL NERVOUS SYSTEM. For clarity,
only the major nerve trunks and nerves are
shown. Actually, if all the nerve branches were
shown, they would solidly fill this outline of the
body, so that if a pin were put anywhere on
the outline it would strike a nerve. The central
nervous system includes the cerebrum (1), cerebellum (2), and spinal cord (3). Groups of peripheral nerves shown include the cervical plexus (4), the brachial plexus (5), the lumbar plexus (8), and the sacral plexus (9). The sciatic
nerve (10) is shown. The sympathetic ganglionic
chain (6) runs the length of the spinal cord on
both sides.

make effective use of the "principles approach" to human physical performance. While it is impossible to do little more than introduce the topic here, a brief discussion of some basic concepts follows.

STABILITY The problems encountered in maintaining efficient stance, whether static or dynamic, begin with the area of the supporting base. In general, the broader or wider the base of support the more stable the stance. This principle is illustrated by the football lineman who prepares to meet the charge of his opponent by assuming a position with either one or both hands in contact with the ground. The position has the added advantage of significantly lowering the center of mass (or the **center of gravity**) of the body, which also improves his stability. The illustration in Figure 9.19 shows how both the area of supporting base and height of the center of gravity affect the stability of an object or a person.

It should be noted that the closer the gravity line (a line drawn from the center of gravity perpendicular to the earth's surface) is to the geometric center of the base of support the more stable the object will be. Conversely, as the center of gravity approaches the edge of the base of support, the object —or the individual—becomes progressively more unstable. The moment the gravity line falls outside the base of support the object will fall. Actually, this situation, on a controlled basis, may be entirely desirable. Walking is a good example of this phenomenon. As the body sways forward, the center

of gravity falls forward of the front edge of the base of support, the body begins to fall only to be saved by the forward swing of the trailing leg. As a matter of fact, this sequence, which we call *walking,* has been described aptly as "a series of disasters, narrowly averted."

Similar conditions prevail in the stances assumed by athletes in various sports. The sprinter raises his center of gravity by raising his hips higher than his shoulders, then leans forward over his hands (see Figure 9.20) in order to become as *unstable* as possible in the direction in which he intends to move. As the gun sounds, no time is wasted in getting his body moving forward, driven by the force of his hard-driving legs. The wrestler, on the other hand, assumes a stance (when standing) with a lowered center of gravity and a gravity line directly over the center of the base of support. The reason for the difference here is that the wrestler does not

FIGURE 9.20 Effect of location of gravity line on stability. Sprinter wishes to be "off balance" in order to move forward quickly; the wrestler may need to move suddenly in any direction.

Base of Support

Base of Support

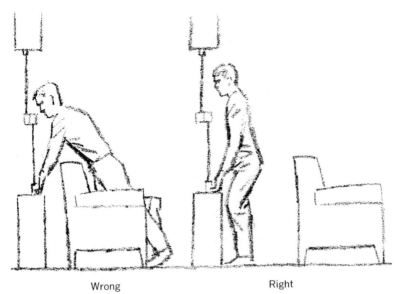

Wrong   Right

FIGURE 9.21 Correct and incorrect ways of raising a window.

know in exactly which direction he will need to move at any given instant; therefore he assumes a position that gives equal advantage to any move that he must make. His low center of gravity is obviously necessary because he must be prepared to resist the charge of his opponent. If he lowers the center of gravity he will become proportionately more difficult to upset.

The stance assumed by the football lineman differs from that of the wrestler in that the lineman knows the direction from which he will be attacked. To prepare for this change he shifts his center of gravity toward the edge of the supporting base that is closest to his opponent. This gives him maximal stability in the specific direction in which it is needed.

Sometimes game strategy will dictate compromises in certain otherwise desirable practices in the interests of deception. Thus a team using plays that require linemen to pull out and move in directions other than straight ahead will have to sacrifice something in terms of mechanical efficiency at times in order to avoid tipping off the opponent as to which play is going to be run.

FORCE Very closely related to stability is *force*, which also deserves consideration in any discussion of the mechanics of human physical activity. It has been pointed out that the human body is capable of generating great amounts of force when the occasion demands. Occasionally this great capacity that some of the large muscles develop can work to the detriment of the total body if certain principles are violated.

Some time ago a well-known major league batter was involved in a serious home accident. His home was equipped with an air-conditioning unit designed to fit into a window opening, and one day he decided to move the unit into another room where it was more urgently needed. The unit was relatively heavy, but this athlete was a huge, strapping physical specimen with biceps so large that he was unable to wear the usual baseball shirt comfortably. In lifting the air-conditioner he was forced to reach across a radiator in front of the window. He bent over, grasped the unit with both hands and lifted suddenly. But as he did so the small muscles of his lower back were unable to resist the tremendous strain

placed upon them, and they gave way, resulting in an injury that shortened his major league career.

Year after year many strong, healthy people suffer similar injuries because of ignorance or carelessness in lifting and carrying heavy objects (Figures 9.21 and 9.22). In order to avoid such senseless injuries, a few fundamental principles need to be observed.

First, when lifting, it is important to allow the strongest muscles we have to do the job, that is, the muscles of the legs. In this connection it is interesting to note two important facts that have emerged from the study of lifting injuries. Morris, Lucas, and Bressler (404) have calculated the amount of force that must be borne by the lumbar

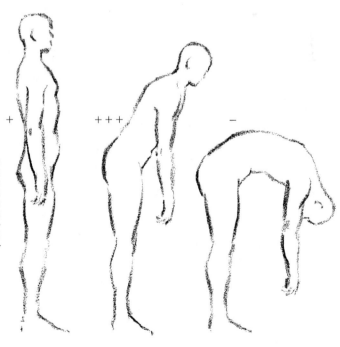

FIGURE 9.22 The erector spinae muscles are active in extending the spine except in a position of complete trunk flexion, as indicated. Even in the initial stages of heavy lifting these muscles remain relaxed when this position is assumed. The dangers to the vertebral ligaments and joints when lifting "with the back," are apparent. Source: J. V. Basmajian, "Man's Posture," *Archives of Physical Medicine and Rehabilitation*, 46:32, 1965.

+   + + +   −

FIGURE 9.23 Sitting, rising, and lifting. Above, proper placement of the feet provides a base of support permitting graceful sitting and rising. Below, placement of the feet and proper use of the legs result in a lifting technique that is both safe and attractive. Source: Ellen Davis Kelly– ADAPTED AND CORRECTIVE PHYSICAL EDUCATION–Fourth Edition–Copyright © 1965 The Ronald Press Company, New York.

sacral disc in bending from the waist (see Figure 9.22) to lift an object weighing 200 pounds. For a man of average dimensions (170 pounds) this force was calculated to be 1483 pounds. It is clear that under such conditions the spinal column needs strong support from the muscles in order to maintain its integrity. The irony of this situation is that these muscles (*erector spinae*) are almost completely inactive (apparently due to inhibition) when the back is fully flexed as shown in Figure 9.22. Basmajian reports that this situation persists during the initial movements of back extension (186). Thus, the lift must be initiated without the aid of the intimate supporting musculature. In this case it is easy to see the wisdom of bending the knees and performing the lift with the spine erect for greatest support.

In addition to remaining erect, it is important to channel the lines of force along the longitudinal axes of the spinal column and the long bones of the body rather than at right angles to them (see Figure 9.23). This means that any heavy object should be carried as close to the body as possible in order to avoid the necessity for small-muscle groups, which are not well designed for lifting, to counteract forces built up by leverage. In addition, the base of support should be made as wide as is practical. By avoiding sudden lifts, by keeping the forces parallel to long bones, including the spinal column, and by not attempting loads clearly beyond one's normal capacity, one should be able to go through life without ever suffering this kind of injury.

Pain Avoidance

Another way in which faulty mechanics can contribute to malfunction of the body is often observed as a secondary or indirect result of an injury. People are reluctant to place themselves in positions where pain or discomfort is likely to occur. In fact, most people will go to considerable lengths to avoid this kind of discomfort. It should not be surprising, then, to learn that one of the frequent causes of muscular strain and spasm is a prior injury. Football trainers have for years been concerned with the rehabilitation of ankle and knee injuries sustained by athletes in this sport. One of the most frequently observed complications is the development of serious discomfort to the knee joint as a result of favoring an ankle injury. The injured player tends to walk with the affected foot turned outward with a limp, which causes the knee on that side to bend slightly during the weight-bearing phase. As this occurs, the ligaments on the medial or inner side of the knee joint are forced to bear the weight of the body in an unnatural manner, causing them to become strained and irritated. Similarly, low-back pain may result when a player favors an injured knee in such a manner as to throw an unusual amount of strain on the muscles of the lumbar region.

Dizzy Dean is a familiar name to baseball fans. This colorful, former professional baseball player was one of the truly great pitchers. He and his brother Paul pitched the St. Louis Cardinals to prominence in the late 1930s. During an all-star game in 1937, Dizzy Dean was struck on the foot by a batted ball. The injury was not serious, and he was soon pitching as usual. He felt some pain in his foot as he threw the ball, but Dizzy found that if he stepped slightly differently as he completed his delivery he had no pain in his foot. However, almost immediately an extremely serious inflammation developed in his arm and shoulder. A series of treatments helped to some extent, but his pitching effectiveness dropped rapidly, and he was forced to retire from the game. A slight alteration in his normal pitching pattern had thrown sufficient strain onto muscles unaccustomed to such a burden that they became severely injured.

Such substitution patterns are the rule rather than the exception wherever pain exists, whether the injury is slight or of major proportions. If the afflicted individual is aware of the dangers of such substitution patterns, he can take the necessary precautions to avoid further complications. Generally, such precautions must include the acceptance of the fact that some pain must be expected and endured if the injured limb is to be returned to full function.

EFFERENT EFFECTS

EFFECTS OF PHYSICAL ACTIVITY ON NEUROMUSCULAR AND SKELETAL FACTORS

We have outlined the basic structure and function of the neuromuscular and skeletal systems and have pointed out how human performance is limited by the capacities of these systems. In other words, we have shown how one's exercise capacity is affected by one's levels of strength, endurance, power, flexibility, and the way in which one coordinates these elements into purposeful activity.

It is the purpose of this section to examine the other side of the coin, namely, how does exercise affect the organism?

You will remember that there are two broad categories of effects attributable to exercise or physical activity. The first is the immediate or *acute* effect. Examples would be such things as increased heart rate, increased respiration, perspiration, and similar systemic responses. In addition, the fatigue resulting from a bout of hard work, and even the muscle soreness experienced twenty-four hours later, are also generally classified as acute effects.

Chronic, or long-term, effects of exercise are, on the other hand, usually called *training effects.* Such effects would be observed over a relatively long period of time during which a series of exercise bouts occurred. Although it is possible for training effects to be observed in a very short period of time (perhaps only two or three days), in certain cases the term *training* usually refers to a period of several weeks or even several years.

Examples of chronic effects would be such things as increased strength, decreased heart rate for a given task, improved muscular coordination, and improved flexibility. Sometimes it is difficult to strictly separate training effects from learning. Indeed, in one sense, some kinds of motor learning

might be considered to be effects of training because they are relatively permanent changes, and they have resulted from repeated exposure to a task. It should not be thought that "learning" and the chronic effects of exercise are synonymous. In most instances we are able to differentiate clearly between these two phenomena. Learning will be discussed in some detail elsewhere in this book.

Strength

The immediate effect of exercise on strength, muscular endurance, and power is quite obvious. During vigorous participation, at least, there is a significant decrement in each of these parameters. As the recovery period progresses, the original levels are gradually regained. It is not expected, however, that a single experience will significantly improve strength or endurance levels. When a second trial does appear to be substantially better than the first, this disparity is usually explained as being due to "learning" rather than to any actual physiological change.

One of the problems frequently encountered in designing strength studies is that most test procedures involve the manipulation of testing apparatus requiring a certain amount of skill. Frequently, brief experience with such apparatus can produce significant increases in scores, even in the absence of any real "training effect." Figure 9.24 shows how such "practice" can affect scores on four successive days of testing. The lesson to be learned from this illustration is that if a group were to be tested only once and then subjected to a training period, it would be impossible to determine how much of the improvement was due to actual strength gains and how much to the "learning" aspect of the test itself. (Of course, the use of a control group provides at least a partial solution to the problem. See Chapter 4.) Some investigators have adopted the practice of pretesting until a plateau is reached before beginning the actual training period.

Chronic Effects of Exercise on Strength

In recent years a great deal of research has gone into the study of the most effective ways of developing strength, power, and muscular endurance in man. This has been prompted primarily by those interested in improving the performance of athletes and by others working in physical rehabilitation.

ISOMETRIC STRENGTH TRAINING The work of two German physiologists, Theodore Hettinger and E. A. Muller, published in 1953, triggered a widespread interest in strength training systems based upon isometric contraction (479). Picked up by the popular press and promoted by equipment manufacturing concerns, "isometrics" has almost become a household word. So many claims have been made for exercise systems falling into this category that the original findings of Drs. Hettinger and Muller, as well as a wealth of information made available more recently, have been disregarded.

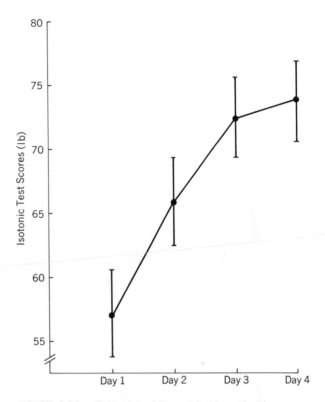

FIGURE 9.24   This plot of isometric strength scores of six men shows that strength appeared to increase on tests administered over four successive days. Gains of this kind in the absence of training are usually attributed to "learning" rather than physiological improvement. Source: Irwin (263).

In the original Hettinger and Muller report, which dealt with the muscles of the forearm that flex the wrist, it was concluded that a single six-second contraction involving two thirds of maximal effort, performed once a day, would develop the strength of the muscles involved as rapidly and to as great an extent as they were capable of attaining. Under this program an increase in strength of 5 percent per week was reported. Subsequent studies, however, indicated that this rate of increase does not always occur. In 1958 Hettinger found only a 3.3 percent increase per week, and in 1961 he reported a 1.8 percent increase. In these cases, however, a training program requiring only a single, one-second maximal contraction once a day was followed. One other important factor was discussed by Muller and Rohmert in 1963. This factor, called "endkraft," is the actual "limit" or ultimate strength potential of the individual. It was shown that the rate of strength increase was related to how close the subjects were to their "endkraft." Those who were close failed to improve as rapidly as others who were farther below their potential.

ISOMETRIC VERSUS ISOTONIC TRAINING
In recent years a great many other studies have been conducted in the area of isometric or static strength training. Although most of these studies have

tended to confirm the basic findings of Hettinger and Muller, others have contradicted them (373, 449, 479, 606). Petersen (449) for example, using an experimental design similar to those of his predecessors, reported no such gains in strength as had been observed by Hettinger and Muller. Mayberry (373) also indicated that a program including a once-daily maximal contraction had no effect on strength.

In general, most studies have indicated that, at least for the average person or for those not close to "endkraft," isometric training can effectively increase isometric strength levels.

There is lack of general agreement on the relative merits of static and dynamic training procedures in strength development. Apparently the strength gains originally reported by Hettinger and Muller are somewhat higher than have generally been encountered by others, but this may be due to the fact

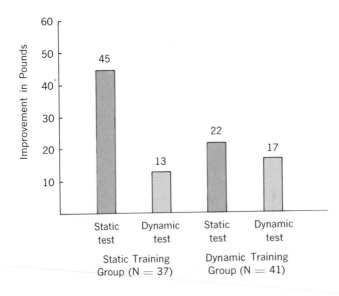

FIGURE 9.25 A comparison of the relative effects of isometric and isotonic tests. Data from Berger (51).

that their subjects were untrained individuals who were a long way from their peak potential, whereas subjects in other studies were often individuals in better than average physical condition.

One of the most important criticisms of isometric methods is that strength is not increased throughout the range of motion of the joint involved. Because there is no limb movement in this type of training, tension is exerted by the muscles involved only at certain angles of joint flexion. It has been demonstrated by Gardner (202) that very often strength improves at the particular training angle involved but is not changed at other points in the range of motion. It is probably for this reason that studies such as that reported by Berger (51) have found that if a person is trained by isometric methods and then tested by isometric methods, he will show the expected increases; if, on the other hand, he is tested by isotonic or dynamic methods (as in lifting a weight), his strength is relatively unaffected by isometric training. It is not so easy to explain why the reverse is also true. According to Berger (Figure (9.25), a person who trains by isotonic methods improves more when tested isotonically than when tested isometrically. This has been partially substantiated in a study in our own laboratory, where men training isotonically showed much greater gains on isotonic tests than on isometric tests (Figure 9.26).

Such phenomena as these are commonly observed when human adaptation to exercise stress is studied. The

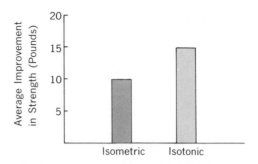

FIGURE 9.26 Average improvement in a group of men engaged in isotonic training as measured by both isotonic and isometric means. Data from Irwin (263).

term used to describe this process is *specificity of training,* which simply means that a person gets what he trains for. This applies not only to static or dynamic strength but also to all the other factors we have described.

The use of eccentric contraction for building strength has received little attention as a means of strength development except, perhaps, in rehabilitation and therapeutic applications. The question has been raised, "Can eccentric training improve strength?" Theoretically, there is no reason to presume that it would not. Logan (350) concluded that there was little difference between the training effects of concentric and eccentric contractions of the quadriceps muscle groups. There has, however, been some work that indicates that eccentric training is not an effective method of increasing strength. Petersen (449), for example, concluded that eccentric training was not effective in increasing strength. The training load used in his study was approximately 20 to 30 percent over the maximum *isometric* value obtained in testing. Subjects were simply required to lower this load slowly for a given number of times during each training session and were tested for maximum isometric strength before and after the training.

In order to shed more light on this question of strength development through eccentric training, a study was conducted in our laboratory (265), in which subjects were required to train with a load that constantly *exceeded* their maximal isotonic lifting ability to 20 percent. It was discovered that this training program was definitely effective in producing strength increases. The graph in Figure 9.27 shows the amount of improvement experienced by the experimental group as revealed by both isotonic and isometric tests. It is interesting to note that great-

er improvement resulted in the isotonic measure than in the isometric measure. The training task was performed on the same isotonic apparatus that was used for the isotonic strength test.

Muscular Endurance

As was true of strength, it is doubtful whether there is such a thing as an acute effect of exercise where muscular endurance is involved. Some of the same problems of measurement are encountered, and the learning effect may compound the training effects.

The chronic effects of exercise on muscular endurance are sometimes quite startling. This is particularly true from the viewpoint of the layman who has failed to understand the important distinctions between strength and endurance. An example will serve to il-

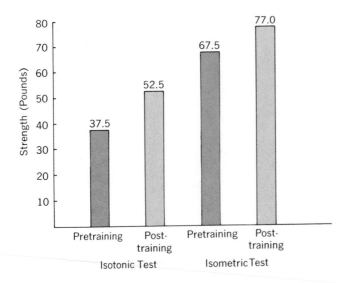

FIGURE 9.27 Strength improvement resulting from eccentric muscular training as measured by both isotonic and isometric tests. Data from Irwin (263).

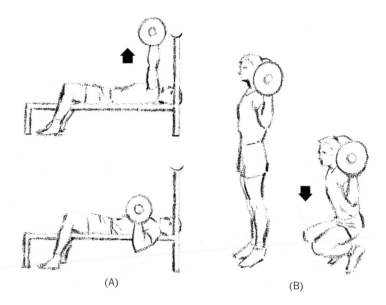

FIGURE 9.28 Illustration of the bench-press exercise (A) and the half-squat (B).

(A)

(B)

lustrate this concept: If a person desired to increase the strength of his triceps (the muscles that enable him to straighten his elbow), he could perform an exercise called "bench presses." In this exercise he lies on his back on a narrow bench and raises a barbell from his chest to a position above the chest with the arms fully extended (Figure 9.28).

Assuming that you could begin this exercise with about sixty-five pounds for four or five repetitions, you might reason that adding one or two repetitions each day should certainly increase the strength of the muscles involved in this task. If you were serious about your exercise program, highly motivated and conscientious, you could probably increase the number of repetitions of which you are capable from five to 100 in a relatively short training period. The question is, have you increased your strength? You will recall

that strength was defined as the maximum force an individual is capable of exerting under a set of prescribed conditions. It is easy to see that in this situation the force necessary to raise the weight each time has not changed. We have seen that you would probably be able to raise the weight many more times than was previously possible (that is, muscular endurance has improved), but we do not know whether you would be capable of raising any greater weight. Experimental evidence indicates that you probably would not be able to lift a much greater weight than you would have been able to lift before the training period began.

In one recent experiment (583) subjects were asked to sit on the edge of a table and extend the lower leg to which a weight had been attached. As soon as all subjects could lift a maximum weight of sixty pounds once, they were

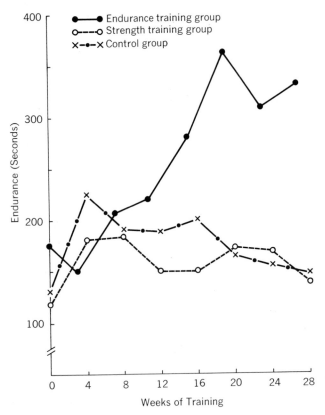

FIGURE 9.29 Illustration of the specific effects of muscular endurance training. After the eighth week subjects training for endurance (isometric holding time) continued to improve; strength-training and control groups did not. Source: E. R. Vanderhoof, C. J. Imig, and H. M. Hines, "Effect of Muscle Strength and Endurance Development on Blood Flow," *Journal of Applied Physiology, 16*:873, 1961.

divided into two groups. Group I continued to lift the sixty-pound weight an increasing number of times each day for five weeks, eventually reaching 100 repetitions. Group II continued with ten repetitions of maximal weights each day (10 *RM*) for the five weeks. At the end of the experimental period, Group I was found to have no significant increase in strength, whereas the members of Group II had doubled their strength. Unfortunately, tests were not conducted to see whether this "overload" group (Group II) had also increased in endurance.

In another study that employed isometric strength and isometric endurance, it was demonstrated that subjects who participated in strength training increased in strength but not in endurance (Figure 9.29). On the other hand, it was found that subjects who trained for endurance (static holding time) increased in strength just as much as did the strength-training group (581). The finding would seem to imply that all endurance training also increases strength. It should be recalled, however, that many research studies of isometric training have demonstrated strength gains resulting from contractions well below maximum. This would seem to be another bit of evidence in support of a submaximal strength training concept.

In general, the available research indicates that if one wishes to increase the strength of a muscle or muscle group, it is necessary to *overload* the movement the muscles produce. As strength increases, the overload must be constantly adjusted upward in order to assure continued improvement. As generally used, the term "overload" is somewhat inappropriate, but it does refer to the application of resistance that is substantially greater than is *normally encountered* by the muscles involved.

It should be noted that there is a number of ways in which an overload can be applied in training. The means utilized will depend upon the goals desired. And because the law of specificity is so important, considerable attention needs to be given to the training design.

If strength is desired, the resistance or weight should be progressively increased. Repetitions should be kept to a minimum, possibly to as few as two or three in a set, with sets repeated only after a rest period.

For the development of endurance, "repetition" becomes the key. Increasing the number of repetitions at a constant resistance, or the time of "holding" in the case of static work, is the type of overload indicated.

It is also possible to create an overload by increasing the rate at which work against a constant resistance is

performed. From a theoretical standpoint this should be an effective type of overload for producing strength increases (237). From a practical standpoint, however, this approach has not been adequately demonstrated.

One of the arguments for isometric exercises has been that the overload is always at a maximum because every repetition was performed at the greatest force that the subject could exert. One of the early problems was the fact that the subject himself could never be sure that he was not deceiving himself

(A)

(B)

FIGURE 9.30 Overload training techniques utilized in the experiment described in the text: (A) standard squats; (B) jumping with weights held in hands.

because there was no "feedback" in terms of how much force he was actually exerting. A number of devices with scales and dials for recording force have recently appeared on the market. With such apparatus, goals can be more easily set and progress assessed.

Another innovation has been recently advocated for strength development, particularly muscle rehabilitation (448, 579). This technique called "isokinetic" training involves a motor-driven resistance that permits movement of the limb at a constant rate and that simultaneously records the force being exerted by the limb. Among other features, this has the advantage of forcing the muscle to work at or near its greatest capacity throughout its entire range of motion. A recorder provides continuous feedback as well as permanent records of the performance. Whether this technique has any real advantages over more traditional techniques remains to be determined.

PAIN THRESHOLDS   Intimately tied up in the matter of muscular endurance is the problem of an individual's ability to continue an activity despite feelings of pain and discomfort. Most of us, when engaged in any attempt to perform up to our maximal capacity in muscular endurance activities, cease long before our theoretical physiological limits have been reached. The reason for this is that we are simply unable to stand the pain. One adaptation resulting from training in any type of physical activity, particularly that which involves muscular endurance, is an increased tolerance or ability to en-

dure discomfort, commonly termed an "increased pain threshold." That pain thresholds vary considerably among people has long been apparent. Women are often considered better able to endure pain than are men. The threshold and tolerance are not yet understood. Several recent studies have produced evidence that "suggestion" and other motivational variables can result in great improvement in performance of strength and endurance (see Chapter 14).

It is interesting to note that training one leg has been found to increase the muscular endurance of the other *non-exercised* leg as much as 200 percent (236). It is extremely doubtful that such dramatic gains could be due to physiological changes.

Individuals who train to develop great muscular endurance also benefit from an elevated pain threshold as well as a distinct increase in the number of functioning capillaries that supply blood to the muscle tissue. The commonly accepted theory (450) is that these capillaries are not entirely new, but have simply been dormant until the increased demand for oxygen has caused them to open up and become functional. Whatever the explanation, the net effect is to make possible increased ability to persist in muscular contraction for greater periods of time with less discomfort and more rapid recovery.

Power

Relatively little research concerning the effects of training on muscular power was available until recent years. Little is known about the acute effects of exercise, but considerable attention has been devoted to the improvement of power (particularly jumping activities) by means of weight training.

Not long ago most athletes shunned any type of weight training because of the fear of becoming "muscle-bound." Some people refused to be taken in by the myth that weight training produces a loss in flexibility and in freedom of movement, however, and O'Connor (432) at the University of Iowa applied some of the research findings by adopting a program of heavy resistance exercises for the development of leg strength in his basketball players. The success of this and similar programs was so great that weight training today has a prominent place in virtually every major athletic activity.

As was pointed out previously, power is dependent on speed of movement as well as on strength. In one of our own studies (275) a group of subjects trained by traditional heavy resistance exercise methods involving squats and toe raises with a heavy barbell on the shoulders while members of another group trained by jumping while holding dumbbells in their hands. Although both groups improved in jumping ability, the group that overloaded the specific task they were trying to improve showed greater improvements than the group that used the traditional generalized techniques.

Similar results were achieved in a study (549) involving the rope climb. In this investigation it appeared that men who already had sufficient strength and power to climb the rope profited more from specific power overload than did those who initially had insufficient strength and power to make it to the top of the rope. These latter subjects apparently profited more from endurance (not power) training exercises. The interpretation here is that if sufficient strength or muscular endurance is not available for the task to begin with, the minimal amount must be developed before the specific power training involving the explosiveness of the movement can be profitably utilized.

Flexibility

As has been previously stated, joint flexibility is largely dependent on the extent to which the joints are used (see Figure 9.41). Any joint that is immobilized for any length of time (as is the case when a broken arm is placed in a cast, for example), will become inflexible. In such instances, the muscles that operate the joint develop contractures, or a condition of "permanent" shortening that makes extensive movement extremely difficult and frequently very painful. By persistent, active stretching of contractures, muscles can be returned to their normal condition in reasonably short periods of time. In cases of severe injury, or when an older person is involved, to return joint flexibility to normal after long periods of immobility is more difficult. Occasionally it is necessary to take special steps to reduce pain associated with stretching exercises. The use of drugs and hypnotic suggestion in such cases is quite common. However, the successful rehabilitation of such patients is almost always directly dependent on the persistence and determination of the patient.

Of course, all joint problems are not restricted to the condition of the surrounding musculature. Sometimes changes take place within the joint itself. Injury or disease can cause difficulties affecting joint surfaces, cartilage, ligaments or other surrounding tissues. Degenerative changes can also result from lack of movement. It is partly for this reason, if for no other, that physicians insist upon moderate exercises for patients suffering from diseases and injuries affecting the joints, even though pain is invariably involved.

Acute Effects of Exercise

Most of us have experienced the fact that the ability to stretch and bend is considerably improved by some preliminary warming up exercises. Indeed, one of the criticisms of the Kraus-Weber tests was that children who were unable to touch their toes (and therefore flunked the test) were discovered to be able to perform this task satisfactorily after a brief practice or warm up period. While scientific documentation is lacking, the belief persists among experienced athletes and coaches that insufficient warm up before certain running and jumping events tends to increase the probability of "muscle pulls" and other injuries. (It should be noted that

there is some evidence that this belief may be unfounded in fact) (292). In any case, it is evident that all of us (whether our joints are normal or impaired in some way) find our flexibility significantly improved after engaging in a few moments of preliminary activity during which muscles are stretched and "warmed up."

Chronic Effects

As has already been indicated, the prescription of exercise for the improvement of flexibility is common. The fact is that flexibility can be tremendously improved over a reasonably short period. Although most of us tend to develop only the amount of flexibility required in our daily tasks, others have purposely utilized exercise to produce unusual ranges of joint motion. Practitioners of Yoga are good examples of people who fall into this category, as are some athletes, particularly swimmers, hurdlers, and gymnasts. Such extremes in flexibility are obviously not necessary for most of us, but the fact remains that normal flexibility is important and is relatively easy to attain through training. (Some simple tests of joint flexibility are presented on page 303.)

Body Mechanics

The basic structure of the body cannot be altered as an acute effect of one or two exercise bouts. Of course it is sometimes possible to momentarily correct faulty alignment by the assumption of certain positions (see Figure 9.31), but as soon as such postures are dropped, the alignment problem reappears.

It is also true, of course, that a single lesson or demonstration can result in the learning of more efficient ways of performing some coordinated activity. This could be considered an improvement in body mechanics, and this is a desirable sort of end product.

In general, however, substantial improvement in body structure or in the mechanical efficiency of the body does not occur without considerable effort over a period of time. A lateral curvature of the spine (scoliosis), for example, can sometimes be markedly improved by repeatedly stretching muscles on one side and strengthening muscles on the other. Such a program, requiring progressive overload training and active stretching exercises, usually requires quite some time to be effective. Similarly, certain faulty movement patterns require time and practice before they can be corrected satisfactorily. This may be because of the time required for a learning phenomenon to occur or simply because the required strength or endurance cannot be developed overnight.

Certain mechanical characteristics can never be altered by exercise. Although it may be argued whether basic body types (somatotypes) can ever be changed, it is apparent that a person with a small skeletal frame cannot make any extensive changes in this structure through exercise. In such cases the most that could be expected would be that a

certain amount of muscular hypertrophy might give the appearance of a larger skeleton. Conversely, exercise can contribute to an apparent reduction in body size by means of weight reduction. This has no real effect on basic body structure. Such structure is determined by hereditary factors and can be altered little, if any, by exercise programs. The one exception to this rule might occur during the growth years, when it is conceivable that excessive exercise, or inadequate activity, might affect normal growth and developmental patterns (see Chapter 16).

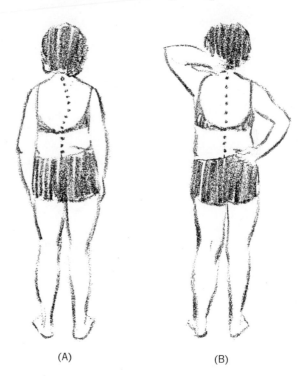

(A)   (B)

FIGURE 9.31   The Key Position is used to obtain an indication of whether scoliosis is due to permanent structural deviations or to other, more easily correctable factors.

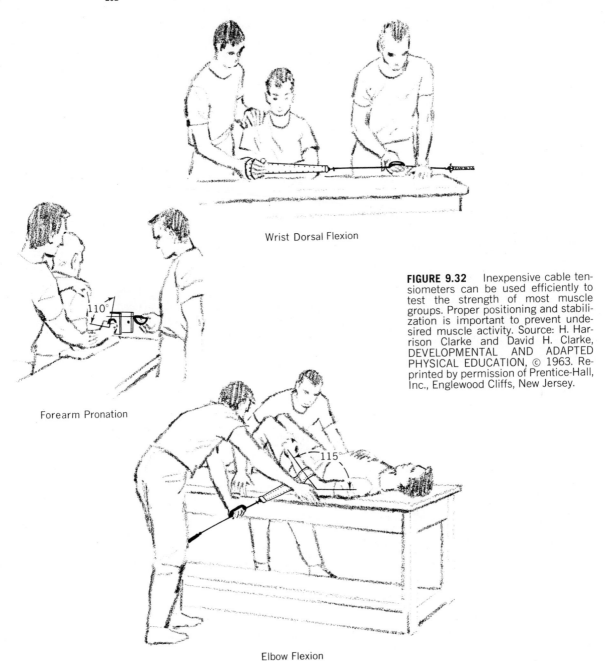

Wrist Dorsal Flexion

Forearm Pronation

Elbow Flexion

FIGURE 9.32   Inexpensive cable tensiometers can be used efficiently to
test the strength of most muscle
groups. Proper positioning and stabili-
zation is important to prevent undesired muscle activity. Source: H. Harrison Clarke and David H. Clarke,
DEVELOPMENTAL AND ADAPTED
PHYSICAL EDUCATION, © 1963. Reprinted by permission of Prentice-Hall,
Inc., Englewood Cliffs, New Jersey.

EVALUATION TECHNIQUES FOR NEUROMUSCULAR FUNCTION

MUSCLE STRENGTH APPRAISAL

In terms of health, it appears to be much less important to appraise one's strength than to test CR capacity and flexibility, but it is of some importance as an index to general physical degeneration through the years. The techniques of measurement will be described briefly here. Strength measurement must involve equipment of some kind. Some of this equipment is so relatively inexpensive that one can generally find some means of evaluating strength on a continuing basis.

Isometric Strength

Measurement of isometric strength requires some means of actually measuring the force exerted. In the laboratory, strain gauges, cable tensiometers, and dynamometers are utilized. It is not practical to discuss these instruments here. Commercial devices are available at most sporting goods stores at low cost that will suffice for isometric testing. With some knowledge of muscle groups and their actions and with some ingenuity one can devise a method to measure the isometric strength of almost any muscle or muscle group. Dr. H. Harrison Clarke, a pioneer in the science of isometric strength testing, has developed very objective and reliable techniques for measuring isometric strength of most large-muscle groups of the body (104).

There are some precautions to be followed if isometric testing is to be reliable and meaningful to you over the years:

1. The state of "fatigue" at time of test (general or local fatigue) will affect the results. Try to minimize this.
2. The position of the body must be the same and should eliminate other muscle groups as much as possible (see Figure 9.32).
3. Because your reading of isometric force will depend upon the angle at which you pull (Figure 9.33), keep this

FIGURE 9.33 Maximum isometric force at various angles of pull and maximum isotonic force exerted continually through the range of motion for elbow flexors. Adapted by permission from W. Doss, and P. V. Karpovich, "A Comparison of Concentric, Eccentric, and Isometric Strength of Elbow Flexors," *Journal of Applied Physiology*, 20:352, 1965.

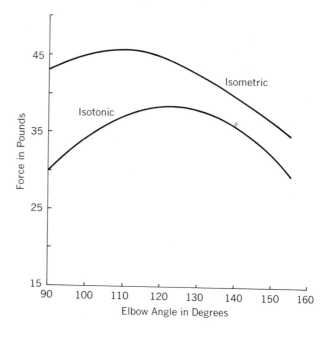

the same each time you test a particular muscle or muscle group.

4. You should test-retest several times to establish the reliability of your scores.

Dynamic or Isotonic Strength

Measurement of dynamic strength must involve either weights or some kind of laboratory equipment. To test for 1 RM, simply standardize body position and, by trial and error, establish the greatest weight you can move through the full range of motion. For the most reliable results, follow the precautions laid down for isometric tests—in other words, standardize as many environmental variables as possible. Allow at least five minutes between trials; when you know you are approaching your maximum, ten minutes' rest is advisable.

Muscular Endurance (ME) Appraisal

In any attempt to evaluate **muscular endurance,** it is important to remember

that muscular endurance is specific only for a given load. That is, for the same individual, moving a resistance of twenty pounds repeatedly is certainly not equivalent to an effort involving eighty pounds. Any test of ME will, by definition of strength, involve a resistance that is *less than maximal.* The number of times a movement can be repeated before "fatigue" sets in will depend, in addition to the actual ME and motivation, upon two factors: (1) the percentage of maximal involved (see Figure 9.34), and (2) the rate of contraction. Thus, if all other environmental and internal factors remain constant, the lighter the load and/or the slower the rate (up to a point), the greater will be the measured ME. A complicating factor must be considered, however. A slow rate, if it necessitates slow eccentric lengthening "contractions," will serve to shorten ME because of the additional work load involved in slowly lowering the weight. The procedure for testing ME must

FIGURE 9.34 Effects of rate of contraction and percentage of maximal strength on muscular endurance. Data from Tuttle and Schottelius (573) and Adams and McCristal (2).

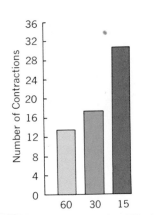

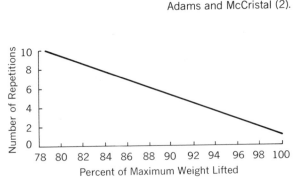

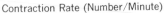

therefore account for a standardized method of lowering the weight—either by gravity or by slow eccentric contractions. This factor becomes more critical as the rate of repetition is decreased.

It is a relatively simple matter to test isotonic endurance. Weights can often be employed but when these are not available, the traditional tests using the subject's own body weight as the resistance can be substituted (pull-ups,

TABLE 9.2 Standardization of Muscular Endurance Tests

MUSCLE GROUP	TEST(S)	PROCEDURES TO BE STANDARDIZED
Elbow flexors	Biceps curl	Grip on bar (forward or reversed).
		Distance between hands.
		Back and shoulders fixed—back of head, shoulders, and hips against wall and heels 6 in. from wall.
		Always use same cadence or rate (30 to 36 per min).
Elbow flexors and shoulder extensors	Pull-ups[b]	Grip (forward or reverse).
		Distance between hands.
		Chin to bar level.
		Full return to arm extension.
		No kicking or kipping although break at hip permissible.
		Always use same cadence or rate (18 to 24 per min).
Elbow extensors	Overhead[a] press	(Grip palms away when bar is before chest).
		Distance between hands.
		Full elbow extension.
		Push, don't thrust.
		Always use same cadence or rate (30 to 36 per min).
	Push-ups[b]	Distance between hands (shoulder width for most people).
		Back and knees straight.
		Touch only chest or chin.
		Always use same cadence or rate (35 to 40 per min).
	Dips on parallel bars[a]	Width of bars.
		Full extension at "top" and "down" to form 90° angle with upper and lower arm.
		No kicking or kipping.
		Always use same cadence or rate (24 to 32 per min).
Abdominals	Bent knee[b] sit-ups	Knees bent to 45° angle.
		Do not hit floor or mat and "bounce up."
		Hand position:
		a. lace fingers behind head, or
		b. at sides, or
		c. across chest.
		May require something or someone to hold feet down.
		Always use same cadence or rate (24 to 32 per min).

[a]Not generally considered as applicable to women.
[b]For persons unable to perform even one of these, there are several ways to work up to them (see page 296).

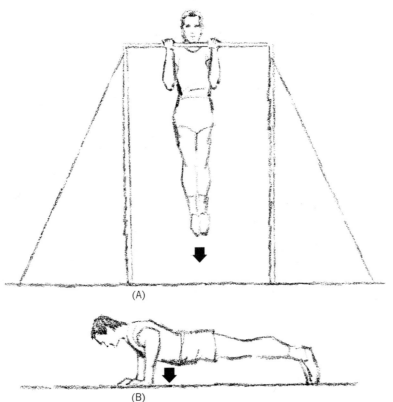

(A)

(B)

FIGURE 9.35 "Holding" exercises for those unable to execute one pull-up (A) or one push-up (B). Get to the desired position any way you can and then hold as long as you can. (Think ahead to prevent injury when you reach the "end point"; a broken nose could result from falling to the floor from the push-up position if the head is not pulled back or turned to the side.) "Eccentric" exercises, denoted by the arrows, involve a slow release after reaching the "up" position. The same principles of "holding" and "eccentrics" can be applied to other ME exercises.

sit-ups, push-ups, or dips on parallel bars). Barbells and dumbbells enable one to test more different muscle groups. The important standardization procedures for tests that are reasonably practical as home tests are given in Table 9.2. For the most reliable results, resistance and rate should *always* be standardized, preferably with a metronome, for all ME tests.

Many other muscle groups can be tested (for example, leg extensors with "squat jumps," dumbbell tests for deltoids, pectorals, and so on), but with knowledge of the basic standardization principles and joint actions one can test almost any muscle group regularly over the years.

Isometric Endurance Tests

Complex mechanical or electronic equipment (such as that used to record the isometric force in the study illustrated on page 264) is needed to measure isometric force exerted over a period of time, but holding time is a practical self-testing technique if one wishes to test isometric endurance: holding time in the "up" position for pull-ups, holding dumbbells out to the side for "time," and so on.

This kind of testing has not been particularly practical and has received little attention except from an academic standpoint in the study of muscular strength and endurance. The one notable exception to this is the use of the flexed arm hang for girls in the AAHPER test.

Isometric and Eccentric Training for Those Unable to Accomplish One Repetition of ME Tests

Performing three bouts of endurance isometric "holding" of position after using any means of getting *to* that position, as illustrated in Figure 9.35, is one possibility for working up to these tests. A second or possibly supplementary technique is to get to the position desired by some means and then to utilize eccentric or lengthening muscle work to return *slowly* to the starting position (see Figure 9.35B). Do this as often as possible before fatigue begins to set in.

Modified ME Exercises for Women

There are "modified" pull-ups and push-ups for women (see Figure 9.36). It has been our experience that girls *can* learn to do regular push-ups. As soon as possible the regular exercise should replace the modified form.

Anthropometric and Body Mechanics Appraisal

The following tests may be valuable in estimating total health and fitness. The value that a person attaches to these measurements depends on his accept-

FIGURE 9.36 Modified knee push-ups (A) and leaning pull-ups (B) for women.

(A)

(B)

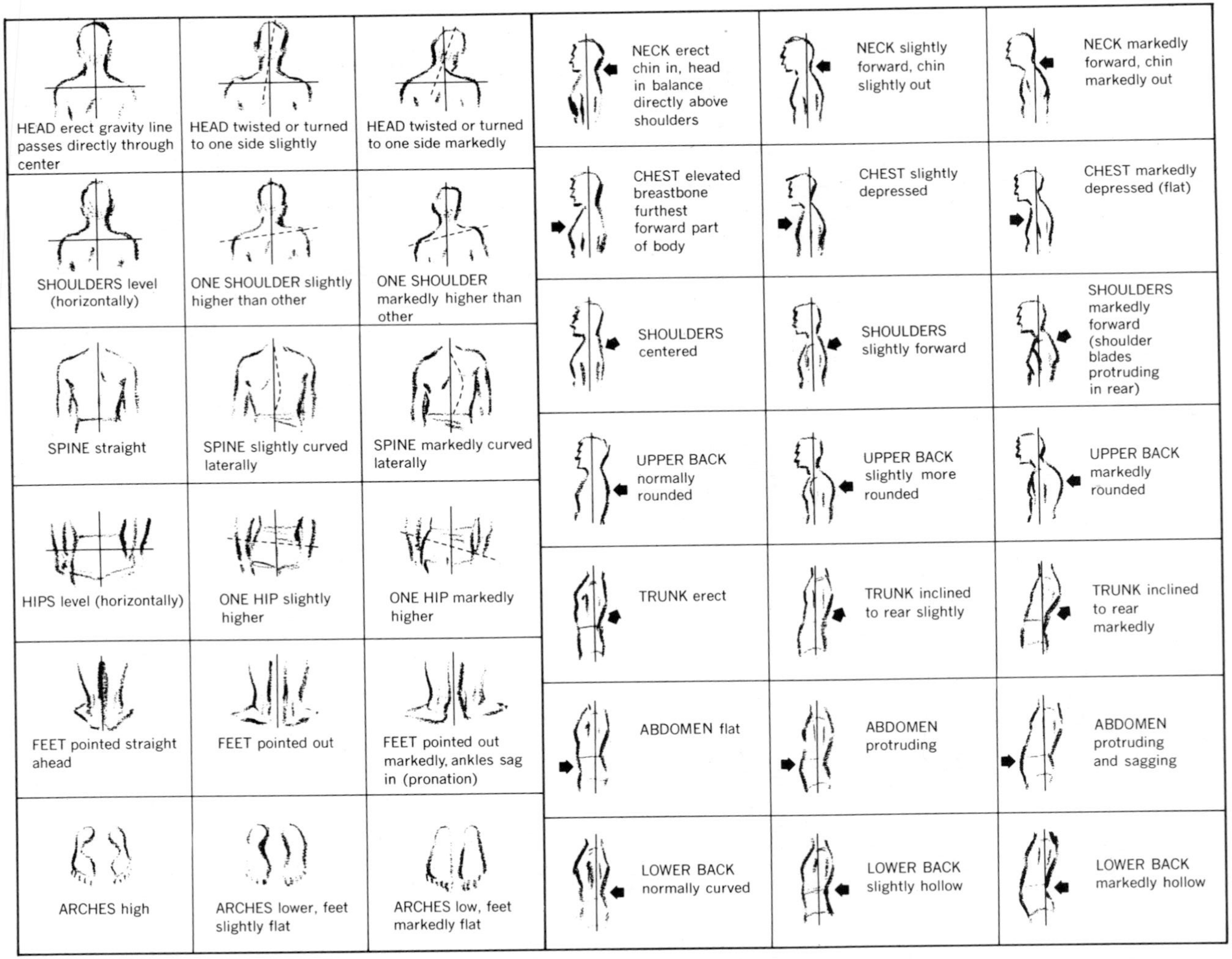

FIGURE 9.37 Subjective analysis of postural and foot alignment. Source: New York State Education Department, New York State Physical Fitness Test. Reprinted by permission of the New York State Education Department.

ance of the principles previously discussed. It is our view that these measures are extremely important as a preventive technique. Some involve a partner or professional assistance.

POSTURAL ALIGNMENT In the typical class situation, postural alignment can often be evaluated by one of several photographic techniques or by an expert's rating scales, or by a variety of other techniques involving some specialized equipment. The use of polaroid photographs has been found to be one of the most practical techniques. Students are able to view themselves immediately, and the teacher's comments can be made on the spot. Lighting is much less of a problem with this technique than other photographic systems, and cameras are simple for an inexperienced person to operate.

Subjects should be photographed in front of a grid (or through a grid of tightly stretched strings) against a sharply contrasting background. Clothing being worn should be minimal (bathing suits or shorts are good) and at least two views should be taken (back and side are most useful). Up to four students can be photographed at one time, but care must be taken to ensure that each subject is aligned correctly with respect to the camera. Careful explanation of the purpose of the evaluation will make it much easier to avoid unnatural poses.

If the less objective methods of evaluation are used, attention to particular factors will facilitate the procedure. Check-lists such as that found on page 298 will be found helpful (Figure 9.37).

FEET Semiobjective means of appraising the functional state of the bone, ligamentous, and muscular structure of the feet are also illustrated in Figure 9.37.

APPRAISAL OF FLEXIBILITY

There are laboratory tests of joint flexibility that involve some mechanical means of recording or measuring actual degrees of flexion, extension, or rotation. Without these devices it is difficult to test the exact flexibility of the important "joints," but there are some valuable "pass-or-fail" techniques and some objective and semiobjective methods available for self-testing. Some may require the aid of a mirror or a "partner" or helper.

1. The *trunk flexion* test ascertains the length and elasticity of the back and hamstring muscles (see Figure 9.38).
2. The *trunk extension* test determines the ability to hyperextend the spine (see Figure 9.39).
3. The *Kraus-Weber Test of Minimal Strength and Flexibility* (325) is a battery of tests designed primarily for children. Failure in any of these tests, with the possible exception of toe touching, in an adult is almost inexcusable unless there is irreversible muscle or joint pathology.

As shown in Figure 9.40, the test consists of (1) a sit-up with the legs held straight; (2) a sit-up with the knees bent and the feet held flat on the floor; (3) a ten-second leg lift with knees straight and heels held ten inches off the floor; (4) from a face-down position,

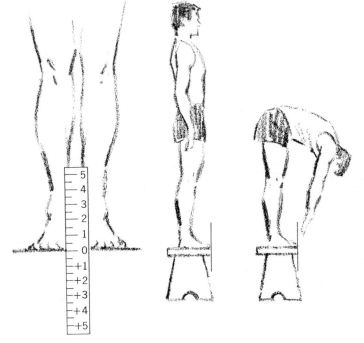

FIGURE 9.38 Trunk flexion test. (1) Heels together and toes pointed to side at about 45° angle; (2) toes near or even with edge of bench; (3) bounce gently down twice (be careful not to pull too hard); (4) hold the third bounce (with hands together and fingers on ruler) for at least 2 seconds so that your partner can read your score; (5) record as minus above bench and plus below bench to nearest half inch.

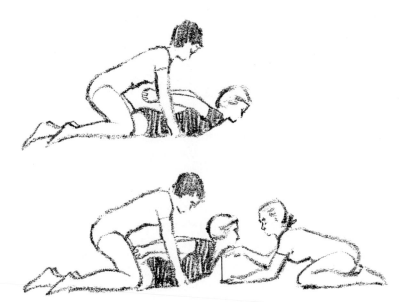

FIGURE 9.39 Trunk extension test. (1) One helper holds down legs and hips while a second prepares to stretch a string vertically from top of sternum to the floor; (2) take two bounces, carefully arching up as high as possible; (3) on third bounce, hold; (4) partner measures distance from sternal notch to floor with string (read from a ruler or yardstick after getting distance on string).

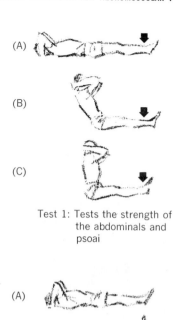

(A)

(B)

(C)

Test 1: Tests the strength of
the abdominals and
psoai

(A)

(B)

(C)

Test 2: Further test for abdominals

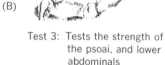

(A)

(B)

Test 3: Tests the strength of
the psoai, and lower
abdominals

(A)

(B)

Test 4: Tests the strength of the
upper back muscles

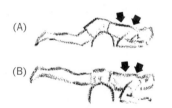

(A)

(B)

Test 5: Tests the strength of
the lower back

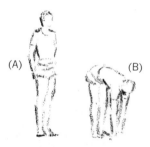

(A)   (B)

Test 6: Tests the length of back
and hamstring muscles

FIGURE 9.40 Kraus-Weber tests for minimal strength and flexibility. Arrows indicate where partner should hold you down. Use a pillow as shown for (4) and (5). (1) and (2) roll up slowly to sitting position; (3) keep knees straight, hold feet off the floor for ten seconds; (4) raise chest, head, and shoulders from the floor and hold for ten seconds; (5) keep knees straight and hold feet off the floor for ten seconds; (6) keep knees straight and feet together, slowly try to reach down and touch the floor for a count of three seconds (do not force unnecessarily). Adapted from Kraus and Hirschland, *Research Quarterly,* American Association for Health, Physical Education, and Recreation (325).

raising the head, shoulders, and chest off the floor for a ten-second count, using a pillow as fulcrum under the pelvis; (5) from a face-down position, raising the legs and thighs off the floor for a ten-second period, again using a pillow for a fulcrum; (6) from a standing position, bending forward without bending the knees and touching the toes — the fingers must stay in contact with the toes for a three-second count.

The sit-up portion of this test (as well as the toe-touching item) has been criticized by some experts as failing to measure the characteristics for which it was designed: abdominal strength. In performing either of these sit-ups it is essential that the low back be kept pressed to the floor and that the subject *roll* up to a sitting position. If the back is allowed to arch as the sit-up is performed, the abdominal muscles are not being utilized and the **hip flexors** (the iliopsoas group and the rectus

femoris) actually accomplish the work. Similar difficulties are inherent in the back-lying leg lift. In such cases actual weakness of the abdominal muscles might go undetected. In order to avoid this difficulty physical therapist Florence Kendall has suggested a modification of these tests that would substitute a leg-lift test for all three of the usual items used to evaluate abdominal strength.

. . . *the legs should be raised to the 90 degree angle, the subject should direct his effort to holding the low back down on the table as the legs are slowly lowered, and the angle of the legs with the table [or floor] should be noted the moment the low back begins to arch and the pelvis starts to tilt forward. A 60 degree angle constitutes 60 percent; a 40 degree angle, 80 percent; and the 10 inches from the table, which is about 20 degrees, would be about 90 percent if the back were held flat (201, p. 141).*

FIGURE 9.41   Leg lowering exercise advocated by physical therapist Florence Kendall. As legs are lowered from the vertical, the lumbar area is carefully monitored. When the low back begins to arch away from the reclining surface, the angle of the legs is noted and a percent of optimal abdominal strength estimated. Test is based on the ability of the abdominal muscles to prevent rotation of the pelvis.

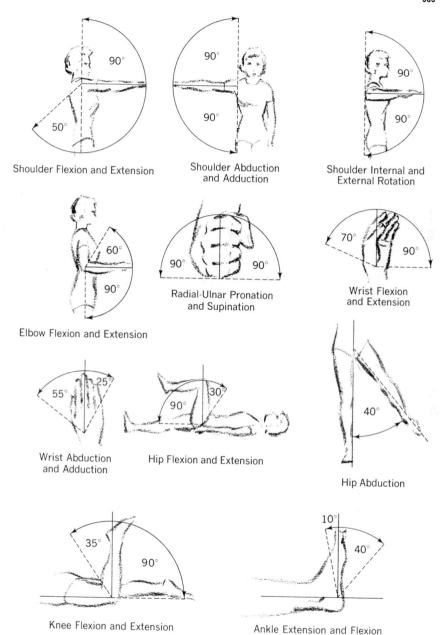

FIGURE 9.42 Normal range of motion for various joints. Solid line represents zero point for degree notations; dotted lines represent limits for normal range. Range of motion figures adapted from L. Daniels, M. Williams, and C. Worthingham, *Muscle Testing*. Philadelphia: W. B. Saunders Company, 1956.

4. *Pass or fail tests* are simple tests that can generally be self-administered, although some may require another person to observe. *Remember:* do not force a joint movement abruptly. Sometimes several gentle, bouncing efforts will safely stretch or increase the measured range of motion. Anything short of the full range shown in the diagrams in Figure 9.42 is generally considered to be less than normal. Any drastic deviation from normal in either direction should certainly be checked for possible serious impairment of joint function.

It is important to remember that *no single test of flexibility is suitable as a measure of total body flexibility.* Joint flexibility is highly specific, and each joint must be tested individually if a total evaluation is to be made.

MOTOR ABILITY APPRAISAL

Many tests of motor ability items are available, although it is not really clear what they measure, other than the ability to perform the specific tasks involved (see Chapter 5). A course in tests and measurements will assist you in making choices from among the several batteries commonly administered (38, 67, 332). Some examples of the types of items frequently found in these batteries are listed following. These should be regarded as being

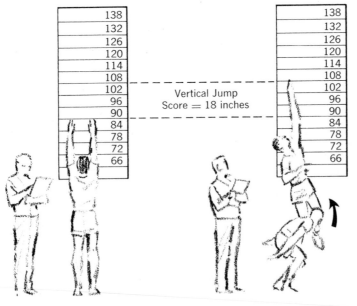

| 138 |
| 132 |
| 126 |
| 120 |
| 114 |
| 108 |
| 102 |
| 96 |
| 90 |
| 84 |
| 78 |
| 72 |
| 66 |

Vertical Jump
Score = 18 inches

FIGURE 9.43   Test of leg power: vertical jump. Subject standing flat footed reaches as high as possible on the board. From a crouch the subject leaps high and touches the board. The difference between the standing reach and the jumping reach is observed and recorded. Average score: men, 20″; women, 13″.

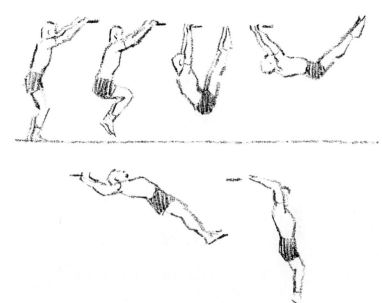

FIGURE 9.44 Test of agility, power, and coordination: bar snap. The subject stands grasping the horizontal bar at shoulder height. Jumping and swinging under the bar he extends his body, releases his grip and lands on his feet. Distance traveled beyond the bar is measured and recorded. Average score: men, 5′0″; women, 3′4″.

Bar Snap Score

representative of commonly used tests; they are not necessarily the best available.

Vertical jump (Figure 9.43). This test of leg power requires that the subject jump from a stationary position (no running or stepping). Score is equal to the difference between the standing reach and highest point touched in the best of three trials.

Bar snap (Figure 9.44). The bar snap is a test of several factors involving power, coordination, and other factors. It is a challenging item and is responsive to changes with practice. Subjects are scored on their ability to thrust themselves in a horizontal direc-

tion. The bar is positioned at 4′6″ (may be adjusted to 5′0″), and distance is measured from a point directly beneath the bar to the point of landing (heel nearest the bar).

Figure **8** *run* (Figure 9.45). Agility is often tested by a run designed to test one's ability to change direction quickly. It is important to minimize "straight" running in a test of agility. The diagram shows the path to be followed by the subject in the figure 8 run. Score is total time for one excursion.

Balance beam test. One of several balance tests, the TU Balance Beam Test is designed to test elements of

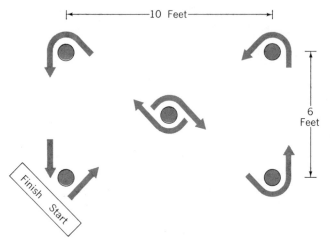

FIGURE 9.45   Test of agility: figure 8 run. The subject is timed to the nearest tenth of a second on his ability to run (from a standing start) once around the obstacles placed as diagramed. Average score: men, 8 sec; women, 12 sec.

balance combined with other factors. On a two-inch-wide beam, twelve feet long, the subject performs a sequence of five moves for which he is awarded two points each (ten points total). Walk the length forward; walk the length backward; turn around; do a full squat and rise on both feet; do a full squat and rise while balancing on one foot. One point is subtracted for every time the subject needs aid in correcting his balance.

Other balance tests. Other balance tests are also commonly used (183, 371). Some of these are quite complex and require considerable expenditure for equipment. However, because tests on a stabilometer are challenging and interesting, and because the apparatus is relatively easy to construct, it is recommended that these devices be used when possible. One such device is illustrated in Figure 9.46.

Speed. Speed is generally tested by running 50 or 100 yards in as little time as possible.

"True" speed. This test eliminates the starting problem and attempts to measure top speed. Subjects are given a running start of at least fifty feet and *then* are timed for a twenty- or thirty-yard distance. The use of two watches would enable this test to be made at the same time as the regular speed test. Photoelectric cells can be used to good advantage in this type of testing.

Reaction time (see page 308). The measurement of reaction time requires special equipment that can be constructed or purchased. The timing device must be capable of measurement to at least 1/100 second. The Dekan Automatic Performance Analyzer and the Hale Reaction Timer are only two of the many devices available for this work. Reaction time can be simply measured for many different and specific actions, ranging from a simple response of the thumb up to total body response.

Norms. Average performances for men and women on the TU Balance

FIGURE 9.46   Tests of balance: (A) The TU Balance Beam Test is described in the text. Points are subtracted for errors committed during the walking routine. (B) The stabilometer is a device that records failure to maintain balance around a central pivot. Total time on balance is recorded for a specified period. (C), (D), and (E) The stork stand, the diver's stance, and the stick balance are all timed tests of ability to maintain balance. Subjects, with eyes closed, are required to maintain the illustrated position for as long as possible.

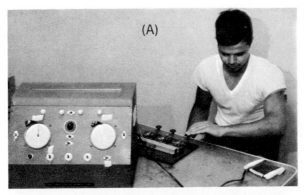

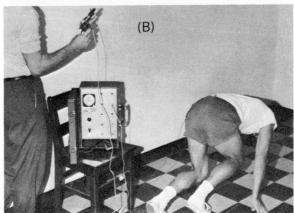

FIGURE 9.47 Tests of reaction time: (A) A single test of "small muscle" reaction time requires the subject to release a key when the buzzer and/or light is observed. (B) "Large muscle" reaction time can be tested by requiring subjects to initiate movements such as the sprint start when the stimulus is heard or seen. Movement time and response time can be tested in similar ways.

Beam Test, their speed, and their reaction time are recorded in Appendix B; Figures 9.43, 9.44, and 9.45 include this information for the tests depicted. Other tests for fitness and motor skills are available from many sources. Fleischman (184) has analyzed many tests and makes several suggestions for interesting tests. Norms are available.

COMMON DISORDERS OF THE NEUROMUSCULAR SYSTEM

Although it is not expected that physical educators or health educators will have a great deal of personal contact with serious disorders of the neuromuscular system of the body, it is their responsibility to educate the public about many of these conditions. In addition, some of these disabilities will be observed in school children, and special physical education programs need to be conducted on their behalf. Such programs are discussed in Chapter 17.

Cerebral palsy is caused by damage to the motor control centers of the brain. Such damage may occur before or during birth, or at any time afterward. Any factor that deprives the brain cells of oxygen for any length of time can cause this kind of damage. The results can range from a slight muscular deviation to a total muscular disability. About one in every one thousand children will be affected with cerebral palsy. Generally, cerebral palsy produces one of the following types of disability:

1. Spasticity: a condition in which muscular movement is restricted because of **contracture** of the muscles. The muscles that support the body against gravity are commonly involved; hence maintenance of good posture is difficult. Mental impairment is more often associated with spasticity than with any other kind of palsy.

2. Athetosis: unlike the spastic, the athetoid has no difficulty in moving, but has a great tendency to move too much with many undesired movements.

3. Ataxia: a less common form of cerebral palsy, and is acquired rather than congenital. This individual would have a poor sense of body and limb position (**kinesthesis**).

4. Rigidity: a stiff, tense musculature resulting from hypertension of the muscles on both sides of a given joint and preventing movement in either direction.

5. Tremor: an involuntary, alternate contraction of the flexor and extensor muscles, producing a rhythmic motion.

Epilepsy is characterized by a short, sudden seizure of unconsciousness accompanied by **convulsions.** There are three major classifications: *grand mal,* which are infrequent, but severe seizures; *petit mal,* which are less severe but more frequent (the person may simply look blank and stare into space for a few seconds); and psychomotor seizures, which consist of episodes during which certain acts may be performed without the individual's being aware of them or remembering them. Epilepsy can be diagnosed by means of an **electroencephalogram** (EEG) in which characteristic brain wave patterns are observed.

Hernia is a protrusion of a loop of an organ through an opening in the abdominal wall. Frequently hernias are acquired by injuries or strains due to the lifting of heavy objects. Surgery is generally able to correct the abdominal weakness.

Multiple sclerosis is a disease once thought to be relatively rare. Onset occurs in the majority of cases between the ages of twenty and forty; the cause has not yet been discovered. A slow, scattered degeneration of nerve cells in the brain and spinal cord produces numbing, tingling sensations and eventual paralysis, blindness, loss of speech, and so on. This disease progresses slowly and may last for twenty-five years.

Muscular dystrophy (progressive muscular dystrophy) is a disease of early childhood in which there is a progressive muscular weakness accompanied by increased size of some of the weak muscles. Onset of the disease, generally found in boys, usually occurs between the ages of two and six. By age ten most patients have become unable to walk and by twenty most have died of respiratory infection.

Other less common dystrophies can affect both males and females. All types are progressive and result in relatively early death.

Parkinson's disease is a slow, progressive disorder of the central nervous system, which affects the life span. It is characterized by slowness of movement, weakness, muscular rigidity, and tremor.

Myasthenia gravis is characterized by a progressive weakness of the muscles, especially those of the throat, neck, and face. Although the cause is unknown, it appears to be related to the inability of the nerve impulse to cross the junction between the nerve and the muscle. Symptoms are always worse in the evening than in the morning because the muscles grow weaker with use. In 80 percent of the cases the disease does not affect the normal life span.

Polyneuritis, an inflammation of many nerves, is really a symptom rather than a disease per se. Mononeuritis is a similar inflammation of a single nerve. The causes may be manifold, and symptoms vary according to whether the fibers affected are primarily sensory (pain, tingling, and so on), or motor (paralysis). By prompt treatment the specific symptoms can usually be relieved, but in order to effect a cure the original cause must be determined and treated. Although recovery is usually rapid in mild cases, more severe involvement may result in chronic sensory, motor, or vasomotor disturbances.

Raynaud's disease is a condition in which the autonomic nervous system becomes hyperactive to the extent that **spasm** occurs in the blood vessels of the superficial tissues, resulting in a decrease in their diameter. Causes may be organic or nonorganic. Sensitivity to certain substances, such as arsenic, ergot, or tobacco, or even certain kinds of injuries may produce the syndrome. Emotional upsets or other psychological problems are frequently involved in this disease. Sometimes **psychotherapy** is successful in treatment. **Gangrene** may be present, but limited to the superficial tissues.

Tetany is a condition in which there are rhythmic spasms of the muscles in the ankles, feet, wrists, hands, and larynx. Sometimes convulsions also occur. The condition, which is due to a lack of calcium **ions** in the blood, is observed most often between the ages of three months and two years.

COMMON DISORDERS OF THE SKELETAL SYSTEM

There are several classifications of arthritic conditions as well as a number of other diseases that are characterized by pain in and around joints leading to joint immobility. The cause of *rheumatoid arthritis,* which is one of the most severe and disabling of the joint diseases, is still unknown. Seventy-five percent of rheumatoid arthritis cases are women and onset begins before age forty.

Osteoarthritis is associated with aging and usually attacks those joints that undergo the most wear and tear. The splintering and disintegration of the cartilage covering the ends of bones leaves the bone exposed and movement becomes painful.

Gouty arthritis (gout), a disorder affecting men chiefly, is characterized by attacks of acute arthritis and by the formation of chalky deposits in the joints. These deposits are made up chiefly of uric acid salts. Patients with gout have high concentrations of uric acid in the tissues and blood. Indications are that relief is almost immediate when meats, particularly sweetbreads, are limited.

Bursitis is the inflammation of the bursae, or pads that act to cushion the joint parts against friction. It may be caused by injury, infection, tuberculosis, or gout. There is local pain, swelling, and tenderness, with recovery usually spontaneous in one to two weeks unless the condition becomes chronic, in which case it will recur.

Rickets is a disease of the bones resulting from a deficiency of vitamin D. The child affected becomes irritable, weak, restless, anemic, flabby, and susceptible to infections. Characteristic deformities are bowlegs and pigeon breast, which occur as a result of the bones bending under weightbearing.

The Arthritis and Rheumatism Foundation indicates that persons who work outdoors and work with their hands are more susceptible. Farmers are particularly A-R—prone; factory workers are next in line. Professional and technical workers are least prone (172). In a review of the epidemiology of rheumatoid-arthritis, Cobb concludes:

Currently the following factors seem to be relevant: faulty immune mechanisms plus infection and/or joint injury, and a personality plus a social environment that lead to low self-esteem and resentment. Just how these things interact to produce arthritis is not as yet known. (108, p. 78).

Factors Associated with Arthritis and Rheumatism

AGE AND SEX   The Arthritis and Rheumatism Foundation reports that more than half of those affected are under forty-five and also reports that there are three times as many women suffering from forms of this disease than men (172).

GEOGRAPHIC FACTORS   In America, **arthritis** and **rheumatism** are more prevalent in the rural than in the urban population (578).

GENETICS   At least one of the forms of A-R disease, **gout,** appears to be highly familial (172).

OTHER FACTORS   Precipitating but not necessarily causative factors appear to be emotional and physical stress and strain, fatigue, injury, shock, exposure to cold, and chronic infections.

Gout is characterized by deposition of **uric acid** and crystals in the joints and a **"clinically silent"** increase in serum uric acid from a normal of 4 mg percent to as high as 12 mg percent almost invariably precedes the joint infection and acute inflammatory reaction (172).

After years of working with experimental "stress" in animals and consideration of clinical histories in human beings, Hans Selye concluded:

All this makes it quite clear that the rheumatic maladies are really typical diseases of adaptation, because if the body's defenses are adequate the disease is suppressed without any intervention by the physician. Here the primary disease-producer (whatever it may be) is certainly not very harmful in itself. When the inflammatory barricade against it is removed by hormones—be they secreted by the glands or administered by the physician—the causative agent (germ, poison) of the rheumatoid diseases does not produce much tissue-destruction. These diseases are essentially due to inadequate adaptive reactions against comparatively innocuous injuries. They are due to maladaptation (505, p. 165). [See Chapter 18.]

In their text *Psychosomatic Medicine*, Weiss and English summarize their section on chronic arthritis by saying:

We believe that there are, within the individual, certain emotional factors that may express themselves through tension and spasms of the voluntary muscular system and thus influence the working of the joints. If this occurs in an individual who for some reason is predisposed to the development of chronic arthritis, then the emotional factor may be important. In other words, if there are numerous interacting factors such as predisposition, fatigue, (which may also be psychologically determined), specific infection, and perhaps even other factors, then arthritis may develop (601, p. 510).

SUMMARY

Without the intimate interaction of three distinct systems, the human body would be unable to function. Although these systems (nervous, muscular, and skeletal) are readily differentiated from one another structurally, they cannot function as separate entities.

The jobs of communication and decision-making are the responsibility of the nervous system. The muscular system is concerned with movement and maintenance of the upright posture. The skeletal system collaborates with the other two to produce movement by its action as a system of complex levers. Its other functions of protection and blood cell production are distinct from its roles in support and locomotion.

A knowledge of the anatomy and physiology of these three fundamental systems is essential to the understanding of human learning, movement, fitness, health, and disease. The explanation and prediction of behavior, and the influencing of behavior, depend upon this kind of understanding.

The exact mechanism by which muscle tissue contracts is not well understood, although great strides have been made recently in identifying important factors in its function. The contractile substance (proteins called actin and myosin), its arrangement, and the means by which it is excited have all been topics of productive investigation.

The fundamental unit of neuromuscular function consists of a single motor neuron together with all the muscle fibers that it innervates. Activity in the central nervous system modifies the activity of the motor unit to control coordinated movement and the appropriately graded force of muscular activity. Functions of increasing complexity are controlled by progressively higher centers of the brain, with voluntary actions initiated in the cerebral cortex representing the most sophisticated activity. Other areas of the brain serve in complexly interrelated ways, to initiate, monitor, modify, and react to the activity of skeletal muscle.

Cardiac and smooth muscle (as well as glandular tissue) are controlled at relatively low levels by the function of the autonomic nervous system. The separate divisions of this system (sympathetic and parasympathetic) serve to prepare the organism for emergencies as well as to maintain homeostasis. Intimate interaction between nervous stimulation and hormonal activation of body tissues provides a dual mechanism by which many body functions can be controlled and modified.

Terminology used in studying the activity of neuromuscular function includes such words as isotonic and isometric contraction, static and dynamic strength, as well as terms like contracture, summation, and facilitation. Concepts of training include an understanding of specificity and overload, fatigue, substitution patterns, and many other important ideas. Distinctions among the various expressions of neuromuscular function, such as strength, muscular endurance, and power are important in dealing with practical problems of preventive medicine, rehabilitation, fitness, and performance. Intimately involved in all

such considerations is the function of joints and articulations. Trauma and degeneration of joints and surrounding tissues are common problems with which physical educators and health educators become involved. Some understanding is basic to any ability to prevent or aid in the amelioration of such conditions.

The efficiency with which the body is able to move depends not only upon strength and related capacities, but also upon the mechanical principles of application. Such principles are as important to the safe performance of everyday tasks as they are to success in competitive athletics.

While it is evident that the nature of the structure and function of the nervous, muscular, and skeletal systems places certain strictures and constraints upon the functional ability of the individual, it is equally apparent that physical activity can have substantial effects upon the development and condition of these systems. These *efferent* effects are the substance of the science of training and physical conditioning; they are also central to many systems devised for the education of children and adults suffering from neurological impairment.

Knowledge of appropriate techniques is important for effective development of strength, muscular endurance, power, and flexibility. Potentialities as well as limitations of such techniques need to be carefully studied if realistic objectives are to be established and achieved through training.

Central to any scientific program for producing changes in the structure and function of the neuromuscular system is the matter of adequate appraisal of status and progress. Knowledge of appropriate tools and techniques of measurement is prerequisite to success in any educational or physical training program.

PRINCIPLES

1. Under the proper circumstances, practically anyone can substantially increase his strength and muscular endurance.

2. In general, the activity of one division of the autonomic nervous system is antagonistic to the activity of the other. The sympathetic system acts to prepare the body to respond to emergency situations, whereas the parasympathetic is concerned with maintaining homeostasis.

3. In cases where movement of any kind is involved, initiation and coordination are the functions of the somatic system.

4. If a given stimulus is of sufficient strength to cause a neuron to fire, the application of a stronger stimulus would have no greater effect insofar as the intensity of the discharge is concerned. This is called the all-or-none law of neural transmission.

5. At a synapse, impulses are permitted to cross in one direction only: from afferent neurons to efferent neurons.

6. Whenever a muscle fiber is stimulated by the neuron (nerve fiber) that innervates it, it shortens to its maximum capacity. This is called the all-or-none law of neuromuscular function.

7. The gradation of force exerted by a muscle may be accomplished in either of two ways: (a) recruitment of additional motor units or (b) increased rate of fire of participating motor units.

8. Gross alterations in required muscular force are achieved by recruitment, whereas fine adjustments are achieved by means of frequency changes.

9. Low threshold motor units are involved in most movements, whereas high threshold units may be activated only rarely when extreme force is required.

10. One theoretical means of increasing strength would be to involve somehow the very high threshold motor units that are seldom or never activated.

11. Central inhibition and facilitation exert great influences on the strength levels achieved by an individual.

12. Unlike certain other limitations imposed upon us by nature, the neuromuscular limits are, to a large extent, under our own control.

13. Approximately half of the work done in most lifting movements involves eccentric contraction of muscles.

14. Flexibility is a highly specific factor; full range of motion in one joint is no indication of the status of other joints of the body.

15. Contrary to common belief, weight training (properly practiced) does not lead to muscle-boundness but can actually increase joint flexibility.

16. Whereas man-made machines wear out with use, the human "machine" becomes more efficient with use.

17. Whenever one body segment deviates from a position directly over its point of support, compensation must

occur elsewhere in the body in order to prevent the whole body from becoming unbalanced in that direction. (For every zig there must be a zag.)

18. Stability of an object or individual is increased:

    a. in direct proportion to the area of supporting base;

    b. in inverse proportion to the height of the center of gravity;

    c. in direct proportion to its mass;

    d. in direct proportion to the closeness of the gravity line to the center of the base of support.

19. Mechanical efficiency must sometimes be sacrificed in competitive performance in the interests of strategy or deception.

20. The phenomenon of pain-avoidance is frequently responsible for the creation of secondary impairment.

21. Isometric training can be effective in increasing the strength levels of most people, but the amount of potential increase is dependent upon how close subjects are to "endkraft."

22. "Specificity of training" simply indicates that one gets the kind of results he trains for. Training methods must be specific to the desired outcomes.

23. In general, if one wishes to increase the strength (or endurance) of a muscle it is necessary to overload the movement produced by the muscles involved. For strength, resistance must be increased beyond levels normally encountered; for endurance the number of repetitions or holding time must be increased.

24. Basic body structure is largely determined by heredity and can be altered little by exercise programs, particularly after the growth years.

EXPERIMENTS AND EXPERIENCES

1. Divide the class into two groups by some random procedure. Test both groups on maximal strength of a given muscle group (biceps brachii, for example) either by determining 1 RM or by use of a static test such as a cable tension test. Also test the maximum number of full contractions (at a controlled frequency) that each subject can perform against a resistance of 40 percent of his maximum. (A standard load can be used by all subjects if preferred.) Calculate a rank order correlation of strength and endurance scores. Make a scattergram plot of the scores. What conclusions can you draw about the relationship between strength and muscular endurance?

2. Select two groups of volunteers of at least six subjects each. Test subjects for maximum strength of a given muscle group (biceps or quadriceps) using either dynamic or static methods. Test each subject for maximal muscular endurance on a standard load.

Subjects in one group should be assigned to training every other day for at least four weeks (six to ten would be better) in which they use a 4 RM system. Attempt to increase by at least one pound each session.

Members of the second group should also train every other day in an attempt to increase the number of repetitions with the standard weight. (Training time should not exceed five minutes a day for either group.)

All subjects should be retested for both strength and endurance at the end of the training period. Comparative changes should be noted.

If sufficient subjects are available, a third group could be added to serve as a control. This group should have no weight training experience during the training period. If desired, a fourth group, training by isometric techniques, could be utilized.

3. Using a goniometer or a protractor with an attached arm, measure the range of motion of the knee in at least ten subjects. Using weights or a cable tensiometer, measure the "maximal" strength of the hamstrings and quadriceps. Make scattergrams of (1) flexibility versus quadriceps strength; (2) flexibility versus hamstrings strength; (3) flexibility versus total of quadriceps and hamstrings strength. Estimate the "line of best fit" for each plot and draw conclusions. Variations: Utilize other joints such as the elbow, wrist, or ankle.

4. For this demonstration use blocks of wood or other substance cut in the shape of a pyramid, cube, rectangle, and so on. Demonstrate the force necessary for tipping each object over. A "tight-rope walker" can be constructed by use of wires and weights which actually places the center of gravity *below* the base of support. A child's toy of this type may be available. Various stances assumed in sports can be demonstrated (track start, football linemen and backs, wrestlers, and boxers) as can positions taken to counteract inertia in subways and on busses, and so on.

5. One subject is sufficient for demonstrating the principles involved in this experiment. Two balance-type scales (or one scale and one platform the same height as the surface of the scale) and a specially prepared board are required. The board should be of measured length (a round number such as 80 inches) and have a vertical marking peg projecting upward at the exact center. Under each end should be a piece fashioned into a knife edge which rests on the scale and platform surface. The empty board should be balanced and the scale(s) zeroed.

A female subject wearing flat heels then stands with both medial malleoli in contact with the marker and the scales rebalanced. The weight indicated on each scale is recorded (or weight on one is recorded and the weight supported by the platform obtained by subtracting from the total weight of the subject). The position of the gravity line with respect to the medial malleoli is calculated:

$$F_a \times F_a A = F_b \times F_b A$$

where F_a = the reading on Scale A; F_b = the reading on Scale B; $F_a A = X$; $F_b A$ = total board length minus X.

The distance X indicates how far the A end of the board is from the gravity line. By subtraction the position of the gravity line from the medial malleoli can be obtained. Similar measurements are made for the same subject immediately after putting on high heels. An observer at the scale should attempt to get a reading as quickly as possible, and if the reading seems to be moving, the direction and the magnitude of the shift should be noted.

Note: Postural adjustments occur very rapidly and the observation of this fact is a part of the experiment. Calculations should be made to see if any "permanent" change has occurred in the position of the gravity line.

SUGGESTED READINGS

Asimov, Isaac, *The Human Body; Its Structure and Operation,* New York: New American Library of World Literature, Inc., 1963. Chapters 2, 3, and 4.

Broer, M. R. and N. R. G. Galles, "Importance of Relationship between Various Body Measurements in Performance of Toe-Touch Test," *Research Quarterly,* 29:253, 1958.

Hellebrandt, F. A. and S. J. Houtz, "Mechanisms of Muscle Training in Man: Experimental Demonstration of the Overload Principle," *Physical Therapy Review,* 36:371-383, 1956.

Mohr, Dorothy R., "The Contributions of Physical Activity to Skill Learning," *Research Quarterly,* 31:321-350, (May) 1960.

Royce, J., "Re-Evaluation of Isometric Training Methods and Results: A Must," *Research Quarterly,* 35:215, 1964.

Digestion
and Metabolism

Chapter 10

One needs only to browse through any recent home magazine or women's magazine to find at least one article, if not indeed several, extolling the virtue of some supposedly new diet or weight reduction scheme. The American public has been literally deluged with advertisement and literature concerning foods and fads, supplements, and low-calorie this-and-that. Almost as prevalent are articles about slimming and weight reduction exercises. In short, the American public is (or, at least, is thought by publishers to be) extremely nutrition conscious. Perhaps, even more, they are weight and calorie conscious. One often wonders how much of the information would be necessary if people once-and-for-all came to really understand the basic, known principles of nutrition and weight control.

Nutrition and weight control education are legitimate and extremely important facets of health education and physical education. You will need a sound understanding of the principles of digestion and metabolism. To that end, an introduction to these topics precedes a somewhat complete presentation of the principles of nutrition and weight control.

AFFERENT CONCEPTS

ANATOMY AND GENERAL FUNCTION

The function of digestion is to prepare food for the process of absorption and metabolism. This, of course, includes both the mechanical and the chemical aspects of digestion. The former involves chewing, swallowing, movement of food through the esophagus into the stomach and on through the intestines (peristalsis) and, finally, defecation or elimination. Chemical digestion includes all the changes in the chemical composition of food as it passes through the alimentary canal:

the breakdown of starches to simple sugars or monosaccharides (mainly glucose), the conversion of proteins to amino acids, the changing of fats to **fatty acids** and **glycerol,** and so on. All these changes, which are necessary to prepare the food for absorption, are dependent upon the activity of a variety of digestive enzymes.

A starch-splitting enzyme in saliva, called ptyalin, begins the process of digestion while food is still in the mouth. The partially digested **starches,** together with the rest of the food, reach the stomach via the esophagus.

Strong muscles in the stomach walls provide the mechanical force for mixing the food with the gastric fluid. These

FIGURE 10.1   Fads: diet, exercise, and weight control.

changes take place in the stomach: digestion of starch continues until the contents of the stomach become acid; an initial splitting of protein occurs and the food is churned to a milklike paste, called *chyme*.

In the small intestine, bile from the liver, juices from the pancreas, and secretions from within the intestinal walls combine with the chyme. Foods are broken down to amino acids, simple sugars, fatty acids, and glycerol, which the cells can use. These are absorbed continually from the small intestine into the bloodstream. As they are absorbed through the intestinal walls, they are carried into the bloodstream and to the cells to be used for energy or to become part of the body. The waste materials not absorbed are carried on into the large intestine to be excreted. Only water is absorbed from the large intestine.

Calorie is the term given to the energy values of food in terms of the large kilogram calorie, the unit customarily used by nutritionists for measuring the energy needs and expenditures of man and the energy value of food. The large or kilogram calorie (kilocalorie) is the amount of heat required to raise the temperature of one kilogram of water one degree centigrade. (You can conceptualize a large calorie very roughly as the amount of heat produced by the flame of a one-half-inch-diameter candle in about one minute.) We shall use the term "calorie" as synonymous with kilocalorie.

The basal metabolic rate (BMR) is the amount of heat expended by the body while in a complete resting state. When a physician determines an individual's basal metabolic rate he does so after instructing his patient not to eat any food for twelve hours prior to the test and to get a good night's sleep. Just before the test the subject rests for thirty minutes in a **supine** position in a quiet room where the temperature is between 68 and 75 degrees Fahrenheit. The basal metabolic rate is usually determined indirectly by measuring the oxygen consumed for a period of from eight to ten minutes. In the postabsorptive state, one liter of O_2 used means an expenditure of about 4.82 calories. Thus the caloric expenditure in calories per hour per square meter of body surface can be estimated. Clinics usually compare a patient's BMR with the age and sex norms, as illustrated in Figure 10.16. They can report the BMR to the person as a plus or minus deviation from the norm. For example, a person with a low metabolic rate may be told his BMR is −22 percent.

The specific dynamic action (SDA) of food exerts a measurable influence on BMR, increasing it for as long as twelve hours after a meal and by as much as 70 percent. Proteins cause the greatest and longest-lasting SDA. A more typical SDA is a 10 to 15 percent increase for five hours. The effect is largely due to chemical reactions involved in digestion, absorption, and storage.

The Liver

The liver (see Figure 10.2 and Plate 7) is not generally considered to be a system but it will be discussed briefly

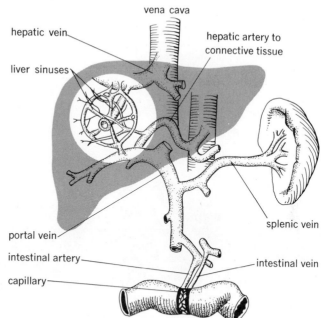

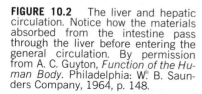

FIGURE 10.2 The liver and hepatic circulation. Notice how the materials absorbed from the intestine pass through the liver before entering the general circulation. By permission from A. C. Guyton, *Function of the Human Body*. Philadelphia: W. B. Saunders Company, 1964, p. 148.

because of its importance in digestion and in exercise. It is difficult to present a simple description of its general functions as there are 500 known functions attributed to the liver. For purposes of simplification, its "metabolic" functions may be categorized as follows:

A STOREHOUSE FOR IMPORTANT MATERIALS The liver stores glucose (in the form of glycogen), fat, and protein. As a storage depot, the liver plays an important role in the regulation of the level of these nutrients circulating in the blood.

A MANUFACTURER The liver manufactures certain antibodies and vitamins, and can manufacture glycogen from amino acids or fats when their blood concentration is high and glucose or glycogen levels are low. Conversely, it can convert glucose to fat. It also produces a substance known as bile, which is stored in the gall bladder until it is needed in the small intestine to aid in fat digestion. The blood proteins are apparently produced in the liver. The endocrine system also plays a role in digestion and metabolism. Certain hormones (for example, enterogastrone, secretin, villikinin, and pancreozymin) play vital roles in the movement, digestion, and absorption of foodstuffs. Thyroxin, of course, has a direct and important effect on total body metabolism. Certain of the hormones secreted by the adrenal cortex are necessary for intermediary metabolic steps; adrenalin, secreted by the

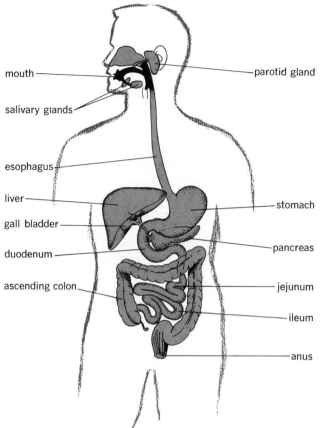

mouth

salivary glands

parotid gland

esophagus

liver

gall bladder

duodenum

ascending colon

stomach

pancreas

jejunum

ileum

anus

FIGURE 10.3 Digestive tract. By permission from A. C. Guyton, *Function of the Human Body.* Philadelphia: W. B. Saunders Company, 1964, p. 8.

adrenal medulla, increases metabolic rate.

We must consider the excretory system (see Figure 8.8) a part of the systems affecting metabolism because it is responsible for the removal of waste produced by metabolic processes.

The gross anatomy of the digestive system is illustrated in Figure 10.3 and in Plate 7. The pancreas and liver, which also serve purposes other than digestive, are very important parts of this system.

FUNCTION IN EXERCISE

Generally speaking, the digestive system has little if any function during the actual exercise period. There may be exceptions to this, as in the case of very long marathon runs or distance swimming during which food may be ingested in order to supply needed energy. Under the usually prevailing circumstances, however, all the energy that will be utilized has already been supplied and stored in one form or another in the body. Because the digestion and absorption of food is a somewhat slow process, it is readily seen that eating immediately before or during a contest would usually have little if any benefit.

Of course, it is important that proper nutritional practices be followed if sufficient energy stores are to be available to sustain vigorous activity. The energy to sustain muscular work is derived from the combination of oxygen with these energy-rich compounds that have been stored in the muscles and elsewhere. Limitations on performance are set by the extent of availability of oxygen and the food-derived energy source (glucose, fats, proteins, and so on) as well as by the accumulation of the waste products of metabolism (CO_2, lactic acid, and so on).

During exercise the rate of metabolism increases as more food is utilized to supply the energy requirement of the specific activity.

HUMAN DIETARY REQUIREMENTS

Protein, Carbohydrates, and Fat

The amino acids that make up proteins are needed to build, repair, and regulate the function of the body's cells. They are found in meat, fish, poultry, eggs, milk, nuts, dried peas and beans, bread, cereals, and vegetables.

There are twenty-three amino acids needed by the body. The thirteen *nonessential* acids are so named because they can be manufactured by the body. The ten essential amino acids must be supplied in the diet. The surest sources

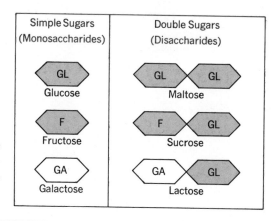

FIGURE 10.4 Schematic diagram of molecular structure of dietary carbohydrates. By permission from Bogert, Briggs, and Calloway, *Nutrition and Physical Fitness.* Philadelphia: W. B. Saunders Company, 1966, p. 22.

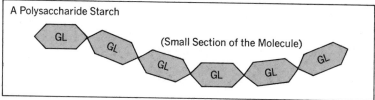

are the meats, although a careful selection of a combination of various vegetable proteins can also provide the essential acids.

Carbohydrates are needed to supply energy, to furnish heat, and to save proteins for building and regulating cells. Carbohydrates, found in fruit, most vegetables, bread, cereal, and milk, are the primary energy source for the body. Carbohydrates are normally ingested as disaccharides (su-

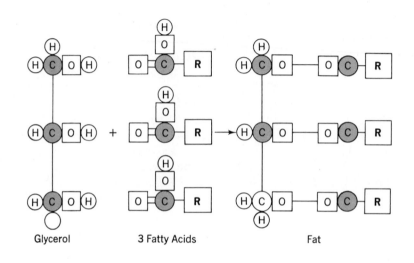

| Glycerol | 3 Fatty Acids | Fat |

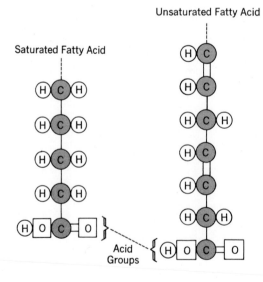

FIGURE 10.5   Schematic diagram of molecular structure of dietary fats. C = carbon, O = oxygen, H = hydrogen, R = fatty acid. By permission from Bogert, Briggs, and Calloway, *Nutrition and Physical Fitness*. Philadelphia: W. B. Saunders Company, 1966, p. 31.

crose, maltose, or lactose) and as highly complex starches (see Figure 10.4).

Fats are a second source of energy and are the primary storage form of foods not utilized immediately by the body. Fat is found in butter, margarine, cream, oils, meat, whole milk, peanuts, nuts, and avocados.

Carbohydrates yield twenty-six percent more calories per liter of oxygen than do fats (5.0 to 4.7), although fat produces more than twice as many calories per gram as do carbohydrates (9.0 to 4.0).

The fats we eat mostly are triglycerides (one molecule of glycerol combined with three molecules of fatty acid). If all the carbon atoms in the long carbon chain of the fatty acid have attached to them as many hydrogen atoms as they can hold, the fat is said to be "saturated." When one or more carbon atoms are not saturated with hydrogen, the fat is said to be "unsaturated." More than one unsaturated carbon atom identifies the fat as "polyunsaturated" (see Figure 10.5). The polyunsaturated fatty acids are essential in human nutrition, because the body needs them and cannot manufacture certain ones. These are known as the "essential fatty acids," and they must be included in the diet. Linoleic acid is the most important of these because the others (linolenic and arachidonic) can be synthesized from it by the body.

Excess nutrients, whether protein, carbohydrate, or fat, are stored largely as neutral fat (triglycerides), which is then available for energy, just as is the stored form of carbohydrate (glycogen).

Vitamins and Minerals

A vitamin is an organic substance that is essential, in very small quantities, for normal metabolism of the body's cells. Figure 10.6 will give you some idea of the general functions and common sources of vitamins, and Table 10.1 lists the most important ones, their functions, the best sources of them, and the results of their deficiencies.

Minerals (inorganic nutrients) are also essential, in small amounts, for normal body function. They have been classified as follows:

1. As components of the hard tissues (bones and teeth)
2. As essential components of soft tissues
3. As constituents of the body fluids

Table 10.2 summarizes the importance of the minerals. Although a balanced diet easily supplies the small amounts of these elements needed by the body, the supply of iron, calcium, iodine, and phosphorous is most likely to be critical (86, 142). The best sources of these are:

1. Calcium: milk and cheese, shellfish, egg yolk, canned sardines and salmon (with bones), soybeans, and green vegetables
2. Iron: liver (best source), heart, kidney, liver sausage, lean meats, shellfish, egg yolk, and dark molasses
3. Iodine: seafood, vegetables grown in iodine-rich soil, iodized salt (surest source)
4. Phosphorous: animal proteins, milk and cheeses, and nuts and legumes (86)

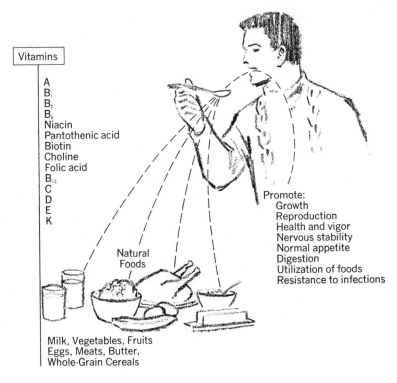

Vitamins

A
B₁
B₂
B₆
Niacin
Pantothenic acid
Biotin
Choline
Folic acid
B₁₂
C
D
E
K

Natural
Foods

Promote:
  Growth
  Reproduction
  Health and vigor
  Nervous stability
  Normal appetite
  Digestion
  Utilization of foods
  Resistance to infections

Milk, Vegetables, Fruits
Eggs, Meats, Butter,
Whole-Grain Cereals

FIGURE 10.6 Different vitamins found in natural foods and their general functions in the body. By permission from Bogert, Briggs, and Calloway, *Nutrition and Physical Fitness.* Philadelphia: W. B. Saunders Company, 1966, p. 205.

Water

Water is essential to maintain life. In fact, we can live longer without food than without water! Water makes up about 75 percent of a newborn infant's total body weight, and it decreases proportionately until adulthood, when some 57 percent of the body is water (224). Water provides a medium for transporting materials and provides a medium within the cell in which its chemical reactions take place. Approximately two to three quarts a day must be ingested to replace the amount excreted via the kidneys, skin, feces, and lungs. The amount lost and the requirement vary with environmental conditions, exercise, and, of course, vary in

health and disease. The scheme of water balance is illustrated in Figure 10.7.

Dehydration is a serious condition that can result from a negative shift in the water balance and is most commonly caused by exercise in a hot, humid environment and by excessive vomiting, especially in children and women nauseated during the first months of pregnancy. Dehydration is discussed further in Chapter 11.

Recommended Dietary Allowances

The United States Department of Agriculture has classified foods according to their contribution of the several nutrients. The guide encourages wide choice in food selection.

TABLE 10.1 Vitamins, Their Sources, Functions; and Deficiency Diseases and Disorders

VITAMIN	SOURCE	BODY FUNCTION EFFECT	DEFICIENCY RESULTS
A	Green leafy vegetables, milk, butter, eggs, liver, fish-liver	Essential to cell function of skin and cells lining the membrane of eye; also night vision	Overgrowth of skin; disease of the eye called xerophthalmia; night blindness
B₁(Thiamine)	Yeast, potato, liver, grains, eggs, meat, vegetables	Influential in stimulating growth; important for proper function of nerves; aids sugar metabolism	Beriberi; heart disease; neuritis
B₂(Riboflavin)	Eggs, milk, liver, meats, cheese	Important in metabolism of all body cells; promotes growth	Overgrowth of skin (keratosis); cracking of skin in corners of the mouth (cheilosis): inflammation of the tongue (glossitis); fear of light (photophobia)
Nicotinic acid (Niacin)	Liver, wheat, yeast, meat	Essential to good health; promotes growth; aids sugar metabolism; important for normal intestinal function	Pellagra (skin disease); inflammation of tongue; nervous disorders
B₃	Liver, cereals, fish, vegetables, yeast	Important for proper protein metabolism; essential to cell function	Nerve inflammation; skin irritation, such as seborrhea
B₁₂	Eggs, milk, liver, meats	Important in fat and sugar metabolism; also in formation of blood; promotes growth	Pernicious anemia; neuritis
C(Ascorbic acid)	Citrus fruits (oranges, lemons, limes, grapefruits), potatoes, tomatoes	Essential to function of blood vessels; healing of wounds; and function of connective tissue	Scurvy with hemorrhages into tissues, from the gums, etc.
D	Fish livers (cod liver oil), milk, butter, eggs, sunlight	Essential to bone metabolism and normal bone formation; also to calcium and phosphorus metabolism	Rickets with bone deformities (bowlegs, pigeon chest, etc.); convulsions in infants (tetany)
Folic acid	Liver, yeast, green vegetables, (lettuce, etc.)	Important in formation of red blood cells	Anemia accompanied by improperly formed red blood cells
K	In intestinal tract of healthy persons on normal diet	Necessary for normal blood clotting	Hemorrhage, especially following surgery

SOURCE: By permission from Otto, Julian, and Tether, *Modern Health*. New York: Holt, Rinehart and Winston, Inc., 1963, p. 313.

The recommended dietary allowances are intended to serve as a guide in planning diets for population groups. Variations are to be expected because activity and energy expenditure levels, body weights, and climatic conditions vary considerably.

A much more general but more complex "rule-of-thumb" may be more useful in determining amount and com-

TABLE 10.2.   Need for Mineral Elements

	ELEMENTS ESPECIALLY NEEDED	RESULTS OF LACK OF THESE ELEMENTS
AS BUILDING MATERIALS:		⎧ Stunted growth
		Weakened or soft bones
Bones and teeth	Calcium and phosphorus	⎨ Malformed or decaying teeth
Hair, nails, and skin	Sulfur	⎩ Rickets
Soft tissues — chiefly muscles	All salts, esp. ⎧ potassium ⎨ phosphorus ⎨ sulfur ⎩ chlorine	
Nervous tissue	All salts, esp. phosphorus	Lack of iron or copper results in less than normal amounts of hemoglobin in blood, a condition called nutritional anemia
Blood	All salts, esp. ⎧ iron ⎨ calcium ⎨ sodium ⎨ phosphorus ⎩ copper	
Glandular secretions	Stomach secretions — chlorine	
	Intestinal secretions — sodium	Lack of iodine results in enlargement of thyroid gland — simple goiter
	Thyroid secretion — iodine	
AS BODY REGULATORS: TO MAINTAIN *NORMAL*		
Exchange of body fluids	All salts	
Contractility of muscles ⎫ Irritability of nerves ⎬	All salts, especially balance of calcium with sodium and potassium	
Clotting of blood	Calcium	
Oxidation processes	Iron and iodine	
Neutrality of body	Balance between: Basic elements — sodium, potassium, calcium, magnesium, and iron Acidic elements — phosphorus, sulfur, and chlorine	

SOURCE: By permission from Bogert, Briggs, and Calloway, *Nutrition and Physical Fitness*. Philadelphia: W. B. Saunders, 1966, p. 132.

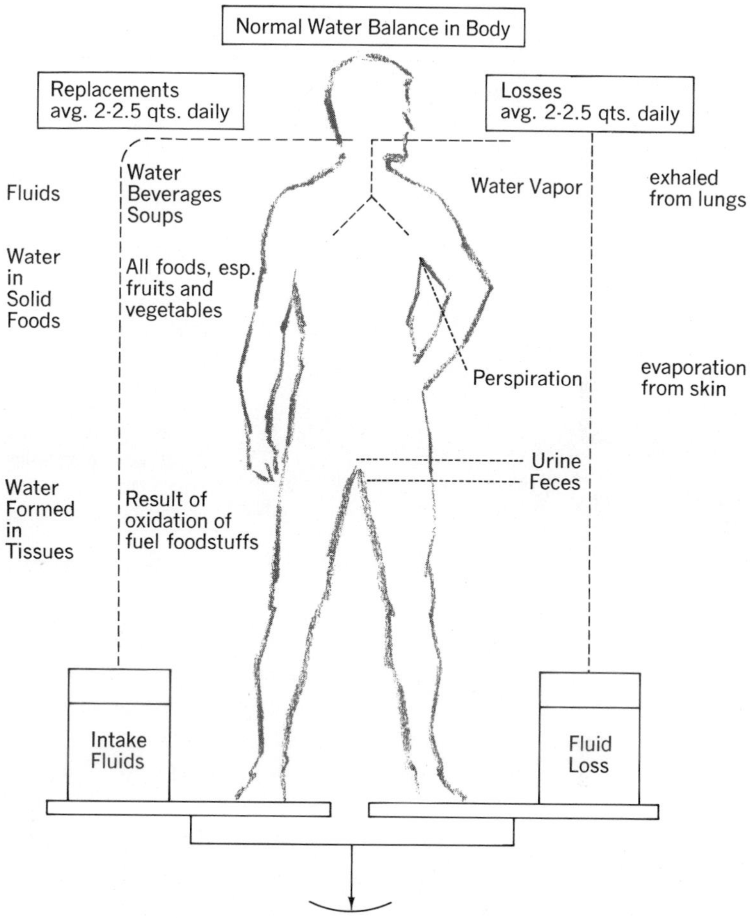

FIGURE 10.7 Normally the intake and output of water from the body are approximately in balance. If much water is drunk, the volume of urine excreted increases. If water intake is low or the amount lost in perspiration is high (with exercise or in hot weather), the urine will be reduced in volume. By permission from Bogert, Briggs, and Calloway, *Nutrition and Physical Fitness*. Philadelphia: W. B. Saunders Company, 1966, p. 142.

position of the diet for the *healthy* adult. (The established minimal vitamin and mineral requirements should, of course, be met.)

1. Determine the caloric intake necessary, depending on the individual's needs to:

a. maintain body weight (intake equals daily expenditure)

b. gain weight (daily intake exceeds expenditure)

c. lose weight (expenditure exceeds intake by at least 500 calories a day with minimal intake of 1500 calories a day)

TABLE 10.3   Recommended Dietary Allowances

GROUP	SERVINGS	INCLUDES
Milk	Some milk daily	Children 3 to 4 cups Teen-agers 4 or more cups Adults 2 or more cups Pregnant women 4 or more cups Nursing mothers 6 or more cups Cheese and ice cream can replace part of the milk.
Meat	2 or more	Beef, veal, pork, lamb, poultry, fish, eggs, with dried beans and peas and nuts as alternates.
Vegetable–Fruit	4 or more	A dark green or deep yellow vegetable important for vitamin A —at least every other day. A citrus fruit or other fruit or vegetable important for vitamin C—daily; other fruits and vegetables including potatoes.
Bread–Cereals	4 or more	Whole grain, enriched, restored.
Other food	Normally included in the daily diet	Butter, margarine, sugars, and unenriched grain products serve to provide the caloric and nutrient allowances.

2. Begin by assuring a daily intake of at least one gram of protein per kilogram of body weight (approximately 2.2 pounds equals one kilogram). Make sure that the ten essential amino acids are included. For gaining weight (for example, for growing children) the excess calories per day should probably be protein.

3. No more than 25 to 30 percent of the total calories should be derived from fats (see Figures 10.8 to 10.10), at least 50 percent of these of the unsaturated variety (soft oils and so forth).

4. The remainder should be from the carbohydrates, with the large majority being of the complex type (starches and so forth) rather than being highly puri-

FIGURE 10.8   Effects of low-cholesterol, low-fat diet on mortality of coronary heart disease patients. Adapted from Katz, Stamler, and Pick (294) after Morrison (407).

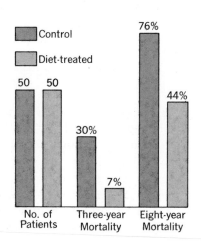

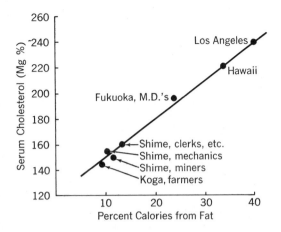

FIGURE 10.9 Diet and serum cholesterol in 284 clinically healthy Japanese men in seven groups. Age range was 40-49. After Figure 2, Ancel Keys, "Diet and the Epidemiology of Heart Disease," *Journal of the American Medical Association,* 164:1912, 1957. By permission.

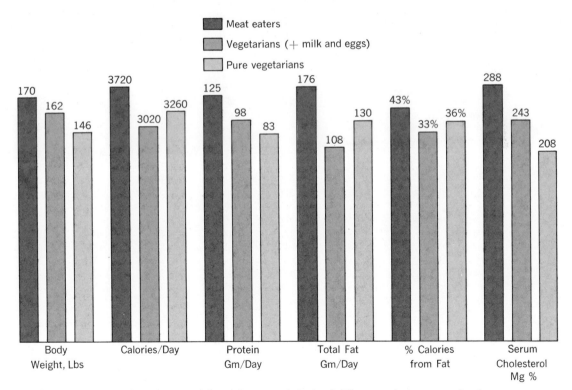

FIGURE 10.10 Nutritional, body weight, and serum cholesterol differences between meat eaters, lacto-ovo-vegetarians, and vegetarians. Adapted from Katz, Stamler, and Pick (294) after Hardinge and Stare (228).

fied sugars (461) (see Figure 8.42). This should not exceed roughly 50 percent of the total caloric intake.

In connection with this recommended diet, it is interesting to note how the United States of America has changed its food intake habits since 1910 (see Figure 10.11 and Table 10.4).

When To Eat

Recent research suggests that, for weight maintenance or reduction, it is best to divide the caloric intake fairly evenly over at least three meals a day (165, 166, 171, 278). In our own laboratory, several experiments have shown

TABLE 10.4 Apparent per Capita Consumption of Major Foods, 1910–1960, U.S.A. (in Pounds per Person)

FOOD	1910	1920	1930	1940	1950	1960
Meats	146	137	129	142	145	161
Fish	—	—	10	11	12	10
Eggs (number)	306	299	331	319	389	334
Poultry	—	—	17	17	25	34
Total milk fat solids	30	29	32	33	29	25
Total nonfat milk solids	35	38	36	38	43	44
Fluid milk and cream	315	348	337	331	349	325
Ice cream (gal)	2	8	10	11	17	18
Fats and oils	—	—	—	46	46	45
Fruits, fresh	138	145	134	142	107	98
Fruits, citrus	18	26	31	57	41	33
Apples	59	63	42	30	23	20
Fruits, canned	4	9	13	19	22	23
Juices, canned	0.5	0.5	0.3	7	13	13
Juices, frozen	—	—	0.5	1	4	9
Fresh vegetables and melons	—	127	145	143	140	132
Canned vegetables	15	19	28	34	42	45
Frozen vegetables	—	—	—	1	3	10
Potatoes	198	140	132	123	106	102
Sugar	75	86	110	96	101	98
Grains						
Corn meal	51	35	28	22	12	7
Oat	3	6	6	4	3	4
Barley	4	3	5	1	1	1
Wheat	214	179	171	155	135	118
Beverages						
Coffee	9	12	13	16	16	16
Tea	1	1	1	1	1	1

SOURCE: *Statistical Abstract of the United States* (578).

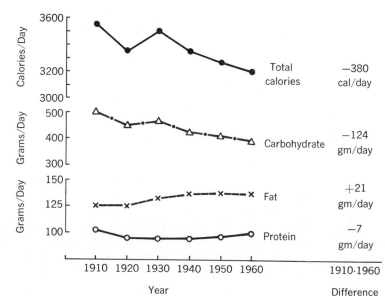

FIGURE 10.11 Nutrients available for civilian consumption per person per day in the United States, 1910-1960. Adapted from *Statistical Abstract of the United States* (578).

that rats fed only once a day gain more weight per gram of food consumed than those fed ad libitum (see Figure 10.12). It appears that the spreading out of the caloric intake may be just as important as the composition of the diet both in terms of efficiency (377) and prevention of obesity and high blood cholesterol (171). Obesity and high blood cholesterol are, of course, statistically associated with heart disease. This concept is discussed further in Chapter 8.

For improved efficiency, meals should be well spaced throughout the day. There is evidence that greater output of work is gained from a five-meal day than from a three-meal day and that eliminating or limiting the composition of breakfast results in decreased work output (377).

FIGURE 10.12 Comparison of assimilation rate of consumed food in "nibblers" and "meal eaters." Ration of weight gained to food eaten. Number was 16 in each group of male albino rats. Data from Johnson and Cooper (278).

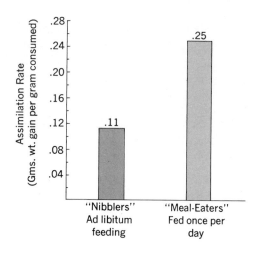

There is a widespread belief that stomach cramps are often responsible for drownings and that they are caused by swimming immediately after eating. There is little if any objective evidence that abdominal cramps are a common swimming hazard. Frequently the causes of drowning accidents have been assumed from the position in which bodies have been found. This is, of course, not objective evidence. Furthermore, it has been reported that efforts to discover swimmers who had ever experienced cramps of this type have been almost completely fruitless. Dr. Arthur Steinhaus quotes an unidentified swimming expert on this subject:

I have never seen a case of so-called stomach cramps. I am familiar with cramps of thighs and legs. These are generally associated with swimming in cold water or when fatigued. Although I have observed hundreds of thousands of persons, among them participants in Red Cross summer institutes, engaged in recreational and instructional swimming immediately after eating, I have yet to see the first case of drowning or near drowning that could be attributed authentically to swimming at this time. Usually drownings are attributable to carelessness or foolhardiness (543, p. 159).

The late Fred Lanoue (328, p. 153), famed swimming coach at Georgia Tech, reported that of more than 30,000 swimmers with whom he had been associated, not one had ever experienced a stomach cramp.

As a result of reports such as these and in the absence of any objective evidence to the contrary, it has been concluded that the "stomach cramp" danger is largely a mythical one. It is further suggested that if there is danger involved in swimming after eating it would probably result from a feeling of discomfort in breathing. This would probably occur only after an extremely large meal. In such cases it would, of course, be wise to refrain from swimming until such time as complete freedom in breathing is restored.

It is not wise to eat just before or immediately following an activity that involves emotions or nervousness—for example, competitive athletics. This type of activity tends to interfere with the digestive process; however, *mild* exercise, not involving competition or emotions, is not harmful and may even act as an aid to digestion.

IDEAL BODY WEIGHT

How much should one weigh? Is there over- or underweight? In trying to answer these questions from height-weight tables, caution should be taken in interpreting them (see Tables 10.5 and 10.6). Underweight or overweight as judged by deviations from the tables does not necessarily indicate undernutrition or obesity. An inherited frame size plays an important part in determining one's weight and most height-weight tables are now designed to include three categories of frames: small, medium, and large (see Tables 10.5 and 10.6). The problem is that most people really have no way of knowing into which category they

TABLE 10.5 Desirable Weights for Men of Ages 25 and Over: Weight in Pounds According to Frame (in Indoor Clothing)

HEIGHT (WITH SHOES ON— 1-INCH HEELS) Feet	Inches	SMALL FRAME	MEDIUM FRAME	LARGE FRAME
5	2	112–120	118–129	126–141
5	3	115–123	121–133	129–144
5	4	118–126	124–136	132–148
5	5	121–129	127–139	135–152
5	6	124–133	130–143	138–156
5	7	128–137	134–147	142–161
5	8	132–141	138–152	147–166
5	9	136–145	142–156	151–170
5	10	140–150	146–160	155–174
5	11	144–154	150–165	159–179
6	0	148–158	154–170	164–184
6	1	152–162	158–175	168–189
6	2	156–167	162–180	173–194
6	3	160–171	167–185	178–199
5	4	164–175	172–190	182–204

SOURCE: Metropolitan Life Insurance Company.

TABLE 10.6 Desirable Weights for Women of Ages 25 and Over: Weight in Pounds According to Frame (in Indoor Clothing)[a]

HEIGHT (WITH SHOES ON— 1-INCH HEELS) Feet	Inches	SMALL FRAME	MEDIUM FRAME	LARGE FRAME
4	10	92– 98	96–107	104–119
4	11	94–101	98–110	106–122
5	0	96–104	101–113	109–125
5	1	99–107	104–116	112–128
5	2	102–110	107–119	115–131
5	3	105–113	110–122	118–134
5	4	108–116	113–126	121–138
5	5	111–119	116–130	125–142
5	6	114–123	120–135	129–146
5	7	118–127	124–139	133–150
5	8	122–131	128–143	137–154
5	9	126–135	132–147	141–158
5	10	130–140	136–151	145–163
5	11	134–144	140–155	149–168
6	0	138–148	144–159	153–173

[a]For girls between 18 and 25, subtract 1 pound for each year under 25.
SOURCE: Metropolitan Life Insurance Company.

fit. As discussed later, there are other means of estimating what one *should* weigh and a combination of several estimates is probably best.

Sheldon (512) is credited with developing the most functional system for classifying the human body. He uses three principal body components designated as **endomorphy** (soft and fat), **mesomorphy** (husky and muscular), and **ectomorphy** (lean and linear), and rates each component on a scale from 1 to 7. Everyone possesses each of the components to some degree but is generally highest in one component with perhaps a second modifying component. One might be basically husky but have many soft characteristics and so be classified as an endomorphic mesomorph. A somewhat muscular but very thin person might be labeled a mesomorphic ectomorph. Somatotyping is discussed further in Chapter 13.

Measuring skin-fold thickness to estimate body fat may provide a good estimate of optimal body weight; however, the reliability of skin-fold measurements has been questioned unless done by an experienced person.

WEIGHT CONTROL AND NUTRIENT ANALYSIS

It is highly recommended that daily diet and activity records be kept as follows:

1. For every member of the family, at least once yearly (perhaps twice, if there is a radical change in diet with the seasonal changes)

2. Any time a child has a weight problem (undue loss of weight or failure to gain)

3. Any time an adult has a weight problem of *any* kind; should be done to ascertain status before initiating any program for change

As many elements as possible should be determined for intake and a thorough record of activities should be kept to estimate energy expenditure. At least five days are necessary and at least two of these should be "weekend" days in order to permit comparison with work days or school days.

Table 10.7 illustrates a completed recall record for one day. By following this procedure, one can get a reasonably reliable estimate. The calculations are made from Tables 10.8 and Appendix E. Calculations based on these tables must, of course, be considered approximate. Caloric expenditure tables are extremely "rough" estimates because many factors affect actual energy cost for a given activity. Table 10.8 presents data on a calories-per-pound of body weight basis because, as you would expect, energy expenditure in activity is strongly affected by body weight. This is an improvement over the absolute calorie tables, but still does not take into account such factors as age, amount of musculature, the range of intensity possible for most of the listed tasks, or the size of the equipment used in the task. For example, individual differences not entirely accounted for by body weight can be quite pronounced. A 195-pound man has been observed to produce calories at a rate of 780 per hour during uphill

TABLE 10.7   Sample Diet and Activity Recall Record

ACTIVITY	TIME	MIN	FACTOR	PRODUCT	FOOD	QUANTITY	CALORIES	PROTEIN (g)	CHO.	FAT	CALORIES FROM SAT. FAT	UNSAT. FAT
Breakfast	8:00– 8:30	30	.0093	.279	Bacon	3	155	8	3	117	37	74
Reading	8:30–10:00	90	.0080	.720	Eggs, scrambled	2	175	11	8	117	37	71
Walking	10:00–10:30	30	.0330	.990	Orange juice, fresh	6 oz	80	1	68	—	—	—
Classwork	10:30–12:00	90	.0110	.990	Toast (white)	1	60	2	47	6	1	5
Lunch	12:00–12:30	30	.0093	.279	Butter	1 pat	70	—	—	70	39	27
Classwork	1:00– 4:00	180	.0110	1.980	Milk	8 oz	165	9	47	79	44	31
Basketball	4:00– 5:00	60	.0470	2.820								
Walking	5:30– 6:00	30	.0330	.990	Hamburger	2	490	41	—	306	146	144
Sitting	6:00– 6:30	30	.0080	.240	Bun	2	240	8	188	24	4	20
Supper	6:30– 7:30	60	.0093	.558	Potato chips	10	115	1	40	67	16	50
Study (writing)	7:30– 9:30	120	.0120	1.440	Soft drink, cola	12 oz	130	—	130	—	—	—
Sleep	11:00– 8:00	540	.0078	4.212	Ice cream	Avg. serv.	205	4	82	109	60	43
(24 hrs. = 1440 − 1290)												
Fill-in		150	.0100	1.500	Ham	Avg. serv.	290	21	—	198	71	117
(Calories expended/pound) = 16.998					Boiled potatoes	2 med.	130	4	120	—	—	—
(Multiplied by weight) × 200 lbs.					Peas, frozen	1/2 cup	55	5	41	3	—	—
3400 cal.					Butter	3 pats	210	—	—	210	117	81
Caloric intake (K) = 3265					Rolls	2	120	4	94	12	2	10
difference = −135 cal.					Milk	8 oz	165	9	47	79	44	31
					Apple pie	1 pc.	410	4	220	151	50	95
					Totals		K = 3265	P = 128g	C = 1135	F = 1548	S = 668	U = 799

Breakfast(B) = 705   Lunch(L) = 1180   Supper(S) = 1380

% CHO calories = C ÷ K = 34.8%

% Fat calories = F ÷ K = 47.4%

$$\% \text{ Fat unsaturated} = \frac{U}{S+U} = \frac{799}{1467} = 55.5\%$$

$$\% \text{ Cal. breakfast} = \frac{(B)}{K} = \frac{705}{3265} = 21.6\%$$

$$\% \text{ Cal. lunch} = \frac{(L)}{K} = \frac{1180}{3265} = 36.1\%$$

$$\% \text{ Cal. supper} = \frac{(S)}{K} = \frac{1380}{3265} = 42.3\%$$

128 (intake)

Wt. (200 pounds) × .45 g/pound =   90 g (required)

+38 g protein excess

walking on a treadmill for five minutes while a 185-pound colleague's rate was only 390—exactly one half (281). Furthermore, fitness or skill in the activity also has an effect. The average cost of a standardized treadmill walk in nine men was reduced from a rate of 500 to 420 calories per hour after four weeks in a relatively moderate exercise program (281).

The point is this: Be careful in attempting energy balance calculations. Absolute figures taken from expenditure tables may be quite misleading, and there may even be individual differences in food absorption related

TABLE 10.8   Approximate Caloric Expenditure for Various Activities

CAL/MIN/ LB. OF BODY WT.	ACTIVITY	CAL/HR/ LB. OF BODY WT.	CAL/MIN/ LB. OF BODY WT.	ACTIVITY	CAL/HR/ LB. OF BODY WT.
.0234	House painting	1.40	.023	Volleyball	1.40
.026	Carpentry	1.56	.026	Playing ping pong	1.56
.031	Farming, planting, hoeing, raking	1.86	.033	Calisthenics	1.98
			.033	Bicycling on level roads	1.98
.039	Gardening, weeding	2.34	.036	Golfing	2.16
.045	Pick-and-shovel work	2.70	.046	Playing tennis	2.76
.050	Chopping wood	3.00	.047	Playing basketball	2.82
.062	Gardening, digging	3.72	.069	Playing squash	4.14
			.100	Running long distance	6.00
.0078	Sleeping	0.47	.156	Sprinting	—
.0079	Resting in bed	0.47			
.0080	Sitting, normally	0.48		Swimming	
.0080	Sitting, reading	0.48	.032	Breast stroke 20 yd/min	—
.0089	Lying, quietly	0.54	.064	Breast stroke 40 yd/min	—
.0093	Sitting, eating	0.56	.026	Back stroke 25 yd/min	—
.0096	Sitting, playing cards	0.58	.056	Back stroke 40 yd/min	—
.0094	Standing, normally	0.56	.058	Crawl 45 yd/min	—
			.071	Crawl 55 yd/min	—
.011	Classwork, lecture	0.66			
.012	Conversing	0.72	.033	Walking on level	1.98
.012	Sitting, writing	0.72	.093	Running on level (jogging)	5.60
.016	Standing, light activity	0.96			
.020	Driving a car	1.20	.01	Fill-in constant for time	0.60
.028	Cleaning windows	1.68		unaccounted for (if not	
.024	Sweeping floors	1.40		completely inactive	
.044	Walking downstairs	—		such as sleeping or	
.116	Walking upstairs	—		resting)	
.014	Lecturing	0.84			

EXAMPLE: 150-pound man sitting and reading for 60 min = 150 × .0080 × 60 = 72 calories expended, or 1 hr = 150 × .48 × 1 = 72 calories.

to, for example, differences in bile available to aid in the digestion of fats (362). One should not be surprised if he does not have success at first. If the intake figures are correct, it is quite possible that there is a need to revise expenditure estimates or to look at the possibility of differences in absorption.

OVERWEIGHT

It is ironic that while much of the world's population suffers from insufficient food supplies, many people of the United States are suffering from an *overabundance* of certain foods in the diet. The American public's most serious nutritional problem is probably excess weight. It is interesting to pause here and note that Russian studies "show convincingly that rats fed on meager but wholesome food, containing all necessary vitamins, amino acids, and salts, live considerably longer than their controls fed on the usual diet." It is also pointed out that, in these studies, the rats on the restricted diet are more active and "their vital indices correspond to a younger age" (370).

Food provides energy for work and heat. If more work is performed than the daily food intake provides for, stored foods are used. If more food is eaten than can be burned, the excess is stored as fat.

Esthetically speaking, stored fat is not desirable; moreover, excess fatty tissue probably has an adverse influence on health. Obesity in children often exposes them to difficult situations and damaging emotional experiences.

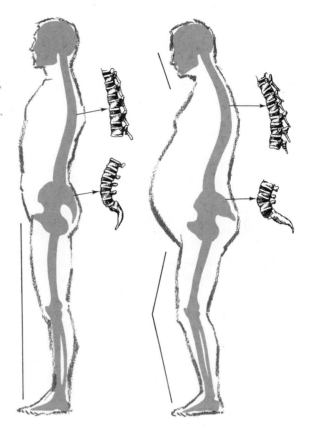

FIGURE 10.13 Normal posture (left) and posture in obesity. By permission from William J. Kerr and John B. Lagen, "The Postural Syndrome Related to Obesity Leading to Postural Emphysema and Cardiorespiratory Failure," *Annals of Internal Medicine*, 10:581, 1936.

Obesity that develops before age 10 or after 16 is difficult to treat, whereas obesity developing just before puberty may be physiologic and is often self-corrective in the next few years. Inactivity often leads to the development and perpetuation of obesity (376).

Environment can play an important role in establishing appetite and eating patterns. Children coming from homes where the mother loves to bake can easily develop an eating pattern that must include desserts. While children are young and active the additional calories are usually burned up, but as this eating pattern continues and their lives become more sedentary the excess calories are stored as fat.

Overweight adults are more susceptible than are those of normal weight to arthritis, cancer, cardiovascular disease, diabetes, gall bladder disturbances, hernia, certain forms of liver disease, and other health impairments (118).

As discussed on page 215, obesity is associated with high blood pressure

FIGURE 10.14 Effect of weight reduction on relative mortality risk. Adapted from Katz, Stamler, and Pick (294) after Shepard and Marks (513).

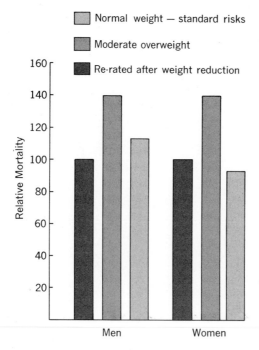

and arteriosclerotic heart disease. Figure 10.14 presents an interesting picture relating weight and mortality.

Cause of Overweight and Obesity

We have noted with a great deal of interest an experimental study on overeating reported by Strong, Shirling, and Passmore (552). Figure 10.15 portrays the calculated results of four days' overeating in sixteen male and female subjects of varying body weights and builds. These data provide evidence that, at least during periods of short-term excess calorie intake, neither the thin nor the obese person "adapts" to the calorie excess by rejecting part of the excess or by burning up a significant proportion of the excess. Fecal loss is not increased nor is BMR increased any more than can be accounted for by the SDA (see page 320). The amount of weight was dependent mostly on variability in water retention. On the average, 9 percent of the excess was stored as protein, 35 percent as fat, and 36 percent as carbohydrate, which means only 20 percent was metabolized and lost via excretion.

A most important phenomenon related to metabolism and weight control is seldom recognized. Changes in activity and the somewhat typical decline in BMR associated with aging can combine to cause unbelievable weight gains.

As one can see by studying Figures 10.16 and 10.17, discontinuance of an activity without a parallel reduction in caloric intake can very subtly but surely cause a substantial deposi-

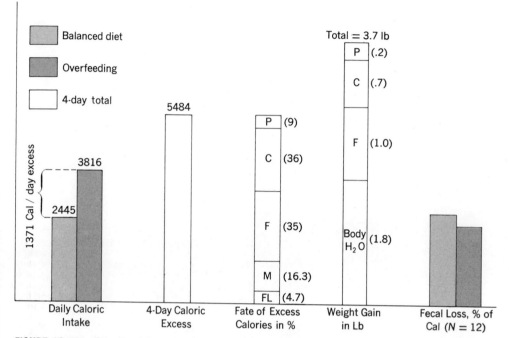

FIGURE 10.15 Results of four days' overfeeding in 16 subjects. Data from Strong, Shirling, and Passmore (552).

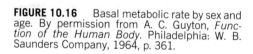

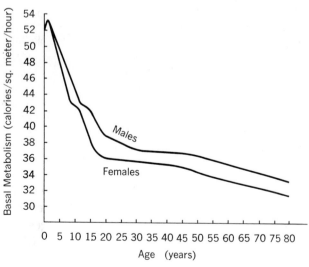

FIGURE 10.16 Basal metabolic rate by sex and age. By permission from A. C. Guyton, *Function of the Human Body.* Philadelphia: W. B. Saunders Company, 1964, p. 361.

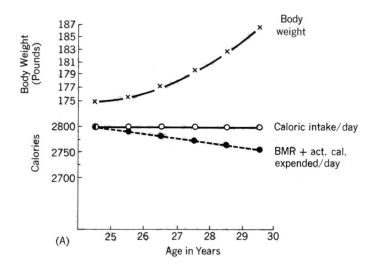

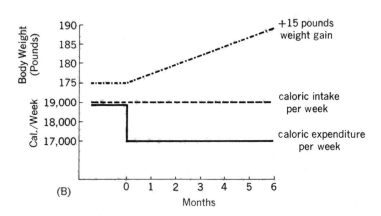

FIGURE 10.17 (A) Theoretical weight gain from normal fall in BMR from age 25-30. Average fall at this age is only 8 calories per day, but this would cause a weight gain of 12 pounds over five years (even if activities stayed same) if intake was not reduced. Assume 3500 calories = 1 pound body weight. (B) Theoretical six-month weight gain resulting from cessation of one hour recreational basketball five days per week and continuation of same caloric intake. Assume 3500 calories = 1 pound body weight.

tion of excess fat. In the example cited in Figure 10.17 the typical 8 percent drop in BMR seen between ages 25 and 30 as illustrated in Figure 10.16 could, by itself, account for a twelve-pound weight gain in five years if intake were not decreased.

The examples are obviously oversimplified. However, the principle is of extreme importance and practicality and should be kept well in mind. There is considerable evidence that this is exactly the sort of thing that happens to many overweight individuals, including former college letter-winners (395) (see Figure 10.18).

Combining our classification system with others proposed in the literature, we have presented what seems to be a logical and understandable means of classifying the causes of obesity (see Table 10.9). The current medical view is that only a very small percentage of obese persons can legitimately attribute their problem to any endogenous cause. In other words, metabolic obesity has not been convincingly demonstrated in the human being. It is important to point out that, *no matter what the cause, one cannot lose weight unless caloric expenditure exceeds caloric intake!* And, conversely, *when intake exceeds expenditure, one will gain weight!*

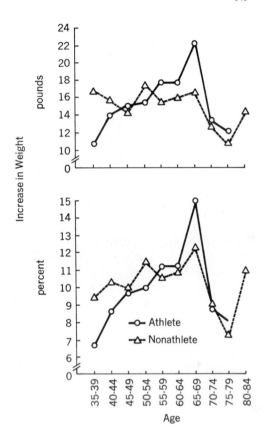

FIGURE 10.18   After 45 years of age, the weight gain of athletes is greater than that of nonathletes. By permission from Montoye and others (395).

TABLE 10.9   Causes of Obesity

	PSYCHOLOGIC	PHYSIOLOGIC
EXOGENOUS: (From "without")	Neurotic overeating Compulsive eating, boredom, and so on	Decreased Energy Expenditure Forced inactivity or immobilization Voluntary inactivity
	Non-neurotic overeating (cultural dietary pattern)	
ENDOGENOUS: (From "within")		Metabolic Obesity Enzyme disorder Endocrine disorder Hypothalamic disorder

EFFERENT CONCEPTS

We shall now take a look at the role that regular exercise plays in digestion, the relationship of nutritional principles to exercise and fitness, and, finally, the very important relationships among food intake, regular exercise, and weight control.

REGULAR EXERCISE, DIGESTION, AND METABOLISM

Does regular exercise increase the size and functional capacity of the digestive organs? There is no support for this claim; in fact, it appears that changes in size and function do *not* occur as a result of training.

Does regular exercise improve digestion and elimination? There is no evidence to support the claim that regular exercise improves actual digestion of foodstuffs. There is some clinical evidence that complete lack of activity in bed-ridden patients often leads to constipation and the medical texts state that exercise is important for "regularity," but there is no experimental evidence to corroborate the view based on the clinical experiences.

Does regular exercise increase the basal metabolic rate (BMR)? Obviously exercise per se increases metabolism, but there is great confusion concerning the effect of training on the basal metabolic rate. The confusion is due, in part, to the difficulty in recording the true BMR. At this time, the best answer appears to be that, in general, regular exercise has no appreciable effect on BMR.

Does regular exercise eliminate body fat? This question will be dealt with later in this chapter. The logical conclusion is that exercise *can* reduce body fat stores provided caloric intake does not consistently exceed caloric expenditures.

Does regular exercise add weight? Again, the complexity of the several factors involved makes it difficult to give a definite answer. If muscle hypertrophy occurs and weight gain is not compensated for by decreased fat stores, appropriate muscle training can increase weight. Obviously, if exercise increases the appetite and this increased appetite is appeased regularly, it is even possible that one might gain weight in this manner. This is not recommended as a means of gaining weight except, perhaps, in an extremely undernourished or thin person. Unless one is extremely thin, it is questionable whether he should even be concerned about "putting on weight," especially if such an increase is primarily an attempt to gain social acceptance by looking more "prosperous"!

EXERCISE, FITNESS, AND NUTRITION

Although a great deal has been written about nutrition and athletic performance and exercise, we see no particular advantage in reproducing such information here. Excellent reviews have been published by Mayer and Bullen (377) and VanItallie, Sinisterra, and Stare (585). The sum and substance of the research is that the great majority of the theories and "fads" do not stand up under scientific inquiry. It can be stated with some considerable degree of confidence that:

1. A normal, well-balanced diet (as described on page 329), increased in keeping with the demands of the increased daily physical activity, is adequate and cannot be improved on by supplementation with any reasonable expectation that performance or fitness will be enhanced.

2. Because glucose as a fuel is more efficient than fat in terms of oxygen needed, there may be some benefit from slightly increasing carbohydrate intake (377, 585), but not at the expense of protein (see entry 3) and not to excess proportions (probably should never exceed 50 to 55 percent of total caloric intake).

3. Protein intake may need to be increased above the minimum recommendation if growth is still occurring or if muscle mass is to be increased (377, 585).

4. Vitamin and mineral supplements have not proven to be of value unless the person has a deficiency. In other words, *excess* vitamin intake in the normal individual does not promote greater physical efficiency. For example, Vitamin B_{12} would not be expected to improve the red blood cell count and the hemoglobin concentration in a man with a normal 14.5 g% hemoglobin concentration (394). Thus, O_2 delivery would certainly not be enhanced by excess Vitamin B_{12} intake.

In summary, the best evidence available supports a cautious and conservative viewpoint. The optimum diet for an athlete or any person exercising regularly "is not different in any major respect from that which would be recommended to any normal individual. The diet should be adequate for maintenance, for growth if the individual is still growing, for increase in muscle mass if need be and for fulfilling of energy requirements . . ." (377). On the other hand, "there is no doubt whatever that performance can be significantly impaired when a less than adequate diet is consumed" (585).

EXERCISE AND WEIGHT CONTROL

(The term "weight control" is used here in its most inclusive sense; it includes the aspects of prevention of weight gain and weight maintenance as well as weight reduction.) It is important to bear in mind that obesity is synonymous with excess body fat, not with "overweight," which may or may not include excess body fat. With respect to the weight reduction aspect of weight control, our discussion is directed toward the condition of slight to moderate obesity and not to the more resistant types of gross, refractory obesity. When discussing exercise and weight control, we assume that exercise is to be combined with a balanced diet, a diet that is balanced with caloric expenditure for prevention of weight gain or maintenance of weight and that is reduced daily by 500 to 1000 calories for weight loss. It is important to remember that, before embarking on a weight reduction program, the degree of obesity, if any, must be properly determined; this means one should use at least the skin-fold method for estimating percent of body fat. For example, a forty-year-old man may be 25 pounds "overweight" according to height-weight tables; if his body is 20 percent fat, because normal for even a twenty-one-year-old male is about 14 percent, he is carrying only about 6 percent of his weight as excess fat; this means only 12.6 pounds to be lost, not 25!

There are apparently three ways in which regular exercise can contribute to weight control. The best known is, of course, an increase in caloric expenditure. Less recognized, but possibly of even greater importance, are: (1) a positive effect on the body's "appestat," which balances food intake with actual need, and (2) promotion of a more optimal body composition (that is, less fat) for a given body weight. There is also greater permanence of weight loss when regular exercise is included as an integral part of a weight reduction program.

Caloric Expenditure

In spite of the poor applicability of caloric expenditure tables to individual situations, such tables do reveal the high energy cost of exercise above the basal rate (see Figure 10.19). It has been estimated that a man can expend the equivalent of sixteen pounds a year through a daily half hour of handball or squash (376). Those who argue against exercise as a means of losing weight cite from the energy tables that it takes seven hours of chopping wood to lose one pound. They fail to state

that one half hour a day will do the same thing in a two-week period as seven hours accomplish all at once. In a year of daily one-half-hour periods, twenty-six pounds can be lost. Therefore, in looking at the hours required to lose weight by exercise, one should think in terms of short daily exercise periods over long periods of time.

There is an abundance of evidence to support the conclusion that regular exercise can reduce body fat; however, exercise is not the only activity that controls weight loss. To reduce fat it is necessary to expend more calories than are consumed. Also, certain individuals may have a hormone or metabolism problem that prevents or limits the amount of fat that can be lost through exercise. Recently there has been advanced a possible explanation for some people's inability to lose weight even though they do not overeat or underexercise. There is a possibility of a temperature control abnormality that makes some persons burn resources other than fat in order to maintain warmth. To maintain body temperature, such persons apparently depend more upon fat's insulating quality than on metabolic processes (378).

Shade and others (509) recently compared the effects of six weeks of "generalized" and of **"spot"** reducing in

FIGURE 10.19 Approximate energy expenditure in various physical activities and "inactivities." Comparison-ranking in calories per pound per 30 minutes and examples calculated for a 120-pound and a 160-pound person. Data from a summary by C. F. Consolazio, R. E. Johnson, and L. J. Pecora, *Physiological Measurements of Metabolic Functions in Man.* New York: McGraw-Hill, Inc., 1963, pp. 330-332.

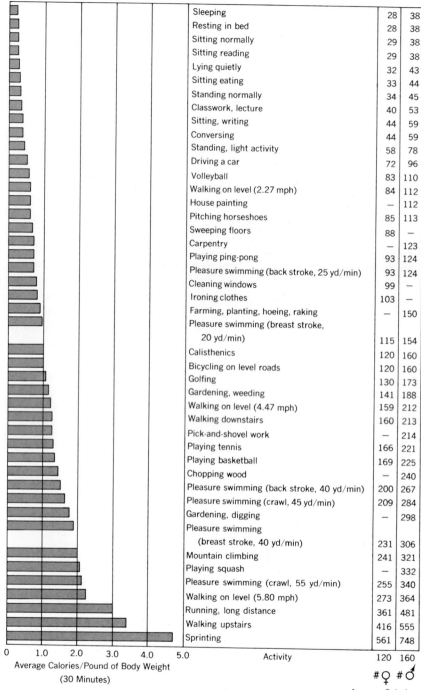

Activity	# ♀	# ♂
Sleeping	28	38
Resting in bed	28	38
Sitting normally	29	38
Sitting reading	29	38
Lying quietly	32	43
Sitting eating	33	44
Standing normally	34	45
Classwork, lecture	40	53
Sitting, writing	44	59
Conversing	44	59
Standing, light activity	58	78
Driving a car	72	96
Volleyball	83	110
Walking on level (2.27 mph)	84	112
House painting	—	112
Pitching horseshoes	85	113
Sweeping floors	88	—
Carpentry	—	123
Playing ping-pong	93	124
Pleasure swimming (back stroke, 25 yd/min)	93	124
Cleaning windows	99	—
Ironing clothes	103	—
Farming, planting, hoeing, raking	—	150
Pleasure swimming (breast stroke, 20 yd/min)	115	154
Calisthenics	120	160
Bicycling on level roads	120	160
Golfing	130	173
Gardening, weeding	141	188
Walking on level (4.47 mph)	159	212
Walking downstairs	160	213
Pick-and-shovel work	—	214
Playing tennis	166	221
Playing basketball	169	225
Chopping wood	—	240
Pleasure swimming (back stroke, 40 yd/min)	200	267
Pleasure swimming (crawl, 45 yd/min)	209	284
Gardening, digging	—	298
Pleasure swimming (breast stroke, 40 yd/min)	231	306
Mountain climbing	241	321
Playing squash	—	332
Pleasure swimming (crawl, 55 yd/min)	255	340
Walking on level (5.80 mph)	273	364
Running, long distance	361	481
Walking upstairs	416	555
Sprinting	561	748

0   1.0   2.0   3.0   4.0   5.0

Average Calories/Pound of Body Weight
(30 Minutes)

Activity

120   160

♀ # ♂

Average Calories
(30 Minutes)

overweight college women. Their concentration was on the hip and abdominal regions. It was found that the mean weight loss was minimal but that the waist, hip, and thigh measurements were reduced significantly by both programs. The authors concluded that "a reduction in body segments was found where fat accumulations had been most conspicuous." There is further evidence that isotonic and isometric exercises can effect small but significant "spot" reductions (392, 582) and that during general weight loss, fat is removed from those areas having the greatest initial deposit (203). Conflicting evidence, however, suggests that "spot" reducing is not effective in accomplishing its goal (95, 475). In summary, it appears safe to say that "spot" reducing (ex-

ercising the area concerned) *may* be effective but probably no more so than general, "nonspot" exercise of equal intensity and duration.

Mayer (376) presents evidence that showed that inactivity was of greater importance than overeating in the development of obesity. The high school girls involved in this study attended summer camp every year and lost weight in spite of the increased food intake because they were involved in a program of strenuous activity.

Mann and others (366) examined the motivational aspect of exercise in weight control programs and concluded from the comments of their subjects that "although the first few days of physical training produced discomforts and fatigue, the men soon experienced

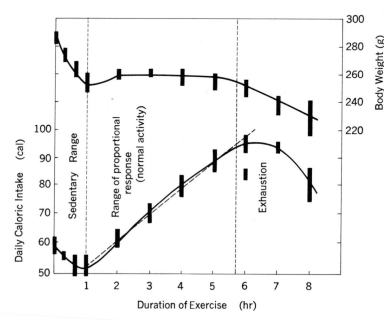

FIGURE 10.20 Voluntary calorie intake and body weight as functions of exercise in normal rats. By permission from The Athletic Institute and Mayer (374).

a sense of well-being and accomplishment that they considered adequate compensation for their troubles." The men in this program also experienced a "continual loss of fat despite an increase in food intake."

Regular Exercise and the "Appestat"

Although the exact mechanisms are not as yet clearly understood, it has been well established that the center for control of food intake is located in the hypothalamus. There is an appetite center, the stimulation of which causes one to want to eat, and a satiety center, which, when stimulated, leads to the reduction or complete extinction of the desire to eat. Together, these centers are often referred to as the "appestat" because they operate in much the same way that a thermostat controls temperature. It is fairly well established that the stimulus to these centers, at least the "appetite center," is in some way related to blood glucose level, although the exact mechanism is not known.

Mayer (375) experimented with the frequent misconception that an increase in physical activity always causes an increase in appetite and food intake that equals, or is greater in energy value than, that of the energy of the exercise. Animal experiments and human population studies provide evidence that such a constant relationship does *not* exist. There appears to be an actual increase in voluntary food intake under very sedentary conditions, which, of course, leads to increased

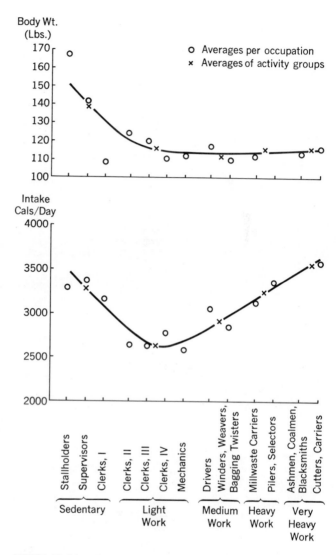

FIGURE 10.21 Body weight and caloric intake as a function of physical activity. By permission from the Athletic Institute and Mayer (374).

body weight (see Figures 10.20 and 10.21). With a normal daily work output or exercise, intake tends to be proportional to output, and weight remains

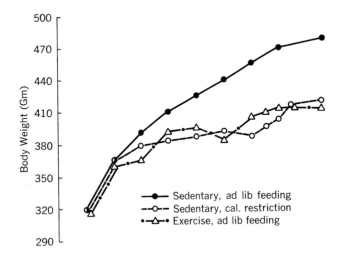

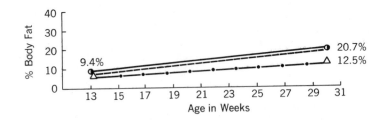

FIGURE 10.22 Comparative effects of fifteen weeks of daily swimming and caloric restriction on body weight, serum cholesterol, and percent body fat in growing male albino rats. Caloric restriction was designed to maintain body weight comparable to that of the exercise animals. Adapted from Jones and others (288).

constant (Figure 10.20). In the animal studies, exhausting daily exercise led to reduced food intake and weight loss, while less-than-normal amounts of daily exercise caused greater food intake than necessary and a subsequent increase in body weight (see Figure 10.21).

This work has led to a hypothesis that an adequate amount of daily physi-

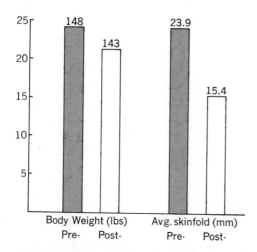

FIGURE 10.23 Effects of six weeks' moderate exercise program (about 500 calories per day treadmill walking and jogging, 6 days per week) on body weight and average skin fold fat measurement; no diet control required. N = 11 overweight college women. Data from Moody, Kollias, and Buskirk (398).

Figure 10.22 provide evidence that body weight and body fat deposition can be controlled by a regular exercise program?

There is evidence that, in response to sympathetic stimulation, there is a greater release of free fatty acids from the adipose tissue of the trained organism than the untrained (443). Furthermore, these free fatty acids, once released, are utilized in response to exercise demands for energy so that they are not restored in fat cells (233). It is also known that exercise following a high fatty meal significantly reduces the level of lipids circulating in the blood, and this also may prevent excess fat deposition.

Summary: Exercise and Weight Control

Exercise, *combined with sensible food intake,* appears to be the most effective, most natural, and probably the safest method of weight control, especially for those who are only moderately overweight. We hypothesize that this is so, at least in part, because exercise and moderate caloric restriction are more *natural* than synthetic and unnatural schemes such as starvation, liquid diets, and drugs. It is our opinion that these methods all involve or produce physiological changes that cannot be maintained indefinitely and, when removed, have in no way "re-educated" the systems of the body. Thus, they are usually doomed to failure in terms of permanent weight loss.

The amount of daily exercise necessary to provide weight maintenance benefits is dependent upon occupa-

cal activity renders the "appestat" more effective, that is, in some way causes it to more closely control appetite and/or intake in keeping with the actual caloric need so that excess food intake does not occur. The evidence presented establishes an adequate base for such a hypothesis.

Exercise and Body Composition

Experiments utilizing animals substantiate the contention that weight loss through exercise is more permanent than loss through caloric restrictions (374). Exercise, even with ad libitum feeding, helps control body weight and, perhaps of even greater importance, controls deposition of body fat, (see Figures 10.22 and 10.23). How does

tional physical activity and most likely upon other individual differences. The amount necessary to contribute to weight loss is, in addition to these factors, dependent upon the amount to be lost and the food intake. The amount is also dependent upon current level of fitness and skill in the exercise task; common sense is helpful when deciding how much exercise to start with.

The composition of the diet should not be altered from the basic diet described on page 330; there should simply be a reduction in total caloric intake, probably not under 1500 calories a day for an adult and not less than one gram of protein a day per kilogram of body weight. In keeping with the concept discussed on pages 332 to 333 and on page 355, it also seems to be important to space the caloric intake over the entire day and not to consume a disproportionately high percentage of the daily intake in only one or two sittings.

WEIGHT REDUCTION SCHEMES OTHER THAN EXERCISE

STARVATION

Lengthy periods of complete starvation are actually ineffective in reducing weight permanently because at least equal amounts of lean tissue are burned by the body after the carbohydrate stores are used up (about thirteen hours). It appears that starvation causes the system actually to become more efficient in absorbing food from the small intestine and in laying down fat deposits! In one recent study, complete starvation in obese patients actually increased the percentage of body fat from 44 to 45 percent (49). The research literature indicates that, in addition to being ineffective, starvation causes certain **histological** and **morphological** changes in the liver, spleen, and heart (3, 268, 279, 389). Other changes have been reported: a reduction in plasma protein and hemoglobin concentration (277); reduced gamma globulin (309) and level of circulating eosinophils (324), which may in turn mean a decreased resistance to infection; increased uric acid levels and arthritic gout (158); significant and consistent depression of ECG waves (60); general endocrine atrophy associated with a failure of the anterior pituitary to secrete its **tropic** hormones (465). Evidence indicates that there is supernormal fat infiltration of the heart, liver, and kidneys associated with an increase in the free fatty acids of the blood (348, 531). In grossly overweight persons, fasting has resulted in low blood pressure and anemia (158).

It now appears that the refeeding period after starvation is even more critical than the actual period of fasting. The effects observed during unregulated refeeding include persistent hypertension and acute cardiovascular stress, even to the extent of heart failure in some cases (153, 530, 531). There is evidence that other changes also occur: acute cardiac **anoxemia** and development of fibrotic patches (530); abnormal glucose metabolism and increased lipogenesis (as much as a ninetyfold increase), in heart and liver; fatty liver and even certain degenerative changes (531); **dyspnea** and **tachy-cardia** on exertion (153).

Skipping breakfast and sometimes lunch, a common practice among teenagers, may border on the starvation-refeeding pattern. By late afternoon they are so hungry they tend to consume the bulk of their daily food intake in the evening hours. Fat storage may tend to be promoted by such eating habits. As was stated before, fewer meals tend to minimize the work output; hence the vicious circle may again come into play—less energy, less activity, more obesity.

Fasting is often the weight-reduction method chosen by grossly obese persons. Obviously such a drastic step should not be taken without a good physical examination beforehand and close medical supervision at all times during the fast. Pregnant women or those who suffer with peptic ulcers, liver trouble, infections, or uncontrolled diabetes should not fast under any circumstances.

A recent study compared the effectiveness of prolonged fasting with low-calorie diets (49). The subjects in the study were starved at one time and at a later date were also studied under a high-fat, 1000-calorie diet of which 82 percent was fat, 14 percent protein, and 4 percent carbohydrates. It was found that of the weight lost during total starvation, 65 percent was from lean-tissue sources and only 35 percent from fat tissue. In contrast, the low-calorie, high-fat diet produced a weight loss of which only 3 percent was from lean tissue; the fat loss was twice as great as that in starvation.

VIBRATORS

It is often said that fat accumulates in the areas used the least. Manufacturers of vibrating machines have promoted this concept into a multimillion-dollar business. Karpovich and Rathbone (292) conducted experiments regarding the effect of vibrating cushions upon the metabolism, body weight, and shape of various parts of the body. There was no weight loss or change in body parts attributable to the vibrations.

Steinhaus (543, p. 153) studied thirteen men, some markedly overweight, during 15 minutes of vigorous vibrator belt massage applied to the abdomen. Based on the data reported, assuming 3500 calories produced per pound of fat burned, and an average 17 percent increase in energy cost when going from sitting to standing, we have calculated energy cost due to the vibrator alone. The average weight loss, over and above that which would have occurred just due to the standing, was about .05 ounces for fifteen minutes. Even if we include BMR and the cost of standing, *one year* of daily fifteen-minute vibrator sessions for these men would bring about an average weight loss of only 1.66 pounds.

LIQUID DIETS

Liquid diets or supplements were believed to have started when a young hospital attendant noticed that a typical comment of the patients after drinking a high-nutrient formula was the feeling of fullness that they had

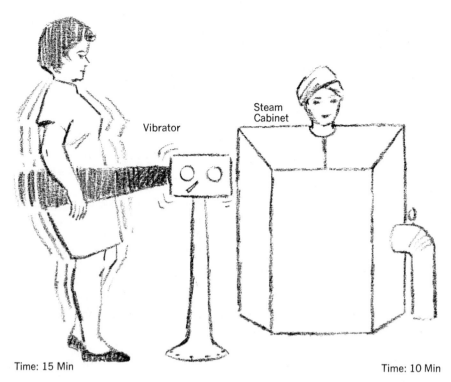

Vibrator

Steam Cabinet

Time: 15 Min

Weight Loss: 0.0046 Lbs

To Regain Weight Loss:
Eat 1 dill pickle or
   1 tablespoon of catsup or
   1/2 of a chocolate cream

Time: 10 Min

Weight Loss: 0.50 to 0.75 Lbs

To Regain Weight Loss:
Drink 1 large glass of water

FIGURE 10.24

from the small quantity ingested. Using this as a basic formula with a new name and a good advertising program, liquid diets became established on the market. To date no deleterious effects of occasional use have been found, and there is some evidence that they can be effective in cases of extreme obesity (221). But longer-range study is needed. Liquid diets are not recommended as "home prescriptions" and should not be used extensively except as advised by the family physician.

STEAM AND DRY HEAT BATHS

The weight loss from the dehydration that takes place in a "steam bath" is quickly recovered upon the ingestion of water. Thirst dictates the amount of water needed and if thirst is ignored and the state of dehydration is allowed to continue, serious health hazards are inevitable. This practice is common in fighters and wrestlers who often attempt to "make weight" just before a bout. Many people feel that steam baths afford an effective means of weight control. It may well have relaxation benefits, but as for weight control, it appears to be absolutely useless.

DRUGS

On the average, drugs used for weight control are not particularly effective, especially those that can be legally sold without prescription. The following drugs and agents are ineffective for significant weight reduction (154): topical anesthetics to dull the taste buds; diuretics to cause initial water loss; bulking agents to expand in the stomach and cause fullness; liprotropic agents to prevent fat deposits; and cathartics to rush the food through the intestines. The regular use of cathartics is also a dangerous practice.

Appetite suppressors may be effective to some limited extent, but the amount that can be sold without prescription is not effective (154). The mechanism involved is not exactly clear, but side effects on the central nervous system, including nervousness and insomnia, at best render the value of such drugs questionable. At any rate, it is certain that such drugs should be used only upon advice of a physician.

"NIBBLING"

Small-animal experiments have provided evidence that intermittent starvation increases the volume of the stomach and small intestine and also increases the rate of fat and glucose absorption from the intestine (204). When daily caloric intake is held constant, rats eating ad libitum all day have only half as much body fat as those force-fed twice daily, even though total body weight is the same in both groups (165, 166). Studies indicate that people eating only two meals per day are more overweight and have higher blood cholesterol levels than those who eat five or more times per day, even though the total caloric intake is greater in the "nibbling," five-meal group (171). Such evidence has led many to the opinion that "nibbling" may be healthier than our established three-meals-a-day pattern, a pattern that may in itself border on an intermittent starvation schedule. Gordon's (215) theory that a 48-hour fast breaks an unfavorable enzyme pattern in the obese has led to his obesity treatment, which involves a 48-hour fast followed by a daily "nibbling" schedule of six meals, 200 calories each meal.

Although "nibbling" has not yet been proven to be an effective obesity preventive or treatment, the evidence is interesting and the concept certainly warrants further investigation (see Figure 10.12).

SPECIAL PROBLEMS

Smoking and Appetite

One of the chronic complaints of men and women trying to stop smoking is the fact that they gain weight when they are not smoking. This may be caused by the nervousness associated with the withdrawal and the desire for something in their mouths and hands. Much of the available evidence substantiates the belief that smoking reduces the appetite (522). Whether such effects are primarily physiological, psychological, or some combination of the two has not been conclusively demonstrated. Dr. McFarland (355), director of the physical medicine program at the Battle Creek (Michigan) Sanitarium, includes several recommendations concerning smoking and food in his "Ten Rules to Help You Quit Smoking." Among these is the admonition to eat regular meals and, after meals, because this is the time when people most want to smoke, get outside and take a walk. He recommends milk or buttermilk rather than alcohol, tea, or coffee as a beverage, in addition to the drinking of six to eight glasses of water between meals. Dr. McFarland urges the smoker who wishes to quit to avoid fish, fowl, meat-rich gravies, fried foods, condiments, and desserts. He suggests, instead, fruit, grains, vegetables, and nuts. He also believes the diet should be supplemented with vitamins, particularly B complex.

"Crash Diets," Physical Performance, and Health

The American Medical Association is opposed to "crash diets" for athletes (133). Its opposition appears to be based on the assumption that repeated periods of starvation and/or dehydration produce essentially the same pathological conditions that natural famine and experimental food restriction have

produced. On the other hand, many wrestling and boxing coaches believe, and there is some evidence to support the belief (520), that rapid weight reductions of about 5 to 7 percent are not only harmless but actually aid performance (156). The two positions are not as incompatible as they seem: the medical opinion relates to health and the coaches' opinion to immediate effects upon performance.

At the present time it appears that small weight losses due to starvation (5 percent of initial weight) do not cause appreciable changes in measured performance. On the other hand, based on the available medical research it must be concluded that submitting to several days of dehydration and/or acute starvation in order to "make weight" is highly questionable practice, especially for growing boys and adolescents.

MISCELLANEOUS DISORDERS

Although you will probably not have direct responsibility for dealing with such diseases and disorders, it is important that you should have some knowledge about them.

INFECTIOUS DISEASES

The following infectious diseases of, or related to, the digestive tract and infectious metabolic disorders are described in Appendix D:

1. Botulism
2. Dysentery

3. Mumps
4. Paratyphoid fever
5. Typhoid fever

Appendicitis is an infection of the appendix, a small worm-shaped and apparently useless projection of the large intestine (see Figure 10.2). It is common, especially during the late teens and middle age, and can be acute or chronic in nature. In acute stages, because of the risk of rupturing and subsequent infection of the lining of the abdominal cavity, surgery is usually required. In the acute stage, there are severe pain, which may become localized in the lower right quadrant of the abdomen, nausea and vomiting, and possibly a fever. A physician should be notified whenever appendicitis is suspected; the patient should *not* be given food, liquids, cathartics, or enemas. Heat should not be applied. In severe cases, sudden cessation of pain may be indicative of rupture of the infected appendix.

IMPORTANT NONINFECTIOUS DISEASES AND DISORDERS

Malnutrition

Adolescent girls often go on self-imposed and ill-advised diet routines that may have unfortunate consequences. *Undernutrition* is accompanied by impaired growth and development, reduced physical and mental efficiency, anemia, increased susceptibility to infectious diseases, such as tuberculosis and rheumatic fever, and, when severe, menstrual and reproductive irregularities, edema, osteoporosis, and other impairments (118).

Attention should be given to the proper nutrition of children, for it is believed that inadequate nutrition in childhood may be a factor in the development of chronic diseases later in life, although the exact influence is not known.

Ulcer

In spite of advances in diagnostic techniques and treatment, death due to ulcers and the prevalence of chronic ulcers has increased since 1920 (578). An ulcer, a disorder of the digestive system, is probably triggered by a disorganization of the autonomic nervous system. Because of their stress-related origin, ulcers will be discussed more in detail in Chapter 18.

An ulcer actually is a sore or open wound in the stomach or upper digestive tract. The oversecretion of gastric and intestinal juices, probably triggered by parasympathetic stimulation (see Table 12.1), when no food is in the system, can cause the hydrochloric acid and digestive juices to actually work on the walls of the intestine or the stomach.

Ulcers may remain dormant for a long time, but when symptoms *do* appear, the distress is similar to a burning sensation or a dull ache or a severe pain that may remain localized in the stomach or travel to the back or move upward beneath the breastbone. The pain, caused by the sore on the wall of the stomach or intestine, may become severe. Bleeding may eventually result and blood may be present in the bowel movement, causing a black coloring. If vomiting occurs, there may be traces of blood.

When the ulcer has progressed to the bleeding stage the victim has a feeling of weakness and nausea, may break out in a cold sweat, and feel faint or dizzy. His face pales and his expression shows his anxiety. If bleeding is severe he may become unconscious.

Ulcers may become perforated, causing agonizing pain in the upper abdomen. Cold clammy sweat appears with nausea and anxiety and the abdominal muscles become rigid. Obviously, a physician should be consulted long before this state is reached. A summary of the factors commonly thought to be associated with gastrointestinal ulcers follows.

1. *Geographic Factors.* There appears to be little relationship between ulcers and rural-urban living (578).
2. *Age and Sex.* Chronic ulcers are most prevalent in the 45 to 64 age group and about three times as prevalent in men. The disease is not, however, limited to middle age as a considerable number of those over sixty-five and under forty-five also develop ulcers (578).
3. *Diet.* The composition of the diet has not successfully been implicated as a causative agent in the etiology of gastric or **duodenal** ulcers.
4. *Emotions.* There is considerable evidence, based on experimental animal and human research as well as clinical research, that prolonged emotional turmoil and conflict, anxiety,

guilt, hostility, anger, and resentment can cause gastric ulcers (68, 391, 493, 619). There is also some evidence that decreased blood supply to the walls of the stomach may be a contributing factor (469).

Chronic Diarrhea

Diarrhea, unless associated with a specific infection, is also a stress-related illness (see Table 12.1 for action of the sympathetic NS on the GI tract). From a nutritional standpoint, it is important to realize that the absorption of nutrients is reduced because of the rapid passage of food through the intestinal tract. It is accompanied by dehydration and mineral loss and is often the precursor of a number of nutritional deficiency diseases. It may deplete the body of water and minerals, causing a number of nutritional deficiency diseases and, of course, dehydration and possibly **acidosis** (see pages 361 and 380).

Chronic Constipation

Constipation occurs in the colon when the flow of fecal movement is slower than normal or something has caused complete cessation of the movement. It may occur as a result of inadequate "roughage" in the diet or it may be stress-related (see Table 12.1). Many persons have severe headaches and others have muscular aches and pains when they become constipated, but there is still disagreement over whether absorption of toxins from the feces remaining in the large bowel or the distention and pressure from constipation cause the headaches and the muscular pains.

One of the major causes of **hemorrhoids** is constipation resulting from digestive malfunction. Much more research needs to be done on the effect of exercise on the colon. It is believed that the propulsive motility is increased by exercise and that strengthened abdominal musculature facilitates defecation, but scientific evidence is lacking.

Diabetes

Diabetes is more than twice as frequent in obese adults as in persons of normal weight. The signs of diabetes can be eliminated in some obese diabetics by weight reduction, and severity can be modified in others, although the eventual course and complications of the disease may not be influenced.

Many diabetics are unable to oxidize fats completely; their urine contains abnormal amounts of products of partial oxidation. Furthermore, the amount of fat in their tissues declines to a very low level. Injections of insulin enable these patients to carry the oxidation to completion and increase remarkably their capacity to synthesize and deposit fat. It seems likely that a block in the enzyme systems involved in the synthesis of fat plays a substantial role in diabetes. In this connection it should be pointed out that the same enzymes that bring about fatty acid oxidation in animal tissues can be made to work in reverse and, under appropriate conditions, synthesize fatty acids (220).

A ten-year-old child who had severe arthritis was quickly relieved by cortisone but immediately developed diabetes; when the cortisone treatment was stopped, the diabetes disappeared but the arthritis reappeared. At last reports her physicians were trying to moderate the dosage to a level that would keep her arthritis mild without making the diabetes acute (219).

In early treatment of diabetes, carbohydrates were limited, but now a patient is allowed a normal carbohydrate diet and then given large quantities of insulin to utilize the carbohydrates. In diabetes, very little carbohydrate is utilized by the body; hence most of the energy is derived from fat. Insulin given to utilize the carbohydrates lowers the rate of fat metabolism and also lowers the high level of blood cholesterol that occurs in diabetes.

Strenuous muscular exertion can increase the rate of metabolism, causing excessive fat metabolism and acidosis. Diabetics should not avoid exercise, but should take precaution while exercising. Some champion athletes, such as Ham Richardson and Ted Schroeder, well-known tennis players, are diabetics.

Cancer

Cancer is the number two killer in the United States today and cancer of the digestive organs ranks first among the causes of death due to cancer (see Figure 5.2). The large intestine, stomach, pancreas, rectum, and liver are most often implicated. Statistically, approximately one person in four will get cancer, and of every six who *do* get it, two will be saved and another one of six *could* be saved with early diagnosis and proper treatment. In other words, half of the cancer cases *can* be saved. Of course, if diagnostic treatment and preventive techniques are improved or developed, these figures could change in a positive direction.

Stomach cancer deaths have declined some 40 percent in the last two decades (496). Cancer of the digestive organs is generally considered to be relatively detectable and highly curable. Because early detection is imperative in order to save lives, a proper examination on a yearly basis is a must!

The primary danger signs for stomach, intestinal, and rectal cancer are (1) a persistent change in bowel habits; (2) rectal bleeding; and (3) persistent gastrointestinal discomfort.

Colitis

The term **colitis** is appropriate only when inflammatory disease of the colon, such as *ulcerative colitis,* is present. The noninflammatory "colitis," associated with tension and anxiety, is more properly called *irritable colon.* The cause of true colitis is unknown, but most often is viral or bacterial in origin, although psychogenically induced spasms of the colon can predispose the tissue to bacterial invasion. The disorder may be acute or chronic, may involve diarrhea, cramps, or bloody mucus in the stools. There may be fever, abdominal tenderness, and distension. Many complications are possible in unattended cases.

In irritable colon, constipation is the rule, with considerable mucus present in the hard stools. Bouts of diarrhea may interrupt the constipation. Some persons exhibit predominantly diarrhea symptoms, in which case they often have diarrhea in the morning with few or no movements the rest of the day. It is obvious that simply giving laxatives or demulcents (depending upon the symptoms) is not the solution to a problem that is psychogenic in nature. In fact, heavy reliance on such unnatural agents may be harmful to normal digestive functions.

Dyspepsia (Indigestion)

Indigestion (with any or all of these symptoms: nausea, heartburn, upper abdominal pain, **flatulence**) usually occurs after the ingestion of food. Simple, nonorganic indigestion can result from improper eating habits, certain kinds of foods, or poorly cooked foods. If these symptoms persist over a period of more than a day or so they may be indicative of some organic disorder. In any case, a physician should be consulted if "indigestion" symptoms persist.

Gastritis

Gastritis, inflammation of the gastric membrane, may be either acute or chronic and results from the ingestion of specific irritant substances or from certain acute infectious diseases, such as influenza, measles, and pneumonia. Irritant substances responsible for acute forms of gastritis range from alcohol and allergenic substances of many kinds to caustic and corrosive agents. The cause of chronic gastritis is unknown, but the inflammation has been linked to the emotions and thus is considered by many physicians to be psychosomatic.

There are certain reasonably effective preventive measures for acute gastritis. Do not ingest substances which, for you, are irritants. A physician can usually help work out a diet to control chronic gastritis.

Because of the difficulty in interpreting the symptoms of gastritis, indigestion, colitis, and irritable colon, a physician should certainly be consulted.

Metabolic Acidosis

Acidosis is not a disease but a condition or symptom that results from a lowered blood bicarbonate and may occur as a consequence of ingesting large quantities of acids. It also may be a result of chronic diarrhea, various metabolic irregularities, or failure of kidney excretion. Severe acidosis can lead to coma and, if not reversed, to death.

Metabolic Alkalosis

Alkalosis is the clinical term used to indicate an increased blood bicarbonate. The first symptom of alkalosis is slow and shallow breathing. Overexcitability of the central nervous system (CNS), with resulting muscular spasms, is another effect of alkalosis. Alkalosis is not very common, but de-

velops occasionally in children from excessive vomiting. Loss of the hydrochloric acid from the stomach causes the reaction of the body fluids to change toward the alkaline side. Treatment involves reversing the body fluids toward the acid side.

BRIEF SUMMARY OF OTHER METABOLIC DISORDERS

Addison's disease results from an insufficient secretion of adrenal cortical hormones. Weakness and early fatigability are characteristic early signs. The skin may acquire a bronzelike coloring or black freckles on various portions of the body. Formerly a progressive, fatal disease, Addison's disease can now be treated so that, with proper care, most patients can enjoy a life that is only moderately restricted.

Cushing's disease is characterized by an unusual accumulation of fat, an elevation of blood pressure, and often a mild diabetes. There may be a purplish streaking of the skin in areas where it is stretched. The disease is caused by an oversecretion of a cortisonelike hormone from the adrenal glands.

Goiter is an enlargement of the thyroid gland resulting from an insufficient intake of iodine in the diet. Consumption of iodized table salt and iodine-rich foods can prevent most occurrences of goiter.

Hyperthyroidism, or overactivity of the thyroid gland, results in nervousness, rapid pulse, rapid breathing, and sometimes nausea and diarrhea. Weight loss may occur despite an increased appetite; metabolism is increased markedly.

Hypothyroidism, the causative factor in goitor, is due to an inadequate iodine intake. Persons suffering from hypothyroidism are inactive, gain weight easily, may have scanty hair, thick, dry, scaly skin, and coarse features.

Myxedema, or lack of the thyroid hormone occurring in adulthood, produces a characteristic puffiness of the hands and face, especially the eyelids. Other common symptoms are drowsiness, mental apathy, and sensitivity to cold. A similar condition in children is cretinism.

EVALUATION TECHNIQUES

If you are to understand problems of weight control and if you are to deal with the subject in your work, either directly or incidentally, you must also understand the principles of determining nutritional status, body proportions, body fat, and so on. You have already seen a method for assaying nutritional status (diet and activity recall, page 337). The following measures are also useful.

GIRTH MEASUREMENTS

Measurements taken "around" body parts can be valuable per se, especially chest and abdominal measures. For example, a nonpathological increase in abdominal girth in an adult obviously indicates fat deposition and *not* skeletal growth. In taking girth measures, it is important to standardize tape

reading procedures and to measure and record the girth while the muscles are contracted as well as in the relaxed state. Try to have the tape at the same point; the degree of "tightness" of the tape should be standardized. Standards are impractical because general body size and type need to be taken into account.[1] However, twice yearly measurements, in combination with abdominal fat measures, will keep you informed as to your rate of unnecessary "middle" growth. Because extra subcutaneous fat can invade normally "taut" and muscular areas as we age, it is also wise to get a base-line measurement at the thigh and upper arm. Full expiration and maximum expanded chest measures may also be useful as a measure of normal chest expansion and, together with the vital capacity test discussed on page 210, could serve as a rough screening measure for normal lung function. Chest expansion and vital capacity generally decrease in several of the lung diseases, for example in emphysema.

FAT MEASUREMENTS

Laboratory techniques involving underwater weighing or fat-caliper measurements to predict total body fat are excellent aids to the total appraisal of

---

[1]As a rough guide, men's chest girth should exceed abdominal girth by at least 5 inches and there should be a minimum of 3 inches expansion. "Average" measurements for young women are waist, 25 inches; bust, 32 inches; hips, 37½ inches.

health and fitness. Although reliability will not be high, one can measure the fat tissue at home with some help. A simple "dime store" divider and a small millimeter ruler will do (see Figure 10.25). Pinch up the fat and skin tissue at the sites illustrated in Figure 10.26 and measure the thickness of the skin-fold with the dividers or some similar device. Record the thickness of the skin-fold and repeat at least twice a year. Norms are also presented in Figure 10.26. Your rough measure may be off as much as 5 to 8 millimeters because it is difficult to standardize the tension on the calipers unless they are made for this purpose. However, it will give you some idea of how you change through the years. The following precautions for taking these skin-fold measurements should be followed carefully.[2]

1. Apply the calipers or dividers about half an inch from the fingers that hold the skin-fold. Make the fold in the most natural way—vertical, oblique, or horizontal.

2. Measurements are best taken early in the morning upon arising in order to reduce the effect of variation in state of tissue hydration (this can cause a variation of 15 percent).

3. Duplicate the measurement, starting with pinching the skin-fold again. Repeat until two consecutive readings agree within 2 mm.

4. It is best, of course, to have someone else take your measurements.

(A)

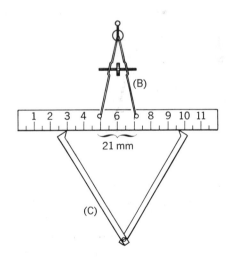
(B)

(C)

---

[2]Adapted from Consolazio, Johnson, and Pecora (122, p. 303).

FIGURE 10.25 Use of fat calipers for skin-fold measures. (B) Improvised fat caliper, using dividers and millimeter scale; (C) improvised width calipers for body segments, using two pieces of wood and a nut and bolt adjusted to hold in position but allow movement.

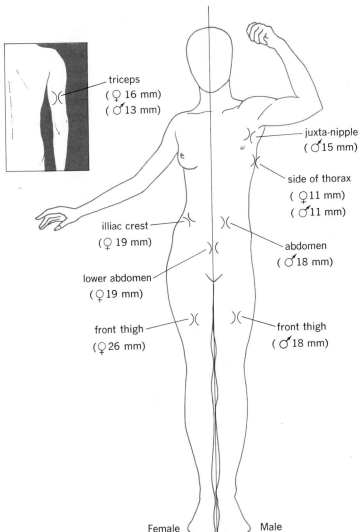

triceps
(♀ 16 mm)
(♂ 13 mm)

juxta-nipple
(♂ 15 mm)

side of thorax
(♀ 11 mm)
(♂ 11 mm)

illiac crest
(♀ 19 mm)

abdomen
(♂ 18 mm)

lower abdomen
(♀ 19 mm)

front thigh
(♀ 26 mm)

front thigh
(♂ 18 mm)

Female   Male

FIGURE 10.26 Sites and approximate averages for skin-fold measurements in men and women. (For taking measurements, see precautions listed on page 363.) Approximate averages are based on data from several sources and on data collected in our own laboratory (appreciation is expressed to Richard Needle and Dr. John Burt).

Equations for predicting body density and percentage of body fat based on skin-fold measurements have been developed. They are probably useless unless based upon measures taken with regular skin-fold calipers. However, in the event you *can* somehow get accurate measurements, the two body density equations and the percent body fat equation presented below will be useful (see example, Table 10.10).

1. For young women, aged 17–25 (525): Density = 1.0764 − .00081 (iliac crest skin-fold, mm) − .00088 (triceps skin-fold, mm).

2. For men (445):
Density = 1.08012 − .007123 (mid. axillary at xiphoid skin-fold, cm) − .00483 (juxta-nipple skin-fold, cm) − .005513 (triceps skin-fold, cm).

3. For converting density to percent body fat (306):

$$\% \text{ body fat} = 100 \left(\frac{4.201}{\text{density}} - 3.813 \right)$$

Average percent body fat at age 20 is about 12 percent for men and 20 percent for women. The average increases up until about age 55 (this is "average" and should not be confused with "normal" or what "should be." It is highly questionable whether the average percentage of fat increase with age is actually unavoidable.)

HEIGHT AND WEIGHT

Height and weight measures, standing alone, do not add a great deal to health appraisal. A standard height-weight table is usually quite unsatisfactory because of differences in build and skeletal size. However, when used in conjunction with others, such as girth, skeletal, and fat measures, such a table can become valuable. There are various methods for estimating what one should weigh. A useful overweight index and a complete method for estimating what one should weigh are presented below.

In addition to height, skin-fold, and girth measurements, one method includes body segment widths or diameters. These diameters can be measured with reasonable accuracy by use of an easily constructed, home-made wooden caliper and a meter or a yardstick (as illustrated in Figure 10.25). The width and girth measurements needed are illustrated in Figure 10.27.

1. Anything 110 percent or greater is considered by Fabry (171) as indicative of overweight (see example, Table 10.10).

$$\text{Overweight index} = \frac{100 \times \text{body weight (kilograms)}}{\text{ht (cm)} - 100}$$

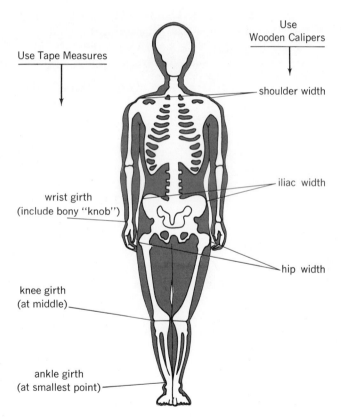

FIGURE 10.27 Bony landmarks for skeletal width and girth measurements. In overweight people and some extremely well-muscled individuals, some of the landmarks for width measures may be difficult to find. Movement of the joint may aid the search.

2. Optimal weight. Willoughby's (611) determination for men and women: (To determine optimal weight per inch of height, enter Table 10.13 with the corrected ankle girth.) (See example, Table 10.12.)

For women:

Corrected ankle girth = [.59 (shoulder width) + .75 (iliac width) + 1.33 (hip width) + 2.70 (wrist girth) + 1.77 (knee girth) + 3.00 (ankle girth)] ÷ 12.

For men:

Corrected ankle girth = [.55 (shoulder width) + .78 (iliac width) + 1.36 (hip width) + 2.28 (wrist girth) + 1.78 (knee girth) + (ankle girth)] ÷ 12.

Perhaps a look at optimal weight predictions based on several methods, combined with the table on page 335, is the best approach. Those who are considerably overweight are advised to include the Willoughby method (611), which is apparently the most realistic

method, and to consult a physician before attempting any weight-losing regimen.

SUMMARY: A USABLE CONCEPT OF WEIGHT CONTROL

1. For weight reduction, first establish a realistic goal for "fat loss," not "weight loss," using appropriate methods to determine the *actual* extent of excess fat tissue.

2. Whether for weight maintenance or weight loss, the diet should be balanced and the calories should probably be spread out evenly over at *least* three meals a day.

3. Systematic and regular exercise causes not only increased Caloric expenditure but also promotes a more desirable body composition (less fat) and may also render the "appestat" more effective.

TABLE 10.10   Examples of Percent Body Fat Calculations

	WOMAN	MAN
Density	= 1.0764 − .00081 (25) − .00088 (15)	= 1.08012 − .007123 (1.0) − .00483 (1.5) − .005513 (1.0)
	= 1.0764 − .0202 − .0132	= 1.08012 − .0071 − .0073 − .00551
	= 1.0430 Density of body	= 1.0602 Density of body
% Body fat	= $100 \left(\dfrac{4.201}{1.043} - 3.813 \right)$	= $100 \left(\dfrac{4.201}{1.060} - 3.813 \right)$
	= 100 (4.030 − 3.813)	= 100 (3.970 − 3.813)
	= 100 × .217	= 100 (.157)
	= 21.7% Body fat	= 15.7% Body fat

TABLE 10.11   Examples of Overweight Index Calculation

	EXAMPLE A	EXAMPLE B
Body weight	= 160 lbs = 160 (.454) = 72.5 kg	= 210 lbs = 210 (.454) = 95 kg
Height	= 70 inches = 70 (2.54) = 178 cm	= 70 inches = 70 (2.54) = 178 cm
O. W. index	$= \dfrac{100 \times 72.5}{178 - 100}$ $= \dfrac{7250}{78}$ $= 93\%$	$= \dfrac{100 \times 95}{178 - 100}$ $= \dfrac{9500}{78}$ $= 122\%$

SUMMARY

Nutrition and weight control education are important aspects of health education and physical education and should also be concerns of recreation agencies.

Professionals in these three fields must have a basic understanding of the digestive and associated systems in order to deal with the concepts of nutrition, exercise, and weight control.

The inclusive term "digestion" includes the process of movement of food, digestion, and absorption into the blood.

The liver, endocrine system, and excretory system are important allies of the digestive system.

The basic nutrients are fats, carbohydrates, proteins, vitamins, minerals, and water. None can be excluded from the diet of the normal, healthy person. Also, certain amino acids and un-saturated fatty acids are "essential."

Metabolic rate is the rate at which the body expends energy, usually measured in calories.

Ideal body weight is best estimated using methods other than standard height-weight tables.

Obesity is associated with many physical disorders.

Obesity is usually caused by exogenous rather than endogenous factors. A subtle but considerable weight gain due to fall in BMR and/or decrease in energy expenditure without concomittant decrease in caloric intake can occur in a relatively short period of time.

There is little experimental evidence that exercise improves digestion or elimination, but neither is there evidence to contradict these claims.

There are no supplements to the normal balanced diet that are known to improve performance or physical fit-

TABLE 10.12   Examples of Willoughby Method for Determination of Optimal Weight and Use in Combination with Percent Body Fat To Determine Actual Extent of Obesity

WOMAN: (65 inches tall, 115 pounds)
Corrected ankle girth =

$$.59 (13) + .75 (12) + 1.33 (13) + 2.70 (6) + 1.77 (12.5) + 3.00 (7.5)$$

$$= \frac{7.7 + 9.0 + 17.3 + 16.2 + 22.1 + 22.5}{12} = \frac{94.8}{12} = 7.9$$

from Table 10.13, 7.9 = 1.80 pounds per inch (for women)
1.80 × 65 = 117 lbs. optimal weight: 115 − 117 = 2 pounds less than optimal

[Assume 18% body fat, a little less than normal, therefore no weight to be lost; could even add a few pounds although certainly not necessary.]

MAN: (70 inches tall, 182 pounds)
Corrected ankle girth =

$$\frac{.55 (15) + .78 (12) + 1.36 (14) + 2.28 (7) + 1.78 (14) + 3.00 (9)}{12}$$

$$= \frac{8.2 + 9.3 + 19.1 + 15.9 + 25.0 + 27.0}{12} = \frac{104.5}{12} = 8.7$$

from Table 10.13 8.7 = 2.37 pounds per inch
2.37 × 70 = 166 lbs. optimal weight; 182 − 166 = 16 pounds excess
[Assume, for example, the man is 23% body fat (23 − 14 = 9% excess fat)
.09 (182) = 16.5 pounds excess fat.]
[Assume, as another example, this man is 17% body fat (17 − 14 = 3% excess fat)
.03 (182) = 5.5 pounds excess fat, therefore his realistic weight reduction
goal should be 5–6 pounds, not 16, since some 10 pounds of his excess weight
is lean tissue.]

ness level. Obviously, caloric intake must be increased when activity is increased. Performance can be impaired by malnutrition.

Obesity is correctly defined as "excess body fat," not excess "weight."

Starvation is not only a potential health hazard, but is ineffective in permanently reducing body fat stores.

Vibrators, steam baths, and drugs are ineffective for significant and permanent weight loss.

The professional physical educator, health educator, and recreation worker should be aware of the typical digestive disorders as well as the obvious "disorder" of obesity.

Skeletal measures and estimated percent body fat are valuable aids to diagnosis of ideal body weight.

PRINCIPLES

1. In terms of oxygen requirement, carbohydrate is a more efficient fuel than fat.

2. At least one gram of protein per kilogram of body weight per day is required for normal maintenance of body tissues.

3. The fat intake in calories should not exceed 25–30 percent of the daily intake.

4. At least 50 percent of the fats should be of the unsaturated variety.

5. Intake of refined carbohydrates should be minimized.

6. There is great individual variability in energy expenditure for a given task.

7. To be valid, a diet recall should be conducted for at least a week (and not during vacations, conventions, and so on).

8. No matter what the cause of abnormal weight, weight cannot be lost unless caloric expenditure exceeds caloric intake, nor can it be added unless intake exceeds expenditure.

9. Principles of weight control:

    a. For weight reduction, first establish a realistic goal for "fat loss," not "weight loss," using appropriate methods to determine the *actual* extent of excess fat tissue.

    b. Whether for weight maintenance or weight loss, the diet should be balanced, and the calories should probably be spread out evenly over at *least* three meals per day.

    c. Systematic and regular exercise causes not only increased caloric expenditure, but may promote a more desirable body composition (less fat) and may also render the "appestat" more effective.

TABLE 10.13 Optimal Weight per Inch of Height for Men and Women

CORRECTED ANKLE GIRTH (IN.)	OPTIMAL BODY WEIGHT, FEMALES	POUNDS PER IN. OF HEIGHT MALES
7.0	1.41	—
7.1	1.45	—
7.2	1.50	—
7.3	1.54	—
7.4	1.58	1.72
7.5	1.62	1.77
7.6	1.67	1.81
7.7	1.71	1.86
7.8	1.75	1.91
7.9	1.80	1.96
8.0	1.85	2.01
8.1	1.89	2.06
8.2	1.94	2.11
8.3	1.99	2.16
8.4	2.04	2.21
8.5	2.08	2.27
8.6	2.13	2.32
8.7	2.18	2.37
8.8	2.23	2.43
8.9	2.28	2.49
9.0	2.34	2.54
9.1	2.39	2.60
9.2	2.44	2.66
9.3	2.50	2.71
9.4	2.54	2.77
9.5	—	2.83
9.6	—	2.89
9.7	—	2.95
9.8	—	3.01
9.9	—	3.07
10.0	—	3.14

SOURCE: Adapted from Willoughby (611) after McGavack (357).

EXPERIMENTS AND EXPERIENCES

1. Determine the extent of body weight that can be lost by means of steam baths. After careful weight measurements are made before and after a

timed bath, the difference in weight should be recorded. Care should be taken to dry off thoroughly before weighing. Weight should be taken again two hours after the steam bath to determine how much has been regained through eating and drinking. Care should be taken to avoid overexposure to the hot, humid conditions.

2. Determine weight losses that can be attributed to a single bout of exercise of various intensities. Utilizing the careful weighing techniques described in the preceding experiment, record the differences in weight loss resulting from participation in normally vigorous sessions of swimming, handball, squash, basketball, softball, and so on. Remember to take the time factor into consideration.

3. Survey adults and contemporaries to determine the status of their knowledge concerning the principles of nutrition, weight control, and exercise.

4. Survey a nearby recreation agency. Ask the professional personnel what facilities and activities they have available for weight reduction. Do the same for a health salon. How many of the *participants* in these places are there to "lose weight"? How do they think they will accomplish this (what activities or machines, and so on)?

5. Complete a "diet recall" for yourself. How does your diet compare with the recommended diet? How can you change it to bring it in line?

6. Write to the FDA and secure information on weight control quackery.

7. Participate in an experiment to compare overweight as determined by percent excess body fat times body weight (see Table 10.12), with overweight determined by standard height-weight tables. Also compare with the Willoughby method for estimating optimal body weight.

SUGGESTED READINGS

The following references are highly recommended: AMA Journal (133) (Crash Diets); Garn (203); Havel (233); Jones, and others (288); Mayer and Bullen (377); Mayer (375); Parizkova and Stankova (443); Shade (509); Steinhaus (543), p. 153.; Van Itallie, Sinesterra, and Stare (585).

Additional recommended references:

Ahlman, K., and J. Karvonen, "Weight Reduction by Sweating in Wrestlers and its Effect on Physical Fitness," *Journal of Sports Medicine and Physical Fitness,* 1:58, 1961.

Banister, E. W., and others, "The Caloric Cost of Playing Handball," *Research Quarterly,* 35:326, 1964.

Bobbert, A. C., "Energy Expenditure in Level and Grade Walking," *Journal of Applied Physiology,* 15:1015, 1960.

Clarke, D. H., "Energy Cost of Isometric Exercise," *Research Quarterly,* 31:3, 1960.

Hashim, S. A., and T. V. VanItallie, "Clinical and Physiologic Aspects of Obesity," *Journal of the American Dietetic Association,* 46:15, 1965.

Johnson, P. B., "Metabolism and Weight Control," *JOPHER,* 39:9, 39, 1968.

Kral, J. A., A. Zenisek, and I. M. Hais, "Sweat and Exercise," *Journal of Sports Medicine and Physical Fitness,* 3:105, 1963.

Logatkin, M. N., "Utilization of Endogenous Fat in Partial Starvation and Physical Exertion," *Federation Proceedings, Translation Supplement,* 23:II: T 1277, 1964.

Margaria, R., and others, "Energy Cost of Running," *Journal of Applied Physiology,* 18:367, 1963.

Mayer, J., "Why People Get Hungry," *Nutrition Today,* 1:2, 2, June 1966.

Nutrition Review, "Present Knowledge of Fat," 24:33, 1966.

Nutrition Review, "Present Knowledge of Carbohydrate," 24:61, 1966.

Ralston, H. J., "Comparison of Energy Expenditure During Treadmill Walking and Floor Walking," *Journal of Applied Physiology* 15:1156, 1960.

Thompson, A. M., and others, "The Relation Between Caloric Intake and Body Weight in Man," *Abstracts of World Medicine,* 30:201, 1961.

Weaver, E. K., and D. E. Elliot, "Factors Affecting Energy Expended in Homemaking Tasks," *Journal of the American Dietetic Association,* 39:205, 1961.

Body Temperature Regulation

Chapter 11

It does not take a genius to perceive that the kinds of deaths illustrated in Figure 11.1 are *preventable* and, as such, are all the more lamentable. It takes only a person who cares about others to see the importance of educating the public so that such needless deaths can be prevented. It should be obvious that you, as physical or health educators, coaches, or recreation workers, are the persons with the greatest responsibility for the prevention of such deaths. This responsibility must be discharged *actively* and *positively*, not by chance but by conducting classes, practice sessions, recreation programs, and so on, so as to effectively *teach* the principles involved. At the same time, you must prescribe the proper conditions to prevent such deaths, as well as the less drastic, but nevertheless damaging, incidents involving nonfatal heat stroke and heat exhaustion. You have greater responsibility for prevention of such tragedies than any other person in our society. (As a matter of fact, when a coach forces his players to practice under conditions of high temperature and/or humidity in full football gear and forbids adequate water replacement, a heat stroke death can leave him seriously vulnerable to a negligence suit or worse!)

It does not take much insight to see that, in order to teach and practice the principles involved you must have knowledge about (1) the body and how its temperature is regulated, (2) the effects of environmental factors and various kinds of clothing on body temperature, and (3) the relationship of exercise to environment, clothing, and body temperature.

AFFERENT CONCEPTS

BODY HEAT

The living body constantly produces heat and constantly loses heat. It is the balance between heat production and heat loss that determines the body temperature (see Figure 11.2). The temperature inside the body (core temperature) is very constant, under normal conditions, for a given person. If taken orally the average temperature is about 98.6°F (about 1°F higher if taken rectally), although the "normal" range is about 97°F to 99.5°F. Because the regulatory mechanisms are not 100 percent efficient, extreme cold can lower the core temperature to less than 97°F, and hard exercise under certain conditions can raise it to as much as 104°F.

Skin temperature, on the other hand, is not so constant and can very considerably from one minute to the next.

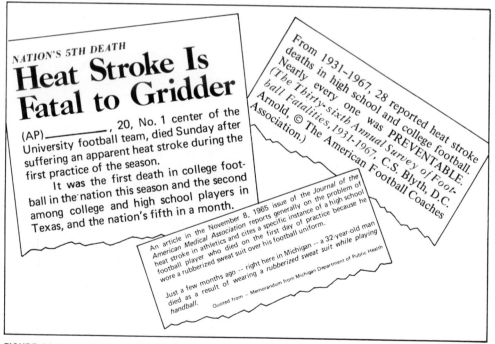

FIGURE 11.1   Heat stroke fatalities.

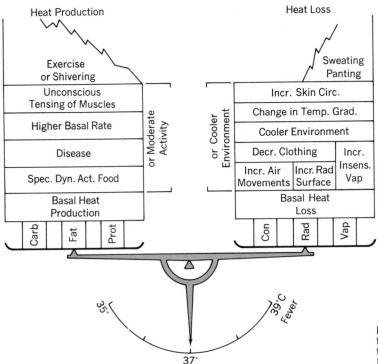

FIGURE 11.2 Balance between factors increasing heat production and factors increasing heat loss. Source: DuBois, *Bulletin of the New York Academy of Medicine*, 15, 1939.

(It can be reduced in the finger tips as much as 15°F in less than a minute by smoking a cigarette.) The reason for this will become obvious as you learn how heat loss is controlled.

Heat Production

The following factors contribute to heat production (see Figure 11.3):

1. Basal metabolism
2. Muscular activity
3. Thyroid hormone
4. Epinephrine (adrenalin) and sympathetic stimulation
5. Temperature of body

Under strictly basal conditions, the liver contributes 20 to 30 percent, the muscles 25 to 35 percent, and the brain some 15 to 20 percent of the total heat production. The amount remaining (15 to 40 percent) is produced almost entirely by the deep, internal organs of the body. Increase in total body muscle tone (short of actual contraction) can increase the metabolic rate some 50 to

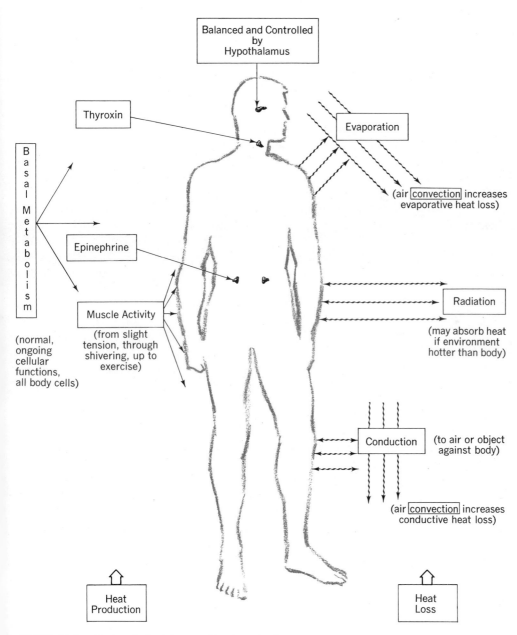

FIGURE 11.3   Factors in heat loss and heat production.

100 percent, and actual shivering can cause as much as a fourfold increase. Vigorous muscular activity can increase the metabolic rate as much as 2000 percent above basal!

Excess thyroxin (thyroid hormone) can double metabolic rate and epinephrine—sympathetic stimulation can very likely increase the rate by as much as 50 percent. It is interesting that the body temperature itself affects heat production; basal metabolic rate is increased about 7 percent per degree Farenheit body temperature increase.

Heat Loss

The following factors contribute to heat loss (see Figure 11.3):

1. Radiation
2. Conduction
3. Convection
4. Evaporation

The body radiates heat rays away from it and thus loses heat in this fashion as long as the temperature of the surroundings is not greater than body temperature. Because all mass that is warmer than absolute zero (including air) also radiates heat rays, it is the temperature differential that determines whether the net effect will be heat loss or heat gain by the body. The amount of heat lost by radiation, then, varies inversely with the temperature of the environment.

Heat loss via conduction (direct contact) is of two kinds, conduction to objects (a chair, for example) and to air. Under ordinary circumstances, far greater amounts of heat are lost by conduction to air. Conduction heat loss varies according to the percentage of the body in contact with objects, the conductive qualities of the objects, the percentage of the body in contact with air, and the rapidity of movement of air across the body. This air movement (convection) plays a vital role in heat loss (see Figure 11.4). If there is literally no air movement, when the layer of air immediately next to the skin reaches body temperature, there can be no further heat loss by conduction to air. Obviously, if the air is constantly moving, there is greater heat loss by conduction.

When water *evaporates* from a surface, heat is dissipated. We lose insensibly about 600 ml of water a day from the skin and lungs. When air temperature is greater than body temperature, evaporation is the only means of losing body heat! The body can increase evaporative heat loss by an increase in sweating, but this will be ineffective if the relative humidity is very high. In fact, when the relative humidity is 100 percent (that is, the air is completely saturated with moisture), there can be no evaporation because there is no place for the moisture to go. Convection is also important for continuous evaporative heat loss because air unsaturated with moisture must be "next to" the skin.

FACTORS AFFECTING HEAT LOSS There are two kinds of factors affecting heat loss that are worthy of your attention, physiological and external. You know that insulation can keep heat in or out, whichever the case may be. The body

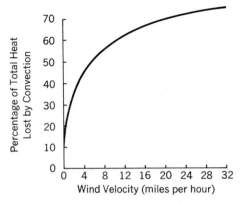

FIGURE 11.4 Effect of wind velocity on the percentage of heat loss that occurs by convection. By permission from A. C. Guyton, *Textbook of Medical Physiology*. Philadelphia: W. B. Saunders Company, 1968, p. 988.

has a layer of insulation—the skin and subcutaneous tissues (mainly fat). The thickness of this insulation certainly affects heat exchange of the body. The second physiological factor is the body's radiator system. If the blood vessels immediately under and in the skin are closed, the deep heat of the body is less effectively transmitted to the skin where it can be dissipated. If these are open, the deep heat can be better transmitted to the surface to be lost. This radiator system is very discretely controlled by the sympathetic nervous system so that heat may be conserved or dissipated in this manner.

In addition to the environmental factors (temperature, humidity, and convection), there is one other external factor that is of considerable importance: clothing. Clothing has an effect on radiation, conduction, and convection heat loss. It has an effect on evaporative water loss. The latter effect is related to the *kind* of clothing worn (clothing pervious or impervious to sweat).

The Body's "Thermostat"

It is apparent that some fine system is constantly and most successfully (at least under normal conditions) working at the task of maintaining "heat balance," so that body temperature is maintained within very narrow limits. That is to say something must be responsible for opening the skin's radiator system to increase heat loss when necessary, for increasing muscle tone or initiating shivering when more heat needs to be produced, and so on. This very delicate control center is located in the hypothalamus (see Figure 11.4) and is sensitive to changes in the temperature of the blood flowing through it as well as to nerve impulses from receptors in the skin. The anterior center and posterior center have a nice reciprocal agreement: when the anterior (temperature-reducing) center is stimulated, it inhibits the posterior (temperature-increasing) center, and vice versa. The anterior center, then, *increases* heat *loss* by increasing sweat rate, opening up the skin's radiator system, and inhibiting the heat-producing posterior center. Conversely, when there is a need to protect against overcooling, the posterior center of this thermostat shuts off the radiator system, reduces or completely abolishes sweating by inhibiting the anterior center's activity, *increases* heat *production* by the cells of the body via the sympathetic nervous system, and increases muscle tone or produces shivering if cooling is great enough.

Temperature Regulation in Exercise

In a cold environment the blood vessels near the surface of the skin become constricted so that the blood does not lose heat to the cold surroundings. In exercise, quite the opposite occurs. As the body produces more heat, the capillaries near the surface become filled with blood (see Figure 8.8), which enables a great deal of heat to be lost to the atmosphere by radiation from the surface of the body. It is important to keep in mind, however, that when external temperature is high, there may be too little difference between body temperature and environmental temperature for heat to be lost by **radiation.** In such cases **evaporation** becomes the chief means by which heat can be dissipated. The sweat glands secrete a watery fluid that, in evaporating from the surface of the skin, causes a very effective reduction of skin temperature. Thus blood that absorbs heat from active muscles can be shunted to the vessels of the skin, where the excessive heat can be lost through radiation and evaporation. Indeed, the ability of the body to dissipate excess heat in this manner is an important factor in exercise under certain conditions. Failure to carry off excessive heat results in **heat exhaustion** and sometimes even in death. Thus, it may be seen that when both environmental temperature and humidity are high, the two major means of heat dissipation are seriously restricted (see Figure 11.5). Under such circumstances one is unable to engage in vigorous physical activity to the extent that would normally be possible.

HEAT STROKE AND HEAT EXHAUSTION

Heat stroke or sunstroke is caused by prolonged exposure to excessively high temperatures or the direct rays of the sun, combined with conditions of high humidity. In this condition there is a serious breakdown of the heat-regulating mechanism. Weakness, headache, dizziness, and nausea are commonly experienced before collapse occurs, but sometimes the onset is sudden. Muscular cramps or twitching may occur, sweating ceases, the skin is flushed, hot, and dry. Body temperature may rise to 106°F or above; collapse and even death may follow. The severe temperatures are of special concern in this condition.

Heat exhaustion, or heat prostration, also results from exposure to excessive heat and humidity. Somewhat less serious than heat stroke, it can nevertheless cause illness, unconsciousness, and, in rare cases, death because of circulatory failure. The victim will usually have a very pale skin, which is cold and clammy. Perspiration is profuse. Body temperature is usually not significantly elevated.

Prevention

The best way to avoid heat stroke and heat exhaustion is to avoid exposing oneself to high temperatures for long

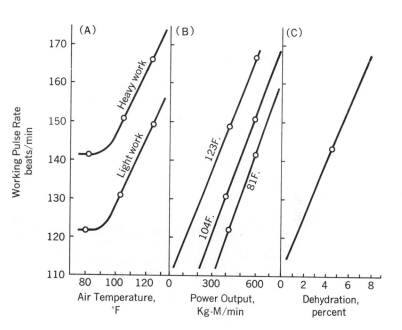

FIGURE 11.5 Simultaneous effects of heat, work, and dehydration. (A) Both light and heavy work cause an increase in pulse rate as the surrounding temperature rises. (B) Rise in surrounding temperature causes decrease in work output. (C) Increased dehydration causes an increase in the working pulse rate. By permission from A. H. Brown and E. J. Towbin, in *Physiology of Man in the Desert*, by E. F. Adolph and others. New York: Interscience Publishers, 1947.

periods. In athletics, frequent breaks, the elimination of any equipment that prevents heat dissipation, and the consumption of adequate amounts of water (see Figure 11.5) and salt are recommended in hot weather.

EFFERENT CONCEPTS

HEAT STROKE AND DEHYDRATION IN ATHLETICS AND WORK

At the end of each summer season, at about the time the public schools open, the papers invariably carry a few terse reports of the death of a high school or college football player. In fact, this happens all too often. Although the cause of the death may occasionally be attributed to violent body contact, too often at this time of the year heat stroke is the direct causative factor. Making such events even more tragic is the fact that in many of these cases ignorance is the real killer. When proper precautions are taken, heat stroke and heat exhaustion can be prevented. Failure to take such precautions is inexcusable.

It is equally inexcusable for YMCA physical directors, coaches of other sports, recreation personnel, and physical educators to permit conditions where persons can succumb to heat stroke or heat exhaustion. You should be aware of potential death or permanent damage possibilities when temperature and/or humidity are high, when persons wish to exercise in rubber suits, and so on. Your knowledge of the facts can prevent such tragedies and your teaching, whether formal or informal, may prevent many more.

WATER CONSUMPTION AND EXERCISE

Common Practices

Until quite recently it was common practice for coaches of athletic teams to forbid their athletes to drink water during practice or competition. During unusually hot or humid weather players were sometimes permitted to rinse their mouths out, but actually swallowing the water was prohibited. The reasons given for such practices were several:

1. To develop a tough, Spartan attitude. It was assumed that punishment of one's self in this manner was good discipline that would somehow carry over into the contest, making the player a tougher, hardier participant.
2. To prevent a water-logged condition. The drinking of water was assumed to contribute to slow, poorly coordinated movements.
3. To prevent excessive salt loss. It was presumed that if too much water was lost through perspiration the salt balance of the body would be upset, leading to dizziness and nausea (the symptoms of heat exhaustion).
4. To hasten the conditioning process.

Many coaches seemed to believe that being deprived of water somehow helped their players to "get into shape" faster. Weight reduction was probably one of the goals here.

Research Findings

Research has done much to dispel many of the misconceptions about the drinking of water during athletic participation.

PAIN IMMUNIZATION The assumption that being deprived of water contributes to the development of an ability to withstand discomfort is not supported by fact. It is doubtful that any beneficial effects (if they do, in fact, exist) could outweigh the harmful ones. The sensation of thirst indicates that the tissues need water. If this need is long ignored, the function of the tissues may be seriously impaired, which in turn, could be detrimental to the function of the whole body. Because enhanced performance, not impaired performance, is the desired outcome of such practices, it would seem logical that the practice of withholding water might well backfire.

"WATER-LOGGED" EFFECT Does ingestion of water produce the so-called water-logged condition? A number of investigations have revealed that there is no decrease in reaction time or movement time associated with drinking large amounts of water. In a study conducted by Little, Strayhorn, and Miller (349) the performance of athletes on a treadmill and in track and swimming events was found to be unaffected by ingestion of as much as 1.5 quarts of water, despite a definite sloshing sensation in the stomachs of the subjects.

In other studies (82, 83) it has been shown that water ingested before and during performance contributes to the length of time that the performance can be sustained. As a matter of fact, in animals it has been shown that water is even more important to the ability to maintain hard work for long periods than is food (624). In one study, six dogs were able to run up hill at 3.6 mph until they had expended 1191 calories under normal circumstances. When they were allowed to drink water during the run, they continued much longer, eventually expending an average of 2141 calories. Even feeding the dogs an energy-rich diet of carbohydrate before a run permitted them to expend only 1299 calories when they were not allowed to drink during the run.

SALT AND WATER BALANCE   The people who have attempted to avoid excessive salt loss by restricting the amount of water taken in are also victims of a serious misconception. It is important for the body to maintain an adequate salt level, but the way to ensure this is to *add* salt to the diet during hot weather, not to restrict water. It should be realized that the function of perspiration is to cool the body. As the water on the surface of the skin evaporates, the temperature of the skin drops, thereby cooling the blood that flows in the

capillaries immediately beneath the surface. As the blood continues to circulate it carries off heat from the deep tissues, thus protecting the body from dangerously high temperatures. In hot weather, when there is greater demand for cooling the body, more water is lost through the skin. If water is not taken in to replace this sweat loss, the body will take water from the fluid portion of the blood, making it difficult for the heart to provide the brain and other tissues with an adequate blood supply. This is a serious condition that could conceivably lead to the death of an individual.

Salt, which is normally found in the tissues of the body, is important for "holding" the water inside the tissue cells. If the supply of salt is low, too much water is allowed to leave the tissues to replace water lost from the blood, and the person becomes dehydrated.

CONDITIONING   Some coaches have told players that if they intend to get into good physical condition rapidly, the excessive drinking of water will be a hindrance. It is difficult to imagine how such a theory could have evolved, unless it is related to the temporary weight reduction due to water loss that frequently results from a vigorous workout.

There is no question that the water portion of the body's composition adds to its weight. It is just as true, however, that bone, muscle, fat, and connective and nervous tissue, which are also body components, also contribute to the total weight of the body. It would seem almost as sensible to remove surgically some bone or muscle in order to lose weight as it does to do it by dehydration. It is obvious that for most sports (with the exception of wrestling and boxing) the *actual* weight of the performer is of little consequence. What is important is his ability to perform efficiently. If, by removal of tissue, the effectiveness of the performance can be improved, then there is some justification for such removal. The only tissue not contributing to the performance in this case is, of course, the fat. In a typical training program this is the tissue normally reduced by oxidation. This would, naturally, produce an overall weight loss. To assume that the weight loss *itself* is the desired

goal is foolishness. The reduction of fat (adipose tissue) is really the important consideration. In addition, this latter type of weight loss is relatively permanent, whereas loss due to dehydration is replaced as soon as the individual resumes his normal drinking habits.

REPLACEMENT   Research has demonstrated that water (see Figures 11.6 and 11.7) and salt replacement is essential during activities that involve high temperatures and considerable sweat production. It is important to know how much water to give and when. Londeree's (353) study provides evidence that prehydration may be the best approach. Generally speaking, performers should be permitted to consume

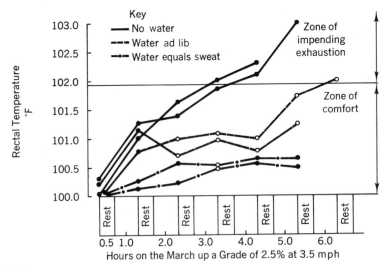

FIGURE 11.6   Effect of water consumption on rectal temperature during heat (temperature, 100° F; relative humidity, 35-45 percent). When no water is given, the temperature rise is sharpest and the subject enters the zone of impending exhaustion. When water is given as desired, the temperature rise is less sharp and the subject is far from exhaustion. When water equal to the amount of sweat lost is given, the temperature rise is smallest and the subject remains in the zone of comfort. By permission from Pitts, Johnson, and Consolazio, *American Journal of Physiology*, 142, 1944.

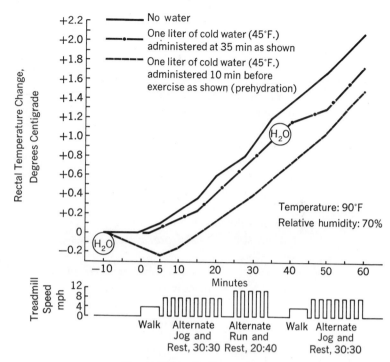

FIGURE 11.7 Effect of fluid replacement on rectal temperature of subjects exercising in full football uniform (including helmet and pads) in hot, humid environment. Data from Londeree (353).

water as they feel the need for it. If this is impractical because of the disruption of practice schedules, a water break should be provided every thirty minutes in average weather, and more often in excessively hot and/or humid conditions. It should be remembered that players will not voluntarily consume nearly as much water as they are losing in hot weather. For this reason it is a wise procedure to encourage them to drink *more* than they actually desire (210). The additional salt needed

can probably best be supplied by slightly increasing the salt in the food. Otherwise salt tablets are recommended or a little salt may be added to the drinking water. If salt is added to the water, care should be taken to see that no more than one level teaspoon per quart is mixed in; otherwise nausea may be produced in some individuals. Some trainers have reported that the addition of a little lemon juice to salted water makes it much more palatable. If the water is cold and the salt sufficiently diluted, however, it is doubtful that players will realize they are drinking salt water.

We strongly recommend field use of a sling psychrometer (approximate cost is $15) to determine relative humidity and an accurate thermometer before and during football practice sessions in late summer and early fall. Murphy and Ashe (412) have provided a useful guide for the protection of players against heat stroke and heat exhaustion.

Wet Bulb Reading[1]

Under 60° — No precaution necessary.

61°–65° — Alert observation of all squad members, particularly those who lose considerable weight.

66°–70° — Insist that salt and water be given on the field.

71°–75° — Alter practice schedule to provide rest periods every thirty minutes in addition to above precautions.

76° and over — Practice postponed or conducted in shorts.

SUMMARY

The professional physical educator, health educator, and recreationist must have knowledge about body tempera-

ture regulation, the effects of environment, and the relationship of exercise to body temperature and environment.

Body temperature is determined by the balance between heat production (which is affected by basal metabolism, muscle activity, thyroxin, epinephrine and sympathetic stimulation, and temperature of the body) and heat loss (which can occur by radiation, conduction, convection, and evaporation). Clothing and environmental conditions obviously affect heat loss.

The body's temperature is regulated by a center located in the hypothalamus; the circulatory system (the vessels of the skin) acts as a radiator system to dissipate heat or to conserve it.

Heat stroke is a serious and often fatal disorder caused by excessive increase in body temperature and is usually the result of high temperature, high humidity, and failure to allow for adequate heat loss.

PRINCIPLES

1. Heat stroke deaths are almost always preventable.

2. The coach or teacher who promotes or permits exercise when conditions for heat stroke are present and/or withholds water is indirectly responsible for any heat stroke which ensues.

3. There is no legitimate reason to withhold water from the organism that requires it; thirst is the mechanism by which this requirement is made known.

4. Work capacity in hot, humid environments is prolonged by the ad-

---

[1]This is not relative humidity. Even when the wet bulb reading is low, high relative humidity dictates extreme precautions. One death occured when the wet bulb was only 64°F but relative humidity was 100 percent (412).

ministration of water before and/or during the activity.

5. When humidity is high, evaporation cannot contribute to heat loss. The other heat dissipation routes *must* be permitted to function (conduction, radiation, and convection).

6. Even when death does not result, heat stroke can cause permanent damage to the individual.

EXPERIMENTS AND EXPERIENCES

1. Observe fluctuations of body temperature throughout a typical twenty-four-hour period, including exercise variations. Beginning on the morning of one day, record the temperature before arising from bed. At regular intervals thereafter take and record oral temperatures. During strenuous activity, take a special "time-out" at the peak of performance to determine temperature change. Plot the fluctuation for the day, observing the effects of various times and activities.

2. Survey football coaches and determine their attitudes toward fall practice in hot, humid weather; what are their solutions, if any? Do they plan for water consumption before and during practice?

3. Drink a pint of water and then jog and sprint. Does the water in any way affect your performance? Repeat at a later time with a quart of water. Is there evidence that water ingestion interferes with performance?

SUGGESTED READINGS

The following references are highly recommended: Little, Strayhorn, and Miller (349); Murphy and Ashe (412); Young (624).

Underlying Psychological Mechanisms

Chapter 12

Not long ago, there appeared in a popular magazine a moving story of a man who amazed witnesses with superhuman efforts utilized in freeing a trapped truck driver from his crushed, burning cab. Three trucks and a wrecker had been unsuccessfully utilized in attempting to free the driver from the twisted wreckage. Men with hammers and crowbars had failed in attempts to open the crumpled doors. As flames licked about the driver's feet, a big man moved out of the crowd and wrenched the door off with his hands. The story goes on to describe how the man "straightened that steering wheel like it was tin." He then proceeded to struggle into the cab until he was in a position to place his feet on the floor boards.

He started rising slowly. His muscles bulged in the half light and the sleeves of his shirt tore . . . . "We actually heard the metal give," reported a farmer who had come to the scene. Discussing the rescue afterward, Deputy Henry shook his head, still baffled. "And he held that top up until we could pull Gaby out . . . If I hadn't witnessed it I'd never believe a lone man could do a job we couldn't do with three trucks and a wrecker" (143).

Documented events such as this, though uncommon, are reported often enough to indicate that such amazing physical feats are possible. Since such performance obviously far exceeds the normal limits of individuals involved, how can it be explained?

For lack of a better explanation, such events are often discussed as being a "psychological breakthrough."

THE NERVOUS SYSTEM

In Chapter 9 the nervous system was discussed in terms of its contribution to movement. There was, however, little reference to the so-called higher function of the brain.

It is important to realize that neurons all operate in the same way, whether they are involved in remembering a poem, perceiving the shape of an object, or kicking a ball. The differences lie in the location of the neurons involved and in the complexity of their organization. Therefore, the previous discussion of the basic components of the nervous system is applicable to

our present discussion. We will, however, need to give a little closer attention to certain aspects of the system.

THE SYNAPSE

In Chapter 9 we discussed the basic system by which nerve impulses are transmitted. It will be recalled that the synapse is a junction between two nerve cells across which the nerve impulse must be carried if the postsynaptic neuron is to become activated. The means by which this occurs is of great importance in controlling all the varied functions of the organism, from thought and memory to fighting and loving.

Although the means by which the impulse is transmitted across the minute space between neurons at the synapse is not completely understood, it is believed to be a neurochemical process involving the release, by the axon endings of the presynaptic neuron, of a substance that affects the membrane potential of the postsynaptic neuron (see Figure 12.1). This "trans-

FIGURE 12.1 Small portion of the receiving area of motor neuron showing a few of the many neurons that synapse with it. The enlarged segment reveals that the end foot of a sending neuron contains sacs filled with a transmitter substance. Source: McKeachie and Doyle (359), p. 50.

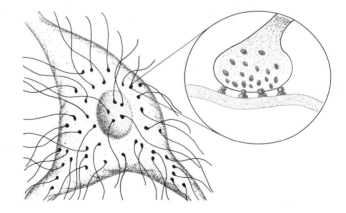

mitter substrate" released by the synaptic vessicles can have one of two effects on the postsynaptic membrane of the receiving neuron. If it is a positive acting (facilitating) substance, it will tend to depolarize the membrane, making it more likely to "fire" and propagate its own impulse. If it is a negative acting (inhibiting) substance, the membrane becomes hyperpolarized and more resistant to firing than it would be in the normal resting state (Figure 12.1).

This system is the basis for two extremely important adjustment mechanisms affecting human behavior: facilitation and inhibition. **Facilitation** is a condition in which excitatory impulses from various sources, including the cerebral cortex, impinge upon the cell bodies of the motor neurons. Although such impulses do not actually cause the neuron to fire, they substantially reduce the **threshold** of such neurons, making them especially susceptible to excitation. Subsequent impulses arriving from any one of a number of possible sources may then be adequate to trigger the action of the facilitated motor neurons.

Inhibition, on the other hand, is just the opposite. This is a condition resulting from the transmission of impulses from the brain (as well as from certain other sources) that actually *increase* the threshold of the motor neurons involved. Thus the motor neuron is prevented from being triggered by normal stimuli. Unusually intense stimulation is required to cancel out inhibitory impulses and cause the motor neuron to fire.

The normal threshold can be thought of as a built-in protective device for the neuromuscular system. If just *any* stimulus, regardless of its strength and duration, could elicit a response, the neuromuscular system would be in almost constant states of activity, much of it random and bizarre. The inhibitory influences, by affecting threshold levels, act as a "governor" to prevent self-damage from muscular contraction that is too vigorous; it may also aid in the timing and control of skilled movements requiring forceful muscular activity.

Sometimes, however, inhibitory impulses can become unusually dominant, even to the extent that an individual is incapable of average performance. A child who has constantly been told to "be careful" and who has never been permitted to exert himself for fear of injury may develop a state of inhibition that significantly reduces observable performance below his levels of capability. Under certain circumstances (hypnotism, hysteria, emergency conditions, and so on) inhibitory mechanisms can be overcome through a process called **disinhibition.**

The learning of any skill (rollerskating, for example) involves facilitation as well as disinhibition. As the appropriate movements are repeated over and over the synapses involved in the neural pathway become easier and easier to cross. Impulses from various sources tend to converge on the appropriate neurons (facilitation), lowering their threshold and permitting them to fire with less conscious effort.

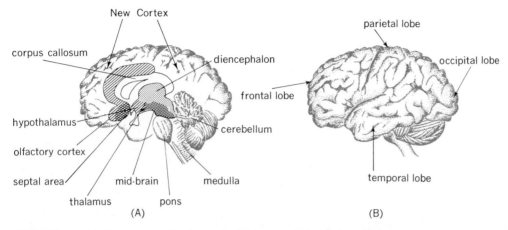

FIGURE 12.2 (A) Major centers in the brain. (B) Lobes of the cerebral cortex.

Such facilitation may persist for years once the pattern has become well established.

Of course, facilitation and inhibition are not limited to motor responses alone. Memory, thought processes, and all other activities of the nervous system are also subject to these phenomena.

THE BRAIN

It will be recalled that the brain consists of several complexly interrelated parts (Figure 12.2). The cerebral cortex sits like a cap or a thick helmet on the top of the other portions of the brain, controlling all of the body's conscious activity, thought, memory, learning, sensations, and many more functions. It is made up of masses of tissue repeatedly folded in upon itself forming two bilaterally symmetrical hemispheres of four lobes each.

Its role in motor function has already been mentioned briefly. Very distinct areas of the frontal lobe have been identified as having control of certain motor activity. As shown in Figure 12.3, the activity of the tongue, the index finger, the foot, and all the other body segments can be initiated by stimulation of specific areas of the brain. (This must not be interpreted as meaning that specific muscles are operated from this level, however.) It is interesting to note that the portions of the body involved in fine or complex activity (such as the tongue or lips) occupy a greater brain area than others involved in more gross activity (such as the trunk), even though the latter may represent much greater body mass. The same principle operates in terms of the sensory areas located in the parietal lobe.

In a general way sections of other lobes have been found to be associated with other functions. The striate area of the occipital lobe is involved with vision. The temporal lobe, when stimulated in one area, produces sensations

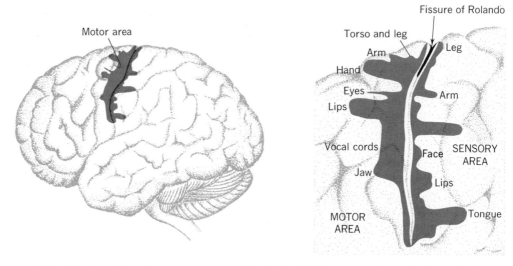

FIGURE 12.3   Location of motor control areas in the brain. The enlarged area indicates the location of several sensory and motor areas. Adapted from McKeachie and Doyle (359), p. 55.

of sound. In another, memories, recollections, or even emotional reactions appear to be centered (Figure 12.4).

Although some functions seem to be distinctly localized, others are much more diffuse. "Association areas" for speech and hearing, for example, are located in the temporal lobe, but specific language behaviors cannot be pinpointed.

At one time it was widely believed that localized areas of the brain controlled the separate types of behavior. Although very little localization had been discovered, it was considered only a matter of time and improved technique before the evidence would be obtained. With the subsequent development of remarkable new techniques, however, it has been discovered that such localization of brain function is not the rule.

It has become evident that no single section of the brain is exclusively responsible for any of the behavioral functions. The various sections of the brain are interconnected by means of a rich, intricate system of circuits, so that activity in any given section is capable of affecting the activity of any other section.

When it comes to locating an activity such as thought or reasoning, it is evident that widely diversified areas of the cortex are involved. Whether, in certain instances, functions of the brain can be transferred from one section to another has not been conclusively demonstrated. There is considerable supposition that such "plasticity" does exist, however, and many programs of learning and rehabilitative therapy are based upon this hypothesis (see Chapter 17).

Relatively extensive areas of the brain have, to date, not been identified with any specific function at all. The frontal lobe has been extensively damaged in many patients without resulting in any discernible alteration in behavior or personality. To say that such areas have no function at all would be illogical. Some have theorized that some of this tissue represents unused capacity and have concluded that man is generally capable of much greater intellectual activity than he normally exhibits. Whether such assumptions are warranted is the focus of considerable physiological and psychological research.

The portions of the brain below the level of the cortex (Figure 12.2) have other interesting functions in addition to those associated with exercise as discussed previously. In the center of the brain (diencephalon), the thalamic structures serve as a major relay station for most of the impulses coming into and going out from the brain. For this reason it is considered capable of influencing nearly all of the brain's activities.

More specific statements can be made about the small cluster of neural centers below the thalamus called the *hypothalamus*. It has already been discussed with respect to its role in temperature regulation, but it also has other very important functions. Emotional behavior, or aspects of thought and behavior relating to emotion, is related to this structure. Eating behavior can also be controlled by the stimulation or removal of certain portions of the hypothalamus. Animals

can be made to eat almost continuously by stimulation, or, conversely, to starve even in the presence of food.

Some recent research has isolated "pleasure" centers in areas anterior to the hypothalamus. Stimulation of such areas has the effect of producing "pleasurable sensations" in humans, and animals have been observed to prefer stimulation of this type to food and sex and will endure considerable pain when this type of stimulation is given as a reward. Some experimentation has been done in utilization of this type of stimulation in reducing aggressive behavior. In one report, electrodes permanently implanted in the brain were connected to a stimulus box that was carried and controlled by the patient. Whenever unpleasant or aggressive feelings were perceived, he could simply press the appropriate button (he had a choice of intensities) and experience feelings of pleasure and tranquillity. Although such procedures

FIGURE 12.4 Areas of the brain to which sensations are "projected."

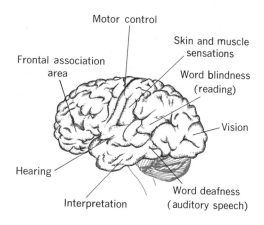

Motor control

Skin and muscle sensations

Frontal association area

Word blindness (reading)

Vision

Hearing

Word deafness (auditory speech)

Interpretation

are rare, they offer exciting possibilities for the future.

The **cerebellum** has been previously described as being chiefly responsible for balance and coordination of the large muscles. It is intimately associated with the learning of motor skills, but the exact manner in which it functions is unknown. It is undoubtedly closely related to the cerebral cortex, and the passing on of correct information about the status of muscles and limbs, and body position, is essential to the organism as it attempts to learn to adapt to specific situations.

The **medulla oblongata,** as you will recall, is the lowest of the brain structures and is continuous with the spinal cord. The vital functions of the body such as blood pressure, heart rate, and respiration are regulated here. Damage to many areas of the brain can be survived (sometimes with remarkable lack of residual difficulty) (206), but damage to the medulla cannot be tolerated.

Passing up through the medulla and the brain stem is a complex formation of offshooting neurons from all the sensory nerves passing upward to the brain. These branches are collectively called the *reticular formation* or the *reticular activating system* (Figure 12.2).

The function of this system appears to be one of maintaining vigilance or alertness of the other systems of the brain. Because fibers pass to all portions of the cortex, all cortical functions are alerted or activated when the system is active. When the reticular activating system is quiescent, the organism is in a state of depressed activity or sleep. It is thus easy to see that the alertness necessary for appropriate reaction and learning is dependent upon the proper function of the reticular formation.

THE PERIPHERAL NERVOUS SYSTEM

As noted in an earlier chapter, the nervous system can be regarded as consisting of two separate divisions: the autonomic and the somatic. Whereas the somatic system deals with the function of the skeletal muscles of the body, the autonomic system is concerned primarily with the control of the **visceral** organs and the circulatory system. Some knowledge of the autonomic system is important to the understanding of many problems relating to psychology. Among these are stress, anxiety, psychsomatic illness, and mental illness, as well as other factors to be discussed later.

The autonomic system is frequently called the "involuntary" nervous system because it is not under the conscious control of the individual. It, in turn, has two separate subsystems: the **sympathetic** and the **parasympathetic.** In general, the action of these two systems is mutually antagonistic. Whereas one may cause increased activity of a gland or organ, the other usually has the opposite effect (see Table 12.1). For example, the heart rate is speeded up by action of the sympathetic nerves, whereas activation of the parasympathetic system slows the heart. Generally speaking, it is the algebraic sum of the effects of these two systems that determines the activity level of organs and tissues at any given moment.

Another way to grossly differentiate the functions of the two divisions of the autonomic nervous system is to note that the sympathetic portion acts to prepare the body to meet emergency situations ("fight or flight"), whereas the parasympathetic portion serves to maintain constant environmental conditions surrounding the cells of the body. These characteristics are especially important in the study of stress and anxiety and their relationships to physical activity.

Inspection of Figure 9.1 shows that the autonomic nervous system can be readily identified by its appearance *outside* the bony structure of the vertebral column. Although most of the **somatic** system is enclosed within the spinal column, the autonomic system is largely composed of two chains of **ganglia** (nerve junction centers) paralleling the spinal column. From these ganglia, branches extend to the internal

TABLE 12.1   Autonomic Effects on Various Organs of the Body

ORGAN	EFFECT OF SYMPATHETIC STIMULATION	EFFECT OF PARASYMPATHETIC STIMULATION
Eye: pupil	Dilated	Contracted
ciliary muscle	None	Excited
Gastrointestinal glands	Vasoconstriction	Stimulation of thin, copious secretion containing many enzymes
Sweat glands	Copious sweating (cholinergic)	None
Heart: muscle	Increased activity	Decreased activity
coronaries	Vasodilated	Constricted
Systemic blood vessels:		
abdominal	Constricted	None
muscle	Dilated (cholinergic)	None
skin	Constricted or dilated (cholinergic)	None
Lungs: bronchi	Dilated	Constricted
blood vessels	Mildly constricted	None
Gut: lumen	Decreased peristalsis and tone	Increased peristalsis and tone
sphincters	Increased tone	Decreased tone
Liver	Glucose released	None
Kidney	Decreased output	None
Bladder: body	Inhibited	Excited
sphincter	Excited	Inhibited
Male sexual act	Ejaculation	Erection
Blood glucose	Increased	None
Basal metabolism	Increased up to 150%	None
Adrenal cortical secretion	Increased	None
Mental activity	Increased	None

SOURCE: Guyton (224), by permission of the author and publisher.

organs such as the heart, liver, kidneys, pancreas, spleen, urogenital organs, and various glands. In addition, the blood vessels serving cardiac muscle and smooth muscle (as found in the digestive tract), are also innervated by this system.

THE SENSORY SYSTEM

The term "sensory system" is probably a misnomer, because the senses are obviously but a portion of the nervous system. On the other hand, the information we obtain from our surroundings through our senses is not only essential to our survival but is also of extreme importance in the acquisition of knowledge, skills, and attitudes.

General Function

The collection of neurons, various kinds of nerve endings, and the higher brain centers in the sensory system are extremely important to health and fitness. Actually this system is a specialized part of the nervous system, but because it is so important to survival and to normal existence, it deserves a special comment. You have probably heard that we have five senses. Persons with uncanny insight or "predictive" abilities are said to have "a sixth sense." But in fact, those of us who are not "uncanny" and are relatively *normal* have more than five senses! It depends upon how one chooses to classify them, but according to our classification, there are eleven senses (touch, pressure, temperature, pain, kinesthesis, muscle

sense, equilibrium, hearing, vision, smell, and taste). Except to point out that there *are* several logical systems of classification (some separating and some lumping together), it seems best *not* to mention all of the various classification systems. We are using a system that appeals to us because it is clear-cut and relatively simple, but there are other perfectly logical classifications.

TACTILE SENSES   *Touch* is the detection of any contact of a part of the body with another object. The touch receptors generally lie very near the surface of the skin. *Pressure* is a type of touch sensation but differs from pure "touch" in that it involves the ability to detect the relative amount of force acting against the skin or other tissues.

TEMPERATURE SENSE   *Temperature* is perceived via the thermal receptors, which enable the human being to distinguish between varying gradations of heat and cold.

PAIN SENSE   The sense of *pain* is a protective mechanism and in most tissues results from even the most minute degrees of tissue damage. Pain receptors, or "free nerve endings," are located in the skin and in most of the tissues of the body.

PROPRIOCEPTOR SENSES   *Kinesthesis* is the conscious recognition of the position of the various parts of the body and the rates of movement of parts of the body. *Muscle sense* involves the awareness of the degree of muscle contraction or stretch and the amount of tension on the tendons. *Equilibrium* or balance involves the vestibular apparatus of the ears to a major extent but also involves information from the sense of vision and the kinesthetic and muscle sense receptors.

SPECIAL SENSES *Hearing, vision, smell,* and *taste* are all referred to as *special senses* in that they perform some very specific function in a very specific area.

THE ENDOCRINE SYSTEM

There is another great coordinating or integrating mechanism in the body besides the nervous system called the *endocrine* system. Because the endocrine secretions enter the blood and remain in the body, they are called *internal secretions* to distinguish them from *external secretions* that are discharged through ducts to internal or external surfaces (the digestive juices and sweat).

Each of the endocrine glands produces a distinctive secretion of its own. All such secretions are called hormones or "chemical messengers." As they circulate through the body they act on the various tissues and organs either to stimulate their action or to inhibit them in specific ways. The various glands work in harmony with each other and with the activity of the nervous system in meeting the changing requirements of the body.

The bodily functions affected most by the endocrine secretions are growth and development, metabolism, sexual function, and the coordination of smooth-muscle activity. In this latter

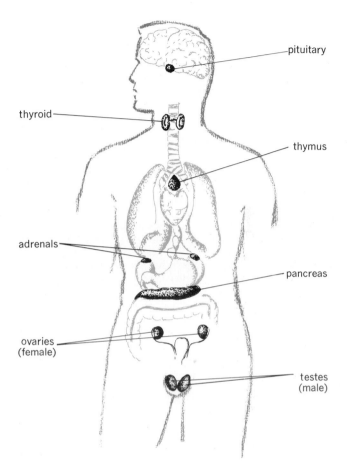

FIGURE 12.5   Location of the endocrine glands.

function the endocrine system works in close conjunction with the autonomic nervous system. Because the secretions of the endocrine system are carried by the blood, their effects are relatively slower in appearing and somewhat longer lasting than the similar effects that result from activity of the autonomic nervous system. Figure 12.5 shows the location of the

TABLE 12.2   Primary Functions of the Endocrine Secretions

GLAND OR HORMONE	PRIMARY FUNCTION(S) OR EFFECTS
Adrenal cortex	
1. glucocorticoids	Controls intermediary metabolism of foodstuffs
2. mineralocorticoids	Controls electrolyte balance
Medulla	
(epinephrine and norepinephrine)	Supports function of the sympathetic nervous system
Gonad	
1. Ovaries	Reproductive functions
(estrogens and progesterone)	Secondary sex characteristics
2. Testes	
(testosterone)	Secondary sex characteristics
Pancreas	
(insulin)	Regulates carbohydrate metabolism
Parathyroid	
(parathormone)	Regulates calcium metabolism
Pituitary (anterior)	
1. growth hormone	Stimulates growth
2. thyrotrophic hormone	Stimulates thyroid gland
3. adrenocorticotrophic hormone	
(ACTH)	Stimulates adrenal cortex
4. gonadotrophic hormones	Control the gonads
Thymus	Possibly associated with development of antibodies in the young
Thyroid	
(thyroxin)	Increases most metabolic activities of all cells

SOURCE: Guyton (224), by permission of the author and publisher.

endocrine glands. Each gland has its particular function, and the size of the tissue is in no way related to its physiological importance.

The regulatory function of the endocrine glands serves to maintain constancy of the internal environment. When this state is not maintained, the individual's behavior is affected, indicating the need for a return to normal functioning of the glands. Table 12.2 summarizes the principal functions of the endocrine glands.

FUNCTIONS OF THE NEUROHUMORAL SYSTEMS IN PHYSICAL ACTIVITY

THE NERVOUS SYSTEM

The responsibility for initiating, coordinating, and directing various movements rests with the central nervous system. Most of the internal adjustments that must be made in order to support exercise, however, are made through the activity of the autonomic nervous system and the endocrine system. Feedback from the systems, either in the form of sensations that are consciously evaluated or impulses that are below the level of consciousness, continuously indicates the status of the body's internal environment. Signals of internal imbalance resulting from such conditions as lack of oxygen and the accumulation of carbon dioxide in the tissue produce sensations of discomfort that normally lead to discontinuance of the activity responsible for these conditions. It is evident, however, that we are capable of continuing performance far beyond the point at which the first signals of distress are experienced. The trained athlete is able to outperform the average person because of his superior ability to deliver oxygen to the tissues and because of greater efficiency developed through the physical conditioning process. In addition to creating improved physiological capacity, however, this repeated exposure to the intense discomfort associated with pushing himself toward greater and greater efforts develops an ability to tolerate distress signals that would cause another person to stop under the assumption that he had reached his absolute limit.

Of course, motivational levels are an important factor in determining the degree to which pain or other signals of internal distress can be ignored. Even untrained individuals are capable of amazing physical feats under certain conditions. In such cases the inhibitory influence of the physiological distress signals is somehow overruled.

Generally speaking, the feedback resulting from the interaction of the various systems during exercise is evaluated by the central nervous system. A judgment based on this information and on past experience is then made as to when the activity should be terminated. It is therefore apparent that the actual limits placed on individual physical performance are partly psychological rather than purely physiological.

THE HUMORAL SYSTEM

The importance of the sympathetic nervous system in physical activity can be demonstrated easily by the observed increase in rate and force of contraction of the heart beat preceding and during exercise. This action is reinforced by the secretion of epinephrine (adrenalin) from the adrenal medulla (or central portion of the adrenal gland). The significant factor to note is that the nervous system and the endocrine system are capable of producing similar kinds of activity within the organs of the body and that they support each other in these actions.

THE SENSORY SYSTEM

It is obvious that vision, equilibrium, muscle sense, and kinesthesis are all important in physical activity. Of these, the proprioceptive senses are the most important; one can more easily perform without visual cues than without balance or an awareness of position and rate of movement. Hearing can be an important cue under certain circumstances. It appears that the senses of touch and pressure, together with the proprioceptors, are essential to optimal strength development. In fact, without the sensory impulses from the limb concerned, it is almost impossible to get an animal or a person even to attempt to contract the muscles of that limb. The sense of pain also plays a role in exercise. There are pain endings in the muscles, and pain certainly is one of the factors that limit performance, although this limitation varies from person to person and also depends upon degree of motivation and level of training. The thermal sense is certainly a limiting factor in exercise, especially in persons who have a low tolerance to heat.

In summary, it is evident that vision and hearing can give cues during exercise and that pain and temperature can be limiting factors in endurance performances. The really critical sensory factors, however, are the tactile senses and the proprioceptor senses, for, without these, one is usually not able to initiate even normal movement. It has been properly said that movement is in reality a "sensory experience."

SUMMARY

While the study of man at the biological level is extremely valuable, it cannot adequately answer all the questions that arise about human beings.

Another approach is to observe how man behaves — to study what he does and says. This approach is the one taken by psychologists.

Because they recognize that all behavior is *caused* by something, psychologists, too, are interested in how men perceive, learn, communicate, and move. In order to even begin to understand such phenomena, however, they must have a good grasp of bodily function, and in particular an understanding of the nervous system.

The phenomena of facilitation and inhibition are directly related to synaptic events. Areas of the brain controlling specific sensory or motor functions are of importance to those who would like to be able to predict or change general behavioral patterns. Ideas regarding the specificity of brain function have been seriously challenged in recent years. Considerable research remains to be done in clarification of such problems.

The function of the autonomic nervous system is important to an understanding of stress and behavior in emergencies, as is the activity of the endocrine system.

The senses also constitute an extremely important area of study for the psychologist because of the limitations this system places upon man's capacity to analyse and interpret events.

EXPERIMENTS AND EXPERIENCES

The following experiment is designed to demonstrate the activity of the autonomic nervous system in preparing the body for vigorous activity. Although manual methods can be used, it is much better for this experiment to have a method of electronically monitoring and recording the heart rate of the subject. Rapid changes cannot normally be detected by manual methods.

The subject should be allowed to sit and relax until heart rate levels off. Record the response to several emotional stimuli. Have the subject stand and, after the rate has leveled off, explain some light exercise he is to undertake and record the rate as the command "get ready to exercise" is given (this is called "anticipatory heart rate") and during exercise; use some form of emotion-evoking stimulus during exercise to see if this has an effect. After the light exercise has continued for several minutes, allow time for return to a near normal heart rate, then repeat, this time using a vigorous, difficult exercise. Study the effects of anticipation of tasks and the other emotion-evoking stimuli on heart rate and explain these effects.

SUGGESTED READINGS

Buchwald, Jennifer S., "Basic Mechanisms of Motor Learning," *Physical Therapy*, 45:314-331 (April), 1965.

King, Barry G. and Mary Jane Showers, *Human Anatomy and Physiology* (5th ed.), Philadelphia: W. B. Saunders Company, 1964.

Reese, W. G. and R. A. Dykman, "Conditional Cardiovascular Reflexes in Dogs and Men," *Physiological Review*, 40:250, 1960 (Suppl. 4, Pt. II).

Scubic, V. and J. Hilgendorf, "Anticipatory, Exercise, and Recovery Heart Rates of Girls as Affected by Four Running Events," *Journal of Applied Physiology*, 19:853, 1964.

Shearn, D. W., "Operant Conditioning of Heart Rate," *Science*, 137:530, 1962.

Wenger, M. A., F. N. Jones and M. H. Jones, *Physiological Psychology*, New York: Holt, Rinehart and Winston, Inc., 1956.

Afferent
Psychological Concepts

Chapter 13

EFFECTS OF PSYCHOLOGICAL FACTORS
ON PHYSICAL ACTIVITY

Although you may not have thought about it in this way before, psychological factors can be viewed in two ways in terms of their relationship to physical activity: (1) How they affect the physical activity of every individual, and (2) how physical activity of the individual affects psychological factors. First, we will identify some important psychological elements and, at the same time, indicate how these factors affect the physical activity of people. Following this we will look at each of these factors again from the standpoint of how one's activity patterns affect the psychological factors (Chapter 14). Not all the topics to be discussed are equivalent in terms of their breadth or importance. Many of them are interrelated, and some are, at least partially, dependent upon others. Each of them, however, has important implications for the health educator, physical educator, or recreation leader.

MOTOR LEARNING

The term "motor learning" is obviously only a modification of the more general term "learning." This implies that learning of a physical skill is somehow different from learning a mathematical relationship or historical fact. A commonly accepted definition of learning would not necessarily support this idea: "Learning is a relatively permanent change in behavior as a result of practice or experience" (400). There is little here that would differentiate between the memorization of a poem and the aqusition of the ability to juggle a handful of plates.

The fact is that no one yet knows whether these are really different processes or not. As the definition of learning just given points out, learning is really never directly observed but is only inferred from observations of overt behavior. It is generally assumed that some physiological or biochemical change has occurred in the nervous system and that these alterations produce the behavioral changes from which learning is inferred.

If you have not already done so, you will encounter various theories that are attempts to explain, at least partially, how learning occurs. Much of the experimental evidence collected in testing these theories has involved gross motor tasks. The assumption has then been made that generalizations from this evidence could validly be made to nonmotor types of learning. The point to be made here is that many of the generalizations or principles of psychology are directly applicable to the learning of motor skills, whether they are generally true for all types of learning or not. Of course, the question remains whether relatively fine motor skills such as holding a stylus in a rotating target (pursuit rotor) or drawing figures as viewed through a mirror are representative of the learning that takes place in athletic skills.

Many psychologists have taken the point of view that there are, indeed, several forms of learning and that each of these should be studied separately; at least care should be exercised in generalizing from one to another. Although there is not universal agreement as to the identification of these forms, one classification system has been proposed by Melton (380). His seven categories include incidental memory and short-term memory, probability learning, perceptual motor skill learning, verbal learning, problem solving, classical and operant conditioning, and concept formation.

A great many theories have been developed in attempts to explain learning. The educator is interested in theories from the practical viewpoint of making learning more efficient. At present there are no theories that have been able to explain adequately all phenomena observed in learning situations. Some theories have been constructed with the intention of explaining only isolated psychological phenomena, whereas others make broader claims. A review of all major theories, both current and historically important, is beyond the scope of this book. However, we can say that much progress has been made since the early attempts to explain behavior on the basis of specific instincts.

Many of the early psychologists, utilizing relatively simple conditions, contributed greatly to the development of modern theories dealing with more complex situations. Pavlov's (446) early experiments with conditioned responses in his dogs have become classic. Education has been strongly influenced by the work of Thorndike (561) and Watson (599) (and many others) whose emphasis was on "connectionism" or the relationships developed between a stimulus and a response. Our ideas concerning the necessity for a reward or reinforcement for desired behavior have sprung from this school of thought.

From the Gestaltists (317, 318, 319) we get the term "insightful learning" and some of our ideas about thought and reasoning. Much productive investigation has resulted from the precisely constructed theories of Hull (258). Ideas concerning the duration and spacing of practice periods have been postulated on his concepts of the accumulation and dissipation of inhibitory potentials. The importance we give to reinforcement comes largely from Skinner (521). More recent theories have expanded our thinking to consider the feedback mechanisms inherent in the nervous system as critical factors in learning. The computer age has not only given us new techniques by which behavior can be studied but has also produced concepts of man-machine similarities that are useful in studying learning. To list a few systems or individuals is probably unwise

because a vast number of others, equally or more important, have been omitted. Courses in general psychology will provide you with opportunities to examine the various theories and their applicability to our profession. Specialized courses in motor learning also provide excellent opportunities to gain valuable information pertaining to the learning of skills. The references listed at the end of this chapter include some interesting discussions of learning theories and other related factors.

Motor Educability

The relative ease with which one is able to learn a new skill, or different kinds of skills, is called motor educability. Obviously, this is important in motor learning, and tests of this characteristic are important if appropriate teaching methods are to be used with the learners involved.

Motor Capacity

Motor capacity (or motor intelligence) affects the rate and extent of skill learning. This factor, together with the ease with which skills can be learned, affects the individual's interest in new activities and his willingness to learn new activities. Both of these factors are affected, to some extent, by his maturation and his early experiences in exploration of his environment.

The question of the relationship between the intellectual and motor capacities has interested people for generations, and we will be spending some time with it later. It is obvious that less-than-normal intelligence would hamper an individual in understanding the requirements of a skill and would probably also affect his interest in it.

Memory

The problems of retention and forgetting are common to both verbal learning and motor skills. It is quite likely, however, that if you learned how to ride a bicycle when you were seven years old you can still ride, even though it may be some time since your last attempt. It is less likely that verbal material learned at that time (unless it has been repeated frequently) has been as successfully retained.

It is interesting that both motor skills and verbal material seem to be subject to forgetting in two different ways. Some material, such as a telephone number, may be recalled for only a moment and forgotten immediately after being dialed (a situation producing exasperation if a busy signal necessitates looking up the number again). Other information (a social security number, for example) may be retained for years, even though it may seldom be needed.

It has become apparent that there are short-term memories and long-term memories. Agranoff (5) has presented evidence that the biochemical events associated with each type of learning are different, at least to the extent that protein systhesis appears to be essential for long-term memory to occur. If something interferes with the essential systhesis, it appears that long-term memory will be impaired. Certainly

the capacity for long-term memory is important to skill retention, and any factors affecting this capacity would be important to know about.

Methods of Organization and Practice

Of all the factors to be discussed, one of the most critical is the topic of the means by which skills are organized and presented to the learner. Although at this point we are primarily concerned with skill attainment, it should be remembered that attitudes, values, and other concepts are also affected by the manner in which the learner is approached. And because much of what is learned is obtained without conscious planning by anyone, it is important to be concerned about the total environment of human beings.

Conditioning

In the simplest situations it is possible to obtain a desired response to a given stimulus by the methods of classical conditioning. As you probably know, this simply involves pairing any stimulus (a bell) with a stimulus that normally produces a reflex response in the organism. Pavlov worked with meat powder and salivation of his dogs. After a number of paired presentations (meat and bell simultaneously) the new stimulus (bell) produced the reflex response (salivation) when presented by itself (446).

Although it is doubtful that such procedures would purposely be used in the teaching of skills, it must be recognized that certain physical and emotional responses (heart rate increases, sweating, fear, anger) may, because of constantly paired association at practice sessions, become associated with new cues (words, sounds, people).

From a more practical point of view, it is more likely that *operant conditioning* (or a modification thereof) would be utilized in producing desired behavior. In this system desired behavior is rewarded and undesired behavior is discouraged, sometimes by punishment (521). Such systems are utilized by animal trainers, and, of course, football coaches. Actually, much of our school experience, from reading to dramatic performance, has been structured in this way. The learning of physical skills is particularly adapted to this reinforcement of appropriate behavior.

Whole-Part Organization

When a specific skill or concept is to be learned, it can be presented in a variety of ways. A decision must usually be made as to whether practice should be begun by practicing the whole skill or by breaking it into simpler parts for concentrated attention on the individual portions. It is important to make a distinction at this point between a "whole skill" and a complete game. A game of basketball is composed of many skills. Dribbling the ball is one, the chest pass another, the jump shot still another. Each of these components of the game may represent a skill in and of itself. As Cratty has pointed out,

"Wholeness" is a subjective term, and relates to the amount of the task a learner can effectively organize motorically and perceptually (136, p. 142).

In practicing a skill by the whole method, the skill in question is repeated over and over again in its entirety. If the part method is used, a skill, such as the jump shot, is broken down into separate phases, and these individual phases are practiced separately. After considerable practice of each, the parts are put together. In some modifications of this procedure, parts may be successively added so that the size of the unit gradually increases; or, emphasis may be made on perfecting each part before moving to the next.

Actually, few teachers use the part method exclusively. Generally, some combination of methods is used in which the individual parts are attempted, then put together, and the whole performance is observed. If analysis reveals faulty performance, the part or parts that are still unsatisfactory are again practiced separately before the whole is observed a second time. This process of analysis and synthesis generally continues until performance reaches a satisfactory level.

Although the literature is not in complete agreement on this subject (424), whole practice appears to be superior for many skills, especially if the task is not too difficult or the learner is not too immature (71, 605). In tasks of greater complexity, especially where memory may be a factor, part methods are usually superior (423).

Massed versus Distributed Practice

Should practice sessions consist of concentrated work with a few rest periods, or should practice be distributed over a longer time with more frequent rest periods? Evidence indicates that for certain motor tasks short practice periods interspersed with brief rest periods are superior to massed practice (10, 274, 568). It is not clear, however, that this is the case for more gross motor skills. In addition, the nature of the task interacts with the method used. When learners are interested, and highly motivated, massed practice is effective. For less attractive tasks, distributed practice appears to be preferable (1, 169, 320).

Mental Practice

Another interesting factor affecting the learning of a physical skill is that of mental practice. When a diver pauses for long moments on the platform before propelling himself in a spinning, twisting arc from the springboard, what is he doing? You may have heard that he is "concentrating" on his dive. What this actually means is that he is mentally rehearsing his movements. He goes over the dive in his imagination, "getting the feel" of the timing of the precise movements he must employ if a successful performance is to result.

A similar type of mental practice can actually improve the execution of a skill over a period of several days or weeks during which no physical prac-

tice occurs (88, 196, 538, 539, 574, 580). Although there can be no doubt that physical practice is superior to mental practice. It has been demonstrated many times that mental practice is superior to no practice at all. This may be one of the factors that enable an individual to sometimes perform better after a lay-off than he did before the interruption of physical practice.

Speed versus Accuracy

There are an almost infinite number of factors that can be varied in the organization and presentation of a learning experience. Regardless of the time distribution of practice, decisions must be made about the subfactors on which the learner should concentrate. In tennis, for example, it is important to be able to stroke the ball with force, as well as with great accuracy. A beginner may be confronted with the problem of whether to concentrate on force and speed or to strive for accuracy. Research in this area indicates that for most activities it is best to attempt to emphasize both equally (196). If, however, this is impossible, it is probably better to sacrifice accuracy at first in favor of speed or force (518).

The indications are that anyone practicing for speed initially will eventually be able to develop accuracy later on at the level of speed desired, but if he chooses to concentrate on accuracy at the outset, he may never achieve as much speed as he would have otherwise. Perhaps one of the reasons for this is related to the matter of specificity of training or practice. If, in attempting to gain satisfactory levels of accuracy early in practice, the beginner adopts habits that are somewhat different from the movement patterns he will need to employ later on when power is added, he will very likely have to learn two separate skills. If he practices the skill at speeds he will be employing when he begins actual participation, his accuracy will be found to improve gradually with practice.

Overlearning

Although overlearning is obviously not a method of organizing or presenting material, it is a characteristic that is often stressed in many types of practice situation. Drills of all types are commonly used to enforce repetition of a simple skill until its execution is not only free from error but also almost automatically performed. Although overlearning results in better retention, the amount of overlearning required for best results may vary. Beyond a certain point, very little improvement in retention will result from continuous drill, therefore, valuable time that could be spent on other matters might be wasted (518).

Transfer

You are probably aware that knowing how to perform a certain skill seems to help in learning a new one. If, for example, you know how to play tennis you may find it relatively easy to learn to hit a badminton shuttlecock effectively. In the same way, skill in throwing a baseball may assist you in learning handball, just as the ability to dive would make the learning of tumbling stunts less difficult. The scientific term attached to this phenomenon is **transfer of training.**

On the other hand, it is possible that being proficient in one kind of activity may actually *hinder* your ability to pick up a new kind of skill (negative transfer). For example, the skillful tennis player who may wish to become proficient in badminton undoubtedly has all the necessary physical characteristics, such as strength, agility, endurance, and coordination. He probably also has developed a pattern of hitting with a rigid wrist. This habit will have to be *unlearned* before the badminton racket can be wielded with the proper wrist snap.

Thus it is that a number of fundamental movement patterns can be developed that are common to many types of skillful performance. If these are appropriately used, the learning of several separate skills can be enhanced. At the same time interfering elements can be anticipated and the appropriate work prescribed to overcome the problem.

MOTIVATION

Early in life, people form attitudes toward physical activity, games, and exercise that predetermine to a great extent whether they will ever become willing participants. Frequently, values change, and people who were once avid participants find other outlets for their

PEANUTS® By Charles M. Schulz

FIGURE 13.1 People differ in their activity preferences. © 1968 United Feature Syndicate.

attention. Sometimes value changes are forced upon people, as in the case of illness or trauma. The threat of heart disease may stimulate one person to take up regular exercise whereas a paralyzing accident may force another into abstinence.

Some motivating factors are quite obvious and forthright, whereas other factors may be operating at the subconscious level of the individual. A desire to lose weight may cause one person to take up jogging. Another person may join the same jogging group as a means of achieving recognition or simply because he somehow thinks he ought to (Figure 13.1). Whatever individual reasons may be given, it is a fact of practical importance for workers in this field to recognize that the socially based motives are much more often responsible for people's participation in physical activity than are any of the others. This would mean, for example, that a person would be much more likely to take up jogging if all his friends were doing it than for any health or fitness reasons (65).

In addition to controlling choices of "whether and what kind" of activity to take up, motivational factors can influence the quality of performance and the retention of the skill he has learned. It is apparent that the interest with which an individual approaches a task will affect his performance and learning. It has already been noted (page 405) that massed practice can be effective when motivation is high, but boredom sets in when interest wanes.

It has also been demonstrated that excessive levels of motivation can produce inferior performance (25, 170). Perhaps most of us can remember "trying too hard" at some time in our lives (see Figure 13.2).

Reward and Punishment

In our country there is no question about the value placed on rewards for accomplishment. Although there is some objection to the terms, we commonly speak of *extrinsic* and *intrinsic* motivation. In the case of the former term, we would be referring to the motivated state produced in an individual because of his desire to secure some reward other than his own self-satisfaction. An increase in salary, a medal, or a trophy; or a kiss from the campus queen or any other external

factor would be termed an extrinsic motivating factor.

Although there is little evidence (192) to substantiate the belief, it is commonly assumed that intrinsic motivation is superior to extrinsic. One of the reasons postulated for this is that intrinsic motivation is less likely to be transitory, so that interest in learning (or other activity) is likely to be more permanent.

The effectiveness of rewards is well known. Even a spoken word of praise or commendation can be a potent reward (8, 550). It is interesting to note, however, that there is some evidence to indicate that rewards given too freely can be less effective than those given only occasionally (175). It is not clear why this should be true of animals, but among human beings it may relate to the individual's perception of the sincerity of the person giving the reward.

At one time it was believed that the effects of reward and punishment were equal and opposite. Today it is recognized that, although punishment does alter behavior, its effects tend to be less permanent than reward. Under certain circumstances it may even lead to an increase in the undesirable behavior. In an experiment in our laboratory we observed marked differences among people in their responses to various motivational factors. Subjects were asked to hang from a horizontal bar for as long as possible under each of four conditions at different times.

In one instance subjects were vociferously encouraged by the cheers of their peers to do their best. In a second situation the promise of a modest monetary reward (five dollars) was made for the best performance (the money was placed in full view of each performer). In the third situation an electrical apparatus was attached to the leg of the subject, and he was informed that upon dropping he would receive a shock but that the longer he held on the less the intensity would be. It was explained that if he held on long enough, he could escape the shock altogether. No specific time was suggested. The final condition was one in which no motivating devices were employed other than a simple request to do his best.

Although the group was not large enough for statistical analyses to be applied, it was evident that particular individuals performed extremely well under certain conditions as compared with others. The individual winning the money more than doubled his best time on the other conditions. One subject did somewhat poorly on all trials except for the shock situation, in which he not only surpassed his own scores on the other conditions but those of his peers as well.

Knowledge of Results

Frequently tasks are assigned to learners who have very little immediate feedback concerning how well they are

FIGURE 13.2 Performance suffers when motivation is either too low (bottom) or too high (top). © 1968 King Features Syndicate.

doing. Supplying knowledge of the results of efforts has resulted in improved performance and faster learning (19, 56, 181, 452). The implications of this fact are that students should be encouraged to carefully monitor their own performances through kinesthetic and visual means, comparing their actions with the model provided. In addition, any additional feedback that can be supplied (movies, TV recordings, verbal comments) by the teacher should be provided. The more immediate such feedback, the better.

Observation by Spectators

We are all familiar with the notorious "home court advantage" enjoyed by some basketball teams. In such instances the spectators are usually very close to the sidelines and take great pride in the thunderous noise they generate in support of their team. Scientific investigations have shown that noise can sometimes be a detriment to performance by means of distracting the performer (360). On the other hand, it can also sometimes cause the performer to concentrate harder, thereby improving performance. It has also been suggested that, to one who is accustomed to noise, its *absence* can be a decided distraction.

It is quite possible that the cheering in such instances is only a small part of the crowd influence. A number of studies has shown that the presence of even a single observer can cause a decided improvement in certain kinds of performance (205, 372, 570). The same has been shown for activities requiring moderate skill, particularly when it is a monotonous or boring type of activity. In such cases the basis of improvement probably lies in the arousal effect produced by the unusual stimulus represented by the observer.

The extreme variability of individual responses to these types of situations makes it difficult to generalize. One study (130) of grade-school children indicated that when observed by various groups of people (mothers, strangers, teachers, peers, experimenter), the "low-anxious" boys showed better average performance than others on a marble dropping task. "High-anxious" boys were poorer in the presence of other people, but improved when watched by the instructor alone. In the presence of the experimenter, the low-anxious group exhibited inferior performance.

Competition

Similar findings have been noted with regard to motivational response to competition. There is also evidence that performance on simple tasks may be more favorably improved by competition than on complex tasks (486). Borridge (53) found that strength measures were substantially improved by competition with peers. In studying effect of various motivational techniques on physical fitness test performance, Strong (551) observed that team competition was more effective than individual competition or suggestions of the desirability of self-improvement.

A recently reported study by Wilmore (613) disclosed a significant improvement in work output on the bicycle ergometer as a result of individual competition. Riding time was also increased over the control situation.

Some of the questions concerning the differential effects of competition and/or cooperation (as in team activities) have not been clearly established. A great deal of research remains to be done in this area.

Suggestion and Hypnosis

The possibility of improving performance through hypnotic suggestion has long been a topic of fascination. As was implied in Chapter 12, some investigators have hypothesized that the inhibitory influences of the cerebral cortex may possibly be reduced through hypnosis, thereby permitting increased ability to exert force and maintain a stressful task. Others have supposed that unconscious inhibitory motives (fear of injury or failure) might be removable by this technique. Several studies have tended to confirm this hypothesis (284, 285, 478).

The reports of Warren Johnson referred to above indicate that hypnosis is apparently more effective in increasing strength and endurance of untrained individuals than of highly trained athletes. Occasional startling exceptions to this "rule" serve only to confuse the issue. Johnson and Kramer report one such exception (284). One of a group of experimental subjects exhibited unique reactions to hypnotic suggestion regarding the pressing of a 47-pound barbell (Figure 9.27). This subject was a professional football player, in a highly trained state with considerable weight-training experience. His nonhypnotic performance consisted of pressing the bar 130 times —an outstanding performance (the next best was 57 times, by another athlete). With the introduction of hypnosis, the subject performed (on separate tests) 180 (where the investigator stopped him), 230 and 233 repetitions. (The maximum number by any of the other athletes was 75.) In addition, this "breakthrough" was maintained following removal from the trance state, much to the amazed consternation of the subject himself. In a later retest he was stopped by the investigator at 350 repetitions! Johnson's discussion of this case makes provocative reading.

Other reports concerning the use of hypnosis by athletes as a means of improving performance have been made, but few have provided any insight into the basic issue (408a, 553). On the other hand, several investigators have reported some very important findings. Levitt and Brady (341) and Barber and Caverley (37) have reported that task-motivating instructions can be just as effective as hypnotic suggestion in improving performance. Barber has written:

A critical evaluation of experimental studies indicates that: (1) "hypnotic induction" per se, without suggestions for improved performance, does not significantly enhance either strength or endurance; and (2) in general, motivational suggestions augment performance on tests of strength and endurance irrespective of the presence or absence of "hypnosis" (36).

Orne (441) has reported that when sufficiently motivated, subjects in the waking state will surpass hypnotic performances. Pain tolerance, for example, was greater among "faking" subjects than among hypnotized subjects. Many of the traditional concepts surrounding hypnotism are challenged by Orne, Barber, and others who have published extensively during the past decade.

Of interest to medically oriented personnel is the matter of injury treatment by means of hypnotism. Ryde (489) has published a series of case studies in which hypnotic suggestion was successfully utilized in treatment of athletic injuries. The implications of this report should be given careful consideration. Is it ethical to relieve pain (thereby permitting return to performance) by hypnotic suggestion? These and similar questions about all aspects of hypnosis point out that this is not a phenomenon to be "dabbled in" by the untrained or irresponsible person.

FIGURE 13.3 The famous Ames rooms were constructed so that the sizes of familiar objects appeared to be distorted. Apparently some perceptual cues were accepted and others rejected to give such impressions.

FIGURE 13.4 Some common optical illusions. (A) Which line looks longer? They are actually the same length. (B) Most people would say that the horizontal lines curve. Do they? (C) Which line looks longer: the horizontal or the vertical? They are actually the same length. (D) Which of these two segments appears longer? They are actually identical. (E) The central circles in the two groups are actually the same size. Do they appear to be so?

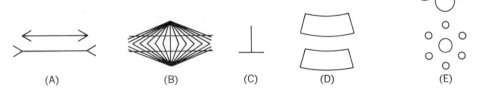

(A)   (B)   (C)   (D)   (E)

PERCEPTION

The organization and interpretation of information from the environment is called **perception.** It is a process including sensation and organization of the stimuli received, but it is more than the simple sum of these processes. *To see* and *to perceive* are not synonomous, because it is theoretically possible to see (or hear, or touch, and so forth) without actually perceiving. On the other hand, it would not be possible to perceive without some source of sensory input, either from *exteroceptors* (sense organs for external stimuli) or *interoceptors* (receptors from sites within the body).

You have probably seen demonstrations of how visual perception can be distorted. The famous Ames rooms that make a boy's dog appear to be larger than he is, or one person to be a giant and the other a midget, are examples of this type of thing (see Figure 13.3). Lines of the same length can be made to appear different, three-dimensional effects can be produced in drawings, and it is possible to produce illusions of movement where lines are

actually stationary ("op art") (Figure 13.4).

Perceptual distortions can be demonstrated that involve almost any of the sense modalities. The study of what cues we use in making interpretations and how such cues can be manipulated and reorganized is a fascinating pastime.

It should be apparent that how we perceive the world around us is extremely important to performance of motor skills. The ability to accurately perceive distances and the speed, size, and shape of objects and to make split-second decisions based upon integrated interpretations of changes in relationships of the stimuli received is certainly a controlling factor in whether one will be successful in such activities.

Perception not only is important to the skill level of the performer but also affects qualities such as stamina and persistence. Studies have shown that levels of pain experienced by individuals are affected by many factors other than the actual intensity of the pain-producing stimulus (see Chapter 18). Some of these are personality, attention, expectations, threat, and anxiety. The discomfort encountered by distance runners, wrestlers, weight lifters, and other competitors can be tolerated better by some people than others; such tolerance may well be the margin between outstanding and mediocre performance.

Another important variable in perception is the *"set"* or *expectation* of the individual. We tend to see what we expect to see. Some people have made the point that most reported sightings of unidentified flying objects (flying saucers) have been based upon a willingness or a desire to interpret natural phenomena or the sight of common objects (usually appearing in other than their normal context) as something supernatural.

More practical applications of this phenomenon occur in games like football where deception is important. When defensive players might logically expect a particular type of play, clever quarterbacks will call a play that gives the *appearance* of such a play but that in reality is another. The "draw" play that develops into a run from what appears to be a passing formation is only effective if the set of the defensive players is appropriate. If the set is strong enough, subjects may actually report "seeing" (or hearing or feeling) things that did not occur. "I could have sworn he had the ball!" might be the puzzled statement of a tackler under such circumstances.

PERSONALITY

As has just been pointed out, personality is one of the factors that affects perception. Eye witnesses to an accident

FIGURE 13.5   These sketches tend to evoke different responses from men and women. What do you see in each of them? Tendencies are for males to see a brush (or a centipede), a target, and a man's head. Women more often report a comb (or teeth), a plate, and a bowl, respectively. From *Sex and Personality* by L. Terman and C. Miles. Copyright 1936 McGraw-Hill Book Company. Used with permission of McGraw-Hill Book Company.

frequently have substantially different versions of the event. The personality of the witness may affect his version of what happened. There is some evidence that men and women perceive ambiguous drawings differently (see Figure 13.5). Many tests of personality (aggressiveness, sensitivity, masculinity, femininity,) are based upon reported impressions experienced when observing ambiguous drawings and ink blots.

In discussing personality, we are dealing with a concept that is familiar to everyone but that is very difficult to define. Textbooks frequently take several pages to describe the components of personality. For the time being, at least, we will define *personality* as the "unique organization of relatively enduring psychological characteristics possessed by an individual, as revealed by his interaction with his environment" (359, p. 410).

What we are concerned with at this point is how personality affects one's physical activity. We have a great tendency to put people into categories (scholar, mother-type, "born loser," rascal, villain, hero, "loner," "politician'') as though each person either has such qualities or does not—a sort of all-or-none proposition. Obviously, such characteristics are possessed to a greater or lesser degree by everyone; we simply tend to emphasize those that appear to be outstanding in comparison to other people of our acquaintance. Therefore, in discussing personality and its relationships to exercise, physical activity, and physical education, we are more concerned with the characteristics that people have in common than we are with their differences.

It should not be surprising to learn that the personality of the individual is related to the types of physical activity he selects. Although studies are by no means unanimous in finding such relationships, it has been reported (230, 563) that weight lifters have different personality profiles than those found in non-weight lifters. On the other hand, personality scores of weight lifters and football players have been shown to be similar (in at least one study) (526), both being more neurotic than the other athletes tested. Differences were also demonstrated between groups comprised of varsity participants in basketball, baseball, and swimming. Johnson, Hutton, and Johnson (286) tested twelve outstanding athletes from different sports by means of two projective tests. Results indicated that, compared with normal populations, these athletes were more aggressive, showed greater anxiety, self-assurance, a greater need to achieve, high levels of aspiration, and a lack of emotional control. Other studies have shown no difference between such groups. Al-

though they used different tests, neither Morgan (402) nor Kroll (324) found significant personality differences between wrestlers and normal populations.

Sometimes the results of such investigations are surprising. Husman (259a) used two separate projective personality tests in evaluating differences in cross-country runners, boxers, and wrestlers. Among other contrasts, he found the boxers *less* extrapunitive (expressing aggression outwardly) than cross-country runners and non-athletes. Whether this is an inherent factor associated with those individuals selecting boxing as a sport or something resulting from participation in the activity, is not known. This question is, quite obviously, one of the most important asked with respect to personality and sports participation.

Of all the studies reported on this topic (and there are relatively few), almost none are concerned with activity selection within physical education class environments. One such study was conducted by Flanagan (182). He was able to detect differences among groups participating in badminton, basketball, boxing, fencing, swimming, and volleyball on certain, selected personality scales. Volleyball players, for example, were found to be less emotionally stable than others, while fencers, although more feminine than basketball players, were higher in dominance than basketball players, boxers, and volleyball players. Before we can accept the position that personality definitely is a factor in activity selection, more evidence is needed.

Another interesting aspect of this problem is the question of whether there are significant personality differences between champions in a given sport and those who do not quite attain championship status. Several studies have demonstrated differences on personality measures between "successful" and "unsuccessful" performers.

Crakes (132) found that of a series of physiological and psychological tests administered to college milers, the psychological tests were at least as effective as the best physiological measures in differentiating between sub 4:17 runners and those running the mile over 4:17. (It should be noted that *none* of the tests utilized were particularly effective in discriminating between the two groups.) Schendel (495) discovered no personality profile differences (CPI) among groups of ninth-grade outstanding athletes, regular players, and substitutes. However, the outstanding athletes in the twelfth grade demonstrated significantly *less* desirable personal characteristics than athletes in the other groups. A parallel situation was found to be true among the college athletes in the study.

In 1966, Morgan (402) tested the English-speaking wrestlers participating in the Amateur Wrestling World Championships. Results of the Eysenck Personality Inventory showed that although neuroticism was not correlated with performance, a significant relationship ($r = .50$) was observed between extroversion and performance.

Although there is little experimental evidence available, clinical observations have led to the belief that some athletes, for various unconscious, deep-seated reasons, actually *avoid* winning. Some psychologists have hypothesized that apparently capable performers who are "losers" may wish to avoid a "competitive relationship" with the father or may even wish to punish others to whom his success could give pleasure or prestige (such as a coach or a parent). On the other hand, his failure may be due to a strong desire to be liked, even by his opponents. To people struggling with conflicting drives, winning may be more of a threat than losing; although he feels compelled to give a good performance, it must not be too good. If somehow he should win, he may find the results intolerable and may give up his participation.

Below are listed some characteristics suggested by Olgalvie and Tutko (433) as being found in outstanding performers:

1. Need for achievement
2. Endurance: ability to apply oneself over a period of time
3. Resistance to stress: ability to maintain poise
4. Dominance
5. Leadership qualities; but a non-joiner, socially
6. Coachability: an openness to learning
7. Intrapunitive: ability to bear pain
8. Self-assertive: bold
9. Intelligence: higher than the college average

Ryan (487) has observed that athletes who are apparently incapable of becoming outstanding performers may exhibit identifiable characteristics.

Some of these characteristics of the poor competitor are extracted below.

1. The poor competitor prefers an atmosphere of friendliness.

2. Many poor competitors tend to arrive at practice either very early or very late.

3. There is a strong evidence that the performances made in the private practices of these athletes are vastly superior to their public performances.

4. Despite great aptitude for his event, the poor competitor seems far more comfortable when working in the manner of the beginner.

5. Related to this workout pattern is one in which the athlete works hard but in such a manner as to preclude achievement.

6. In lieu of attention to principles and techniques the poor competitor makes vague references to some secret and almost magical aspect of form.

7. He is often at his very best in the off-season and his performance diminishes as the competitive season nears.

8. His orientation is toward a distant goal. Even when he is completing his athletic career, his athletic goals remain in the distant future.

9. Many of the poor competitors routinely berate themselves after each practice effort.

10. The poor competitor is constantly fearful of error.

11. Success leads to failure: of some sixty poor competitors, none was reported to follow a good competitive performance with another such performance.

12. The poor competitor is considerably constricted in the expression of his aggression.

13. Individual cases present striking examples of "bottled up" personalities.

14. He tends to speak very little, seldom initiating a conversation.

15. The ability to laugh separates the good and poor competitors. The latter is apparently unable to laugh in a spontaneous or uproarious manner.

16. He does not strike one as shy and bashful. He appears to be poised even in competition. In short, he can perhaps be said to be introverted without being particularly self-conscious.

17. Unlike most athletes, the poor competitors avoid the expression of personal achievement needs. They apparently cannot easily confront their own aggression. Instead, they cite "higher" or more noble motives for participation.

18. The defenses seem deep-rooted and strong. Thus far there is no certain documentation of a poor competitor becoming a good one.

Another aspect of personality is the matter of characteristic mannerism and posture of an individual. Attitudes (arrogance, confidence, shyness, humility) or emotional states (joy, anger, depression, fear) can be communicated by the way we hold our bodies or move our limbs. Although only a little scientific study has been conducted along this line, actors and dancers have made extensive use of the almost universally recognized relationships between personality and the consistent activity patterns of the body.

Somatotypes

Throughout history the idea has persisted that human beings can be classified into types on the basis of their appearance. Shakespeare's *Julius Caesar* expressed this feeling:

Let me have men about me that are fat;
Sleek-headed men, and such as sleep o' nights:
Yond Cassius has a lean and hungry look;
He thinks too much: such men are dangerous.

Then the image of the jovial, fat, easygoing type is contrasted with the thin, studious type of individual. Also universally recognized since earliest civilization is the "athletic" type. Several classification systems have been developed from time to time; one of the most recent and widely known is that of W. H. Sheldon (512).

Sheldon's system of *somatotyping* involves three basic body types: *endomorph, mesomorph,* and *ectomorph* (Figure 13.6). The endomorph is characterized by appearance of softness and roundness; a predominance of the viscera is apparent. The mesomorph is the hard, muscular, rectangular (or triangular) physique. The ectomorph presents a fragile, linear appearance, the thinness accentuated by a large bulbous forehead (indicative of nervous system dominance).

In this system every individual possesses some of each of the three characteristics. An individual's somatotype consists of three numbers representing his ratings on each of the basic components: endomorphy, mesomorphy, and ectomorphy. Ratings can range from one to seven on each component. Thus a 7-1-1 would be the designation assigned to an extreme endomorph. A 1-7-1 would be an extreme mesomorph and a 1-1-7 an extreme ectomorph. An individual rated as a 2-6-2 would be predominately mesomorphic, whereas a 5-4-1 would be a mesomorphic endomorph. In the original sample of college men, Sheldon discovered the most common somatotype to be 3-4-4. In more recent work with college women, it was discovered that women tend to be more endomorphic than men, the most common somatotype being 5-3-3.

The controversial aspect of Sheldon's system is his assertion that extensive correlation studies show that body type is related to temperament or personality. A summary of the claimed characteristics follows:

Endomorphy: *Viscerotonia*—love of pleasure, eating, and comfort; enjoyment of relaxation and social contact
Mesomorphy: *Somatotonia*—characterized by energetic, aggressive activity; courageous, love of risk and power
Ectomorphy: *Cerebrotonia*—characterized by introversion; likes solitude and privacy; inhibited

Despite reports of high correlations between physique and temperament ratings, most psychologists resist the assertion that one can be predicted with any accuracy from the other. A review of the arguments is presented by Anastasi (11).

Sheldon has extended his theory to psychiatric patients and juvenile delinquents with equally controversial, however interesting, results.

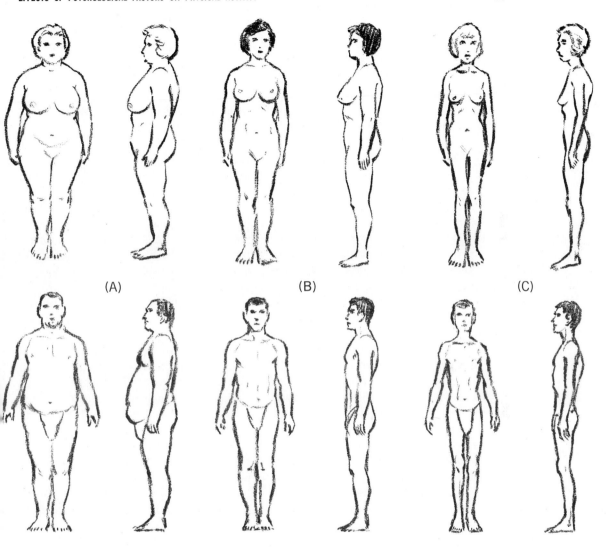

(A) (B) (C)

FIGURE 13.6 Illustration of three extreme body types: (A) endomorph, (B) mesomorph, and (C) ectomorph. Everyone has some of each characteristic, and extremes such as these constitute a very small percentage of the population.

PSYCHOSOCIAL BEHAVIOR

The interrelationships of people is one of the primary concerns of all educa- tors. The facility with which people can live and work together toward common goals is directly related to the achieve- ment of personal fulfilment and happiness. The role of physical activity (including games and sports, as well as physical education in the schools) in our culture is an important one. Discussion of these issues will be found in Chapter 17.

STRESS AND ANXIETY

Like many other terms in psychology and education, "stress" has many different meanings. Most of us tend to equate it with concepts of *tension, pressure,* or *tightness.* It is probably significant that all these words have been derived from the physical sciences and describe conditions that can be directly observed and measured. Obviously, when we speak of psychological stress, we are concerned with a feeling or an experience that is not directly measurable but that is, none-the-less, a situation producing discomfort from which we would like to escape.

Anxiety is not really a synonym for **stress**, although it is sometimes used as though it were. More generally, anxiety is regarded as a by-product of stress or, perhaps more precisely, as the "experience" of stress. In psychology, anxiety is often related to a single aspect of stress, namely **fear.** In such instances **anxiety** is used to describe the feelings of fear when the object of or reason for the fear is unknown.

Stress has a number of effects upon physical activity patterns, from both a personal and a cultural viewpoint; the reverse is also true. However, because the subject of *stress* and related concepts is too important to cover in a

brief paragraph, more complete discussion will be postponed until Chapter 18.

INTELLECTUAL DEVELOPMENT AND INTELLIGENCE

Anyone who has ever worked with retarded children is aware of the fact that they are also generally limited in their capacity to perform in various types of physical activity. A number of studies have been conducted in an attempt to establish the kinds of difficulty suffered and to determine the frequency and extent to which they occur. Although distribution of test results usually overlaps the normal range, scores for strength, endurance, skill, and agility are almost always reported to be substantially lower for retarded groups. Because of limitations in capacity and much slower learning responses, physical education programs and other organized physical activity must be substantially modified for successful implementation among retarded individuals.

The effects of intelligence levels of normal populations has been found to be of little importance. With very few exceptions, research has indicated that there is no substantial correlation between intelligence and motor skill or fitness scores. One interesting exception to this trend is that reported by Ishmail, Kephart, and Cowell (266), in which scores of fifth- and sixth-grade children on certain tasks of coordination and balance were found to correlate with intelligence ($r = .80$), whereas the standard measures of strength, speed, and accuracy did not. It is the contention of these investigators that previous studies had concentrated on static or unchanging measures (strength, speed, endurance), whereas "dynamic" measures were included in their study. The significance of this difference apparently rests in the constant adjustments demanded of the performer in the "dynamic" tasks. Although this may prove to be an important issue, more research is needed to clarify the point.

It is important to note that although few studies have indicated consistent relationships between physical and intellectual aptitude, several investigations have indicated that *academic success* (as indicated by drop-out rates, achievement of expected potential) as distinct from intellectual ability, may be related to measures of physical fitness (104, 109, 232, 291). One of the most often quoted is Appleton's (16) study of West Point cadets over a fifteen-year period, in which it was found that positive relationships existed between physical ability of cadets at the time of entry and such factors as failure to graduate, discharges for any reason, leadership ability, aptitude for military service, emotional maladjustment, and academic failures. Critics point out that the nature of military training, and the military stereotype places a premium on physical performance attributes. This may explain, at least in part, some of the relationships observed. On the other hand, there have been few other studies of this magnitude conducted under more typical circumstances. It certainly is not unreasonable to expect that poor fitness levels might be related to an inability to withstand the rigors of demanding academic life.

Creativity is another area of the psychological makeup of people that is related to their activity patterns. Although little is known about how creativity is developed (or even what it really is), it is obviously related to curiosity and certain factors of personality. The interest in discovery of one's environment certainly affects his activity patterns. The urge to try new things and to actually experience some of the exciting possibilities offered by various sports, games, and other physically demanding tasks is obviously important in the selection of one's life patterns. People who lack this urge may not only prefer sedentary lives themselves but may also frown upon (and refuse to support) the desire of others to engage in such activities.

SUMMARY

This chapter is concerned with examining several psychological factors in terms of their influence on the physical activity patterns of people.

Whether motor learning differs from other kinds of learning has not been satisfactorily determined. Theories to explain learning have been formulated by a great many people, but no theory has been found to account for all the varied learning phenomena.

The problems of the individual's capacity to learn and retain motor skills are of great interest. The effects of various practice and teaching methods must be understood by all potential teachers. The effects that the learning of one skill can have upon the learning of another (transfer) are intimately related to problems of course organization and curriculum development.

One of the most important requisites to learning, motivation, is the focus of much current research. The practical problem of obtaining all-out cooperation and effort is a common one. Discovering how to stimulate individuals to produce their best efforts is a problem absorbing the attention of many psychologists. The effects of competition on the quality of performance have been as little studied as have the effects of cooperation or team effort. Results are still inconclusive, and a great deal remains to be learned about individual differences in these circumstances.

Hypnosis is a topic frequently discussed in connection with motivation. Here again, scientific study has failed to substantiate many commonly accepted suppositions concerning the effectiveness of this practice.

The problem of perception is another that is vital to any educator. Perceptual distortions can involve any of the senses, and efficient learning is directly dependent upon accuracy and consistency of perception. Factors affecting perception are frequently encountered in stressful situations such as athletic competition, illness, emergencies, and in drug and alcohol addiction.

Personality and its effect upon choice of life style or patterns are also of great current interest. Whether people of certain personal characteristics gravitate toward certain activities or whether participation in a given activity produces certain personality changes, is still an undecided issue. Of course, the answer to this question could be a very important one.

Stress and anxiety are so commonly encountered as problems in everyday life that their consideration in the light of physical activity is essential.

Intellectual ability, intelligence, and creativity all effect one's patterns of physical activity and one's attitudes toward it.

PRINCIPLES

1. It is not certain whether motor learning is different from other kinds of learning.

2. Learning is never directly observed but can only be inferred from observations of overt behavior.

3. At present there are no theories that have been able to explain adequately all phenomena observed in learning situations.

4. Reinforcement of desired responses is generally regarded as essential to the learning of motor tasks. Such reinforcement can arise from many sources and take many forms.

5. Motor educability and motor capacity are affected by maturation and early experience in exploration of one's environment.

6. It is apparent that there are two distinct types of memory for skills as well as for verbal material: short-term and long-term.

7. The manner in which material to be learned is presented has a decided effect on the efficiency of learning.

8. Although physical practice of a skill is superior to mental practice, it has been demonstrated that mental practice is superior to no practice at all.

9. Just as the possession of skill in one activity may facilitate the learning of a second skill containing some of the same elements, some proficiencies may interfere with the acquisition of new skill patterns.

10. It is a fact of practical importance that socially based motives (as contrasted with rational thought or logic) are most often found to be responsible for people's participation in physical activity.

11. The degree of interest with which an individual approaches a task has a direct effect on the rate and permanence of learning.

12. There is an optimal level of motivation for any given task. Motivational levels that are either too high or too low result in inferior performance.

13. The effects of reward appear to be more permanent in changing behavior than those of punishment.

14. Feeding information back to the performer concerning the quality of performance is an important factor in the acquisition of skill. Immediacy of feedback and the number of sources of feedback both appear to be important variables.

15. Observation by spectators, as well as cheering or other loud sounds, may contribute to improvement of certain kinds of performance. Personality of individuals is a significant factor in determining the nature of reactions to such situations.

16. Competition may have a significant effect on performance, depending upon the personality of the performer and the nature of the task. Team competition may be more effective than individual competition, and simple tasks may be more favorably affected than complex tasks.

17. Hypnosis is apparently more effective in increasing strength and endurance of untrained individuals than of highly trained athletes.

18. Task-motivating instructions are often found to be at least as effective as hypnosis in improving performance.

19. Levels of pain experienced by individuals are affected by many factors other than the actual intensity of the pain-producing stimulus.

20. An important variable in perception is "set" or expectation. We tend to see (or hear or feel) what we expect to see (or feel or hear).

21. Personality has an effect on the perception of objects and events.

22. The types of activities selected by individuals for participation may be related to personality factors.

23. The chief factors discriminating between a good performer and a great performer are almost certainly personality variables.

24. There is no consistent relationship between static measures of physical fitness or motor ability (for example, strength, speed, accuracy) and intelligence. There is some evidence that "dynamic" measures such as balance and coordination may correlate with intellectual ability.

25. Academic achievement (as distinct from intellectual ability) has been found to have a moderate positive relationship to physical fitness and motor ability scores, at least under certain circumstances.

EXPERIMENTS AND EXPERIENCES

1. Test the efficiency of whole versus part learning, for three groups of five or six each. Using an unfamiliar motor skill (such as juggling, stick juggling, or fencing lunge) test each subject before and after practice. One group serves as control with no practice between tests. (They should not be permitted to observe the others practicing.) One group practices the entire skill; the other practices the skill in as many parts as are reasonable. (A fourth group could be utilized, if desired, in which a combination of whole-part methods would be employed.) Average group improvements are compared and conclusions drawn.

2. Basically the same as the preceding experiment, this one utilizes a group that *watches* others perform the skill and is encouraged to practice the skill mentally before being retested.

3. This experiment is designed to determine the extent to which individuals can improve in motor skill over a period during which no practice is permitted. Generally the term *reminiscence* applies only to short periods ranging from a few seconds up to several minutes. Some studies have been concerned with this phenomenon for periods extending over several weeks. The skill used must be one in which there are no in-herent rest periods; otherwise reminiscence will probably not occur. It is also important to work with a skill which is unfamiliar to all the participants. Suggested skills: one-finger typing (for nontypists) or typing with a stick attached to a head band; tossing and catching a ball that is attached to a small cup by a string; tossing and catching a ring that is attached to a stick by a string; holding a stick across two other sticks held one in each hand, tossing the third stick into the air so that it rotates end for end one time, catching it across the two sticks.

Subjects (at least six) should perform successively or simultaneously but should not be permitted to observe one another. Subjects should perform the skill for a period of at least twenty minutes with rest periods of thirty seconds and three minutes interspersed alternately every five minutes. The number of successful attempts should be recorded for every thirty seconds of participation. These scores should be averaged and plotted in graph form so that the effect of the rest periods can be observed. Compare the difference in scores from the period immediately preceding each rest period to the segment immediately following that rest period with differences observed over other rest periods. Variations: several possible combinations of rest periods could be tried; the effects of varying lengths of work preceding rests could also be investigated.

4. Use several kinds of "negative" motivation (for example, extra laps, library papers, automatic electric shock) for failure to complete a test, and sever-

al kinds of "positive" motivation (tangible reward, peer exhortation) to reward completion or good performance.

Possible tests could include hanging time, holding weights at arm's length, and so on. Use as many subjects as possible in each group to equalize difference between subjects. Remember to standardize all conditions except the variable you introduce; subjects should never be able to see each other perform.

Compare group average performances. Variation: Also test the effects of the same motivational techniques in a *skill* performance. Are the comparative motivational effects the same as those found for the "effort" tasks?

SUGGESTED READINGS

Beisser, Arnold R., *The Madness in Sports*, New York: Appleton-Century-Crofts, 1967.

Bilodeau, E. A. and I. M. Bilodeau, "Motor-Skills Learning: Feed-back," *Annual Review of Psychology*, 12:243-259, 1961.

Espenschade, Anna S. and Helen M. Eckert, *Motor Development*, Columbus, Ohio: Charles E. Merrill Books, Inc., 1967.

Fitts, P. M. and M. I. Posner, *Human Performance*, Belmont, Cal.: Brooks-Cole Publishing Co., 1967.

Frankl, Viktor, *Man's Search For Meaning*, Boston: The Beacon Press, 1959.

Henry, F. M., "Increase in Speed of Movement by Motivation and by Transfer of Motivated Improvement," *Research Quarterly*, 22:219, 1951.

Start, K. B., "Kinaesthesis and Mental Practice," *Research Quarterly*, 35:316, 1964.

Efferent
Psychological Concepts

Chapter 14

EFFECTS OF PHYSICAL ACTIVITY ON PSYCHOLOGICAL FACTORS

We have examined a number of psychological factors and have seen how they influence our interest in and capacity for physical activity and exercise. Now we will turn our attention to the matter of how physical activity contributes to the development and modification of these same psychologically oriented factors.

THE NERVOUS SYSTEM

For many years it has been assumed that, except for disruptive effects of trauma and disease, the nervous system (and the brain in particular) developed in a hereditarily determined manner and that major modifications in its activity or the quality of its function through training programs was impossible. Recently, however, evidence from a number of different sources has begun to accumulate, indicating that perhaps the nervous system is not so impervious to change as was once thought.

Some studies have indicated increase in the size and other characteristics of animal brains because of such simple sensory stimulation as daily handling (340). Rats walking a tight wire to obtain food were found to have greater RNA (ribonucleic acid) content in brain tissues than controls. Similar results have been noted as a result of enriched environments (48). Studies of cortical regeneration (212, 615) and memory-improving drugs (356) have been among those of recent importance.

The whole matter of the dominance of one cerebral hemisphere over the other, and whether functions normally performed by one hemisphere can be transferred to the other, has produced much fascinating research (206, 225, 411) and a storm of controversy in its wake. Certainly brain damage and rehabilitation methods have undergone renewed study, and a flurry of activity in the area of mental retardation has occurred.

One of the problems associated with work in this area is that of the emotional reactions of people who have an interest in the treatment of retarded or brain-damaged people. In addition, wildly speculative articles in the popular press or reports of dramatic neurosurgical breakthroughs that appear to be unsubstantiated (20) cause reputable research specialists to shun involvement with controversial issues. Fortunately, there are those in research who are willing to ignore the emotional claims and counterclaims and to quietly continue their painstaking search for the truth.

SKILL AND MOTOR LEARNING

Learning Skills

What effect do one's activity patterns have on his ability to learn motor skills? As a result of the types of research findings just discussed (as well as for other reasons), schools of thought have sprung up around a concept of *developmental activity*. In this view, certain basic neuromuscular skills must be learned as the infant progresses through early childhood. The order in which these skills are learned is crucial, and if one level should be skipped, efficiency of function at the higher levels will presumably result. As a vastly oversimplified example of this hypothesis, it has been observed that if a child fails to creep and then crawl before learning to walk, he may fail to develop adequate neurological laterality. The result might be an inability to make adequate left-right discriminations so that activities such as reading would be difficult or impossible to learn.

Developmental Theories

Among the chief proponents of such developmental theories are Robert and Glenn Doman and Carl Delacato (Institutes for Human Potential) and Newell Kephart (Purdue University). Their programs are described in Chapter 19.

Because physical educators and health educators are in such advantageous positions to incorporate aspects of these systems into the school situation if they have merit, it is important that the effectiveness of these systems be evaluated. To date, little experimental evidence is available on either. In several cases where investigations have been undertaken, research designs have been such that conclusions were difficult to draw (211). In addition, the obvious bias of the investigators, in some cases, raise questions about the validity of the results (150). Hockey (250) studied the effects of a specially designed exercise program on the reading ability of junior high school children. No difference was found between experimental and control groups. On the other hand, Wilson (614) reported improvement in reading ability of poor male readers subjected to Kephart-recommended exercises. Statistical re-examination of his data confirmed that observed differences were significant. Other investigators have failed to find a relationship between reading ability and laterality (473, 474). Some studies have reported positive relationships (50, 52, 304).

As pointed out in Chapter 19, it is apparent that screening tests designed to detect youngsters who have laterality and dominance problems are important. Because there are many reasons for poor reading, it does not seem reasonable to subject all poor readers to special exercise programs with an expectation of an overall improvement. Indeed, if such improvement is seen, in the absence of screening procedures, attributing it to the effects of exercise is obviously questionable.

Skill-learning Capacity

It has been pointed out that both the ease with which one can learn a skill and his capacity for performance limit his performance. On the other hand, the extent to which he has previously engaged in certain activities can affect his capacity.

Success in many activities may depend upon more than accuracy and coordination of movements. As an example, several sports employ what might be called the "power stroke."

This type of movement is exemplified by the throw in baseball, the swing of the bat, the forehand and backhand tennis strokes, the volleyball serve and spike, the downswing in golf, and so on. All such movements have in common a combination of considerable force exerted over a very short time span.

As you have learned earlier, power is derived from the strength of the muscles involved in any given activity, and such strength can be increased through appropriate overload techniques. The time factor can also be reduced through practice so that power can be improved through two approaches.

SPECIFIC MOVEMENTS   In addition to the *general* improvement of power, however, there is great need to pay particular attention to the specificity of the precise movement required for the task at hand. Development of power for the overhand throw, for example, is not guaranteed to improve substantially your skill in an underhand movement.

On the other hand, proper practice of an underhand power movement may well improve all the skills that employ such a move.

SKILL AND POWER It should be recognized that the development of power in a particular group of muscles is no absolute guarantee of drastically improved **skill** in an activity. If, however, one cannot participate effectively because of a lack of strength or power needed in the efficient performance of the required movements, then it should be obvious that working to increase basic strength and speed of movement is the most logical road to improvement.

In practicing movements for application to a specific skill, a great deal of time and effort can be saved if the actual movements of the skill involved are the ones rehearsed. The addition of more power to these movements is supplied by **overloading** them. This may be done in a number of ways (weighted ball, bat, or racket; weighted vests, wall pulleys, and so on), but regardless of the technique used, it is wise to avoid overloads which are so great that they change the actual pattern of the movement. When this happens, one may find himself practicing an entirely different movement and employing an entirely different set of muscles from the one in which he is interested (507, p. 34). Again, the principle of **specificity** must be carefully coordinated with the **overload principle.**

USE OF IMPLEMENTS Most of our national games involve the use of some object, such as a ball, a puck, or a shut-

tlecock. As we have already noted, success in games of this type often depends upon whether adequate power is available for propelling these objects. Equally important, of course, are other factors, such as **hand-eye coordination** and body orientation with respect to the object. Just as power needed for the specific movements involved can be improved by appropriate practice so can these factors. Learning not to get too close to the ball in tennis is very similar to the type of **orientation** that is also important to such a game as handball or badminton. This skill or ability can be practiced consciously in many different situations, and is one that beginners in these types of sports should understand early.

LEARNING AND FATIGUE

Another factor that frequently affects the ease and efficiency with which a new skill is learned is muscular **fatigue.** It will be recalled from a previous discussion that the amount of force any muscle or group of muscles exerts at a given time is regulated by the number of motor units active at any one time. The classic work of Seyffarth (507) has shown that in precise movements the *same* motor units are always active; even more important is the fact that these motor units always fire in the same pattern for any given movement. Now if an individual practices to the point where his muscles become impaired, the motor units that have been called upon to perform repeatedly will be unable to continue. What apparently occurs in such situations is that the motor pattern is changed slightly (perhaps imperceptibly) so that different motor units have been brought into play. In actuality, an entirely new "skill" has been employed; hence instead of polishing the old one, a new one must be mastered. Such practice is, of course, extremely inefficient. It is for this reason, as well as for some others, short practice periods with frequent rest periods are generally superior to longer periods of practice for the development of neuromuscular skills.

MENTAL PRACTICE

Although mental practice has been shown to improve performance, Corbin (125) has demonstrated that some previous experience with the skill in question is required. Previous information derived from the proprioceptors can then be "read out" of the kinesthetic memory, and the skill can be mentally simulated and rehearsed. An interesting sidelight observed in studying this phenomenon is that sometimes subjects seem to lose control of their practice. Reports of the ball disappearing or sticking to the floor, much to the frustration of the participant, have been made. One experimental subject even refused to participate further in mental rehearsal of foul shooting because the imaginary ball kept disappearing and then striking him in the back of the head! The significance of such near-hallucinatory behavior has not been explained.

Ballistic Movement

Regardless of the method used in the presentation of a skill, there are certain factors that will affect the success of the teaching. One such factor is ballistic movement. If you have ever played golf or baseball, you will probably recognize the truth of the following statement: *Once your swing has started* there is very little you can do to improve it if it feels "bad," but it is an easy matter to spoil a good one. The reason for this is that we are discussing movements generally classified as **ballistic movements.** A ballistic movement is initiated by the powerful contractions of a muscle group and then allowed to proceed to its conclusion driven only by its inertia or accumulated momentum. If the movement is properly "grooved" when the first powerful thrust occurs, it will successfully carry out its job. If it is improperly started, however, there is no time available for feedback information from the eyes or **proprioceptors** to permit any corrections: the ball is sliced.

If movements which are normally ballistic are performed in such a manner that the propelling muscles attempt to "steer" the limbs involved, it will be quickly discovered that consistent performance cannot be developed. It is almost impossible to exert and maintain exactly the same degree of tension in several groups of muscles time after time as would be required in most sports activities. It is much more efficient to *start* the movement with maximal velocity and then relax the driving muscles, allowing momentum to complete the action (257). This *absence* of tension is much easier to duplicate from one trial to the next. This is a skill that can be learned by almost anyone, but it is commonly overlooked. As a neuromuscular skill, it must be practiced if it is to be performed successfully. It should be noted that not all authorities agree about the extent to which ballistic movements occur in motor activities (44).

TRANSFER

It has been pointed out that experience in a given skill may positively (or negatively) affect performance in another activity. It has also been observed (351) that training of one limb may affect the limb on the opposite side, although some studies have contradicted these findings.

More important than "cross education" is the matter of whether the ability to perform a skill is specific to that particular activity or whether there is a generalized motor ability that can be developed that will contribute to the more efficient learning of many or all skills. Most evidence indicates the more similar two tasks are to one another the more likely it is that positive transfer will occur (10, 621). There is little evidence that a general motor ability exists, although it has been demonstrated that general principles of performance can transfer (152). Whether simple tasks should be learned before undertaking more com-

plex ones is not clear (201, 333, 345, 519). More work is needed utilizing physical education activities. The implications for leadup activities and teaching drills may be of great importance.

REMINISCENCE

We have been looking at the effects of activity on learning of skills. A very interesting topic is the effect of *nonactivity* on learning. Improvement in a skill over a period of nonpractice is called *reminiscence*. You may have experienced an improvement in performance after a layoff of a few days or even a few weeks. Coaches frequently give players an unscheduled rest in an attempt to overcome "staleness." Many of the data on reminiscence have come from tasks requiring only fine motor control, so it is not possible to draw definite conclusions at this time. However, it has been shown (597) that more reminiscence occurs under conditions of massed practice than with distributed practice. It is also believed that reminiscence is related to the motivational level (170), at least in some tasks; the higher the motivation during the task, the less the reminiscence. The optimal period of time for reminiscence to occur is not clear, and many of the results involving studies of gross motor skills are confusing. There is some evidence that most sports activities have "built-in" rest periods of sufficient frequency so that reminiscence does not occur to any major extent.

MOTIVATION

There are some ways in which the physical activity of the individual may affect his motivational levels. Psychiatric patients suffering from one of the many forms of extreme depression have been observed to have more energy and feel less tired after being urged to exercise (322). It is interesting to note that such patients who express interest in active recreational pursuits on questionnaires (as opposed to passive pastimes) show better recovery rates and are less likely to require rehospitalization, despite the fact that their actual behavior may include only *passive* pursuits (216).

Common practice reflects the belief that vigorous activity can reduce tensions built up during periods of relative inactivity. Psychiatric theory is strongly based upon the notion that aggressive feelings toward people can be legitimately pursued by transfering them to others in sports such as boxing or football, or even to objects, as in bowling and tennis. (See Chapter 18 for a discussion of mental illness.)

MEMORY

As has been pointed out previously, the success we experience in attempting new activities depends to a great extent on memory. Although no claims are made that memory is improved by general exercise, it is becoming evident that complete lack of activity may be inhibitory to memory as well to other functions (243). On the other hand, increased physical activity may be helpful in extreme cases (that is, retardation, brain damage) with possible increases in RNA, as already noted. Effects of exercise and physical activity have been seldom concerned with memory except as it relates to fatigue. Work with retarded children may prove interesting in this regard.

PERCEPTION

Perception is affected by physical activity in a number of ways. Obviously, the sensory deprivation studies referred to earlier would constitute *absence* of activity and thereby reduce stimuli from the receptors within the body. Absence of all stimuli apparently can lead to hallucinatory behavior and, perhaps, even to insanity. On the more practical side, the experience we gain from participation in activities provides us with information to utilize in future situations. The experienced baseball player has learned to detect cues to tell him when a pitch is going to curve away from him and when it is not. Inexperienced players are universally chagrined to find themselves ducking away from pitches that break neatly over the plate for a strike.

Sprinters learn that if they concentrate their attention on the act of breaking away from the line rather than on the sound of the gun, they will get away more quickly. All athletes learn to develop a "set" in order to respond to the appropriate cues but to ignore those that are not involved. In general, the fewer the cues necessary, the greater the accuracy and rapidity of the response. The ability to detect and respond to cues is readily learned with practice (359).

Herschel Leibowitz (337) has reported that the stress associated with certain kinds of activity can affect both peripheral and central vision. Specifically, it has been observed that under the stress of flying emergencies, warning signals located well within the normal range of the pilot's central vision are not seen. It has been found that practice can significantly reverse this stress effect; that is, with practice, in simulated circumstances the visually narrowing effects can be substantially avoided in the actual situation.

Implications of this finding are obvious. In sports activities where peripheral vision is important, conscious practice of maintainance of a broad visual field can apparently prevent the harmful narrowing of the perceived area under stressful conditions.

One of the most interesting ways in which physical activity affects perception is in terms of autonomic reactions. Faulkner (173) observed that businessmen who were asked to perform a stepping exercise on benches of different heights had *anticipatory* heart rates (immediately *before* exercising) that were proportional to the height of the bench on which they were to perform. In a carefully conducted study, Hockey (250) observed that anticipatory heartrates before a standardized exercise test correlated just as highly with maximal oxygen intake as did the Harvard Step Test score itself. As fitness levels increase with training, anticipatory heartrates reflect the changes, to a certain extent at least.

Communication through Movement

Up to this point the importance of understanding movement in order to improve its efficiency has been emphasized in the discussion. There is, however, another aspect of the movement of human beings that is not frequently discussed, probably because its importance is not realized: the expression or communication of thoughts and ideas, and even of moods, by means of movement alone. An experienced actor playing the part of a disconsolate, discouraged "failure" would not be likely to portray such a person holding his head high and walking in a sprightly manner. Appropriate to this role is a slow, shuffling gait, slouched shoulders, and a downcast gaze.

It is relevant to note that employment agencies instruct their clients how to stand, sit, and carry themselves, for all these factors contribute to the impression an applicant makes.

For years the arts of pantomime and modern dance have employed movement to convey moods and feelings. What may often be overlooked is that unless we ourselves have experienced the sensations associated with similar movements, we are incapable of deriving the intended message from any of these activities. The association of how certain movements *look* and how they *feel* to us when we perform them, as well as the memory of how we may have felt when we were inclined to act in that particular manner, all combine to give meaning to the movements of the performers.

In a similar way our ideas and thoughts are based upon the information our muscles have provided. If we had never experienced space and distance through firsthand movement, such terms as "a foot," "a mile," "twelve inches" would all be meaningless. And is it possible that someone could ever understand a phrase such as "international tension" if he had never pulled hard on something and actually felt tension within his own body? There is a great deal yet to be learned about the contributions the muscle senses make to our personalities and our very attitudes toward life. It may even be that emotional states, such as elation and depression, may be at least partly determined by the so-called muscle senses or proprioceptors (603, p. 120).

Dr. Arthur Steinhaus (545) has expressed many of these ideas in an article entitled "Your Muscles See More Than Your Eyes." Excerpts follow.

Your Muscles See More Than Your Eyes

ARTHUR H. STEINHAUS

The sixty to seventy pounds of muscle that are attached to the skeleton of the average-sized man not only move him but also serve as his most important sense organ. Should this fact and all of its implications become more fully understood and we shape our programs accordingly, physical educators will find their rightful place as one of the most distinguished contributors to the education of man.

For too long educators have considered the eye as the most important sense organ for learning. It is true that man's visual analysers have great powers of discrimination so that he can, for example, detect the difference between the capital C and capital G of the printed page and associate appropriately different meanings with this difference. In this sense man is eye-minded, even as the dog who can discriminate between the sounds of your footsteps and those of a stranger, is ear-minded. But in both man and dog a larger portion of the central nervous system is devoted to receiving and integrating sensory input originating in muscles and joint structures than is devoted to the eye and ear combined. . . .

We can live without eyes, we can live without ears, and probably would sometimes be happier without the sense of smell. But without the messages that come to us from our muscles and joint structures we could not talk, walk, breath, find our mouth to feed it, or follow the printed line while reading—and probably we could not think.

Long before we learn to associate meaning with what comes to us through the eyes and the ears, we learn something about near and far, heavy and light, and how to get things into the mouth because of the sense organs in our muscles and joint structures.

Only relatively recently have the sense organs in muscles and related joint structures received the broad recognition they deserve. Most prominent among these sense organs is the muscle spindle, which next to the eye has been called the most complex sense organ in man. This encapsuled organ lies parallel to the muscle fibers and emits nerve impulses whenever it is stretched. Through its innervation by the gamma fiber system, the sensitivity of this organ to stretch or applied tension can be increased or decreased to ensure muscle tonus at any muscle length and perhaps even to evoke consciously directed, voluntary movement by appropriate modification of the stretch reflex. . . .

A second and far less complex muscle receptor is the Golgi tendon organ which also produces nerve impulses when subjected to tension or stretch. . . .

A kind of Pacinian corpuscle is found between muscles and in joint structures where it is sensitive to pressures and to rapid changes in pressure such as are produced by a vibrating tuning fork. These corpuscles also are unequally distributed in and around various muscles. . . .

The joint surfaces are richly supplied with freely branching, naked nerve endings, known as Ruffini endings, that are sensitive to pressure. These record movement and the extent of movement of bone on bone within the joint. Little is known about their number.

From counts in the rectus femoris taken from nine cats this muscle alone is supplied with 102 spindle endings, as well as 78 Golgi tendon organs and 12 Pacian corpuscles. Such endings together with those found on joint surfaces give rise to sensations that have been variously designated muscle sense, tendon and joint sensibility, kinesthesia, and proprioception. Together they supply "feed-back" from the standing and moving skeletomuscular system to report where the body is and what it is doing, i.e., "self-knowledge" or proprioception, its Latin equivalent. Although much of their activity is responsible for regulating movement with little participation of the cortex, a great deal does activate the cortex to register in consciousness in various ways. Thus the experience of weight, tension, pressure, passive and active movement, fast and slow movement, the location of body parts, and much of the shape or form of three dimensional objects (stereognosis) comes to consciousness with mere impulses originating in them. Such sense endings in and around the muscles that move the eyes, that change our facial expressions, that operate the tongue,

the lips, the vocal cords, and the movements of air that vibrate the cords are in a very special and intimate way related to man's power of formulating words, which are the tools of communication, the substance of thought, memory, and reasoning, that is, those neuromuscular skills that distinguish man from man and human beings from their nearest relatives in the animal kingdom. . . .

Inside the nervous system there are only impulses, but somehow some of them give rise to very specific feelings or awarenesses in consciousness that are called "sensation." Thus the sensations of light or color, of noise or music, of sweet or sour, of discomfort or nausea are very personal experiences resulting from the stimulation of sense organs.

In a similar but also very special way the sense organs of muscle and joint structures convert stimuli of pressure, tension, vibration, and moving parts into nerve impulses that give rise to corresponding sensations. But there is an important difference. Whereas ether waves that strike the retina are produced by the sun or a candle, the air waves that activate the ear by a tolling bell or a lecturer's vocal cords, and the chemical energy that excites taste buds by a crystal of sugar or salt, the tensions and movements that activate the organs of "muscle sense" are produced by ourselves. Thus for the proprioceptors and for them alone we create the energy source that serves as the stimulus. The only exception is the ear for which we may also with our own vocal cords produce stimuli. *So the proprioceptors not only give us information about ourselves; we also stimulate them ourselves.*

The information that comes into the cord and brain from these endings is a kind of "feed-back" or servomechanism of the engineer's world, that serves as cues by which we monitor movements both consciously and without awareness. . . .

Our now rather extensive experience with neuromuscular relaxation has given me some entirely new insights concerning proprioception and the importance of "muscle-sight" in human behavior. It was most astonishing to find that when the voluntary musculature, especially that of the eyes, face, and voice organs, is completely relaxed, the mind goes blank even though we may not be asleep. . . .

Thirty-five years ago Edmund Jacobson published findings showing that just thinking of a word produced tensions in the tongue of the thinker which could be detected by a highly sensitive galvanometer, provided the thinker was otherwise sufficiently relaxed to rule out electrical disturbances from extraneous tensions. When you say "up" or just think "up" not only your tongue but also your lips and jaw muscles participate in the "up" feeling. You can prove this to yourself by trying to say "up" while moving your lips and jaws downward. Or try to say "point" while moving your lips backward rather than pointing them.

Such tensions in the tongue, lips, other voice organs, and in fact all muscles that are associated with words and the meaning of words create nerve impulses in their contained proprioceptors that feed into the brain center for speech. Thus tensions in the muscles used for speech (in a mute these muscles are largely those of the finger and hand) are the conditional stimuli which in the Pavlovian sense reawaken in consciousness the experiences that we have in our lifetime associated with these words. This only happens in man, who has evolved the neuromuscular mechanism of speech. In fact, it is man's most complicated and most minutely monitored muscular skill.

The sound of a bell can become the conditioned stimulus in man and dog for the flow of saliva, for a change in blood pressure, or for a modification of the vasomotor system. This sound is a stimulus of the first system of signals of reality in the Pavlovian sense. But only in man will a picture of the bell or the statement "I will ring the bell" subsequently and without further practice of any kind, produce the same flow of saliva and the same changes in the circulation initially conditioned to the sound of the bell. This kind of response is found only in man. It is because man has the power of speech. The word "bell" has in his lifetime been associated not only with the sound of the bell itself (first signal system) but also with the picture of a bell, with the sound of the word "bell," in fact, with his every sensory experience with bells. In each such instance the tensions in the voice muscles when the word "bell" was spoken aloud or in thought became the conditional stimulus or signal for these sensory experiences. Because the stimulus of tension in the voice muscles has thus come to be the signal that recalls or reinvokes the neural and other responses originally activated by the sound or sight stimulus, this tension stimulus is really a stimulus of a stimulus or a signal of a signal. This so-called signal of the second order is one step further removed from reality. It is a tension created primarily though not exclusively by muscles in man's voice organs that substitutes for the stimulus of sound or sight, originally created by the bell itself. It serves, in fact, as a conditional stimulus for all experiences that the person has had with bells and is therefore the signal that activates the neural paths that form his concept or idea of bell. Each such generalization of experiences (that is, concept) to which we have given a word name in turn may recall another one from the storehouse of memory and this succession of words comprises the "inner speech" which Plato identified as thinking. When by chance a succession of such concepts forms a new and especially useful combination it is called creative thinking.

From what I have presented it should be clear that the eyes contribute to man's experience only what they can see, the ears that which they can hear, the skin sense organs that which they can feel. But the sense organs of muscle and joint structures not only report the movements and position of head, trunk, and limbs as they "see" them but in another and uniquely human way are informed or "tensed in" on all sensory experiences to which man has given a name or ascribed a word. True to the function of this kind of "kibitzer" role, they not only receive information from the ever changing field of mental activity, they are just as quick to send it back to call the next play. Thus in a very special way the muscles provide "motor power" also for moving along the highly complex interplay of current and stored sensorimotor experiences called conceptual thinking. In this sense, the muscles see all — and that is more than the eyes see.

For those of us who work to improve mental health and mental efficiency this peculiarly human role of the muscles takes on new meaning. By enriching a child's neuromuscular experiences in his play life as well as speaking ability we multiply vastly the connections of muscle sense with the thousand and one experiences of daily living, of body in space, of what is left, right, up, down, forward, backward, and what comes before and what comes after in a series of movements. No wonder Newell Kephart and others who concern themselves with helping the slow learner find that such enrichment also provides learnings that hasten the perfection of the neuromuscular skills of reading and writing. . . .

A somewhat different application of the principles here discussed helps us to understand why persons who are taught to relax their skeletal muscles profit healthwise in several ways. Such persons can fall asleep more quickly, can apply themselves more consistently to mental tasks, can reduce or eliminate stress-accentuated headaches and other pains, can at will gain the renewal of mental efficiency that follows a few minutes of completely resting the muscle-mind mechanism, and can ensure for themselves many other advantages that come from reducing the deleterious effects of mental and emotion-based stresses on body functions. Teaching people how to relax their muscles is as much physical education as is teaching them how to contract their muscles!

Further serious thought and research in directions to which I have here but feebly pointed are certain to enhance our special field of education and will bring correspondingly great personal satisfaction to those who undertake the task. It is truly the direction of our future.

PERSONALITY

Claims have often been made for the character development resulting from participation in various types of physical activity. Unfortunately, little objective evidence has been collected to support this point of view. This does not mean that the cultivation of desirable personality characteristics cannot be an outcome of physical education programs and athletic participation, but that is not always observed and probably seldom occurs *automatically*.

A number of studies have indicated that differences in personality exist between participants and nonparticipants in athletics (see Chapter 13). The problem with virtually all such studies is that they are cross-sectional in nature, and there is no means of determining whether the participation is responsible for the differences or whether those who become participants do so *because* they are different to begin with.

Seymour's (508) longitudinal study on Little Leaguers hints that perhaps personality differences between participants and nonparticipants are independent of participation. Schendel (495) found that whereas no differences in personality (CPI) were noted at the ninth-grade level among outstanding athletes, regular players, and substitutes, at the twelfth-grade level the outstanding players showed less desirable personal and social characteristics than the other groups. The same situation was also found to be true for college athletes. Cassel and Childers (96) (using a different instrument) found little evidence to indicate that high school football players differed from other students. In studying major league and minor league baseball players, La Place (330) discovered that, in general, the more successful players (major leaguers) had superior personality traits, as measured by the MMPI (Minnesota Multiphasic Personality Inventory).

Although there is little doubt that professional physical educators have valuable opportunities to influence the personal and social characteristics of youngsters in favorable ways, there is little evidence that they are currently doing so. (See also the discussion of social characteristics in Chapter 15.) There may be at least two possible reasons for this: (1) research studies have not revealed the true picture, or (2) teachers and coaches have neglected to actively strive for such outcomes. Of course, it is possible that we are mistaken in our assumption that physical education can make a contribution to personality development. It seems unlikely that this is the case, however.

Another way in which activity may affect personality is through the modification of one's *body image.* Each of us views himself as having a body, and often our ideas about the adequacy or inadequacy of ourselves as individuals are reflected in how we perceive our bodies (290). Efforts to build our bodies may sometimes reflect feelings of personal inadequacies (230). Some authorities have contended that it is essential for children to develop accurate body images in order to develop normally (180, 413, 414, 497). In order to help them do this, activities must be designed to help them discover their own body-space requirements, and other capabilities of their bodies.

Another program in which modifications of personality are sought through the conscious efforts of the individual is one called *psychocybernetics* (365). This is a widely taught system of positive-thinking techniques designed to help people realize their psychological potential. (This should be distinguished from the general approach to the study of man as a machine-like feedback system called cybernetics) (607). Physical activity is involved in a very general sense (conscious modification of posture and mannerisms), but experimental data on the effectiveness of such efforts are lacking.

Yoga utilizes various exercises and postural attitudes to achieve a tranquility of spirit, which is certainly a desirable characteristic. Here, too, little other than clinical data and personal testimony are available for our consideration (see Chapter 18).

INTELLECTUAL DEVELOPMENT

Claims for improved intellectual development have already been mentioned (see Chapter 13). Several educational systems are founded partially on principles of sequential learning, beginning with gross physical experiences and continuing through maximal utilization of tactile and kinesthetic senses as well as vision and audition. The Montessori system is representative of such constructs. Kephart and Delacato have already been mentioned.

Aside from these attempts to improve performance of normal children through enrichment of experiences, most efforts at improving intellectual capacity have involved retarded and brain-damaged people. As mentioned in Chapter 13, several studies have reported improvement of IQ as well as other factors when structured programs of physical activity were applied.

In one of the better-designed studies, Oliver (436) experimented with matched groups of mentally retarded boys. The experimental group was given a ten-week course in progressive physical conditioning and recreational activities, whereas the control group continued the regular school program (which included some physical education and organized games). Significant differences favoring the experimental group were observed in athletic achievement, physical fitness, emotional stability, and personality adjustment. Twenty-five percent showed increases in IQ, whereas none of the control subjects exhibited improvement in IQ. A similar result was observed by Corder (126). Such studies have great value in assisting the mentally retarded, but extension of generalizations to normal populations is unwarranted.

EVALUATION OF PSYCHOLOGICAL PHENOMENA

As has been pointed out previously, most evaluation techniques in psychology require extensive training and experience. There are a few objective measures used, but even these cannot be interpreted without a background in psychological theory.

TESTS OF INTELLECTUAL ABILITY

Two widely used tests of intelligence are the Revised Stanford-Binet Scale and the Wechsler Intelligence Scale. Our term "IQ" has come from tests such as these. IQ means "intelligence quotient" and is a simple ratio of mental age to chronological age.

$$IQ = \frac{MA}{CA} \times 100$$

Thus, if the mental age and chronological age are the same, the IQ is 100. If the mental age is less than the chronological age, the IQ is below 100; and if the reverse occurs, the IQ exceeds 100.

It must be remembered that "intelligence tests" do not really measure mental *capacity*. They simply reveal performance of an individual on certain tasks (to which it is assumed everyone has had equal exposure). If the subject is optimally attentive and motivated, there is usually a fairly good chance of predicting academic achievement.

TESTS OF PERSONALITY

Several kinds of personality assessment devices are used today. All of them are subject to criticism on certain grounds, and accurate *prediction of individual behavior* on the basis of such tests is not possible.

Personality inventories, such as the Minnesota Multiphasic Personality Inventory (MMPI), the California Psychological Inventory (CPI), the Eysenck Personality Inventory (EPI), and the Cattell 16 Personality Factor Test are pencil-and-paper tests that can be easily and quickly administered to groups or individuals. For this reason they are widely used in correlation studies involving physical activity.

Projective tests are used in clinical settings by psychiatrists and psychologists. Two of the most widely used are the Thematic Apperception Test (TAT) and the Rorschach Ink Blot Test. In the former, a series of ambiguous pictures is observed by the subject or patient, who is asked to interpret them or to tell a story based upon what he sees. The ink blot test is similarly used. It is presumed that the subject will "project" his own feelings into his oral interpretation. The usefulness of such tests is directly dependent upon the skill and experience of the analyst.

ROUTINE PSYCHOLOGICAL EXAMINATIONS

At present our culture is not geared to routine formal psychological examinations. Examinations of this kind, usually more of a psychiatric nature, are almost entirely reserved for those who "need" such testing and are analogous to appraising the status of the barn after it has already begun to burn. Natural evolution may some day lead to routine psychological examination. (Notice the term "psychological," *not* "psychiatric" examination.) Many would argue that such a mass evaluation program, designed to establish conditions ranging anywhere from "normalcy" to deep-seated emotional problems, is useless until and unless more objective and reliable assessment techniques are available. Remember that it was not always the practice to submit to even a routine physical check-up. People went to physicians only when physical problems had already become obvious. It is not our purpose to promote routine psychological examinations, although, with the advent of the nonpersonal computer techniques and the knowledge of the physiological measures that also reflect emotional changes, it is an interesting possibility. We wish to point out, however, that at present the practice is either to ignore or avoid any consideration of psychological examination or to utilize the processes of self-analysis and introspection for this purpose. What we wish to emphasize is this: it should be realized that a psychopathological change is much like heart disease—it may *show* itself all at once, an unannounced and traumatic experience rather than *physical* pain but, like heart disease, it has actually developed over a long period of time. Careful, serious, and constant self-analysis may prevent the "barn from burning," or at least enable one, with proper help quickly secured, to extinguish the fire before irreparable damage has been done.

PERCEPTUAL-MOTOR TESTS

Of great interest to physical educators is the matter of being able to test the perception and motor characteristics of youngsters. Health educators are also concerned with many of these tests, particularly as they may relate to functional abnormalities.

Visual acuity may be easily tested by any of the standard eye charts available, such as the Snellen chart. Depth perception can be tested by means of simple, inexpensive equipment that can be set up almost anywhere. Peripheral vision can also be easily and inexpensively tested. These three variables are critically involved in motor performance, and information concerning them can be extremely helpful in dealing with learning problems.

Another factor of interest is that of fine coordination and ability to reorganize sensory feedback. Examples of devices used to test these characteristics are items such as the Crawford Small Parts Dexterity Test and the Minnesota Rate of Manipulation Test. The Snoddy Stabilimeter (Figure 14.1) is an apparatus on which a star is traced as rapidly and as accurately as possible while viewing it in a mirror. The pursuit rotor is another device that has

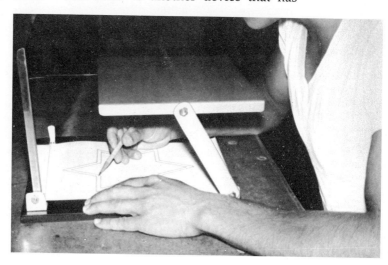

FIGURE 14.1 Stabilimeter or mirror tracing device. The subject attempts to trace a pattern without going outside the boundaries, guided only by a reflected image.

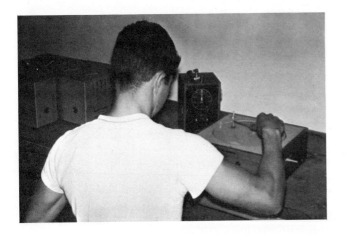

FIGURE 14.2 Pursuit rotor. The subject attempts to keep the tip of a stylus in contact with a nickel-sized point on a rotating disk. Time in contact is accumulated.

been used widely. The subject attempts to keep a stylus in contact with a particular spot on a revolving disc (Figure 14.2). Devices for measuring reaction time and movement time were mentioned in Chapter 9.

SUMMARY

This chapter deals with how physical activity affects psychological factors; these we have named the *efferent concepts.*

In recent years a great deal of interest has centered around the effects of motor activity on the growth and development of the brain and nervous system.

Controversy has arisen over the matter of development of laterality and dominance in the young child. Laterality is the ability to conceptualize the difference between left and right, while dominance involves the development of definite dominance of one side of the body (and one hemisphere of the brain). Both factors are claimed to be positively affected by

appropriate motor activity. Success in activities such as reading and certain other "intellectual" activities is linked to their adequate development.

Adequate experimental analysis of theories of neurological development is lacking. Available studies are contradictory, and a great deal of emotion has been generated by these issues, causing many people to lose sight of the theoretical questions involved.

Several factors besides accuracy and coordination of movements are involved in successful performance of motor activities. Although the specificity of practice for skill development is recognized, certain general factors such as possession of adequate power (and the *concept* of power strokes) are important. The overloading of specific movements is suggested as an ideal way to achieve adequate power without sacrificing too much in the area of specific practice. Hand-eye coordination and orientation of one's body to moving objects are also general factors that appear to be transferable. Evidence for a general motor ability is, however, lacking.

Fatigue obviously affects the ability to perform. It also affects the very nature of the act that is being practiced. Sometimes confounded with fatigue effects is *reminiscence* (improvement during a period of nonpractice). The extent to which reminiscence occurs may have strong implications for selection of teaching techniques.

The effects of physical activity on motivational states have implications for mental health and general well-being. Memory, perception, and even the ability to communicate effectively are all affected by experiences involving gross muscular activity. Claims have also been made for the effects of physical activity and sports participation on personality, but little concrete evidence has been advanced to support this position.

Recent studies indicating a positive effect of physical activity on the intellectual development of retarded youngsters has stimulated other work in this important area.

PRINCIPLES

1. Recently, evidence from a number of different sources has indicated that the nervous system, including the brain, is much more susceptible to change than was once thought.

2. There is little evidence for a general factor of motor educability. Most physical skills appear to be highly specific.

3. Certain generalities do contribute to success in skill development. Adequate strength and power and the concepts of how to apply them are examples.

4. In order to develop power for a given skill, the actual movements required should be overloaded.

5. Orientation to a moving object for purposes of catching or striking it is a general characteristic that appears to transfer.

6. If practice continues beyond the point of fatigue, different muscular patterns become involved and an entirely "new" skill must be practiced.

7. In order for mental practice of a skill to be effective, some previous experience with that skill is required.

8. Many skilled movements apparently require ballistic movement of limbs. During such movement there is no time for corrections based on neural feedback.

9. Experience in a given skill may positively or negatively affect performance in another activity.

10. The training of one limb can have a positive effect on the contralateral limb.

11. Most evidence indicates that the more similar two tasks are to one another, the greater the probability of positive transfer.

12. General principles of performance can transfer.

13. More reminiscence occurs (for certain tasks, at least) under conditions of massed practice than of distributed practice.

14. The level of motivation during the learning of a task is inversely related to reminiscence.

15. Complete absence of physical ability is inhibitory to memory, and

increased activity may be stimulating to memory in retarded individuals.

16. The fewer the cues necessary for a decision, the greater the accuracy and rapidity of the elicited response.

17. Perception of impending physical activity requirements has a profound, selective effect on involuntary body functions such as heart rate, respiration rate, and perspiration rate.

18. Movement, even without other accompanying cues or symbols, is capable of conveying ideas, moods, and attitudes.

19. The association of how certain movements *look* with how they *feel* to us when we perform them, gives meaning to movements.

20. Differences apparently exist between the personalities of participants and nonparticipants in athletics, but it has not been established whether this is an outgrowth of the activity involved.

21. One's concept of his worth as an individual may be related to his perception of the adequacy or inadequacy of his own body.

EXPERIMENTS AND EXPERIENCES

1. "Borrow" a three-, four- or five-year-old child and expose him to cards on which simple words (preferably nouns) have been printed in large letters. Cards should be displayed and the word spoken several times during the day, but exposure must not be prolonged. How many exposures does it take before the child can recognize the word among other words similarly printed (spread out on the floor, for example)? After the word is learned, print it in identical letters on a card of another color or shape. Is the word still recognized? Discuss the implications of the experiment.

2. After determining the limits of the peripheral vision of a subject, place small lights just inside these borders. Instruct the subject to signal whenever either the right or the left light goes on. Then, require the subject to toss balls at a moving target directly ahead of him. Note effects on his peripheral visual acuity. Use other types of distraction including noise, lights, and so on.

3. Secure a book on Yoga (see references) and attempt some of the basic postures. Maintain the suggested poses and attempt to experience the kinds of feelings that the book recommends. What are your reactions? Do you believe it is possible to learn to slow your heart rate below its normal resting rate, for example?

SUGGESTED READINGS

Cratty, Bryant J., *Movement Behavior and Motor Learning,* Philadelphia: Lea & Febiger, 1964.

Delacato, Carl, *The Diagnosis and Treatment of Speech and Reading Problems,* Springfield, Ill.: Charles C Thomas, Publisher, 1963.

Radler, D. H. and Newell C. Kephart, *Success Through Play,* New York: Harper & Brothers, 1960.

Scott, M. Gladys, "The Contributions

of Physical Activity to Psychological Development," *Research Quarterly*, 31:307-320, Part II, 1960.

Shy, Milton G., "The Plasticity of the Nervous System of Early Childhood," *Physical Therapy*, 45:437-443, 1965.

Singer, Robert N., *Motor Learning and Human Performance*, New York: The Macmillan Co., 1968.

Vithaldas, Y., *The Yoga System of Health and Relief from Tension*, New York: Affiliated Publishers, Inc., 1961.

Societal Foundations

Chapter 15

Society may be defined as "any community of individuals united together or related one to another by any common bond." The common bond may be thought of at many different levels: a nation, a school, a neighborhood, a family, a club, and so on. But perhaps the essential aspect of the concept of *society* is "a community of individuals." This simply means that more than one individual must be involved. Thus, societal foundations are those that deal with man's relationship to man, and not with man as an individual. This is not to say that man's individual traits do not affect his relationships with others; in many ways, they *determine* the nature of his societal relationships. But, bear in mind that the association is a reciprocal one: his individual traits, unless he was raised without human contact, were not developed in a vacuum. Individual traits (personality characteristics) are the result of the interaction between an individual and his environment, which environment certainly includes "societal influences."

Thus, it is easy to see that there is but a fine line separating societal foundations from psychological foundations. Perhaps our best hope is to deal here with the phenomena that have definitely to do with "more than one" person and to be fully cognizant of the fact that individual "psychology" can never be completely dissected away from what we will deal with as "societal."

Whereas "society" carries a meaning that can run the gamut from "common purpose and interest" all the way up to an entirely impersonal grouping (such as in a geographic area) in which many persons do not even know each other, the concept of "social integration" or "the group" is more often applied to the group closely knit by common goals and purposes. *Group* may refer to a somewhat permanent situation (family, friends, a college department, and so

on) or may be used to refer to a more transient situation, such as a temporary committee or even an audience at a sports event, theater, or political convention; a group may become a "mob" subject to what is commonly called "mob psychology." The behavior characteristic of "groups" is learned and has application to many of our current social problems.

Social mobility is a concept that involves society's selection, promotion, demotion, and distribution of persons into certain social "groups" or "classes."

The family is the earliest and most profound contributor to social development, but the school is also a social structure, and it includes many sub-

FIGURE 15.1   Social concerns.

groups; as such it is probably one of the most important societies in terms of contribution to social development.

This chapter directs attention to the relationship between certain societal factors and health education, physical education, and recreation. The science known as sociology, although not so "exact" a science as physiology, has identified certain principles that, on the average, tend to characterize societal relationships. Many of these have great meaning for your chosen professions. We will touch upon these principles and their implications and then proceed to a discussion of the effects of health education, physical education, and recreation on the individual's social development and, thus, on society. We will also raise some serious questions and comment upon current social issues and problems. In the end, you will probably have the feeling that there are more problems and questions in this area than irrevocable principles and answers. You will probably be correct! But a concept about what is known and what is unknown is the prerequisite for a *useful* understanding of the forces that relate your professions to society and how they can be utilized to improve your contribution to that society through your profession.

AFFERENT CONCEPTS

GENERAL PRINCIPLES

The concepts and principles that follow are not intended to provide a complete introductory course in sociology. Nei-

ther do we wish to imply that the list is exhaustive; we *do* believe that the principles presented are a reasonably complete sampling of the more important and better-established principles and, perhaps more important, those that have some implication for your professions.

☐ *It has been stated that man is by nature a "gregarious animal";* that is, he is fond of company. There is little question that normal persons are gregarious, at least to some extent; but whether this is "by nature" is difficult to prove. The important concept is that, whether "by nature" or through environmental influences, man does tend to desire association with others and, to go one step further, usually desires and seeks out mutually enjoyable associations.

☐ *Social development is the process through which one learns to be a participant in society.* Although certain hereditary and physiological factors play a role, social development is nevertheless based almost entirely upon learning. As Kenyon (303) points out, children and adults learn to play certain *roles.* Some of these roles are "ascribed," such as that of son, mother, teen-ager, senior citizen, and so on. Others are "achieved," such as that of teacher, athlete, lawyer, hippie, YMCA director, and so on. Each of these roles, ascribed or achieved, is well-defined and quite specific. In contrast, there are the less-defined, nonspecific roles, such as good citizen, natural leader, follower, and so on. Whether specific or nonspecific, it appears that socialization occurs according to a somewhat typical pattern of learning: imitation, identification, and reinforcement (303). That is, individuals tend to imitate and identify with a model (either a person or an ideal that is self-conceived but influenced by experience). The intensity and duration of the imitation and identification is apparently a direct function of the reinforcement received from reasonably pleasant repetition and extrinsic awards bestowed by society.

□ *Adjustment is the "dynamic process" by which one meets his needs.* As Cowell (128) puts it, human personality apparently "cannot be developed apart from the social group"; the "group" has an amazingly strong influence on the individuals within it. In other words, social feedback and aspiration level (which is definitely influenced by the "group") play an important role in personality and social development (134).

□ *It is not the activity itself that is primarily responsible for social development, but, rather, the circumstances associated with the experience* (303).

□ *Social development related to one role does not necessarily carry over to other aspects of social life,* although, where similarity of situations exists, some transfer may be expected (303).

□ *Cooperation and competition, as divergent as they are, both seem to be part of the normal child development process, and both are apparently important to our society.* Cowell cites evidence that children two to three years old generally demonstrate no competitive tendencies. At three to four years of age, they show some tendencies in this direction, but they are still more interested in the social relationships. From four to six, they show a desire to excel and thus to compete (128). Cratty (134) points out, and logically so, that groups *can* work by cooperating with individuals in their own group while at the same time competing with another group.

□ Cratty (134) concludes that *the desire to "dominate or lead one's fellows seems to be a fundamental trait of the human society."* It cannot be assumed, however, that leadership is a general trait; it does not necessarily transfer from one situation to another.

□ *An audience has an effect, of varying kinds and degree, on the individual's responses* (134). We should also point out that the response is related to whether the individual is, at the time, functioning alone or in a group.

IMPLICATIONS OF GENERAL PRINCIPLES

We shall discuss very briefly some implications of these general principles for your professions. You are encouraged to discuss others that come to your mind.

□ *Man is a gregarious creature.* The obvious implication is that your professions, whether involving formal schooling or recreation, can capitalize on the group process. (This does not imply that education and recreation cannot in many instances be effective on a one-to-one basis. Nor does it mean that learning requires another individual "in person.")

□ *Social development is based upon imitation, identification, and reinforcement.* The implications are broad, extremely important, and should be very obvious

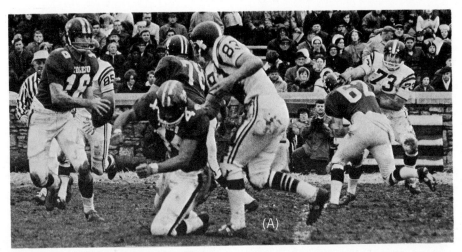

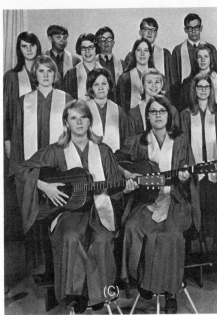

FIGURE 15.2 Illustrations of various conditions under which people participate in activities observed by others: (A) football, where participant is only one of twenty-two; (B) basketball, where participant is usually one of ten but at times stands alone; (C) choral group, where participant is one of many in cooperative activity (courtesy Monroe Street United Methodist Church, Toledo); (D) gymnastics, where participant stands entirely alone; (E) wrestling, where participant is alone in direct competition with another person; (F) dramatics, where leading characters are much alone but there can be great variability in closeness to audience, make-up, age, and intellectual level of audience, and so on (courtesy of City of Toledo, Ohio, Recreation Department).

(D)

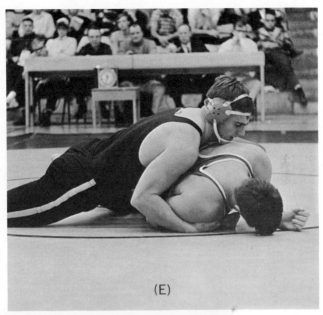

(E)

(F)

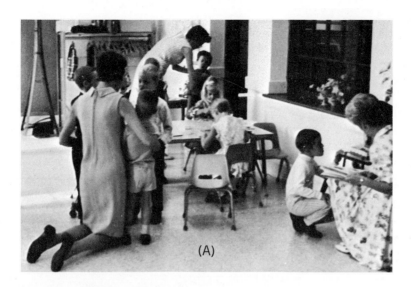

(A)

(B)

FIGURE 15.3 Being "together" seems to be important at all ages. (A) A church-school five-year-olds' class. (B) This church-school class of elderly ladies, most of whom are now widows, has been meeting together for fifty years.

to you. Remember that certain kinds of social development *can* be undesirable; example becomes important (Figure 15.4).

□ *Adjustment means "meeting needs."* Needs are omnipresent and not universal, even in a given situation. As professionals, you can promote posi-

tive adjustment by anticipating and planning for as many group and individual needs as possible.

□ *Human personality is not developed in a vacuum.* Physical education and recreation experiences provide excellent conditions for social interaction because there is quite often more free-

FIGURE 15.4 "Quick, fake an injury, fake an injury!"

dom of movement and verbal expression involved. Therefore, it is possible that a considerable effect is exerted upon the development of personality and upon social development in physical education and recreation settings. But this can be for worse instead of for better if poorly handled!

□ *Circumstances associated with activities are responsible for social development. (It is not the game per se.)* This implies to us that merely allowing a class to play volleyball or basketball, or any other team or group activity, does not automatically provide the best opportunity for optimal social development! Physical educators and recreation workers often act as though they believe this.

□ *Development for specific social roles does not necessarily transfer to other roles.* Behavior adhered to in the gymnasium or in a sports contest will not automatically carry over to all other social situations.

□ *Cooperation and competition are apparently both a natural part of our existence.* We can capitalize on both of these characteristics in promoting learning as well as in specifically planning for social development.

□ *The desire to lead is a fundamental human trait.* Although everyone in a given group cannot be the leader, many persons can be given the op-

FIGURE 15.5 "This is an activity which promotes social development."

portunity to lead some specific activity; notice that we said "given the opportunity," not "required." Why do you suppose we make this point? Where does it have application? Where is it not applicable?

☐ *An audience (or any "onlookers") affects in varying ways and to varying degrees an individual's responses.* This has obvious implications for learning as well as for social development: individual differences, with regard to the effect of onlookers, need to be recognized and taken into account.

From this sampling it should be apparent that many of the principles and concepts isolated by sociologists have direct and meaningful application to health education, recreation, and physical education.

EFFERENT CONCEPTS

RELATIONSHIP TO SOCIAL DEVELOPMENT

In answer to the question "What evidence is there to suggest that physical education classes facilitate socialization?" Kenyon (303) answers, "Very little." But he hastens to point out that there is, likewise, little evidence to support the negative view and that few studies have properly tested the question. The same is certainly true for health education and recreation; little if any objective evidence is available. Yet, we all feel intuitively that these kinds of experiences must have an effect on socialization. That they do is apparent. But the appropriate question is: What is the effect? Predominently positive or negative? Much careful research is needed to answer these questions.

We do have some evidence which is impressive, at least in terms of quantity. However, when we consider the importance of the questions and the magnitude of the problems with which we are concerned, the evidence is unimpressive in terms of both quantity and quality. We see, by way of summary, that athletic ability and participation have been shown to be related positively to social adjustment (55), popu-

FIGURE 15.6 "Now who can we lead?"

larity, social prestige and status (67, 70, 185, 358, 439, 572), choosing friends (610), and leadership (547, 632). Superiority in physical abilities and skills has been demonstrated to be somewhat related to social adjustment (64, 114, 528, 602), popularity and social status (571), general behavior (229), choosing friends (594), and leadership (632). Strength is apparently positively related to adjustment (64, 289, 602), social status (289), and behavior (229). Physique and body size have been positively correlated with positive adjustment (64, 602), social status (90), and leadership (547). Vitality and health are related to adjustment (64, 602), popularity and social status (229), and leadership (547, 632).

One study has shown a relationship between adjustment and recreation skills (470) and between adjustment (as judged by teacher and classmates) and the physical education grade (129). There is some evidence that those who are active adults were active in play as children (81) and that "meager play experiences as a youngster" is quite common among mental patients (516). High school drop-outs are apparently inactive in extracurricular activities (560), and youngsters labeled "most likely to succeed" are significantly more interested in play (590).

There are, of course, contradictory studies. For example, one study showed that in the sixth grade "skillful in games" was no better than sixteenth on a list of criteria for choosing friends (26). A recent study demonstrated no improved behavior adjustment in first through third graders who had been both behavior deficient and poor in motor skill, even though the six-week program significantly improved their motor skill (438).

The same searching and, in a sense, damning question can be asked in reference to every single one of the studies just summarized: has there been cause and effect demonstrated? For example, have these positive social traits developed because of physical education classes or athletic participation? Or do the youngsters excel in athletics and physical skills because they are strong and because they are socially inclined to begin with?

Another important question might be asked: What about those who are not strongest, not best athletically, not healthiest? Are they necessarily doomed to poor social adjustment, to lack of social esteem, and so on? We should strenuously hope not. Fortunately, most of the studies listed indicate that there are factors completely unrelated to physical prowess that also contribute to adjustment, social status, leadership, and so on. The problem is, for the physical educator, health educator, and recreation planner, *to meld the two kinds of contributions (physical and nonphysical) into a positive environment where they will not operate as opposing forces interfering with social development!*

INFLUENCE ON SOCIETY

Inasmuch as health education, physical education, and recreation can affect social development, they obviously affect society. But let us look at this from a slightly different angle. How do your professions and their activities influence society *in general?* That is, how do they affect what people talk about and what people do? It is obvious, if one looks carefully and thoughtfully, that sports, health education, and recreation are, to varying degrees, intimately bound up in, and contributing forces to, our society. We will suggest but a few; perhaps you can add many more. You should be aware of how these tie in with the principles on pages 480 and 481.

☐ The concept of "excellence" may be at least partly attributed to athletics. Athletics are also a means by which parents can reap the satisfaction of seeing their children "excel" (see the Little League discussion in Chapter 19).

☐ The Negro in sport is an established part of our culture and is at the time this is written intimately caught up in the black man's struggle against discrimination.

☐ We see athletic hysteria in many towns and sections of large cities, wherein a large and influential segment of the community (booster clubs, and so on) supports and often, as a result, dictates to some extent athletic policy to the school or college.

☐ There is a staggering number of persons who attend sporting events at all levels of competition. This phenomenon, although it may be a healthy sign that people are "recreating," may also be an unhealthy sign that far too many people are watching instead of participating in some form of recreational activity of their own.

FIGURE 15.7   "We really did it, didn't we, Son?"

☐ Competition of others (and even animals such as horses and dogs) is exploited and turned into big money by those who capitalize on man's apparent need for competition; if man cannot compete directly, he can compete (once removed) by wagering with a friend or an establishment on somebody else's competition.

☐ People are sensitive to and talk a great deal about obesity, weight control, and calories.

☐ Smoking education and sex education are apparently beginning to make their mark on society in terms of frankness of discussion, if not yet in terms of gross changes in behavior.

☐ The need for recreation is quite commonly understood and readily discussed by individuals, as well as by community leaders. This need is receiving special attention in connection with upgrading the lives and experiences of inner-city inhabitants.

As you can see, some of these effects are good, and others are perhaps bad. We must work to irradicate the bad. But we can hardly deny that health education, physical education, athletics, and recreation are integral and dynamically contributing forces in our society.

ISSUES AND PROBLEMS

We wish to advance for your careful consideration and further discussion eight issues and problems interrelating society with one or more of your professions. These are complex problems, some of which are on the lips and minds of a major portion of our

FIGURE 15.8 "Weight fluctuation is my 'thing.'"

society, others which are more specific to our professions. Solutions are not clear-cut and simple, and our intent here is only to lay these problems before you. (We will offer some suggestions for solution to certain of the problems in the final section of this chapter.)

☐ *Sexual attitudes and practices, according to statistics and surveys, have changed toward greater permissiveness, with a resultant increase in premarital intercourse, illegitimate births, illegal abortions, and venereal disease.* Some of the results of Packard's (442) recent survey are featured in Figure 15.12, and these require no further comment. Some people argue that there has been no real change, that there is just greater honesty in reporting; others even go so far as to claim that, because sexuality has become a kind of status symbol, many

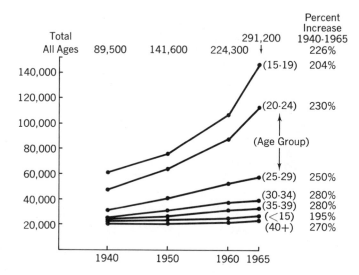

FIGURE 15.9   Illegitimate live births reported in U.S.A., 1940–1965, by age group. Source: *Statistical Abstract of the United States*, 1967 (578).

respondents either claim sexual activity that has never taken place or grossly exaggerate it. To be sure, there may be some of both involved, but when one views the objective data depicted in Figures 15.9 through 15.13, it is difficult to attribute all of the reported increase in premarital sex to greater honesty and/or boastful dishonesty! It is interesting to note the considerably greater increase in females experiencing coitus before age 21 (from 27 percent to 43 percent). Packard (442) also reports that, in general, the college girl's attitude is that premarital sex should be based on a meaningful relationship with some reasonable expectation that marriage will eventually ensue. The college men do not so enthusiastically share this attitude. Only about half of the some 1400 students (male and female) surveyed at twenty-

one colleges and universities of the United States felt that ideally it is "true that a man and girl who marry should have their first full sexual experience together." Only 35 percent of the males felt that the first experience should be reserved until after marriage, compared with 47 percent of the girls. Packard is quick to point out that his data do not necessarily reflect attitudes and practices of groups other than the one he sampled—college and university students. But he does lean toward the view that, because college students are coming from a wider social and economic slice of our society, data from college students are becoming more and more representative of young people in general.

Although the data on premarital intercourse are informative, interesting, and, most assuredly, related to the other problems mentioned, it is the resultant picture presented by the increase in illegitimate births, venereal disease, illegal abortions, and that silent social eroder "divorce" that represents the most tangible and gravest social problems. There can be little argument that sexual behavior and attitudes toward sex have a direct bearing upon the first three problems. It is more conjecture (although certainly not at all illogical) that these attitudes and behavior are at least one prominent factor contributing to the increased divorce rate (see Figure 15.11). And the cycle is vicious, because the home is the institution most responsible for personal and social development. Reflect for a moment on this speculation: Decreased family tranquility, more "broken families," and divorce cause less stable attitudes toward love,

sex, and marriage; this, in turn, causes greater premarital promiscuity; this, in turn, results in greater incidence of illegitimate births, venereal disease, and illegal abortion; this, in turn, collectively causes less stable marriages.

The home can hardly be replaced by the school when it comes to sex education—the home is the key. But it is our opinion that health education can help to bridge the gap between ignorance and knowledge by beginning appropriate and effective sex education at the beginning of a child's formal school experience. But assimilation of such knowledge brings forces to bear against only a part of the problem. The *moral* use of this knowledge can be supported by health educators and the church school but *must be developed, nurtured, confirmed and reconfirmed by example and teaching in the*

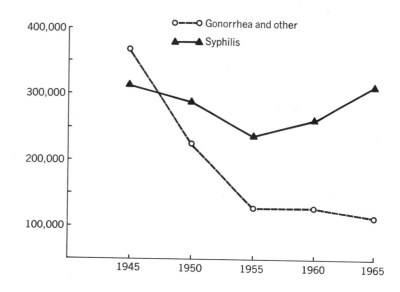

FIGURE 15.10 Reported venereal disease in the United States, 1945–1965 (civilian only). Source: *Statistical Abstract of the United States*, 1967 (578).

FIGURE 15.11   Comparison of marriage rate and divorce rate in U.S.A., 1910–1965, and ratio of divorces to marriages. Source: *Statistical Abstract of the United States*, 1967 (578).

home! Still, health education, including strong emphasis on family-life education, is perhaps one of our best hopes for an ultimate solution to the problems relating to human sexuality.

TABLE 15.1   Incidence Rate of Syphilis per 100,000 Persons, 15–19 years Old

YEAR	PERCENT OF TOTAL CASES
1956	10.1
1957	10.5
1958	10.2
1959	12.9
1960	19.9
1961	24.2
1962	24.8
1963	22.8

SOURCE: U.S. Health, Education and Welfare Trends, 1964.

☐ *Crowds in attendance at athletic contests are becoming more aggressive and* *less sportsmanlike; high school athletic contests are apparently precipitating more postgame hostility and more frequent physical violence.* There are no statistics to corroborate or refute this statement, but we venture to estimate that few if any of you have reached college age without being in, seeing, or, at least, reading about a postgame riot or "brawl" in your community. Perhaps you have even been party to or have witnessed examples of crowd aggressiveness during a contest. Whether or not a statistical increase in such occurrences can be demonstrated, and whether or not the athletic contest per se is entirely responsible (it obviously is not), this kind of phenomenon is of very real concern to us and should be to you and to our society. We cannot control all the factors involved—many are beyond our immediate jurisdiction or responsibility—but we can come to grips with at least one tangible and obvious factor. The *coach and his players, by conducting themselves in an exemplary manner, can often prevent, or at least reduce the severity of, many such disturbances.* When a crisis is building or when first signs appear, the coach involved, whether or not he has himself, by example, set the stage for such a crisis, can often avoid or arrest crowd aggressiveness by stepping to the public address system to request cooperation and to announce his intention to forfeit the contest if necessary.

Of course, his chances for success are considerably greater if he has been setting a good example. But even if he has personally "slipped," preceding his remarks with the admission that he himself has been out of order, an apology may get the job done. But this takes courage and a conviction to do what is right, in spite of a desire to win! Spectator *education* in the schools and via the public media, (*not* just announcements that fans should try to be more sportsmanlike) is another positive and concrete action which can be taken. It is a problem that the

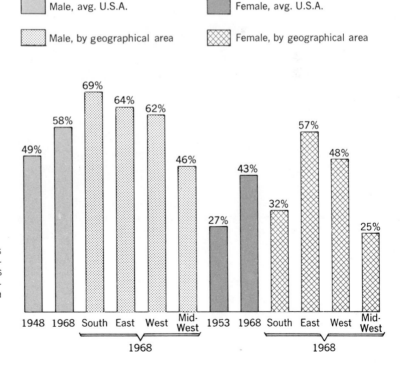

FIGURE 15.12 Percent college males and females reporting coital experience. Comparison of the Kinsey reports and Packard's data (442), 1968. Geographical breakdown for 1968 data only.

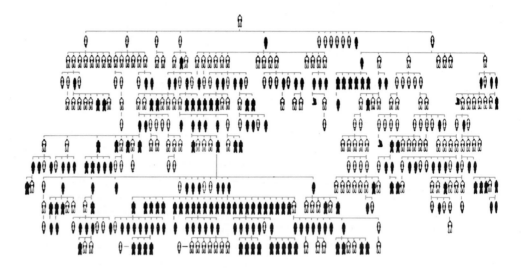

FIGURE 15.13   Persons involved in a typical syphilis epidemic. White figures represent adults; black figures represent persons under twenty; small black figures represent infants. From U.S. Public Health Service Task Force on Eradication of Syphilis, 1962.

school and especially the coach can ill-afford to ignore, whatever the cause! □ *The fantastic increase in "spectating" is a double-edged phenomenon; it indicates that people are recreating, and at the same time it probably means less active recreation participation.* It is literally an impossible task to determine the total number of spectators and total number of active participants for a given year in this country.

A study by Kenyon (302) is worth noting in this respect. His survey of Wisconsin adults indicated that, by their own admission, 84 percent of the men and 89 percent of the women never engage in vigorous physical activity even during the summer months (51 percent of the men and 64 percent of the women never engaged in even moderate activity). During the winter

months over 50 percent never engaged in even light physical activity.

Based on figures reported, we have made an estimate that may give some idea of the magnitude of the army of spectators in this country (see Table 15.2). This estimate does not take into account family bicycling and walking, backyard sports, beach swimming (only actual swimming should count), bowling (which we have seen is far from active anyway) and other less-common private kinds of activity; nor does it account for attendance at high school athletic events, college athletics other than football, or professional spectator sports other than baseball, basketball, and football. Actually, our estimating procedure, admittedly incomplete, is very conservative in favor of physical participation.

TABLE 15.2   Partial Estimate of Spectators and Physical Activity Participants in U.S.A., 1960

Estimated annual attendance (includes movie attendance and conservatively low estimate of home TV viewing)[a]	46,000,000,000
Estimated annual physical participation (outdoor and indoor)[b]	725,160,000
Ratio: PARTICIPATION: SPECTATION = 1:75[c]	

[a]Includes only professional football (NFL), baseball, basketball (NBA), boxing, college football, horseracing, and greyhound racing.
[b]Does not include cycling, jogging, beach swimming, and so on.
[c]Estimates all conservatively high for participation and low for spectating.
SOURCE: Calculations based on data from *Statistical Abstract of U.S.A.*, 1967, and assumptions based on maximal utilization of physical facilities.

As encouraging as it is to see the growth in outdoor recreation areas and facilities and the growth in camping, it is our belief that, in the first place, the ratio of participation to spectating is entirely too low (1:75, one participator to 75 spectators) and indicates too much vicarious experience and far too little personal participation. In the second place, even the recreation that is offered by municipalities, schools, Y's and so on is most often incomplete and inappropriate. Not only are more facilities for active participation needed, but they need to be more imaginative, more diverse, provide for more real physical activity and, perhaps most important, need to be much more accessible to the public in terms of location, cost, and utilizable hours per day. Although lack of available facilities is not the only cause for this deplorable 1:75 ratio, we believe it to be the most critical. It is our opinion that municipalities and counties, through expansion of public facilities and utilization of school facili-

ties, can significantly alter this ratio in the right direction.

☐ *The individual is handicapped by our society's overemphasis on conformity and the group's concept of "average equals normality."* We have already pointed out that personality is not usually developed apart from society, and certainly that is not undesirable. But it is our firm conviction that schools and homes have fostered the concept of being at least average and hopefully better than average to the point that *average* and *typical* have come to mean *"normal."* Thus, any "downward" deviation from what is considered typical is naturally assumed to be abnormal. We seem to have lost sight of a truth: Abnormality is the antithesis of "nor-

FIGURE 15.14   "Let's see now; that's 75 spectations, I guess I'm due for a participation."

mality," *not* of "average." Yet young-sters who appear different from what peers consider to be average or typical (be it size, eyeglasses, protruding teeth, different haircut, different dress style) may be considered peculiar or abnor-mal. If less than average ability in physical or academic skills accompanies this different kind of appearance, his fate may really be sealed. He may be teased and physically put upon and ostracized until his personality devel-opment and possibly even his learning may be seriously impaired or retarded. He may never realize the potential he has. Or he may compensate by means of any one of many adjustments — some of which may be for better, some for worse.

It is our contention that society, the home, and the school can no longer plead innocent and hide behind the "it's just natural for kids to pick on cer-tain of their peers — it's just the way kids are." It is "natural" only when society presents and promotes to an extreme the concept of "average equals normality." At this juncture let us say that, regardless of who is responsible, the school is in a position to begin the long haul toward overcoming this prob-lem; and health education, physical education, and recreation should be right in the thick of the effort. Right from the beginning, children can be shown that there is a wide deviation on either side of average that is per-fectly normal in appearance, abilities, and personal characteristics. But it can-not be left to chance. It must be planned for, and every "teachable moment" needs to be utilized to help youngsters

see that individuality up to a point is not only normal but also desirable; that average does not equal normal; and that an individual should be respected for what he is, not always degraded for what he is not. There is no better time than the present to begin to make this change; there is no better place to begin than in health education, physical edu-cation, and recreation. You may even lead the effort and attempt to encourage each school to formulate a positive plan of attack in this effort to eradicate this kind of small-mindedness that does not allow for negative deviation from the "average." When youngsters are raised and educated in an environ-ment where such bigotry is frowned upon, they can all then benefit from an opportunity to unashamedly and real-istically evaluate themselves and thus to develop a more realistic self-image. Many defense mechanisms will become unnecessary. We are convinced that such an atmosphere would substanti-ally contribute to a reduction in be-havior problems and dropouts and would significantly contribute to im-proved personality and social develop-ment as well as to better mental health and physical fitness.

☐ *Very few physical education classes and recreation experiences, as currently struc-tured and operated, make an optimal con-tribution to social development.* All too many classes (and recreation programs are not totally dissimiliar) are con-ducted either in a completely auto-cratic manner, "by the numbers and stay in line," or as "commando physi-cal education," where nearly anything goes. Neither of these situations promote optimal social development, and this should be painfully obvious. So it is that we must begin to plan for social development. Yes, the development should be as natural as possible, but being natural does not mean we can leave such development to "incidental" or accidental learning. To be sure, some social development *must* automatically occur, no matter what you do. But unless you believe in "survival of the fittest" as the best possible approach to social development for each and every member of the group, then you must concede that the best chance for optimal development is to *plan* for social development, to be sensitive to the need, and to be alert to every moment during which the need can be met.

There is no simple prescription for social development planning. Prescription or not, it is our belief that when a physical educator, health educator, or recreation worker, having been exposed to the concept of the importance of social development, fails to implement some specific plan for such development in his program, he is guilty of malpractice!

☐ *The excellent benefits of sports participation are all too often negated by well-meaning but short-sighted athletic department personnel and the administrations that either support or judiciously ignore what is happening.* This is a strong statement; it is certainly not original in its tone; it will not win us a popularity contest with many coaches. But it is the way we see it, and, furthermore, we are not alone! We believe it needs to be said, and we have been as fair as we can in saying it. The benefits to be

reaped from sports participation are excellent, and we believe that most of the coaches who allow their enthusiasm for success to dominate their better judgment are well-meaning but, unfortunately, short-sighted; they do not see the long-range effect on the athlete in any terms other than what they have come to accept as the almost automatic benefits that come to nearly every hard-working athlete.

There are many good arguments supporting the appropriateness of athletics in educational programs. We agree with Cole (112): "Athletics . . . have a legitimate place in American colleges and universities; interest and participation in sports is both normal and desirable." Few of the critics of college athletics challenge the rightful place of athletics in the program. It is not a question of "whether" but "how." How shall they be conducted? There can be little argument that college and high school sports are heavily emphasized in our society; one might even say *overemphasized*. As Beisser (47) points out in his book *The Madness in Sports* (which is not an indictment), the sports sections in both our daily newspapers and *The World Almanac* occupy more pages than the sections on politics, entertainment, business, or science. In a speech, an educator included a cryptic comment to this effect: " . . . in the same newspaper that editorially attacks present day big-time college athletics, we find sixteen times as many sports reporters as we do educational or science reporters." Why would this be so? The reason is obvious: firm belief in a principle notwithstanding, it is economically sound to give the readers what is believed to be what they want. One can cite many examples that illustrate the emphasis our society places on athletics. We have no quarrel even with overemphasis; it is not in and of itself the problem, but it may well be partly responsible for what might be some of the real problems. Perhaps, because of the emphasis placed upon athletics, it is, as Coleman (115) phrases it, "castigated as the antithesis of scholastic activity by intellectuals—many of whom have never taken part in interscholastic sports. It is defended and praised as the builder of men by coaches and athletes—most of whom have a vested interest in this proposition."

Based upon his experience at some one-hundred institutions in thirty-eight states over a five-year period, Foster (189) feels that "athletics are conducted either for education or for business." He maintains that, in general, success in accomplishing the educational aims is "inversely proportional to success in attaining the aims of athletics as business." He also believes that most of what is to be said on this subject is as applicable to high schools as to colleges. He does not advocate the demise of college or high school athletics; he maintains a position that if the business aspects of athletics "can be conducted as incidental and contributory to the main (educational) purposes of athletics, well and good. But first of all the question must be decisively settled: Which aims dominate—those of business, or those of education?"

Dr. A. R. Beisser (47), a psychiatrist whose sports career was cut short by polio, draws our attention to some of the paradoxes of modern sport. "Americans tend to be somewhat embarrassed by the intensity of their feelings about sports. They express concern about the priority of sports in schools and idolization of sports heroes, but this concern does not diminish their fervor." He also points out as another paradox that it is not unusual to explain modern sports as the natural outgrowth of play. But *play* is defined as an activity that is *not* serious, that should not be considered *too* important. Work is something to be taken seriously, but sports that "began as play, such as ball games, . . . have assumed instead [for the athlete] all the qualities of serious, hard work. Hunting and fishing, in contrast, began as the soul of work [for survival], serious and productive. But in our culture, hunting and fishing have assumed the true spirit of play. . . . "

Beisser (47) further comments on the application of one of Freud's observations: " . . . people are reluctant to make any penetrating examination of activities which give them pleasure . . . [deeper understanding] is vigorously resisted for fear that the understanding will deprive one of the pleasure." His observation that the United States of America is the "second great nation in history to spend great amounts of time and resources in elaborately produced spectator sports" is especially interesting when he follows this up by pointing out that Rome, during the period of its decline, was the first.

Because most high school and college players will not make a living from sports, Beisser feels that many young hopefuls prepare for roles they will never realize and that they often become "has-beens" by their late teens or early twenties. Beisser concludes this chapter with a pinpointed statement: "The effect of these paradoxes on the personality development of the individual is that the transition from boy to man becomes a contradictory journey to nowhere." Whether or not one is in agreement with Beisser's ideas, they provide some interesting food for thought.

There are more direct and more serious criticisms. As quoted in an article by Furlong (198), an educator at a leading university feels that wanting to win is not wrong but that what is wrong is using this as an excuse for dishonorable practices that betray the reasons for the university's existence. A former All-American football player expresses the view that "the athletes are being cheated, and in some cases corrupted, by the win at any cost program administered, not by educators, but by persons whose principal objective is to provide effective competition for professional sports" (296).

You have been exposed to a representative sampling of the criticisms. Except to state that we believe the benefits inherent in sports competition to be real and significant, we have said little else of a supportive nature. Let us say here and now that we are firmly convinced that organized sports participation can be a most meaningful

and significant force in a youngster's life. The necessity to work hard to improve, the tenacity required to stay with it, the opportunity for leadership and fellowship; these, when they occur, are priceless experiences. But whether or not these experiences are counteracted by morally crippling negative kinds of experiences is almost entirely dependent upon the coach or coaches. There are two ways in which the coach is responsible: first, by his personal example as a person on and off the field, as trite and old-fashioned as it may sound; second, and equally important, by what he promotes or allows to happen "behind the scenes," and what he allows (or causes) to happen to the youngster's character both on and off the field. It is not our idea of character building, for example, to allow the youngster no quarter through the physically and mentally demanding requirements of practice and games and then allow or help him to slip by in some questionable way in his studies or in other school obligations. Whereas he sees that there is no short cut to success on the practice field, he learns that short cuts off the field in certain other activities are condoned and perhaps even encouraged.

In short, we are of the following mind regarding high school and college athletics:

1. Let us always have strong athletic programs, with good and carefully screened coaches and for as many youngsters as wish to participate.

2. At the college level, let us award scholarships to deserving young men

who are legitimately qualified, or at least who are nearly so, for college work. But make them to understand that the *scholarship* is to be their aid and their *only* aid, financial or otherwise.

3. Let the high school and college athlete be expected to participate fully in good health and physical education programs because they are not replaced by athletic competition.

4. Let the athlete be expected to pursue a normal course sequence toward completion of a legitimate degree. Most, if not all, could succeed if they fully understood that it was expected of them. There is no objection to a somewhat lighter academic load during the active season, but the college athlete who is admitted legitimately can succeed academically if he so wills.

5. Provide tutoring, but do so from among the better-scholar athletes and coaches—not at the expense of the school's budget.

6. In no way, except for the aforementioned scholarship (room, board, and laundry) and within-the-ranks tutoring, give the athlete any advantage that other students do not get.

7. Provide for books and supplies as part of the scholarship for whoever needs the extra financial assistance, but permit them to keep at least the professional books for their future use.

8. Provide ample opportunity for real and meaningful leadership among upper-division players. Give the game back to the players!

It would seem logical that when these policies are adhered to faithfully, the character-building benefits that can accrue to the youngster have the best chance to do so—because he is getting something over and above the other students, not in terms of the financial assistance (at the college level), but in terms of what he is required to put out daily. If he has this experience in addition to his academic experiences, and if nothing is made easier for him in the classroom, then he really has reaped the maximal benefits of athletic participation. But what has he profited if something is taken away from his full academic responsibility, or if he is given academic "gifts"? He has merely, in that instance, received a different kind of experience than the nonathlete, and there is no evidence that under such deplorable circumstances his total experience has been any more valuable in preparing him as a person and as a useful member of society.

Now, if these policies or similarly sound ones are not soon instituted and vigorously carried out, we favor a second course of action. Simply and boldly stated, it is this: at the college level, openly employ athletes for the big-business sports, the only requirements being a minimum age of, let us say eighteen, and reasonably good moral and ethical character. The only restriction would be on the maximum number of seasons, and perhaps five would be reasonable; in this time a man could earn a degree. If he is not by this time ready for the professional league, chances are he will never be and that he should go to some other means of earning a living. Of course this plan would require details to be worked out, but it would remove most, if not all, of the hypocrisy that many persons believe surrounds college athletics today. The athlete could in this manner either prepare for a career in professional athletics or, with the money he earns during his particular sports season, attend college full-time during his off-season and earn a degree.

Except for the age limitation (which would be intended to eliminate raiding of high schools) and the five-year limitation, this plan is basically the same as one recommended by a former college president who has written a provocative article entitled "College Athletics, Education or Show Business?" Stoke (548) submits that the first and most crucial step toward solution of the problem is to admit "both inside and outside the universities, that our programs of inter-collegiate athletics are operated primarily as public entertainment and not as educational responsibilities." He maintains that a policy essentially like the one we have just described would place responsibility for rules concerning recruitment, eligibility, discipline, and so on with those most concerned about them: the athletic managements. He further states that "the relinquishment of formal academic—not institutional—control over athletics will have very substantial advantages both for athletics and education. Such honesty will free athletics as well as education from the schizophrenia from which they both now suffer." Pointing out very logically that physicians re-examine their diagnosis when a certain treatment does not work and that scientists revise their basic hypotheses when experiments produce unexpected results, Stoke concludes by saying:

Educators now find that what was once the recreation of students in school has been transformed into a responsibility of the educational system to supply the public with entertainment. It is essential that educators carry through a fundamental revision of concepts of athletic management appropriate to this transformation (p. 548).

We have directed much attention to college athletics, but, make no mistake about it, college athletic practices and policies have a most profound and direct effect on all forms of organized athletics below that level. Whatever continues to happen in college athletics or whatever program of reform is instituted will have a far-reaching effect on philosophy and attitudes toward sport and fitness, on athletic practice and policy, especially at lower levels, and even on the overall value system of our society. But, most certainly, it will affect high school athletics directly and indirectly, and perhaps this makes careful analysis and reform in college athletics even more essential.

We are of a somewhat divided opinion regarding the question of athletic reform. One of us favors first an attempt at the reform aimed at keeping college athletics within the context of its educational objectives. The other favors an immediate admission that at least basketball and football are primarily "show business" for outsiders, alumni, and students and, as such, should be reformed more in line with the alternative plan described—players in those sports employed by the university. We both agree, however, that should the first plan fail or be deemed impractical by educators and/or athletic managements, some form of the alternative plan is the only intellectually honest, and at the same time practical, reform at the university's and college's disposal.

☐ *Whether their claims are completely, partially, or not at all justified, the fact that the Negro in sport feels that he has problems associated with his being black demands that society must honestly and objectively address itself to the problems.* "What people feel becomes reality for them" (437). This is not meant to imply that there is in reality no problem. It simply points out a simple and basic truth: one cannot solve a problem by saying to another "you really have no problem, it's all in your mind." *Any problem is reality to the person or persons who claim it, and it is quite impossible to prove that it is fantasy unless it is recognized and analyzed.* With specific reference to the problem at hand:

Sport has long been comfortable in its pride at being one of the few areas of American society in which the Negro has found opportunity—and equality. But has sport in America deceived itself? Is its liberality a myth; its tolerance a deceit? Increasingly, black athletes are saying that sport is doing a disservice to their race by setting up false goals, perpetuating prejudice and establishing an insiduous bondage all its own (437).

It has been suggested that white society has created what is at this writing called "black athletic power," that the "explanation for black preeminence in sport is social, not scientific" (426). There is evidence that there are some anthropometric and motor capacity differences (368) which may favor the Negro in specific skills. But whatever the explanation, physiological or social, "For the militant Negro college athlete, talent on the playing field has become a means toward an ideological end: nothing less than an attack on racial injustice in American life" (426).

The specific charges and their counter-charges are many, but they boil down to this: the Negro athlete feels he has been "used," and the white defenders feel that the Negro has "used" sports and that sports has been good to the Negro. Olsen (437) says "the world of professional sport has offered great opportunity to the Negro in recent years, but it has not offered him equality. He still gets less for doing more on behalf of a white athletic establishment that appreciates him most when he knows his place." Prentice Gautt, a successful college and professional fullback, is quoted by Olsen (437): "It's a sad thing to face, but racial prejudice is almost a tradition in sports."

There is little question that sports have "made" a good life for some Negro athletes. In fact, according to a *Newsweek* article (426), some of the older Negro sports stars, among them Jesse Owens and Willie Mays, insist that sports have been good to the Negro and that sport should not be a target for Negro militants. Yet Jesse Owens, just two years after he had won four gold medals in the 1936 Olympic Games at Berlin, was "reduced to racing against horses and motorcycles in order to eat" (426). The white defense against the claim that the Negro has been used by sport usually includes these arguments: (1) The Negro has profited as much as sport. Without sports, where would they be? (2) Sport has been good to the Negro, and if he complains, he is ungrateful and bites the hand that feeds him. (3) The Negro professional athlete is in the upper 1 percent of the per-capita income of all Negroes— what right has he to complain?

A college coach is reported by Olsen (437) to have told a Negro athlete, "I think this university's athletic program has been damn good to you." The young man, after voicing his feeling that he had likewise been good to the university, added, obviously with reference to his recruitment, "I want you to remember one thing: you came to me, I didn't come to you." *White recognition of the truth in this simple and pointed statement may provide some of the insight essential to an understanding of and solution to the problem.* At least for big-time college athletics, it may help answer the question "Who seeks whose help first?" even if it does not settle the argument "Who helps whom the most?" The latter is a childish and irrelevant question anyway. The more appropriate questions are "Is it right to help any athlete in return for his services; if so, under what conditions?" "It is right for any athlete to provide his services to the institution in return for an education; if so, under what conditions?" If the answer to both questions is yes and if the conditions are morally and ethically acceptable, then the question of who benefits most, Negro or sport, is pointless. What is relevant then is this: How is the Negro athlete to be treated? The answer to this question is obvious: Like a man. This will not be easily carried out by some people, but difficulty of execution does not change what is known to be right! This much can be clearly established.

☐ *Leadership is a term often misunderstood and misused in connection with physical education, health education, athletics, and recreation.* It is a term which is often encountered in education. Careful examination of the term leads to the realization that, from an educational viewpoint, leadership has two entirely distinct but related facets. It is concerned with "provision" and "development." In formal education we strive to *provide* leadership while at the same time hoping to *develop* leadership among our students. Whether physical education, athletics, health education, or recreation provides good leadership is debatable, but it is certain that the answer must take into account some understanding of the term itself. The term is constantly and very casually bantered about. It is a term applied to innumerable social undertakings of various and sundry kinds (song leader, discussion leader, squad leader, group leader, patrol leader, "our" leader, team leader, and so on). Yet, as casually and knowingly as we apply and assign to individuals the descriptive term leader, it is questionable whether many of us have ever paused to reflect on its real meaning and on how one can develop leadership qualities.

Whether one is talking about providing or developing leadership, one definite concept needs to be underscored: *true leadership cannot be appointed, elected, delegated, or in any other way "officially" bestowed upon an individual. One must earn the descriptive title of "leader."* Very simply stated, even though the term leader may be included in the title of a permanent position (such as squad leader) or a transient task (such as discussion leader) and may be implied by other titles such as director, teacher, coach, or team captain, leadership is descriptive and not titular. In a sense, the term leader describes an individual more than it names him. Thus it is clear that one can be a supervisor, teacher, coach, recreation director, team captain, and so on, but not necessarily be a leader. The reason is clear if one looks closely enough: to lead is to *precede*, not to direct, and implies that there is something toward which people are being guided.

Other terms implying leadership have meanings similar to "leader", but we see in all of them important shades of difference (see Table 15.3).

With reference to developing leadership in your programs, it must be recognized that leadership can develop in a very informal, unplanned and natural

TABLE 15.3   General Definitions of Terms Typically Applied to Formal Roles

ROLE OR POSITION	DEFINITION
Captain	one who has command over others
Chairman	one who presides over a group such as an assembly, meeting, department
Coach	one who prepares others for an examination or contest
Coordinator	one who works to bring different elements together for a common goal
Director	one who drives others in a straight line, who points out with authority
Guide	one who shows the way, especially on a tour
Instructor	one who furnishes others with orders and directions
President	one who presides over an assembly, corporation, sect, or republic
Professor	one who publicly teaches any branch of knowledge
Superintendent	one who controls others, one who oversees
Supervisor	one who oversees
Teacher	one who informs, who causes others to learn
Trainer	one who draws another along, who disciplines, who forms or molds another to a given form or function
Educator	(dictionary and traditional): one who imparts knowledge
Educator	(more definitive and distinguishes better from the term "teacher"; it is difficult to conceive of one person imparting knowledge to another): *one who facilitates learning for others*
Leader	*one who through his assistance and guidance precedes others toward some goal*

way. This kind of informal leadership is typified by the "neighborhood" leader, the team leader, the person who assumes leadership of a group in a common emergency, and so on. This is more likely to be the kind of leadership that can be developed in association with your programs. It is inappropriate to say that the experiences and activities per se develop leadership; but they do provide situations in which leadership can be developed—*if the program is structured in such a way that leadership among the participants is needed.*

What is the meaning of this for your professions and for you as a professional? First, you must recognize that leadership describes one, not names him. This means that if you are appointed teacher, coach, director, or supervisor, you are not *ipso facto* a leader. It means that a person whom you delegate or is elected by the group as captain, squad leader, chairman, or whatever it may be, is not necessarily going to be an effective leader. Second, it should draw your attention to the fact that, in a similar fashion, the title of teacher, coach, director, and so on, may also be abused in the sense that the function, as defined, does not necessarily result from the assignment of a title. For example, a teacher is supposed to be "one who causes to learn." In actual fact he may be nothing more than a guide who shows the way on a tour, or a supervisor who oversees, or a director who points out with authority. Whether one is truly a teacher or coach or educator depends in large measure upon his methods (acquaint-

ance, domination, classic conditioning, indoctrination, or facilitation, Table 15.4) and the goals he sets for the participants in his program.

We cannot deny that one *can* be a leader, as defined, without even a semblance of the qualities of the educator. This makes it rather obvious that leadership is *not* necessarily related to subject matter and content per se. Some of history's most famous and infamous leaders have been anything but educators or facilitators—they have often been dominators, conditioners, threateners, and so on. Likewise, there are coaches and physical educators who have been leaders without qualifying as facilitator-educators or even, for that matter, as teachers or coaches! This makes another point clear: leadership is *not* a general quality but *specific* to some task or goal. For example, a dominant coach may be able to *lead* his team to victory, but not to other accomplishments which he by his example is *not* identified with.

We have agreed that leadership *can* be exerted when formal education is not even remotely involved, when the leader is not even functioning as a real teacher or coach. But it is apparent that a good teacher or coach or recreation director who practices his profession according to the fullest extent of the definition of his position is much more likely to be an educator (facilitator). As an educator, he is then more able to lead his participants to educationally sound goals.

The first question to ask is: "Am I as a teacher (or coach or recreation leader) carrying out my appointment in keep-

TABLE 15.4   Methods Employed by Persons in Various Positions of Authority[a]

METHOD A: ACQUAINTANCE (WITH PROCEDURE OR FACT)	METHOD B: DOMINATION-THREAT	METHOD C: CLASSIC CONDITIONING	METHOD D: INDOCTRINATION	METHOD E: FACILITATION
"Here it is; what you do with it is up to you."	"You *will* do this because I say to and since I am in a position of authority you had better not dissent. I will judge you and rate you, therefore I control your future in some way; you had best conform to my principles and my ways."	"You respond in this way to this situation. We will repeat it again and again until you can react and respond as I want you to without thinking."	"This is the way; there is no other. See how excellent the results are? Isn't this best? Of course it is. This is the way; there is no other. See how excellent . . . etc., etc., etc."	"This appears to be so. You do not believe it? Then we shall try it for ourselves. "This is the problem; How shall we solve it? "Here is a problem and some data and some opinions; what are your conclusions?"
Under certain circumstances may be acceptable; probably best used only in isolated instances and most applicable to older persons.	Never acceptable in educational setting or where some kind of educational goal is involved.	May have application to certain kinds of learning, especially to physical skills related to motor performance or safety. Never acceptable if only method or if used for unethical purposes.	Never acceptable in educational setting.	The distinguishing characteristic of true education. Most acceptable method for all kinds of learning.

[a]These methods are often used in various combinations.

ing with the full definition of the position? Or, am I something less?" (See Table 15.3.)

The second question should be: "What are my methods? (See Table 15.4.) Am I an educator (facilitator)?"

The third question follows: "Am I a leader? Do I 'precede' and do I avoid use of methods B and D? (See Tables 15.3 and 15.4.) Do I qualify as a leader according to the principles outlined on page 477?"

In short, one must be certain that he is first of all a teacher or coach or recreation director in the proper sense of the term. Then he must stop to ask "How do I operate?" and "Is there something beyond my immediate goal?" The teacher can settle for "causing to learn," the coach for "preparing for a contest," the recreation director for "pointing out with authority the way it is to be done." They have each done their jobs according to the definitions set down. But how? What methods were employed? Was there something more important than "causing to learn" and "preparing for a contest?" If not, sound *educational* leadership has not likely been the result. Some shorter-sighted, more immediate and specific goal may have been attained and, to this extent, there may have been successful leadership, but not with respect to the broad, more permanent goals of *total* education. Furthermore, chances are that very little leadership among the participants has been *developed* in such a program.

A theory of the teacher's, coach's, or recreation director's leadership role has been presented: You would be well advised to apply a "methods and leadership test" to persons in authority you have known, past and current, and to yourself current and future. It is a challenging and worthwhile exercise with improved understanding and professional self-enrichment as natural outgrowths. As additional food for thought and as examples of the use and misuse of leadership opportunities, we present for your analysis (without comment) some excerpts from an article by an educational psychologist and an article by a sociologist.

. . . the professor or coach should pass judgment only on the level of performance, not on the method of preparation for that performance. A student who gets an A on an examination deserves that grade regardless of what his study habits are. And an athlete who is the best runner on the team should be able to compete for his school regardless of how he trains.

. . . .

Herb Elliott has written, " . . . the more I speak to athletes, the more convinced I become that the method of training is relatively unimportant. There are many ways to the top, and the training you choose is just the one that suits you best." The finest scientific investigators, after examining various training methods, have reached essentially the same conclusion as Elliott.

Most university coaches are either unfamiliar, or disagree, with Elliott for they seem to believe they have the method. How else could they justify dismissing those students from the team who do not follow their every dictate. If coaches believe they have the only correct method, they are wrong scientifically. And if they know they do not have the only correct method, but still force students to train under their direction, they are being sadistic and are morally wrong.

. . . .

A student who is attempting to be a serious scholar while at the same time trying to participate in athletics would find it to his advantage to be schizophrenic. A good university student is inquisitive, argumentative, and one who accepts nothing without a thorough investigation. However, sports psychologists Bruce Ogilvie and Tom Tutko, in their book *Problem Athletes and How to Handle Them,* a book widely praised by most American coaches, say athletes are resisting coaching when:

1. They try to catch the coach making inconsistent statements and to find flaws in his arguments.
2. The athlete will use other authorities in an attempt to refute the coach's arguments.
3. There is a tendency to be argumentative . . .

Our students are supposed to question the most intelligent members of the academic community, the professors, but they risk the stigma of being branded "uncoachable" if they rigorously question their coach.

. . . .

. . . Under the present system, being coachable means nothing more than being willing to conform to your coach's prejudices.

. . . .

. . . Cerutty writes, "Indeed, immediately, when I find that an athlete is a conformer, a respector of authority, who is diligent in doing exactly as he is told, just as soon do I know such an athlete is limited in his capacity and never can become truly great."

Our best educators do not have to require students to attend their lectures. Only those professors who feel they have nothing to offer require class attendance for they know no one would come if attendance were voluntary. If our university athletic coaches have something to offer their athletes, they will not have to require students to train under them. Could it be that these coaches realize that, in fact, they have nothing to offer?[1]

An Appraisal of Leadership and Group Structure in Volleyball*

SIDNEY J. KAPLAN

For a period of approximately six years the writer has played volleyball with a

---

[1] Quotes from Jack Scott's "College Track Uptight" (Opinion '68), *Track & Field News,* 21:3, 21, March 1968. (Scott was a 9.6, 21.1 college sprinter in the early sixties and received his AB degree *Magna cum laude* before going into coaching and eventually entering a PhD program in educational psychology.)

*© The Physical Education Association, 1961. All rights reserved. Reprinted by permission from *Physical Education,* July, 1961. (Professor Kaplan is a sociologist and has been an active sports participant.)

group of university faculty members and graduate students. About half the players, faculty members, have been playing regularly. The other half are graduate students who because they are transient have played for periods of time varying from several months to three years. Over the years a relatively stable core of players has emerged who for various reasons—fun, catharsis, escape from academic tasks, and exercise— have maintained a high level of interest in volleyball.

Professionally the players, both faculty and graduate students, are in the fields of Education, Physical Education, Sociology and Agriculture. Recruitment generally has been by informal word-of-mouth.

As might be expected there have developed structural relationships among the players based upon personality factors, competence in volleyball, and to some limited extent academic status. These structural relationships vary from game to game since team membership and team size vary with the number of people who show up on a given day, and the results of choosing up or assignment to a team based upon a desire to obtain balanced team ability. In actual practice there has been a variation of four teams of three members each to two teams of seven men each. In this latter instance one man stands by and "rotates in" as a point is lost by the competing team.

Among those who have played volleyball regularly are a number of individuals who may be termed leaders. These persons choose up or assign players to teams and when playing either assume a leadership role or are deferred to when guidance seems to be called for. This guidance ranges from minor advice or reassurance like "play back further" to arranging the players in their positions before a game begins and making additional structural changes as games are won and lost.

Two of these leaders are worth singling out for examination since in their relationships to others one appears to exhibit successful leadership and the other unsuccessful leadership in terms of contemporary leadership theory.

According to several students of leadership theory who appraise leadership within a "situational framework" the following principles appear to be associated with successful leadership:[†]

1. A successful leader must have "membership character" in his group. That is, he must have "the pattern of attitudes and reaction common to the group."

2. The leader must represent a "region of high potential" in his group. That is, in terms of group goals he must be a superior performer. In the instance of volleyball he must be a superior player.

3. To be effective the leader must understand his followers — their attitudes, fears, values, frustrations, goals, and so forth.

4. An effective leader must be adept at creating and maintaining his group's morale in the sense of keeping individual purposes and activities harmonious with the goals of the group.

5. In the maintenance of discipline the leader will be less concerned with inflicting punishment than with creating conditions in which the group will discipline itself.

If then these are some of the basic principles of effective leadership the following question may be raised: To what extent do the two leaders singled out — the successful one and the unsuccessful one — either conform to or depart from these principles of leadership in their relationships to their teammates? In short, the attempt here is to appraise these two leaders against commonly accepted principles of situational leadership. In no sense does such an appraisal represent a crucial test of the relevance of these principles. It rather can serve only as an impressionistic assessment, useful groundwork for a subsequent and more rigorous examination.

GROUP STRUCTURE AND SUCCESSFUL LEADERSHIP

Leader #1 is a competent volleyball player who spikes and plays the field with uniform reliability. Ordinarily he "chooses up" to form the teams and in doing so oftentime deliberately selects an inferior player to promote competitive balance. Sometimes when an odd player turns up late this leader will voluntarily take him although the inclusion of such a player will be frequently disadvantageous to his team. Self-effacing, unobtrusive, and competent he is immediately deferred to and makes position assignments in consultation with his better teammates. From the viewpoint of the other players he is a desirable teammate since he is steady and carefully "covers" his teammates when they are off balance or out of position. In his relationships to others this leader is acceptant, affable, and even-tempered. When mistakes are made he exhibits no anger, engages in no reproach, and only on rare occasions does he offer advice and this only to players who are new to the game and in obvious need of reassurance or help. From time to time he exhibits a marked playfulness and reduces tension not only in his own team but in the competing team as well by yelling some witty

[†]See J. F. Brown, *Psychology and the Social Order* (New York: McGraw-Hill Book Co., Inc., 1936), pp. 342ff. See also G. C. Homans, *The Human Group* (New York: Harcourt, Brace & Co., 1950), p. 435, and S. S. Sargent and R. Williamson, *Social Psychology* (New York: The Ronald Press Co., 1958), Chapter 14.

or incongruous remark, and it might be added, usually at no one player's expense. When his team is far behind and demoralized he draws them almost spontaneously to the center of the court and leads them in a kind of mock "rally round" hand clapping which seems to break up their tension and encourage them for further effort. From the point of view of team morale nothing could be more calculated to revive their spirits than this playful demonstration of mock "college spirit."

There is on his part no apparent conscious effort to understand the other players. What seems to be operating is a kind of intuitive understanding and a concomitant behavioral response which serves to provide assurance and enthusiasm to his teammates. Less conscious than empathic, his understanding and response seem to be borne of "membership character" in his group. There is little question but that his oneness with his group is shared by his teammates, so effective is he as a symbol of their efforts and goal aspirations.

In a very limited sense does this leader reward and punish. He does not blow up, show his displeasure or reproach his colleagues in play. What his teammates do appears to be an almost automatic response to his leadership. Whereas an individual will on occasion break the pattern of set and spike either because he thinks he can make a point or because he is dissatisfied with his own or his teammate's playing, when playing with this leader he tends despite his inclination to break the offensive pattern to conform and play his expected role. When a person does break pattern for some reason he, as some players have admitted, may have some feeling of guilt for having let his teammates down. Self-reproach in this instance is manifest by expressions of apology or sometimes by what appears to be explosive intrapunitive or extrapunitive hostility. In effect what

occurs is that the player out of deference to this leader and his expectations tends to play a tightly patterned game, not because of fear of punishment or expectations of reward but because of the leader's capacity to "create conditions in which the group disciplines itself." In a very real sense this leader helps to establish a democratic nonpunitive atmosphere for his teammates which enhances their performance.

GROUP STRUCTURE AND UNSUCCESSFUL LEADERSHIP

To label a player an unsuccessful leader may appear to be a contradiction in terms. How one may ask does Leader #2 maintain his position as leader? In part the answer to this question is that this leader has prestige in the academic hierarchy. That is, there is in part a carryover of leadership from the leader's academic position to the volleyball court. Secondly, and more important, this leader because of his vast experience in sports knows the game and is in general an extremely able performer. Despite his knowledge and ability however the teams he directs—and "direct" is quite appropriate—are commonly characterized by low morale, backbiting, and suppressed and expressed resentments, sometimes to such an extent that performance obviously suffers.

While this leader does have membership character in the group, he assumes a directive capacity that is not in keeping with the generally equalitarian and somewhat individualistic character of these casual volleyball games. Quite commonly he sets himself apart from his teammates by a presumption of authority which is manifest not only in gratuitous advice but also in terms of the self ascription which he uses, namely, "captain." Frequently this is manifest not by explicit self reference but rather by reference to the leader of the other team as "your captain;" thus implicitly he singles himself out as the other "captain's" counterpart. Such a self ascription rather than calling up respect from his teammates serves rather to antagonize them and set them apart. What he does unwittingly is divorce himself from his group by shattering his membership character.

There is in this leader apparently little understanding of his teammates and their difficulties or their self expectations. Instead of offering reassurance he criticizes and directs. Quite often in his efforts to correct his teammates in their play he abandons his own position thus permitting the opposing team to make a point at his expense. This has occurred with such frequency as to occasion no little embarrassment on the part of this self styled captain and ill disguised delight on the part of the competing team as well as his own team. Quite often this leader breaks the pattern of expected play to engage in a personal rivalry with some member of the opposing team. This takes the form of unexpected soft shots or long arching shots all calculated to throw his rival off balance and by so doing to achieve a personal victory. Such rivalries often appear petulant and from the point of view of his teammates are at the expense of patterned play and the more probable success associated with patterned play. What this leader does is destroy the structure of the group not only by gratuitous criticism but also by departing from his own role as a functioning member of the group. Morale deteriorates and individuals unable to find satisfaction in coordinated group play seek personal satisfactions by non-patterned idiosyncratic play which further weakens the group structure. In effect, tightly patterned play, the key to effective volleyball, is shattered and the possibility of winning is immeasurably diminished. As a con-sequence of the deteriorated group structure individuals do not discipline themselves and the "captain's" attempt to discipline by advice or criticism is completely ignored and the team's performance deteriorates.

CONCLUSION

What is evident in the preceding characterization of the two leaders is the extent to which group performance is a function of structural unity and the extent to which leadership can contribute to or destroy this unity. Leadership, in short, appears to be a function of both the personality traits which inhere in the leaders and the situation in which the leader acts. In the instance of volleyball, where a tightly knit structure is conducive to success, the relationship between leader and structure is clearly discernable. Leader #1 in his relationships to his teammates conformed to commonly accepted principles of leadership. Leader #2 departed markedly from these principles. This appraisal, then, extends our understanding of informal volleyball leadership by clearly showing the relationship between leadership, group structure and performance.

REFERENCES

L. Carter, "Leadership and Small Group Behavior," in M. Sherif and M. O. Wilson, *Group Relations at the Crossroads* (New York: Harper, 1953).

C. A. Gibb, "Leadership" in G. Lindzey, *Handbook of Social Psychology* (Cambridge: Addison-Wesley Publishing Co., Inc., 1954), Vol. II.

F. Redl, "Group Emotion and Leadership," *Psychiatry*, 1942, 5. 573–596.

W. F. Whyte, *Street Corner Society* (Chicago: University of Chicago Press, 1943).

SUMMARY AND RECOMMENDATIONS

The sum and substance of this chapter is centered about the question, "Can health education, recreation, and physical education play a role in social development?" The answer is, "The experiences involved not only can but do play a role." But the real professional will not be content with this sum because it has no substance! For he knows in the depths of his mind and feels in his heart that the mere existence of the programs, albeit accepted that social development naturally occurs in any social atmosphere, does not insure optimal opportunity for social development. He knows that optimal development is not automatic, that incidental and random experiences are not enough; he knows that under any circumstances, even the best planned, social development will be both bad and good. So the question becomes "What improvements can be made to create greater odds in favor of "good" social development? There is one general but essential first step for the professional: recognize and be constantly conscious of the need for and importance of taking regular, planned, and specific action, even though it may often be indirect or subtle as far as the participants are concerned. Then, more specifically, it seems that the following steps constitute a reasonable beginning.

☐ Strengthen and expand health education programs to include sex education, family life education, and emphasis on the importance of individuality, as well as planning for social develop-ment through classroom and community experiences.

☐ Promote and develop more imaginative and diverse recreational facilities and programs, making facilities highly accessible to all persons, and in all programs endeavor to stress the importance of individuality, and consciously create an atmosphere for positive social development.

☐ In physical education, plan for both indirect and direct experiences to promote the odds in favor of positive social development. Lay reasonable emphasis on the concept of acceptance of the individual and the development of realistic self-image. Specifically direct attention to spectator education both within the school and in the community.[2] Work forcefully for the full attainment of educationally sound intramural and interscholastic athletic programs at both the high school and college level. To this end, better screening and licensing of coaches is recommended.[3] Administrators must

---

[2]The American Association for Health, Physical Education, and Recreation has published an excellent pamphlet, *Spectator Sportsmanship* (536), which includes a discussion of the responsibilities of the administrator, athletic director, coach, player, officials, student council, cheerleaders, and sports editor.

[3]The 1963 Platform Statement *Athletics in Education,* (23), prepared by the Division of Men's Athletics, American Association for Health, Physical Education, and Recreation states that athletics should be conducted by "professionally prepared personnel of unquestioned integrity," who should, in addition to possessing a knowledge of athletics, "have a knowledge of (1) the place and purpose of athletics in education, (2) the growth and development of children

have the courage to give no quarter when it comes to maintaining sound educational practice in athletic programs; in this they can receive encouragement by support of physical educators and coaches. Work toward full (but within reason) school financial support for athletics so that community financial support and its often attendant evils will not be necessary. Finally, at all levels of sports competition and education, honest and sincere attention must be directed to the problems of the Negro; dissect objectively and without bias the fact from the exaggeration. Take positive indirect action, and direct action where necessary, to contribute to the long-range solution to this problem that goes above and beyond the gymnasium and the athletic contest.

☐ Be constantly mindful that we, in one role or another, provide a model for the youngsters we lead, be it in classroom, gymnasium, field, or recreation setting.

PRINCIPLES

1. The family is the earliest contributor to social development, and the school is usually the second.

2. Most people are gregarious in nature.

3. All persons assume certain roles in society; some are ascribed, some achieved.

4. Social development is in large measure dependent upon imitation, identification, and reinforcement.

5. Social development in one role does not necessarily carry over to all other roles.

6. To compete and to cooperate both seem to be human needs.

7. Onlookers have an effect on an individual's response, but the effect is highly variable among individuals and is influenced by the setting.

8. An activity per se is not the factor which contributes to social development; it is the circumstances associated with an activity which provide for social development; they may be "positive" or "negative" in nature.

9. Participation in physical activities and recreational activities, especially when "required" or forced, does not automatically insure positive or optimal social development.

10. Many aspects of physical education, health education, and recreation play an important, often even a dominant role, in molding social value systems.

11. Leadership is a role which must be achieved or earned; it cannot, in actuality, be "appointed."

EXPERIMENTS AND EXPERIENCES

1. Relate experiences from your own past which attest to the validity of the principle that social development in one role does not necessarily carry over to other roles. Share these experiences with others in your class and analyze

---

and youth, (3) the effects of exercise on the human organism, and (4) first aid." There is a trend in the direction of establishment of state certification for coaches. See "New Minor for a Major Profession" (587) and "Certification of High School Coaches" (168) in the *Journal of Health, Physical Education, and Recreation.*

the role society played in such inconsistency.

2. Design and carry out a small-scale situational research study to determine whether young children in play situations are naturally competitive, cooperative, or both. If you have enough colleagues, have each study a different age level and compare results.

3. Conduct a survey to determine the impact of health science, athletics, physical education, or recreation on society's code of ethics, modes of communication, or activities.

4. Determine the attitude of various segments of society toward interscholastic and intercollegiate athletics. Direct questions toward certain supposedly beneficial aspects of athletics and to supposedly detrimental aspects as well. Determine whether goals of the participants' or of the spectators' pleasure seem to come out in the answers to questions (do *not* lead the respondents to give answers which sound good, but which are not true expressions of their real feelings).

5. Plan a specific learning experience or series of experiences for adoption by a nearby elementary school or recreation program which would promote the concept of the "value of the individual" while at the same time accomplishing testing or learning objectives in health education, physical education, or recreation. Through proper channels, attempt to secure permission for actually implementing your plan. It would be advisable to arrange for some simple but valid pre- and post-test of the concepts involved to see whether learning has actually occured.

SUGGESTED READINGS

Bishop, L. F., "Sportsmanship — Medical Evaluation," *Health and Fitness in the Modern World,* Chicago: Athletic Institute, 1961.

Cowell, C. C., "The Contributions of Physical Activity to Social Development," *Research Quarterly,* 31:2 (Part II), 286, 1960.

Frederickson, F. S., "Sports and the Cultures of Man," *Science and Medicine of Exercise and Sports,* New York: Harper & Brothers, 1960.

Kenyon, G. S., "Sociological Considerations," *Journal of Health, Physical Education, and Recreation,* 39:9, 31, 1968.

Shaw, J. H., and H. J. Cordts, "Athletic Participation and Academic Performance," *Science and Medicine of Exercise and Sport,* New York: Harper & Brothers, 1960.

Steinhaus, A. H. "A Biologist Looks at Delinquency," Reference (543:356).

Steinhaus, A. H., "Some Psycho-Social Aspects of Physical Education," Reference (543:45)

The following references are highly recommended: Beisser (47); Cole (112); Coleman (115); Foster (189); Olsen (437); Packard (442); Stoke (548).

Growth
and Development

Chapter 16

WITH WHOM ARE WE WORKING?

If a person is genuinely interested in the people with whom he will work as *recipients* of the benefits of his teaching, coaching, or recreational leadership and is not more interested in how these people will contribute to his ego and his personal success, then he should be intensely interested in *understanding* the people with whom he will work. He must understand something of their general physical capacities and limitations, their social needs, their psychological and emotional capacities and limitations, and, perhaps above all, their individual differences. When the persons with whom you will work are children (let us say ages five to eighteen), two additional factors need to be considered: (1) *The general or so-called normal capacities and limitations change, often drastically, from one age to the next.* (2) *It is perhaps more important to understand and deal with the individual differences, because it is during these ages (perhaps even more specifically, the early school ages) that lifelong self-concepts are formed.*

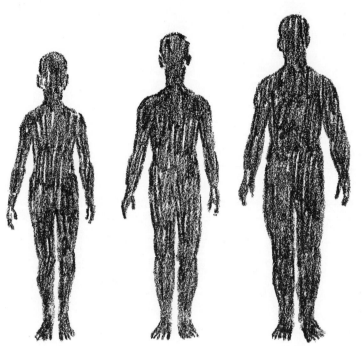

Age: 14.2
Ht: 5'0
Wt: 95 Lbs.

Age: 14.1
Ht: 5'5
Wt: 115 Lbs.

Age: 14.2
Ht: 5'9
Wt: 150 Lbs.

FIGURE 16.1 Typical differences in three ninth-grade classmates.

The true professional in our field of endeavor realizes the importance of understanding the "raw material" with which he works. He further recognizes that in children this "raw material" is extremely complex and dynamic, so he sees that a knowledge of what we call "growth and development" is essential in the fullest sense of the word. Without this knowledge (or the desire to get it), he will never be able to creatively practice his profession. He will be limited to conducting traditional programs with-

out knowing (and probably without being capable of *caring*) whether they meet the needs of the persons involved. In fact, without these fundamental concepts, it is doubtful whether a person can ever be more than a technician in our fields, because he then prescribes or conducts programs without *intelligently directed concern for his charges.*

Let us look at examples of questions that can be properly answered only with some knowledge of growth and development. At what age level should an activity (for example, basketball) be introduced into a recreation or physical education program? Is a given age level appropriate in terms of physical capacity and motor capacity (so that negative attitudes caused by failure will not develop)? What about the level of emotional stability (in the light of failure)? If an activity is introduced, what should be expected of the participants at this age level? How strenuously (intensity and duration) can children participate at this age? What is the attention span for physical activity? For classroom activity? What methods will capitalize on the characteristics and interests of learners at this age? What is "normal" for this age, and how much deviation can there be before there is cause for concern?

In short, it seems to us that the facts and concepts of growth and development are essential to the physical educator, health educator, and recreation worker because:

1. They provide the only sound basis for *program planning* (curriculum, recreation programs, corrective programs, and so on).
2. They provide the only sound basis for *selecting and modifying methods* of teaching and leadership.
3. They provide the best basis for *understanding persons* involved in the program, their *capacities* and their *individuality.*
4. They enable the teacher or leader to help the *persons* involved *understand themselves.*
5. They provide a sound basis for *recognizing significant deviations* from what is "normal."

PURPOSE OF THIS CHAPTER

It is not the intent of this textbook to *complete* your education and training for your profession, and so this chapter does not purport to provide you with all the concepts of growth and development you will someday need and want. In the first place, all the principles are not known. Much is yet to be learned. Second, it is expected that you will, in your training, have a course or two that deal specifically with the principles of growth and development. Third, when you begin the practice of your profession, you will need to constantly collect and classify information of your own in order to add to the general principles you have learned. This will be necessary because there is much unknown, because what is general may not apply to a specific situation, and because society's goals are ever-changing.

We attempt in this chapter to accomplish three things: (1) to provide insight into the kinds of growth and development concepts that are applicable; (2) to identify, as a somewhat extensive sample, some of the applicable facts and concepts that are known or estimated; and (3) to discuss briefly the effects of exercise and training on growth and development.

AFFERENT CONCEPTS

DEFINITIONS

Although there are differences of opinion about some of these definitions, the following seem to us to be acceptable.

Development: increase in capacities and complexity of function

Growth: quantitative increase in size or weight

Maturation: qualitative physiological change (not the result of "learning")

Learning: change brought about by "experience"

As a child becomes older, he normally is "growing" (becoming heavier and taller); he is "developing" (increasing his capacities and his ability to carry out more complex functions); he is "maturing" (his digestive system is becoming better adapted to handling different foods, his sensory system is becoming more "useful", his perceptions are improving, and so on); and he is "learning" (daily experiences, planned and unplanned, formal and informal, are increasing his knowledge and contributing to his attitudes toward life in general and toward specific aspects of living). It is obvious that these are not completely separate activities. They are complexly and intimately entwined. We might conclude that growth, maturation, and learning all contribute to the development of the child. In fact, for optimal development it is clear that growth, maturation, and learning are essential.

Growth and development, then, occur as the result of the continuous interaction between the individual and his environment. In summary, growth and development are affected and influenced by (1) genetic factors, (2) nutrition (affected by geographical factors, economic status, and so on), (3) hormones, (4) environment (culture, home,

school, mass media, and so on), and (5) activities.

STAGES OF GROWTH AND DEVELOPMENT

For purposes of discussion of the concepts, the following will serve as a useful base in terms of the *stages* of growth and development (598):

Infancy: first year

Preschool: one to six years (also called "early childhood")

Prepuberty: six to ten years (also called "later childhood")

Adolescence: girls, eight or ten to eighteen years old; boys, ten or twelve to twenty years old

Puberty (average): girls, thirteen years old; boys, fifteen years old

TYPES OF GROWTH AND DEVELOPMENT

It seems reasonable to divide growth and development into four basic types: (1) *physical* (growth), including subclassifications: lymphoid, neural, general, and genital, each of which normally proceeds at a different rate (see Figure 16.2).

(2) *motor* (development), including general body control, fine motor skills such as writing and cutting with scissors, and large muscle motor skills such as running, jumping, and throwing; (3) *sensory, perceptual, cognitive* (development), such as weight discrimination, depth and distance perception, learning, imagination and creativity, reasoning ability, and so on;

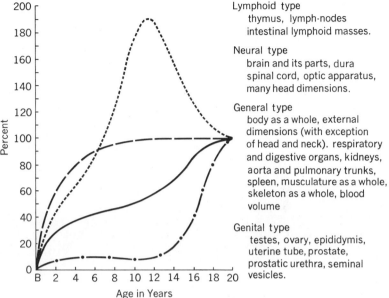

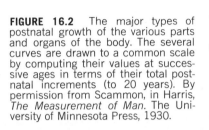

FIGURE 16.2 The major types of postnatal growth of the various parts and organs of the body. The several curves are drawn to a common scale by computing their values at successive ages in terms of their total postnatal increments (to 20 years). By permission from Scammon, in Harris, *The Measurement of Man.* The University of Minnesota Press, 1930.

and (4) *social* and *personality* (development).

APPLICATION OF DATA AND OBSERVATIONS

Basic data are presented, and some are discussed in terms of the concepts that evolve from them and in terms of their implications for health education, physical education, and recreation. Six basic figures and tables are used to present data and information as follows: (1) growth (height and weight) and growth and development of circulatory and respiratory systems (Figure 16.2); (2) miscellaneous factors (body temperature regulation, skeletal and mechanical, nervous system, excretory system)

(Table 16.1); (3) primary and secondary sex characteristics (Table 16.2); (4) behavioral characteristics (cognitive, personality, social skills) (Table 16.3); (5) muscular and circulorespiratory capacities (Table 16.4); and (6) motor skills and abilities (Table 16.5).

We can conclude, by simple inspection of Figure 16.1, that girls are generally larger than boys from about ten to fourteen years of age but that after age 13.5 boys begin to catch up and become larger, on the average, by fifteen years of age. We can see from Tables 16.4 and 16.5, however, that even though girls tend to be larger from ten to fourteen, they do not have as high a level of gross motor skills nor do they have the functional-muscle and

TABLE 16.1 Miscellaneous Growth and Development Factors

TEMPERATURE REGULATING MECHANISM
May not be mature at age 5–6 (more information needed).

SKELETAL
1. Epiphyseal union and fusion normally not complete until:

Shoulder girdle and arms	♀18	
	♂19	
Legs	♀18	
	♂19	
Vertebrae	♀	♂early 20's (See 7 below.)
Pelvis: Hip	♀10	
	♂14	
Sacrum	♀	♂25
Hands and wrists	♀17	
	♂19	
Feet and ankles	♀14½	
	♂16½	

2. In young, larger spaces between bones; longer and less firmly attached ligaments; greater flexibility.
3. In young, more water and protein-like substance in bones and less minerals; less easily broken but more easily deformed.
4. Growing bone has better blood supply; bones more prone to blood borne infection.
5. Racial differences: Negro more rapid skeletal maturation than Caucasian.
6. Onset of menstruation more related to skeletal age than chronological (13.5–14.5 skeletal age).
7. Pull of muscles and body position can influence vertebral curves considerably until early 20's; it is believed that children and young adolescents should be protected from lifting very heavy loads and from long periods of standing.

POSTURE AND AGE

5	6	7	8	9	10	11	12	13	14	15

←Protruding abdomen normal ─────────────────→
←Exaggerated lumber curve normal ─────→ Should become less exaggerated
←Shoulders rounded ─────────→

Prominent shoulder
blades typical →

Pelvis tilted slightly downward in front ───────────────→ Tilted slightly upward in front

---

(Lateral curvatures at any age are abnormal.)
 (Knock knees, bowlegs, flat feet and pronation, pigeon-toed, although normal in preschoolers, should be improved or gone by 6–7 yrs.)

BODY CENTER OF GRAVITY
5–6 yrs.: just below umbilicus; 7–12 yrs.: moving downward; 13 yrs.: should be below crest of ilium

NERVOUS SYSTEM
1. By 5–7 yrs., development of reflexes (knee jerk, Achilles' tendon, and so on) complete although they may be very exaggerated.
2. Sensory system and CNS about 90% developed by 6 yrs., 95% at 8, 97% at 10, 99% at 12, and 100% by 13.
3. Perception: accurate perception of space, distance, depth, size, weight, and so on, may not be complete until 12–15 yrs. even though these capacities begin in preschool and early school age; there is considerable variability in perceptual capacity.

EXCRETORY SYSTEM
Best evidence is that urinary system is mature by 5–6 yrs.

---

circulo-respiratory efficiency that boys do. We also note that the sexes tend to "voluntarily" separate at about age eight or nine (Table 16.3) and that, sexually, girls mature earlier than boys (Table 16.2). It is therefore quite traditional to separate boys and girls for physical education beginning in the fifth grade (about age ten). This separation is usually continued throughout

TABLE 16.2 Development of Primary and Secondary Sex Characteristics in Boys and Girls

	AGE										
SEX CHARACTERISTIC	8	9	10	11	12	13	14	15	16	17	18
Growth spurt, general (height and weight)					♀ ▬▬▬	♂ ▬▬▬					
Pelvis	♀Female contour and fat deposition begins										
Breasts			♀First hypertrophy ▬▬		♀Enlargement and nipple pigmentation / ♂Some hypertrophy normal		♂Disappearance		♀Maturity ▬▬		
Vagina					Secretion begins						
Penis and testes				Increase in size			Rapid growth				
Pubic hair				♀Initial appearance ▬▬	♀Becomes abundant and curly / ♂ Initial appearance ▬▬		♂Becomes abundant and curly				
Auxillary hair and sweat glands increase secretion					♀▬▬▬	♂▬▬▬					
Acne					♀▬▬▬ / ♀ ♂Acne varies considerably; present in 75–90% before age 18		♂▬▬▬				
Voice							♂Deepens				
Menstruation begins			▬▬▬ Average age about 12.5–13.0; was 14 in 1900								
Mature sperm				▬▬▬ Average = 15 yrs. ▬▬▬							

TABLE 16.3   Behavioral Characteristics of Children, Age Five through Adolescence

AGE	ATTITUDES	SKILLS
5	Poised and controlled Serious and concerned about his ability Wants some responsibilities Gets along well with adults Good memory for past events Play may follow domestic pattern in both sexes	Some discrimination Draws recognizable picture of person Reconstructs rectangular card divided into two triangles
6	Age of great physical and psychological change Constant activity Poor at finishing what is started easily Vocabulary may include slang and swearing Temper tantrums common Rudeness common Explosive and unpredictable Vigorous and imaginative at play Most like school and want to learn Parental love and praise *vital* at this difficult stage	Vocabulary of 2500 Counts to 20 or 30 Knows right and left parts of body Knows number combinations to 10 Differentiates AM and PM
7	Play approached more cautiously Less of a problem child Aware of and sensitive about sex—avoids self exposure Introspective and desires approbation of peers and parents "Pensive" year	Counts by 2's and 5's Tells time Copies diamond shape Has basic addition and subtraction concepts
8	Increased smoothness and poise Unsupervised play may become rowdy Wants to be in group and needs peer interest Segregation by sex becomes apparent Enjoys school, often more than home Great individual differences Broader experiences and intellectual exploration	Counts backward from 20 to 1 Skeptical of characters in stories, movies, etc. Describes differences and similarities between things from memory
9	Better self control, seeks independence Can better complete tasks Can look at future and can plan ahead for play and work Can accept blame	Describes objects in detail Arranges weights in order of heaviness Can do simple multiplication

Essentially honest
Obeys well and can assume responsibilities
Hero-worship prominent
Self-sufficient, self-critical, anxious to
    please
Sexes remain separate

10   Change in attitude toward sex   Knows simple fractions
     Girls more mature and poised   Copies simple design after 10 sec.
     Begins to think about and discuss social   examination
         problems
     Power of suggestion about good and evil is
         great
     Good or bad characteristics may be most
         readily established at this age
     Concept of individual, in self and others,
         better developed
     Personal traits give fair indication of adult
         personality
     Teamwork, submission to fixed rules of play
         now possible

11   Girls somewhat behind boys in strength and   Can define abstract terms such as
         endurance   justice, honesty, revenge
     Joins clubs and groups   Sees moral in fables
     Takes part in drives, etc.   Underestimates need for basic hygienic
     Team games popular   measures
     Shyness may become increased in shy child   Great individual variability
     More critical of his own work

Adolescence Social acceptance important
     Conforms to group own age and achieves
         more independence from parents
     Greater emphasis on looks and physique
     Society's view of "normality" makes many
         anxious about own body and capacities
         and yet unwilling to discuss them
     Easily hurt when criticized
     Romantic ideas about people; may be
         obsessed with certain ideals
     Girls may have "crush" on teachers
     Some social differences owing to girls'
         2-year advancement in physical and
         emotional development
     Conflict between his and others' aims for
         him
     May be aggressive and rebellious
     Will withdraw if not accepted
     Some pressure, if compatible with ability,
         is probably desirable

TABLE 16.4   Development of Muscular and Circulo-Respiratory Capacities

CAPACITY		AGE										
	6	7	8	9	10	11	12	13	14	15	16	17
STRENGTH												
Grip (in pounds)[a] ♂								65	78	93	106	109
♀								42	43	55	59	63
Composite (in pounds: isometric, shoulder extension, ankle plantor flexion, trunk extension, knee extension)[b] ♂				323	356	399	429					
MUSCLE ENDURANCE												
Pull-ups (number)[c] ♂					3	3	3	4	5	6	7	8
Sit-ups (number)[c] ♂					48	50	56	65	70	72	72	69
♀					33	32	32	32	30	29	29	29
POWER												
Leg: Jump and reach (in inches)[d] ♂	6.1	7.0	8.8	7.9	11.1	11.7						
♀	5.7	7.1	7.6	8.5	10.2	10.5						
Standing broad jump (in feet and inches)[c] ♂					5'0	5'2	5'5	5'8	6'4	6'9	7'0	7'2
♀					4'8	4'9	5'0	5'0	5'2	5'4	5'4	5'5
Shoulder: Softball throw for distance (in feet)[c] ♂					99	110	121	140	158	172	180	188
♀					53	61	68	73	78	80	79	78
MUSCULATURE												
Greatest development (% of body)					33%							40%
CR CAPACITY												
600 yd run-walk (minutes:seconds)[c] ♂					2:35	2:31	2:28	2:15	2:06	2:00	1:55	1:56
♀					2:48	2:55	2:56	2:58	2:57	2:50	2:52	2:58

[a]SOURCE: Fleishman (184).
[b]SOURCE: Clarke, Bailey, and Shay (105).
[c]SOURCE: Hunsicker (257).
[d]SOURCE: Johnson (282).

TABLE 16.5 Development of Motor Skills and Abilities

SKILL (IN GENERAL)

5 years Alternate feet on stairs, up and down; hop on one foot; (some can skip)

6 years Galloping, skipping, hop on two feet; (some master dance steps); jump rope, balance on beam or walk line, ride bicycle; steady improvement in reaction time

7 years Roller skate

8 years Most can master dance steps

SKILL		5	6	7	8	9	10	11	12	13	14	15	16	17
KICKING BALL[a]	♂		23	27	30	33	34	33						
	♀		22	26	25	30	31	33						
THROWING AND CATCHING[a]	♂		16	27	31	39	44	47						
	♀		14	22	25	33	40	42						
BATTING[a]	♂		2.7	3.1	3.1	4.9	5.7	6.2						
	♀		2.1	2.1	2.9	4.2	4.8	5.6						
AGILITY:														
Zig-zag run (in seconds)[a]	♂		11.3	10.1	9.6	8.5	8.5	8.5						
	♀		12.1	10.4	9.8	9.9	9.2	9.2						
Shuttle run (in seconds)[b]	♂						11.3	11.2	11.1	10.7	10.4	10.1	10.0	9.9
	♀						11.8	11.8	11.7	11.6	11.5	11.5	11.5	11.4
SPEED														
50 yd (in seconds)[b]	♂						8.3	8.1	7.8	7.5	7.2	6.9	6.7	6.7
	♀						8.5	8.4	8.3	8.3	8.3	8.3	8.4	8.4

[a]SOURCE: Johnson (282). Numbers refer to scores on standardized tests.
[b]SOURCE: Hunsicker (259).

the school years and, indeed, even into "required" college physical education classes. There is little question that beginning with age seven or eight there are progressively more and greater differences between boys and girls in strength, endurance, and motor performance (Tables 16.4 and 16.5), but one must question whether this means complete segregation of the sexes for all physical education activities at all ages after age ten.

A possible clue to girls' comparative CR inefficiency and lack of muscular endurance is illustrated in Figure 16.2. We see that girls' RBC count, hemoglobin, and hematocrit (all of which relate to the O_2 carrying capacity of the blood) increase very little after age ten, while these measures in boys increase considerably. The question becomes, "Is this difference inevitable or can it, at least in certain individuals, be reversed?"

Figure 16.1 also would seem to provide some evidence that, as children grow, their capacity for strenuous work also increases. Heart weight and volume and aortic cross-sectional area increase steadily, as does the lung capacity. The resting heart rate and respiration rate decrease steadily; this also implies greater CR efficiency (see Chapter 8).

The self-explanatory items 1, 2B, 2C and G, 3, and 5C in Table 16.1 are of

particular importance to physical educators and recreation leaders. Item 4 implies that balance may be more difficult for the younger child.

Table 16.2 certainly has serious and important implications for the health educator in terms of sex education, and for the physical educator and recreation leader in terms of understanding and coping with children's physical and emotional problems related to development of primary and secondary sex characteristics.

Table 16.3 is literally "loaded" with developmental characteristics that can

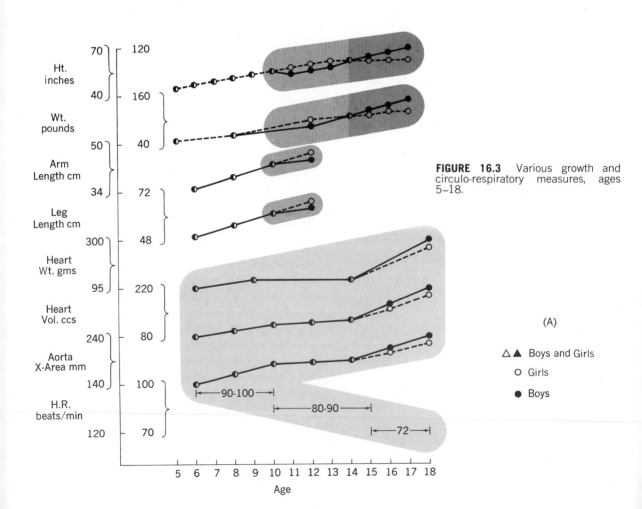

FIGURE 16.3 Various growth and circulo-respiratory measures, ages 5–18.

(A)

△▲ Boys and Girls
O Girls
● Boys

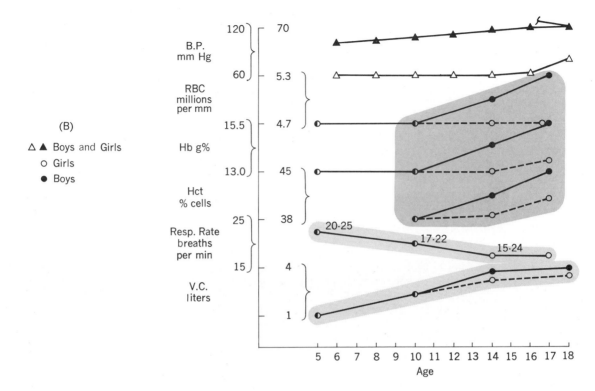

B.P.
mm Hg

RBC
millions
per mm

Hb g%

Hct
% cells

Resp. Rate
breaths
per min

V.C.
liters

120
60
15.5
13.0
25
15

70
60
5.3
4.7
45
38
4
1

20-25   17-22   15-24

5 6 7 8 9 10 11 12 13 14 15 16 17 18
Age

aid immeasurably in program and curriculum planning, in creating methods of instruction, and in understanding individuals.

Table 16.4 provides data that might help the physical educator to evaluate children in terms of normal development of motor capacities. The data from Table 16.5 provide the physical educator with some rough guidelines for average performance on certain tests of strength, muscular endurance, and CR capacity. These should, of course, be replaced by or supplemented with data collected in the teacher's particular setting. On the basis of the data presented in these two tables, it appears that girls tend to reach their maximum muscular endurance and CR capacity by age ten, their best performance in gross motor ability (at least in agility

and speed) by age ten, and their peak power performance (softball throw and standing broad jump) by age fourteen or fifteen. For boys, the comparable ages are apparently sixteen to seventeen, fifteen to sixteen, and sixteen to seventeen. It would be interesting to know whether this difference between boys and girls is physiologically, psychologically, or culturally based.

A final word of caution: in presenting the data and characteristics in these figures and tables, we are not promoting the concept of the importance of "normality" and of being "average." These figures and characteristics should be viewed as an aid to understanding children at a given age *in general* for purposes of program planning, but, even more importantly, these characteristics and norms should be viewed as *an aid to understanding the individual child so that he can be treated as an individual and helped as much as possible to grow and develop within his own range of "normality" and within his own capacities.*

EFFERENT CONCEPTS

GROWTH

With respect to physical growth, an excellent and concise summary has been prepared by Professor G. Lawrence Rarick:

In respect to the lasting effects of exercise on growing organisms, controlled experimentation in which animals have been exercised throughout a lifetime has shown that only limited differences in general body size occur between the exercised animals and the unexercised controls. Studies of exercised animals show a lower percentage of body fat, a correspondingly greater weight of the musculature, and a positive effect on certain of the internal organs. With discontinuation of exercise during the growing years, the gains achieved tend to be partially retained for the remainder of the growth cycle. In general the data on animals indicate that some increase in mineralization of bone occurs as a result of exercise during the period of growth, but the increase seems to be in the direction of greater bone diameter with little effect upon bone length.

The limited data available on exercise and human growth tend, by and large, to parallel the findings on animals. The evidence suggests that a childhood devoted to heavy muscular activity tends to ac-

centuate lateral growth, i.e., increase in breadth and girth measures, with little noticeable effect on height. On the other hand, long bone growth in those segments which do not support the body weight appears to be positively influenced by extended periods of use. Experience has shown that children who lead an active and vigorous childhood have firmer, stronger, and more supple muscles, with sturdier physiques and less adipose tissue than children who follow a more sedentary existence. From the evidence now available it appears that exercise promotes the nitrogen retention and protein-building powers of the body, thus contributing to the effective use of the nutrients supplied to the cells.

The critical question as to the amount and intensity of activity which is needed for optimal growth cannot be answered conclusively at this time. Present knowledge indicates that a given exercise program will not have the same effect on all children and may vary from one developmental period to another.[1]

DEVELOPMENT

The effects of physical education experiences and physical activity per se on perception and on personality are discussed in Chapter 14 and effects on social development are covered in Chapter 15. With respect to sensory

---

[1]From G. L. Rarick, "Exercise and Growth," in W. R. Johnson (ed.), *Science and Medicine of Exercise and Sports.* New York: Harper & Row, Publishers, 1960, pp. 440–441. Reprinted by permission.

development, there is no evidence that regular physical activity during childhood has any appreciable effect on the senses.

It is quite obvious that physical activity has an effect on motor development. For example, a child who participates in a given skill or activity will almost certainly be superior in that skill to a child who has never attempted that skill, and there is a tendency for very active children who try to participate in many physical activities to be more advanced in general motor development than children who are physically very inactive. There is some evidence that "early learning" (that is, learning as soon as possible for a given concept or skill) is superior to later learning (see Chapter 5). But here there is a serious lack of knowledge that hampers us considerably. What is the "ideal" age or general developmental level at which a given motor skill can best be learned? In other words, when is a given person ready to learn a given skill? Is there a danger in attempting to learn a skill too early, so that negative learning will result? When, for example, does the average youngster best learn the skills involved in tennis or badminton or basketball? From a very practical standpoint, what do we do when a number of students have reached a given readiness level in either an academic class (like health education) or activity class and others have not? The answers are not available, but you should be aware of these questions and should be alert in your professional reading for answers or partial answers. A great deal of good

research is needed to answer such questions. In the interim, you can at least be aware that there is such a thing as *learning readiness* and that individual differences in learning readiness do exist. You should be sensitive to this awareness and should be inquiring enough to seek further knowledge about readiness level in the various learning experiences you set up as part of your program. Keep in mind that a given skill, activity, or concept may be more quickly and better learned at a time later than the time at which *you*, for some personal reason or for convenience, would like to introduce it.

SUMMARY

Knowledge of the facts and concepts of growth and development is essential to the *professional* in physical education, health education, and recreation.

Growth, maturation, and learning (as defined) are essential aspects of optimal development.

The four basic types of growth and development are physical growth, motor development, sensory and perceptual development, and personality and social development.

Data and characteristics that identify and describe various growth and developmental levels can be used to plan curricula and programs and to better understand and work with individuals.

There are a great many gaps in knowledge about growth and development that urgently need filling.

The importance of individuality has intentionally been stressed; there is no more important concept to be derived from this chapter.

PRINCIPLES
General principles

1. There is a wide range of individual growth and developmental differences which are well within the limits of normality.
2. Capacities and limitations can change rapidly during the developmental years.
3. Growth and development are affected by genetic factors, nutrition, hormones, environment, and activities.

Sample of specific principles

1. Girls generally begin and complete their growth spurt earlier than boys.
2. Children's capacity for exercise increases as they grow and develop.
3. Development of adult perceptual capacities is not complete until about age twelve to fifteen, and there is considerable developmental variability in perception.
4. *On the average,* boys are superior to girls in motor skills beginning at about age seven or eight.
5. Rapid growth changes are often accompanied by equally rapid changes in personality and social development.
6. Physical activity is an important contributor to optimal growth and development.

EXPERIMENTS AND EXPERIENCES

1. Design and carry out a study to investigate the apparent motor skill superiority of boys beginning at age seven. Is this a physiological or sociological phenomenon?
2. Study children's attitudes about differences in body size and propose a specific plan whereby you could improve their understanding of individual differences in growth.
3. Survey parents' attitudes about the value of exercise in growth and development.
4. Survey children's and parents' knowledge of the factors determining growth rate and final body height and weight.
5. Select any developmental characteristic which can be objectively and reliably measured and establish a developmental curve according to sex and age. You will have to use a cross-sectional design (a given random sample from each grade for each sex). Balance is a possibility, and it could also be related to the measurement of center of gravity.

SUGGESTED READINGS

Beach, F. A. and J. Jaynes, "Effects of Early Experience upon the Behavior of Animals," *Psychological Bulletin,* 51:239, 1954.

Espenschade, A. S., "The Contributions of Physical Activity to Growth," *Research Quarterly,* 31:2 (Part II), 351, 1960.

Espenschade, A. S., "Motor Development," *Science and Medicine of Exercise and Sports.* New York: Harper & Row, Publishers, 1960.

King, J. A., "Parameters Relevant to Determining the Effects of Early Experience upon Adult Behavior of Animals," *Psychological Bulletin,* 55:46, 1958.

The following references are highly recommended: Breckenridge and Vincent (69); Rarick (466); Watson and Lawrey (598).

Concepts Underlying
Special Programs

Chapter 17

Although this chapter is directed toward the school physical education program and its potential for working with handicapped children, health education and recreation cannot afford to remain aloof from the concepts and principles involved. The health educator should be intimately involved as he teaches about handicapping disorders and diseases and as he aids in referral of students to physicians for special examinations. He can also work hand-in-hand with the physical educator in solving problems concerning handicapped students. Contacting health agencies, communicating with physicians and parents, and helping to arrange for special programs and equipment are some of the ways in which he can contribute.

The recreation leader must recognize the importance of providing the opportunity for handicapped persons to continue, after graduation, what may have been initiated in the school or college special programs. Therefore, his attention to this topic is most essential.

ATYPICAL CONDITIONS AND
PHYSICAL ACTIVITY

One of the great problems that has always plagued people in education is that of how to provide programs that will satisfy the requirements of all children. For obvious practical reasons, most curricula are designed for the "average" student; and because almost no individual is really "average," our

One-Legged Youngster Plays Basketball, Football

KALAMAZOO, Mich. (AP)—Donald Webster filled out a physical education class form at Milwood Junior High School last fall. A space marked "list all handicaps" was left blank.

His teacher, Carl Burress, noticed what he thought was an oversight and handed the form back to Donald. The husky 13-year-old penciled in "broken leg."

Burress didn't say anything. He just watched the boy pick up his crutches and move off. Donald's right leg was amputated just below the hip five years ago.

Donald plays touch football, soccer and baseball with the aid of his crutches. He plays basketball without them.

A Top Scorer

Burress says Donald was one of the leading scorers in Milwood Intramural Basketball League this winter, played tenacious defense and rebounded with the rest of the boys.

Donald hops up and down the court, dribbling, passing and shooting with dexterity.

"Don has a good chance of making our eighth grade team next year," said Burress.

He said Don gets no special consideration on the court because defenders have to work hard to stop him. His best shot is a one-handed set, lofted with the left hand. But he can dribble with either hand.

In touch football, he plays end and does the punting. He moves out for passes with his crutches, discards them to catch the ball and hops up the field on one leg.

The crutches are needed more when Don punts. He steadies himself with his crutches and booms left-footed punts down the field.

Don, still growing, has had four artificial legs fitted, but his parents, Mr. and Mrs. Donald Webster Sr., said he seldom uses them.

"He hardly ever wears the artificial leg," says Mrs. Webster. "The only time he's worn his present one was to a dance at the school several weeks ago."

Living With Tragedy

Donald broke his right leg when he slipped and fell on the ice on Jan. 12, 1961. Subsequent tests revealed the youngster had osteogenic sarcoma of the femur, a bone cancer doctors said would eventually prove fatal if the leg was not amputated.

Basketball coach Carl Burress watches Donald Webster practice his shooting at Milwood Junior High School gym in Kalamazoo, Mich. At right, Donald works on dribbling.

Despite loss of right leg to a bone disease, Donald is a leading scorer on basketball team, also plays soccer and touch football. (AP)

Figure 17.1 News story dramatizes the need to provide challenging opportunities for handicapped individuals. Copyright AP; photos, Wide World Photos.

curricula fall short of meeting the needs of many students—particularly those at the extreme ends of the school population distribution.

Certain aspects of the school curriculum have received a great deal of attention in recent years, as experts have attempted to develop programs of instruction that would more specifically apply to students of varying ability. The use of reading materials of differing levels of difficulty for a given grade is commonplace. For students who have special problems, classes with specially trained teachers are often provided. Other programs for slow learners, retarded children, and especially intelligent or talented youngsters are also provided in many modern schools.

The problems of physical education and health education are no different from other subjects in terms of the need to provide students with experiences and information that will satisfactorily meet their particular needs. In some respects, however, physical education differs from other areas in the curriculum in the degree to which the needs of atypical students are met. Whereas many subject-matter areas do an adequate job with the average group, frequently an excellent job with the low-capacity groups, and almost nothing with the youngsters of special talent, physical education is almost the opposite.

In our profession, the best job is done with a small group of highly gifted students on varsity teams. The expenditures involved in programs serving these students are enormous. The programs designed to serve the majority of students (falling in the "average" category) range from moderately good to poor. What is done in terms of special education for the students on the low end of the scale? Almost nothing!

Of course, the fact that students have certain handicaps means that traditional programs and activities must be modified if they are to be of any real value. The extent to which modifications are necessary is directly dependent upon the type and degree of disability possessed by the students involved.

Probably the chief reason for lack of modified physical education programs is that they cost extra money. Although there may be some necessity for equipment expenditures, most of the added cost is related to personnel requirements. Properly trained teachers are not really more expensive to hire than others, but the fact that an additional person above basic requirements is usually needed compounds the problem. The class size is usually smaller when special physical education is made available to students because of the limited number of students having disabilities and because of the problems of scheduling students with compatible difficulties at convenient times.

When we speak of "modified" physical education programs, we really mean any one of several different kinds of specialized activity programs designed especially for atypical students.

Adapted physical education is a term used to describe programs in which games and other activities are changed (either slightly or drastically) so that

FIGURE 17.2 Young paraplegics are frequently capable of participation in extremely vigorous activity if opportunities are made available. Photo courtesy of Rehabilitation Education Services, University of Illinois.

handicapped students are able to participate. Wheelchair basketball, baseball with auxillary runners, and archery from a seated position are only a few of the less imaginative kinds of adaptation that can be made. (Figure 17.2)

Whereas the aims of adapted physical education may not include any goal of actual *improvement* of the handicap, *corrective physical education* has the amelioration of the defect as its primary aim. For this reason, although modified games and sports may be included in the program, there is usually some emphasis on specific exercises such as calisthenics, weight training, or even instruction in relaxation techniques. This type of program is also refered to as *remedial physical education.*

Developmental physical education, as its name implies, is similar to corrective physical education in that it seeks to make an improvement of the disability of the student. These disabilities are frequently related to a lack of adequate levels of physical fitness and/or motor ability regardless of the cause (inactivity, illness, operation, obesity, lack of experience). The techniques used usually are similar to those employed in corrective physical education, with emphasis on total physical improvement rather than on the correction of a specific defect.

Special physical education is a term that has been used to include all of the programs just mentioned plus some others (such as those designed for the intellectually gifted) either within or outside the school environment.

Of course, some schools have attempted to have handicapped students incorporated into regular classes with activities especially adapted to their limitations. For some handicaps this approach is entirely satisfactory and has the added advantage of making the atypical youngster feel less "different." On the other hand, when dealing with relatively severe handicaps, such an approach is impossible, and when it is attempted, the youngsters involved usually find themselves assigned to routine chores such as score-keeping, handing out towels, and similar functions. Some value may be derived from this kind of activity, but it is certainly far below the value that physical education can hold for handicapped students.

One of the greatest ironies observable in our profession today is that where the greatest rewards are to be found, there are the fewest people working. Physical educators who are accustomed to teaching and coaching in traditional circumstances know that overt, sincere expressions of gratitude from students or parents are extremely rare. On the other hand, anyone who has ever taught a paralyzed child to swim across a pool or who has helped a blind student to master a difficult gymnastics routine has also seen the tears of joy and excitement in a parent's eyes and has felt the student's handclasp of gratitude.

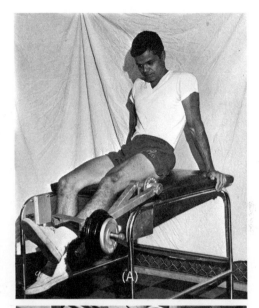

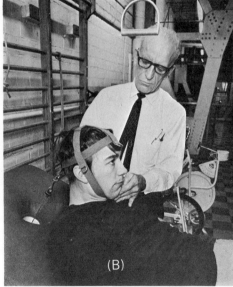

FIGURE 17.3 Corrective physical education. (A) Special devices like this unit are valuable in providing carefully controlled exercise routines for knee rehabilitation following surgery or injury. (B) More elaborate equipment is available for treatment of a wide variety of problems requiring exercise.

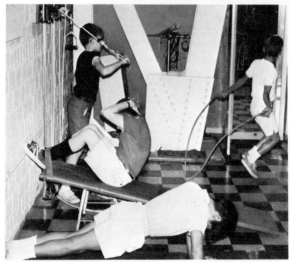

FIGURE 17.4 Developmental programs concentrate on improvement of general body function and condition. Systematic programs are utilized to insure adequate attention to all underdeveloped muscle groups.

It is of utmost importance to recognize at this point that the real reasons for absence of special programs for handicapped students in public schools are not the extra equipment required or the additional expense. The real problem is a lack of ability of teachers to communicate comfortably with handicapped students. Even interested, dedicated teachers often find themselves uneasy and unsure of themselves when confronted with the necessity of working for the first time with a severely handicapped child. Until you have been closely involved with such situations personally, it is almost impossible to see atypical youngsters simply as persons and only secondarily to notice the brace, or the limp, or the wheelchair. On the other hand, the inexperienced teacher cannot help being conscious of the handicap first and, as a consequence, cannot react easily and naturally to the person involved.

Most of us have known handicapped people who seemed especially courageous and determined in the face of their difficulties. Occasionally you might also meet such a person who is unpleasant, selfish, and bitter. What is it that makes the difference? One important thing is the attitude of the people around these handicapped persons. Parents and friends who are able to encourage the handicapped to be as independent as possible and who firmly refuse to allow the youngsters to indulge in self-pity, contribute greatly to the development of dignity and self-respect that any person, handicapped or otherwise, needs.

Technical training in how to modify and present games, exercises, and other activities can be given to anyone. There is no way to insure that this know-how will be utilized, however. If a prospective teacher is uncertain and ill-at-ease in the presence of a handicapped child, or if he feels sorry for the child, it is almost a certainty that he will be unable to establish a normal pupil-teacher relationship. It is for reasons based on this problem that atypical youngsters in the public schools are almost always excused from physical education classes, sometimes even when they would much prefer not to be excused.

It has become clear that it is absolutely essential for every prospective physical education teacher to be intimately associated with at least one severely handicapped person. This is the only way that he will actually become able to view handicapped people simply as people. In no other way can he come to see a youngster hobbling down the hallway as a *person* who has fitness and skill problems and therefore ought to be in physical education class. With such an outlook, the brace being worn, or the paralysis, or the lack of sight, become merely technical problems to be dealt with, and do not appear as emotion-tinged obstacles preventing effective interaction with youngsters.

FIGURE 17.5 Effective teachers have learned to see handicapped youngsters as individual children—the handicap is noted only secondarily. Photo courtesy of Toledo Society for Crippled Children.

There are many excellent sources from which information can be obtained about how to work with handicapped students (139, 299, 467). Despite the validity of such advice, most of us are hesitant to act on information that is secondhand. Following are some statements from individuals who themselves have various handicaps. They represent different levels of disability and have differing opinions about the kinds of activities they believe to be important. But you will see that each of them has similar overall attitudes and viewpoints.

Judy S. is a 21-year-old college sophomore who sustained an injury resulting in quadriplegia while still in high school. This statement was made after completion of two semesters of physical education at the college level.

First encounters with a disabled student may be stressful experiences for everybody concerned. However, they need not be frustrating, nor should the teacher feel unduly apprehensive. Basically, the best procedure is to approach such a situation directly. Openly discuss the student's physical limitations, evaluate the potential therein, and together establish realistic and attainable goals. Avoiding the confrontation hinders both teacher and student by permitting each to escape from the reality of the situation.

The medical term which describes my physical condition is quadriplegia. In my case, paralysis was sustained as a result of an injury. In essence, I have "minimal" muscular function up to, but not including the wrist and fingers. However, with the aid of adaptive devices I am able to perform functional activities.

In my opinion, there is no valid reason why *anyone,* regardless of impairment, should be entirely exempt from physical education or health requirements. Each person is unique in terms of his physiological, psychological, and sociological composition. The disabled student is no different from anyone else in that he too, must be objectively viewed in totality.

Obviously, specific considerations, course requirements, and adaptations will depend on the individual's personal needs. Ultimately, however, the disabled student's psychological and sociological attitudes, needs, and values are comparable to those of the physically normal student.

Disabled people resist participation in physical education because they lack confidence in themselves and their impeded ability. Generally, this insecure or inadequate attitude is representative of the *newly* disabled.

The opportunity to engage in self-adapting physical education and health courses motivates the disabled student and promotes a greater degree of self interest. In addition, these experiences can result in the development of a rewarding rapport between the student and the teacher.

It is important to understand that after sustaining a paralysis, the individual undergoes a period of adjustment. Duration of this period varies with each person. However, a favorable prognosis (in terms of good physiological, psychological, and social adjustments) is dependent upon his psychological stability before paralysis occurred, as well as upon the attitudes of people around him, including family, friends, and associates in general.

This adjustment period is much like the developmental and formative years of childhood. The disabled person must redevelop not only attitudes, beliefs, and morals, but also an entirely new self concept. The self concept, however, will invariably be sharply modified and difficult, if not impossible, for some to accept. Consequently, the individual may display a marked reluctance to engage in activities where he feels alienated from the physically normal student.

Sensitive instructors can be instrumental in motivating and counseling the disabled student and modifying the curriculum to comply with each individual's specific impediments.

It is, however, not sufficient for the disabled student merely to recognize and accept his physical limitations. It is imperative for him to become better acquainted with the physiological, psychological, and sociological components of total health and fitness. Considerable importance must be attached to the development of *personal* fitness. Individual limitations should be determined and evaluated, but de-emphasized. Instead, emphasis should be placed upon areas where potential is feasible, especially in intellectual pursuits and physical activities within the disabled student's capabilities.

Essentially, it is the educator's responsibility to encourage and motivate the disabled student to become actively involved in physical education and health.

Because states provide special educational facilities for blind youngsters, it is only rarely that a blind student is enrolled in the public primary or secondary schools. Beyond the high school level, however, the blind student must generally pursue his education in the regular educational institutions.

John F. is a college sophomore who entered college after attending a state school for the blind.

As our highly developed culture progresses, machines are doing more of our work all the time. Consequently, the need for some type of physical education program is increasing. Most high schools are making efforts to meet this demand. Ironically, however, blind students (people who sometimes need physical activity more than others) are not permitted to attend physical education classes in far too many of these high schools. Because blind people are often less active than others, our co-ordination is sometimes awkward, and our need for physical activity is acute.

Why then, are blind people not required to take physical education classes? Perhaps the most significant reason is that administrators and instructors are unaware of our capabilities. Although playing baseball is impractical because of the obvious need for vision, one need not see to do any of the ordinary calisthenics or even to run track if he follows someone. Only those activities which relate directly to one's ability to see, watching an airborne baseball for example, should not be expected of one who is blind. Above all, instructors and administrators should never feel sorry for a person simply because he cannot see. A good workout will hurt him no more than it does the other members of the class. His doctor should be consulted, however, in case some types of activity could harm his eyes. If there are no such complications, he should be expected to attend classes and to participate in as many activities as possible. He will benefit not only physically, but mentally and socially as well.

Some blind students are quite apathetic because their friends help them too much. Because exceptions have always been made for them, they expect to be exempted from vigorous physical activities as well. Fortunately, about 50% of Ohio's blind students attend a state school for the blind where instructors, being aware of their capabilities, make very few exceptions for them. The other 50%, however, are in the public schools where they are given few opportunities to even attend physical education classes. Their legitimate needs can be met only if physical education programs are opened to them. Expect as much from them as from their classmates, and treat them not as helpless people, but as *individuals* who just happen to be blind!

Ken C. entered the university while still recuperating from an automobile accident. Although other injuries had healed, he was still forced to breathe through a tube that was inserted into the trachea at the base of the throat (tracheotomy).

Just because a person has a tracheotomy doesn't mean he is special. He should take some physical education (although I would not suggest track, football or, of course, swimming).

Even though I have to breathe completely through the tube I am luckier than many people since I can still talk reasonably well. The biggest problem I have is shortness of breath. I don't know whether this is caused by my tube or lack of exercise. . . .

The idea of being in an "adapted" physical education class didn't appeal to me; I wasn't interested in riding an exercise bicycle or working with the rowing machine. I found that learning to play badminton was not only fun and good exercise, but it gave me a chance to *compete*.

I appreciate being able to compete in a game without needing to have the rules changed for my benefit. I would like to play games like basketball but I just can't run as much as I used to.

As far as making adjustments is concerned, I find that most people are pretty reasonable. Once in a while when someone says something stupid like "Why do you have to wear that dog collar all the time?" I do get irritated, though.

Of course some have more trouble with these tubes than I do and this should be taken into consideration by these instructors. However, I think a teacher should come forward and push those with a tube to activity. It is easy for a person to become

lazy and hide behind his tube and say he is handicapped.

In his book *Adapted Physical Education*, Arthur S. Daniels reports on a case study that clearly reflects the inadequacy of physical education programs in our public schools. He reports the case of a young male polio paraplegic, J. O.:

"They tell me I have to see you about physical education."

"Good. Won't you have a seat?" John got himself arranged in a chair.

"I want to be excused from physical education."

"Why?"

"I can't do anything, can't you see my braces?"

"Can you swim?"

"I just told you I can't do anything."

"Would you like to learn to swim?"

John reflected a little, then "Do you think you can teach me?"

"With those big arms and shoulders, it will be easy."

John reported to the pool the first day, disrobed, but wearing his braces and using his crutches. He apparently didn't mind. Besides, there were several artificial legs and various kinds of leg braces standing against the wall—they belonged to some of the men already in the pool. He sat down, removed his braces and crawled into the pool. He asked the instructor to hold him steady until he controlled his balance. "This is the first time in my life I have ever been in the water, except in the bathtub," he said.

John learned to swim and later he took a course in archery. He knew his way around the physical education department now and he had some friends. One day he asked his adviser, "Why is it I never had a chance to learn anything like this in high school? Why did I have to wait all these years to find out I could do some things like everybody else? Why did I always have to go to study hall when the other kids went out to play?" The adviser just shook his head. He couldn't give John a single reason why it had been necessary for him to take the psychological and social beating all through the elementary and secondary school years. There wasn't any.

While the possessors of certain types of handicaps can speak with eloquence for themselves, there are others who cannot. However, it is obvious that the mentally retarded child or the child who cannot speak or write also has needs and desires, even though he may not be able to verbalize them. Perhaps it should not be surprising that in recent years more attention has been given to the development of programs for children suffering from these disabilities than for others. In any case, special schools (as well as camps and other facilities) have been established for children with serious physical or mental disabilities. And although academic and "daily needs" types of activities have predominated, the value of organized physical education has steadily gained recognition. Many schools specializing in the education and training of handicapped students employ physical educators.

In such camps and schools the types of activities that are utilized are designed to meet at least two specific objectives. First, the general fitness needs of these students are stressed. Such youngsters are generally extremely sedentary if left to their own devices, and such behavior sets up a cycle leading to progressively less

activity on the part of the child. The second objective often stressed is that of developmental experiences. Because many handicapped children have been deprived of the wide range of experiences enjoyed by normal children, they have failed to develop the neuromuscular and perceptual acuteness that we all need. Special activities are frequently employed to provide experiences that may have been missed by the youngsters involved.

Some of the claims that have been made for some kinds of programs have been strongly criticized. Others have been well documented by scientific experimentation. Programs of various types will be discussed subsequently.

MENTAL RETARDATION AND OTHER LEARNING PROBLEMS

AFFERENT CONCEPTS

Although some attention was being given to the special needs of mentally retarded children by the public schools as early as 1900, it was really not until the mid 1950s that government figures began using their influence to impress the public with the necessity for special programs for mentally retarded individuals in our society. Much of the credit for this interest must be given to the family of the late president John Kennedy. The diligent efforts of Eunice Kennedy Shriver, sister of the President, and the establishment of the Joseph P. Kennedy Foundation were major factors in the development of progressive programs for aid to the mentally re-

FIGURE 17.6 Sheltered workshops provide retarded persons with an opportunity to achieve some economic self-sufficiency and an increased sense of worth and dignity. Photo courtesy Lucas County (Mich.) Association for Retarded Children.

tarded in both public and private sectors.

Among changes that have occurred in dealing with the problem of retardation has been the change in terminology and classification systems used. Formerly, individuals having IQ scores below 20 were termed *idiots*. *Imbecile* included persons between 20 and 50 in IQ, and *moron* included those having scores between 50 and 70. The newer terminology describes retardation as being *profound, severe, moderate,* or *mild*. As a means of functional classification, the terms *totally dependent, trainable,* or *educable* are used.

Persons who are considered totally dependent are unable to communicate effectively with others and can never be

expected to care adequately even for their own personal needs. They are unable to profit from any training designed to make them useful in an economic sense, and they will never become able to participate in any social activities.

Those who are classified as trainable have some capacity for profiting from training for some social adjustment, self-care, and economic usefulness of a limited nature. In addition to being able to care for some of their own personal needs, they are able to learn to handle simple tasks around the home or in a situation such as is often available in a "sheltered workshop." In such workshops, mentally retarded people are employed in closely supervised, simple (but nonetheless productive) tasks for which they are paid modest wages. Such programs have been developed in order to give retarded people as much independence and dignity as possible.

The educable person is one whose mental development is approximately one half to three fourths as fast as that of the normal child. Such a child would find the regular school curriculum beyond his capacity but could profit from a program that would eventually include simple number concepts and some reading. Self-support in adulthood is possible, although difficulty in communication places definite limitations on potential in this area.

There is another type of learning difficulty that is sometimes mistaken for mental retardation but that is actually not due to a limitation in intellectual capacity. In such cases a youngster may have a normal or even above-average IQ but still have extreme difficulty in reading and other skills. Because every child is a unique individual, there are doubtless many different conditions that could result in similar symptoms.

Excluding what might be generally called the psychiatric or emotionally based problems, we are left with children who seem to have difficulty in perceiving relationships between things in the actual world, which produces difficulty in relating their own bodies to their surroundings. Such problems might arise because of difficulties in sensory pathways (including the sense of body position in space, called *kinesthesis*) or it may be due to failure of the motor pathways to perform the in-

tended acts in the proper manner. Such flaws as these are generally grouped under the heading of *perceptual-motor dysfunction*.

Special tests and training programs have been developed for individuals with perceptual problems (135, 150, 195, 305, 527, 554). Few of these programs have been adequately tested, and there is considerable controversy about their effectiveness (190). Because of inadequate controls, even when improvement has been demonstrated, it has been impossible to determine exactly which element or elements of the program have been responsible.

EFFERENT CONCEPTS

Effects of Physical Activity Programs

It has been recognized by clinicians for some time that physical activity can produce desirable changes in mentally retarded individuals. The benefits claimed usually fall into three general categories:

1. *Improved physiological function.* This includes improved physical fitness and vigor, coordination and motor ability, and posture and body weight. Most of the scientifically documented positive effects have been in this category.

2. *Improved intellectual function.* This is usually not interpreted as an increase in actual intellectual capacity but, rather, as an improved ability to utilize inherent capabilities to a fuller extent. Several studies have indicated that those who are exposed to experiences involving some physical activity also

appear to improve in their ability to perform on intellectual tasks (see Chapter 14). Although the actual reasons for such improvement are not well understood, it is apparent that the additional stimulation to the central nervous system of the body has a beneficial effect.
3. *Improved social-emotional function.* Although there is not a great deal of scientific evidence to support this asertion, it is widely held that moderately vigorous programs of play and recreation can do much to help the retarded person learn how to relate to other people more acceptably. Theoretically, there are several ways in which this might be accomplished. Through such participation he may be led to feel less different. He may learn to feel less threatened by loud noises or sudden

movements of others about him. Some retarded youngsters may develop greater courage, an improved sense of worth and self-respect. By whatever means and to whatever degree such objectives are attained, their pursuit is extremely worthwhile.

Programs for the Mentally Retarded

Because of the extensive range of disability associated with retardation, it is obvious that the types of programs utilized will be dictated by the capacities and needs of the individuals involved. For this reason it is important to be able to accurately diagnose the degree of impairment suffered by individuals. In recent years several test batteries have been developed for the

FIGURE 17.7   Swimming is one of the important vigorous activities that many retarded persons can learn to enjoy. Photo courtesy Lucas County (Mich.) Association for Retarded Children.

assessment of perceptual-motor dysfunction, but few of them have had time to be adequately evaluated, and none has, as yet, proven to be universally satisfactory.

A considerable amount of specialized training is necessary for the proper administration of any diagnostic instrument or technique. Many systems of treatment involve evaluation procedures that are unique to one particular system of treatment. For this reason we will point out only two or three general approaches and will not deal specifically with evaluation techniques except where treatment and evaluation techniques are similar or identical to one another.

THE DOMAN-DELACATO SYSTEM (148) One of the most widely known "systems" for the treatment of retarded youngsters as well as others possessing perceptual-motor problems (reading difficulty being one of the most widely recognized) is that developed by the founders of the Institutes for Human Potential at Chestnut Hill, Philadelphia, Pennsylvania. Inspired by the ideas of neurologist Temple Fay, Glenn and Robert Doman (physical therapist and M.D., respectively) together with Carl Delacato (Ed. D.) constructed a theory of treatment based upon the hypothesis that most treatments commonly employed were really directed at the peripheral symptoms rather than the real causes of perceptual-motor difficulty. In their view, much, if not all, of this type of problem is really due to brain damage of varying degrees of severity. Their contention is that the

site of such damage needs to be ascertained as early as possible and that the functions of these areas need to be stimulated as rigorously as possible in order to enable undamaged cells to perform these essential functions. Much of their theory is dependent upon the hypothesis that the nervous system is extremely "plastic" and capable of adapting itself to a number of different kinds of functions under appropriate conditions.

The Doman-Delacato system places great deal of emphasis upon the necessity for development of strong dominance within the nervous system. Thus, they maintain (in oversimplified terms) that a child should not be permitted to be right-eyed, left-handed, and right-footed. Rather, he should be oriented either entirely all to the right or all to the left. Ambidexterity, in young children, is not permitted; the child is "forced" to make a choice.

Another concept that is important in this system is that of parallel between the **phylogenetic** and **ontogenetic** development of each individual. The incorporation of the primitive reflexes into the behavior patterns of the child is deemed to be of considerable importance, and out of such considerations certain "patterning" exercises are employed. It is presumed, in this theory, that each developmental stage of the organism is dependent upon preceding stages. Thus, if the child is permitted to walk without the previous experience of creeping and crawling, vital stages in his neurological development will be omitted. For this reason, children exhibiting certain problems are required to crawl in certain prescribed patterns for specified periods each day.

Another technique used (for more severely afflicted youngsters) involves passive "patterning" of limbs and head. In this procedure all four limbs and head are moved through a specific creeping sequence by therapists or parents. The duration of such exercises may reach several hours each day (in combination with other treatments), requiring a great deal of time and expense (this is one point that has received a great deal of criticism). Through constant repetition of such passive movements it is theorized that sufficient neurological stimulation can be elicited in the affected areas to gradually enable these cells to function more normally.

Although a great deal of criticism (17) has been leveled at the Doman-Delacato system, very little of it has been directed at the underlying theories. This is not to say that the neurological basis for these procedures has been clearly spelled out; it has not been. Most critics have been concerned with the heavy responsibilities placed on parents for the eight hours of patterning each day and the possible effects this may have on other children in the family or on the parents themselves in terms of guilt feelings if their efforts do not seem to be productive. Other critics have pointed out the lack of experimental evidence in support of the system. Of course, this criticism could be leveled at virtually every other method used in the treatment of children with perceptual-motor problems.

Because of the nature of the disabilities being treated, it is difficult for either the proponents or the opponents of the system to remain objective. Parents whose children have improved tend, understandably, to become disciples. Others who have little first-hand knowledge of the system are offended by sensational articles published in the popular press by professional journalists. Intemperate claims made in such articles are sometimes presumed to be approved by the operators of the Institute, although this may not be the case at all.

Emotional reactions on both sides of the issue have tended to cause reputable individuals to avoid involvement with the problem simply because it is controversial. Although this is not unusual in medically related matters, it is unfortunate because it only delays the solution of the problem as to whether the system has any real merit. It is doubly unfortunate from the viewpoint of the physical educator and the health educator because of the obvious implications that such a system would have (if it were found to be at least as effective as traditional methods) for those working with retarded and minimally brain damaged children in schools and other institutions.

THE KEPHART PROGRAM In 1960 Dr. Newell Kephart, of Purdue University, published a book called *The Slow Learner in the Classroom* (305). His concern was not primarily with youngsters of low native intelligence, but, rather, with those who apparently had difficulty in learning despite adequate

IQ's. As was true with Doman and Delacato, Kephart's ideas were not all new by any means, but his approach was imbued with enough freshness and promise to attract the attention of a great many people, particularly those interested in reading problems.

Kephart placed a great emphasis on the necessity of development within the individual of an adequate awareness of the difference between right and left (laterality). This ability to discriminate meant much more than the simple ability to distinguish the right hand from the left, but was a directional conceptualization basic to the interrelationship of the individual and his environment. If there is no difference between the directions of left and right, then it should make no difference whether a sentence or word is read from right to left or left to right. Because many poor readers do have this tendency of reversing words or phrases, it was hypothesized that they may have inadequate laterality. The same people would then be expected to have difficulty in distinguishing between certain letters such as a *b* and a *d*, because both are simply "circles attached to the bottom of a stick." If a child really had no concept of the difference between left and right, he would actually perceive these two letters as being the same. It can be seen how confused a child might become when teachers insisted that the figure must be sometimes called one name and sometimes another.

As a means of developing laterality, Kephart favored the acquisition of strong dominance. Activities neces- sitating the use of one hand or one side of the body were emphasized.

Another interesting aspect of Kephart's program was the integration of time concepts with concepts pertaining to space. Activities emphasizing appropriate sequences and time judgment were stressed. And because most of the children that Kephart was interested in were in the normal school situation, many of the activities advocated came directly from the repertoire of the physical educator.

Kephart's system involves the manipulation of body parts in space under a variety of conditions designed to force the child to make adjustments that will involve integration of the sensory and motor systems. Two devices strongly advocated for use are the balance beam and the trampoline. Graded routines on both of these appliances have been designed to challenge the youngster to continually changing gravitational circumstances. Similar emphasis is given to work in the water, where the effects of gravity are substantially altered.

The kicking and bouncing of balls, hopscotch-like games, and calisthenics involving coordinated movement of arms and legs in unusual patterns are all prominent in Kephart's program. In addition to these types of activities, pencil-and-paper tasks, chalk-board drills, eye-tracking exercises, and other procedures are utilized in the development of the desired abilities.

Although there has been a great deal of interest in programs of the type just described, there has been very little experimental evidence of its effective-

FIGURE 17.8 Systematic training in simple movements requiring balance adjustments and certain patterns of coordination has become popular. Programs are designed to assist slow learners, poor readers, and others.

ness (see Chapter 14). Although some studies have been conducted and some favorable results have been reported, one of the great difficulties is that reading difficulties may result from any one of a great number of possible causes. Although it may well be true that some children lack the dominance and laterality required for appropriate spatial conceptualization, there are undoubtedly other children whose difficulties lie in entirely different areas. For this reason it is extremely important that diagnostic tests be developed that will

aid in determining when a youngster possesses these deficiencies. Until such time as adequate diagnostic tests are available, it is doubtful that significant experimental results can be expected when treatments are applied to heterogeneous groups of poor readers, regardless of the cause of their difficulty. Of course, this does not mean that programs of this nature should not be used as a means of helping youngsters who do have such difficulty. And it is possible, although not yet demonstrated, that the thoughtful incorporation of some of these activites into the early elementary physical education programs may be instrumental in the prevention of some reading problems.

TRADITIONAL SYSTEMS Although the foregoing systems have been widely used recently in working with retarded children, more traditional programs of physical education have also been strongly advocated (540). It has been demonstrated repeatedly, particularly with retarded children, that proficiency on certain fitness and motor ability measures is related to intellectual and academic attainment (see Chapter 14). It is obvious that such correlations are by no means perfect and that, in individual cases, there may even be strong negative relationships.

In dealing specifically with retarded children, however, it is now commonly accepted that the stimulation of physical activity (so often absent when retarded children are left to their own devices), in conjunction with other experiences, can be extremely helpful in aiding such people to become more capable human beings.

The kinds of programs found to be specifically helpful are usually those involving only the simplest rules (514). Moderate self-testing activities such as obstacle courses (159, 352) and tumbling stunts have been found useful. With some retardates, simple relays or dual contests may have some appeal. Swimming has been found to be extremely popular (200) with many youngsters, in both camp situations and schools. Because the degree of retardation can vary so greatly, the kinds of appropriate activities and exercises are almost infinite.

Although it is impossible to point out exactly what aspects of physical activity are particularly important in the improvement of the retarded person's ability to function in society, there are a number of factors that are of obvious importance. The purely physical changes, such as increased muscular strength and endurance, improved cardio-respiratory function, and decreased body fat, can all be important. How much the attainment of such qualities contributes to improved ability to interact with others is impossible to determine, but the social benefits, whether related to physical changes or not, are certainly of utmost importance.

There can be little doubt that physical activity programs, whether of a traditional, general nature or of a highly specialized type, have great potential in the education and training of retarded children and adults. It is imperative that the fundamental concepts underlying the use of these methods be made clear to those who are in (or will be in) positions to utilize them.

HEART DISTURBANCES

AFFERENT CONCEPTS

As we have discussed elsewhere in this book, heart disease is the greatest single cause of death in the United States today. It should be recognized, however, that there are a great many different kinds of heart disease, and only certain kinds are likely to be encountered in youngsters who are in school.

Degenerative Heart Disease

The much discussed "heart attack" is an event resulting from years of degeneration of the cardio-vascular system. The suspected causes of this degeneration are reviewed in detail in Chapter 8. The heart disorders suffered by young people are very rarely of this type.

Congenital Heart Disease

Abnormalities in the structure of the heart and/or blood vessels occur with great enough frequency for most of us to be aware of them. There are currently at least thirty-five different kinds of inborn defects of the heart. Fortunately, only a fraction of 1 percent of all babies are born with defective hearts, and with advanced surgical techniques many of these can now be corrected or vastly improved.

Infectious Heart Disease

The type of heart disese most likely to be encountered among school-age children is that resulting from rheumatic fever. Up to two thirds of all childhood heart disease is of this type. Although the exact cause of this disease has not yet been discovered, it is clear that the streptococcal infection that may lead to rheumatic fever causes antibodies to be formed in the victim. Apparently, these antibodies attack not only the strep organism but also the tissues of the heart valves and leave them scarred and unable to function properly (191). Inability of these valves to open fully is called *stenosis*. The blood must be forced through a small opening, creating the necessity for the heart to work unusually hard. When the valves are damaged in a manner to prevent their proper closure, a process called *regurgitation* results. In such instances the blood simply flows back into the heart after having been pumped out.

The development of artificial heart valves and improvements in surgical techniques have made it possible for many victims of rheumatic fever to resume normal lives. While it will always be necessary for such patients to exercise caution, the restrictions will be minimal in comparison with those formerly imposed.

EFFERENT CONCEPTS

Physical Activity Programs

In general the physical educator will be dealing with two different types of activity programs with regard to the cardiac patient. For those whose cardio-vascular system can be improved by judicious exercise, he must design and administer physician-approved programs involving progression in large muscle activity. On the other hand, the activities proposed for nonremediable cases must stress quiet activities of a recreational or diversional nature. It should be remembered that even

NEUROLOGICAL AND ORTHOPEDIC PROBLEMS

AFFERENT CONCEPTS

When we speak of neurological handicaps we are usually referring to some condition in which portions of the central nervous system are damaged. A spastic paralysis resulting from cerebral palsy would be an extreme example of this kind of difficulty. Orthopedic handicaps are generally thought of as being more peripherally located, such as would be true in the case of an amputation or a club foot. There is, however, an area where considerable overlap may exist. Paralysis resulting from poliomyelitis is usually classified as an orthopedic difficulty, even though it is obviously a result of a lesion or break in the nervous system.

Braces, supports, wheel-chairs, and other devices to stabilize and assist the persons involved are usually identified with orthopedic handicaps. It should be clear, however, that although many neurological conditions require bracing or support of some kind, not all conditions requiring such devices are of a neurological origin.

Cerebral Palsy (CP)

Damage to the brain from trauma, infection, or lack of oxygen (as well as from other causes, either before birth or at any time thereafter) can result in a type of difficulty called cerebral palsy. This disease can take several forms, and each can range from mild to severe. In some cases only one part of the body

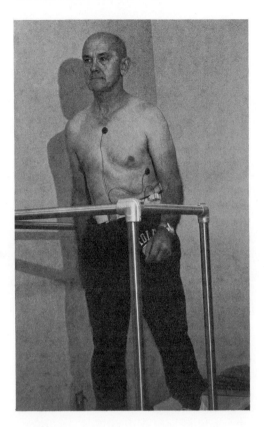

FIGURE 17.9 The treadmill and electronic monitoring of the electrocardiogram provide techniques of carefully controlling exercise in cardiac rehabilitation.

though vigorous or strenuous activity involving the whole body may need to be avoided, it is often possible to maintain desirable levels of strength and muscular endurance by mildly overloading separate body parts separately. If appropriate rest is provided for and care is taken not to overload the heart it is possible for exercise to be of both physical and psychological benefit. Of course *any* program must have the approval of the student's physician.

may be affected, whereas in other cases the affliction may be considerbly more extensive. The term *monoplegia* refers to involvement of only one limb, whereas *diplegia* usually indicates involvement of both legs, the arms being affected to a slight degree only. *Paraplegia* means the involvement of both legs only; *hemiplegia* refers to involvement of the limbs on one side of the body. When all four extremities are afflicted the term *quadriplegia* is used.

The most commonly occurring type of cerebral palsy is that producing *spasticity* of the limbs involved. Here the muscles are tightly contracted, and movement is difficult and jerky. The characteristic scissors gait results from tension in the antigravity muscles of the legs. Of all the types of CP, the most commonly observed is that of spastic hemiplegia.

Athetosis is a form of cerebral palsy in which there is uncontrollable, excessive movement of a body part. Desired movements must be superimposed upon the unwanted movement.

A third type of palsy is called *ataxia*. In this type of disability the individual has a poor sense of equilibrium and kinesthesis. He may have difficulty in estimating distances when reaching for an object or stepping up or down. In more severe cases, walking without support may be impossible.

A fourth general classification of cerebral palsy is *rigidity*. Both the antagonistic and the agonistic muscles of a given joint have a tendency to contract simultaneously, so that no

movement whatever can occur. Sometimes, however, movement in one part of the body will stimulate involuntary movement in another part.

A condition called *tremor* is the fifth type of cerebral palsy. As the term suggests, uncontrollable trembling of the involved limbs is the predominant characteristic.

In addition to the neuromuscular involvement of sections of the body, a high percentage of persons afflicted with cerebral palsy also have other problems such as deafness, blindness, or some degree of mental retardation. It should not be inferred, however, that persons exhibiting the most severe neuromuscular symptoms are necessarily retarded. One of the great tragedies of this desease is that intelligence may be unaffected although means of communication and expression may be seriously hampered. It is not surprising that under these conditions of literal "imprisonment," extreme frustrations and adjustment difficulties are often encountered.

Epilepsy

A second neurological disability likely to be encountered in school-age children is that consisting of several types of epilepsy. Because of widespread misunderstanding of the nature of the disease over the years, epileptics, until relatively recently, were commonly witheld from society in general and school in particular. The social stigma attached to the disease has actually caused greater distress to epileptic individuals than have the physical symptoms. Although the exact cause is unknown, great progress in the treatment of epilepsy has been made in recent years (420).

The most severe form of the disease (*grand mal*) is characterized by sudden and sometimes violent convulsive seizures. The seizures may last for several minutes, during which the person undergoes synchronous, convulsive movements of the body; bladder and bowel control are lost, and biting injuries to the tongue and cheeks, as well as other injuries to thrashing limbs, may occur if preventive measures are not taken. A deep sleep, sometimes lasting three or four hours, follows the seizure, from which the person awakes with no memory of the event.

A second form of the disease known as *petit mal* results in less severe types of behavior. Unconsciousness of short duration accompanied by staring or rolling of the eyes or muscular twitching is characteristic. Although conscious mental activity is suspended during these brief episodes, the interruption of activity may be so slight as to go unnoticed by both patient and his associates. It is possible for this type of seizure to recur several times (even a hundred or more in extreme cases) in a given day.

Other types of seizures causing bizarre behavior or emotional outbursts (of which the person has no recollection) rather than convulsions are called *psychomotor seizures.* Other types of symptoms related to epilepsy also exist but will not be discussed here.

One of the chief factors making it possible for the epileptic to assume a more normal role in society has been the discovery of drugs that will control and often completely eliminate seizures. This, together with better education of the lay public concerning the nature of the disease, has created a much more favorable atmosphere for the social integration of people afflicted with epilepsy.

Muscular Distrophy and Multiple Sclerosis

Neurological conditions such as *muscular dystrophy* and *multiple sclerosis* are not commonly seen in the public schools but do frequently occur in the population. A degeneration of the insulating sheath (myelin) of the nerve cells causes difficulty in both sensory and motor function in *multiple sclerosis.* Usually this disease strikes people only after the teen-age years, so that few would be encountered in high schools, and virtually none among youngsters of elementary school age. Although the disease is generally a progressive one (becoming gradually more severe), people contracting the disease have approximately the same life expectancy as those of the general population.

Individuals afflicted with *muscular dystrophy* are not so fortunate. This, too, is a progressive disease, but it strikes much earlier, and certain forms of the disease are frequently fatal within five to ten years from the time of onset. There are several types of the disease, but all result in the loss of muscular function of legs, arms, and/or shoulder girdle. In some forms, the atrophy of muscles is not apparent because of the development of fat deposits within and around the weakened musculature.

Although bracing and wheel chairs can prolong mobility for a time, victims of this disease eventually become rapidly weaker until they are no longer able to be out of bed. It should be emphasized that some types of muscular dystrophy are not as severe as other types, and frequent remissions of considerable duration are relatively common. Some patients may have a virtually normal life expectancy.

Poliomyelitis

Since the advent of the Salk polio vaccine, the incidence of polio in the United States has dropped markedly (see Figure 17.10). Unfortunately, not all children are receiving one of the

currently available vaccines, despite the fact that the protection provided is almost 100 percent assured. For this reason, there is still an occasional postpolio case encountered in the school system.

The paralysis produced by polio is the flaccid type in which the limb is limp and in which extreme atrophy occurs. Sensory function is usually not lost in the affected limbs in the most common type of polio. Braces are often effective in restoring locomotive function in the polio victim.

Bone and Joint Abnormalities

Although there is a whole host of bone and joint diseases, few of them will be listed. Most such disorders require avoidance of weight-bearing and trauma.

Perthe's hip (Legg-Calvé-Perthe's disease) is an example of this type of condition. The epiphyseal (growth) line

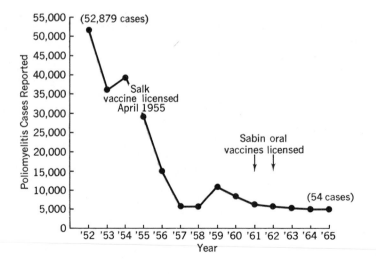

FIGURE 17.10 Introduction of polio vaccines has resulted in a dramatic drop in the incidence of poliomyelitis. Source: U.S. Public Health Service, Department of Health, Education and Welfare.

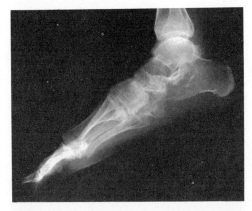 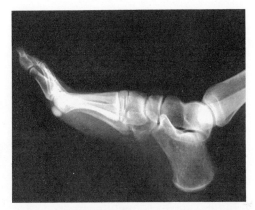

FIGURE 17.11 Arthritis is not a disease reserved exclusively for old people. Compare the foot of a fifteen-year-old boy who is suffering from an arthritic disease (left), with a normal foot. Notice how the joint spaces have begun to disappear as the bones actually have begun to fuse together.

of the femur at the hip joint tends to degenerate and disintegrate. With rest (no bearing of weight) the condition generally reverses itself within two years. Similar conditions occur at other epiphyses and are identified by the names of physicians who first recognized and described the characteristic symptoms. Osgood-Schlatter's disease affects the knee joint (tibial tubercle), and Scheuermann's disease is seen in the vertebral column. Actually, the overall term given to all of these specific diseases is *osteochondrosis.*

Osteomyelitis, a bacteria-caused inflammation of the bone, is another disease commonly occurring among children of elementary school age. Drug treatment is effective in its control, but the disease may become chronic, and flare-ups may occur throughout the lifetime of the individual. Mickey Mantle, of the New York Yankees, is reported to suffer from this disease.

Public misunderstanding of the nature of this problem led to some controversy over the fact that such an apparently healthy physical specimen should not be eligible for military service.

To some people, it comes as a surprise to learn that *arthritis* is not a disease limited to elderly people. Actually, arthritis strikes thousands of people in all age categories, including children. The causes of this disease are still not known, and a cure has not yet been discovered. Treatments of various kinds have been designed to relieve painful, crippling symptoms and, in many instances, to reduce the severity of the disease. The pain, heat, and swelling of the joints lead to ultimate restriction of mobility and physical deformity of the involved body segments. Where pain is severe, strength of surrounding musculature suffers from disuse atrophy, and ankylosis (rigid fixation) of joints may occur.

Foot Defects

It has been estimated that most people, at some time in their lives, suffer from some sort of foot difficulty. Unreasonably designed footwear has been given much of the blame for many types of foot discomfort, as have other products of civilization such as concrete sidewalks and unyielding floors.

In addition to weak feet and feet distorted by shoes with high heels and pointed toes, congenital defects are also common. The most serious of these are frequently correctable through surgery; others may be improved by exercise and corrective footwear or other types of bracing. Plantar warts (caused by a virus), calluses, corns, bunions,

blisters, athlete's foot, and other difficulties are commonplace. All of these conditions are correctable and generally preventable with reasonable care.

Amputations

Although a very small percentage of school children undergo amputation of a limb, their number is sufficient to warrant mention. Such youngsters frequently have few, if any, limitations on their activity except those directly imposed by the absence of the limb. Cardiovascular and muscular capacities and needs remain high, and the major bar to participation in a wide variety of activities is usually the fear of appearing to be "different."

FIGURE 17.12   The desire to excel in athletics has overcome handicaps as serious as limb amputations in some cases. Pete Gray became famous as a one-armed outfielder for the old St. Louis Browns during the 1940s. Photograph courtesy of the *Toledo Blade*.

Postural Deviations

Many different kinds of disabilities contribute directly or indirectly to unsightly and restrictive postural deviations. Neuromuscular diseases in which some muscles are paralyzed permit stronger muscles to pull the body out of normal alignment. Abnormal tension in muscles (as observed in spasticity) has similar effects. Apart from these considerations, however, are some deviations that are not in any way connected with specific illnesses or diseases. Poor fitness levels or faulty habits of walking, sitting, or standing may sometimes be responsible for serious postural deviations.

The most common postural deviations (lordosis, kyphosis, scoliosis) are described in Chapter 9. Others, such as winged scapulae, forward head, elevated shoulder, and elevated hip, are examples of postural conditions that can often be detected and improved by a competent physical educator.

Low Back Pain

In Chapter 9 we discussed the prevalence of low back pain and the fact that much of this kind of discomfort is directly due to insufficient strength of abdominal musculature. Children of school age are not so susceptible to this difficulty as are their parents, but the basis for this type of difficulty is laid during the early school years. Adequate attention to the strength of abdominal muscles, postural habits, and appropriate means of maintaining these attributes will pay big dividends in later years.

EFFERENT CONCEPTS

Effects of Physical Activity

Physical activity programs for youngsters suffering from neurological and orthopedic conditions are effective in several ways.

1. Stretching of tight muscles and strengthening of weak muscles
2. Improving and maintaining strength and endurance of musculature not related to disability
3. Improving and maintaining of circulo-respiratory capacity in afflicted individuals
4. Maintaining and/or restoring joint mobility in affected limbs
5. Aiding in the maintenance of body weight through expenditure of energy involved in exercise
6. Providing for rest and relaxation through special techniques not ordinarily employed
7. Providing facilities and supervision for implementation of corrective exercises

It must be remembered that the school program in adapted and corrective physical education is not a substitute for physical therapy or other professional medical treatment, nor is it expected that the physical educator will become a therapist. It is designed to complement such programs and to add another dimension to the lives of the students involved.

ABDOMINAL EXERCISES AND LOW BACK PAIN To many people the discussion of abdominal exercises as a therapeutic measure for low back pain seems pointless. They have reasoned, rather logically, that back pain must result from weakness of the back muscles. The fact is, that although certain back injuries do occur which involve strain or other damage to back muscles, much of the widespread back pain in the United States today can be traced to flabby, sagging *abdominal* muscles.

Lordosis, for example, is an exaggerated curvature of the lumbar area that may result in inefficient weight-bearing on the spine, together with muscular imbalance and a predisposition to back pain and injury. As shown in Figure 17.13, the abdominal muscles are connected on their upper ends to the lower ribs and at their lower attachments to the front of the pelvis. If, when these muscles shorten, the rib cage is held up firmly, the front of the pelvis rotates downward and under,

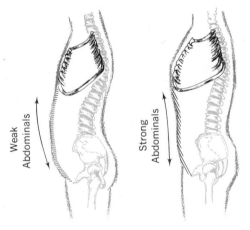

Weak Abdominals

Strong Abdominals

FIGURE 17.13 Attachments of the abdominal muscles. It should be noted that the abdominal muscles do not attach to the legs but to the pelvis and the ribs. Sit-ups and leg lifts are only "indirectly" effective in strengthening abdominal muscles.

causing the lumbar area to become flattened out somewhat. It is with the aim of reducing lordosis that abdominal strengthening is stressed by physical educators and orthopedic specialists.

Ironically, certain exercises often recommended for reducing lordosis by strengthening the abdominal muscles can actually contribute to the aggravation of lumbar curvature. Reference is made here specifically to leg-lifts and sit-ups in which care is not taken to keep the low-back flat.

It should be carefully noted once again that abdominal muscles are not connected to the legs. The muscles therefore directly responsible for lifting the legs off the floor as shown in Figure 17.13 are the hip flexors (the iliopsoas and the rectus femoris, primarily). The rectus femoris and iliacus portion of the iliopsoas both attach to the pelvis. The psoas portion of the iliopsoas attaches to the lumbar vertebrae of the spine. Therefore, when the legs are raised from the floor in the back-lying position, the contraction of the hip flexors tends to tip the front of the pelvis forward and downward, and to pull the lumbar spine forward! The only muscles in a position to stabilize the pelvis and prevent this undesirable tilting action are the abdominals. If the abdominals are relatively strong they may be reasonably successful in stabilizing the pelvis, although most people would certainly not be able to hold the back to the floor throughout the movement. If, on the other hand, the abdominals are weak, the pelvis may not be stabilized at all and the strong hip flexors, by excessive tilting of the pelvis, may actually *accentuate* the condition the exercises are designed to correct!

In an effort to reduce this problem it has been widely recommended that leg-lifts be eliminated as an abdominal exercise. Instead, many authorities have advocated the use of the "bent-knee" sit-up. With the knees flexed and the feet flat on the floor the hip flexors are already partially contracted, and it is reasoned that these muscles will not now be in as strong a position to cause undesirable tension on the low back. It is obvious that such a procedure does make it easier to keep the back from arching during the sit-up. It should be recognized, however, that it by no means eliminates the action of the hip flexors. If such were the case, it would be impossible to come to a sitting position at all.

If care is taken to flex the knees strongly and to keep the lumbar area in contact with the floor throughout the exercise by "curling up" a vertebra at a time, minimum difficulty should be encountered and maximal benefit for the abdominals should be drived.

After one has had a chance to evaluate his own condition as a result of performing the suggested test items, he should have a sounder basis on which to make a decision as to whether or not his strength, endurance, and flexibility are sufficient to ensure avoidance of the low back syndrome.

EXAMPLES OF ACTIVITY PROGRAMS The exercise programs for students having neurological or orthopedic disorders are usually of two types. The first in-

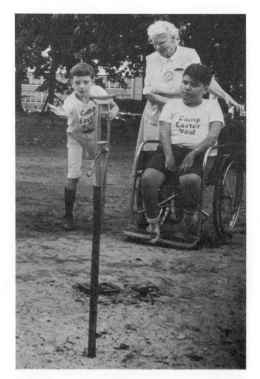

FIGURE 17.14 Competition in activities requiring physical skill can be very important to handicapped youngsters. Photo courtesy of Toledo Society for Crippled Children.

volves modified games and sports, altered in ways that permit participation of the handicapped student. Such activities may be individual sports such as archery, golf, or swimming, or they may be dual or team games. Examples of the latter range from horseshoes and table tennis through basketball and even football. For students whose disability does not make them especially vulnerable to further trauma, participation in extremely vigorous activities requiring high degrees of skill is not only possible but also desirable. Other students may need to restrict their particpation to inactive games, but they can still benefit from the socialization in such activities.

The second kind of activity program is built around more formal kinds of exercise such as calisthenics and weight training and other kinds of resistive exercise. Included in such programs would be running, rope skipping, walking, and cycling, as well as other activities designed to benefit the cardiovascular system. Such activities have the advantage of ease in regulating the amount of exertion involved. In addition to maintaining desirable progression, it is simple to evaluate progress by keeping records of the number of repetitions the student can perform or the amount of weight he can lift.

Circuit training. Although useful in working with many kinds of handicaps, circuit training has been found especially useful as a means of combining controlled amounts of exercise with the motivational variable of competition. In circuit training (see Chapter 21) a series of stations is set up at which specified exercises are to be performed. A given station may involve a particular calisthenic exercise, a specific weight-lifting routine, or even some type of gymnastic activity. The total number of repetitions is specified, and the time required to complete the circuit is recorded. Running between stations can be an integral part of the system or can be eliminated by appropriate grouping of the stations. As students progress, the difficulty of the exercises can be increased as desired. The keeping of accurate records serves as an excellent motivational device,

whether used to compare performances of different individuals or simply used as a self-competetive device.

OTHER COMMON DISORDERS

Following are several specific disabilities commonly observed among students in the public schools. Although the list is by no means exhaustive, it is suggestive of the kinds of conditions a competent physical educator should know how to deal with effectively by the time he enters the teaching profession. Some possible effects of exercise on each condition are also noted, along with certain suggested techniques.

ALLERGIES

Although allergic conditions may sometimes prevent participation of individuals in certain kinds of activities in the normal physical education curriculum, they are usually not thought of as causing enough difficulty to require a special program of activity. On the other hand, dust from mats or athletic fields may trigger allergic reactions in some people and make participation in regular programs most impractical.

Although the hay fever type of allergic reaction (swelling and watering of eyes, nasal congestion) may sometimes be an adequate reason for modifying curricula for certain individuals, other more severe reactions *demand* that modification be made.

Bronchial asthma is an allergic condition that can cause extreme distress. In addition to pollens, dust, and other irritants, an asthmatic attack can sometimes be triggered by physical overexertion or emotional upset. Because of difficulties encountered in breathing, the asthmatic tends to avoid physical activity. As fitness levels diminish, tolerance to exercise also becomes less, so a vicious cycle develops. Because of this, and other factors, carefully monitored exercise is frequently prescribed for even relatively severe cases of asthma.

The types of exercise usually recommended for asthma sufferers center around muscular endurance and strength exercises. Running is generally minimized, or at least kept well within the comfort limitations of the student. Activities in which social interchange and growth are possible are highly desirable, although those in which great excitement is commonly aroused may need to be avoided.

Among the few studies of the effects of exercise on asthmatic conditions is that of Itkin (267). From his work with adolescent asthmatics in physical activity programs, he concluded that "physical conditioning of asthmatic subjects is practical in many cases and can lead to physically more useful lives." As a result of this kind of work a number of programs have been developed in various communities in an effort to give youngsters the healthful physical and social benefits that can result from such activity.

ANEMIA

If the blood has too few red cells or too little hemoglobin, the condition is called anemia (see Chapter 8). Typical symptoms are fatigue, lack of energy, shortness of breath, and a general "washed-out" feeling. Because the body is already unable to handle its oxygen delivery requirements, exercise is generally contraindicated during treatment. After the acute stages, however, graduated exercise can be beneficial to the manufacture of new cells and the return of the individual to optimal fitness levels.

DIABETES

Diabetes mellitus is a disease characterized by the inability of the body to properly utilize carbohydrates because of failure of the pancreas to produce enough insulin. Injection or the use of an oral form of insulin enables patients to overcome this problem and to live a relatively normal life. Of course, medication must be taken regularly, and diet carefully watched.

Regular physical activity is beneficial for most diabetics provided that proper precautions are taken. Vigorous exercise may be unusually fatiguing to a diabetic and appropriate rest must be provided. With the change of metabolic demands presented by vigorous exercise, there is always the possibility of undesirable fluctuation of blood sugar levels. When proper precautions are taken, however, most diabetics can successfully participate in virtually every type of physical activity.

DYSMENORRHEA

Dysmenorrhea is defined as painful menstruation. Backache, nausea, headache, aching legs, and abdominal cramps are some of the symptoms suffered by many, if not most, girls and women at some time in their lives. Although there is some evidence (251) that the general pain threshold of women who suffer most from dysmenorrhea is low, there is nonetheless considerable other physiological justification for this discomfort (187).

Despite the fact that exercise of an appropriate nature can be beneficial in relieving much of the discomfort, or perhaps because of ignorance of this fact, girls have frequently been customarily excused from physical education during the menstrual period. Although in some cases this may be justified, it is probably more often true that some positive activity would be more beneficial than simple dismissal.

Several specific exercises have been recommended for prevention and relief of dysmenorrhea, some of which have been subjected to experimental study.

The purpose of most recommended exercises is to increase the efficiency of the circulation to the pelvic area and to relieve congestion and pressure that presumably contribute to the experienced discomfort. One of the oldest exercises is that of "abdominal pumping," known as the Mosher exercise (299). The subject rests on her back with the knees flexed. With one hand applying pressure, the abdomen is massaged from the pubic area up toward the sternum while the abdomen is retracted and the breath forcefully expired. The exercise should be repeated several times.

FIGURE 17.15 The Billig Stretch is designed to stretch the ligamentous structures of the pelvic area as an aid in the prevention of dysmenorrhea.

The *Billig stretch* (Figure 17.15) has become one of the most widely advocated exercises in the literature. Emphasis is placed upon the stretching of the hip and abdominal region under the assumption that the ligamentous bands through which the sensory nerves pass will be stretched and will produce less tension on these nerves. Standing with one side toward the wall, and about 12 inches away from it, the forearm is placed against the wall at about shoulder height. The opposite hand is placed on the hip, pressing the hips against the wall. The body position is reversed and the exercise performed on the opposite side. Eight or ten repetitions, executed slowly and firmly, are recommended.

Leib Golub reported in 1959 (214) that an exercise consisting of twisting and bending was effective in reducing dysmenorrhea in his sample of women. This exercise is initiated from a standing position with the arms extended straight out from the shoulders (Figure 17.16). The subject then twists and bends, keeping the knees straight, reaching across and around toward the heel of the opposite foot. The exercise is then repeated on the opposite side.

The second maneuver involves swinging the arms forward and upward to a reaching position overhead while one leg is extended backward vigorously. After returning to the standing position, the exercise is repeated on the opposite side. Each part of the exercise is to be performed four times on each side.

EMOTIONAL MALADJUSTMENT

Although physical activity has been utilized in mental and corrective institutions as a therapeutic measure for

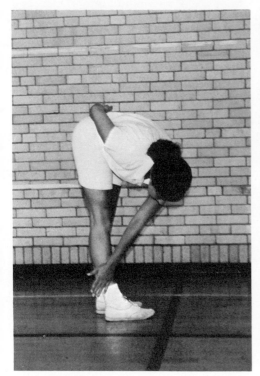 

FIGURE 17.16 Twisting and bending exercises such as this modification of the Golub exercise have been found useful in prevention of dysmenorrhea.

some time, the effectiveness of programs has not been adequately evaluated. In the school situation, where emotional instability of only relatively minor proportions is generally encountered, the effects of physical activity are even less well known. There is a logical presumption, however, that the physiological by-products of stressful situations can somehow be "worked off" by vigorous physical activity. And, certainly, aggressive tendencies can be given expression through some sports and games more readily than through classroom activities. It is extremely important to recognize, however, that *physical education classes should never be permitted to be regarded by anyone as simply a place to "blow off steam."* Although certain activities may sometimes be deliberately planned with this objective in mind, the overall purposes and goals are much broader and more educationally oriented. The gymnasium experience should provide a positive contribution to the educational process; *it should not ever be permitted to play a negative role chiefly characterized by the celebration of the absence of classroom tensions.*

NUTRITIONAL DISTURBANCES

Malnutrition has been one of man's serious problems since antiquity. While there is concern about the overall problem of feeding the world's rapidly growing population, other nutritional problems afflict even the affluent Western society. Children from underprivileged areas are still frequently the victims of inadequately balanced diets. Minimal nutritional requirements and the essential foods are discussed more fully in Chapter 10.

Overweight and obesity comprise one of the most frequently seen nutritional problems in the schools today. Because it is so difficult for youngsters who become obese ever to resume normal body weight, it is extremely important for the physical educator and health educator to assist overweight youngsters with this problem as early as possible.

All programs for weight reduction must be initiated with the approval of a physician. Of course, dietary restrictions are of paramount importance, and the development of an adequate understanding of energy balance and of the caloric values of food is an important (but often neglected) function of the school. Such information should not be confined to special classes composed of overweight students, however.

Obese students, whether in special classes or not, require assistance in designing exercise programs that will be effective in helping them to lose weight and maintain desirable body proportions. In general, activities involving as much of the body musculature as possible are desirable. This will have the dual effect of maintaining general body suppleness and tone while at the same time burning sufficient energy to make a meaningful contribution to weight reduction.

Care in the selection of activities is important. Activities in which the bearing of total body weight is required (running, jumping) may be so exhaustive for the overweight student that he will be unable to continue them for sufficient time for any real benefit to be derived. For this reason, cycling, rowing, swimming, and weight training are popular types of exercise. Running should not be avoided entirely in most cases but should be prescribed in appropriate doses.

It is desirable to utilize groups or teams whenever possible in the exercise sessions. Socialization can be extremely important in maintaining enthusiasm and in relieving boredom. On the other hand, care must be exercised that the socializing process does not replace the exercise!

Simply prescribing exercises and providing a place for their pursuit will seldom, if ever, result in satisfactory progress. The necessity for faithful, daily maintenance of the diet and exercise prescriptions for a lifetime (hopefully at modified levels) must be made clear to the obese person. Once the basic concepts of weight control are clear (as outlined in Chapter 10), the road should be less difficult for him.

The underweight individual may also find appropriate exercise programs beneficial. To some people, it seems paradoxical that exercise should be recommended for both losing and gaining weight. Once it is recognized that the quality of the exercises differs depending upon the goals sought, the logic is readily seen. As a general rule, great resistance (rather than many repetitions) is employed in an effort to gain weight. This type of overload acts as a strong stimulus to the hypertrophy of muscles, thereby increasing the bulk of the body. Additional protein intake is probably essential (see Chapter 10).

POOR PHYSICAL FITNESS

It is generally assumed that the improvement of physical fitness is one of the primary objectives for all students in physical education. Sometimes, however, the fitness levels of students are so poor that special attention to fitness is required before participation in regular classes can be beneficial.

Prescribed exercise programs, including running, weight training, calisthenics, and swimming, may be combined with games and contests of various kinds. If such programs are to be effective, a good testing system must be utilized to keep both student and teacher appraised of progress.

POST ILLNESS

Frequently students returning to school after prolonged illness or surgery are not prepared to participate in the regular physical education curriculum. Attention to general fitness levels can best be given in special classes where time for adequate testing and individual supervision is available. Where such classes are available, return to normal condition can be substantially accelerated. The specific programs utilized will depend upon the nature of the individual conditions and upon the physician's recommendations, but in most cases they will parallel closely the activities prescribed for students of low general fitness.

SENSORY DISORDERS

FIGURE 17.17   With encouragement and proper instruction and supervision, blind people can find great enjoyment in activities normally thought to require vision. Photos courtesy of the Toledo Society for the Blind.

Blind and deaf students are only infrequently encountered in schools below the college level because most states have provision for special schools to assist them in the difficult problems they face. On the other hand, students with poor vision or hearing who may not qualify for (or prefer not to attend) state schools, are quite often part of the general student population. More and more blind students are found in colleges today. This is apparently not true for deaf students, probably because of the emphasis on lectures, which are primarily designed for listeners rather than viewers.

Programs for blind students obviously must be adapted to avoid the necessity for utilizing visual cues. In many cases auditory or tactile stimuli can be substituted, resulting in satisfying kinds of activity. Buzzers attached behind targets make archery a challenging game, and guide rails used on the approach provide adequate orientation for blind students to be able to develop remarkable bowling success. Some students have developed proficiency in golf and even ball games such as soccer (in which a bell is located inside the ball).

Although the activities just listed are somewhat unusual for blind students, vigorous activities such as wrestling, swimming, weight lifting, and some types of gymnastics are very commonly enjoyed. The circulo-respiratory requirements of such students can readily be met through programs of running (guidance being provided by a rail, guide rope, or a partner), jumping rope, or similar activities. The fitness needs of blind students are frequently greater than normal (see page 507), but, given the opportunity, their eagerness to participate is unsurpassed.

Activity programs for deaf students are actually quite simple to prescribe. If the student is able to read lips, problems in communication are greatly simplified. But in any case, with a little care any competent instructor can make his explanations clear, and students need little, if any, modification of general activity programs.

Of course, there are sometimes complicating factors with deaf students that must be understood and evaluated in terms of their effect on the physical education program. Sometimes balance problems are encountered because of inner-ear involvement. In these and other cases, the appropriate corrective or adaptive programs need to be worked out with the student's physician.

AGING AND THE ELDERLY

AFFERENT CONCEPTS

The discussion of modern physical education, health education, and recreation would be incomplete without mention of the somewhat special needs of the older members of our society. This problem has become more acute simply because of the sheer weight of numbers. Although the population has doubled in the last fifty years, the number of persons over sixty years of age has quadrupled. From 1920 to 1966, life expectancy increased from fifty-three to sixty-six years for males and from fifty-four to seventy-four for females, an average increase of some thirty percent.

Largely because of advances in medical science, we now have an older population—and it is hypothesized that man has the physiological potential for living at least a hundred years (542).

FIGURE 17.18   Wrestling is one of the few extremely vigorous competitive activities in which blind youngsters can compete. Photo courtesy of the Ohio State School for the Blind.

It is obvious that these years added to one's life can be a burden rather than a blessing, unless they are productive, enjoyable years. The implications, both afferent and efferent, for physical education, health education, and recreation are obvious and present a very real challenge to professionals in these fields.

Typical Changes Associated with Aging

Physiological aging occurs at different rates for different functions, but some are apparently age resistant. Although there is considerable individual variation, the four most common disorders associated with aging are cardio-vascular degeneration, cancer, arthritis, and nervous system diseases involving the cardiac, vascular, skeletal, muscle, and nervous tissues.

The period from eighteen to thirty years of age is normally the period of greatest physical and mental vitality. From this point on, strength, muscular endurance, and coordination tend to decrease, and maximum O_2 utilization and maximum ventilation also begin to decline. From age twenty to seventy-five, maximum heart rate decreases about forty beats a minute, and there is a slowing of recovery from exercise (431). There is evidence that systolic blood pressure rises higher during sub-maximal exercise and recovers more slowly (87). Sexual vigor begins to decline during middle age, although the exact age for a given individual may vary from the average considerably. This gradual loss of libido can have serious psychological effects on certain individuals and thus affects other functions as well (542).

Other changes commonly associated with aging are (542) the need for eye-glasses, often bifocals; some loss of hearing; a definite tendency to put on weight; less mental and emotional adaptability (more rigid, closed mind); menopause or climacteric (discussed further in Appendix C); slower urination in men due to some prostate gland enlargement; and failing memory. Osteoporosis, the increased brittleness of bones, is quite typical (62), and a decreased blood volume is not uncommon (370).

Out of this presentation of typical changes associated with aging, a searching question most naturally arises: Is there cause and effect? Because these changes are typical, does this mean that aging *causes* these changes? Scientists and physicians are beginning to suspect that many of these changes may be typical, but they are certainly not normal! Many agree that certain of these changes are "caused and accelerated to a large extent by senile inactivity, by lack of sufficient physical activity" (370). Bortz argues that, "clinically, persuasive evidence exists that osteoporosis in the elderly is accentuated by disuse; muscles become flabby (and minds, too) from lack of exercise; . . . " (62). The phenomenon of "retirement shock" has been oft observed, and Bortz maintains that "when a man retires out of life, life retires out of him. To keep mentally and physically fit, action and incentive are essential. Disuse and decay are close relatives."

In short, there is much logic and some evidence (see next paragraph) to suggest that all changes typically identified with aging are not inevitable, at least not as early as they are appearing.

EFFERENT CONCEPTS

Exercise and Aging

There is widespread evidence, most of it indirect, that regular physical activity can, by and large, prevent or delay the onset of certain of the degenerative processes typically associated with aging. Most of this evidence is found in the relationship between activity and coronary artery disease (review Chapter 8). There is no evidence that regular exercise provides protection against the other three major age-related disorders (cancer, arthritis, and nervous system diseases). There is little question that muscular strength and endurance and the other physiological parameters mentioned in connection with work capacity can be maintained if a reasonably active exercise program placing these demands upon the body is continued into and through the adult years. There is no evidence to support the claim that physical activity affects either positively or negatively the decline in sex drive (87).

Mateef (370) argues that Vogt and Vogt's conclusion that preservation of cerebral activity is the best protection against senile degeneration of the brain cells provides sound support for the anti-aging value of physical activity. He reasons that "physical exercises are actually intensive cerebral activity,

which unlike onesided mental activity, stimulates metabolism, respiration, blood circulation, and the activity of the endocrine glands. . . . Physical exercises therefore are the best physiological means of controlling the phenomenon of senescence." He concludes his position: " . . . the control of . . . senescence . . . should begin as early as possible, before man has completed his development. It is considerably more difficult to control the phenomena of old age when they have already set in. . . . [it is] more difficult then to postpone or retard their occurrence." His point concerning prevention is certainly well made; and logic, indirect evidence, and clinical observation (if not direct evidence) are strongly lined up behind his and others' strong belief in the physical activity prescription for prevention or delay of senescence.

IMPLICATIONS FOR PHYSICAL EDUCATION, HEALTH EDUCATION AND RECREATION Properly consummated, health education and physical education can contribute to well-being by providing a sound base for health and exercise habits. These habits can then contribute to both productivity and enjoyment throughout the aging process. Recreation can most certainly add to both productivity and enjoyment.

Health education can teach about aging so that people will come to understand the typical changes and what they as educated persons might do to postpone those that are not inevitable. Physical education, in addition to promoting the role of physical activity in postponing senescence, can, of

FIGURE 17.19   Modern retirement communities make extensive provisions for creative and recreational activities for their residents. Photographs courtesy of Crestview, Sylvania, Ohio.

course, teach the skills that can be used to provide that physical activity. Finally, recreation can provide for and stimulate appropriate exercise and relaxation experiences so that people can put into practice what they have learned about postponement of "old age." Recreation personnel must also be trained and prepared to provide special programs for older citizens, programs in which they can participate freely and regularly without embarrassment in activities appropriate to their psychological and physiological needs. The increase in the number of self-contained communities for the aged and for retirees may well provide a totally new and special field for the physical activity and recreation specialist of the future.

SUMMARY

The problem of dealing with atypical children in physical education programs has many implications for both health education and recreation. The welfare of such students depends upon cooperation of health personnel for coordination of screening tests and referral of students to appropriate agencies. Provision of adequate recreation opportunities for handicapped youngsters involves a knowledge of common disabilities together with an understanding of appropriate activities.

One of the greatest obstacles to the inclusion of more modified physical education programs is the cost of properly trained personnel and additional facilities. Ultimately, however, the underlying reason for failure to provide good physical education for handicapped students resides in the lack of ability of teachers to communicate comfortably with handicapped people. Until one has had experience in being closely involved with handicapped students, he cannot really see such people as simply *people.*

Governmental interest in mental retardation has prompted increased activity in this field in recent years. In many respects, programs designed to benefit retarded children are much more widely pursued than are programs for other handicapped children.

Consistent with the general change in public attitude toward mental retardation are changes in terminology and classification of retarded persons. The aim of integrating as many retarded people as possible into normal society has created many new opportunities for them.

Benefits claimed for physical activity among retarded individuals fall into three general categories: (1) improved physiological function; (2) improved intellectual function; (3) improved social-emotional function.

Among systems devised to help those who suffer from psycho-motor difficulties are the Doman-Delacato system and the Kephart programs, as well as more traditional kinds of activities. These systems are designed to produce specific neurological changes, whereas the activities are utilized in the hope of improving general fitness and function which, in turn, are expected to indirectly improve performance of intellectual activities. Claims for improvement of function of individuals falling into *normal* classifications have aroused considerable controversy.

Other severe disabilities commonly encountered include heart disease and neurological and orthopedic problems. In all cases, the disability affects the quantity and quality of activity possible (or desirable) for the individual, just as the quantity and quality of physical activity engaged in can affect the disability. Awareness of the limitations imposed as the principles appropriate for dealing with each problem is extremely important.

Types of activities utilized in activity programs are usually divided into two general categories: (1) modified sports or games; (2) calisthenics, weight training, and other forms of more formal exercise.

A great many common disorders are encountered in the schools that are serious enough to prevent a youngster from participating actively in the regular physical education program. Anticipation of these contingencies and adequate general preparation (particularly the development of a positive professional attitude) can enable the physical educator or recreation leader to make great contributions to the welfare of handicapped students.

PRINCIPLES

1. Probably the chief reason given for the lack of modified physical education programs is the simple fact that they cost extra money.

2. A crucial factor underlying the failure to provide adequate programs of special physical education is the lack of ability of teachers to communicate comfortably with handicapped children.

3. Even interested, dedicated teachers often find themselves uneasy and unsure of themselves when confronted for the first time with the necessity of working with a handicapped child.

4. It is absolutely essential for every prospective physical educator, health educator, and recreation leader to be intimately associated with at least one severely handicapped person.

5. Physical activity programs of various kinds can produce improvement in the ability of retarded individuals to interact with their environment.

6. The mechanisms by which retarded persons are aided through physical activity are not understood, but it is apparent that the additional stimulation of the central nervous system has a beneficial effect.

7. A considerable amount of specialized training is necessary for the proper administration of any diagnostic instrument or technique.

8. Any program prescribed for an atypical student must be approved by his physician before it is implemented.

9. The school program in adapted and corrective physical education is not a substitute for physical therapy or other professional treatment. It is designed to complement such programs and to add another dimension to the lives of the students involved.

10. Much of the back pain reported today can be traced directly to weakness of abdominal musculature.

11. Accurate record keeping is essential to the success of any special physical education program. Records serve as an excellent source of motivation for students, as well as assuring maintenance of an appropriate program.

12. Whereas it is a legitimate assumption that sports and games can provide an acceptable context for the expression of aggressive feelings, physical education classes should never be permitted to be regarded by *anyone* as simply a place to "blow off steam."

13. Simply prescribing exercises and providing a place for their pursuit will seldom, if ever, result in satisfactory progress for any student.

EXPERIMENTS AND EXPERIENCES

1. Arrange to have all students in the class blindfolded for at least one hour (and preferably longer). During this time they should learn to find their way around a gymnasium which has been prepared in advance without their observation. (Use of an *unfamiliar* room of adequate dimensions would be even better.) Students should familiarize themselves with the location of objects and dimensions of the room by feel.

Participate in activities set up for this purpose. Examples: Duck pin bowling; ball catch; basketball free throwing (place noise-maker on the basket); tumbling; relay races (with rope guides and safety barriers); rhythmic games; clay modeling.

Record and discuss your feelings and reaction to this experience.

2. Arrange to do a case study on a single handicapped youngster. Spend

at least ten hours with him over a period of no less than five weeks. Work up a medical history, family history, and other pertinent data. If possible, work with him in his therapy program (under competent direction) as well as in skills instruction. Keep a daily record of pertinent events and your reactions. Upon completion of the time, write a report of your reactions to this experience.

3. Visit a facility for the training of the blind. Observe training equipment, techniques and recreational programs. If possible, attend a training session in "mobility" (teaching blind individuals to be independent in moving about the community, on busses, and so on).

4. Visit a school, camp, or home for the mentally retarded. Observe the gradations of disability. Work with some of the youngsters in a game situation. Prepare a report on your reactions.

5. Volunteer to work with a group involved in assisting a stroke victim or a retarded youngster by means of "patterning" his limbs. Report your observations and reactions.

SUGGESTED READINGS

Activity Programs for the Mentally Retarded (reprint), AAHPER, 1201 Sixteenth Street N.W., Washington, D.C., 20036.

Baker, Louise M., *Out on a Limb*, New York: McGraw-Hill, Inc., 1946.

Barton, Betsy, *And Now To Live Again*, New York: Appleton-Century-Crofts, 1944.

Erickson, Marion J., *The Mentally Retarded Child in the Classroom*. New York: Crowell-Collier and Macmillan, Inc., 1965.

Mason, J., "What You Can Do with What You Have," *Life*, 56: 75–88, 1964.

The Concept of Stress[1]

Chapter 18

AFFERENT CONCEPTS—EFFECTS ON ACTIVITY AND WELL-BEING

In recent years a great deal of attention has been directed toward the question of how stress affects human well-being. During this period a great many aspects of the problem have been studied, from a number of different viewpoints. As a result, the term **stress** has acquired several definitions, some of which have little relation to the layman's understanding of the term.

Traditionally, stress has been described in terms of difficult or trying situations that "put pressure" on people. Feelings of uneasiness and discomfort resulting from such circumstances have commonly been called anxiety, fear, tension, restlessness, and so forth. Scientists have found it necessary to create more precise definitions of stress in order to study it. Because such definitions (called operational definitions) are arbitrary, at least two general ways of defining stress have become widely

---

[1]We wish to acknowledge the contributions of Donald C. Stolberg.

recognized. One of these views stress as being closely related to anxiety, and perhaps, producing anxiety. Anxiety, in turn is defined as "a vague, objectless fear." Other, more technical definitions would point out that anxiety is a condition of "heightened arousal" and an "energizer of other responses." Sometimes it appears as though extreme levels of anxiety are called stress, although stress is seldom defined in this way.

One of the problems that has been encountered with the use of the term **anxiety** is that it has been used to describe so many different conditions. "Manifest anxiety," "harm anxiety," "bound anxiety," "failure anxiety," and "free anxiety" are only a few of the ways in which this concept has been modified.

Although most psychologists in clinical and experimental fields do not appear to be disturbed by problems such as these, physiological psychologists and scientists in related fields have objected to the practice of using the same words to describe widely differing phenomena.

Another, more biologically oriented, view of stress has become widely recognized as a result of the work of Hans Selyé, world-famous Canadian physician and endocrinologist.

THE STRESS CONCEPT

Informally described as consisting of the "rate of all wear and tear on the body caused by life," stress, more technically, is the state manifested by a specific syndrome that consists of all the nonspecifically induced changes within a biological system. Dr. Selyé has made a sharp departure from the conventional use of the term "stress" in that he chooses to use this word to identify the body's *reaction* to trying circumstances. The stress-producing circumstances or conditions he calls "stressors." Stress may be produced either by the more direct physical stressors, such as extreme environmental temperatures, or by extreme and prolonged pain. However, we can never have anything that can be called "psychological stress" without physiological involvement. Simply stated, any situation that makes the body mobilize its resources and increase its energy expenditure may be considered a stressor.

Selyé (505) is convinced that whatever the stressors, the body reacts in a consistent manner. Patterns of adaptation are predictable and the degree of the response is determined by the type and quantity of the impinging forces and the effectiveness and efficiency of the body's internal organization. The response of the body is local and general, whatever the stressor may be. The general response, or the General Adaptation Syndrome (GAS), consists of three states: (1) the alarm reaction, (2) the resistance stage, and (3) the exhaustion stage.

The alarm reaction results in a local response to the stressor and a general response through the nervous system to the pituitary gland. The resistance stage consists of the balancing of the **"pro-inflammatory" hormones** and the **"anti-inflammatory" hormones** secreted by the adrenal cortex. These hormones are controlled by the secretions of the pituitary gland and are influenced by other hormones, nervous reactions, diet, heredity, and tissue memories of previous exposures to stressors.

The delicate balancing of these facilitating and inhibiting body forces is crucial to the health of the organism in two ways: in resisting the stressor and maintaining the internal homeostasis; and in preserving proper internal functioning. Inability of the organism to adjust to the stressor results in the third state—exhaustion—which im-

plies nonadjustment of the organism and leads to death (505, p. 3).

Stress cannot be measured or described by the external circumstances with which man must contend, but rather by his *reaction* to these circumstances. Individual differences and chance factors make it impossible to predict with reasonable accuracy the effect of a stressor by knowing its character. The effect may be a continuing one, or the stressor may be unidentifiable. In fact, one man's stress may be another man's pleasure (see Figure

FIGURE 18.1 One man's stress is another man's pleasure.

18.1). For example, the stress effect of business (buying, selling, dealing, deciding, speculating, waiting, planning, observing, meeting deadlines, and so on) in today's world is recognized; yet some face the situation and thrive whereas others face it and overrespond dangerously.

Drs. M. Friedman and H. Roseman, physicians in San Francisco, conclude that some men are born to lead stress-filled lives and others are not (426). The unfortunate group become heart-attack-prone, and are called "Type A" individuals. Those who can tolerate the situation are called "Type B" individuals. A statistical evaluation of a large group of businessmen has produced profile descriptions of the two groups. It is possible to identify a reasonably high percentage of each group through careful investigation. Friedman and Roseman suggest that deficiencies in vital hormone levels might be the differentiating factor of major importance. Such a hormone has yet to be identified, however.

Physiologist Stanley J. Sarnoff (565) pointed to the paradoxical nature of the stress concept when he stated that stress is the process of living and the process of living is the process of reacting to stress.

Mental stress today is probably no more severe than in the days of the frontiersman. In spite of the fact that life appears to be more stable today, even for the underprivileged, new stressors have replaced the old. In the past, continued day-to-day existence was uncertain for many people. Disease, war, accidents, thieves, mau-

rauders, and political and religious upheavals all contributed to people's insecurity. Today our threats come from different sources. Social mobility, advanced communication techniques, terrifying weapons of war, and "an explosion of personal expectations" have produced stressors that have seriously affected the adaptability of this generation.

TENSION

"Tension" as something that is experienced as a result of stressors is familiar to all of us. It is, perhaps, mere-

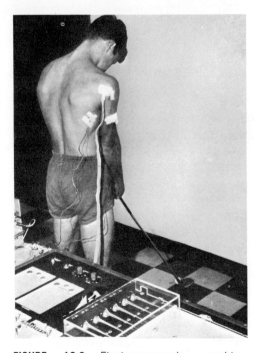

FIGURE 18.2 Electromyography provides recordings of the electrical activity of muscles. With subjects at rest it can be used to assess levels of tension in the musculature.

ly coincidental that the term we use to describe this general personal feeling or experience also describes a physiological phenomenon that is taking place in the muscles of the body.

Stressors produce emotional changes, and when profound emotion is experienced, tension or **tonus** in skeletal muscle also increases (364, 417). The condition can be likened to applying more stretch to a rubber band already in a condition of moderate stretch. This increased tension in the muscles reflects psychological states facilitating greater overt activity. The more muscle tension, the greater the degree of wakefulness; conversely, the more muscle relaxation, the greater the depth of sleep.

The mechanism of increased muscle tension resulting from profound emotion is not known. Suffice it to say that if you become frightened or angry, not only will your autonomic nervous system respond but so will the skeletal musculature. Muscle contraction is usually measured by attaching electrodes to the skin or inserting electrodes into the muscle itself. The electrodes pick up the small electrical changes or **action potentials,** which can be amplified and recorded. Recordings of action potentials from muscles have not produced any sure system of determining general muscle tension within the body on the basis of measurements of isolated muscle groups. In other words, patterns of differential relaxation are so great, even in supposedly tense individuals, that we cannot base our judgments on any one group of muscles (603, p. 371). An in-crease in skeletal muscle tension will facilitate mental activities to a certain extent, but beyond that it will interfere with efficiency. Muscle tension in itself is not of utmost importance.

STRESS-RELATED ILLNESSES

Selyé's theory of stress postulates that almost any disease can be caused by emotional tension. He points out that the function of the pituitary and adrenal hormones is to combat stress and ward off threats to body processes. He indicates that in our competitive life our glands help us adjust to stressful living by producing excess hormones. Finally, after constant exposure to stress, this defense system may break down. He cites stress as a factor involved in hardening of the arteries, in high blood pressure, and in inflammatory diseases, such as arthritis. He lays the blame for obesity on stress, especially in those persons to whom eating has become an emotional release. At the same time he also states that loss of weight is one of the most apparent consequences of chronic stress.

According to Selyé's theory, stressful activity prepares us for rest and sleep. On the other hand, emotional stress before going to bed or emotional stress that wakes a person during the night is the cause of insomnia. He suggests that in dealing with stress disorders, the diagnostic terms and conceptual framework of mechanistic medicine have outlived their usefulness, but that, as yet, no satisfactory new terms have appeared (505).

PSYCHOSOMATIC DISORDERS

One term used to describe the nature of certain stress-related disorders is *psychosomatic*. **Psychosomatic disorders** are the bodily or somatic changes that a mental or **psychic** attitude can produce. Disorders that can be psychosomatic include peptic ulcer, diarrhea, constipation, asthma, hives, hay fever, and high blood pressure. Certain forms of heart, kidney, or gall bladder disease, many skin disorders, and many disorders of sexual function are psychosomatic in origin.

Many illnesses have been recognized for some time as "nervous" or "functional" disorders (in other words, disorders for which no organic bases have been found). Chronic fatigue is a classic example of this type of disorder. Another example is general psychosomatic tension. It is characterized by general tiredness associated with inability to sleep, lessened desire to eat resulting in loss of weight, muscle tension increase, and headaches. "Nervous indigestion," insomnia, and worry are all well known (603, p. 365). Functional disturbances are unique because even the finest study of the tissues involved does not reveal any discernible **morphological** changes. The anatomical structure of the organ is not changed; only the coordination and the integrity of its functions are disturbed. Such disturbances are more readily reversible, and are considered less serious, than diseases in which the tissues show a definite morphological alteration, which frequently signifies irreversible damage (7, p. 42).

Less generally appreciated in considering functional disorders are the **psychogenic** factors. "Psychogenic" is defined as all integrated or partial activities stemming from perception, memory, learning, ideation, and thought. These activities of the body are involuntary and largely unconscious, such as the effect of worry upon facial expressions, posture, and the viscera. They affect vision and other senses, as well as glandular and other biochemical imbalances. The manner in which mental activity can influence the course of organic disease, such as tuberculosis or cancer, is, as yet, unknown, as is the psychogenic factor in some "accidents" (603, p. 365).

In almost all psychosomatic disturbances induced by life situations the disordered physiology is in the nature of **hypersecretion, hyperemia,** and **hypermotility.** Such excessive activity of organs results from the inability of the systems of the body to handle a stress situation.

Psychosomatic disorders can be treated indirectly by the use of surgery or drugs. In the case of an ulcerated stomach, portions of the stomach can be surgically removed. The pain resulting from the ulcers is therefore alleviated. The associated functional disorders may remain, as will the basic underlying emotional cause of the disorder. Drug treatments can successfully reduce the severity of the atypical situation that disturbs the patient most, and perhaps produce a momentary sense of total security. However, psychotherapy is generally necessary to resolve the recurring underlying anxieties and to allow a reasonable chance for physiological reorientation.

PSYCHOLOGICAL DISTURBANCES

Although most psychologists would not accept Selyé's, stress concept (or any other biological interpretation) as an explanation of neuroses or psychoses, they have recognized a parallel between the General Adaptation Syndrome and the symptoms associated with motivational conflicts.

The initial reaction is a heightened state of arousal which may be manifested as aggression, flight from the situation, or diffuse anxiety. None of these reactions normally change the frustrating situation. However, the organism now has an additional problem to cope with—the anxiety which results from his inability to reach his goals. People often diminish this anxiety by distorting some aspect of their thinking. Such a distortion is called a defense mechanism. *The use of defense mechanisms corresponds to the stage of resistance in the general adaptation syndrome. However, if the psychological stress situation is extremely serious, then the defense mechanisms are insufficient, a person's psychological resources are exhausted, and he becomes maladjusted (359, p. 380).*

FRUSTRATION AND MOTIVATIONAL CONFLICT

It was mentioned earlier that many forms of mental illness or psychological disturbances are actually the result of adjustments to intolerable situations. Frequently these extreme kinds of adjustment involve an attempt to escape from conflicts or frustrations.

From childhood on we are constantly confronted with obstacles of one kind or another. Many are environmental barriers, such as laws prohibiting certain actions or physical distance that separates us from some place we would like to be. Such obstacles are a source of frustration in that they tend to thwart one's desires or needs.

Another source of frustration is the inability to attain goals one sets for himself. Such frustrations may occur in connection with vocational ambitions, financial status, or social position. In each case the person is frustrated by his own inability to reach the goals he has set for himself.

Motivational conflict is another source of frustration. Whenever there is a conflict of motives within a person, he is faced with the necessity of making a choice. Sometimes the choice may be between two equally desirable alternatives, such as going to a ball game or attending a party, both of which are scheduled for the same time. On the other hand, neither of the possible alternatives may be desirable. The necessity of either paying income taxes or going to jail is an example of a conflict between negative goals. The choice of whether to go to work day after day when one dislikes his job must be weighed against the alternative of facing the loss of income.

The motivational conflicts most difficult to resolve are those in which the same goal or object both repels and attracts. One of the common illustrations of this type of situation involves sexual behavior. Strong sexual urges may be in conflict with social mores. Achievement of success and recognition, which usually involves competition, may also place us in a position of conflict. If we are successful in achieving our particular goal we may lose the friendship or companionship of those who have lost out in the pursuit of the prize.

The usual reaction to situations of conflict and frustration is to develop feelings of anxiety or aggression. Because, in our society, overt aggressive behavior is frequently punished, we may learn to become anxious about possible punishment when we even *feel* aggressive. Thus anxiety is the most notable effect of the frustration of motives or desires. Technically, anxiety is a rather vague, objectless fear; a general state of apprehension or uneasiness that occurs in many different situations and that can be acquired through learning and through generalization. Fear is distinguished from anxiety in that it is a reaction to actual things or specific situations (429, p. 101). A very strong irrational fear that apparently has no real justification is called a **phobia.**

Reactions to Frustrations and Anxiety

Each of us has experienced anxiety to some extent and has developed his own ways of attempting to reduce or eliminate anxiety. Most of us are successful in making adjustments that do not seriously interfere with our ability to function as social beings. Psychologists have used various terms to describe the adequacy of the defense

mechanisms adopted in attempting to cope with anxiety.

When anxiety levels rise in intensity and are prolonged, a **neurotic** state exists. **Neurosis** or **psychoneurosis** is a personality disorder in which a person is usually anxious, miserable, troublesome, or incapacitated in his work and in his relations with other people (429, p. 637). It represents inability to cope with frustration.

Neurosis may reflect an adjustment state in a person's life. It can result from being truly misunderstood or unappreciated. It can result from socioeconomic situations that restrict creative or intelligent development. Possibly the anxieties that stem from insecurity of youth, maturing, and the pressures exerted by the tide of social conformity and imposed goals, set the scene for a confused and neurotic teenager or young adult. Feelings of guilt, restlessness, unfulfilled desires, and general insecurity characterize the neurotic condition.

Neurotic symptoms may be reversed as the vastness of life is appreciated and a solidity resulting from physical and emotional maturity is achieved. This is not to say that all neurotics are just going through a phase, but to suggest that high levels of anxiety are not entirely abnormal and that it is possible that highly intelligent or creative people are particularly susceptible to feelings of insecurity.

Psychoneurotic behavior ranges from forms of minor **hysterias**, through **obsessions** and **compulsions,** to various types of anxiety reactions. Possession of the symptoms of imagined diseases (hypochondria) is characteristic of this condition, as are general nervousness, fatigue, and insomnia. Although these characteristics reflect an unstable personality, there is a good chance that appropriate changes in the individual's life and attitudes can result in return to normal stability.

MENTAL ILLNESS

The extent to which mental illness afflicts the population is not widely appreciated. Some estimates have indicated that at least one out of every three families has or will have some member who requires psychiatric help. The Cornell study (Figure 18.3) revealed that nearly 40 percent of the women sampled, as well as 21 percent of the men, exhibited "clear psychiatric disorders" (234). One interesting aspect of this particular study (that may have far-reaching implications) is that people holding jobs with the highest status

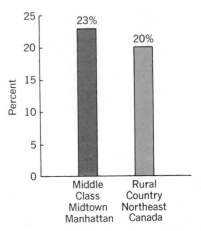

FIGURE 18.4 Percent of urban (middle-class, midtown Manhattan) and rural (rural county in Canada) populations in need of psychiatric help. The difference is insignificant. Data from *Health Bulletin* (234).

were the least susceptible, and that the more education one had, the less likely he was to develop emotional illness (Figure 18.4).

It is difficult to determine the exact percentages of the psychiatric population suffering from the various kinds of mental illness because of serious differences in diagnostic techniques and terminology. Apparently, however, the most frequently encountered disturbances are schizophrenia and personality disorders related to alcoholism and arteriosclerosis (see Figure 18.5).

The initial phases of mental illness are characterized by the escape of "dangerous, destructive impulses" leading to "outbursts, attacks, assaults, and social offenses." There is a disruption of orderly thought as well as behavior. This regression is called **psychosis**, which can be defined as a profound disturbance of behavior that

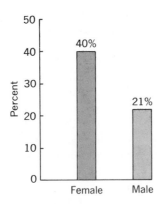

FIGURE 18.3 Percentage of males and females exhibiting clear psychiatric disorder in Cornell University study. Data from *Health Bulletin* (234).

renders an individual unable to adjust to normal life in an even passably satisfactory manner. The façade of propriety cannot be maintained. A psychosis is a psychiatric disorder which so manifests itself in an individual's behavior, thinking, or feeling that it is grossly different from others of the social group and frequently requires hospitalization for the patient's protection.

Although there is considerable difference of opinion regarding diagnostic criteria for mental illness, there are two traditional classifications of psychosis or insanity. The first is *functional*—a state in which there is no known disease of the brain. Three subclassifications are manic-depressive, paranoia, and schizophrenia. The manic-depressive state represents a fluctuating state in which the patient has extreme ups and downs in mood. In the manic state he is extremely active, engaging continuously in vigorous and often destructive pursuits. He may sing, dance, talk incessantly, run, and perhaps even throw things or attack people. At another time the same individual may be hopelessly melancholy and depressed. He may refuse to communicate or care for himself in any way. Attempted suicides are common for persons in this state.

Paranoia is a classification used to describe a person who suffers from certain delusions and hallucinations. Frequently he believes himself to be some famous person and almost always believes someone is plotting against him. Because his delusions of persecution are so strong the paranoid may become so aggressive and dangerous that it is often necessary to keep him in custody.

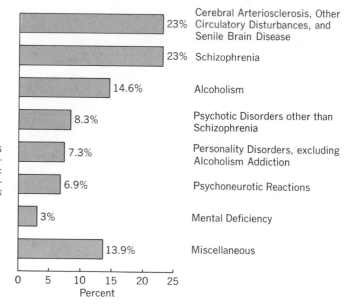

FIGURE 18.5 Percentage of patients in mental hospitals according to underlying cause, United States. Source: *Facts on the Major Killing and Crippling Diseases in the United States Today* (172).

Schizophrenia is a state in which a person cuts himself off from the outside world. Like the paranoid the schizophrenic may have delusions of grandeur and persecution, but his delusions are much less organized and permanent than those of the paranoid. In its purest form schizophrenia is characterized by withdrawal from the world. It may become so severe that the patient becomes absolutely immobile, refusing to move, speak, or care for himself in any way. The state of muscular rigidity sometimes exhibited is called **catatonia.**

The second classification is *organic* psychosis. These disorders are primarily caused by damage or disease in the brain. They can also result directly or indirectly from physical disease or physical changes in the body. General paresis (resulting from syphilis), senility, and acute alcoholism are forms of organic psychosis.

There has been considerable controversy about the designations and diagnosis of mental illness in recent years. Dr. Karl A. Menninger, cofounder of the world's most famous hospital for the mentally ill, rejects all present labels as being unjustified and harmful. He suggests that "all the names so solemnly applied to various classical forms and stages of mental illness be discarded" (566). In their place he suggests a breakdown of mental illness into five levels in ascending order of severity:

1. Nervousness, a slight but definite disturbance, a slight but definite failure in coping.
2. Increased disorganization, marked by "painful symptoms," which "some-

times pain the environment almost as much as the patient." It calls for "expensive tension-reducing devices" on the part of the patient. The devices may range from crazy-clean tidiness to untidy drinking. Such illnesses have recently been called "neurosis" and "neurotic syndromes."
3. Regression, which is characterized by the escape of "dangerous, destructive impulses" leading to "outbursts, attacks, assaults, and social offenses."
4. Disruption of orderly thought as well as behavior "these are . . . the 'lunacies' of our great-grandfathers, the 'insanities' of our grandfathers, the 'psychoses' of our fathers."
5. Abandonment of the will to live, "an extremity beyond 'psychosis' in the obsolescent sense." A penultimate step to suicide.

From Stage 3 on, almost all mental illness is likely to require some hospitalization, but whatever the severity of the illness, Dr. Menninger refuses to accept any psychotic state as being hopeless.

Coleman (113) shares Menninger's optimistic outlook. He has estimated that nearly 90 percent of the schizophrenics and an even larger percentage of the manic-depressives receiving early treatment are sufficiently improved to be discharged from mental hospitals.

COPING WITH STRESS

Psychoanalysis

When our individual attempts to cope with anxiety and stress become inadequate we have at our disposal extensive facilities and several kinds of professionally trained people to assist us. People such as psychiatrists (M.D., with a specialty in mental disease) and clinical psychologists (non-M.D. with graduate training in clinical psychology) have a number of tools at their disposal. One of these often used is that of psychoanalysis. Utilizing one of the several basic theories underlying psychotherapy, an attempt is made to help the patient identify and interpret factors (usually residing in the subconscious mind) that may be responsible for conflict and subsequent anxiety. Once the conflict is identified, it is theorized, the patient can be helped to deal with it in constructive ways.

Psychotherapy

Other therapeutic techniques used include behavioral therapy (conditioning and other reinforcement techniques) group therapy (in which patients are encouraged to communicate with each other about their problems under the guidance of a therapist), play therapy (used with children to gain insight into their frustrations), and psychodrama (acting out problems on the stage, sometimes with role reversals).

Shock Therapy

Other more drastic treatments include electroshock or insulin shock therapy. Convulsion-producing shocks are administered in an effort to reduce the depression of afflicted patients. Shock therapy is used much less today than in previous years, but why it sometimes has desirable effects is still not understood.

One of the factors most responsible for the decreased use of electroshock therapy is the advent of drug therapy. The adjustment of depressed patients by means of stimulants or the use of tranquilizers with anxious patients has dramatically reduced the hospitalization rate for certain types of illnesses and shortened stays of those who do require institutionalization.

Sedatives

Sedatives generally reduce nervous system activity, produce a state of relaxation, and generally depress the action of the vital organs of the body. Sedatives or hypnotics are basically sleep-producing drugs.

The most commonly used sedatives are barbiturates; there are at least twenty drugs in this group. Under proper medical supervision, the barbiturates serve a useful purpose. However, to use these drugs indiscriminately as an easy, quick, readily available method of reducing conscious activity of the brain is very unwise. The danger in using barbiturates lies both in long-continued use and in overdosing. A person intoxicated by barbiturates is likely to consume more of the drug than he realizes, and the result can be fatal. Barbituric acid compounds are taken in either capsule or pill form. Upon prescription, they may be purchased under a variety of names, such as Sodium Amytal, Allonal, Barbital, Phenobarbital, Seconal, Nembutal, Tuinal, and Veronal (273, p. 410).

Chloral hydrate is a synthetic drug and acts as a strong sedative. The usual therapeutic dose produces five to ten hours of sleep. Overdoses will cause longer sleep and may lead to coma and death. This drug is not widely used by the medical profession. However, criminals have been known to use it to render their victims unconscious. The drug is known more popularly as "knockout drops" or a "Mickey Finn" (273, p. 95).

Tranquilizers

Tranquilizers work by reducing the sensitivity of the nervous system, thus allowing the individual to withstand pressures that might otherwise emotionally incapacitate him. As previously noted, tranquilizers have significantly reduced the number of mental patients in this country since 1956, when their use became generally

accepted (see Figure 18.6). Anyone admitted to a mental hospital today has twice the chance of getting out that he would have had before the use of the drugs became accepted practice.

Three of the major tranquilizers in use today are chlorpromazine, reserpine, and meprobamate. Chlorpromazine (trade name, Thorazine) is useful in suppressing the delusions of paranoid patients, as it relieves deepseated anxieties of chronic mental disturbances. Reserpine (trade name, Serpasil) is similar to chlorpromazine but less rapid in initial action and the effect is more sustaining. Meprobamate (trade names, Miltown and Equanil) affects the nervous system to relieve tensions without impairing the higher thinking capacities of the individual. Miltown and Equanil can successfully relieve tensions, but also can produce a psychological dependence in the individual (273, p. 95).

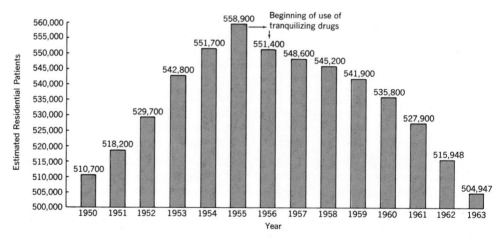

FIGURE 18.6   Estimated residential patients in mental hospitals, United States, 1950–1963. Source: *Facts on the Major Killing and Crippling Diseases in the United States Today* (172).

Research is continually producing more usable tranquilizers. Their usability is determined by the level of undesirable side effects and the degree of sedation produced. The psychological effect of tranquilizers, as in the case of any pill ingested by self-prescribing individuals, can relieve a condition of compulsion neurosis for a time, especially if the individual can easily identify with a drug type of agent. In some cases, sugar pills or placebos can accomplish the same results.

PLACEBO EFFECTS

One of the most interesting aspects of the pharmacological aspects of medicine is that of the "placebo effect." A placebo is a biologically inert substance that is sometimes given to patients under the pretense that it has true medical properties. Most physicians have, at one time or another, prescribed sugar pills or capsules containing distilled water or syrup (restrictions have recently been placed upon this practice by the U.S. Food and Drug Administration) (174). Under certain circumstances it has been conclusively demonstrated that such procedures can be effective in producing remission of symptoms.

The placebo effect of painkillers like morphine has been studied in order to determine their actual worth as analgesics. Melzak (383) has reported that about 50 percent of the painkilling effect of morphine was due to this effect. In other words, pain would be reduced half as effectively by the administration of *any* substance under

those exact circumstances. Because of this phenomenon, any tests of new medicine or a new treatment of illness must be compared with a "control" situation (in which a treatment known to be noneffective is given) if a valid analysis of its effectiveness is to be determined. This sometimes poses some extremely difficult problems in terms of ethics and philosophy ("Who gets the *real* cancer-curing experimental drug and who doesn't?")

The placebo effect has other names in other situations. In 1941 the National Research Council reported a now-famous investigation conducted at the Hawthorne Plant of the Western Electric Company (120). One of the problems studied was the effect on work output of altering illumination. Tests over several months revealed that output increased steadily regardless of the treatment. It became evident that the very fact that some special procedure was being applied to them was sufficient stimulus for the workers. The implication is that in any experimental situation an experimental variable of any type may affect motivation or arouse the interest of subjects sufficiently to have an affect on the performance of the individuals involved.

Many experimental studies in physical education and health education have suffered from deficiencies in design in terms of possible Hawthorne effects. Even when control groups are employed, it is possible for improvements to be observed that are really due to differences in the amount of *attention* paid to the experimental group rather than any effect of training or practice. This is particularly likely to be true if eager volunteers for an experiment are assigned to a group to be tested once at the beginning and again at the end of a long period of time, while others of their acquaintance get solicitous daily attention from an authority figure. Some studies have avoided this problem by providing equal attention to control subjects or by administration of placebos (described as "pep pills") at regular intervals.

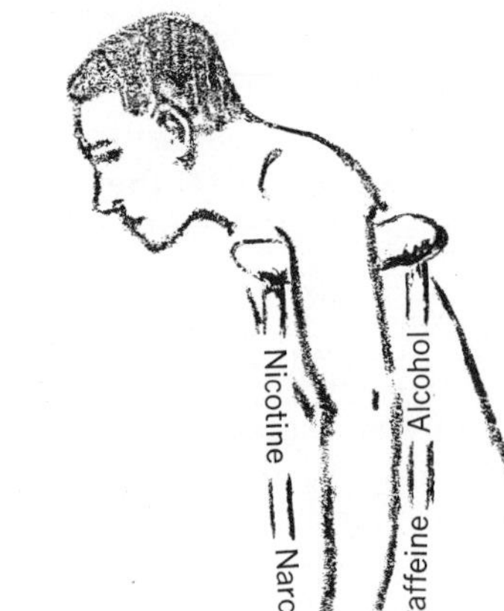

PSYCHOSOCIAL CRUTCHES

Although few of us have had extensive experience with the kinds of drugs utilized in the treatment of mental illness, we are all familiar with the use of drugs to produce anesthesia for surgical procedures, and, of course, we are all constantly reminded that there are a number of products available for the alleviation of headache and minor aches and pains.

Drug Addiction

Lying between these two examples is a large number of nervous system manipulators or drugs, most of which fall into one of two categories: stimulants or depressants. The application of the two terms in classifying these chemical agents is difficult because their action may be dependent upon the psychic state of the person. Some drugs produce a stimulating effect, initially, and then a period of depression. The amount of stimulation and depression is dependent on the individual's physiological capacity. Also, the amount of drug necessary to initiate a measurable response varies with individuals. Cases of reverse effects have also been reported. For example, it is even possible for some people to be put to sleep by substances normally classified as stimulants.

FIGURE 18.7   For some people, the use of certain substances has become a psychological crutch.

The unpredictable effects of stimulants and depressants constitute a serious disadvantage to their use. Overstimulation can cause serious physiological damage. The depressing effect of drugs on some people can contribute to an unrealistic evaluation of their physical ability or capacity and result in accidental injury. This effect is in addition to the possibility of inducing a psychotic depressive state.

Narcotics

Narcotics are drugs that generally produce stupor, complete insensibility, or sleep. They cause addiction when their use is not completely controlled.

According to common usage, there are three classifications of narcotics: opium and its derivatives, cocaine, and marihuana. There is some support for the addition of barbiturates and alcohol to the list. The classification of so-called narcotics is dependent upon the addiction qualities of the material and its general depressant effect. The confusion is apparent when the stimulating effect of cocaine is considered, along with the potentially addicting qualities of barbiturates and alcohol.

The initial, early effects of the opiate drugs are to relieve pain and produce a sense of false well-being (euphoria). Opium is an extract of the opium poppy. It produces depression of the central nervous system, dulls pain, and induces sleep. It may excite the nervous system for a time, as may all narcotics. It reduces body secretions, except those of the skin. A large dose can depress the respiration and thus cause death. Morphine, codeine, papaverine, and heroin are derivatives of opium (603, p. 397).

Morphine's action is similar to that of opium, but it is not as likely to be followed by headache and nausea. Once the body economy has been accustomed to opium or morphine a new equilibrium is established, the upset of which is more profoundly motivating than was that of the previous normal level.

Heroin is the most dangerous in terms of producing drug addiction. It is an outlaw drug having no legitimate medical uses. Probably three fourths of all confirmed drug addicts use heroin. The increased use of heroin in the United States in recent years has caused a great deal of concern. The underlying causes of drug usage are probably related to a general confusion and unrest concerning human and social values. Crime associated with drug traffic has led some groups to advocate the free dispensation of drugs to registered addicts. Where this has been tried, however, it has not met with notable success (463).

Cocaine is a powerful, quick-acting drug that is capable of producing an addiction as difficult to break as that of heroin. Cocaine is derived from the coca leaf, a shrub indigenous to Bolivia and Peru. Unlike most narcotics, which act as sedatives tending to depress the spirit, a moderate dose of cocaine actually stimulates the central nervous system, accelerating the respiratory and circulatory rates. Taken in excess, cocaine can produce psychotic symptoms of great excitement and peculiar sensations of crawling on the skin that are referred to as "cocaine bugs" (595).

Marihuana is an intoxicating drug obtained from the flower and leaf of an Indian hemp plant that grows wild and can be cultivated in many parts of the world, including the United States. Commonly smoked in the form of thin cigarettes, known as "reefers," "joints," or "sticks," the drug produces an unpredictable variety of effects, including exaltation or a violent delirium. Marihuana, however, is not habit-forming in the same sense as other narcotics.

A great deal of controversy has centered around the issue of legalizing marihuana. Supporters of legalization claim that the effects of marihuana are less dangerous than those resulting from the consumption of alcohol. Opponents contend that whereas addiction is not a problem, psychological dependency does develop. In addition, it is claimed, use of marihuana leads to experimentation with other drugs that are addictive. Much more evidence is needed before this argument can be effectively settled.

Most important is the addiction potential of these drugs. It is possible to develop a body need that can escalate into a greater need as the drug is used. This physiological need—or **addiction** —is reflected by extreme states of mental anxiety that can be relieved only by an adequate dosage of the drug, or by long-term rehabilitation.

Stimulants and depressants, of course, serve certain definite medical purposes. Medical applications are based on medical needs, ranging from surgical uses, through psychosomatic treatments, to the treatment of minor cases of anxiety. Such uses involve a doctor's supervision of dosage and evaluation of the drug's effectiveness. Implicit in this type of use is the regulation of dosage through prescriptions.

Of course, most of us, when we feel "below par" in certain ways, want to "take something" to get back to normal and do not always feel it necessary to go to a physician. With some people, however, this goes considerably beyond the aspirin-or-seltzer stage. Drugs taken to speed up functions must be countered by others to depress them sufficiently if relaxation and sleep are to occur. This kind of manipulation of the systems seriously disrupts the delicate natural balance of the body. The individual may be affected to the extent that he completely loses his ability to estimate what the "normal" level is and therefore can miscalculate the dosages required to return his functions to that level. Such inevitable errors in judgment can lead to serious health problems and even to death.

In the case of some stimulants, such as caffeine or nicotine, people may not really be aware of their stimulating effects. Here the reason for indulgence is often related more to social behavior patterns than to any consciously felt physical need and may simply be a matter of joining in a socially approved group activity.

It is undoubtedly true, however, that the use of stimulants and depressants, regardless of their potency, is related to one's self-concept and how he perceives himself in terms of his relationship with the rest of society. All of us feel inadequate and uncertain at times. There are many, however, who dwell in an almost constant state of anxiety because of conflicts of self-image and the perceived demands of society. In such cases an individual may seek out the immediate (though temporary) tranquillity supplied by artificial system manipulators. It is easy to see how the anxious person who is forced to be socially active may come to rely on the use of stimulants and depressants. The use of such psychosocial "crutches" may be incorporated into his life as habits or, in the case of certain drugs, he may become addicted to their use.

Alcohol

Alcohol is a sometimes addicting beverage that generally reduces the efficiency of virtually every physiological function. Primarily, however, alcohol is a depressant, and seems to act first on the higher brain centers, then work its way downward. Cortical functions are inhibited first and then those of lower areas, so that the medulla oblongata is the part affected last. Thus the more complex activities involving judgment, memory, learning, self-criticism, and environmental awareness are the first impaired. The influence of the cortex on the lower areas of the brain also becomes diminished, and their release from cortical control is evident in the excitement characteristic of one phase of alcoholic intoxication (248, p. 549). Alcoholic beverages have a tension-reducing effect. Because alcohol works most strongly against the higher functions of the brain, anxiety is diminished.

Alcohol is a combustible substance yielding in the body about 7 calories for each gram, or 200 calories per ounce. It provides heat and some energy but contributes nothing to the upbuilding or repair of tissue. Ingestible alcohol (ethyl alcohol) is obtained from fermentation of starches and sugars, such as corn or molasses. Pure ethyl alcohol has virtually no odor or taste, so that any differences in flavor among alcoholic beverages results from the various other compounds that may be present. The amount of alcohol in a given beverage is ordinarily designated by "proof," which, in American usage, can simply be divided by two to give the percent volume. Thus 100 proof is 50 percent alcohol by volume; a wine with 20 percent alcohol is 40 proof (10, p. 39).

Before ingested alcohol can reach the tissues, it must be absorbed. Absorption rate can vary with the concentration, with the content of the stomach, and according to individual differences. Concentrations of alcohol of 50 percent (100 proof), or greater, exert a depressant effect on absorption, a sort of local narcosis. In addition, high concentrations are irritating to the mucosa and evoke the secretion of mucus, which also delays absorption. But with small concentrations, below 10 percent, absorption is again slowed by the low percentage of alcohol in the total volume ingested. It would seem, then, that concentrations of alcohol of from 10 to 30 percent, as found in wines and highballs, provide the most rapid rate of entrance of alcohol into the bloodstream. Food is a deterrent to the absorption of alcohol. Milk, fat, and meat all slow the absorption rate. On a full stomach, therefore, the reaching of the peak level in the blood is delayed, thus providing a longer period for the process of elimination (248).

Tolerance for alcohol depends upon individual susceptibility, or, rather, resistance, and apparently is inherent. Habituation differs from tolerance; it is acquired by practice. The facts on habituation are somewhat surprising. We know that the practiced drinker usually takes alcohol with comparatively fewer and less marked effects. Yet we find he absorbs alcohol more rapidly than the abstainer, and, for that reason, the peak level in his blood tends to be higher. There is no reason to believe that alcohol enters the brain of the habituated individual more slowly or that he detoxifies the substance more rapidly, whether by oxidation or by elimination through the kidneys, lungs, and skin. There is, however, good evidence for the conclusion that habituation is an adaptive reaction whereby the central nervous system reacts to a lesser degree as a result of exposure to alcohol (for a given concentration of alcohol the intoxication is more severe when the alcohol level is rising than when it is receding). Moreover, a single dose of alcohol provokes such signs of intoxication as incoordination, which gradually becomes less severe with time. With successive doses each dose again intensifies the signs of acute alcoholism, which again disappear despite the higher levels of alcohol in the bloodstream of the individual (48).

Addiction can occur even in individuals with tolerance or habituation. Addiction becomes obvious when the withdrawal of alcohol produces such serious disturbances that it constitutes a problem both for the individual concerned and for others.

Amphetamines

Amphetamines (trade names, Benzedrine, Dexedrine, Desamine, and Methedrine) produce effects similar to those caused by the activity of the sympathetic nervous system. The effect of a small dose on most people is an increase in alertness and a quickness of reaction. The drug may be used to allay the effects of sleepiness in times of emergency. There are, however, dangers in the use of amphetamines because of the toxic side effects and the possibility of overstimulation. There is also some evidence of auditory nerve degeneration from prolonged use of amphetamines (603, p. 398).

There has been some interest in determining whether athletic performance can be improved by the use of amphetamines. As the pressure to break records and achieve international recognition becomes more and more an integral part of the life of an athlete, he will consider using any legal device that may help him. Medically speaking, the practice of using stimulating drugs for performance purposes is not recommended. However, no legal or moral obstruction now stands in the way of using certain amphetamines under a doctor's supervision. The lack of controls by the various sports governing bodies has caused widespread experimentation by participants, especially at the higher levels of competition, including the Olympic Games (155, 464). The best evidence presently available indicates that amphetamines do *not* produce superior performance but do tend to cause the participant to *perceive* his performance as being outstanding.

Caffeine

Caffeine, a true stimulant, is present in tea, coffee, cocoa, and certain soft drinks. Body activity is ordinarily speeded up with moderate dosages of caffeine. Repeated doses of caffeine lead to the development of a tolerance, so that the same dose produces fewer and fewer effects. Large doses, especially if continued over a long period of time, can interfere with sleep, produce nervousness, and may lead to indigestion.

Smoking

Tobacco nicotine is an oily, colorless, volatile alkaloid that physiologically produces a temporary stimulus for an increase of sympathetic nervous system activity. Physiologically, the heat resulting from smoking does not produce any adverse effects. However, there is a slow, steady increase in heart rate (15 to 20 beats per minute) and a rise in blood pressure. There is a drop in peripheral skin temperature. Basically, nicotine stimulates the following adjustments in body function:

1. An increase in breathing rate

2. Vasoconstriction of systemic and pulmonary circulation

3. An increase in the force of cardiac contraction

4. An increase in arterial blood pressure

In most people the stimulating effect is overshadowed by the symbolic period of rest that a cigarette may suggest, that is, the "smoke break." The pharmacological response of the whole organism at any one time, therefore, represents the algebraic sum of stimulation and depression effects resulting from many direct reflex and chemical mediating influences on the autonomic nerve transmission and excitability of virtually all organ systems (532, p. 69).

The habitual use of tobacco is related primarily to psychological and social drives, reinforced and perpetuated by the pharmacological actions of nicotine on the central nervous system. The latter is being interpreted subjectively either as stimulant or depressant, depending on the individual response. Nicotine-free tobacco or other plant materials do not satisfy the needs of those who acquire the tobacco habit.

The tobacco habit should be characterized as an habituation rather than an addiction, in conformity with accepted World Health Organization definitions, because, once it is established, there is little tendency to increase the dose. Psychic but not physical dependence is developed, and the detrimental effects are primarily on the individual rather than on society. No characteristic abstinence syndrome is developed upon withdrawal.

The difficulties encountered in the discontinuation of smoking are more psychological than physiological. The physiological changes that result when nicotine is withheld are usually reversed after two or three days of total abstinence. The urge to smoke persists, however, particularly whenever situations arise that have been associated with the act of smoking. Thus the difficulties attendant upon the extinction of any well-established habit are encountered when one attempts to stop smoking. Probably the best means of approaching this problem is to reinforce factors that interrupt the underlying motives or drives that make

smoking an attractive or satisfying from of behavior. The use of a nicotine substitute or supplementary medications have not been proven to be of major benefit in breaking the habit.

Very little experimental work has been done in the area of tobacco smoking and performance. The results of several studies are reported in Chapter 8.

The effect of smoking on health is currently a matter of widespread concern. The issue has rapidly become national in scope, encompassing legal, economic, moral, and philosophical considerations. The recent report of the Advisory Committee to the Surgeon General of the Public Health Service has given impetus to many projects that are concerned with the curtailment of cigarette smoking. The report officially supports the stand that smoking leads to the development of cancer of the lungs and that it generally results in earlier death from other diseases (see Figure 18.8).

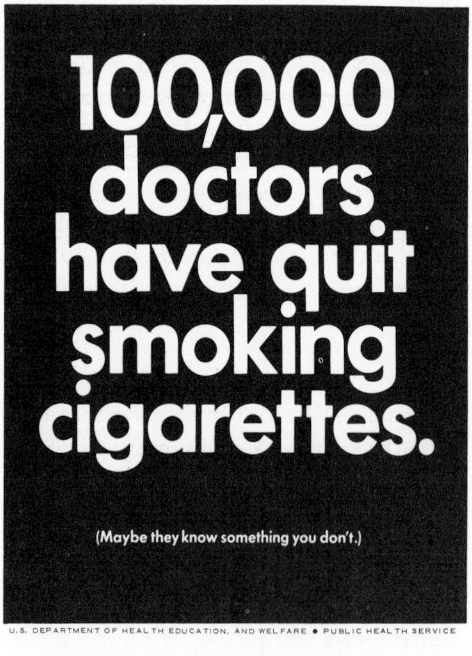

In medical circles, the harmful effects of cigarette smoking have precipitated the antismoking recommendation of many organizations and individual physicians. One might ask, "Why, then, do many physicians continue to smoke?" No definitive answer can be given. Many physicians *have* ceased to smoke both for reasons of personal health and because they believe they have a responsibility to set an example in health practices. Others have recognized the danger but simply prefer to take their chances. Others have apparently not been convinced that the evidence is absolutely conclusive. It should be remembered also that it is

100,000 doctors have quit smoking cigarettes.

(Maybe they know something you don't.)

U.S. DEPARTMENT OF HEALTH EDUCATION, AND WELFARE ● PUBLIC HEALTH SERVICE

FIGURE 18.8 Governmental health agencies have shown increasing concern over the relationship between smoking and health. From U.S. Public Health Service.

no easier for a physician to break the smoking habit than it is for anyone else. Some doctors have simply not been successful in their attempts to give up smoking. In short, physicians are *people*, with problems, biases, and prejudices; they have the same basic needs and desires as the rest of us. The same factors that cause *any* reasonably intelligent person to persist in behavior that provides immediate gratification, but is ultimately harmful, operate equally effectively in layman and physician.

Curtailment of advertising is an initial goal of many antismoking groups. They reason that once the social acceptability is destroyed the initiating stimulus will be reduced. Smokers who begin early smoke more and inhale more deeply; hence the importance of removing the initial stimulus is obvious. The more deeply rooted and fixed adult habituations must be approached from a strong philosophical base or from the application of psychotherapeutic techniques.

There remains a real need, however, to study the factors that cause people to smoke. Some research has been reported on this important topic (145, 256), but the question is far from answered. We also need to know whether smoking meets any important psychological need, and if so, what kinds of behavior may result if smoking is avoided.

FATIGUE

It has been frequently observed that we are all involved in a perpetual adaptive effort to maintain a "vital balance" by mutual interaction between ourselves and our environment. Because the environment is always in flux, so also must be the person: he changes to meet change, changing the outside world or changing himself in accordance with his own capacities.

In one sense, practically all forms of mental disease are really "adjustments" of an extreme nature that have resulted from certain internal or external changes. Most of us, however, do not find it necessary to make such drastic adjustments to the pressures of life. There are, nevertheless, many subtle effects of our reactions to the assumption of responsibilities, interpersonal friction, and struggles to achieve or maintain status. One such effect is chronic **fatigue.**

Fatigue implies tiredness, inability to continue, and lack of energy. Defining fatigue is difficult because its use is so inconsistent (501) and its precise measurement is practically impossible. By examining the term from two viewpoints it is possible, however, to identify the factors involved and to describe their effects.

Quite commonly various modifiers are employed to indicate what is meant when the word "fatigue" is used. Such terms as physical fatigue, psychological fatigue, emotional fatigue, battle fatigue, and even metal fatigue (sometimes responsible for aircraft accidents) have become commonplace.

Certain scientific investigators, notably Bartley (41, 42), have objected to such indiscriminate use of the term "fatigue" on the grounds that it merely confuses the real issues and impedes orderly investigation of the subject. Bartley reserves the term for the *feelings* of tiredness, or disinclination to continue a task, which are experienced by the individual. It is a perceptual matter involving evaluation of the situation. He would use the term **"impairment"** to indicate any state of tissue that disrupts normal active body function. In this construct a separate body part could never be said to be "fatigued"; only the *person* can experience fatigue. Although the degree of impairment may be related to the extent of fatigue experienced, it is by no means a one-to-one relationship. As a matter of fact, serious impairment may exist in the complete absence of fatigue, or fatigue may be present without any metabolic or chemical changes (such as when one thinks about an unpleasant task that needs to be completed). It can be readily seen that a person's attitude toward his job in such a scheme may be more important in determining how fatigued he is after his day's work than is his actual energy expenditure.

Unfortunately, the orderly concept suggested by Bartley has not achieved widespread acceptance. Attempts to measure "fatigue" by studying work output continue and textbook descriptions of "muscular fatigue" continue to appear.

Traditionally the physiologist has been interested in studying the ability of man to perform various tasks and in relating this ability to the amount of energy required. It has been possible to make a distinction on this basis among *moderate, hard,* and *maximal* levels of work. Moderate work, for the average person, is defined as the amount of activity requiring energy expenditure of approximately three times the basal rate. A mean metabolic requirement of about eight times the basal rate is as much as can be maintained for eight hours. Up to this level the circulatory and respiratory systems effectively provide the body with the necessary oxygen. In moderate and hard work only minor blood changes occur; lactic acid concentrations and alkaline reserve are apparently unchanged, and the heart rate, respiratory volume, and circulation rate remain in linear relationship with the metabolic rate. In maximal work a person enters the **overload** zone, in which a **steady state** cannot be maintained and he will soon be unable to continue.

Research on fatigue indicates that even chronically tired people can do much more than they think they can, and that chronically tired businessmen are driven more by fear of failure than by pride of past accomplishments. This half effort at work does not, in any way, allow for body efficiency or integrity.

Some believe that, in our modern culture, social and occupational attitudes may have something to do with lack of incentive to work. The resulting fatigue is a reflection of boredom. If this is the case, physical exercise might produce better results in combating fatigue than does rest (see Chapter 16).

In his book, entitled *Fatigue: Mechanism and Management*, Bartley points out the factors that contribute to fatigue and reviews the evidence pertaining to the means by which it can be relieved. In this concluding remarks he states:

There are five different types of things that may be involved in the management of fatigue: (1) some clarification as to what fatigue is and then what it is that is to be dealt with and achieved; (2) the treatment of disease, if present . . . (3) The establishment of a reasonable physiological hygiene which, for example, may consist in the following: (a) an activity rest cycle suitable for the particular individual involved . . . ; (b) the temperate use of stimulants and alcohol; (c) the elimination of any chronic self-medication that may have become habitual, though not wholly believed in by the person himself; (d) the use of warm and cold baths to produce relaxation and toning; (e) the regulation of eating times and the avoidance of foods that may not be well tolerated; (f) the possible use of formal physiotherapy; (g) the development of a program of exercise to develop a better cardio-circulatory system . . . . (4) Another factor is the discarding of habits of either hurry or of indolence and sluggishness . . . . (5) The development of an improved and more wholesome outlook on life in general (42, p. 85).

Dr. Selyé has suggested that each of us inherits his fatigue pattern. He also recommends that each of us should appraise his energy store and that everyone should sit down and ask himself:

1. What are the main stress factors in my life?

2. At what time of the day or night do I have the most energy? the least?
3. When fatigue strikes me, how long does it last?
4. How long can I keep adapting to trying circumstances without growing weary?

Once you have established your fatigue pattern, "try to space out jobs, and reserve energy-demanding tasks for the time when you have the greatest strength," advises Dr. Selyé. "Also it is important to change your pace. If you are too tired to think well, stop and walk around a bit; if you are muscle-tired, sit down and think or listen to music" (103, p. 63).

EFFERENT CONCEPTS—EFFECTS OF ACTIVITY ON STRESS

EXERCISE AS A STRESSOR

In Selyé's stress theory, exercise is classified as a potent stressor, along with such elements as cold and heat. You will recall that exposure to stressors results in first an alarm reaction, followed by an adaptation stage. Because stress is a generalized reaction producible by any number of separate kinds of stressors, it was hypothesized that the development of the resistance mechanisms by one stressor might enable the body to better resist a second stressor. As a matter of fact, it has been discovered that some kinds of stressors may be antidotes for the harmful effects of other kinds. Exercise, for example, can be considered a stressor. The body responds to the demands of exercise, and, in training, to progressive *amounts* of exercise. If the level of work is reasonable or if the training is not excessive, an efficient response to the exercise results. This adaptation, which is the result of healthful body functioning, can facilitate and economize body responses to other stress-producing stimuli and can help to prevent the exhaustion phase of the stress syndrome.

One implication of Selyé's stress theory is that the person who exercises regularly should be better able to resist another stressor, such as extreme temperatures or other personal discomfort. In one study laboratory animals were subjected to leg fractures. In those animals that had been sedentary there was a considerable amount of heart damage, apparently associated with the trauma of the fracture. No such damage was found in the hearts of animals that had been subjected to regular exercise (31).

Despite some criticism, the stress concept remains a solid attempt to describe the process of living in a meaningful way. Selyé's approach may not entirely resolve the problems associated with the potentially dangerous effects of stressors today, but there is some reassurance in the statement that "one cannot be cured of stress but can only learn to enjoy it" (565).

MODIFIERS OF STRESS

As was mentioned earlier, psychologists recognize that frustrating situations may lead to the employment of certain defense mechanisms. Among such mechanisms is the mechanism of displacement, frequently associated with feelings of aggression. Some inaccessible or threatening object of aggressive feelings is replaced by a substitute. Contact sports have long been regarded as serving this function. Where else is it possible to gain social approval in attempts to "kill" (as has been reported by boxers) (47)? Under what circumstances is it possible to physically assault peers with the full approval and encouragement of authority figures (as in football)? Ample opportunity exists for the transference of aggression to inanimate objects in sport. The extent to which this occurs is not well known, but psychiatrists have long recognized this possibility and, as a result, have utilized such activities in therapy programs.

From a cultural viewpoint, it has been suggested that sport participation, as well as watching, may serve as an efficient and a necessary substitute for unacceptable aggressive behavior of people (178). Chapter 15 deals with these and other cultural implications of physical activity.

SLEEP

Another way in which human activity can influence the effects of stress is through sleep. Sleep is so fundamental a need that some might be led to question whether wakefulness is the more natural and fundamental state, in which sleep is only a restorative interlude, or whether sleep is the truly normal condition. Apparently man does not have a "sleep center" that must be activated to produce sleep. Rather, the principle mechanism involved in sleep is a "wakefulness center" or system whose activity induces and maintains wakefulness and whose inactivity leads to sleep.

Aristotle was convinced that a heavy meal leads to sleep by the action of heavy vapors rising from the stomach. Physicians used to believe that it was merely a matter of temperature change. By lowering body temperature sleep could be induced. The practice of reducing room temperature for this purpose was not entirely successful, since the body would adapt by raising its temperature accordingly. It is a fact, however, that the state of sleep results in a slight drop in body temperature. Neurologists suggest that sleep is caused by complex integrations of various nerve bundles. "Nonsense to all these claims," says Dr. Nathaniel Kleitman, the grand old sandman of science, "Man goes to sleep when his muscles are so tired they have to relax." He admits, however, that this is complicated by the tensing effects of emotions on muscles (564).

Listed below are some of the physiological changes occurring during sleep:

1. Heart rate slows from 70 to 60 beats per minute.
2. Breathing rate slows from 16 to 12 per minute.
3. Blood pressure falls.
4. Sweating increases.
5. Liver stores glycogen.

6. Kidneys continue working, endlessly filtering metabolic poisons out of the blood.

Relaxation is the key to sleep. Tense muscles represent the most serious obstruction to relaxation. Muscle relaxation is the most effective general technique in producing sleep. Stomach contractions, resulting from hunger, sometimes interfere with sleep. Hot milk, Sanka, Ovaltine, cocoa, or hot buttered rum can sometimes solve this problem if ingested in small quantities. Small portions of vodka, Scotch whisky, or gin do not interfere with sleep, but brandy, bourbon, or rye will keep most people awake. Caffeine in the form of coffee or tea may, in some individuals, reverse its normal stimulating effect and produce sleep. Sleeping pills and hypnotics usually are extremely effective; however, they affect different people in different ways. These differing effects of usually predictable drugs are generally unexplainable. In fact, some amphetamines have been known to put people to sleep. However, tranquilizers are usually effective in setting the stage for the sleep state.

For people who find themselves unable to relax and sleep readily there are cleverly designed, mechanical sleep-inducing aids. The adjustable bed and the vibrating bed are two of these. Earplugs and face masks are others. "Blend noise," providing sea sounds or a pleasant hum, is sometimes used to drown out intermittent noises. Whatever the set of conditions, only when complete relaxation is achieved can a state of sleep be realized.

PROGRESSIVE MUSCULAR RELAXATION

Relaxation, derived from the Latin word *relaxare,* "to loosen," is both popularly and scientifically interpreted as the "release of tension" (311, p. 23). Relaxation is the opposite of movement. It is marked by reduction or complete absence of muscle tone in a part or in the entire body. Relaxation of the musculature is accompanied by reduced circulation, but its greatest value probably lies in the lowering of brain and cord activity resulting from a reduction of the nerve impulses arising in postural muscles, sense organs, and other sense organs located in tendons and joint structures (543, p. 321). Relaxation, or reduction of tension, can be classified as follows:

1. *Pseudo relaxation* consists of merely sitting or lying down for the purpose of resting; no other deliberate attempt is made to reduce tension. Certain signs of tension, such as slight movement of facial muscles, frowning, and irregular breathing, may be evident during pseudo relaxation.
2. *Complete relaxation* is a state immediately preceding sleep in which tension is reduced to the lowest possible level in the waking state.
3. *Differential relaxation* is a state in which muscular tension is restricted, insofar as possible, to those parts directly involved in the activity. Complete relaxation is the goal in all other body parts (311, p. 25).

Dr. Edmund Jacobson, who has contributed much to the study of relaxation, has used the term "residual tension" to describe the phenomenon of excessive muscle tenseness. **Residual tension** appears to be a fine, continued contraction of muscle along with slight movements or reflexes. Often it is reflexly excited, as by distress or pain, but usually it is the product of nervous tension (270, p. 54). Jacobson also reports similarity between the actions of skeletal muscles and internal muscles. If you relax your skeletal muscles sufficiently (those over which you have control), the internal muscles also tend to relax. The person whose visceral muscles are overtense, as is often the case in certain states of nervous indigestion, spastic colon, palpitation, and other common internal symptoms, shows clearly to any experienced observer that his external muscles are also overtense. Electrical measurements support this statement. Relaxation of skeletal muscles is effective in the treatment of certain internal disorders because it removes the cause or an essential part of the cause (270, p. 58).

Dr. Jacobson (269) has developed a method of reducing residual tension that he has called "progressive relaxation." He holds that a man who can control a muscle can also relax it. Muscle relaxation means letting go and doing absolutely nothing with your muscles. Actually, as Dr. Jacobson sees it, "relaxation isn't something you do; it is something that happens when you stop doing something else." In Dr. Jacobson's system of relaxation, you are told to contract a group of muscles tightly, and then let go. Contract one group and then another. Various intensities of contraction are followed by complete relaxation. The individual soon learns the feel of tensions and how to let go completely. Dr. Jacobson suggests that you lie comfortably on your back on a cot or bed with your arms at your sides and your legs not crossed. Then, one by one, you can tense your muscles and relax them, the biceps, triceps, hand flexors, elevators of the shoulders, even the face muscles of smiling and frowning, of mouth opening and of swallowing.

The aim of this method is to train the individual to use his own initiative. He learns to localize tensions when they occur during nervous irritability and excitement and to relax them away by this means of nervous re-education. Josephine Rathbone (467, p. 128) favors a technique of inducing relaxation that is similar to Jacobson's technique of progressive relaxation. Rathbone's method consists of trying to relax different parts of the body separately by imagining that relaxation is occurring in every muscle, then trying to relax more than one part at the same time, with concentration on the parts being relaxed. The subject is next required to observe his own breathing and to aim to increase the regularity and volume so that inhalation and exhalation take equal amounts of time.

Eleanor Metheny (388, p. 59) has designed a three-step procedure for teaching relaxation. The first step is the development of kinesthetic awareness, or the feeling of relaxation, by distinguishing between states of tension and relaxation in muscle groups and in the body as a whole. The second involves practicing muscle relaxation until the feeling can be produced at will. The third consists in eliciting the feeling at will in potential tension-producing situations. Such reactions as becoming extremely tense, twisting and stretching, and coming to an extremely tense sitting position on hearing a sudden sound are alternated with the relaxed state. The final step involves the performance of an activity, such as writing, while constantly endeavoring to relax those parts not required for the activity.

Another interesting relaxation technique has been developed by Sweigard. By visualizing the body as an empty suit of clothes, or a rag doll, positions of "constructive rest" can be assumed from which relaxation procedures are initiated. Much visual imagery is used to induce reduction of muscle tension (555). Maja Schade's (494) method, while similar in many ways to other techniques, also employs the shaking and swinging of limbs.

Progressive relaxation produces a reduction in mental imagery, attention level, recollection capacity, thought processes, and emotions (269, p. 188). Therefore, it is definitely of value in partial adaptation to emotional stressors. However, in terms of changes in physiological functioning, whether relaxation inhibits or improves adaptation under stressful conditions has not yet been shown (311, p. 43).

YOGA

Another method that can be applied to reduction of muscle tension result-

Lotus Pose

Plough Pose

Twist Pose

Inverted Pose

FIGURE 18.9 Some of the typical positions adopted in the practice of Yoga.

ing from emotional sources is Yoga, an ancient Indian system of health that lays stress on bodily and mental poise and is designed to produce an equanimity of spirit that is beneficial to the whole nervous system (589, p. 7). Some moderns think of Yoga as an extended system of psychotherapy; others regard it as an excellent technique to gain relief from tension. Many European and American concert artists practice Yoga. Whether it is used to gain relief from tension or as a system of psychotherapy would depend on the individual involved.

In *The Yoga System of Health and Relief from Tension*, Yogi Vithaldas writes:

Yoga raises the mind to its highest level in order to study its activities on lower levels of consciousness. Yoga aims at that command over the body that is the state of individual existence in which the mind, working smoothly in a physically fit body on a high level of consciousness, can observe and control all mental activities on the lower level (589, p. 18).

Thus Yoga seems to be a combination of physical exercise and mental concentration. It uses strength exercises to gain adequate strength to support the prescribed body positions that stress high levels of body flexibility (Figure 18.9). Yoga sees therapeutic value in the inverted body and the physical stress of extending joint structures to the fullest. These programs are progressive and the tolerance of the exercises constitutes part of the concentration faculty. Mental concentration which allows a Yoga performer to lose track of time during an exercise requiring support of part of the body weight is impressive. Masters of the art of Yoga have some voluntary control over body functions that are usually the responsibility of the autonomic nervous system. They have been known to reduce heart and respiration rates practically to zero, for short periods of time, without any adverse effects.

RECREATION

Refreshment, relaxation, and **recreation** are concepts often confused. Refreshment and relaxation are two of the desired outcomes of recreation. "Recreation," however, is a broader term representing the individual state related to the environment over a period of time.

"Recreation" is defined by some as being any activity, apart from one's occupation, taken for pleasure (533, p. 139). Others say that it is not an activity but a state of mind. All agree that no single activity is sure to produce positive effects for all members of a group, nor is there assurance that the value will be duplicated on another occasion. The value of recreational activities is directly related to the level of personal involvement. The activity should completely engross the individual (543, p. 322).

Recreational activities that are too competitive or aggressive may tend to intensify the anxieties and pressures they are supposed to relieve. Basically, the effectiveness of an individual's recreational program is proportional to the completeness of his momentary escape from less than satisfactory reality. The person whose work provides a sufficient variety of activities, each completely absorbing, often feels little need for special recreation.

Recreation, with all its implications and variety of applications, is being re-evaluated by many groups of people who have not been overly concerned with its influence on the productive, economically striving population of today. Increased leisure time for the worker resulting from advancing technology causes the concern: the work-week has been constantly shortened, life expectancy has lengthened, retirements come earlier, holidays multiply, and paid vacations lengthen.

Increasing wealth and leisure have produced problems, both social and individual in nature. Socially, the welfare state and its implications of care, service, and support have removed the need to work to survive.

Individually, the joy of working, for the majority of workers, has been removed. The automated or semi-automated production line is boring. The build-up of the service areas provides work, but little of it is creative. Work on useless products or on items planned for early obsolescence seems meaningless. The joy of accomplishment is shifting to recreational activities, where the degree of personal commitment and involvement is at a maximum. The time is past when recreation could be regarded as a source of brief, pleasant diversion. For ever-increasing numbers of people recreational activities are providing substance and meaning to life—qualities often found lacking in an automated culture.

PSYCHOLOGICAL DISTURBANCES

We have just discussed the role of recreation in helping people to adjust to the everyday stressors of life. As was pointed out, recreation may become a state of mind, which is a desirable thing in terms of acceptable adjustment. On the other hand, "recreation" can also become a way of life, and this may not be so desirable. In this case the term is distorted to include the tendency to adjust to tensions by *escaping* from them and by never constructively treating their source. It has been said that Western man is preoccupied with seeking diversion. "Those who can afford it are perpetually moving from place to place," observes Bertrand Russell, "carrying with them as they go gaiety, dancing, and drinking, but for some reason always expecting to enjoy these more in a new place" (485, p. 39).

We can seek this kind of distraction in a number of ways. Some have done so in drugs. One of the greatest drug controversies of modern times has arisen over whether the use of certain drugs such as LSD are mere escapism or whether there is some "mind-expanding" quality, as is claimed by Timothy Leary and others (336, 425).

As has been pointed out by Beiser (47) (see also Chapter 17), sports are sometimes used to refuse to face other issues and responsibilities in life. Some sports fans quite routinely seem to regard the outcome of the baseball game involving the local team (professional or otherwise) with more concern and interest than their jobs or even the problems of their own families. Certainly the awareness of world affairs among our citizens suffers during the World Series each fall.

It is often noted, with considerable validity, that many boys would have been drop-outs from school if it had not been for sports and their love of competition. Is it not also true, however, that many capable youngsters may have been permitted (or even *encouraged)* to substitute *excessive* activity in the gymnasium (shooting baskets or "working out") for other kinds of activity required for the meeting of important responsibilities?

All mature individuals (including professional athletes and even some sports journalists) recognize that sport is not life; it is only one small aspect of life. Bill Russell, player-coach of the famous Boston Celtics refers to professional basketball players as "a bunch of men playing a kid's game" (47, p. 13).

Howard Cosell, ABC television sports-caster says: "Face it. Sport is the toy department of life." On the day of the assassination of New York Senator Robert Kennedy, Cosell refused to report the baseball scores on his nightly newscast. "When people view outlet, escape, and entertainment as the be-all and end-all of human existence," he explained, "then I have to wonder how sick this society really is" (218).

MENTAL ILLNESS

The question of whether exercise programs or recreational activities (either active or passive) are of any real value in alleviating the symptoms of mental illness, is an important one. Although it has been reported that well-adjusted persons engage more extensively in hobbies than others (385), does this really mean that such activity is preventive or therapeutic?

There is no question about the fact that activity programs of various kinds are almost universally employed in the "total push" kinds of therapy that are employed in modern psychiatric treatment. Mohr has observed that:

There is no such thing as a purely psychic illness or a purely physical one, but only a living event taking place in a living organism which is itself alive only by virtue of the fact that in it psychic and somatic are united in a unity (393, p. 772).

In his review of scientific and clinical evidence, Johnson has come to the conclusion that "the personality as a whole functions better when its physical competence is at least adequate" (283, p. 168). One of the observations that led to this statement was Menninger's contention that good mental health is directly associated with the individual's desire and capacity to play (386). The results of a series of studies at the University of Illinois prompted Cureton to state that "It is certainly suggestive that personality deterioration and physical deterioration parallel one another, and it follows that improvement of physical fitness should minimize both types of deterioration" (138).

A dissenting view was presented by Stern and McDonald in 1965 when they pointed out the lack of convincing evidence of physiological variables that appeared to be capable of causing mental illness. They state: "To the best of our knowledge, no physiological bases for any of the major mental diseases have been found, if by mental disease we mean principally psychotic states" (546). They point out that one of many possible causes for this situation is the lack of reliable psychiatric diagnoses.

Several studies (252, 382, 628) have been reported in recent years utilizing exercise as a variable in treatment. Frequently, however, exercise is confounded with the other treatments so that specific effects are difficult to assess. Bamford and Swan (35), for example found that adapted physical education in a group of chronically regressed schizophrenic patients was "rendered more effective by concurrent treatment with Thorazine."

Because fatigue is a complaint that is common to many types of mental disease (particularly the depressive illnesses), some study has been directed at its causes in patients. It has been observed that neither sleep nor rest is capable of alleviating this feeling of fatigue in the depressed patient. Kraines has pointed out that even though it may require a great deal of effort to arise, "the patient may feel much stronger once he is at work; . . . though fatigability may be great, many patients in the terminal or initial stages may be encouraged or urged to mild exercise; and many will report feeling better after walking for an hour, even though they were 'dead tired' when they started" (322, p. 150).

Hellerstein (239) has worked for several years with the rehabilitation of nonpsychiatric cardiac patients. In administering the MMPI he has discovered that scores on depression have decreased as physical working capacity increased. In summarizing the clinical case studies and experimental research, Dr. E. M. Layman concludes: "Individually prescribed physical exercise as an adjunctive therapy may result in behavioral improvement in psychiatric patients who do not respond well to other therapies" and "exercise helps some patients to profit more from other therapies" (334, p. 722).

MEASUREMENT OF STRESS

One of the great problems in research has been that of detecting and measuring stress. Selyé's approach has had great appeal because it restricts stress to the cellular level where distinctions are made in terms of tissue changes. When we begin to think in terms of the anxiety associated with stressful situation, however, we begin to get into a situation that closely resembles the problems relating to the discussions and studies involving fatigue.

One way to decide on measures is to place subjects in situations that are judged to involve stress (examinations, jumping from airplanes, competing for championships) and then to monitor certain responses. Some of the techniques that have evolved from this kind of investigation include electromyograms (recordings of muscle action potentials), heart rate, blood cell counts (eosinophils), respiration rate, galvanic skin response (perspiration on skin measured electrically), excretion of hormones and other substances, hand steadiness, blood pressure, eye-blink rate, pupil dilation, and various visual perception tests. Some investigators have concluded that the best measure is to simply ask the subject about the level of stress he is experiencing. One of the reasons for this is that measures of stress do not seem to correlate very well with each other. It is entirely possible that some measures may be more effective with one type of stressor than another (acute versus chronic), or that certain individuals exhibit different kinds of stress symptoms.

Although it is readily conceded that exercise of a vigorous nature is a stressor, some concern has been expressed about how much stress is associated with the emotional aspects of competi-

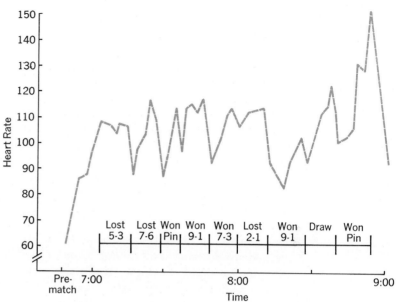

FIGURE 18.10 Continuous monitoring of a coach's heart rate during a wrestling meet indicates the degree to which emotional involvement affects physiological function. Source: D. L. Castill and P. B. Samuels, "Heart Study Shows Emotional Involvement of Wrestling Coach," *Amateur Wrestling News*, 12:6 (February 22), 1967.

tion. It was discovered, for example, that although measures of blood changes in competing crewmen indicated significant stress, the coxswain (who does not row, of course) was found to exhibit similar changes (471, 247). Similar observations have been made on coaches when studied in conjunction with their players (127).

Under the assumption that too much emotional stress may be harmful to youngsters, many people have criticized aspects of competitive sports for youngsters. Using galvanic skin response measures, Skubic (522) concluded that Little League and Middle League baseball participants experienced no more stress than players in physical education classes. Hanson (227) monitored the heart rates of Little Leaguers during competition and observed that heart rates were greatest during batting (see Figure 19.3), but no conclusions were drawn about the emotional effects of this experience. Ulrich's (576) study of college women was interesting (eosinophil counts) because of her finding that inexperienced girls exhibited greater stress (postgame) if they had participated, whereas experienced girls showed greater stress if they had not been permitted to play.

Controversy over the advisability of encouraging certain kinds of competition at young age levels continues, but it is not likely to be settled (in the near future, at least) by conclusive physiological or psychological evidence of detrimental effects on a large scale. The fact is that measurement techniques are currently inadequate for detecting the effects of such short-term effects. Techniques for the evaluation of personality, psychological disorders, and related phenomena are presented in Chapter 14.

SUMMARY

The concept of stress has assumed increased importance in recent years. In order to study the topic, scientists have constructed definitions formulated from differing viewpoints. Some people regard stress in terms of circumstances or events that create feelings of anxiety, fear, and uncertainty. Others view stress as a biological response to certain kinds of stimuli called *stressors*. Stress, in this sense, is viewed as a nonspecific response of the body to several different kinds of situations, ranging from infections caused by invading organisms to perceptions of danger and fear of approaching events.

Increase in skeletal muscle tension is only one indicator of the presence of stress, but it is commonly monitored as a stress sign. Many common illnesses and disorders are thought to be caused, or at least triggered, by stress.

Psychosomatic illnesses are often said to result from the body's responses to stress. In such cases treatment of symptoms will probably give only temporary relief. Discovery and re-

moval of the stressor would appear to be the only permanent cure for such problems.

Psychological disturbances are usually not explainable on the basis of hormonal activity, but some of the biologically oriented stress concepts are related to other views concerning psychological disturbances.

Conflicting motivations and the frustrations of goals are increasingly implicated as causative factors in psychological disturbances. Inability to express aggression without violating strong social codes is a common example of the kind of motivational conflict blamed for many of our psychological disorders.

Psychological disorders exist at many different levels of severity. Inability to cope with frustration may lead to anxiousness or inability to get along with others. These and related phenomena are usually labeled neuroses. More severe symptoms that prevent one from dealing effectively with the real world (often involving outbursts, attacks, and social offenses) are called psychoses. Hospitalization is frequently required.

Two problems of effectively treating mental illness are the lack of uniformity of terms and disagreement concerning diagnostic characteristics.

Many techniques have been utilized in the treatment of mental illnesses, including psychoanalysis, psychotherapies of various kinds, shock therapy, neurosurgery, and drug treatments. The success associated with drug treatments of certain difficulties has greatly stimulated research in chemotherapy.

Illustrative of the intricate relationship between so-called psychological and physiological phenomena is the "placebo effect." Apparent pharmacological effects have often been demonstrated for biologically inert substances under appropriate circumstances. This and a nonmedical extension of the principle called the Hawthorne effect, have led to the necessity of greater care in the design of experiments studying drugs, effects of working conditions, and school problems.

Other problems relating to psychological dependency have taken on urgent overtones, particularly in terms of hallucinogenic drugs. Smoking behavior and alcohol addiction are other topics of great importance and interest. Many interested groups are concerned with finding effective means of dealing with these problems.

The problem of fatigue is not new, but very few definitive answers are yet available. Implications for health as well as personal and economic well-being are evident in learning to understand the mechanisms underlying acute and chronic fatigue.

Examination of the ways in which physical activity affects stress indicates that some kinds of stressors may act as antidotes for the effects of other kinds. Other ways of modifying stress are seen in the substitution of socially acceptable means of exhibiting aggression for unacceptable means.

The effects of stress can be influenced in other ways as well. Sleep, techniques of muscular relaxation, and recreational activities can all have significant effects on reactions to stress.

Psychological disturbances and mental illness are also affected by patterns of physical activity, including exercise and recreation.

The difficulty in measurement of stress has been one of the greatest drawbacks in studying this problem. The confounding effects of exercise and competition make studying either one separately (by means of current techniques) rather difficult.

PRINCIPLES

1. It is impossible to have something called "psychological stress" without physiological involvement.

2. Individual differences and chance factors make it impossible to predict with reasonable accuracy the effect of a stressor by knowing its character. One man's stress may be another man's pleasure.

3. Although the sources of stressors have changed considerably, it is doubtful that man today faces a more stressful existence than he ever has. His responses to it may be considerably different, however.

4. Increased muscular tension (at rest) is associated with heightened emotional involvement

5. Whenever there is a conflict of motives within a person, he is confronted with the necessity of making a choice. The choice may be between two desirable or two undesirable alternatives.

6. The usual reaction to situations of conflict and frustration is to develop feelings of anxiety or aggression.

7. Most therapeutic approaches to mental illness involve an attempt to

discover underlying sources of conflict. In the meantime, drugs may be relied upon to reduce the severity of symptoms.

8. The expectations of people have a profound effect on the effectiveness of drugs and other treatments.

9. The use of stimulants and depressants, regardless of their potency, is related to one's self-concept and how he perceives himself in terms of his relationship with the rest of society.

10. While there is no reason to believe that alcohol enters the brain of the habituated individual more slowly or that he detoxifies the substance more rapidly, there is good evidence that habituation is an adaptive reaction whereby the central nervous system reacts less acutely to the exposure to alcohol.

11. The effect of a small dose of amphetamines on most people is to produce an increase in alertness and a quickness of reaction.

12. Research indicates that amphetamines cannot produce superior performance but do tend to cause the participant to perceive his performance as being outstanding.

13. The habitual use of tobacco is related primarily to psychological and social drives, reinforced and perpetuated by the pharmacological actions of nicotine on the central nervous system.

14. The difficulties encountered in the discontinuation of smoking are more psychological than physiological.

15. Valid investigations of fatigue cannot be based on observations of work decrement alone.

16. Fatigue is basically a matter of perception rather than a strictly energistic phenomenon.

17. Some kinds of stressors may be antidotes for the harmful effects of other kinds.

18. Contact sports may serve to provide individuals with opportunities for transference of aggression.

19. Only when complete relaxation is achieved can a state of sleep be realized.

20. Practice in qualitatively tensing and relaxing skeletal muscles, as well as in specific concentration of attention, can lead to the achievement of relaxation levels beyond those otherwise possible.

21. Recreational activities that are too competitive or aggressive may intensify the anxieties and pressures they are supposed to relieve.

22. While no physiological basis for any of the major mental illnesses has been found, it is widely acknowledged that the personality as a whole functions better when its physical competence is at least adequate.

EXPERIMENTS AND EXPERIENCES

1. Obtain a device for detecting changes in skin resistance (galvanic skin response). Test three subjects while they are resting, alone, in a comfortable room. Retest all three immediately before and immediately after participation in a card-sorting contest performed before the entire class. Note and explain any differences.

2. Administer a pencil and paper test that purports to measure anxiety levels (work through your guidance and testing center or department). Compare the mean anxiety level of a small sample of athletes with an equal number of students who have never performed at a varsity level.

As an alternate experiment test athletes before and after performance in a varsity contest. Compare scores with control scores obtained at another time, if possible. (Tests with at least two equivalent forms must be used.)

3. Spend one period undergoing progressive relaxation techniques as described in the chapter references. Someone with experience should conduct the sessions. A relatively quiet, comfortable area must be provided.

4. Make arrangements to have a psychiatrist explain and demonstrate psychodrama. If possible, make arrangements to visit a clinic where psychodrama is conducted.

SUGGESTED READINGS

Bajusz, E. and H. Selyé, "Adaptation to the Cardiac Necrosis-Eliciting Effect of Stress," *American Journal of Physiology,* 199:453, 1960.

Bartley, S. Howard, "Some Things to Realize about Fatigue," *Journal of Sports Medicine and Physical Fitness,* 4:153–157, 1964.

Brady, J. V , "Ulcers in Executive Monkeys," *Scientific American,* 199:24, 1958.

Clark, M., "How to Live without Fatigue," *Reader's Digest,* 80:63, 1962.

Jacobson, E., *You Must Relax,* New York: McGraw-Hill, Inc., 1948.

Selyé, Hans, *The Stress of Life,* New York: McGraw-Hill, Inc., 1956.

Smoking and Health, Report of the Advisory Committee to the Surgeon General of the Public Health Service. Public Health Service Publication No. 1103, Washington, D.C.: 1964.

PART IV

Special Considerations

Selected Issues

Chapter 19

In this chapter we wish to raise and discuss briefly some very important problems and issues that do not rightfully belong in any one of the foundations chapters. Each issue has physiological and sociopsychological ramifications, and yet, when the dust settles from all of the arguments pertaining to these aspects, there is still a strong, inherent philosophical question to be dealt with. Furthermore, all the issues have important implications for health education, physical education, and recreation. These issues are

1. The continued shift in the direction of greater automation with its attendant benefits and drawbacks; this is related to the question: Should science be directed more toward man's "living better" or "living longer"?

2. The question of the wisdom of continuing the "Little League" impetus that has reached enormous proportions in many sports for pre–high school boys.

3. The closely related questions of the advisability of athletic competition and heavy physical exercise for girls and women.

AUTOMATION

That we have become more and more an automated or at least highly mechanized society is undeniable. A society as radically mechanized and controlled as Aldous Huxley's *Brave New World* (260) seems a little less remote, a little less science fiction than it did when first published in 1932. In that book, while extolling the merits of this "new world" where all babies are produced by artificial means, the Controller at one point explains:

The world's stable now. People are happy; they get what they want and they never want what they can't get. They're well off; they're safe; they're never ill; they're not afraid of death; they're blissfully ignorant of passion and old age; they're plagued with no mothers or fathers; they've got no wives, or children, or lovers to feel strongly about [sex is free and requires no real attachment]; they're so conditioned that they practically can't help behaving as they ought to behave (260, p. 149).

And later:

. . . truth's a menace, science a public danger. [Referring to the twentieth century:] People were ready to have their appetites controlled then. Anything for a quiet life. We've gone on controlling ever since. It hasn't been very good for truth of course. But it's been very good for happiness. One can't have something for nothing. Happiness has got to be paid for (p. 155).

As we read Huxley's words, we see some ideas that are not too far removed from what our world seems to be blindly striving for. And science now predicts that by 2020 (within the normal life span for most of you beginning a college career) we will likely see: cheap and effective fertility control, computor language translation, implanted plastic and electronic organs, use of nonnarcotic drugs to change personality, some form of primitive artificial life, regional weather control, blanket immunization against infectious diseases, chemicals to stimulate growth of new organs and limbs, drugs to increase intelligence, drugs to increase life span by fifty years, breeding of intelligent animals for low-grade labor, and education by direct recording on the brain. Certain aspects of Huxley's brave new world look less and less like fantasy! You may even say, after reading the list of scientific predictions, that "these are all to be desired; bring them on now!" There is little argument that some of these are certainly desirable; perhaps even all are. But such a world does mean massive adjustment, and we have not in the past shown ourselves to be overly adept at adjusting smoothly and effectively to such changes. The physiological and sociopsychological effects are obvious and numerous: lack of physical activity could become even more pronounced; lack of real-life mental stimulation could become a serious problem; society cannot help but be affected. Assuming that these things can be made to come to pass, and even if they are physiologically desirable, the philosophical issues remain: For the good of mankind, *should* such a life be eagerly sought after? Can man ef-

FIGURE 19.1 "Fish eye" view provides a panoramic glimpse of the British European Airways Reservation Hall in the West London Airport Terminal. More than 200 operators handle reservations using data communication terminals. Said to be Europe's largest civil computer network, this system is used in integrated passenger reservations, flight operations, management information system applications, flight and crew scheduling, load control, message switching, and automatic ticketing. Photograph courtesy of UNIVAC Division, Sperry-Rand Corporation.

fectively make the transition and compensate for certain needs that mechanization and control will not fulfill?

You should be aware of this problem of the present and future and perhaps begin thinking about your role as a professional and as a member of society in meeting this challenge; the challenge appears destined to make itself even more intensely and persistently felt.

LITTLE LEAGUE

Twenty years ago there was no sport highly organized for competition among youngsters less than fourteen years of age. (American Legion baseball for the most part utilized players fourteen to seventeen years old.) Today there is hardly a competitive sport that is not highly organized for youngsters. (Baseball, basketball, football, and swimming are the prime examples; soccer, track and field, and tennis are

beginning to be heard from.) It is not that youngsters did not take part in any of these sports, especially baseball (or softball), football, basketball, and swimming (depending upon the section of the country). They just did their own organizing on more of a neighborhood basis.

The proponents of organized athletic competition for children (and many activities are provided for those as young as six) argue that organization is desirable because there is better control and thus greater safety. But there is no evidence that such has been the case. In fact, with the intense competition involved, there may be more injuries. The proponents also argue that more children are participating now that these things are organized and publicized. Perhaps so; we will never know how many would participate just for fun if adequate facilities and some leadership were provided and if there

FIGURE 19.2 "Little League" baseball action. Photograph courtesy of City of Toledo, Ohio, Recreation Department.

were no organized league competition. Furthermore, now that the organized competition has provided a new status symbol, these leagues and teams often have more eager applicants than they can keep on their teams; so the "product has been sold." Many youngsters want to participate but either "ride the bench" or do not make the team.

Another argument is often heard. Little Leagues and their counterparts provide earlier coaching and thus produce better-skilled athletes. Such is apparently only partly true. Many high school and college coaches have been known to complain that poor habits are learned and fostered by Little League and similar competition. It has also been claimed that these early experiences develop and promote sportsmanship. At least one objective study (298), as well as many testimonies, bears witness to the contention that, on the average, no such thing occurs.

"Physical fitness is an important concommitant of competition," says the proponent. "Not so for baseball," says the opponent, and a study of telemetered heart rates by Hanson (227) backs him up. Hanson concludes that "the exercise involved in the ½ to 2 hours of a Little League baseball game, excluding . . . pitching and catching, is minimal. So minimal in fact that it should not be considered a major contributing factor to the development of cardiovascular respiratory fitness."

"Organization to a point is desirable," argue the opponents, "so that leadership and opportunity to participate can be increased. But," they also argue, "super organization and an almost exclusive emphasis on winning has negated this potential benefit; not all who want to play can because there aren't enough sponsors or uniforms or because there aren't enough managers." They maintain that the need for sponsors could be minimized and more of the money put into equipment if uniforms were not required and that more men would manage if so much importance were not placed upon almost professional level skills, which means many minutes of extra team and individual practice. The fear of failure that operates as a deterrent to recruitment of coaches and managers could be reduced if more fun and less serious competition were involved. But the proponent argues that more fun and less emphasis on winning would foster mediocrity and less team and individual skill development. The opponent retorts, "How in the world did Babe Ruth, Joe DiMaggio, Bob Feller, Bob Cousey, Jim Thorpe, Otto Graham and the like ever develop their skills?" And the proponent rebuts, and so it goes on ad infinitum—almost!

Critics are also concerned about the physiological and psychological effects. Are children nine through thirteen years of age physically ready for tackle football? How about the much publicized "Little League elbow"

(12), a serious and often permanent injury that, if extreme enough, involves the tearing away of the bony knob called the "epicondyle" from the long bones of the upper arm? Are the Little Leaguers harmed by the emotional stress at such a tender age? (see Figure 19.3.) Have they achieved at age eight things that then leave them little to look forward to? Critics feel that overemphasis is the cause for most of the ills (and herein lies what seems to be the soundest argument of all). They shudder at incidents such as one in which the pitcher hit his head on the dugout roof only a half hour before the game, was rushed to a hospital where five stitches were taken and drugs administered to relieve the pain, then was sent in to pitch "while still unsteady from the blow on his

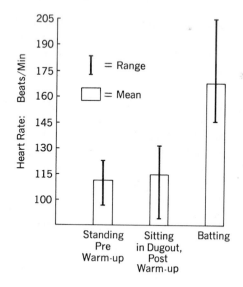

FIGURE 19.3 Effects of batting on Little Leaguers' heart rates. $N = 10$; average for batting computed on basis of four at-bats while at plate only. Data from Hanson (227).

head" (271). Joey Jay (271), the first Little Leaguer to make good in the major leagues, reports a case of ulcers in a twelve-year-old, the case of one youngster's need for sleeping pills, and that coaches and even the fathers are yelling insults at boys who make mistakes; he also describes fathers that are paying for hits and home runs (the same is true for tackles and recovered fumbles in football). Critics argue that such occurrences would seldom occur if it were not for the overemphasis placed on organization and winning.

Jay describes the cases of two star players, one of whom had even had his picture in a national magazine. One never went out for his high school team; the other tried out and did not make it. But, on the other side of the coin, there are others who have been helped by their experiences in organized competition; the debate could rage on forever on this particular topic.

In essence, it appears to be at least partly a philosophical issue. There is much to be drived from organized competition, but much damage to be inflicted, physically and psychologically, when sound physiological and educational policies are ignored or skirted! In summary, it appears that it is not the games per se, or the competition, or the fact that there is some organization. *It is a question of degree and emphasis.* It seems that competition for youngsters ten and over may be relatively harmless, but certain guidelines need to be established and closely followed. We feel the following recommendations are sound and worthy of serious consideration:

1. Effect a close working relationship with schools and recreation departments.

2. Screen and select managers from trained personnel, persons experienced in working with youngsters.

3. Curtail extensive promotion and publicity.

4. Provide "spectator and supporter" education directed toward improving sportsmanship of fans and father-son relationships.

5. Use municipal and school fields whenever possible to avoid the expense of special "miniature big-league parks."

6. Prohibit commercialism and advertisement; merchants who are unwilling to support minimal equipment needs without advertisement are interested in the wrong objective anyway. Caps are adequate for team differentiation in baseball, "pinneys" for basketball. Tackle football represents a serious financial problem where boys cannot afford their own personal equipment, but commercialism must be avoided at all costs. Other solutions are dictated—perhaps tackle football is inadvisable before age fourteen anyway.

7. Teams must be numerous enough to allow every applicant to become a team member, and teams should be required to use every boy at least two innings in baseball, one quarter in basketball, and so on.

8. Awards should be inexpensive and given only to teams and not to individuals.

9. Trips of more than one mile should not be allowed except when competi-

tion is not available within the one-mile radius.

10. All-star teams and all-star games should be discouraged.[1]

ATHLETICS AND PHYSICAL ACTIVITY FOR WOMEN

Willowdale Girl Smashes World Record

Maureen Wilson, 80 pound teenager, placed sixth in distance marathon for

[1]Some of these recommendations are based upon Jay's (271) suggested reforms.

men Saturday. Unbelievable achievement was questioned by American Sportscasters with U.S. networks asking for medical proof that Maureen is a girl and suggesting that she may have covered part of the distance by car . . . (567).

The story above appeared in the Willowdale, Ontario, *Enterprise* on May 10, 1967. Little (four feet, ten inches) "Mo" Wilson, age thirteen, had run in a twenty-six–mile marathon against twenty-nine experienced male runners and had finished sixth in a time of 3 hours, 15 minutes, and 22.8 seconds. (She ran the last mile in six minutes.)

FIGURE 19.4   Vigorous and intensive action in a women's field hockey contest. Photograph courtesy of Mrs. Richard Schaefer, Valley Farm Summer Hockey Camp, Brooklyn, Michigan.

Reaction to the feat was mixed. Along with incredulous inquiries from around the world, there were caustic criticisms. Former British olympic coach (now head of the Canadian Legion Training Plan) Geoff Dyson commented: "It's like pushing peanuts uphill with your nose. She did it, but so what?" "A ridiculous effort," said the chairman of the women's committee of the Canadian AAU, "I'm surprised her parents would allow it. I've talked to many doctors and my conclusion is that nobody knows yet what may happen in the future, when a child this age is older. Then damage may show."

This entire episode epitomizes much of the problem of competitive sports for women. The history of women's athletics is replete with controversy over problems imagined and real. In the United States the idea of girls competing in sports more vigorous than synchronized swimming and weekend bowling is relatively new.

The question of competitive athletics for women has been around for some time. (Of course, no one is advocating competition between men and women.) The Division of Girls' and Women's Sports (DGWS) of AAHPER has been active in studying the problems and in making recommendations for a number of years. Conservation has been the watchword in most instances.

But these times are new times. The problems have not changed, but attitudes have: social attitudes, attitudes of girls, parents, administrators, and teachers alike. The question keeps coming up, and some of the answers may be changing.

COMMON OBJECTIONS

As indicated by the reaction to Maureen's run (obviously an extreme case), the objections offered fall into several categories.

Physiological Damage

Traditionally it has been assumed (in the United States) that women were physiologically unable to stand the rigors of hard training and competition. The phenomenon of the girl swimmers has begun a revolution in this area. Most of the world records and olympic championships have been set by girls in their early teens. Training schedules that once would have been rejected by male college swimming teams are now common among youngsters of both sexes.

An excellent study (22), conducted in Sweden by a distinguished group headed by P. O. Åstrand, has reported swimming schedules for thirty young (twelve to sixteen years old) girl swimmers of up to twenty-eight hours, and as many as thirty-four miles a week. Such training schedules are not uncommon in the United States in age-group swimming programs. The question of how they are tolerated is an important one.

Åstrand's group studied the Swedish swimmers from several points of view, including complete assessments of medical history, family and social background, body growth, gynecological aspects, social adjustment and psychiatric aspects, and physiological status and reaction to training. From the standpoint of growth and development, no differences from the normal population could be detected except for a slightly earlier average age of menarche (12.9 years). This was not attributed to the training, however, because it appeared to be consistent with a progressive trend toward earlier menstruation of the Swedish female population.

A survey of former champion swimmers (a part of Åstrand's study) revealed no body weight deviations that might be attributable to having ceased competing. Subjects ranged from twenty to forty years of age in this part of the study. No grounds for increased illness of any kind was found among this group.

Gynecological Problems

One of the questions most frequently raised is the effect of vigorous participation on menstruation and childbirth. Several studies (13, 167, 488) have indicated that former athletic participants have no greater difficulty in childbirth than others, and at least one study has indicated that average labor is considerably shorter among this group (451). Dr. Evelyn Gendel has observed that women who have never participated in sports or moderate physical activity at any time may have greater postpartum problems of back pain and other discomfort (207). Strength of abdominal muscles appears to be one of the significant factors.

With respect to menstruation, Dr.

Gendel has said: "We have been overprotective about this phenomenon for years. Facts about menstruation, although well documented and understood, have been colored by the folklore of the female subculture and the influence of women on men . . . (207).

In a study of 729 female Hungarian athletes, Erdelye found that about one third declined in performance during their menstrual periods, that half experienced no change, and that the rest improved (167). It is significant that in the 1956 Olympics at least six gold medals were won by women competing during their menstrual periods.

Similar results have been observed by others studying the problem. The fact that discomfort is an individual matter (but not worsened by training and competition) was confirmed by Åstrand's group. Some girls trained during their menstrual periods, and others did not. However, all girls competed if events coincided with their menstrual periods, with thirteen of the thirty reporting that they felt their performance was adversely affected.

Dysmenorrhea has not been found to be greater among female athletes or former athletes (167), but some evidence has indicated that those who are regularly active enjoy an advantage in this regard (207).

Although there has been no evidence of increased gynecological diseases due to swimming during the menstrual cycle, Åstrand's group made recommendations discouraging this practice on the basis of possibly increased susceptibility to infection during this time.

Safety

The danger of traumatic injuries to the breasts or of damage to the face has prompted most authorities to rule out sports where the probability of such injury is high. Protective devices are sometimes advocated for those who do participate in such sports (46). The safety problem does not appear to be acute.

Masculinization

There can be no doubt that one of the greatest deterrents to participation in sports by girls is their aversion to "getting muscles." In the last decade the influx of attractive young ladies into activities such as track and gymnastics has done much to dispel this myth. One could point to any number of feminine, attractive women in competitive athletics, as well as in such other vigorous activities as ballet and modern dance, as evidence. The fact of the matter is that most girls could not develop large muscles by intensive training if they set out to do so. The limited amount of muscle hypertrophy that may occur usually serves to improve the appearance of the participant rather than to detract from it.

It is true that masculine characteristics of size and breadth may provide advantages in certain kinds of competition. For this reason, female competitors with such characteristics are frequently encountered. In order to put the twelve-pound shot, the participant must have considerable mass. In such cases it is the selection factor that

has attracted this type of individual to the activity; the activity has not produced the characteristics in the performer. If one would care to make the effort, he could observe many of the same types (who have never touched a shot or discus) pushing a shopping basket in a supermarket. No one has raised objections to grocery shopping.

Emotional Aspects

Another argument commonly expressed is that women are more emotional than men and, therefore, unable to control themselves adequately in competition. There is no question about the greater freedom of women to express certain kinds of emotion in our culture. Crying is approved for children and women, but not for men. One wonders, however, whether the male animal's self-control is superior to that of his mate. One of the arguments used in favor of athletics for boys is that it increases his ability to deal with emotional stress. Perhaps if girls were given similar opportunities, their emotional stability would be improved. It is obvious that the leadership involved in these programs is important in dealing with problems such as this.

Administrative Considerations

The DGWS has developed a strong organization that is determined to avoid the many pitfalls that have beset the athletic programs for boys. A system for the training and certification of officials has been successfully worked out (38), and operating policies have been formulated to insure careful control of interscholastic athletic programs for girls. One of the big problems has been inadequate funds. With no gate receipts to rely upon (and no desire for such), women's programs have been severely limited. With more pressure from students and others for this type of activity, it appears that the future holds considerably more opportunity for the girl who would like to compete.

A legitimate concern of female administrators is the avoidance of exploitation of girls' teams for entertainment purposes. Past experience, in areas where competition in sports like basketball are played, has indicated that women's sports can engender the same kind of community enthusiasm (and lack of rational behavior) that has characterized male competition. No one is anxious to enter an era of high pressure recruitment of female athletes for the local university.

The training of coaches is another problem that once appeared to be formidable. Gradually, however, female coaches are gaining experience and recognition. If women wish to retain control of athletics, however, more must be done to prepare female teachers for this responsibility. In many cases men have taken the responsibility for girls' teams, but this is viewed as a temporary arrangement. As professional classes in coaching techniques are opened up to women and as cooperation grows between men and women in the profession, greater numbers of women will be prepared to handle interscholastic programs.

As has been pointed out in Ulrich's review (577), cultural and philosophical considerations are probably more important than biological differences in resolving the problem of competitive athletics for women. "The standards of the culture and the biological structure of the participants will undoubtedly direct the future of women's sports."

The biological mythology has been largely dispelled; the cultural "rules" are apparently changing. It will be interesting to watch the growth of athletic competition among women in the United States during the next decade.

SUMMARY

EXPERIMENTS AND EXPERIENCES

1. Identify as many labor-saving devices as you can and estimate the daily reduction in caloric expenditure for their average use.
2. Identify automated devices which have replaced workers and estimate the number of persons replaced by each single device.
3. Survey adult opinion concerning the "little league" concept. What are their major concerns? Determine what percent of little league coaches have a policy that: (1) every boy who tries out makes the team, and (2) every boy on the team is given a chance to play in every game.
4. Survey high school students' opinion about the "masculinizing" effect of exercise on girls. Survey parents of sixth- to ninth-grade girls.

SUGGESTED READINGS

The following references are highly recommended: Hanson (227); Huxley (260); Jay (271).

Additional recommended references:

Charles, A. H. "Women in Sport," *Injury in Sports,* Springfield, Ill.: Charles C Thomas, Publisher, 1964.

Ryde, D., "The Effects of Strenuous Exercise in Women," *Practitioner,* 177:75, 1956.

Steinhaus, A. H. Reference 543, "Contribution of Sports to Women's Fitness," "Exercise and the Female Reproductive Organs."

Ulrich, C., "Women and Sport," *Science and Medicine of Exercise and Sports.* New York: Harper & Row, Publishers, 1960.

Essential
Emergency Procedures

Chapter 20

In physical education and recreation, the most common injuries are those involving the muscles and joints. Because there is still widespread misconception concerning treatment of muscle injuries, we feel it essential to deal with these procedures. And because any person who deals daily with large numbers of persons is more likely to have to deal with injuries, we shall also briefly describe general emergency procedures: mouth-to-mouth resuscitation, external cardiac massage, and treatment for hemorrhage and shock. It is not our intent to provide a first-aid course, which you will certainly get as a part of your training, but to provide you with the details of the emergency life-saving measures.

GENERAL EMERGENCY PROCEDURES

1. If the injury is serious, send for medical aid quickly if someone is available, but do not leave the patient to do so until you are sure you can do nothing more for him.
2. Whether or not the person is conscious:
   Check to see that he is breathing; if not, begin mouth-to-mouth resuscitation (page 601).

Next, check for bleeding; if it is excessive, initiate some appropriate form of hemorrhage control (page 605).

Next, check for fractures.

Always, in case of serious injury, or if the victim is particularly frightened, suspect and treat for shock (page 608).

Loosen tight clothing, remove loose objects (especially from mouth if victim is unconscious), keep person quiet and comfortable (added warmth in cool weather and plenty of air in hot, close weather). Reassure him as much as possible.

Be prepared to allow the victim to vomit freely without choking. This will prevent him from sucking the vomitus into his own lungs.

3. *Don'ts.*

Don't give anything by mouth, except as specified in certain poison treatment, or *as indicated* in hemorrhage or shock (page 608).

Don't give aspirin, drugs, and so on.

Don't move person unless his position endangers him.

Don't allow him to get up and move until you are absolutely sure he can do so safely.

SPECIFIC EMERGENCY AND FIRST-AID THERAPY

Someone who enjoys and participates in active sports runs a somewhat greater risk of incurring injuries from accidents than does the inactive person. Moving at high speeds, making sudden starts and stops and quick changes in direction, coming in contact with various objects and implements as well as with other participants—all these increase the risk of personal injury. But such risks are unavoidable. In fact, they are part of the attraction of the activity. Whether we are conscious of it or not, they contribute to the general challenge of the game or contest.

Consider the sports of auto racing, mountain climbing, and boxing, for example. In all of these the risk involved has the strongest attraction for many. But few of us actually desire to be injured or to spend time recuperating from an accident or an injury, regardless of how it was sustained. Therefore, because injuries are such a real possibility, you need to know how best to prevent them and how to treat them if they occur.

MUSCLE SORENESS

One of the most universal complaints after vigorous physical activity is muscle soreness. The individual who is active only occasionally is, of course, more subject to this discomfort than are people who exercise regularly. In any case, muscle soreness can be a real problem. At one time or another most of us have found ourselves unable to bend our legs or arms comfortably after a session of strenuous exercise. The actual cause of such soreness is still not completely understood. There is evidence (481, p. 355) that an excessive concentration of potassium in the tissues in some way is involved with the pain. The actual pain mechanism may be due to an accumulation of fluids in the area that causes pressure on nerve endings, especially when the muscles in the area are asked to contract.

Probably the most effective single treatment for dispelling muscle soreness is moderate activity. If one can bring himself to engage in some gentle stretching and bending exercises, gradually increasing the intensity of the activity, he will discover that the soreness will disappear quickly. Of course, rest will eventually result in a cure, but this may take several days.

MUSCLE PULLS

Another commonly encountered condition, closely related to muscle soreness is the muscle pull or tear. In activities where all-out sudden starts, stops, and turns are demanded, the attachments of muscles can actually be partially torn away from the bones. Sometimes such tears occur within the belly of the muscle itself. In either case a great deal of pain and discomfort are felt and prompt treatment is required.

PREVENTION Many athletes and coaches believe that adequate warm-up before actual competition begins aids in preventing muscle pulls. Although this technique appears to "make sense," experimental evidence (293, p. 13; 569) does not support it. There does, however, seem to be no doubt that an adequate conditioning program preceding participation has a direct effect on reducing the incidence of such injuries. It is clear that if proper attention is given to the training of specific mus-

cles before they are called upon to produce the very great forces needed to propel the body or its parts, much of the difficulty could be avoided.

TREATMENT Once this injury has occurred, a cold pack should be applied immediately. This treatment should be continued for one or two hours, and repeated at regular intervals for twenty-four hours. Following the first day, hot packs and whirlpool treatments may be used to stimulate circulation to the area involved, although some trainers prefer to continue the cold treatment through the first week. Ultrasound or other deep-heat treatments may also be helpful when properly administered. Protective taping may be indicated, depending upon the type and location of the injury. The healing of such injuries is notoriously slow and before participation is resumed it is important for the patient to undergo a thorough reconditioning program.

SPRAINS

Next to bruises and abrasions probably the most commonly observed athletic injury is the sprained ankle. Sprains to other joints, such as the wrist, are also commonplace. The treatment for such accidents is essentially the same as for a muscle tear. The joint should be immediately packed with ice or immersed in cold water to prevent excessive swelling. Athletic trainers frequently wrap the joint with an elastic bandage during this cooling period to further inhibit swelling. Such bandages should not be too tight and should be frequently loosened in order to ensure adequate circulation to the limb involved. The joint should then be taped firmly for support and given as much rest as is necessary for healing to take place. Unless the sprain is severe it is usually possible for the victim to get around without crutches, provided the joint is properly immobilized by taping. Further treatments with cold and hot baths, as well as the whirlpool, are desirable.

TORN LIGAMENTS — THE KNEE

The knee has been described as the most vulnerable joint in the body. Probably the most common serious injury in football is the tearing of knee ligaments and cartilage. Whenever a player is blocked from the side, and even when he simply pivots suddenly, tremendous strains are thrown onto the ligaments that secure the lower leg to the femur. Whenever an injury of this type occurs it is extremely important to have an immediate diagnosis to determine whether permanent damage has been done. Because ligaments are not elastic, if one is torn it must be repaired surgically if normal function is ever to be regained.

DISLOCATIONS

Dislocations of the shoulder, elbow, finger, toe, hip, and sometimes other joints are not uncommon. A dislocation involves the slipping of the bones of a joint out of their usual places and al-

ways causes great pain. Sometimes such displaced bones slip back into their proper positions by themselves, but at other times they lodge in such positions that they must be reduced by a physician. A dislocation is always a serious injury and should be reduced only by a qualified and experienced person.

Ordinarily, a dislocation should be treated like a broken bone. The patient should be kept quiet and treated for shock. He should be placed in the horizontal position with the head slightly lower than the body and kept warm. All tight and restrictive clothing should be loosened.

BROKEN BONES

Of course broken bones are a common hazard of many types of athletic activity. In all cases of breaks or suspected breaks the bone should be splinted with a cushion, a padded board, or one of the new pneumatic splints. Movement of the part must be avoided. If the broken end of the bone protrudes through the skin any bleeding must be controlled. This can usually be satisfactorily accomplished by placing pressure above or below the wound. In rare cases a tourniquet may be necessary. Whether the fracture is simple or compound, treatment for shock is important (page 608). A physician should always be summoned immediately.

BLISTERS

Not all injuries sustained by active people are major ones. Blisters are equally familiar to the week-end gardener and the professional athlete. Although most often found on the feet and hands, blisters will form wherever there is persistent friction between the skin and another surface. The pain resulting from blisters may be considerable, but the most serious problem associated with them is the very real possibility that they may become infected.

PREVENTION   In order to prevent blisters on the feet it is recommended that special care be taken to wear only properly fitting shoes. Wearing two pairs of socks will help to reduce friction against the surface of the shoe itself. (Care should be taken to be sure that the sock does not bunch up under the foot.) The use of a good talcum powder in the shoes and socks also serves to reduce friction effectively.

TREATMENT   If a blister should form on the foot it must be carefully protected from dirt as well as from further injury. A thick coating of petroleum jelly covered with a "doughnut" pad, with the hole placed over the blister, will be found helpful. For blisters on the hands, petroleum jelly spread over the blisters and covered with a light bandage should help to prevent further aggravation. The use of a golf glove or a similar protective glove is suggested for the person who frequently develops blisters on his hands.

Scratches and abrasions, as well as blisters that have ruptured, require the same treatment: cleansing the injured area with clean, soapy water. The prevention of infection is the primary consideration. If dirt has been ground into the wound, more complicated measures may have to be taken and a physician should be consulted. Of course, for deeper wounds, such as lacerations or puncture wounds, a physician should determine whether a tetanus shot is indicated.

ATHLETE'S FOOT

Another skin problem is a fungus infection commonly associated with people who are active in sports and athletics. Dubbed "athlete's foot," this disease causes cracks in the skin between the toes and sometimes blisters around the toes and on the bottoms of the feet. Severe itching and pain generally are present. Research (89) has indicated that certain chemicals used in foot baths can aid in the prevention of athlete's foot. However, the simple expedient of keeping the feet dry is also helpful. Careful drying between the toes following showers and the use of powder in the socks can help prevent this condition.

TREATMENT   This is another case in which the best "cure" is prevention. Once the condition has been contracted, however, a number of effective medicines are available for its control. A physician should be consulted in order to be sure the correct medicine is used: any one of several types of fungus may be responsible for a case of athlete's foot.

"CHARLEY HORSE"

Another condition universally identified with athletics is the deep muscle bruise that goes by the name of "charley horse." At times a bruise of the bone may also be involved in such injuries. The treatment for this type of injury is similar to that advocated for muscle tears and sprains. The injury should be first treated with ice, followed (after at least twenty-four hours) with heat treatments and whirlpool. Deep heat, such as diathermy or ultrasound, would probably also be indicated in these cases.

CRAMPS AND MUSCLE SPASMS

When any muscle contracts vigorously it produces a certain amount of discomfort. Sometimes muscles go into a spasm or cramp spontaneously. Such occurrences are frequently quite painful and may even be dangerous, depending upon the activity being engaged in when they develop. When muscles are called upon to contract vigorously and for long periods of time, as in athletics or very heavy work, cramps are much more likely to occur. Certain muscles seem to be more susceptible to cramps than others. The calf muscles (triceps surae), for example, seem to cause difficulty quite often. Another area frequently afflicted involves the muscles of the front of the thigh (quadriceps). A particular type of cramp, known as "stitch in the side," is frequently experienced by runners. It is thought by some that this moder-

ately painful sensation is produced by a spasm or spontaneous contraction of the muscles of the diaphragm. Others attribute it to a stretching of the ligaments that support the abdominal organs (543, p. 130).

Although the actual cause of cramps is not clear, the condition occurs whenever the muscle tissue becomes especially irritable. There is some evidence that such irritability may be caused by an insufficient amount of salt (sodium chloride) in the body, but this has not been substantiated for all types of cramps.

RELIEF OF CRAMPS Regardless of whether a cramp occurs during rest or in the midst of physical activity, the pain is intense. The immediate treatment for a cramp (except abdominal "heat" cramps) calls for a stretching of the involved musculature. If, for example, a cramp develops in the calf, the muscle can be stretched by lifting the toes up vigorously toward the shin. Another technique that seems to help in some cases is to vigorously knead the afflicted area with the fingers. In the case of extreme cramps that result from excessive salt losses relief can be obtained only through the administration of salt by infusion or by ingestion.

SWIMMERS' CRAMPS A swimmer who is stricken with a cramp may be in considerably more difficulty than a runner. The same procedures may be used for relieving the cramp, but it is obviously much more difficult to carry out these maneuvers in deep water than on land. If it is possible to withstand the discomfort until one can reach the shore or some support, this should be done. Sometimes changing to another stroke or to a float will help. In any case it is essential to avoid panic and its accompanying flailing movements. Experienced swimmers can usually deal with cramps successfully because they are able to avoid panic.

MOUTH-TO-MOUTH RESUSCITATION

Anytime breathing has stopped, from any cause, or when breathing is so shallow or difficult that stoppage or even unconsciousness is imminent, begin mouth-to-mouth resuscitation *immediately*. If possible, no more than ten seconds should be spent in preparation. This means you must be prepared and well rehearsed in the procedures.

1. Check to make sure victim is not a "neck breather" (a surgical hole in the windpipe). This requires a different procedure.
2. Remove foreign material from throat and mouth of victim (including false teeth) and keep tongue pulled forward. (See Figure 20.1.)

FIGURE 20.1

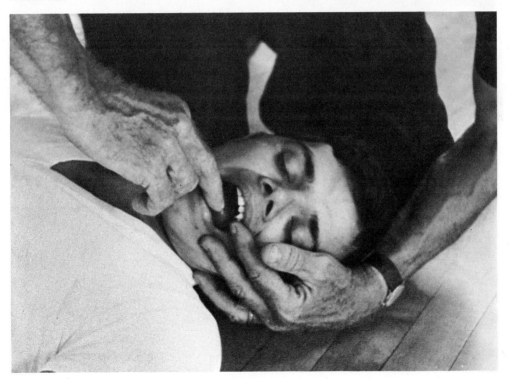

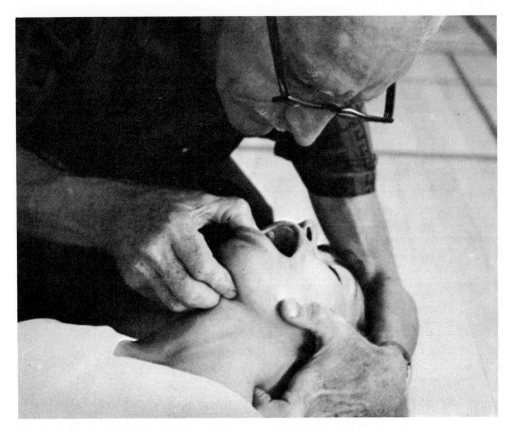

FIGURE 20.2

3. Keep air passage open by tilting victim's head back and pulling up on his jaws; place yourself to the side. (See Figure 20.2.)

4. Prevent air leakage from victim's nose and around his mouth by pinching nostrils shut with your free hand and blow forcefully into his mouth after a deep breath with your mouth pressed tightly over the victim's.

(Note: Blow gently into child's mouth, covering both nose and mouth with your mouth.) (See Figure 20.3.)

5. When you see the victim's chest rise, take your mouth away and allow natural exhalation.

6. When exhalation is completed, repeat the blowing procedure; repeat about every two to five seconds.

7. Be sure air exchange with the lungs is actually taking place.

8. Continue until the victim recovers breathing or until he is pronounced dead by a physician.

9. Be prepared for vomiting. If it occurs, remove debris from throat and mouth immediately and begin again.

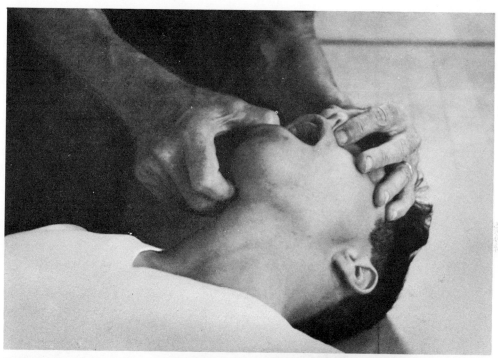

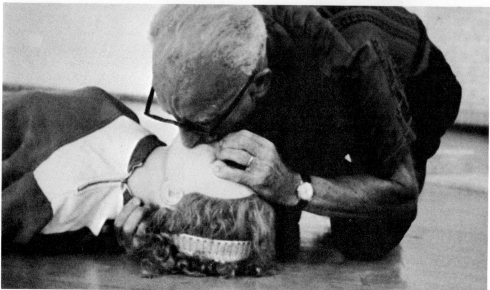

FIGURE 20.3

EXTERNAL CARDIAC MASSAGE

Henderson (240) states that "Between 7,500 and 9,000 people die in the United States each year from cardiac arrest—

which need only have been temporary had the proper resuscitative measures been applied quickly." It is known that in many instances the heart can be "restored" by properly squeezing

FIGURE 20.4

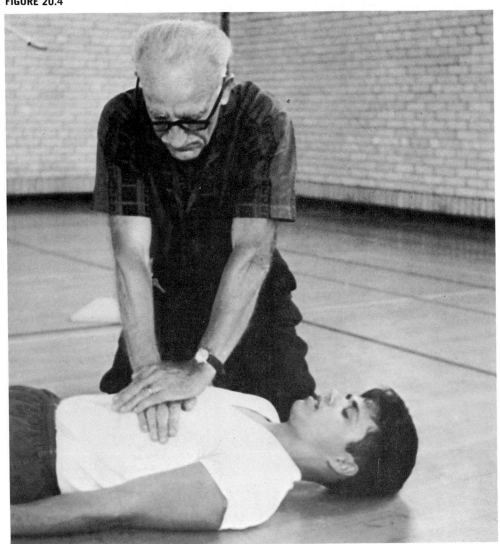

it rhythmically between the breastbone and spinal column. In order to apply external cardiac massage, the following procedures should be carried out.

1. Place victim on his back.
2. Place yourself at right angles to his chest, kneeling.
3. Prepare him for mouth-to-mouth resuscitation.
4. Blow air into his lungs three times.
5. *For adults,* use heel of hand only (with heel of other hand on top of it), on lower one-third of breast bone, and press firmly down so that breast bone is depressed about two inches. *Do not press with fingers on ribs.* Repeat once every second. *For babies* and *young children,* use only the finger tips, applied to the center of the breastbone, and do not press too hard. For children nine to ten and up, use heel of one hand only.
6. Have someone give mouth-to-mouth resuscitation. *Cardiac massage is useless without respiratory resuscitation measures.* If no one else is available, stop massage every one-half minute and give mouth-to-mouth resuscitation for four deep breaths.
7. Continue until relieved or until the victim has recovered or is pronounced dead by a physician.

HEMORRHAGE

Direct pressure with a clean gauze pad or other soft cloth (not cotton) will stop bleeding from most minor cuts unless an artery or large vein is involved. Permanence may be attained by bandaging the pressure pad into position. Make sure flow to the rest of the area (leg, for example) is not also restricted.

If direct pressure does not work and bleeding is profuse, use of pressure points may be necessary. The major pressure points are illustrated in Figure 20.5. They are used to control bleeding by applying pressure between the heart and the point of bleeding. The following cautions are very imporant.

Apply pressure to those points *only as a last resort.*

Apply only as much pressure as is necessary to stop bleeding.

At the carotid artery point (B in Figure 20.5), be careful to avoid pressure on the windpipe and to use pressure discriminately, as this is the major blood supply to the brain. Unconsciousness may result from the pressure near the carotid body.

If pressure does not stop bleeding after a short period of time, a tourniquet may be needed. If applied (see example in Figure 20.6), certain rules are *extremely important:*

1. Place it as close as possible to the wound, between the wound and the heart, without actually touching the wound's edges.
2. Tighten only enough to reduce bleeding, no more!
3. Use a pad over the artery to be compressed.
4. Do *not* use something that will cut into the flesh (wire, rope, and so on).
5. *Do not release tourniquet pressure until medical assistance is present.*
6. Note the time the tourniquet was

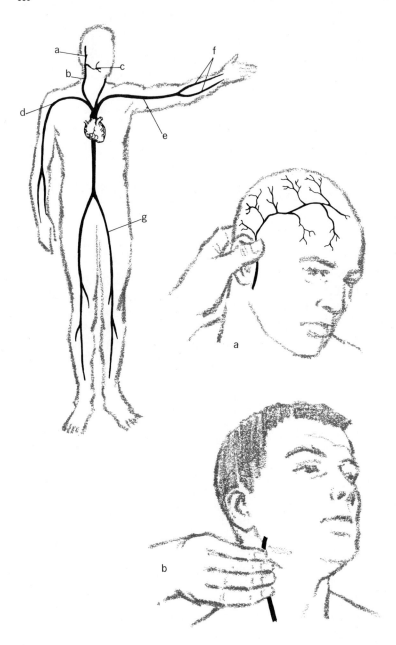

FIGURE 20.5 Diagram of available pressure points for control of arterial bleeding. By permission from John Henderson, *Emergency Medical Guide*. New York: McGraw-Hill, Inc., Blakiston Division, 1963.

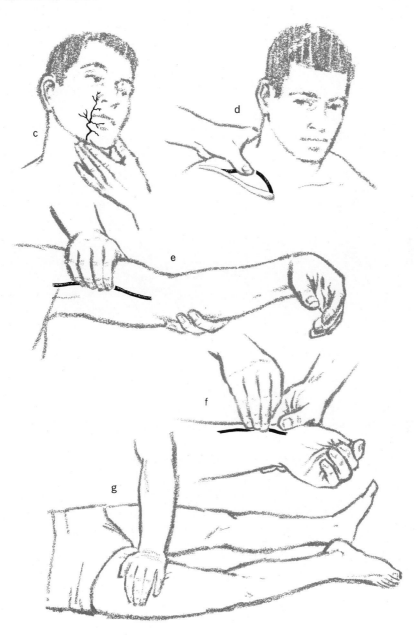

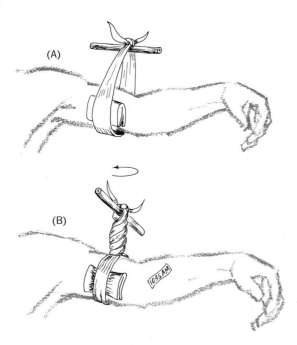

(A)

(B)

1045 AM

FIGURE 20.6 Use of a tourniquet. Padding is essential.

placed on the victim (Figure 20.6).
7. If the victim is conscious, water or other liquids can be given by mouth to help replace lost fluids. Hot coffee and stimulants should be avoided.

SHOCK

As mentioned earlier, all seriously injured or emotionally upset victims should be treated for shock, whether or not it has set in. The symptoms are (any or all): faintness; weakness; clammy skin; pupils dilated; rapid and irregular, deep or shallow breathing; nausea; thirst; fast irregular and weak pulse (may even be too weak to feel in severe cases); may or may not be unconscious.

Keep the victim lying down.

Make him comfortable; conserve body heat (blankets *under* and over him in cool or cold weather); do *not* cover him if weather is warm or hot unless victim complains of chills.

Unless victim has a head injury, chest injury, or respiratory difficulty, raise feet to level above head. With a head injury, keep him flat; with chest injuries or breathing difficulty, raise his head and shoulders if possible.

Give fluids if victim is conscious; urge him to take as much as possible.

Selection
of Exercise Programs[1]

Chapter 21

In keeping with the approach of this book, it would be inappropriate to list and describe for the physical educator and recreation worker all the techniques available as "conditioning" programs. Up to this point our approach has been to stress the importance of *concepts* and individual responsibility for health and fitness. We do not intend to deviate from our original position—that the individual, all-important in health and fitness, must have the knowledge and the opportunity to make his own decisions about fitness; it is the physical educator's task to educate persons so as to be able to make effective use of this opportunity. This opportunity must also include the freedom to select *how*, once the decision to exercise regularly has been reached. It is the purpose of this chapter to present certain principles and considerations for conditioning work, to describe very briefly and in a general way some of the techniques and "gimmicks," and to present a very general framework upon which one can build his own program. For

---

[1]We wish to acknowledge the contributions of Donald C. Stolberg to the development of the concepts presented in this chapter.

those interested in specific programs, references are cited at the end of the chapter.

(A word of caution would be in order for those who wish to begin exercise, as a part of an AHD prevention program, after some years of sedentary existence. To be told that what he needs is "exercise" is like having a physician tell him that what he needs is "medicine." Important questions, in each instance, such as "What kind? How much? How often?" must be answered. If one is health and fitness educated and his physician approves, moderation and a knowledge of exercise as related to health and fitness can carry him to a successful exercise prescription.)

TRAINING PRINCIPLES AND CONSIDERATIONS

An intelligent person, about to enter into a life of regular exercise, should probably consider certain important and fundamental factors before commencing. Each person must decide for himself whether these factors are related to *his* health and fitness goals and how. How much independence one is capable of is dependent, of course, upon age and health and fitness knowledge.

PRIOR PHYSICAL EXAMINATION

Whether one needs a physical exam prior to beginning an exercise program is dependent upon (1) age, (2) known health status, (3) current level of physical activity, and (4) nature and intensity

of the exercise program to be adopted. In other words, the older one gets, the poorer the health status, the more sedentary his life, and the more vigorous his intended activities are, the more logical it becomes for him to get a physical checkup first.

PRIOR FITNESS TESTING AND APPRAISAL

If one wishes a general program and desires to work on particular weaknesses, some testing and appraisal are essential. For details see Appendix B and appropriate chapters.

WARM-UP

Depending on the intensity of the activity or exercise program, it is generally advisable to work into the activity gradually, especially during the early sessions. One might actually apply the same four factors described under "Prior Physical Examination" as determining the need for warm-up. Injury, obviously, can occur even after warm-up, but the stretching and pulling kind of muscle injury can be minimized and rendered less probable after some gentle and thorough stretching exercises.

SCHEDULE

Such considerations as time of day, length of workout, and number of sessions per week are important, but usually depend upon environmental, social, family, and similar factors. Nobody has definitely established the "best" time of day. The length of the exercise session needed for benefit depends in part upon the intensity of exercise. For example, rope jumping for five minutes may be equivalent to walking for two hours. Level of aspiration will also have some bearing upon establishing the number of times to exercise per week. With knowledge, some common sense, and some experimentation, one can readily determine what exercise program best fits into the daily schedule. Experience leads us to conclude that at least thirty minutes, three times per week, is minimal, but such factors as age, current physical state, personality, and intensity of exercise could modify this.

OVERLOAD CONCEPT

One should keep in mind that, in order to elicit gains in the function of any system, an overload must be applied to that system. The heart cannot become stronger and more efficient if it is never taxed. The muscles and the respiratory system cannot improve their adaptability to work unless they are, in fact, worked. This concept is often referred to as the "law of use and disuse." In other words, a normal, healthy system functions roughly in proportion to the regular demands placed upon it; thus we conclude that we must "tax" or "overload" the circulo-respiratory system, the muscles, the ligaments, and the tendons if we are to improve CR capacity, muscle performance, and flexibility. For ex-

ample, one would be foolish to expect CR changes if his heart rate is never accelerated and is maintained for some time beyond 120 beats per minute. Dramatic examples of disuse are exemplified best by examples such as those illustrated in Figure 21.1. Opposite effects of "overload" are also illustrated, not to promote a "bulging muscles, strong heart, rubber-man fad," but to illustrate the overload principle and the "law of use and disuse."

SPECIFICITY

The principle of specificity has been discussed previously; its application appears to find its way into all phases of conditioning. In short, "you get what you train for, and *relatively* speaking, little other than that." Obviously there is a possible carry-over, but you are cautioned against assuming that one activity will automatically prepare you for *any* activity. Perhaps endurance running or swimming, as general CR conditioners, come as close to nonspecific entities as any, but even here we find great specificity, as the swimmer who tries to run two miles will testify.

MOTIVATION

The personal reason or motivation for adopting an activity program may ultimately determine its success or failure. Some commitment is necessary to initiate a program, but an even greater commitment is needed to continue!

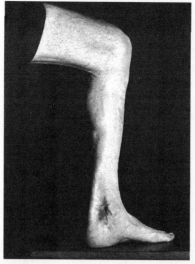
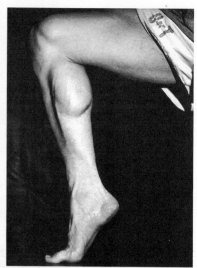

FIGURE 21.1 Examples of "use" and "disuse." Muscle atrophy resulting from injury or disease is compared with the hypertrophied calf muscle of a highly trained jumper. Poor flexibility (not at all unusual in adults) is contrasted with the flexibility of the modern dance performer. Average heart weight in wild animals is almost always greater than that in their domestic counterparts. The data from many experimental laboratory animal studies lend additional support for exercise-induced cardiac hypertrophy. The means illustrated are from an experiment conducted in the University of Toledo laboratory.

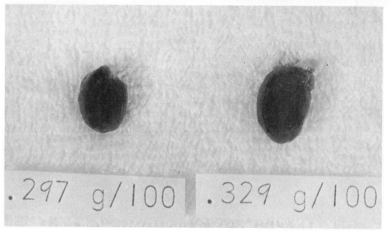

.297 g/100   .329 g/100

Depending upon the level of attainment desired (from general minimal fitness to some kind of championship competition in a given sport), some physical discomfort and boredom or staleness may have to be tolerated and somehow dealt with. An understanding as well as acceptance of the fact that annoyances and discomfort may occur helps the individual react realistically to a program of home exercise; the temptation to quit at times may be strong. It appears to us that dedication or motivation is truly the basic factor underlying successful health and fitness attainment.

TECHNIQUES, PROGRAMS, EQUIPMENT, AND "GIMMICKS"

TECHNIQUES

General calisthenic exercises usually do not require elaborate equipment or "partners." They emphasize muscular endurance (very little resistance), flexibility, CR capacity (if duration is extended), and some degree of grace and coordination. They are often used in shortened form for "warm-up." They include familiar and rather natural activities such as jumping exercises (side-straddle hops, jumping jacks),

FIGURE 21.2 Selected general exercises.

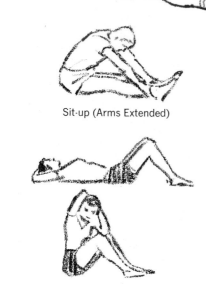

Sit-up (Arms Extended)

Sit-up (Fingers Laced, Knees Bent)

Sit-up (Arms Extended, Knees Up)

Flutter Kick

Push-up

Leg Raiser (On Extended Arm)

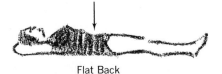

Hump Back
(Attempt to Arch Back
like an Angry Cat:
Repeat at least
ten times)

Flat Back
(Flatten Lower Back
against Floor:
Repeat at least
ten times)

FIGURE 21.2   (continued)

push-ups, toe touching, arm circling, trunk bending in all directions, sit-ups, back arching, running-in-place, and many others (see Figure 21.2).

Modern dance is not only an art medium; it is particularly useful in developing flexibility and balance as well as grace and coordination (see Figure 21.3); if participated in vigorously and often enough, it can also contribute somewhat to CR fitness.

Isometric and isotonic resistance exercises and circuit training, interval training, rhythmic exercises, sports

Leg Raiser

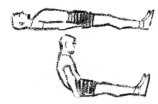

Head and Shoulder Curl

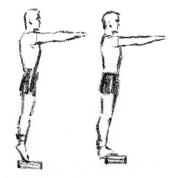

Ankle Stretch

Toe-touch

Jump Rope

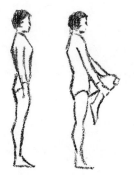

Knee-lift

Half Knee Bend

Body Bender

Prone Arch

Knee Push-up

FIGURE 21.3 Flexibility (top), balance, grace, and body control (bottom) can be highly developed through the medium of modern dance.

TABLE 21.1   Examples of Application of Interval Training to Improvement of Fitness and Motor Ability
Components

COMPONENT	SIT-UPS (ME)	JUMPING ENDURANCE (POWER ENDURANCE)
Rate	30/min	10 max jumps/min
Work interval	½ min	1 min
Rest interval	3 min	3 min
Bouts	3	5
Variations	When 3d bout becomes easy, decrease rest interval to 2 and increase work interval to ¾ min	When all jumps, including the last of each bout, are actually "maximal," decrease rest interval to 1½ min

activities, and "aerobics" are discussed in previous chapters. (Examples of application of interval training are presented in Table 21.1.)

SPECIFIC PROGRAMS

Numerous exercise programs are published by various private and public agencies. The Canadian 5BX and XBX programs and the U.S. Government Adult Physical Fitness programs involve general calisthenics and CR activity. We recommend that you secure a copy of one of these booklets as a guide to the selection of specific exercise programs. There are, however, certain important items other than specific exercises and activities that we deem important to good fitness programming and that are not included in any of these programs. You will find those nonexercise items described in the section beginning on page 618.

SPECIAL EQUIPMENT AND GIMMICKS

There are probably more gimmicks and pieces of special equipment on the market than there are special programs. Vibrators, bicycle-type exercisers, isometric gadgets, weights, and so on, are common items on the consumer market. Many of the gimmicks are integral parts of the "health-salon" programs. Some are valuable aids to exercise although few, if any, are by any stretch of the imagination actually essential. Careful inspection and experimentation will show that some do not give the benefit claimed (they may have other values); some, in our opinion, are nearly worthless. If you have the opportunity, observe and experiment with many of the gimmicks so that you can evaluate them. A knowledge of basic mechanics and physiology, reinforced with some logical reasoning, will help you to reach a decision concerning the usefulness of any piece of exercise equipment or any health salon program. It is not only a question of what is good and what is harmful. To be sure, there have been, and will continue to be, health and medical hoaxes that are actually harmful. But with the exercise gimmicks and health salons, it is more a question of whether *real* benefits are derived.

You should ask these questions: Do scientific principles suggest that this gimmick or this program will accomplish what it claims? If not, is there any *other* value in it? If a gimmick or a health studio program is useless but currently fashionable, one may wish to go ahead and sacrifice the time and money to be "in." However, let us hope that as a professional person, you will recognize the difference between value and fraud and recommend accordingly.

It should be made clear that our intention is not to discredit health studios. Our point is that one should carefully analyze the situation and choose a program, whether it be for a class, at home, or in a health studio, based on scientific principles and not a fad. As a professional, you can aid in such decisions.

It should not be difficult for a person educated in health and fitness to evaluate techniques, programs, and special equipment in terms of overall fitness benefits. Experience in the activity itself and common sense should quickly lead one to decide whether, in fact, the activity improves each or any of the components of fitness. It is an interesting personal experiment to evaluate a list of such programs and techniques. (You may wish to experiment with specific techniques and programs.) After completing such a list, you may wish to compare your estimates with those in Table 21.2.

Educating people so that they know the available techniques and programs is essential but, before the most useful and effective continuing program of physical activity can be selected by the individual (or recommended by a professional), personal and environmental factors must be taken into consideration. Changes in personal needs or environmental changes can modify the basic desire to exercise in either a positive or a negative direction. Some of the more important of these personal and environmental factors will be discussed briefly.

PERSONAL FACTORS INFLUENCING PROGRAM SELECTION

Any of the various types of programs for individuals ranging from home exercise programs to highly organized and competitive team sports, requires a certain amount of critical analysis. Questions like "Will I succeed?" "Will I enjoy myself?" "Will I be embarrassed?" "Can I do it?" and "Is it all worth the trouble?" are asked of oneself. Past experience and the deep-seated desire for success and achievement add to the complexity of evaluating the individual personal factors.

BODY TYPE

One very important personal factor is body type. An obese person, for example, would not usually select tennis, especially if he has difficulty starting and stopping quickly. On the other hand, swimming is an activity to which such a person might very nicely adapt. The extremely thin person must evaluate his limited force potential when

TABLE 21.2 Rating of Sports and Activities

ACTIVITY	CR CAPACITY[a]	MUSCULAR ENDURANCE[a]	STRENGTH[a]	FLEXIBILITY[a]	OTHER[b]	AGE RANGE RECOMMENDED[c]
Archery	0	3	1.5	(0)		All ages
Badminton (singles)	2.5	1.5	0	(0)	A,C	Under 50
Badminton (doubles)	1	1.5	0	(0)	A,C	Under 60
Basketball	2.5	2.5	(0)	(0)	A,C,P,B	Under 30
Baseball	1	2	(0)	(0)	C,P,B	Under 45
Bicycling (recreation)	2.5	3	1.5	(0)		All ages
Bowling	0	1	0	0	C,B	All ages
Calisthenics	1.5–3.0	2–3	1	1–3	C,B	All ages
Canoeing, rowing (recreation)	2–3	2–3	1–2	(0)	C	All ages
(competitive)	3	3	2–3	(0)	C	Under 30
Field hockey	3	2–3	1	(0)	C,B,A	Under 30
Football	1.5	2–3	1–2	(0)	C,A,P	Under 30
Golf	1–2	(0)	0	(0)	C,P	All ages
Handball (singles)	2.5	1.5	0	(0)	C,P,B,A	Under 45
Handball (doubles)	1	1.5	0	(0)	C,P,B,A	Under 60
Apparatus	0	2–3	2.5	1–2	C,B,A	Under 45
Tumbling	0	2	1.5	2–3	C,B,A	Under 50
Hiking	2	2	(0)	(0)		All ages
Skating, speed	2.5–3	2–3	1	(0)	C,B,A	Under 45
Skiing	1–3	1–3	1–2	1	C,B,A	Under 45
Soccer	3	2–3	1	(0)	C,P,A	Under 45
Softball	1	1–2	(0)	(0)	C,P,A	Under 50
Swimming (recreation)	1–3	1–3	1	(0)		All ages
(competitive)	2–3	1–3	2	1–2		Under 30
Tennis, singles	2.5	1.5	(0)	(0)	C,P,A,B	Under 45
Tennis, doubles	1	1.5	(0)	(0)	C,P,A,B	Under 50
Jogging	2–3	2–3	(0)	(0)		All ages
Running	3	2–3	(0)	(0)		Under 45
Rope skipping	2–3	2–3	(0)	(0)	C,B	Under 40
Volleyball	(0)	1–2	(0)	(0)	C,B,P,A	All ages
Wrestling	2–3	2–3	1–2	2–3	C,B,P,A	Under 30

[a] 3 = high; 2 = medium; 1 = low; (0) = doubtful; 0 = none. All activities rated 1, 2, 3 are variable, depending upon regularity, intensity, and duration.
[b] C = Coordination; P = Power; A = Agility; B = Balance.
[c] Recommended age is dependent upon physical fitness and health of individual.

considering activities that require considerable strength. Very short and very tall individuals have advantages in certain activities but also have disadvantages in others. Basketball has become a tall man's game, provided that the tall man has the leg power and the endurance to exploit his height around the basket. Short people with superior coordination can compete favorably in practically all recreational activities, and can excel in such sports as gymnastics and diving as well. Except for the very active games, however, body type is not usually a critical factor involved in selection of the *physical fitness* phase of the program.

FITNESS LEVEL

Any very strenuous activity requires an appropriate level of fitness. If the skill potential is to be realized, resulting in a pleasurable experience, a fitness requirement must be met. This conditioning process may well take several weeks of dedicated and regular effort. Normally, the fitness level improves along with the skill level as the activity is practiced. If personal performance goals are set at a reasonable level and a *gradual* increase in physical fitness and skill is expected, participation should prove to be a stimulating and satisfying experience. The fast-rising sport of judo represents an interesting example of parallel requirements in fitness and skill over a period of participation. The judo performer must be fit in order to absorb the falls, and he must be skilled in throwing and countering. In addition, the challenge level is high because he is striving for a level so remote that chances are he will never reach it.

Modern dance is another activity requiring a realistic analysis. Without a high level of fitness, including exceptional flexibility, the dancer cannot express himself or herself creatively in a manner that will produce the ultimate satisfaction.

EMOTIONAL TEMPERAMENT

Just as children can play and compete to the point of physical exhaustion and psychological overstimulation, so can the immature adult. Such a person is less likely to go to *physical* extremes but is more likely to exceed emotional propriety. The resulting emotional escalation is not always good and can result in nervous tension and psychosomatic disorders as well as some post-performance feelings of guilt or embarrassment. It is therefore quite possible that overinvolvement for some people should be discouraged. If a man finds that his experiences on the golf course or in bowling so disturb him that he may take hours to "unwind," it is doubtful whether he should continue this activity. If his problem is simply a matter of learning to exercise a little self-control, then perhaps the activity can be of real service to him. He may be able to consciously set goals and behavioral boundaries for himself in order to improve his personal qualities.

If, on the other hand, he is actually unable to overcome this problem, he might do well to change activities, for there are many in which overt aggressive behavior is permitted and even essential to success. If suppression of aggressive tendencies in the less active sports continually results in explosive verbal or physical outbursts, he may well be able to profit from learning a sport such as handball, tennis, squash, judo, swimming, or any number of other activities in which vigorous overt activity is called for.

MOTOR ABILITY

Before anyone takes up a new sport or recreational activity, he should analyze it carefully, including the basic motor skills required. Past experience in similar activities may provide some basis for an estimation of potential success. The common requirements of the various court games and racket sports (table tennis, badminton, squash, paddle ball, and tennis), such as basic similarities in movement patterns, visual cues, and strategy, result in a facilitation in the learning of any of these activities if a high level of proficiency has been previously developed in one of the others.

MOTOR EDUCABILITY

Although there are certainly hereditary differences in motor skill, the basic issue in motor educability is quite often dedication. Most people can participate actively, if not efficiently, in almost any activity of their choice. People's rates of learning, however, vary greatly. In such activities as bowling, golf, fly and bait casting, or badminton, some can achieve phenomenal

early success, whereas others can engage in the sport for years, and improve only slightly. However, the patterns of improvement, even for the gifted, level off, and the ultimate physical skill is primarily the product of time, effort, proper practice, and patience.

ENVIRONMENTAL FACTORS

Because most motor skills are taught within the framework of a social institution (that is, the school), it would appear that considerations of program selection would require more than just an evaluation of personal factors. Appropriate environmental factors must exist if participation in the popular activities learned in school is to continue. Absence of any one of the essential factors, such as appropriate facilities, can stifle any desire to participate. Equally important are the social environmental factors. For many people, difficulties in securing teammates, the lack of spectators, or the absence of public acclaim may serve to reduce motivation to the level of indifference. An understanding of the *need* for exercise and familiarity with nonsocial, individualized activities may be essential if problems of this kind are to be avoided.

AVAILABILITY OF FACILITIES

Community facilities for very popular activities are usually provided because of public demand. Multiple-use facilities satisfy most of the demands of the public, especially if the facility is used by all age groups. Park developments and school athletic and physical education plants are examples. Generally, however, small, special-interest groups are handicapped and must build their own facilities or rely on the multiple-use public facilities which may be in constant demand. Many church, social, commercial, and labor organizations fall into this category. Tennis, swimming, archery, firearm, and skating groups frequently incorporate and build their own facilities. Public facilities, important as they are, do not need to be involved in an exercise program, and their inaccessibility is not really a valid excuse for failure to maintain an adequate physical fitness level.

ORGANIZATION

Team sports require extensive organization and generally reflect patterns of play established in school. The organized activities demand conformity to certain rules. They require strict adherence to time and position, and reward the participant with a multitude of physical and emotional experiences and pleasures. But they are *not* the only means of achieving optimal physical fitness and, in many cases, are not even the *best* means. This is especially true for circulo-respiratory fitness: few of the organized community sports in this country are good CR conditioners.

COMPETITORS

Team sports need a homogeneous group of competitors in order to be suc-

cessful. Progressive levels of competition give maximum opportunity for a complete physical experience and consequently result in a deeper emotional involvement. This involvement, in itself, can counteract a great many other disadvantages to participation for many people who, for various reasons, may need this kind of achievement. Most individual sports require two closely matched competitors if any real exercise benefits are to be realized. Activities involving no great organizational difficulties can provide satisfying levels of competition, self-expression, and exercise for many years.

PROGRAM CLASSIFICATIONS

The extent to which the selection of a regular program of physical activity is neglected by some people appears to be related to their lack of understanding of the basic need for exercise. Another problem is their inability to evaluate realistically their past experiences in terms of their current and future needs. For example, not all activities in which a person is skilled or has participated are appropriate for later stages of life. Team sports, such as basketball, baseball, field hockey, softball, hockey, soccer, football, and volleyball, are usually not convenient or available for most adults. The problem is complex. First, organization cannot function without facilities, and most gymnasium and field facilities are used to capacity by schoolchildren. The time required, in the light of family and job responsibilities, creates difficult problems and represents a second major concern. Finally, personal pride in past achievement levels may sometimes cause an individual to avoid any activity in which he may, even temporarily, appear unskilled or awkward. In other words, the psychological need of an individual to excel might, in later life, result in a disproportionate amount of practice necessary for achievement of the skill level necessary to satisfy his ego.

Practical adult programs should be tailored to personal requirements. They should allow for continuous progress and improvement, especially in fitness, and should allow the participant to evaluate his changing status in both fitness and skill. The aim of such programs is to provide an experience that will lead to personal satisfaction in terms of physical improvement and total well-being. A brief discussion of the various major program classifications follows.

The *basic conditioning program* is specifically designed for a person who wants to place his confidence in a standard conditioning program. Such programs entail regular daily participation, stressing physical fitness activities, ranging from minimum to maximum levels of effort. Application of standards and self-evaluation principles have to be incorporated into these programs to ensure their success. The Canadian 5BX and XBX programs and the U.S. Adult Fitness Program are examples of this basic approach.

The *integrated conditioning program* is for those who have good motor skill backgrounds and interests and who

desire physically competitive situations but lack the time or opportunity to schedule regular sports activities. Under this program the sporadic sports skill participation is complemented by a conditioning program in order to meet basic exercise needs. The conditioning program could be designed to perfect a particular skill, or it could serve to improve general endurance or power. For example, a person could hunt and fish when able, and could keep up his daily conditioning program as a means of maintaining general fitness as well as preparing him for periodic wilderness expeditions. Many ski enthusiasts have wisely made it a practice to condition themselves prior to the ski season in order to receive full benefit of the ski day or week-end.

This kind of program may actually be the only practical one for the individual who prefers team or individual sports. Despite his interest in regular participation, family and business commitments continually interrupt his schedule. The idea of parallel programs of sports participation and conditioning activities can enable the individual to satisfy his personal desires and physiological needs and still meet his social obligations without completely sacrificing his favorite sports activity.

The *prescribed conditioning program* is directed to satisfying a real or an imaginary physical need, and is usually administered and evaluated by a qualified person.

Preoperative and postoperative exercises fall into this category. Weight reduction and improvement of body image are examples of such programs supervised by physicians. Physical therapists are commonly active in this work, especially in orthopedic cases. Qualified physical educators also prescribe these programs in corrective physical education classes.

The professional person directing the program must first completely evaluate the physical status of the patient and must understand the process of physical change. He must also instill in the patient confidence and faith.

Work-supplementing recreational activities are found in programs designed to meet the needs of the person engaged in a nonchallenging, sedentary occupation who needs an exercise program involving large expenditures of energy. The activities used should be quite vigorous and should probably involve some social interchange. The energy cost factor is necessary for the prevention of physical degenerative changes just as the recreational elements are needed for psychological rejuvenation. The recommended activities in this program are all active games. All the racket type of sports fall into this category. Tennis, handball or paddle ball, and squash are very active sports and provide the desired competitive interchange. Swimming, ice skating, and bicycling are also active and, although they do not necessarily involve competition, can be performed in groups. *Fastmoving* golf three times a week or more can provide moderate activity. Bowling may fill the social need but hardly qualifies for the fitness need.

Basketball is an excellent activity, requiring high-energy expenditure

and good competitive opportunities. Volleyball can be very active if it is played at a highly competitive, high-skill level.

Work-complementing recreational activities are part of a program utilizing physical activity to assist in the psychological adjustment of a worker whose job demands a high expenditure of energy. In other words, he is physically fit as a result of his work. Very active sports are not necessary to complement this person's life, but if the individual desires them, he should not be discouraged. However, low-energy cost, recreational activities such as golf, bowling, and boating are recommended to provide relaxation and emotional fulfillment.

INDIVIDUAL PROGRAM SELECTION

The pertinent points regarding selection of individual physical activity programs may be summarized as follows. (The same basic principles apply to selection of group programs.)

1. If one can participate in and enjoy some vigorous sport or activity, analyze it carefully to determine whether it meets all of the needs for *physical fitness* (see Table 21.2). If it meets all these needs, one need only be sure that he can continue to participate in the future as he ages and as facilities may become less accessible.

2. If such an activity does not fulfill all needs (for example, does not provide CR overload), then one must sup-

plement the sport with appropriate activities from Table 21.2.

3. If one is not highly skilled in some activity for which he can find facilities and opponents, then he will need to adapt to this situation by learning a new sport or by adopting some kind of *complete* conditioning program.

4. Do not neglect the nonphysical aspects of functional fitness. Also, remember that complete relaxation may be as important as vigorous activity.

5. Do not assume that regularly "working up a sweat" automatically means that an optimal physical fitness level is being maintained. Use appropriate tests regularly to measure physical fitness.

6. For a successful and regular exercise program, it seems that one must develop either an "exercise habit" or the same attitude toward exercise that he has toward eating: he knows he *must* eat regularly even if for some reason it becomes unenjoyable!

GENERAL FRAMEWORK FOR PROGRAM SELECTION

We recommend that each individual should learn how to design a program that can meet his personal needs better than any general or prepared program. This requires some knowledge of certain fundamental principles and an awareness of personal needs. Our "framework" is just that—it is *not* a complete and specific program but a basis for the self-designed program, the program that can best meet an individual's needs. In addition to the rather distinct advantage of meeting

individual needs, the concepts of continuing self-appraisal, weight control, and the relaxation components are part of the framework. The general framework follows.

1. Have a *physical exam yearly.* This will establish one's systemic health base. (See pages 123 and 130.)

2. Begin your fitness program slowly and, after age thirty, only after a thorough physical exam. *"Underdo" rather than overdo at the start.*

3. *Flexibility.* Use gentle stretching exercises for joint flexibility. Try to involve all joints, especially those where testing indicates excessive tightness. (See pages 299 and 303.)

4. *Muscular endurance.* Use repetitions to increase muscular endurance of specific muscle groups (push-ups, sit-ups, pull-ups, or submaximal weight work). Easy does it at first. (See page 295.)

5. *Walking.* At first do plenty of walking and walk briskly. Later, one can jog or, if one must exercise at home, use bench-stepping (8–12-inch bench or stool) in rhythm, 24–36 steps per minute for 1–3 minutes, depending on the initial level of fitness. After adaptation to this work, rope-skipping is excellent. Vigorous sports can substitute here (handball, swimming, tennis singles, and so on) if one is "ready," and the systemic health base is sound. As an index to control progression, take a post-exercise heart rate; count for a period from 5 to 20 seconds immediately after cessation and multiply by four. As a rough gauge, if the exercise is at least three minutes long and

recovery heart rate based on the 5–20 second count is over 150 beats per minute, one should continue *that* exercise. When it drops below 150, one should increase the intensity or add another "bout" of the same exercise. A rate over 170 should lead one to decrease intensity temporarily, especially if he is over thirty-five years of age, or there is extreme discomfort. *Err on the side of moderation and use common sense* in selecting and carrying out or recommending CR work.

6. *Relaxation* is equally important. If they relax a person, hobbies, cards, bowling, golf, and so on are good; if they do not, try progressive muscular relaxation. (See page 568.)

7. Twice yearly use some form of exercise recovery heart rate test, such as a step-test, to *check CR capacity.* Each time you test use a bench of the same height and make the same number of steps per minute for the same length of time. Once a person has become reasonably fit, this score can be used as a standard and be maintained through the years with regular exercise. (For details of method and norms, see pages 210 and 213.)

8. *Weight.* Adults should weigh every morning and keep a graph of their weight. If one is not underweight and sees a persistent two-pound gain, it is best to take care of it "now." This is far easier than taking off a ten- or twenty-pound gain later. A daily weight chart can also serve as an index of health in that gradual or sudden weight loss is associated with many chronic as well as acute disease states. Periodic fat measures and girth measures are also recommended (see pages 362 through 367).

9. *Specific individual weaknesses.* Add items designed to correct any special weakness one wants to improve, such as the strength of a specific muscle group, postural correction, motor ability weaknesses, for example.

10. *Reading.* Keep current on evidence concerning diet and nutrition, heart disease, weight control, cancer, and so on. Evaluate this evidence critically in the light of what you have learned about exercise, health, and fitness. You may find something worthwhile to add to your program; equally important, you may see a need to subtract from it!

You will notice that the selection of specific exercises has been left entirely up to you. Likewise, any general item could conceivably be eliminated if it is necessary. A sample of a record is illustrated in Table 21.3.

Our program requires some knowledge and thought on the part of the "exerciser" and thus involves some time for initial planning. But there is really no other avenue leading to one's ability to develop a truly personal program.

We have included some exercises, on pages 613–615, but specific exercises may be selected from any number of pamphlets and books, some of which you will find in the list of references at the end of the chapter. Exercises may also be designed on the basis of one's knowledge of muscle and joint action and the overload and specificity principles.

TABLE 21.3   Example of Form for Health and Fitness Appraisal Records

TEST	DATE					
	1–10–63	7–14–63	1–15–64	8–1–64	1–7–65	7–14–65
1. Physical exam	Positive	Positive	Positive	Positive	Elevated Bl. Press.	Bl. Pr. Normal
2. 3 min step test (30/min, 12 in.) 1–1:30 count × 2	120	98	96	102	124	108
3. Push-ups	12	25	25	25	25	18
Pull-ups (reverse grip)	2	10	10	9	11	6
Sit-ups (knees bent)	12	40	40	40	41	32
4. Trunk flex. (in.)	−1″	+2″	+2″	+2″	−½″	+1½″
Trunk ext. (in.)	8″	15″	16″	16″	10″	15″
	All pass	All pass	All pass	All pass	Failed two	All pass
(mm)	22	18	18	19	27	20
Iliac crest fat (mm)	25	21	21	22	29	23
6. Waist girth (in.)	32	31	31	31	33	31½
7. Biceps curl	75#	75#	70#	75#	75#	75#
8. Overhead press	80#	80#	80#	80#	80#	80#
9. Body weight	175	172	173	170	185	177
10. Comments:	Sedentary, no regular exercise No overt psychological or social problems	Reg. ex. 3 × wkly., no strength work Includes running	Cont. maint. program	Cont. maint. program	Stopped running and flex. work, new job, less time to exer. Some difficulty in home relations, assoc. with new job & more pressures.	Sac. ME exercises for rope jumping and flex. work. Checked food intake carefully, added prog. relax. & hobby. Began daily weighing & wt. chart.

Assenting to the idea that "fitness is a personal matter" is really of little value to someone who cannot determine for himself what activities are appropriate for him. To design an adequate program for himself he must know what activities are available, and all other relevant factors previously discussed must also be considered. The following cases are presented to give you practice in helping to design a program for someone else. List specific activities you think would meet each individual's needs and interests. (Assume these are all young adults in their twenties or early thirties.)

CASE 1. Female endomorph; forty pounds overweight but enjoys social activities and competition; is almost completely sedentary throughout the day in her work; has average motor ability; has participated in and enjoys bowling and table games.

CASE 2. Male endomorph; considerably overweight, and shy and retiring; sedentary occupation; no experience in sports or games; motivated to exercise because of a concern about overweight and possible heart disease.

CASE 3. Male mesomorph; works in heavy construction with lots of climbing and lifting; good fitness level; former football player; has plenty of leisure time with only household responsibilities to occupy his nonworking hours; gregarious and outgoing; good motor ability but experience in only team sports.

CASE 4. Female of average build; within normal weight limits but has fat accumulations on hips, back of legs, and upper arms, no athletic experience, is friendly and enjoys people; occupation, homemaker with two children, ages two and four.

CASE 5. Male ectomorphic-mesomorph; impatient and nervous, busy, with little leisure time; reads a great deal; enjoys competition; occupation is not sedentary but provides no vigorous activity.

CASE 6. Slightly overweight male; has history of circulatory ailment but is not seriously impaired; enjoys people and competition; even temperament, good sense of humor; reasonable motor ability but little experience in motor activities.

CASE 7. Female of average build, has tendency to put on weight; occupation is college student, works as salesgirl three hours daily; little leisure time; little or no interest in athletics.

CASE 8. Female ectomorph, taller than average; subject to moderately severe asthma attacks during summer months; occupation, college student; average motor ability; interested in sports and games but little experience in motor activities.

CASE 9. Male ecotomorph; flabby muscles, extremely unfit, weak, sagging abdominal muscles; absolutely no interest in exercise or sports; occupation, college professor; little leisure time; advised by physician to exercise.

EXPERIMENTS AND EXPERIENCES

1. Explain the results of a study which showed that as many muscle pulls occurred in varsity sprinters after full warm-up as occurred following no warm-up.

2. Determine why most people would rather "play" for fitness than "work" for fitness.

3. Locate and evaluate as many quack exercise gimmicks and programs as you can.

4. Think critically about the "general framework" concept as presented on

page 624, do you prefer a more regimented program for most people? Why?

SUGGESTED READINGS

Adult Physical Fitness. Washington, D.C.: Government Printing Office, 1900.

Casady, D. R., D. F. Mapes, and L. E. Alley, *Handbook of Physical Fitness Activities.* New York: Crowell-Collier and Macmillan, Inc., 1965.

Cooper, K. H., *Aerobics.* New York: Bantam Books, Inc., 1968.

Hooks, G., *Application of Weight Training to Athletics.* Englewood Cliffs, N.J.: Prentice-Hall, Inc., 1962.

Murray, J., and P. Karpovich, *Weight Training and Athletics.* Englewood Cliffs, N.J.: Prentice-Hall, Inc., 1956.

Summary of Relationship of Systems and Organs to Exercise and Training

Appendix A

SYSTEM OR ORGAN	GENERAL FUNCTION	CONTRIBUTION TO EXERCISE	PARAMETER AFFECTED	EFFECT OF EXERCISE[a]	EFFECT OF TRAINING[a,b] RESTING / EXERCISING	
Circulatory	Transports materials	Provides increase of supplies to cells and re- moves waste products from cells accord- ing to increased metabolic de- mands	Cardiac muscle	NA	Strengthens	
Heart	Pump		Cardiac vascularization	NA	(Increases)	
			Heart rate	+	—	—[e]
Vascular bed	Transport network for delivery and removal		Stroke volume	+[c]	+	+[e]
			Cardiac output	+	0	+
			Hemoglobin, Hct	+[d]	(+)	( )
			Blood volume	—	(+)	( )
			Blood pressure	+	0	—[e]
			CR capacity and max. $\dot{V}O_2$	NA	NA	+
Respiratory	O_2 and CO_2 gas exchange	Increases availa- bility of O_2 and removal of CO_2	Ventilation	+	—	—[e]
			Maximum ventilation	NA	NA	+
			Vital capacity	NA	(+)	NA
			Respiration rate	+	—	—[e]

SYSTEM OR ORGAN	GENERAL FUNCTION	CONTRIBUTION TO EXERCISE	PARAMETER AFFECTED	EFFECT OF EXERCISE	EFFECT OF TRAINING[a,b] RESTING / EXERCISING
Nervous	Communication and integration		Motor capacity (coordination, agility, balance, power)	(All involve nervous and muscular system and specific activities can be improved through repetition or training)	
Voluntary	Initiation of conscious activity	} Same	Nervous system, general	(See page 426)	
Autonomic	Control of involuntary functions		Strength	(Improvement in strength is probably partially attributable to nervous system)	
Sensory	Input, feedback				
Muscular	Movement; producing body heat	Same	Strength	NA	+
			Muscular endurance	NA	+
			Connective tissue in muscle	NA	(+)
			Stored glycogen	—	+ Less depletion
			Flexibility	—	+
Skeletal	Framework for locomotion; protection; blood cell production	Same	Rbc production	NA	(+)
Endocrine	Regulation of processes	Same			
Pituitary	Master gland; controls many other endocrine glands (gonads, thyroid, adrenal cortex), water restoration by kidneys, and growth	Especially adrenal cortical stimulation and water reabsorption	Pituitary function	f	No consistent conclusive evidence available to support meaningful effects
Thyroid	Metabolism	Very little acute effect during exercise	Thyroid secretion		
Parathyroids	Mineral metabolism; Ca, P retention	Very little acute effect during exercise	Parathyroid function		
Pancreas (Islets of Langerhans)	Insulin (necessary for glucose transport across cell membranes)	Same	Insulin secretion	f	

SYSTEM OR ORGAN	GENERAL FUNCTION	CONTRIBUTION TO EXERCISE	PARAMETER AFFECTED	EFFECT OF EXERCISE	EFFECT OF TRAINING[a,b] RESTING / EXERCISING	
Adrenal medulla	Epinephrine stimulates heart (coronary blood flow, force, and rate), increases metabolic rate, liver and muscle glycogenolysis, decreases renal blood flow and thus decreases urine formation	Same	Adrenal function	f		
Adrenal cortex Mineralocorticoids	Controls electrolyte balance, promotes tubular reabsorption by kidneys of Na^+ and H_2O	Same	Mineralocorticoid secretion	f	No consistent conclusive evidence available to support meaningful effects	
Glucocorticoids	Necessary for intermediary metabolism of foodstuffs (conversion) for energy	Same	Glucocorticoid secretion	f		
Testes	Primary and secondary sex characteristics; protein deposition in muscle; initiation of sperm		Testicular function			
Ovaries	Primary and secondary sex characteristics; preparation for pregnancy and lactation		Ovarian function			
Excretory (lungs, kidneys, skin, alimentary tract)	Waste removal (CO_2; H_2O; nitrogenous; indigestibles)	Same (CO_2 and H_2O in increased quantities); effect on blood volume	Kidney function	(Conserves water)	0	0
Digestion and metabolism	Energy	Same (increased demand)	Metabolism	+	0	—e

SYSTEM OR ORGAN	GENERAL FUNCTION	CONTRIBUTION TO EXERCISE	PARAMETER AFFECTED	EFFECT OF EXERCISE	EFFECT OF TRAINING[a,b] RESTING / EXERCISING	
Liver	About 500 known functions; categories: 1. Manufacturer 2. Storage 3. Blood reservoir 4. Purification of blood 5. Body heat 6. Assist endocrine glands	Glycogenesis; lactate conversion; gluconeogenesis	Liver function	Increases certain functions	( )	( )
Skin	Barrier; waste removal; heat loss	Waste removal and heat loss considerably increased	Skin function	Increased	0	0

[a]+ = increases or improves; — = decreases or depresses function; 0 = no change or no effect; NA = not applicable; ( ) = uncertain or, when placed around symbol, probable effect although not strongly documented
[b]Assuming specificity of training (see page 611)
[c]Up to a point and, even then, not so much in untrained person
[d]Concentration increases, may be solely due to this and not due to reserve red blood cells, as some believe
[e]Assuming standard exercise
[f]Secretion increased in response to exercise

Summary of Health, Physical Fitness, and Motor Ability Appraisal Methods

Appendix B

QUALITY	TEST OR MEASURE	SYSTEMS OR CLASSIFICATION INVOLVED								AVG. OR NORM.	REFER TO PAGE(S)[a]
		Circ.	Resp.	Nerv.	Musc.	Metab.	Anthrop.	CA[c]	Skel.		
Health	1. Sensory										
	Visual acuity			X				X			441
	Depth perception			X							441
	Peripheral vision			X				X			441
	Perception and discrimination			X				X			
	2. Posture				X				X	NA	298
	3. Bl. pressure	X								120/80	
	4. Hct, Hb	X								♂45; 15g% ♀40; 13.5g%	
	5. Vital capacity		X							♂4.6L. ♀3.1L.	210
	6. Maximal br. cap.		X							⟶	210

QUALITY	TEST OR MEASURE	SYSTEMS OR CLASSIFICATION INVOLVED								AVG. OR NORM.	REFER TO PAGE(S)[a]
		Circ.	Resp.	Nerv.	Musc.	Metab.	Anthrop.	CA[c]	Skel.		
	7. % Body fat					X	X			♂14% ♀20%	362
	8. O.W. index					X	X			100%	365
	9. Wt. prediction					X	X			NA	366
Physical fitness	10. CR Capacity										
	Max. V̇O₂	X	X			X				⟶	209
	Step tests	X	X							⟶	210
	12-min field test	X	X							⟶	214
	11. Strength										
	Minimal				X			X		One each[b]	
	Isotonic				X			X		Biceps curl: ♂75; ♀42	294
	Isometric				X			X		grip (dom. hand) ♂125; ♀65	293
	12. Muscular Endurance										
	External resistance				X					Biceps curls at 50% max. resist. ♂23	294
	Body wt. (pull-ups, dips, sit-ups, push-ups, etc.)				X					Bt.knee sit-ups ♂40; ♀20; Pull-ups ♂8	294
										Push-ups ♂25	294
	13. Flexibility				X			X	X	Trunk flexion: ♂+1"; ♀+3.5" Pass-fail: Pass all	299

QUALITY	TEST OR MEASURE	SYSTEMS OR CLASSIFICATION INVOLVED								AVG. OR NORM.	REFER TO PAGE(S)[a]
		Circ.	Resp.	Nerv.	Musc.	Metab.	Anthrop.	CA[c]	Skel.		
	14. (Also % body fat, posture, VC)						X			(see 2,5,7 above)	
Motor ability	15. Coordination: bar snap			X	X			X		⟶	305
	16. Agility: figure-eight run			X	X					⟶	306
	17. Balance: TU Bal. Beam Test			X	X			X		♂8 ♀8	307
	18. Power: Leg: vertical jump			X	X					⟶	304
	Arm and shoulder: softball throw			X	X					♂165'; ♀85'	
	19. Speed: 50-yd dash			X	X					♂6.7 sec ♀8.4 sec	
	"True speed"			X	X					♂24.2 ft/sec ♀20 ft/sec	306
	20. React. time: small muscle (thumb)			X	X					♂.16 sec ♀.17 sec	308

[a]Discussion and/or methods are located on these pages.
[b]At least one bent-knee sit-up (feet held down), one reverse grip pull-up, one complete dip on parallel bars or one floor push-up with back straight; also see Kraus-Weber test on page 301.
[c]Corrective-adaptive

The Reproductive System

Appendix C

Obviously the primary purpose of the reproductive system is procreation of the species. The major biological purpose of sexual intercourse is reproduction, but man, the highest of animals, has taken this biologically simple act and implicated it deeply with social, physical, and mental health problems. To support this rather bold statement, we need ask you to look no further than the problems of prostitution and venereal disease and the medical literature on the incidence of sex-related problems in the pathogenesis of many mental and psychosomatic illnesses. It is not the purpose of this book to discuss the moral and social issues, as important as they are. We *do*, however, want to point out the need for a thorough understanding of the physical and mental health problems that can be associated with human sexuality. It is folly to ignore such problems, for all of us must face up to the fact that our children will inevitably be perplexed by questions concerning sex. Where will we, their parents, be? And will we be there and with the correct approach when these problems occur? It is our responsibility to meet the health needs of our children—and to meet their needs in such a manner and at such a time that "the barn door is locked *before* the horse is stolen." The nature of this particular text does not allow a thorough treatise on sex education. We recommend that either a course in sex education or a good text on the subject be placed high on your priority list of "elective" things to do.

GENERAL FUNCTION AND ANATOMY

In both the male and female, reproduction is the primary and almost single function of the reproductive system. Practically speaking, the following organs are considered as part of the reproductive system in women (Figure 1A): vagina, **uterus, Fallopian tubes, ovaries** and breasts; in men, the penis, **prostate,** and **testes** are the primary reproductive organs (Figure 1B). Because

the anterior pituitary gland secretes several hormones that are essential to the normal growth and function of both the male and female reproductive organs, it should be considered an integral part of this system.

We mentioned that reproduction was the "almost" single function of this system. It should be borne in mind that the hormones secreted by the testes and ovaries are also responsible for primary and secondary sex characteristics.

The male hormone testosterone is, first of all, responsible for sex differentiation in the **fetus** (a **placental** hormone formed during pregnancy triggers its secretion). After birth, the placental stimulus is lost and the testes become relatively dormant until puberty. Then testosterone, under the stimulating effect of the **gonadotropins** from the pituitary, is again secreted by the testes and rapid development of the male sex organs begins. It causes growth of the

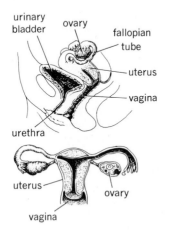

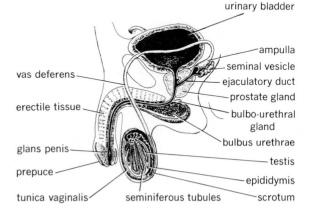

(A)

(B)

FIGURE 1

testes and, together with one of the pituitary gonadotropins, is essential for the formation of the **sperm.** Testosterone is responsible for secondary male characteristics, such as the distinctive hair distribution and deeper voice; it also increases the deposition of protein in the muscles and thus apparently plays an important role in the development of muscular strength.

The principal ovarian hormones, the estrogens, cause proliferation of particular specialized cells and so are responsible for the primary and secondary female sex characteristcs, such as the development of the vagina and uterus, hair distribution, broadening of the hips, growth of the breasts, and deposition of fat in the thighs and hips. The estrogens also promote rapid bone growth, but apparently they also cause the growth to cease after a few years, perhaps because of the rate of growth itself. Thus the girl grows faster than the boy after puberty but her height is usually less than his. He grows more slowly but for a longer period of time and therefore usually reaches a greater height. Another ovarian hormone, progesterone, is concerned primarily with the readiness of the uterus to accept and implant a fertilized **ovum;** it is also a stimulant to the breasts to prepare to secrete milk after birth. The oscillation of the ovarian hormones and the gonadotropic hormones is responsible for the female sexual cycle (ovulation through menstruation).

Androgens, which are, in effect, male sex hormones, are secreted by the adrenal cortex in men and women, but to such a limited extent that they are, under normal conditions, entirely ineffectual. In the female, hypersecretion of androgens can cause masculine characteristics such as a deeper voice, atrophy of breasts, and increased musculature.

ROLE OF REPRODUCTIVE SYSTEM IN EXERCISE

Although it is obvious that testosterone is important in the development of the musculature of the male and thus at least in part a determinant of strength, there is little else one can say about the positive contribution of this system in exercise. It is interesting to note that Slonaker[1] found normal rats ran more (9 to 11 miles per day), ate more, and lived longer than castrated or ovariectomized rats, who ran only 0.10 to 0.15 miles per day and ate less but still grew longer and heavier, probably because of their almost complete lack of activity. However, castration and ovariectomy (removal of testes and ovaries) are complete extremes, and whether various degrees of function in the intact gonads would affect the desire for activity so dramatically as complete removal is pure conjecture.

The question of the effects of the menstrual cycle on exercise (and vice versa) are discussed in Chapter 19.

---

[1]Slonaker, J. R., "The Effect of Excision of Different Sexual Organs on the Development, Growth and Longevity of the Albino Rat," *Amer. J. Physiol.,* 90:307, 1930.

Common Infectious Diseases

Appendix D

DISEASE	CAUSE	HOW SPREAD	USUAL SITE OF INFECTION	INCUBATION PERIOD
Athlete's foot	Various fungi	Contact with contaminated floors and other objects; showers and swimming pools	Feet, especially between toes	Undetermined
Botulism	Bacterium	Improperly canned nonacid foods contaminated with soil and eaten before cooking	Nervous system	12–36 hours
Brain fever (encephalitis)	A specific virus	Droplet infection and as a disease complication	Brain substance	Variable; depends on virus
Bronchitis (acute bronchitis)	Various bacteria, including streptococcus	Droplets, nasal discharge	Lower trachea and bronchi	Variable

DANGER SEASON	SYMPTOMS AND SIGNS	TREATMENT	OUTLOOK, OR PROGNOSIS	IMMUNITY
Summer	Cracks and itching sores; raw and inflamed areas	Fungicides keep feet dry, change shoes and socks frequently	Usually not serious	None
Any season	Fatigue, dizziness, double vision, muscle weakness, paralysis	Antitoxin in large doses	Very poor; mortality 65%	None
Winter months, can be any season	Headache, vomiting, drowsiness	Spinal puncture to relieve headache; intravenous glucose	Mortality 10–50%	Depends on virus
Winter and spring	Cough, chills, fever, pain in back and muscles	Aspirin, antibiotics, absolute bed rest, force fluids	Recovery in 4–5 days unless complications set in	Probably none

DISEASE	CAUSE	HOW SPREAD	USUAL SITE OF INFECTION	INCUBATION PERIOD
Chickenpox (varicella)	Virus	Droplets, contact with infected articles	Blood stream and skin	2–3 weeks; usually 14 days
Common cold (coryza)	Various viruses	Droplets, nasal discharge	Nasal passages, sinuses, pharynx	Probably 12–72 hours
Cystitis	Bacteria, especially colon bacillus	From intestine to urinary bladder; from kidneys to urinary bladder	Urinary bladder	Variable
Diphtheria	Bacterium	Droplets, infected articles	Throat, upper trachea	2–5 days
Dysentery, amoebic	Protozoan	Food and water, feces of infected persons and carriers	Large intestine, liver	3 days to several months; usually 3–4 weeks
Epidemic jaundice (acute infectious hepatitis)	Virus	Not known; may be food, water, direct contact or blood of infected persons	Liver and blood stream	Long and variable, usually 20–120 days
Gonorrhea	Bacterium	Direct contact with lesions; occasionally infected articles	Mucous membranes, especially of genital organs	1–14 days, usually 3–5 days

DANGER SEASON	SYMPTOMS AND SIGNS	TREATMENT	OUTLOOK, OR PROGNOSIS	IMMUNITY
Winter and spring, especially during childhood	Mild fever, weakness, skin eruptions in different stages at same time	Relief of itching and prevention of infection and scarring of pustules	Usually not serious	Permanent after recovery No immunization known
Winter and spring	Nasal congestion, running nose, sneezing, sore throat, fever, headache	Bed rest 3–4 days; force fluids	Not serious without complications	Probably none Vaccines largely ineffective
Any season	Soreness in bladder; frequent, painful urination	Sulfa drugs, antibiotics; force fluids	Usually not serious unless kidneys are involved	None
Fall and winter	Sore throat, pain, fever, hoarseness, nasal discharge	Antitoxin serum and antibiotics	Good, with serum and antibiotics	Permanent after recovery Antitoxin for passive Toxoid for active
Summer	Abdominal pain, severe diarrhea, blood and mucus in stools	Iodine and arsenic compounds; antibiotics	Serious; very dangerous in infants	None
Any season	Jaundice, fever, nausea, headache, pain over liver, reddening and itching of hands and feet	Bed rest; fat-free diet, high in carbohydrates and proteins	Rarely fatal; often lasts several months	None after recovery Gamma globulin for passive (6 weeks)
Any season	Pus discharged from genital opening; various symptoms which spread through body	Antibiotics	Few deaths or complications with early treatment	Questionable after recovery No immunization

DISEASE	CAUSE	HOW SPREAD	USUAL SITE OF INFECTION	INCUBATION PERIOD
Heart valve infection (bacterial endocarditis)	Various bacteria, especially streptococcus	Secondary infection, often following previous heart valve damage	Heart lining and valves	Variable; depends on organism and primary infection
Hydrophobia	Virus	Saliva of infected animals, esp. dogs	Central nervous system and brain substances	10 days to 2 or more years
Impetigo	Bacteria, usually streptococcus or staphylococcus	Contact with lesions or infected articles	Face, less often hands	2–5 days
Influenza	Virus of several types, usually A or B	Droplets and nasal discharge, contact with contaminated articles	Respiratory organs	1–3 days
Laryngitis (croup in children)	Cold viruses; various bacteria, especially streptococcus	Droplets and nasal discharge; often a complication from a cold	Larynx and upper trachea	Variable; depends on organism
Malaria	Protozoan (four distinct forms)	Bite of infected female Anopheles mosquito	Blood stream, especially red corpuscles	Usually 6 days
Measles (rubeola)	Virus	Droplets and nasal discharge, contact with contaminated articles	Respiratory organs and skin	10–15 days

DANGER SEASON	SYMPTOMS AND SIGNS	TREATMENT	OUTLOOK, OR PROGNOSIS	IMMUNITY
Depends on organism	Chills, sweats, pain in tips of fingers and toes; shortness of breath	Penicillin; absolute bed rest during active infection	Formerly fatal; 10–30% fatality with penicillin	None
Spring and summer	Mental depression, insomnia, convulsions, spasms, general paralysis	None	Probably 100% fatality	Vaccine given in Pasteur treatment to produce immunity during incubation period
Any season	Circular, raised lesion, usually on face; becomes crusted	Local application of salves containing antibiotics and other drugs	Highly contagious but not dangerous	None
Winter and spring; epidemics at any season	Sudden fever, weakness, ache in back and limbs, sore throat	Bed rest; force fluids	Good, unless complications develop	Possibly temporary after recovery Vaccine effective few months
Winter and spring	Harsh, metallic cough; hoarseness; swelling of pharynx	Bed rest; inhalation of steam	Usually not serious	None
Spring, summer, and fall	Chills followed by high fever and sweats; attacks daily, every other day, or every third day	Quinine, quinacrine (atabrine), or pentaquine	Few deaths except in one (24-hour) form	Possibly temporary to one type after recovery
Spring	Fever, cough, red swollen eyes, rash spreading from face to body; Koplik's spots in mouth	Bed rest, protection of eyes, antibiotics to prevent complications	Less than 1% mortality unless complications develop	Permanent after recovery Serum for passive immunity

DISEASE	CAUSE	HOW SPREAD	USUAL SITE OF INFECTION	INCUBATION PERIOD
Measles, German or 3-day (rubella)	Virus	Droplets and nasal discharge, contact with contaminated articles	Respiratory organs and skin	10–21 days, usually 18 days
Mumps (epidemic parotitis)	Virus	Saliva and droplets	Parotid salivary glands	8–35 days, usually 17–25 days
Osteomyelitis	Bacteria, usually staphylococcus	From a wound or skin infection through the blood stream	Bone	Indefinite; severe symptoms within 10–14 days
Paratyphoid fever	Bacteria; several salmonella forms	Contaminated food and water, flies, feces of human carriers	Intestine, blood stream	1–10 days
Parrot fever (psittacosis)	Virus	Nasal discharge and droppings from infected birds, esp. parrots, parakeets, and pigeons	Lungs	7–15 days
Pneumonia, bronchial	Various bacteria from respiratory organs	Complication from upper respiratory infection	Lungs	Usually 1–3 days
Pneumonia, lobar	Bacterium (pneumococcus of several types)	Droplet infection; complication following other respiratory infections	Lungs	Probably 1–3 days

DANGER SEASON	SYMPTOMS AND SIGNS	TREATMENT	OUTLOOK, OR PROGNOSIS	IMMUNITY
Early spring; epidemics 3–4 years apart	Slight fever, swollen glands; rash resembling scarlet fever	Bed rest until rash has faded	Not serious unless complications develop	Usually permanent after recovery
Winter and spring	Fever, pain, and swelling in parotid salivary glands	Local applications; gamma globulin and serum to prevent complications	Usually not serious unless complications develop	Permanent after recovery Gamma globulin for passive immunity
Any season	Fever, chills, redness, pain, and swelling over infected bone; muscle spasms	Penicillin	Rarely fatal	None
Summer	Fever, diarrhea, enarlgement of spleen	Antibiotics	Usually not fatal	Permanent after recovery Vaccine gives active immunity for 2 years
Any season	Headache, backache, cough, fever for 2–3 weeks, general weakness	Penicillin of some benefit	20% fatality if contracted from parrot family	None
Winter and spring	Cough, chest pain, fever, aching	Antibiotics, sulfa drugs	Usually not fatal	None
Winter and spring	Sudden, prolonged fever, chest pain, chills, cough, rust-colored sputum	Penicillin, sulfa drugs	5% fatality with antibiotics	Possibly temporary after recovery Vaccine seldom used

DISEASE	CAUSE	HOW SPREAD	USUAL SITE OF INFECTION	INCUBATION PERIOD
Pneumonia, virus	Several viruses	Droplet infection; complication following other virus infections	Lungs	7–21 days
Poliomyelitis	Virus	Discharges from nose and throat, and feces of carriers	Spinal cord and motor nerve roots; spinal bulb	5–35 days, usually 10 days
Pyelitis	Various bacteria, especially colon bacillus	From blood or by way of ureters	Kidney pelvis	Variable
Rheumatic fever	Reaction to streptococcus bacteria	(See "Strep throat")	(See "Strep throat")	(See "Strep throat")
Rocky Mt. spotted fever	Rickettsia	Infected ticks	Blood stream, skin, internal organs	3–10 days

DANGER SEASON	SYMPTOMS AND SIGNS	TREATMENT	OUTLOOK, OR PROGNOSIS	IMMUNITY
Winter and spring	Fatigue, muscle pain, cough, chills, fever	Antibiotics	Recovery usual but often slow	Active immunity after recovery Many develop gradual immunity
Summer	Headache, stiffness of neck and spine, fever about 100° F, paralysis of limbs after acute stage in some cases	No specific treatment; therapy to regain use of limbs	1–4% fatal; higher in bulbar polio	Usually permanent after recovery 3–4 weeks with gamma globulin Salk vaccine permanently effective in 90% of paralytic cases
Any season	Sudden chills and fever, pain in kidney region; bacteria, pus, and albumen in urine	Antibiotics, sulfa drugs, soft diet, force fluids	Few fatalities; recovery after 1–2 weeks	None
(See "Strep throat")	Red, swollen, tender, painful joints; fever	ACTH or cortisone	Recovery usual with antibiotics; heart damage a grave danger	Probably temporary after recovery
Spring, summer	Sudden chills and fever; headache and general aching; rash with bleeding under skin	Antibiotics	Good, with antibiotics	Active for long period after recovery

DISEASE	CAUSE	HOW SPREAD	USUAL SITE OF INFECTION	INCUBATION PERIOD
Scarlet fever	Bacterium, streptococcus	Droplet infection	Throat	2–5 days
Shingles (Herpes zoster)	Virus	Probably by droplet infection	Sensory nerves	Undetermined
Smallpox (variola)	Virus	Droplet infection, contact with skin lesions	Blood stream and skin	8–12 days
"Strep throat" (acute pharyngitis)	Bacterium, streptococcus	Droplet infection, infected milk	Pharynx	Variable
Syphilis	Spirochete	Contact with lesion	Genitals, then blood, then any organ in body	10–90 days, usually 21 days
Tetanus (lockjaw)	Bacterium	Puncture wound	Wound	4–21 days

DANGER SEASON	SYMPTOMS AND SIGNS	TREATMENT	OUTLOOK, OR PROGNOSIS	IMMUNITY
Fall and winter	Severe sore throat, high fever, chills; nausea, vomiting; bright scarlet rash on second day	Antibiotics, sulfa drugs	Good, with antibiotics	Usually permanent after recovery
Any season	Pain along a nerve followed by a blister-like eruption which itches and burns	No specific treatment	Good, but pain may remain for long period	Usually permanent after recovery
Most common in winter but may appear at any season	Severe headache, chills, high fever; rash over body developing into raised, pus-filled pustules	Penicillin; prevention of itching; cleanliness	Fair or poor, depending on degree of fever	Permanent after recovery Vaccination effective for about 7 years
Winter and spring	Severe sore throat, high fever, general aching	Antibiotics, sulfa drugs	Not dangerous without complications; rheumatic fever a hazard	None
Any season	Primary lesion in form of running sore	Antibiotics	Good, with antibiotics started early	None
Any season	Muscle spasms, first local then general; paralysis	Antitoxin	Highly fatal: outlook improving	Many years after recovery Toxoid gives protection 5–7 years

DISEASE	CAUSE	HOW SPREAD	USUAL SITE OF INFECTION	INCUBATION PERIOD
Trench mouth (Vincent's disease)	Two associated bacteria— bacillus and spirillum	Direct contact and contaminated articles	Gums; mucous membranes of mouth and throat	Undetermined
Typhoid fever	Bacterium	Water, food, feces of infected persons and carriers; contaminated articles	Large intestine; blood stream	3–40 days, usually 7–14 days
Typhus fever	Rickettsia	Body louse	Blood stream and skin	6–15 days
Tuberculosis, pulmonary	Bacterium	Droplet infection, sputum	Lungs	Variable
Undulant fever (brucellosis)	Bacterium	Direct contact with cattle, infected milk	Blood stream and any body organ	5–21 days
Whooping cough (pertussis)	Bacterium	Droplet infection, contact with contaminated articles	Lower respiratory organs	7–10 days
Yellow fever	Virus	Bite of infected female Aëdes mosquito	Liver and kidneys	3–6 days

DANGER SEASON	SYMPTOMS AND SIGNS	TREATMENT	OUTLOOK, OR PROGNOSIS	IMMUNITY
Any season	Painful ulcers of gums and mouth; slight fever; sore throat	Antibiotics	Usually not serious	None
Summer	Continued high fever; abdominal pain and cramping; diarrhea, blood in stools; rose spots on abdomen	Antibiotics	Good, with antibiotics	Permanent following recovery Vaccine for active immunity
Winter	Chills and fever, general aching, skin eruption	Antibiotics	Good in children; up to 60% mortality in older people	Permanent after recovery Vaccine for active immunity
Any season	Cough, loss of appetite and weight, night sweats, low-grade fever, chest pain, blood in sputum	Antibiotics, esp. streptomycin, drugs, pneumothorax, surgery	Fair, but improving with antibiotics and chemotherapy	None
Any season	Fever, sweats, pain in joints	Antibiotics, sulfa drugs	Good, but many remain chronic	Probably none
Fall and winter	Cough, followed by a "whoop" and lasting 1–2 months; fever, vomiting	Immune serum, antibiotics, sulfa drugs	Dangerous in infants; less serious in older children	Permanent after recovery Vaccine for active immunity
Any season	Fever, face and tongue red, vomiting	None	Highly fatal	Vaccine effective for about 2 years

SOURCE: J. H. Otto, C. J. Julian, and J. E. Tether, *Modern Health*. New York: Holt, Rinehart and Winston, Inc., 1963. By permission.

Approximate Caloric and Nutrient Content of Common Foods

Appendix E

FOOD	APPROXIMATE MEASURE	CALORIES	PROTEIN G	MINERALS CALCIUM MG	IRON MG	VITAMIN A I.U.	THIA-MINE MG	VITAMINS RIBO-FLAVIN MG	NIACIN MG	ASCORBIC ACID MG	CARBO-HYDRATE	CALORIES FROM FAT	SAT. FAT	UNSAT FAT
Almonds, shelled	12–15 nuts	90	3.0	35	0.7	0	0.04	0.14	0.5	tr.	12	67	5	59
Apples Fresh, E.P.	1 med. large, 3 in. diam.	90	0.3	11	0.5	140	0.05	0 03	0.2	6	79	8		
Baked, un-pared	1 large, 2 tbsp sugar	195	0.5	12	0.6	180	0.04	0.05	0.3	2	176	2		
Apple juice. fresh or canned	½ cup, scant	50	0.1	6	0.6		0.01	0.02	0.1	1	43	0		
Applesauce Sweetened	½ cup	115	0.3	5	0.6	50	0.03	0.01	tr.	1	108	1		
Unsweetened	½ cup	50	0.3	5	0.6	50	0.03	0.01	tr.	1	47	3		
Apricots Fresh	2–3 medium	50	1.0	17	0.5	2700	0.03	0 04	0.6	10	47	2		
Canned, heavy syr-up pack	4 halves, 2 tbsp juice	105	0.7	13	0.4	1990	0.02	0.02	0.5	5	94	1		
water pack	4 halves, 2 tbsp juice	40	0.7	12	0.3	1830	0.02	0.02	0.4	4	36	1		
Dried, sul-fured, raw	4–6 medium halves	80	1.5	20	1.7	3270	tr.	0.05	1.0	4	72	2		

FOOD	APPROXIMATE MEASURE	CALORIES	PROTEIN G	MINERALS		VITAMINS					CALORIES FROM			
				CALCIUM MG	IRON MG	VITAMIN A I.U.	THIA-MINE MG	RIBO-FLAVIN MG	NIACIN MG	ASCORBIC ACID MG	CARBO-HYDRATE	FAT	SAT. FAT	UNSAT. FAT
Apricots (cont'd) unsweet-ened (cooked)	½ cup fruit and liquid	120	2.0	31	2.5	4200	tr.	0.07	1.4	4	108	3		
Apricot nec-tar, canned	½ cup	70	0.4	11	0.3	1180	0.01	0.01	0.3	4	65	1		
Artichokes French, A.P.	1 large, cooked	50	5.5	102	2.2	300	0.14	0.08	1.4	16	72	3		
Asparagus Fresh, green, cooked	½ cup cut, 6–7 spears	20	2.0	21	0.6	900	0.16	0.18	1.4	26	14	2		
Canned, green	½ cup cut. 6–7 spears	20	2.0	19	1.9	800*	0.06	0.10	0.8	15	11	3		
Avocados Fuerte, California	½ pear, about 4 in. long	170	2.0	10	0.6	290	0.11	0.20	1.6	14	22	143	29	99
Florida	½ pear, about 4 in. long	160	2.0	13	0.8	360	0.14	0.25	2.0	18	40	118	24	81
Bacon, broiled, drained	3 strips, crisp	155	8.0	4	0.8	0	0.13	0 09	1.3		3	117	38	74
Bananas, E.P.	1 medium	105	1.5	10	0.9	240	0.06	0.08	0.9	12	112	3		
Beans, Canned, with pork and tomato sauce	½ cup	160	8.0	70	2.3	170	0.10	0.04	0.8	3	100	25	9	13
Canned, with pork and sweet sauce	½ cup	195	8.0	82	3.0		0.08	0.05	0.7		108	50	19	26
Lima, fresh, boiled	½ cup, drained	90	6.0	38	2.0	220	0.14	0.08	1.0	14	64	3		
Red, canned, solids and liquids	½ cup	115	7.0	36	2.3	tr.	0.06	0.05	0.8		84	4		
Snap, green, fresh or frozen, cooked	¾ cup, drained	25	1.5	50	0.6	540	0.07	0.09	0.5	12	20	2		
Snap, green, canned	¾ cup, drained	25	1.0	45	1.5	470	0.03	0.05	0.3	4	20	2		
Soy, dry weight	½ cup, scant, after cooking	120	10.0	68	2.5	20	0.33	0.09	0.7		41	42	8	32
Bean sprouts, cooked	⅔ cup	15	2.0	10	0.5	10	0.05	0.06	0.4	4	12	1		

			MINERALS				VITAMINS				CALORIES FROM			
FOOD	APPROXIMATE MEASURE	CALORIES	PROTEIN G	CALCIUM MG	IRON MG	VITAMIN A I.U.	THIA-MINE MG	RIBO-FLAVIN MG	NIACIN MG	ASCORBIC ACID MG	CARBO-HYDRATE	FAT	SAT. FAT	UNSAT. FAT
Beef,														
Corned, canned	3 slices, 3×2×¼ in.	185	21.5	17	3.7		0.02	0.20	2.9	0	0	90	43	42
hash, canned	½ cup	230	10.0	30	1.4	tr.	0.03	0.16	3.3	0	35	153	73	72
Dried, creamed	½ cup	210	16.0	106	2.1	440	0.07	0.30	1.6	0	23	117	56	55
Hamburger, broiled market ground	4 from pound	245	20.5	9	2.7	30	0.08	0.18	4.6		0	153	73	72
lean ground	4 from pound	185	23.0	10	3.0	20	0.08	0.20	5.1		0	90	43	42
Roast, chuck, braised or pot roasted	2 slices, 4×1½×½ in.	375	24.0	10	3.1	60	0.04	0.19	3.8		0	270	130	130
oven, relatively lean	1 slice, 4½×3×½ in.	345	23.5	10	3.1	50	0.06	0.18	4.3		0	243	117	114
rib, choice grade	1 slice, 4½×3×½ in.	440	20.0	9	2.6	80	0.05	0.15	3.6		0	351	169	165
Steak, round, broiled	1 piece, 4½×3½×½ in.	260	28.5	12	3.5	30	0.08	0.22	5.6		0	135	65	63
sirloin, broiled	1 piece, 4½×2½×1 in.	410	22.0	10	2.9	60	0.06	0.18	4.6		0	315	151	148
Beets, cooked or canned	½ cup, drained solids	30	1.0	12	0.4	20	0.03	0.03	0.3	5	24	0		
Beet greens	½ cup, boiled, drained	20	1.5	99	1.9	5100	0.07	0.15	0.3	15	12	2		
Biscuits, baking powder, from mix	3 biscuits, 2 in. diam.	325	7.0	68	2.3	tr.	0.27	0.25	2.0	tr.	205	76	11	58
Blackberries, dewberries, boysenberries, and youngberries, fresh	⅔ cup	60	1.0	32	0.9	200	0.03	0.04	0.4	21	47	8		
Blueberries, fresh	⅔ cup	60	0.7	15	1.0	100	0.03	0.06	0.5	14	54	4		
Bread,														
Boston brown	3 slices, ½ in. thick	210	5.5	90	1.9	70	0.11	0.06	1.2	0	182	8	1	6
Corn, from mix.	1 piece, 2 in. square	95	2.5	34	0.5	110*	0.06	0.08	0.5	tr.	51	25	4	19
French or Vienna, enriched	1 slice	70	2.0	10	0.5	tr.	0.06	0.05	0.6	tr.	51	6	1	5
Raisin	1 slice	60	1.5	16	0.3	tr.	0.01	0.02	0.2	tr.	47	5	1	4
Rye, American	1 slice	55	2.0	17	0.5	0	0.04	0.02	0.3	0	47	3	.4	2
White, unenriched	1 slice	60	2.0	19	0.2	tr.	0.02	0.02	0.3	tr.	47	6	1	5
enriched	1 slice	60	2.0	19	0.6	tr.	0.06	0.05	0.6	tr.	47	6	1	5
Whole wheat	1 slice	55	2.5	23	0.5	tr.	0.06	0.03	0.7	tr.	44	6	1	5
Broccoli	⅔ cup, boiled, drained	25	3.0	88	0.8	2500	0.09	0.20	0.8	90	20	3		

*No vitamin A if made with white cornmeal.

FOOD	APPROXIMATE MEASURE	CALORIES	PROTEIN G	MINERALS CALCIUM MG	IRON MG	VITAMIN A I.U.	THIA-MINE MG	VITAMINS RIBO-FLAVIN MG	NIACIN MG	ASCORBIC ACID MG	CALORIES FROM CARBO-HYDRATE	FAT	SAT. FAT	UNSAT. FAT
Brussels sprouts	5–6 sprouts, boiled, drained	25	3.0	22	0.8	360	0.06	0.10	0.6	61	16	3		
Butter	1 pat, 45 per pound	70	tr.	2	0	330				0		70	39	28
	1 tbsp	100	tr.	3	0	460				0		97	53	38
Cabbage, headed Raw	1 cup shredded	25	1.5	49	0.4	130	0.05	0.05	0.3	47	20	2		
Cooked	1⅓ cup	20	1.0	42	0.3	120	0.02	0.02	0.1	24	16	2		
Cakes, Angel, from mix	2 in. sector of 8–in. cake	105	•2.5	38	0.1	0	tr.	0.04	tr.	0	98	1	.1	1
Chocolate fudge icing	2 in. sector of 8–in. cake	370	4.5	70	1.0	160	0.02	0.10	0.2	tr.	230	144	62	82
Gingerbread, from mix	2×2 inches	150	1.5	50	0.9	tr.	0.02	0.05	0.4	tr.	115	34	5	26
Plain cake or cupcake, iced	2 in. sector of 8–in. cake or 2 medium cupcakes	370	3.5	50	0.3	200	0.02	0.07	0.1	tr.	258	101	14	77
Pound cake, plain	1 slice, 2¾× 3×⅝ in.	125	2.0	12	0.2	90	0.01	0.03	0.1	tr.	66	50	7	38
Yellow cake, iced, from mix	2 in. sector of 8–in. cake	335	4.0	91	0.6	140	0.02	0.08	0.2	tr.	238	92	13	70
Candy, Caramels, plain or chocolate	1 oz	120	1.0	44	0.4	3	0.01	0.05	0.1	tr.	90	27	15	10
Chocolate, milk, plain	1 oz	155	2.5	68	0.3	80	0.02	0.10	0.1	tr.	66	88	48	34
with almonds	1 oz	160	3.0	69	0.5	70	0.02	0.12	0.2	tr.	59	97	32	28
Fudge, with nuts	1 oz	130	1.0	24	0.4	tr.	0.01	0.03	0.1	tr.	82	45	45	18
Hard	1 oz	115	0.0	6	0.6	0	0	0	0	0	113	3	2	1
Marshmallow	1 oz	100	0.6	5	0.5	0	0	tr.	tr.	0	94			
Peanut brittle	1 oz	125	2.0	11	0.7	0	0.05	0.01	1.0	0	98	25	6	18
Cantaloupe, See Melons														
Carrots Raw	1 carrot, 5½× 1 in. or ½ cup grated	20	0.6	19	0.4	5500	0.03	0.03	0.3	4	20	1		
Boiled, drained	⅔ cup, diced	30	0.9	33	0.6	10500	0.05	0.05	0.5	6	28	2		
Cauliflower, Raw	1 cup flower buds	25	2.5	25	1.1	60	0.11	0.10	0.7	78	20	2		
Boiled, drained	¾ cup	20	2.5	21	0.7	60	0.09	0.08	0.6	55	16	2		
Celery, Raw	2 lg. stalks or													

FOOD	APPROXIMATE MEASURE	CALORIES	PROTEIN G	MINERALS			VITAMINS					CALORIES FROM			
				CALCIUM MG	IRON MG	VITAMIN A I.U.	THIA-MINE MG	RIBO-FLAVIN MG	NIACIN MG	ASCORBIC ACID MG		CARBO-HYDRATE	FAT	SAT. FAT	UNSA FAT
Celery *(cont'd)*															
	1 cup diced	15	0.9	39	0.3	270*	0.03	0.03	0.3	9		16	1		
Boiled, drained	¾ cup, diced	15	0.8	31	0.2	240*	0.02	0.03	0.3	6		12	1		
Cereals, Ready to eat Bran Flakes, 40% added nutrients	¾ cup	90	3.0	21	1.3	0	0.12	0.05	1.9	0		98	4	1	3
Corn Flakes, added nutrients	1 cup	95	2.0	4	0.4	0	0.11	0.02	0.5	0		86	1	.1	1
Rice, puffed, added nutrients	1 cup	55	0.8	3	0.3	0	0.06	0.01	0.6	0		53	1	.1	1
Wheat Flakes, added nutrients	1 cup	90	3.0	10	1.1	0	0.16	0.04	1.2	0		82	3	1	3
Wheat, puffed, added nutrients	1 cup	45	2.0	3	0.5	0	0.07	0.03	0.9	0		37	2	.2	1
Wheat, shredded	1 large biscuit	140	4.0	17	1.4	0	0.09	0.04	1.8	0		131	7	1	5
Cooked (figured from 1 oz. dry weight) Cornmeal, white or yellow, un-enriched	½ cup	60	1.0	1	0.2	70†	0.02	0.01	0.1	0		53	2	.2	1
enriched	½ cup	60	1.0	1	0.5	70†	0.07	0.05	0.6	0		53	2	.2	1
Corn grits, white, de-germ., un-enriched	½ cup	60	1.0	1	0.1	tr.	0.02	0.01	0.2	0		51	1	.1	1
enriched	½ cup	60	1.0	1	0.4	tr.	0.05	0.04	0.5	0		51	1	.1	1
Oatmeal	⅔–¾ cup	65	2.0	11	0.7	0	0.10	0.02	0.1	0		49	8	2	6
Wheat, Cream of, reg. (Farina) unenriched	⅔–¾ cup	50	2.0	5	0.2	0	0.01	0.01	0.1	0		40	1	.1	1
enriched	⅔–¾ cup	50	2.0	5	0.4	0	0.05	0.04	0.5	0		40	1	.1	i
Wheat, whole meal (e.g., Ralston)	½ cup	55	2.0	8	0.6	0	0.07	0.02	0.7	0		44	3	1	3
Chard, Swiss, boiled	½ cup, stalks & leaves	20	2.0	73	1.8	5400	0.04	0.11	0.4	16		12	2		
Cheeses, Natural Cheddar, American	1 oz. or 4 tbsp, grated	120	7.5	225	0.3										

*Based on green variety; if bleached, only 140 I.U.
†Based on yellow cornmeal; white cornmeal contains only a trace of vitamin A value.

FOOD	APPROXIMATE MEASURE	CALORIES	PROTEIN G	CALCIUM MG	IRON MG	VITAMIN A I.U.	THIA-MINE MG	RIBO-FLAVIN MG	NIACIN MG	ASCORBIC ACID MG	CARBO-HYDRATE	FAT	SAT. FAT	UNSAT. FAT
Cheeses, *(cont'd)*														
Cottage, large or small curd, creamed	¼ cup or 2 rounded tbsp	60	7.5	52	0.2	390	0.01	0.14	tr.	0	2	88	48	34
uncreamed	¼ cup or 2 rounded tbsp	50	9.5	50	0.2	90	0.02	0.14	tr.	0	8	18	10	7
Cream	1 oz or 2 tbsp	110	2.5	19	0.1	5	0.02	0.15	tr.	0	8	2	1	1
Swiss, domestic	1 oz	110	8.5	278	0.3	460	0.01	0.07	tr.	0	2	97	53	38
Pasteurized processed						340	tr.	0.12	tr.	0	2	70	39	28
American	1 oz	110	7.0	209	0.3	370	0.01	0.12	tr.	0	2	79	44	31
Cheese food (e.g., Velveeta)	1 oz	95	6.0	171	0.2	290	0.01	0.17	tr.	0	8	62	34	24
Cheese spread, American	1 oz	85	5.0	170	0.2	260	tr.	0.16	tr.	0	12	53	29	21
Cherries, Raw, sweet	15 large, 20–25 small	70	1.5	22	0.4	110	0.05	0.06	0.4	10	61	3		
Red, canned, heavy syrup	½ cup, pitted, with syrup	95	1.0	18	0.4	70	0.02	0.02	0.2	4	94	2		
Red, canned, water pack	½ cup, pitted, with juice	50	1.0	15	0.3	60	0.02	0.02	0.2	3	43	2		
Chicken, Broiler	3½ oz, flesh only	135	24.0	9	1.7	90	0.05	0.19	8.8		0	36	12	23
Canned, flesh only	3½ oz	200	21.5	21	1.5	230	0.04	0.12	4.4	4	0	108	35	69
Creamed	¾ cup	310	26.5	124	1.6	490	0.06	0.27	5.7	tr.				
Fryer, breast	Approx. ½ breast, fried	205	32.5	12	1.7	90	0.05	0.22	14.7		8	54	17	35
thigh and drumstick	1 of each, med. size, fried	235	29.0	13	2.3	200	0.06	0.48	6.8		12	99	32	63
Roasted	3½ oz, flesh and skin	250	27.0	11	1.8	420	0.08	0.14	8.2		0	135	43	86
Chickpeas or garbanzos, dry weight	½ cup, after cooking	110	6.0	45	2.1	15	0.10	0.03	0.6		72	8	1	7
Chicory or endive, curly	10 small leaves	5	0.5	22	0.2	1000	0.02	0.03	0.1	6	4	1		
Chili con carne, canned														
With beans	1 cup	335	19.0	80	4.3	150	0.08	0.18	3.3		123	126	15	102
Without beans	1 cup	500	26.0	95	3.5	380	0.05	0.30	5.5		59	311	37	251
Chocolate (beverage), all milk	1 cup, small, 6 oz milk	210	7.0	222	0.5	295	0.08	0.32	0.1	1	125	70	39	27

| FOOD | APPROXIMATE MEASURE | CALORIES | PROTEIN G | MINERALS | | VITAMIN A I.U. | THIA-MINE MG | RIBO-FLAVIN MG | NIACIN MG | ASCORBIC ACID MG | CALORIES FROM | | | |
				CALCIUM MG	IRON MG						CARBO-HYDRATE	FAT	SAT. FAT	UNSAT. FAT
Chocolate, bitter or baking	1 oz or 1 square	150	3.0	23	2.0	20	0.02	0.07	0.5	0	35	141	77	54
Clams, canned, solids and liquid	½ cup	50	8.0	55	4.1		0.01	0.11	1.0		12	6	3	3
Cocoa (beverage), all milk	1 cup, small, 6 oz milk	174	7.0	224	0.9	295	0.08	0.34	0.3	2	78	79	44	30
Cola type beverages, See Soft Drinks														
Coconut, dried, sweetened	2 tbsp, shredded	80	0.5	2	0.3	0	0.01	tr.	0.1		33	50	43	4
Collards, boiled, drained	½ cup	30	2.5	152	0.6	5400	0.14	0.20	1.2	46	20	5		
Cookies, assorted, commercial	3 small or 1 large, 3 in. diameter	120	1.5	9	0.2	20	0.01	0.01	0.1	tr.	74	42	6	31
Corn, sweet Fresh	1 small ear, cooked	90	3.5	3	0.6	400*	0.12	0.10	1.4	9	86.1	8	1	7
Canned, drained	½ cup, scant	85	2.5	5	0.5	350*	0.03	0.05	0.9	4	82	7	1	6
Cream style, canned	½ cup, scant	80	2.0	3	0.6	330*	0.03	0.05	1.0	5	82	5	1	4
Cornmeal, See under Cereals														
Corn syrup, light or dark	1 tbsp	60	0	9	0.8	0	0	0	0	0	60			
Cowpeas or blackeye peas, Immature, fresh	1 cup, cooked	170	13.0	33	3.4	560	0.48	0.18	2.2	27	118.9	8	1	7
Mature, dried	½ cup, cooked	95	6.5	21	1.6	12	0.20	0.05	0.5		69.7	3	.3	3
Crabmeat, canned or cooked	⅝ cup	100	17.5	45	0.8		0.08	0.08	1.9		3.9	27	12	14
Crackers, Graham, plain	1 cracker, 2½ in. sq.	25	0.6	3	0.1	0	tr.	0.01	0.1	0	20.5	6	1	5
Ry-Krisp	2 wafers, 1⅞× 3½ in.	45	1.5	7	0.5	0	0.04	0.03	0.2	0	41	2	.2	1
Saltines	1 cracker, 2 in. square	17	0.4	1	0.1	0	tr.	tr.	tr.	0	12.3	4	1	3
Soda, plain or oyster	2 crackers, 2½ in. sq. or 10 oyster	45	0.9	2	0.2	0	tr.	0.01	0.1	0	28.7	8	1	6

*Yellow corn. White corn has trace only.

FOOD	APPROXIMATE MEASURE	CALORIES	PROTEIN G	MINERALS		VITAMINS					CALORIES FROM			
				CALCIUM MG	IRON MG	VITAMIN A I.U.	THIA-MINE MG	RIBO-FLAVIN MG	NIACIN MG	ASCORBIC ACID MG	CARBO-HYDRATE	FAT	SAT. FAT	UNSAT. FAT
Cranberry, jelly, sweetened	1 level tbsp	30	tr.	1	tr.	4	tr.	tr.	tr.	tr.	28.8			
Sauce, un-strained	1 level tbsp	25	tr.	1	tr.	3	tr.	tr.	tr.	tr.	25.2			
Cream, Half-and-half	¼ cup or 4 tbsp	80	2.0	65	tr.	290	0.02	0.10	0.1	1	11.7	62	34	24
Heavy or whipping	¼ cup or 4 tbsp	210	1.5	45	tr.	920	0.01	0.07	tr.	1	7.8	202	111	79
Light, coffee or table	¼ cup or 4 tbsp	130	2.0	61	tr.	500	0.02	0.09	0.06	1	11.7	106	58	41
Cucumbers, raw, pared	½ medium	7	0.3	9	0.2	tr.	0.02	0.02	0.1	6	7	1		
Custard, See under Puddings														
Dandelion greens, boiled	½ cup, drained	35	2.0	140	1.8	11700	0.13	0.16		18	22	5		
Dates, dried or fresh	½ cup pitted or 12 average	275	2.0	59	3.0	50	0.09	0.10	2.2	0	263	4		
Doughnuts, Cake type	1 average	120	1.5	12	0.4	24	0.05	0.05	0.4	tr.	62	50	7	38
Yeast	1 average	125	2.0	11	0.5	20	0.05	0.05	0.4	0	45	67	9	51
Eggs, Raw, whole, E.P.	1 large, 24 oz per doz.	80	6.5	27	1.2	590	0.06	0.15	0.1	0	2	54	17	33
white	1 white	16	3.5	3	tr.	0	tr.	0.09	tr.	0	1			
yolk	1 yolk	64	3.0	24	0.9	580	0.04	0.07	tr.	0	.4	50	16	30
Omelet or scrambled	2 small eggs with milk	175	11.0	80	1.7	1080	0.08	0.28	0.1	0	8	117	37	71
Eggplant, raw	2 slices or ½ cup pieces	25	1.0	12	0.7	10	0.05	0.05	0.6	5	23	2	1	1
Fats, Cooking, vege-table,	½ cup	885	0	0	0		0	0	0	0		880	202	634
solid or oil	1 tbsp	110	0	0	0		0	0	0	0		117	29	82
Figs, Fresh	2 large or 3 small	80	1.0	35	0.6	80	0.06	0.05	0.4	2	78	3		
Canned, heavy syrup	3 figs and 2 tbsp. syrup	85	0.5	13	0.4	30	0.03	0.03	0.2	1	86	2		
Dried	1 large	55	0.9	25	0.6	20	0.02	0.02	0.1	0	55	3		
Fish, Cod, steak, baked	4 oz, before cooking	170	28.5	31	1.0	180	0.08	0.11	3.0			45	11	32
Fish sticks	5 sticks, or 4 oz, cooked	195	18.0	12	0.4	0	0.04	0.08	1.8		27	90	22	64
Flounder or	4 oz, before													

FOOD	APPROXIMATE MEASURE	CALORIES	PROTEIN G	CALCIUM MG	IRON MG	VITAMIN A I.U.	THIA-MINE MG	RIBO-FLAVIN MG	NIACIN MG	ASCORBIC ACID MG	CARBO-HYDRATE	FAT	SAT. FAT	UNSAT FAT
Fish (cont'd)														
sole	cooking	200	30.0	23	1.4		0.07	0.08	2.5	2		72	17	51
Haddock, cooked, fried	4 oz, before cooking	165	19.5	40	1.2		0.04	0.07	3.2	2	23	56	13	40
Halibut, broiled	3½ oz, cooked	171	25.0	16	0.8	680	0.05	0.07	8.3			63	15	45
Mackerel, Atlantic	3½ oz, cooked with butter	235	22.0	6	1.2	530	0.15	0.27	7.6			144	27	111
Salmon, fresh, broiled	3½ oz, cooked	180	27.0		1.2	160	0.16	0.06	9.8	0		63	10	50
Canned, pink	½ cup	155	23.0	216	0.9	80	0.03	0.20	8.8			63	10	50
Canned, sockeye or red	½ cup	190	22.0	285	1.3	250	0.04	0.18	8.0			90	14	71
Sardines, Atlantic, packed in oil	3 oz, drained solids	175	20.5	371	2.5	190	0.03	0.17	4.6			81	15	62
Swordfish, broiled	3½ oz, cooked with butter	175	28.0	27	1.3	2050	0.04	0.05	10.9			54	10	42
Tuna, canned, in oil	⅝ cup, drained	195	29.0	8	1.9	80	0.05	0.12	11.9			72	18	50
water pack	⅝ cup, solids and liquids	125	28.0	16	1.6	—	—	0.10	13.3			7	2	5
Flours, Rye, light	1 cup, sifted	285	8.0	18	0.9	0	0.12	0.06	0.5	0	245	7	3	4
Wheat, patent, all purpose, unenriched	1 cup, sifted	400	11.5	18	0.9	0	0.07	0.06	1.0	0	332	8	1	6
enriched	1 cup, sifted	400	11.5	18	3.2	0	0.48	0.29	3.9	0	332	8	1	6
whole grain	1 cup, stirred	400	16.0	49	4.0	0	0.66	0.14	5.2	0	336	17	3	13
Fruit cocktail (heavy syrup)	½ cup, scant	75	0.4	9	0.4	140	0.02	0.01	0.4	2	72	1		
Gelatin, dry, plain	1 tbsp	35	8.5											
Gelatin dessert, Plain	½ cup	70	2.0								61			
With fruit	½ cup	80	1.5							4	72	1		
Grapefruit, Raw, pulp only	½ med., 4¼ in. diam.	40	0.5	16	0.4	80	0.04	0.02	0.2	38	40	1		
Canned, in syrup	½ cup, scant, solids and liquid	70	0.6	13	0.3	10	0.03	0.02	0.2	30	65	1		
Grapefruit juice, canned, Unsweetened	6 oz, ¾ cup	75	0.9	14	0.7	20	0.05	0.04	0.4	61	65	2		
Sweetened	6 oz, ¾ cup	95	0.9	14	0.7	20	0.05	0.04	0.4	56	83	2		
Grapes, American type (slip-skin)	22–24 avg. size	70	1.5	16	0.4	100	0.05	0.03	0.3	4	58	8		

FOOD	APPROXIMATE MEASURE	CALORIES	PROTEIN G	MINERALS CALCIUM MG	IRON MG	VITAMINS VITAMIN A I.U.	THIA-MINE MG	RIBO-FLAVIN MG	NIACIN MG	ASCORBIC ACID MG	CALORIES FROM CARBO-HYDRATE	FAT	SAT. FAT	UNSAT. FAT
Grapes (*cont'd*)														
European type (adherent skin)	22–24 avg. size	65	0.6	12	0.4	100	0.05	0.03	0.3	4	61	3		
Grape juice	6 oz, ¾ cup	130	0.4	21	0.6	—	0.08	0.04	0.4	tr.	115			
Griddle cakes, from mix, with milk	1 med., 4 in. diam.	50	1.5	55	0.2	30	0.04	0.06	0.2	tr.	31	9	5	3
Ham, smoked Cooked	3½ oz, 2-3 small slices	290	21.0	9	2.6	0	0.47	0.18	3.6	—		198	71	117
Canned	3½ oz	195	18.5	11	2.7	0	0.53	0.19	3.8	—	4	108	42	64
Heart, beef, braised	3 oz	160	27.0	5	5.0	30	0.21	1.04	6.5	1	2	45	22	21
Honey, strained	1 tbsp.	60	0.1	1	0.1	0	tr.	0.01	0.1	tr.	62			
Ice cream, plain, factory pack	¾ cup (12% fat)	205	4.0	123	0.1	520	0.04	0.19	0.1	1	82	109	60	43
Ice milk (dessert)	⅔ cup	150	5.0	156	0.1	210	0.05	0.22	0.1	1	86	44	24	17
Ices, water, lime	½ cup	80	0.4	tr.	tr.	0	tr.	tr.	tr.	1	119			
Jams, jellies, preserves, marmalade	1 tbsp	55	0.1	4	0.2	tr.	tr.	0.01	tr.	tr.	50			
Kale, boiled, drained	½ cup, leaves only	20	2.5	103	0.9	4570	0.06	0.10	0.9	51	12	3		
Kidney, Beef, raw	3½ oz	130	15.0	11	7.4	690	0.36	2.55	6.4	15	4	63	30	29
Lamb, raw	3½ oz	105	17.0	13	7.6	690	0.51	2.42	7.4	15	4	27	15	11
Kohlrabi, boiled, drained	½ cup diced	20	1.5	25	0.2	15	0.05	0.02	0.2	32	16	1		
Lamb, (choice grade) Chop, loin, broiled, lean and fat	1 avg., 3½ oz, ¾ in. thick	360	22.0	9	1.3		0.12	0.23	5.0			261	146	104
lean only	2.4 oz	125	19.0	8	1.3		0.10	0.18	4.0			35	20	14
Leg. roasted lean and fat	3½ oz, 2 sl. 4×3×¼ in.	280	25.5	11	1.7	0	0.15	0.27	5.5			171	96	68
lean only	3 oz	160	24.0	11	1.9		0.14	0.26	5.3			54	30	22
Shoulder, roasted, lean and fat	3½ oz	340	22.0	10	1.2		0.13	0.23	4.7			243	136	97
lean only	2.7 oz	155	20.0	9	1.4		0.11	0.21	4.3			72	40	29

FOOD	APPROXIMATE MEASURE	CALORIES	PROTEIN G	MINERALS		VITAMINS					CALORIES FROM			
				CALCIUM MG	IRON MG	VITAMIN A I.U.	THIA-MINE MG	RIBO-FLAVIN MG	NIACIN MG	ASCORBIC ACID MG	CARBO-HYDRATE	FAT	SAT. FAT	UNSAT. FAT
Lard	½ cup	990	0	0	0	0	0	0	0	0		126	54	52
	1 tbsp.	125	0	0	0	0	0	0	0	0				
Lemon juice	½ cup, scant	25	0.5	7	0.2	20	0.03	0.01	0.1	46	29	2		
	1 tbsp	5	0.1	1	tr.	tr.	0.01	tr.	tr.	7				
Lemonade con-centrate, frozen	1 cup, diluted as directed	110	0.3	3	tr.	tr.	tr.	0.02	0.2	18	104			
Lentils, dried, cooked	½ cup	105	8.0	25	2.1	20	0.07	0.06	0.6	0	76			
Lettuce, raw Compact head	2 lg. or 4 small leaves	7	0.5	17	1.0	485	0.03	0.03	0.2	4	4	1		
Iceberg type	1/5 head, 4¾ in. diam.	12	0.8	18	0.5	300	0.05	0.05	0.3	5	12	1	35	34
Loose leaf	2 lg. or 4 small leaves	9	0.7	34	0.7	950	0.03	0.04	0.2	9	8	2	45	32
Liver, Beef, fried	2 slices 3×2¼× ⅜ in.	170	20.0	8	6.6	40050	0.20	3.14	12.4	20	16	72	35	34
Lamb, broiled	2 slices 3×2¼× ⅜ in.	195	24.0	12	13.4	55880	0.37	3.83	18.7	27	8	81	45	32
Pork, fried	2 slices 3×2¼× ⅜ in.	180	22.0	11	21.8	11180	0.26	3.27	16.7	17	8	81	26	51
Lobster, canned or cooked	⅔ cup meat	95	18.5	65	0.8		0.10	0.07			1	18	8	9
Loganberries, Fresh	⅔ cup	60	1.0	35	1.2	200	0.03	0.04	0.4	24	54	5		
Canned, juice pack	½ cup, scant, solids and juice	55	0.7	27	1.2	150	0.02	0.03	0.3	12	47	4		
Macaroni or Spaghetti, Unenriched, tender	1 cup, cooked 14–20 min	155	5.0	11	0.6	0	0.01	0.01	0.4	0	126	5	1	4
Enriched, tender	1 cup, cooked 14–20 min	155	5.0	11	1.3	0	0.20	0.11	1.5	0	126	5	1	4
Baked with cheese	1 cup	475	19.0	398	2.0	950	0.22	0.44	2.0	tr.	174	211	116	82
Margarine, fortified*	1 pat, 1/45 lb	70	0.1	2	0	330				0		72	31	38
	1 tbsp	100	0.1	3	0	460				0				
Melons, E.P. Cantaloupe or muskmelons	½ of 4½ in. melon	30	0.7	14	0.4	3400	0.04	0.03	0.6	33	29	1		
Casaba	3½ oz, 1 avg. serving	35	0.8	14	0.4	40	0.04	0.03	0.6	23	29	3		
Watermelon	½ cup, balls or cubes 1/6 of a 10×	25	0.5	7	0.5	590	0.03	0.03	0.2	7	22	3		

*Almost all margarines now on sale are fortified to contain 15,000 I.U. of vitamin A per pound.

FOOD	APPROXIMATE MEASURE	CALORIES	PROTEIN G	MINERALS CALCIUM MG	IRON MG	VITAMINS VITAMIN A I.U.	THIA-MINE MG	RIBO-FLAVIN MG	NIACIN MG	ASCORBIC ACID MG	CALORIES FROM CARBO-HYDRATE	FAT	SAT. FAT	UNSAT. FAT
Melons (cont'd)														
	16 in. melon	235	4.5	63	4.5	5310	0.27	0.27	1.8	63	209	17	3	13
Milk,														
Whole, fresh	8 oz, 1 cup or full glass	165	8.5	285	0.1	370	0.07	0.41	0.2	2	47	80	44	31
Skim or but-termilk	1 cup	85	9.0	298	0.1	tr.	0.10	0.44	0.2	2	51	2	1	1
Half and Half	1 cup	325	8.0	261	tr.	1160	0.07	0.39	0.2	2	43	246	236	96
Evaporated	½ cup or 1 cup reconstituted	170	9.0	318	0.1	400	0.05	0.43	0.3	1	47	88	48	34
Condensed (sweetened)	1 tbsp	65	1.5	52	tr.	70	0.02	0.08	tr.	tr.	43	18	10	7
Dried, whole	1 tbsp	40	2.0	73	tr.	90	0.02	0.12	0.1	1	12	18	10	7
skim (nonfat solids)	1 tbsp	25	2.5	98	tr.	tr.	0.03	0.14	0.1	1	16	1	1	.3
Malted, plain, dry	1 tbsp	35	1.0	23	0.2	80	0.03	0.04	tr.	0	23	6	3	2
Chocolate drink com-mercial	1 cup (skim milk used)	190	8.0	270	0.5	200	0.10	0.40	0.3	3	105	53	29	21
Yogurt, low-fat	1 cup	125	8.5	295	tr.	170	0.10	0.44	0.2	2	51	35	19	14
Molasses,														
Light	1 tbsp	50		33	0.9		0.01	0.01	tr.		51			
Medium	1 tbsp	45		58	1.2			0.02	0.2		47			
Blackstrap	1 tbsp	40		137	3.2		0.02	0.04	0.4		43			
Muffins,														
Bran	1 medium	90	2.5	50	1.3	80	0.05	0.08	1.4	tr.	62	25	4	19
Cornmeal (yel-low, enriched)	1 medium	140	3.0	47	0.8	140	0.09	0.10	0.7	tr.	86	42	5	34
White flour, enriched	1 medium	120	3.0	42	0.6	40	0.07	0.09	0.6	tr.	16	126	18	96
Mushrooms, raw	3½ oz	30	2.5	6	0.8	tr.	0.10	0.46	4.2	3	16	3		
Mustard greens, boiled, drained	⅔ cup	25	2.0	138	1.8	5800	0.08	0.14	0.6	48	16	3		
Mustard, pre-pared, brown or yellow	1 tbsp	11	1.0	13	0.3						4	8		
Noodles, egg														
Unenriched	⅔ cup, cooked	125	4.0	10	0.6	70	0.03	0.02	0.4	0	90	18	6	11
Enriched	⅔ cup, cooked	125	4.0	10	0.9	70	0.14	0.08	1.2	0	90	18	6	11
Nuts, mixed, shelled	8–12 average nuts	95	2.5	14	0.5	tr.	0.09	0.02	0.6	tr.	12	76	6	66
Oils, salad or cooking	½ cup	970	0	0	0	0	0	0	0		990	426	525	
	1 tbsp	125	0	0	0	0	0	0	0					
Okra, boiled, drained	9 pods, 3 in. long	30	2.0	92	0.5	490	0.13	0.18	0.9	20	24	3		

FOOD	APPROXIMATE MEASURE	CALORIES	PROTEIN G	MINERALS		VITAMIN A I.U.	VITAMINS				CALORIES FROM			
				CALCIUM MG	IRON MG		THIA-MINE MG	RIBO-FLAVIN MG	NIACIN MG	ASCORBIC ACID MG	CARBO-HYDRATE	FAT	SAT. FAT	UNSAT. FAT
Olives, E.P.														
Green	1 large or 2 small	5	tr.	3	0.08	15					.4	5	1	4
Ripe (Mission)	1 large or 2 small	10	0.1	5	0.09	5	tr.	tr.			1	8	1	7
Onions, green (scallions), raw	1 medium, without tops	5	0.1	3	0.05	tr.	tr.	tr.	0.03	2	4			
Onions, mature, dry														
Raw	1 onion, 2½ in. diam.	40	1.5	27	0.5	40	0.03	0.04	0.2	10	36	1		
	1 tbsp, chopped	4	0.2	3	0.05	5	tr.	tr.	0.02	1				
Boiled, drained	½ cup, 3–4 small	30	1.0	24	0.4	40	0.03	0.03	0.2	7	63	1		
Oranges, raw, E.P.	1 medium, 3 in. diam.	75	1.5	62	0.6	300	0.15	0.06	0.6	75	65	3		
Orange juice,														
Fresh or canned	6 oz, ¾ cup, 1 sm. glass	80	1.0	20	0.4	370	0.17	0.06	0.7	93	69			
Frozen, con-centrate (as diluted)	6 oz, ¾ cup, 1 sm. glass	80	1.0	17	0.2	370	0.17	0.02	0.6	83	72			
Oysters, raw														
Eastern	5–8 medium	80	10.0	113	6.6	370	0.17	0.22	3.0		16	18	8	9
Pacific and Olympia	5–8 medium or 3½ oz Olympia	110	13.0	102	8.6		0.14		1.6	36	31	27	12	14
Oyster stew (1 part oysters, 3 parts milk)	1 cup, 3–4 oysters	200	11.0	269	3.2	640	0.14	0.41	1.6		43	108	48	55
Pancakes. See Griddle cakes														
Papayas, raw	½ cup, cubed	40	0.6	20	0.3	1750	0.04	0.04	0.3	56	40	1		
Parsley, raw	1 tbsp, chopped	2	0.1	7	0.2	300	tr.	0.01	tr.	6	1			
Peaches,														
Raw, yellow, E.P.	1 med. peach, 2 in. diam.	45	0.7	10	0.6	1530	0.02	0.06	1.2	8	40	1		
Canned, heavy syrup	2 halves, 2 tbsp juice	95	0.5	5	0.4	520	0.01	0.02	0.7	4	86	1		
water pack	½ cup, sliced, with liquid	40	0.5	5	0.4	540	0.01	0.04	0.7	4	36	1		
Dried, sul-fured, cooked, unsweetened	½ cup, 5–6 halves, 3 tbsp liquid	110	1.5	20	2.6	1650	tr.	0.08	2.0	3	104	3		

FOOD	APPROXIMATE MEASURE	CALORIES	PROTEIN G	MINERALS CALCIUM MG	IRON MG	VITAMIN A I.U.	THIA-MINE MG	VITAMINS RIBO-FLAVIN MG	NIACIN MG	ASCORBIC ACID MG	CALORIES FROM CARBO-HYDRATE	FAT	SAT. FAT	UNSAT. FAT
Peanuts, shelled, roasted	15–17 nuts (without skins)	90	4.0	11	0.3		0.05	0.02	2.6	0	12	68	15	48
Peanut butter	1 tbsp	90	4.0	10	0.3		0.02	0.02	2.4	0	12	67	15	48
Pears, Raw, including skin	1 pear 3×2½ in. diam.	110	1.5	14	0.5	40	0.04	0.07	0.2	7	101	6		
Canned, heavy syrup	2 halves and 2 tbsp syrup	90	0.2	6	0.2	tr.	0.01	0.02	0.1	1	86	2		
water pack	2 halves and 2 tbsp juice	40	0.2	6	0.2	tr.	0.01	0.02	0.1	1	36	2		
Peas, Green, fresh or frozen	½ cup, boiled, drained	55	4.5	18	1.4	430	0.22	0.09	1.8	16	41	3		
Canned, drained	½ cup	65	4.0	20	1.4	550	0.09	0.05	0.8	6	49	3		
Split, dry, cooked	½ cup (from 1 oz dry wt.)	145	10.0	14	2.1	50	0.19	0.11	1.1		107	3	1	2
Peas and carrots, frozen, cooked	½ cup	40	2.5	19	0.8	6980	0.14	0.05	1.0	6	32	2		
Pecans	12 halves or 2 tbsp chopped	105	1.0	11	0.4	20	0.13	0.02	0.1	tr.	8	92	7	78
Peppers, Green, raw, E.P.	1 medium shell	15	0.8	6	0.5	270	0.05	0.05	0.3	83	12	1		
	1 tbsp, chopped	5	0.1	1	0.1	40	0.01	0.01	tr.	13	2			
Red, canned (pimientos)	1 medium	10	0.4	3	0.6	920	0.01	0.02	0.2	38	4	2		
Pickles, cucumber Dill	1 large, 4× 1¾ in.	15	0.9	35	1.4	140	tr.	0.03	tr.	8	12	3		
Sweet	1 pickle, 2¾× ¾ in.	30	0.1	2	0.2	20	tr.	tr.	tr.	1	28	1		
Relish, sweet or mixed	1 tbsp	20	0.1	3	0.1	0	0	0	0	0	16	1		
Pies, Apple	1/6 of 9-in. pie	410	3.5	13	0.5	50	0.03	0.03	0.6	2	220	151	50	95
Blackberry	1/6 of 9-in. pie	390	4.0	30	0.8	140	0.03	0.03	0.5	6	198	151	50	95
Cherry	1/6 of 9-in. pie	420	4.0	22	0.5	700	0.03	0.03	0.8	tr.	220	151	50	95
Chocolate meringue	1/6 of 9-in. pie	405	7.5	110	1.1	300	0.05	0.19	0.3	tr.	194	160	55	100
Custard	1/6 of 9-in. pie	350	10.0	154	1.0	370	0.03	0.26	0.5	0	133	151	50	95
Lemon meringue	1/6 of 9-in. pie	360	5.0	20	0.7	240	0.04	0.11	0.3	4	191	118	42	70
Mince	1/6 of 9-in. pie	435	4.0	45	1.6	tr.	0.11	0.06	0.6	2	238	200	65	130
Pumpkin	1/6 of 9-in. pie	320	6.0	77	0.8	3710	0.50	0.15	0.8	tr.	133	143	45	93

FOOD	APPROXIMATE MEASURE	CALORIES	PROTEIN G	CALCIUM MG	IRON MG	VITAMIN A I.U.	THIAMINE MG	RIBOFLAVIN MG	NIACIN MG	ASCORBIC ACID MG	CARBOHYDRATE	FAT	SAT. FAT	UNSAT. FAT
Pineapple, Raw	⅔ cup, no sugar	50	0.4	17	0.5	70	0.09	0.03	0.2	17	50	2		
Canned, crushed, heavy syrup sliced	½ cup, solids and liquid	95	0.4	14	0.4	70	0.10	0.03	0.3	9	90	1		
	2 small or 1 large slice, 2 tbsp juice	90	0.4	13	0.4	60	0.10	0.02	0.2	8	83	1		
water pack	2 small or 1 large slice, 2 tbsp liquid	40	0.3	12	0.3	50	0.03	0.02	0.2	7	36	1		
Pineapple juice, canned, un-unsweetened	6 oz, ¾ cup, 1 sm. glass	100	0.7	28	0.6	90	0.09	0.04	0.4	17	90	2		
Pineapple and grapefruit juice	6 oz, ¾ cup	100	0.4	9	0.4	20	0.04	0.02	0.2	30	90			
Pinenuts, Piñón	2 tbsp	95	2.0	2	0.8	5	0.19	0.03	0.7	tr.	12	76	8	74
Plums, Raw, hybrid type	2 medium	50	0.5	12	0.5	250	0.03	0.03	0.5	6	43	2		
Canned, purple (Italian) heavy syrup	3 med., 2 tbsp syrup	100	0.5	11	1.1	1450	0.02	0.02	0.5	2	94	1		
Popcorn, with oil and salt	1 cup	70	2.0	1	0.3			0.01	0.3	0	36	25	3	21
Pork, Chops, broiled, E.P. lean and fat	1 medium thick chop	245	15.0	7	1.9	0	0.33	0.15	3.2			180	68	104
lean only	(from above serving)	110	13.5	6	1.8	0	0.29	0.13	2.6			54	21	31
Loin, roasted lean and fat	2 slices, 3½ × 3¼ in.	335	20.0	9	2.6	0	0.45	0.21	4.4			252	98	146
lean only	(from above serving)	165	20.0	8	2.5	0	0.43	0.20	3.9			81	31	47
Potatoes, Baked	1 medium	95	2.5	9	0.7	tr.	0.10	0.04	1.7	20	84			
Boiled, pared before cooking	1 medium	65	2.0	6	0.5	tr.	0.09	0.03	1.2	16	60			
French-fried	20 pieces, 2×½×½ in.	275	4.5	15	1.3	tr.	0.13	0.08	3.1	21	144	109	25	33
frozen (re-heated)	20 pieces, 2×½×½ in.	220	3.5	9	1.8	tr.	0.14	0.02	2.6	21	136	67	47	19
Mashed, milk and table fat added	½ cup	95	2.0	24	0.4	170	0.08	0.05	1.0	9	48	34		

| FOOD | APPROXIMATE MEASURE | CALORIES | PROTEIN G | MINERALS | | VITAMINS | | | | | CALORIES FROM | | | |
				CALCIUM MG	IRON MG	VITAMIN A I.U.	THIA-MINE MG	RIBO-FLAVIN MG	NIACIN MG	ASCORBIC ACID MG	CARBO-HYDRATE	FAT	SAT. FAT	UNSAT. FAT
Potato chips	10 chips, 2 in. diam.	115	1.0	8	0.4	tr.	0.04	0.01	1.0	3	40	67	16	50
Prunes, dried Softened	4 prunes, medium	80	0.7	16	1.2	510	0.03	0.05	0.5	1	79	2		
Cooked, un-sweetened	8–9 med., 2 tbsp juice	160	1.5	32	2.4	1010	0.04	0.09	0.9	1	151	3		
Prune juice, canned	6 oz, ¾ cup	140	0.7	25	7.4		0.02	0.02	0.7	4	122	2		
Puddings, Apple Brown Betty	½ cup	150	1.5	18	0.6	100	0.06	0.04	0.4	1	108	34	10	10
Chocolate, cooked or in-stant (from mix)	½ cup	160	4.5	133	0.4	170	0.03	0.20	0.1	tr.	117	35	19	14
Custard	½ cup	115	5.5	112	0.4	350	0:04	0.19	0.1	tr.	43	53	29	21
Junket (mix) with milk	½ cup	125	4.0	152	tr.	200	0.04	0.21	0.1	1	66	44	24	17
Prune whip	½ cup	100	3.0	14	0.8	300	0.01	0.09	0.3	1	86	1		
Rice, with raisins	⅔ cup	210	5.0	142	0.6	160	0.04	0.20	0.3	tr.	140	42	25	27
Tapioca, cream	½ cup	135	5.0	105	0.4	290	0.04	0.18	0.1	1	68	42	24	18
Vanilla, home recipe, with starch	½ cup	145	5.0	152	tr.	210	0.04	0.21	0.1	1	84	42	24	18
Pumpkin, canned	1 cup	40	1.0	30	0.5	7680	0.04	0.06	0.7	6	40	3	1	3
Radishes, raw, common	4 small	7	0.4	12	0.4	5	tr.	tr.	0.1	10	4			
Raisins, natural unbleached	¼ cup	115	1.0	25	1.4	4	0.02	0.01	0.1	tr.	112	1		
	1 tbsp	30	0.1	6	0.3	1	tr.	tr.	tr.	tr.	29			
Raspberries Black, fresh	⅔ cup	75	2.0	30	0.9	tr.	0.03	0.09	0.9	18	58	8		
Red, fresh	⅔ cup	55	1.0	22	0.9	130	0.03	0.09	0.9	25	50	4		
Red, canned, water pack	½ cup, solids and liquid	35	0.7	15	0.6	90	0.01	0.04	0.5	9	32	1		
Rhubarb, cooked, with sugar	½ cup, fruit and syrup	190	0.7	105	0.8	110	0.03	0.07	0.4	8	176	1		
Rice, Brown, cooked	⅔ cup	120	2.5	12	0.5	0	0.09	0.02	1.4	0	104	5	1	4
White, en-riched, cooked	⅔ cup	110	2.0	10	0.9	0	0.11		1.0	0	96	1	.1	1
Precooked, instant	⅔ cup	110	2.0	3	0.8	0	0.13		1.0	0	96			

| FOOD | APPROXIMATE MEASURE | CALORIES | PROTEIN G | MINERALS | | VITAMINS | | | | | CALORIES FROM | | | |
				CALCIUM MG	IRON MG	VITAMIN A I.U.	THIA-MINE MG	RIBO-FLAVIN MG	NIACIN MG	ASCORBIC ACID MG	CARBO-HYDRATE	FAT	SAT. FAT	UNSAT FAT
Rolls and buns (enriched) Plain (pan rolls)	1 small	85	2.5	21	0.5	tr.	0.08	0.05	0.6	tr.	54	17	2	13
Hamburger bun	1 large	115	3.0	28	0.7	tr.	0.11	0.07	0.8	tr.	79	17	2	13
Hard	1 large	160	5.0	24	1.2	tr.	0.14	0.12	1.4	tr.	123	17	2	13
Rutabagas, boiled, drained	½ cup, diced (yellow turnip)	30	0.7	47	0.2	440	0.05	0.05	0.6	21	28	1		
Rye wafers, See Crackers														
Salad dressings, avg. commercial Blue Cheese	1 tbsp	80	0.8	13	tr.	30	tr.	0.02	tr.	tr.	4	70	39	28
French	1 tbsp	60	0.1	2	0.1						12	53	29	21
low-calorie	1 tbsp	15	0.1	2	0.1						8	5	3	21
Mayonnaise	1 tbsp	100	0.2	3	0.1	40	tr.	0.01	tr.		1	97	53	38
Salad dressing (mayonnaise type)	1 tbsp	65	0.2	2	tr.	30	tr.	tr.	tr.		8	53	29	21
low-calorie	1 tbsp	20	0.2	3	tr.	30	tr.	tr.	tr.		3	18	10	7
Thousand Island	1 tbsp	75	0.1	2	0.1	50	tr.	tr.	tr.	tr.	8	70	39	28
Salad dressings, Boiled, home recipe	1 tbsp	30	0.7	15	0.1	80	0.01	0.03	tr.	tr.	12	18	10	7
Sauces, Butterscotch sauce	2 tbsp	205	0.5	41	1.4	300	tr.	tr.	tr.	tr.	160	59	32	23
Cheese sauce	2 tbsp	65	3.0	88	0.1	210	0.01	0.08	0.1	tr.	8	42	23	16
Chocolate syrup, thin	2 tbsp	100	0.9	7	0.6	tr.	0.01	0.03	0.2	0	98	67	37	26
Fudge type	2 tbsp	165	3.0	64	0.7	80	0.02	0.11	0.2	tr.	105	59	32	23
Custard sauce, avg.	2 tbsp	40	2.0	39	0.2	120	0.01	0.12	0.1	tr.	20	17	9	7
Hard sauce	2 tbsp	95	0.1	2	tr.	230	tr.	tr.	tr.	0	47	50	28	20
Hollandaise, true	¼ cup, scant	180	2.5	23	0.9	1030	0.03	0.04	tr.	tr.	2	160	88	62
Tartar sauce	1 tbsp	105	0.3	4	0.2	40	tr.	tr.	tr.	tr.	3	101	55	39
Tomato catsup or chili sauce	1 tbsp	20	0.3	4	0.1	240	0.02	0.01	0.3	3	2	1	1	.3
White sauce, medium	½ cup	215	5.0	153	0.3	610	0.05	0.23	0.3	tr.	47	143	79	56
Sauerkraut, canned	⅔ cup, solids and liquid	20	1.0	45	0.6	60	0.04	0.05	0.3	18	20	3		
Sausages, Bologna, all meat	1 oz, 1 slice 4¼×⅛ in.	85	4.0	–	–						4	63	23	37
Frankfurter	1 average, cooked	150	6.0	3	0.8		0.08	0.10	1.3		3	118	43	70
Liverwurst, fresh	1 oz	90	5.0	3	1.6	1910	0.06	0.39	1.7		2	72	26	43

FOOD	APPROXIMATE MEASURE	CALORIES	PROTEIN G	MINERALS CALCIUM MG	MINERALS IRON MG	VITAMINS VITAMIN A I.U.	VITAMINS THIA- MINE MG	VITAMINS RIBO- FLAVIN MG	VITAMINS NIACIN MG	VITAMINS ASCORBIC ACID MG	CALORIES FROM CARBO- HYDRATE	CALORIES FROM FAT	CALORIES FROM SAT. FAT	CALORIES FROM UNSAT. FAT
Luncheon meat, pork, cured, canned or pkg.	1 oz	90	5.0	3	0.7	0	0.09	0.06	0.9		2	72	26	43
Pork sausage, link, cooked	3 links	285	11.0	4	1.4	0	0.47	0.20	2.2			243	92	141
Salami, dry	1 oz	135	7.0	4	1.1		0.11	0.08	1.6		2	99	36	58
Vienna sau- sage, canned	2 oz, ½ can	145	8.5	5	1.3		0.05	0.08	1.6		1	108	39	64
Scallops, Raw	3½ oz	80	15.5	26	1.8			0.06	1.3		12	2	1	1
Frozen, breaded, fried	3½ oz, reheated	195	18.0	—	—						43	72	26	43
Sherbet, orange	½ cup	135	0.9	16	tr.	60	0.01	0.03	tr.	2	112	8		
Shrimp, canned	3 oz, meat only	100	20.5	98	2.6	50	0.01	0.03	1.5		2	8	4	41
Sirup, table, cane and maple	1 tbsp	50	0	3	tr.	0	0	0	0	0	51	0	0	0
Soft Drinks, Cola type	1 bottle, 6 oz	65	0	—	—	0	0	0	0	0	65	0	0	0
Dietary drink (less than 1 Cal./oz)	1 bottle, 6 oz	—	0	—	—	0	0	0	0	0		0	0	0
Ginger Ale	1 bottle, 6 oz	50	0	—	—	0	0	0	0	0	55	0	0	0
Root Beer	1 bottle, 6 oz	70	0	—	—	0	0	0	0	0	70	0	0	0
Soups, canned, diluted, ready to serve Asparagus or celery, cream of, made with water	¾ cup	70	1.0	38	0.4	150	0.02	0.04	tr.	tr.	28	34		
made with milk	¾ cup	130	5.0	154	0.6	300	0.04	0.21	0.6	2	47	62	19	13
Bean, with pork	¾ cup	125	6.0	46	1.7	480	0.09	0.06	0.7	2	66	34	13	20
Bouillon, broth or consomme	¾ cup	20	4.0	tr.	0.4	tr.	tr.	0.02	0.9		8	0	0	0
Chicken, cream of,	¾ cup	75	2.5	19	0.4	320	0.02	0.04	0.4	tr.	23	45	14	29
with rice	¾ cup	40	2.5	6	0.2	110	tr.	0.02	0.6		16	8	3	5
Clam chowder (Manhattan)	¾ cup	60	2.0	27	0.8	680	0.02	0.02	0.8		39	18	8	9
Mushroom, cream of	¾ cup	105	2.0	32	0.4	60	0.02	0.10	0.6	tr.	32	34		
Pea, split	¾ cup	110	7.0	22	1.1	330	0.19	0.11	1.1	tr.	66	17	6	10
Tomato	¾ cup	65	1.5	11	0.6	760	0.04	0.04	0.9	9	48	17		
Vegetable beef	¾ cup	60	4.0	9	0.6	2040	0.04	0.04	0.7		28	17	8	8
Soups, de- hydrated, add water as di- rected Chicken noodle	¾ cup	40	1.5	6	0.2	40	0.06	0.04	0.4	tr.	23	9	1	7
Onion	¾ cup	30	1.0	7	0.2	tr.	tr.	tr.	tr.	2	16	8		

FOOD	APPROXIMATE MEASURE	CALORIES	PROTEIN G	CALCIUM MG	IRON MG	VITAMIN A I.U.	THIAMINE MG	RIBO-FLAVIN MG	NIACIN MG	ASCORBIC ACID MG	CARBO-HYDRATE	FAT	SAT. FAT	UNSAT. FAT
						MINERALS			VITAMINS		CALORIES FROM			
Spaghetti, canned, in tomato sauce, with														
Cheese	⅔ cup	75	2.0	16	1.1	370	0.14	0.11	1.8	4	59	5	3	2
Meat balls	⅔ cup	100	5.0	21	1.3	400	0.06	0.07	0.9	2	43	36	17	17
Spinach, fresh or frozen, boiled	½ cup, drained	20	3.0	84	2.0	7290	0.06	0.13	0.5	25	12	3		
Squash, Summer, boiled, drained	½ cup	15	0.9	25	0.4	390	0.05	0.08	0.8	10	12	1	.2	1
Winter, baked	3½ oz (yellow)	65	2.0	28	0.8	4200	0.05	0.13	0.7	13	60	3	1	3
boiled, drained	½ cup	40	1.0	20	0.5	3500	0.04	0.10	0.4	8	36	3	1	2
Starch, pure (arrowroot, corn, etc.)	1 tbsp	30	tr.	0.	0	0	0	0	0	0	28			
Strawberries, Fresh	⅔ cup	35	0.7	21	1.0	60	0.03	0.07	0.6	59	29	4		
Frozen, sweetened, whole	3½ oz	90	0.4	13	0.6	30	0.02	0.06	0.5	55	86	2		
Sugar, Brown	½ cup, firmly packed	410	0	94	3.7	0	0.01	0.03	0.2	0	413	0	0	0
White, granulated	½ cup	385	0	0	0.1	0	0	0	0	0	390	0	0	0
	1 tbsp or 3 level tsp	45	0	0	tr.	0	0	0	0	0	47	0	0	0
powdered	1 cup, stirred before meas.	495	0	0	0.1	0	0	0	0	0	495	0	0	0
	1 tbsp	30	0	0	tr.	0	0	0	0	0	31	0	0	0
loaf	1 cube or domino	30	0	0	tr.	0	0	0	0	0	27	0	0	0
Sweet potatoes, cooked														
Baked, skinned	1 small	140	2.0	40	0.9	8100	0.09	0.07	0.7	22	144	4		
Boiled in skin	½ medium	115	2.0	32	0.7	7900	0.09	0.06	0.6	17	104	3		
Candied	½ medium	170	1.5	37	0.9	6300	0.06	0.04	0.4	10	136	25	12	12
Canned, vacuum pack	½ cup	110	2.0	25	0.8	7800	0.05	0.04	0.6	14	100	2		
Tomatoes, Fresh	1 medium, 2× 2½ in.	35	1.5	20	0.8	1350	0.09	0.06	1.1	35	28	3		
Canned or cooked	½ cup, solids and liquid	25	1.0	7	0.6	1080	0.06	0.04	0.8	20	20	2		
Tomato juice, canned	6 oz, ¾ cup	35	1.5	13	1.6	1440	0.09	0.05	1.4	29	32	2		
Tomato purée, canned (sauce)	½ cup	50	2.0	16	2.0	1920	0.11	0.06	1.7	40	44	2		

FOOD	APPROXIMATE MEASURE	CALORIES	PROTEIN G	MINERALS		VITAMINS					CALORIES FROM			
				CALCIUM MG	IRON MG	VITAMIN A I.U.	THIA-MINE MG	RIBO-FLAVIN MG	NIACIN MG	ASCORBIC ACID MG	CARBO-HYDRATE	FAT	SAT. FAT	UNSAT. FAT
Tongue, Beef, fresh, simmered	3½ oz, cooked	245	21.5	7	2.2		0.05	0.29	3.5		2	153	73	72
Canned or cured, beef, lamb, etc.	3½ oz, cooked	265	19.5	—	—						1	180	101	72
Tuna, See Fish.														
Turkey, roasted (flesh only) Light meat	3½ oz, 3 slices (3½×2× ½×¼ in.)	175	33.0	—	1.2		0.05	0.14	11.1		0	36	10	24
Dark meat	3½ oz	205	30.0	—	2.3		0.04	0.23	4.2		0	72	21	48
Turnips, white boiled, drained	½ cup, diced	20	0.6	26	0.3	tr.	0.03	0.04	0.2	17	16	2		
Turnip greens, boiled, drained	½ cup	15	2.0	138	0.8	4730	0.11	0.18	0.5	52	12	2		
Veal, Cutlet, broiled	3½ oz	215	27.0	11	3.2		0.07	0.25	5.4		0	99	48	47
Shoulder, oven braised	3½ oz	235	28.0	12	3.5		0.09	0.29	6.4		0	117	56	55
Vinegar, cider	1 tbsp	5	tr.	1	0.1						3	0	0	0
Waffles (from mix), with milk and eggs	One, 4½× 5½×½ in.	205	6.5	179	1.0	170	0.11	0.17	0.7	tr.	105	67	29	34
Walnuts, English	1 cup, halves	650	15.0	99	3.1	30	0.33	0.13	0.9	2	66	538	38	479
	2 tbsp, chopped	100	2.0	15	0.5	10	0.05	0.02	0.1	tr.	8	84	6	75
Watercress, raw	10 average sprigs	2	0.2	15	0.2	490	0.01	0.02	0.1	8	1	fr.	fr.	fr.
Watermelon, See Melons.														
Wheat germ, crude	1 tbsp, rounded	35	2.5	7	1.0	0	0.20	0.07	0.4	0	20	8	1	7
Yeast, Baker's, moist	1 cake, compressed	10	1.5	2	0.6	tr.	0.09	0.20	1.3	tr.				
dry, active	1 tbsp	20	3.0	4	1.3	tr.	0.19	0.43	2.9	tr.				
Brewer's (debittered)	1 tbsp	23	3.0	(17)	1.4	tr.	1.24	0.34	3.0	tr.				
Yogurt, See Milk.														

SOURCE: Bogert, Briggs, and Calloway, *Nutrition and Physical Fitness* (Eighth Edition), Philadelphia: W. B. Saunders Company, 1966, and calculations based on information from *Composition of Foods*, Agriculture Handbook No. 8, U.S. Dept. of Agriculture.

Conversion Table for Weights, Measures, and Temperature

Appendix F

---

1 inch = 2.54 centimeters (cm) = 25.4 millimeters (mm)
1 centimeter = 0.3937 in.

1 mm ___

1 foot = 30.48 cm = .3048 m

1 cm _____

1 meter = 39.37 in. = 3.281 ft

1 inch _____

1 meter = 1000 mm = 100 cm

1 ounce = 28.35 gr = .028 kilogram (kg)
1 gram = .035 oz = .002 lb
1 pound = 454 gr = .454 kg
1 kilogram = 1000 gr = 35.27 oz = 2.205 lb

1 cubic inch = 16.39 cubic centimeters (cc)
1 cubic centimeter = .061 cubic inches = approximately 1 milliliter (ml)
1 liquid quart = .946 liter (l)
1 liter = 1.057 liquid qt
1 fluid ounce = 29.57 ml
100 milliliters = about ½ a "Coke" bottle

5 lb bag is
about 2.3 kg

150 lb man,
about 70 kg

1 cc (1 ml)
actual size

1 small "Coke," filled
to top, is about 200 ml

1 ft-lb = .000324 Calories (kilocalories)
1 Calorie = 3087 ft-lb

To convert °C to °F: 1.8(°C) + 32°
To convert °F to °C: .555(°F − 32°)

Glossary

acidosis a disturbance in the acid-base balance of the body tissues in which pH is lowered (the tissues become more acid). See also pH.

action potentials changes in electric potential at the surface of a nerve or muscle cell, occurring at the moment of their excitation.

active exercise exercise initiated and carried through by a patient without aid from a therapist (as opposed to passive exercise).

addiction the habitual use of a drug or other substance due to a physiological adaptation that produces seriously disturbing symptoms if the substance is not supplied.

adrenalin (epinephrine) a commercial name for the hormone secreted by the medullary (inner) portion of the adrenal gland.

afferent neurons nerve cells that conduct impulses toward the CNS.

agility the ability to shift direction quickly while moving at nearly full speed or, in dance, to move upward or downward quickly.

agonist the muscle directly responsible for any particular joint action.

AHD arteriosclerotic heart disease.

albumin a protein found in nearly every plant and animal tissue; in the blood, it contributes to plasma osmotic pressure and thus helps regulate the volume of plasma water.

alkalosis increase of pH of the body due to excessive alkaline substances or removal of acids or chlorides from the blood.

allergy an abnormal sensitivity of the body to certain foods, pollens, drugs, etc.

all-or-none term used to describe the manner in which nervous tissue responds to a stimulus: it either responds by propagating an impulse or it does not; the strength of the impulse elicited is not proportional to the strength of the stimulus; also applied to muscle fiber.

alveoli (singular, alveolus) tiny air sacs of the lungs where CO_2 and O_2 exchange with the pulmonary capillaries takes place.

amino acids compounds, present in proteins, from which the body builds parts of most of its tissues and that *can* be utilized for energy. See page 323.

amphetamines a class of drugs used as central nervous system stimulants: Benzedrine, Dexedrine, etc.

anaerobic without oxygen.

analysis separation of an activity or process into its component parts in order to determine how it operates.

anemia a condition in which there is insufficient hemoglobin or red blood cells (or both).

angina pectoris pain in the chest; usually associated with heart disease. See page 226.

anorexia loss of appetite.

anoxemia lack of O_2 in the blood.

antagonist a muscle that has an action directly opposite to that which is responsible for a given joint action.

anthropometry measurement of the body and its parts.

antibodies substances existing in the blood, either naturally or by "immunization," that combat bacteria and other poisons entering the body.

antidiuretic exerting an influence that decreases urine formation.

anti-inflammatory hormones hormones produced by the adrenal cortex that inhibit the defense reaction of the tissues called inflammation; another name for glucocorticoids.

anxiety a vague, objectless fear; the awareness of the physiologic reactions to the perception of a dangerous situation calling for fight or flight responses.

apoplexy ("stroke") loss of consciousness and paralysis caused by inadequate blood supply to a portion of the brain.

arrhythmia irregular heart rate. See page 226.

arteriosclerotic heart disease heart disease caused by degeneration and hardening of the walls of the arteries of the heart.

arthritis a metabolic (noninfectious) or infectious (rheumatic, tuberculosis, gonorrhea) inflammation of a joint.

assistive exercise a movement in which a patient is aided by a therapist.

asthma difficulty in breathing usually caused by allergy. See page 233.

atherogenesis the process of fatty degeneration of the arterial wall.

atherosclerosis fatty degeneration, with fat and fibrin deposits, of the walls of the arteries.

atrophy a reduction in size of an organ or other body structure or part.

autonomic (nervous) system the nervous system supplying and exerting a regulatory influence over involuntary muscle, glands, viscera, etc.; divided into sympathetic and parasympathetic nervous systems. Also called the involuntary nervous system.

bacteria one-cell, plantlike microorganisms, some of which cause infectious disease.

balance maintenance of equilibrium.

ballistic movements rapid movements of limbs *started* by the driving muscles (prime movers) but completed by their own momentum.

basal metabolic rate the minimum energy expenditure required for life in the resting, postabsorptive state. See page 320.

bile a liver secretion, usually stored in the gall bladder until needed to aid in the digestion of fats in the small intestine.

body density actually the relative weight of the body, compared to an equal volume of water; or the weight of the body per unit volume, for example, kilograms per liter.

cable tensiometer a device used to measure the amount of tension present in a cable.

calorie a unit used to express the amount of heat liberated from food.

cancer the name applied to a group of diseases characterized by wild and uncontrolled cell growth.

capillarization the property of possessing capillaries.

carbohydrates a major energy-yielding

food, contained in sugars, starches, cellulose.

cardiac output the amount of blood pumped by the heart per minute (usually refers to left ventricle only). Also called minute-volume.

center of gravity the theoretical point at which the entire weight of the body (or a body part) can be considered to be acting.

central inhibition inhibitory impulses originating in the central nervous system.

central nervous system that portion of the nervous system which lies within the skull and spinal column; the brain and spinal cord.

cerebellum the part of the brain occupying the area at the base of the skull, behind the pons and below the cerebrum.

cerebral vascular disease disease of the blood vessels of the brain. See page 230.

cholesterol a waxy organic alcohol, classed as a lipid because it reacts like a fat; present in animal fats; one of the building blocks of body tissue, especially the brain and spinal cord.

circulo-respiratory capacity the ability of the body to perform strenuous total body tasks for long periods of time; work capacity. See page 183.

clinically silent a disease for which no obvious symptoms exist or which exists for some length of time before the symptoms occur.

coagulation (blood clotting) the formation of fibrin, a threadlike clot or clump of solid material in the blood.

colitis inflammation of the colon. See page 360.

collateral circulation additional, anastomosing, supplementary, or "substitute" vessels that increase circulation to a part of the tissue.

compulsion an act performed on irresistible impulse.

congenital heart defects "inborn" defects of the heart.

congestive heart failure "failure" of the heart, caused by its inability to pump a sufficient proportion of the blood it contains, with subsequent congestion.

constipation sluggish action of the bowels; inability to defecate.

contractility the property of shortening in response to a stimulus.

contracture a "permanent" shortening of a muscle such as occurs following immobilization of a limb.

convulsions a series of involuntary muscular contractions of a very generalized nature.

coordination the summation of several individual movements into one smooth resultant action. See page 97.

coronary occlusion blockage of a coronary artery.

coronary reserve the capacity of the heart to perform maximally under overload conditions; the difference between resting cardiac output and the maximal cardiac output that can be attained without heart failure.

coronary thrombosis partial or complete blockage of a coronary blood vessel by a clot.

cortex a surface layer of cell bodies on some organ—cerebral cortex, adrenal cortex, etc.

cyanosis a blue-gray discoloration of the skin or lips caused by an oxygen deficiency.

degenerative diseases diseases involving gradual deterioration and impairment of a tissue or organ.

depressant a medicine that diminishes the functional activity of the body, particularly the nervous system.

diabetes insipidus a disease in which there is excessive urination; not caused by insulin lack.

diabetes mellitus insulin deficiency which leads to inability of the cells to receive glucose from the blood.

diarrhea frequent and usually loose, watery defecation; usually results from increased peristalsis. See page 358.

diastolic blood pressure the lowest pressure attained during the relaxation phase of the cardiac cycle.

disinhibition the reduction of inhibition or the canceling out of inhibitory impulses.

distributed practice periods of rehearsal or training that are frequently interrupted by rest periods.

diurnal variation daily variation or change.

dualism the state of consisting of two parts as seen in the theory that mind and body are two separate, irreducible entities or principles.

duodenal pertaining to the duodenum (the section of the small intestine that receives the chyme from the stomach).

dynamic stance all nonstatic postures; the positions assumed by the body as it moves in performing its tasks.

dynamic strength the maximum force that can be exerted by a muscle or group of muscles as they shorten *throughout* the full range of joint motion involved. Also called isotonic strength.

dysmenorrhea difficult or painful menstruation.

dyspnea difficult breathing.

early learning a relative term referring to specific learning which occurs as early as possible for that task but *not* prior to the "ideal" age.

eccentric contraction a lengthening of a muscle against resistance; the muscle attempts to shorten but the resistance actually causes it to lengthen.

ectomorphy the thin, linear body build component.

edema excessive retention of fluid in the tissue spaces causing a swelling; commonly called dropsy.

efferent neurons those neurons that conduct impulses from the brain and spinal cord to the muscles and glands.

efficiency in physiology, refers to the mechanical efficiency of accomplishing work. See page 187.

ego in psychoanalytic theory, that part of the personality in conscious contact with reality.

electrocardiogram (ECG) a recording of the action potential or electrical activity of the heart muscle; used to study certain aspects of cardiac function; not all-inclusive but a valuable tool.

electroencephalogram (EEG) a record of the electrical activity of the brain recorded from outside the skull; brain waves.

electromyographic (EMG) pertaining to the process of recording action potentials from muscles as they contract.

embolism obstruction of a blood vessel by a foreign object (usually a "loose" clot floating about and lodging in a vessel); can also be caused by air bubbles and other substances.

emphysema a stretched, overinflated, and inefficient condition of the lungs. See page 234.

endomorphy the heavy, round, and fat body build component.

enzymes important organic catalysts that aid many body processes and conversions, such as digestion, oxidation, etc.

epidemiology literally, the science or study of epidemic disease; the study of "widespread and prevalent" diseases, not necessarily infectious in nature.

erythrocytes the red blood cells.

etiology literally, the study of the causes of disease.

evaporation the process of changing from a liquid to a gaseous state.

extension increasing the angle at the joint between two bones or two body segments, as in straightening the elbow.

extensor a muscle which extends a joint.

facilitation the increased ease of carrying out an action or function; the furtherance of neural activities by previous or simultaneous stimulation.

fallopian tubes the ducts that pass from the ovaries to the uterus.

fat a major energy-yielding food, composed of one glycerol and three fatty acid molecules.

fatigue a feeling or perception of tiredness that may be elicited by various circumstances; a disinclination to continue a particular activity.

fatty acid a component of fats, composed of

glycerine and an acid, such as stearic, palmitic, oleic; some "free" fatty acids circulate in the blood and are found in the tissues; can be used for energy.

fear an emotion marked by dread, apprehension, or alarm.

fetus the baby, in the uterus, after the third month of development.

fibrin a whitish, elastic substance formed by the action of thrombin on fibrinogen; a blood clot is composed of fibrin and blood cells.

fibrinogen soluble protein in normal plasma that is rendered insoluble fibrin (a clot) in the presence of thrombin and adequate calcium.

fixator a muscle or group of muscles that supports one part of the body in order to provide a firm base for the movement of another part.

flatulence gas in the digestive tract.

flexibility literally, the quality of being bent without breaking; pliability; in the body, range of joint motion.

flexion the decreasing of a joint angle.

flexor a muscle that functions to flex a given joint of the body.

frustration the thwarting of desires or goals of an individual.

functional deviations abnormalities of posture or stance that can be corrected by a conscious repositioning of the body; not due to the permanent bony structure.

functional fitness the capacity to successfully and fully respond physically, mentally, and emotionally to the "forces of life" without undue debilitation.

gall bladder a sac, near the liver, that stores bile.

ganglion (plural, ganglia) cluster of nerve cell bodies lying outside the central nervous system.

gangrene death and putrefaction of tissue, especially applied to large areas of the soft tissues.

gastric pertaining to the stomach.

glial cells fibrous, nonnervous supporting elements of the nervous system.

globulins proteins in the blood that are primarily concerned with resistance to infection.

glucose one of the simple sugars, an end product of carbohydrate digestion; the primary form of sugar in the bloodstream.

glycerol a clear, syrupy liquid that is a component of fats.

gonadotropins pituitary hormones that exert a specific and purposeful influence on the gonads.

gout a recurring metabolic disorder of the joints (often the great toe); associated with high levels of uric acid in the blood.

hand-eye coordination the ability to estimate distances and speed of movement in order to reach objects efficiently by use of the hands, as in catching or striking objects.

health a state of physical and mental well-being that includes, but is not limited to, freedom from disease and defect.

heart murmur a blowing sound, heard through the stethoscope during auscultation of the heart (listening to heart sounds); although not *necessarily* pathological, quite often caused by serious vascular defects.

heart rate number of times the heart contracts ("beats") in one minute.

heat exhaustion a condition resulting from excessive exposure to high temperature and humidity; characterized by moist, cold skin, poor circulation, restlessness, anxiety, and sometimes nausea or dizziness; also called heat prostration.

hematocrit the volume of red blood cells per unit volume of blood, usually about 40–45 percent.

hemoglobin the iron-containing red pigment in the red cells that carries nearly all the O_2 and almost half the CO_2.

hemophilia an inherited inability of the blood to clot properly; transmitted by the mother, although women seldom have it themselves.

hemorrhoids enlarged (varicose) veins in the anal region, commonly called piles.

hernia an imperfection or tear in a muscle layer that allows a part of the body to project from its natural cavity; usually a bulging out of the intestine; commonly called rupture.

hip flexors the muscles that serve to flex the femur on the pelvis; primarily the rectus femoris, the iliacus, and the psoas (together called iliopsoas).

histological pertaining to microscopic tissue analysis.

homeostasis the maintenance of internal equilibrium of the organism by coordinated physiologic processes.

hormone a chemical product, produced by an endocrine gland, secreted into the blood and exerting a distinct and usually powerful effect on some body function or organ.

humoral pertaining to the substances that serve as agents to transmit nervous impulses across synapses and muscle-nerve junctions.

hyperemia (hyperdemia) increased content of blood in a part, with distention of the blood vessels.

hypermotility increased motility as of the stomach or intestines.

hypersecretion excessive secretion.

hypertension abnormally elevated blood pressure; "essential" hypertension is the name given to this condition when the cause cannot be determined.

hypertrophy increase in the size of a muscle, organ, or other body part due to an enlargement of its constituent cells.

hypotension low blood pressure.

hypothalamus the most anterior portion of the part of the brain stem called the diencephalon.

immunization a means of protection against a communicable disease; natural immunity often results from having the disease; artificial immunity for some diseases through vaccines that stimulate natural body resistance (diphtheria, smallpox, whooping cough, red measles, polio, etc.).

impairment the inability of certain tissues to function because of physiological changes (accumulation of metabolic wastes, deprivation of oxygen or nutritional substances).

inhibitor a neuron whose stimulation stops or suppresses the activity of the part it innervates or of a neuron with which it synapses.

inner ear the innermost portion of the "organ of hearing," including the semicircular canals; intimately involved in maintenance of equilibrium.

internuncial neurons a connecting or intermediate nerve cell between two others in a neural pathway.

interstitial literally, lying between the essential parts of the tissue.

intraocular tension pressure within the eyeball.

ion an electrified or charged (positive or negative) particle.

ischemia local and temporary anemia caused by insufficient blood flow to the part or area.

isometric pertaining to a type of "attempted" muscle contraction in which tension increases but length remains constant; static.

isometric strength also called static strength; the maximal force that can be exerted by means of an isometric contraction.

isotonic pertaining to a type of muscle contraction in which the muscle length changes but the tension remains constant; dynamic.

isotonic strength also called dynamic strength; the maximum force that can be exerted by a muscle or group of muscles as they shorten throughout the full range of joint motion involved.

kinesthesis muscle, tendon, and joint sensitivities; the sense or perception of movement, weight, resistance, and position.

kyphosis an excessive posterior curvature of the upper (thoracic) spine.

lactation the formation or secretion of milk.

lactic acid an end product of glucose oxidation, a buildup of which is associated with muscle impairment, and which is converted to glucose again in the presence of oxygen.

lean tissue nonfat tissue.

leukemia abnormal and persistent excess of white blood cells, usually resulting from disease of the bone marrow (probably cancerous).

leukocytes white blood cells.

ligament a band of tough, white, fibrous tissue connecting the articulating ends of the bones.

lipid a comprehensive term for all fats and fatlike substances.

lordosis an excessive forward curvature of the lumbar spine.

lumbar pertaining to the low back; there are five lumbar vertebrae located just below the thoracic vertebrae and just above the sacrum.

lymph a clear fluid bathing the cells, returned to bloodstream via the special lymphatic system.

lymph nodes glandlike structures, located in the lymphatic system, that filter the lymph and produce lymphocytes.

lymphocyte a form of leukocyte (white blood cell).

lysis literally, the dissolving of.

macroscopic large enough to be seen with the naked eye.

malnutrition literally, poor or improper nutrition; usually associated with undernutrition but should include also overnutrition or any kind of improper nutrition.

massed practice long periods of participation that are not interrupted by rest periods.

maximal oxygen intake the greatest volume of oxygen that can be used by the body (extracted from the blood by the tissues) per minute; usually increases with CR training (see page 182).

medulla oblongata that portion of the brain stem lying just above the spinal cord.

menstruation the recurrent monthly sloughing off of cells and blood from the uterus; occurs during the period of a woman's sexual maturity from puberty to menopause.

mental practice the conscious mental rehearsal of an activity occurring in the absence of actual physical practice.

mesomorphy the stocky, muscular body build component.

metabolism the sum total of all body processes, including the building up and breaking down processes.

millisecond one thousandth of a second.

miometric a shortening, as in an isotonic concentric contraction of a muscle.

monistic the concept of unity or "one-ness" as opposed to dualistic.

morphological pertaining to body, organ, and tissue structure and form without regard to function.

motive an internal organismic state that initiates or otherwise determines behavior; often used synonymously with need or drive.

motor area the specific location of the part of the cerebral cortex where movement is controlled.

motor cortex area of the brain that controls body movement.

motor neuron an efferent neuron.

motor unit a single efferent nerve fiber, together with all the muscle fibers it innervates.

movement time time lapse between the actual beginning of a movement and its completion.

muscular endurance the ability to persist in (repeat more than once) a specific muscular movement.

myocardial infarction pathological blockage of a coronary artery.

nerve a bundle of nerve fibers (neurons), usually outside the brain or spinal cord, that may contain both afferent and efferent neurons.

neuron a single nerve cell.

neurosis a psychoneurotic disorder, a type of disorganization characterized by anxiety and nervousness. There is no gross disorganization of personality in relation to external reality.

neurotic pertaining to a neurosis; an emotionally unstable individual.

noradrenalin (norepinephrine) one of the adrenal medullary hormones similar in action to epinephrine (Adrenalin).

obsession an idea or emotion that persists in an individual in spite of any conscious attempts to remove it.

occlusion a neural reflex phenomenon due to overlapping connections of efferent neurons so that stimulating two efferent nerves simultaneously leads to a response less than the sum of the responses obtained individually.

orientation the process of properly positioning oneself for purposes of efficiently manipulating objects used in sports and games, as in preparing to strike a tennis ball.

orthopedics that branch of surgery concerned with corrective treatment of abnormalities of bone, muscle, and joints.

osmotic pressure a measure of the tendency of water to move across a membrane permeable to water but not permeable to certain particles dissolved in the water; the "pressure" or tendency is created by a difference in concentration of the particles in solution; the water then attempts to restore concentration equilibrium by moving across the membrane from the area of low particle concentration to one of high concentration.

ovaries two glands in the female, producing the ovum (egg) and at least two hormones.

overload any resistance greater than that usually encountered.

overload principle in order for improvement to occur in strength or endurance, the intensity (in the case of strength) or the duration (endurance) must exceed those levels ordinarily experienced.

ovum the female sexual cell (egg), which, if fertilized by the male sperm cell, can develop and "reproduce" another living organism.

oxygen debt the amount of oxygen used, during recovery after effort, over and above the amount that would have been used at rest.

oxygen debt tolerance the greatest O_2 debt a given person can tolerate before terminating the effort.

oxygen requirement the amount of O_2 actually required, per minute, for a given effort.

oxygen utilization the amount of O_2 actually *used* by the body per minute; synonyms: O_2 intake, O_2 uptake, O_2 consumption.

pain avoidance the tendency to behave in a manner that deviates from normal patterns in order to prevent or avoid pain.

palpate to attempt to locate muscle activity (or other nonvisible characteristics) by feeling with the fingers.

parasympathetic nervous system that part of the autonomic nervous system predominately concerned with the maintenance of homeostasis within the organism.

parturition the act of giving birth.

passive exercise the movement of a patient's body part or limb through a range of motion by a therapist or other person.

pedagogical pertaining to the science or art of teaching or instruction.

perception the interpretation of sensation.

perineal pertaining to the anatomical area between the anus and vulva in the female and between the anus and scrotum in the male.

peripheral nervous system all nerves and ganglia outside the skull and vertebral column of the body.

personality the unique organization of relatively enduring psychological characteristics possessed by an individual, as revealed by his interaction with his environment.

pH the symbol for hydrogen ion concentration or degree of acidity; 7.0 is exactly neutral, below 7.0 is acid and above 7.0 is alkaline; normal blood pH, which is about 7.3, must be maintained within very narrow limits.

phobia an irrational fear.

physical fitness a state of the organism in which all body systems are functioning optimally in terms of individual requirements, particularly those involving great muscular effort; it is not necessarily related to skill or motor ability.

physiological fatigue reduction in the capacity of an organism to do work as the result of previous activity; impairment.

placental pertaining to the structure in the uterus, formed during pregnancy, through which the fetus derives its nourishment.

plasma the solvent or liquid portion of the blood.

platelets small blood cells necessary for coagulation.

pliometric eccentric or lengthening contraction of a muscle.

postprandial after-meal.

posture characteristic positions assumed while standing, sitting, and moving; one's natural static and dynamic stance.

power explosive muscular contraction; force exerted over a very short period of time.

power stroke the coordinated arm and body movements characteristically employed in tennis, handball, squash, baseball, golf, and similar sports.

prime mover a muscle directly responsible for a particular movement; also called principal mover.

pro-inflammatory hormone hormones produced by the adrenal cortex that produce the defense reaction of the tissues called inflammation; another term for mineralocorticoids.

proprioceptors sense organs located in the muscles, joints, tendons, and the non-auditory inner ear that are sensitive to stimuli associated with movement, changes of direction, and body position.

prostate gland a small glandular-muscular organ about the size of a horse chestnut, surrounding the bladder opening in the male; glandular portion secretes fluid that becomes part of the seminal fluids in ejaculation.

psychic pertaining to the mind.

psychogenic a term applied to behavior initiated in the cerebrum.

psychological fatigue a feeling or perception of tiredness that usually increases with work output and with time elapsed after rest and sleep.

psychoneurosis a psychoneurotic disorder characterized chiefly by anxiety, which may be directly felt and expressed or unconsciously controlled by means of a defense mechanism; there is no gross disorganization of personality in relation to external reality.

psychoneurotic relating to or affected by a psychoneurosis.

psychosis a profound disturbance of behavior that renders an individual unable to adjust to normal daily life in an even passably satisfactory manner; true insanity.

psychosomatic disorders physical disorders believed to be of psychogenic origin.

psychotherapy any systematic treatment of psychological disorders that depends on interaction with a therapist.

psychotic descriptive of profound disturbances of behavior characteristic of true insanity.

pulmonary pertaining to the lungs.

pulmonary gas exchange O_2 and CO_2 exchange between alveoli and pulmonary capillaries.

radiation the emission of rays in all directions from a common source; energy (heat) is propagated through space from the body (one form of heat loss); specifically, also refers to x-ray, infrared, ultraviolet, etc., emission.

rationalism the theory that reason, by itself, is a source of knowledge, independent of the senses.

reaction time time required for an individual to begin his response to a stimulus; more complex than simple reflex time.

recreation any activity, apart from one's occupation, taken for pleasure.

reflex a relatively simple innate response to a particular stimulus.

reflex time time required for a nerve impulse to traverse the reflex arc from the initiation of the stimulus to the beginning of the response.

reminiscence the improvement of skill or performance that may occur during a period of nonpractice.

residual tension the amount of tension present in the skeletal muscles at rest.

respiratory efficiency mechanical efficiency of breathing.

response characteristic reaction to a stimulus.

response time total time measured from initiation of stimulus to completion of the response.

rheumatism a disease of the joints involving fever, pain, inflammation, and swelling.

RM (repetitions maximum) the maximum number of repetitions that can be performed with a given weight.

roughage edible but indigestible fiber of certain foods that acts to stimulate peristalsis and thus aids elimination.

saturated fats "hard" fats, usually animal, in which the molecules are highly hydrogenated (the molecules are "saturated" with as many hydrogen atoms as can combine with the molecule).

scoliosis a postural abnormality in which the spine exhibits a lateral curvature.

sedatives drugs that depress CNS activity in general; agents that reduce activity of an organism.

sensory neurons neurons that carry impulses from the sense receptors to the CNS; also called afferent neurons.

serum the clear, yellowish fluid of the blood that remains after blood has clotted and the clot is removed.

serum cholesterol see cholesterol and serum.

sinus a space, cavity, or hollow, as in the bones of the head, in the liver, etc.

skeletal muscles the striated, voluntary muscles of the body that are responsible for movements of limbs and other body parts; distinguished from smooth muscle and cardiac muscle.

skill an act requiring some degree of neuromuscular coordination and dexterity; also the ability to perform tasks requiring these qualities.

sociometric pertaining to measurement of social characteristics.

somatic (nervous) system the division of the nervous system which is responsible for the activity of the skeletal muscles.

somatotype a body type as classified by application of certain observable criteria; the three basic components are endomorphy, mesomorphy, and ectomorphy.

spasm a sudden muscular contraction of an involuntary nature.

specificity of training systems of practice or training in which the particular outcomes desired are rehearsed; contrasted with generality in which many kinds of general activity constitute practice; in weight training, the use of many repetitions for endurance and great resistance for strength.

speed the ability of an individual to run fast; may also refer to the velocity with which a given limb may be moved.

sperm the male germ cell, produced by the testes, that fertilizes the ovum.

spinal reflex reflex that does not involve activity of CNS structures above the spinal level.

spleen a highly vascular, oval organ, located near the stomach, that contains blood and is extra-rich in red blood cells. It appears to form blood cells, but its function is not well understood.

"spot" reducing generally refers to an *effort* to eliminate or reduce fat deposition in a specific area by exercising or massaging the muscles in that area. See page 346.

staphylococci pus-forming germs involved in many common infections; particularly resistant to modern drugs.

starches noncrystalline carbohydrates; polysaccharides (containing many simple sugar molecules) that must be broken down by enzymes to simple sugars in order to be absorbed and utilized.

static stance all nondynamic posture; the positions assumed by the body while at rest, sitting, or standing.

static strength the maximal force that can be exerted by means of an isometric contraction (under the conditions specified).

statistically significant not likely to have occurred because of chance alone; "significant at .05 level" means there are only five chances in a hundred that an occurrence was due to chance; likely to be real and not due to chance.

statistics numbers or figures representative of some population (or sample) characteristic.

steady state that condition where the oxygen requirement of the body is equaled by the oxygen utilization.

stimulant any agent that acts to excite or increase functional activity.

stimulus any energy that excites or irritates a cell.

strength the maximum force that can be exerted by an individual under a prescribed set of conditions.

stress the total physiological response that occurs in abnormally intense or prolonged stimulation.

stressor any agent capable of producing a stress reaction within an organism.

stroke *see* apoplexy.

stroke volume the amount of blood pumped by the heart per beat.

structural deviations abnormalities of posture or stance that are due to faulty bone growth.

substantive elements those parts or factors that make up the "substance" or essential nature of a thing or idea.

substitution patterns unusual or unnatural movements utilized in order to avoid pain or because of impairment (physiological fatigue) in the muscles normally responsible for the desired movement.

suggestion the artificial production of a certain psychic state in which the individual experiences such sensations as are suggested to him, or ceases to experience those he is instructed not to feel.

supine lying on the back, face upward.

sympathetic nervous system that portion of the autonomic nervous system primarily responsible for body adjustments to emergency situations.

synapse the point of functional contact between two neurons.

synaptic delay the time required for a nerve impulse to cross the junction between two neurons.

synchrony the simultaneous contraction of several motor units; units normally contract asynchronously, or out of phase with one another.

syndrome a pattern of symptoms characterizing some disorder, as in low back syndrome.

synergist a muscle that cooperates in performing a movement but is not primarily responsible for it.

synthesis the formation of a complex concept by the combination of separate ideas.

systemic health the level of functional capacity of the organs and systems of the body.

systolic blood pressure the blood pressure attained during the peak of the contraction phase of the cardiac cycle.

tachycardia abnormally fast heart rate.

tactile pertaining to the sense of touch.

terminal disease a relative term concerning a disease for which there is no cure and for which death is the most likely prognosis.

test battery a group or series of individual tests.

testes (testicles) the male gonads that produce sperm and testosterone.

thalamus a mass of gray matter at the base of the brain; it receives fibers from all parts of the cortex.

therapeutic pertaining to treatment; having medicinal or healing properties.

threshold minimal level of stimulation that will produce a response in a cell or system.

thrombus a blood clot that obstructs a vessel or cavity.

tidal volume the volume of air breathed per breath in the normal, resting state.

tonus the slight state of tension present in normal muscle even when it is completely relaxed.

tranquilizers drugs used to reduce the sensitivity of the central nervous system.

transfer of training facilitation of the ability to learn one activity or skill as the result of practice in another; also the improvement of strength or endurance in one limb as a result of training another.

triglyceride "neutral fat," composed of three fatty-acid molecules and one molecule of glycerol.

tropic exerting a specific effect on a specific organ.

ulcer a sore on the skin or the mucous membrane of an internal organ.

unsaturated fats "soft" fats (usually liquid at room temperature); not saturated with hydrogen atoms.

uremia a disease state in which wastes accumulate in the blood; it is usually due to kidney failure.

uric acid end product of metabolism of proteins high in purine bodies.

urogenital pertaining to the urinary-genital organs.

uterus (womb) a muscular, hollow female organ where the fertilized ovum is implanted and where growth of the fetus takes place.

varicose veins bulging, dilated, and swollen veins that usually occur on legs. See page 236.

vascular pertaining to the blood vessels.

vasoconstriction narrowing of the lumen of a blood vessel, usually referring to arterioles.

vasodilation opening or widening of the lumen of a blood vessel.

ventilation breathing.

vertigo dizziness.

vital capacity the greatest volume of air a person can exhale following as forceful and deep an inhalation as possible.

vitamin a nutrient furnishing no calories but essential to some normal body function.

References

1. Abbey, S. David, "Age Proficiency and Reminiscence in a Complex Perceptual-Motor Task," *Percept. Mot. Skills,* 14:51–57, 1962.
2. Adams, W. C., and K. J. McCristal, *Foundations of Physical Activity.* Champaign, Ill.: Stipes Publishing Co., 1965, p. 137.
3. Addis, T., L. J. Poo, and W. Lew, "The Quantities of Proteins Lost by the Various Organs and Tissues of the Body during a Fast," *J. Biol. Chem.,* 115: 111, 1936.
4. Adler, J. Mortimer, "The Meaning of a Liberal Education," address delivered to the second general session, AAHPER National Convention, Chicago, 1966.
5. Agranoff, Bernard W., "Memory and Protein Synthesis," *Sci. Amer.,* 216: 115–122, (June) 1967.
6. Alderman, M. H., and R. P. Davis, "Hyperuricemia in Starvation," *Proc. Soc. Exp. Biol. Med.,* 118:790, 1965.
7. Alexander, F., *Psychosomatic Medicine: Its Principles and Applications.* New York: W. W. Norton & Company, Inc., 1950.
8. Allen, Sara, "The Effects of Verbal Reinforcement on Children's Performance as a Function of Type of Task," *J. Exp. Child Psychol.,* 13:57–73, 1965.
9. Ammons, R. B., "Effects of Distribution of Practice on Rotary Pursuit 'Hits,'" *J. Exp. Psychol.,* 41:17–22, 1951.
10. Ammons, R. B., C. H. Ammons, and R. L. Morgan, "Transfer of Skill and Decremented Factors along the Speed Dimension in Rotary Pursuit," *Percept. Mot. Skills,* 11:43, 1958.
11. Anastasi, Anne, *Differential Psychology* (3d ed.). New York: Crowell-Collier and Macmillan, Inc., 1958.
12. Anderson, K. N., "How Your Own Strength Can Hurt You," *Today's Health,* 43:18, 1965.
13. Anderson, Theresa W., "Swimming and Exercise during Menstruation," *JOHPER,* 36:66–68, (Oct.) 1965.
14. "The Angry Black Athlete," *Newsweek,* July 15, 1968, p. 56.

15. Antor, M. A., M. A. Ohlson, and R. E. Hodges, "Changes in Retail Market Food Supplies in the U.S. in the Last Seventy Years and the Relation to the Incidence of Coronary Heart Disease, with Special reference to Dietary Carbohydrates and Essential Fatty Acids," *Amer. J. Clin. Nutr.,* 14:169, 1964.

16. Appleton, Lloyd O., and others, "A Fifteen Year Summary of the Application of Physical Aptitude Examinations for Selection of West Point Cadets," multilithed manuscript, Office of Physical Education, U.S. Military Academy, West Point, New York, 1965.

17. *Archives of Physical Medicine,* 49:183–86, (April) 1968.

18. Aristophanes, *The Clouds* (introduction and notes by L. L. Forman). New York: American Book Company, 1915.

19. Arps, G. F., "Work with Knowledge of Results vs. Work without Knowledge of Results," *Psychol. Monogr.,* 28:125, 1921.

20. Associated Press, "Spinal Repair, Thought Impossible, Performed with Aid of Unique Tool," *Toledo Blade,* Sept. 17, 1967, p. 1.

21. Åstrand, P. O., *Experimental Studies of Working Capacity in Relation to Age and Sex.* Copenhagen: Munksgaard, 1952.

22. Åstrand, P. O., and others, *Girl Swimmers* (Erica Odelberg, Tr.). Stockholm: Svenska Trychereaktie-bolaget, 1963.

23. *Athletics in Education.* Washington, D.C.: AAHPER, 1963.

24. Atkinson, John W., *An Introduction to Motivation.* Princeton, N.J.: D. Van Nostrand Company, Inc., 1964.

25. Atkinson, John W., "Motivational Determinants of Risk-Taking Behavior," *Psychol. Rev.,* 64:359–372, 1957.

26. Austin, M. C., and G. G. Thompson, "Children's Friendship Study of the Bases on Which Children Select and Reject Their Best Friends," *J. Educ. Psychol.,* 3:101, 1948.

27. Autio, L., O. Eranko, and E. Jalavisto, "Vasomotor Reactions in Valsalva's Experiment," *Acta Physiol. Scand.,* 17:130–149, 1949.

28. Bachman, J. C., and S. M. Horvath, "Pulmonary Function Changes which Accompany Athletic Conditioning Programs," *Res. Quart.* 39:235, 1968.

29. Baetjer, A. M., "The Effect of Muscular Fatigue upon Resistance," *Physiol. Rev.,* 12:453, 1932.

30. Bailey, J. A. "Treatment of Underweight Patients," *J. Amer. Med. Assoc.,* 187:790, 1964.

31. Bajusz, E., and H. Selye, "Adaptation to the Cardiac Necrosis-Eliciting Effect of Stress," *Amer. J. Physiol.,* 199:453, 1960.

32. Bajusz, E., and W. Raab, "Early Metabolic Aberrations through Which Epinephrine May Elicit Myocardial Necrosis," *First International Conference on Preventive Cardiology,* University of Vermont, 1964.

33. Baker, J. A., "Comparison of Rope Skipping and Jogging as Methods of Improving Cardiovascular Efficiency of College Men," *Res. Quart.,* 39:240, 1968.

34. Balke, B., and R. T. Clark, "Cardio-Pulmonary and Metabolic Effects of Physical Training," in *Health and Fitness in the Modern World.* Chicago: The Athletic Institute, 1961.

35. Bamford, D., and D. W. Swan, "A Study to Ascertain the effects of Thorazine on Chronically Regressed Schizophrenic Patients Receiving Adapted Physical Education," *J. Assoc. Phys. Ment. Rehab.,* 12:23–24, 1958.

36. Barber, T. X., "The Effects of Hypnosis and Suggestions on Strength and Endurance: a Critical Review of Research Studies," *Brit. J. Soc. Clin. Psychol.,* 5:42–50, 1966.

37. Barber, T. X., and D. S. Caverley, "Hypnotic Behavior as a Function of Task Motivation," *J. Psychol.,* 54:363–389, 1962.

38. Barnes, Mildred, "Officiating and Amateur Status in Girls' and Women's Sports," *JOHPER,* 39:24–27, (Oct.) 1968.

39. Barrow, Harold, "A Test of Motor Ability for College Men," doctoral

dissertation, University of Indiana, Bloomington, 1953.

40. Barrows, Isabel C. (Ed.), *Physical Training*. A Full Report of the Papers and Discussions of the Conference Held in Boston in November, 1889. Boston: Press of George H. Ellis, 1890. Cited by Janet Felshin in *Perspectives and Principles for Physical Education*. New York: John Wiley & Sons, Inc., 1967.

41. Bartley, S. H., and E. Chute, *Fatigue and Impairment in Man*. New York: McGraw-Hill, Inc., 1947.

42. Bartley, S. H., *Fatigue: Mechanism and Management*. Springfield, Ill.: Charles C Thomas Publisher, 1965.

43. Basmajian, J. V., "Man's Posture," *Arch. Phys. Med. Rehab.*, 46:26–36, 1965.

44. Basmajian, J. V., *Muscles Alive: Their Functions Revealed by Electromyography*. Baltimore, Md.: The Williams & Wilkins Company, 1962.

45. Basowitz, H. H. Persky, S. J. Korchin, and R. R. Grinker, *Anxiety and Stress, An Interdisciplinary Study of a Life Situation*. New York: McGraw-Hill, Inc., 1955.

46. Bayne, J. D., "Pro + Tec Protective Bra," *J. Sports Med. Phys. Fit.*, 8:34–35, (March) 1968.

47. Beisser, A. R., *The Madness in Sports*. New York: Appleton-Century-Crofts, 1967.

48. Bennett, Edward L., Marion C. Diamond, David Krech, and Mark Rozenzweig, "Chemical and Anatomical Plasticity of Brain," *Science*, 146:618, 1964.

49. Benoit, F. L., "Prolonged Fasting: Physiologic Undesirability Studied," *Med. Trib.*, 6:16, (May 15–16) 1965.

50. Benton, Curtis, D., J. W. McCann, and M. Larsen, "Dyslexia and Dominance," *J. Ped. Opth.*, 2:53, (July) 1965.

51. Berger, R. A., "Comparison of Static and Dynamic Strength Increases," *Res. Quart.*, 33:329, 1962.

52. Berner, G. E., and D. E. Berner, "Reading Difficulties in Children," *Arch. Opth.*, 20:838, 1938.

53. Berridge, Harold L., "An Experiment in the Psychology of Competition," *Res. Quart.*, 37:42, 1935.

54. Bevans, Bonnie Jo, "The Future of Interscholastic Sports for Girls," *JOHPER*, 39:39–41, (March) 1968.

55. Biddulph, L. G., "Athletic Achievement and the Personal and Social Adjustment of High School Boys," *Res. Quart.*, 25:1, 1954.

56. Bilodeau, Edward A., and Ina M. Bilodeau, "Variable Frequency of Knowledge of Results and the Learning of a Simple Skill," *J. Exp. Psychol.*, 55:379–383, 1958.

57. Bjurulf, P., "Atherosclerosis and Body Build, with Special Reference to Subcutaneous Fat Cells," *Acta Med. Scand.* (Suppl.), 349:1, 1959.

58. Bland, J. H., and R. L. Lipson, "Comprehensive Management of the Common Rheumatoid Diseases," *Phys. Ther.*, 44:592, 1964.

59. Bode, R., *Ausdruckgymnastik* (Expressive Gymnastics). Munich, 1922.

60. "Body Weight and Electrocardiographic Patterns," *Nutr. Rev.*, 12:305, 1954.

61. Bogert, L. J., G. M. Briggs, and D. H. Calloway, *Nutrition and Physical Fitness*. Philadelphia: W. B. Saunders Company, 1966.

62. Bortz, E. L., "Exercise, Fitness and Aging," in *Exercise and Fitness*. Chicago: The Athletic Institute, 1960.

63. Bouchier, I. A. D., and B. Bronte-Stewart, "Alimentary Lipemia and Ischaemic Heart Diasease," *Lancet*, 1:363, 1961.

64. Bowen, P. A., "The Relation of Physical, Mental, and Personality Factors to Popularity in Adolescent Boys," doctoral dissertation. University of California, Berkeley, 1941.

65. Bowerman, J. W., and W. E. Harris, *Jogging*. New York: Grosset & Dunlap, Inc., 1967.

66. Brace, David K., "Studies in Motor Learning of Gross Bodily Motor Skills," *Res. Quart.*, 7:242, 1946.

67. Brace, David K., "Sociometric Evi-

dence of the Relationship between Social Status and Athletic Ability among Junior High School Boys," Professional Contributions Number 3. Washington, D.C.: American Academy of Physical Education, 1954.

68. Brady, J. V., "Ulcers in Executive Monkeys," *Sci. Amer.*, 199:24, 1958.

69. Breckenridge, M. E., and E. L. Vincent, *Child Development*. Philadelphia: W. B. Saunders Company, 1966.

70. Bretsch, H. S., "Social Skills and Activities of Socially Accepted and Unaccepted Adolescents," *J. Educ. Psychol.*, 43:449, 1952.

71. Briggs, George E., and W. J. Brogden, "The Effect of Component Practice on Performance of a Lever-Positioning Skill," *J. Exp. Psychol.*, 48:375–380, 1954.

72. Brightbill, Charles K., *Man and Leisure*. Englewood Cliffs, N.J.: Prentice-Hall, Inc., 1961.

73. Brody, A. J., "Master Two-Step Test in Clinically Unselected Patients," *J. Amer. Med. Assoc.*, 171:1195, 1959.

74. Brooks, F. P., D. J. Sandweiss, and J. F. Long, "The Relationship between Peptic Ulcer and Coronary Occlusion," *J. Amer. Med. Sci.*, 245:277, 1963.

75. Brown, C. E., and others, "Observations on Blood Vessels and Exercise," *J. Geront.*, 11:296, 1956.

76. Brownell, Clifford L., and E. Patricia Hagman, "Physical Education: Foundations and Principles," New York: McGraw-Hill, Inc., 1951.

77. Brumbach, W. B., "Changes in the Serum Cholesterol Levels of Male College Students Who Participated in a Special Physical Exercise Program," *Res. Quart.*, 32:147, 1961.

78. Brunner, D., and G. Manelis, "Myocardial Infarction among Members of Communal Settlements in Israel," *Lancet*, Nov. 12, 1960, p. 1049.

79. Bucher, Charles A., *Foundations of Physical Education* (3rd ed.). St. Louis: The C. V. Mosby Co., 1960.

80. Bucher, Charles A., *Foundations of Physical Education* (5th ed.). St. Louis: The C. V. Mosby Company, 1968.

81. Bunker, H., "The Selective Character of the Active and Non-active Student in Physical Education," *J. Amer. Assoc. College Registrars*, 20:350, 1945.

82. Burt, J. J., and C. S. Blythe, "Effect of Water Balance on Ability to Perform in High Ambient Temperatures," *Res. Quart.*, 32:301, 1961.

83. Burt, J. J., C. S. Blythe, and C. L. Wrye, "An Evaluation of Four Schedules of Fluid Replacement during Physical Activity under Extremes of Temperature," paper presented to the American College of Sports Medicine, Oklahoma City, May 5, 1962.

84. Burt, J. J., and R. Jackson, "The Effects of Physical Exercise on the Coronary Collateral Circulation of Dogs," paper presented at American College of Sports Medicine Meetings, 1964.

85. Burt, J. J., C. S. Blyth, and H. A. Rierson, "The Effects of Exercise on the Coagulation - Fibrinolysis Equilibrium," *J. Sports Med. Phys. Fit.*, 4:213, 1964.

86. Burton, B. T., *The Heinz Handbook of Nutrition*. New York: McGraw-Hill, Inc. (for H. J. Heinz Co.), 1965.

87. Buskirk, E. R., and J. E. Counsilman, "Special Exercise Problems in Middle Age," in *Science and Medicine of Exercise and Sports*. New York: Harper & Row, Publishers, 1960.

88. Buxton, C. E., "Reminiscence in the Acquisition of Skill," *Psychol. Rev.*, 49:191–196, 1942.

89. Byrd, O. E., and E. M. Bloner, "Footbath Solutions and Athlete's Foot in High Schools," *Res. Quart.*, 33:3, 1962.

90. Cabot, P. S., "The Relation between Characteristics of Personality and Physique in Adolescents," *Genet. Psychol. Monogr.*, 20:3, 1938.

91. Campbell, D. E., "Effect of Controlled Running on Serum Cholesterol of Young Adult Males of Varying Mor-

phological Constitution," *Res. Quart.*, 39:47, 1968.

92. Campbell, D. E., "A Study of the Influence of Several Physical Activities upon the Blood Serum Cholesterol," unpublished Ed. D. dissertation, Colorado State College, 1961.

93. Campbell, W. R., and R. H. Pohndorf, "Physical Fitness of British and United States Children," in *Health and Fitness in the Modern World*. Chicago: The Athletic Institute, 1961.

94. Cantone, A., "Physical Effort and Its Effect in Reducing Alimentary Hyperlipaemia," *J. Sports Med. Phys. Fit.*, 4:32, 1964.

95. Carns, M. L., and R. B. Glassow, "Changes Accompanying Weight Reduction in College Women," *Hum. Biol.*, 28:305, 1957.

96. Cassel, Russell, and Richard Childers, "A Study of Certain Attributes of High School Varsity Football Team Members by Use of Psychological Test Scores," *J. Educ. Res.* 57:64–67, 1963.

97. Cattell, Raymond B., "The Nature and Measurement of Anxiety," *Sci. Amer.*, 208:96–104, 1963.

98. Chandler, Harriet M., and R. W. Hyde, "A Socialization Activity Index for a Mental Hospital," *Nursing World*, 125:343, 1951.

99. Chapman, C. B., and J. H. Mitchell, "The Physiology of Exercise," *Sci. Amer.*, 212:88, 1965.

100. "The Chemistry of Thought," *Time*, Feb. 10, 1961, p. 51.

101. Chidsey, C. A., E. Braunwald, and A. G. Morrow, "Studies of Sympathetic Activity and Cardiac Norepinephrine Stores in Congestive Heart Failure," *First International Conference on Preventive Cardiology*, University of Vermont, 1964.

102. "Childhood Eating Habits May Determine Obesity," *J. Amer. Med. Assoc.*, 200:31, (May 29) 1967.

103. Clark, M., "How to Live without Fatigue," *Reader's Digest*, 80:63, 1962.

104. Clarke, H. Harrison, *Application of Measurement to Health and Physical Education* (4th ed.). Englewood Cliffs, N.J.: Prentice-Hall, Inc., 1967.

105. Clarke H. H., T. L. Bailey, and C. T. Shay, "New Objective Strength Tests of Muscle Groups by Cable-Tension Methods," *Res. Quart.* 23:136, 1952.

106. Clarke, H. Harrison, and Boyd O. Jarman, "Scholastic Achievement of Boys 9, 12, and 15 Years of Age as Related to Various Strength and Growth Measures," *Res. Quart.*, 32:155–162, 1961.

107. Clarke, H. H., and T. G. Schopf, "Construction of a Muscular Strength Test for Boys in Grades 4, 5 and 6," *Res. Quart.*, 33:515, 1962.

108. Cobb, S., "The Epidemiology of Rheumatoid Arthritis," *Arth. & Rheum.*, 8:76, 1965.

109. Coefield, John R., and Robert H. McCollum, "A Case Study Report of 78 University Freshmen Men with Low Physical Fitness Indices," master's thesis, University of Oregon, 1955.

110. Cofer, C. N., and W. R. Johnson, "Personality Dynamics in Relation to Exercise and Sports," in *Science and Medicine of Exercise and Sports* (W. R. Johnson, Ed.). New York: Harper & Row, Publishers, 1960, pp. 525–559.

111. Cohen, A. M., "Fats and Carbohydrates as Factors in Atherosclerosis and Diabetes in Yemenite Jews," *Amer. Heart J.*, 65:291, 1963.

112. Cole, F. C., "Intercollegiate Athletics and Higher Education," in *Current Issues in Higher Education*. Washington, D.C.: NEA, 1961.

113. Coleman, J. C., *Abnormal Psychology and Modern Life* (3d ed.). Glenview, Ill.: Scott, Foresman and Company, 1963.

114. Coleman, J. C., J. F. Keough, and J. Mansfield, "Motor Performance and Social Adjustment among Boys Experiencing Serious Learning Difficulties," *Res. Quart.* 34:516, 1963.

115. Coleman, J. S., "Athletics in High

School," *Ann. Amer. Acad. Polit. Soc. Sci.*, 33:338, 1961.

116. Collingwood, R. G., quoted in A. Castell, *The Self in Philosophy*. New York: Crowell-Collier and Macmillan, Inc., 1965.

117. Collins, J., "Philosophy and Religion," in *The Great Ideas Today* (R. M. Hutchins and M. J. Adler, Eds.). Chicago: Encyclopaedia Britannica, Inc., 1962.

118. Commission on Chronic Illness, *Chronic Illness in the United States;* Vol. I, *Prevention of Chronic Illness.* Cambridge, Mass.: Harvard University Press, 1957.

119. Commission on Goals for American Recreation, *Goals for American Recreation.* Washington, D.C.: AAHPER, 1964.

120. Committee on Work in Industry of the National Research Council, "Fatigue of Workers—Its relation to Industrial Production," bulletin. New York: Reinhold Publishing Corporation, 1941.

121. Comroe, J. N., Jr., "The Physiological Effects of Smoking," *Physiol. for Physicians,* 2:1, 1964.

122. Consolazio, C. F., R. E. Johnson, and L. J. Pecora, *Physiological Measurements of Metabolic Functions in Man.* New York: McGraw-Hill, Inc., 1963.

123. Cooper, K. H., *Aerobics.* New York: Bantam Books, Inc., 1968.

124. Cooper, K. H., "The 12-Minute Field Performance Test as a Measure of Cardiovascular Fitness," paper presented at American College of Sports Medicine Meeting, University Park, Pa., 1968.

125. Corbin, Charles B., "The Effects of Covert Rehersal on the Development of a Complex Motor Skill," *J. Genet. Psychol.*, 76:143–150, 1967.

126. Corder, W., "Effects of Physical Education on the Intellectual, Physical, and Social Development of Educable Mentally Retarded Boys," *Except. Children*, 32:357, 1966.

127. Costill, David L., and Peter B. Samuels, "Heart Study Shows Emotional In-

volvement of Wrestling Coach," *Amateur Wrestling News,* 12:6, (Feb. 22) 1967.

128. Cowell, C. C., and A. H. Ismail, "Relationship between Selected Social and Physical Factors," *Res. Quart.*, 33:40, 1962.

129. Cowell, C. C., "Validating an Index of Social Adjustment for High School Use," *Res. Quart.*, 29:7, 1958.

130. Cox, F. N., "Some Effects of Test Anxiety and Presence or Absence of Other Persons on Boys' Performance on a Repetitive Motor Task," *J. Exp. Child Psychol.*, 3:100–112, 1966.

131. Cox, F. N., "Sociometric Status and Individual Adjustment before and after Play Therapy," *J. Abnorm. Soc. Psychol.*, 48:354, 1953.

132. Crakes, James G., "The Anatomical, Physiological and Psychological Differences between Distance Runners of Varying Abilities, Ph.D. dissertation, University of Oregon, Eugene, 1960.

133. "Crash Diets for Athletes Termed Dangerous, Unfair," *Amer. Med. Assoc. News,* 2, (Jan. 26) 1956.

134. Cratty, Bryant J., *Social Dimensions of Physical Activity.* Englewood Cliffs, N.J.: Prentice-Hall, Inc., 1967.

135. Cratty, Bryant J., *Developmental Sequences of Perceptual-Motor Tasks.* Freeport, Long Island: Educational Activities, Inc., 1967.

136. Cratty, Bryant J., *Movement, Behavior, and Motor Learning.* Philadelphia: Lea & Febiger, 1964.

137. Cureton, T. K., "Improvement of Psychological States by Means of Exercise Fitness Programs," *J. Assoc. Phys. Ment. Rehab.*, 17:14–25, 1963.

138. Cureton, T. K., *Physical Fitness of Champion Athletes.* Urbana: University of Illinois Press, 1951.

139. Daniels, Arthur S., *Adapted Physical Education.* New York: Harper & Row, Publishers, 1954.

140. Daniels, L., M. Williams, and C. Worthingham, *Muscle Testing.* Philadelphia: W. B. Saunders Company, 1956.

141. Darcus, T. L., and N. Salter, "Effect

of Repeated Muscular Exertion on Muscle Strength," *J. Physiol.,* 129:325, 1955.

142. Davidson, S., and R. Passmore, *Human Nutrition and Dietetics.* Baltimore, Md.: The Williams & Wilkins Company, 1966.

143. Davis, Elsie Miller, "A Man Don't Know What He Can Do," *Reader's Digest,* October 1952, pp. 23–25.

144. Davis, J. E., and N. Brewer, "Effect of Physical Training on Blood Volume, Hemoglobin, Alkali Reserve and Osmotic Resistance of Erythrocytes," *Amer. J. Physiol.,* 113:586, 1935.

145. Davis, R., *Cigarette Smoking Motivation Study.* London: Research Services, 1956.

146. Dawber, T. R., F. R. Moore, and G. V. Mann, "Coronary Heart Disease in the Framingham Study," *Amer. J. Public Health* (Suppl.), 47:4, 1957.

147. Dawber, T. R., W. B. Kannel, and G. D. Friedman, "Vital Capacity, Physical Activity and Coronary Heart Disease," *First International Conference on Preventive Cardiology,* University of Vermont, 1964.

148. Delacato, Carl H., *The Treatment and Prevention of Reading Problems.* Springfield, Ill.: Charles C Thomas, Publisher, 1959.

149. Delacato, Carl H., *The Diagnosis and Treatment of Speech and Reading Problems.* Springfield, Ill.: Charles C Thomas, Publisher, 1964.

150. Delacato, Carl H., *Neurological Organization in the Classroom.* Chicago: S.F.E., Inc., 1966.

151. Delacato, Carl H., *Neurological Organization and Reading.* Springfield, Ill.: Charles C Thomas, Publisher, 1966.

152. Denny, M. R., and J. M. Reisman, "Negative Transfer as a Function of Manifest Anxiety," *Percept. Mot. Skills,* 6:73–75, 1956.

153. "Diet and Hypertension," *Nutr. Rev.,* 6:295, 1948.

154. "Dieting Drugs: How Good and Safe?" *Good Housekeeping,* Jan. 1966, p. 131.

155. Dirix, Albert, "The Doping Problems at the Tokyo and Mexico City Olympic Games," *J. Sports Med. Phys. Fit.,* 6: 183–186, (Sept.) 1966.

156. Dorscher, N., "The Effects of Rapid Weight Loss upon Physical Profiency of College Students," *Res. Quart.,* 15: 317, 1964.

157. Drenick, E. J., I. F. Hunt, and M. E. Swendseid, "Influence of Fasting and Refeeding on Body Composition," *J. Am. Public Health Assoc.,* 58:477, 1968.

158. Drenick, E. J., "Prolonged Starvation as Treatment for Severe Obesity," *J. Amer. Med. Assoc.,* 187:100, 1964.

159. Drowatzky, John N., *A Research Report; Evaluation of a Residential Camp Program for Mentally Retarded Children.* Toledo, Ohio: University of Toledo, 1967.

160. DuBois, E. F., "Heat Loss from the Human Body," *Bull. N.Y. Acad. Med.,* 15:143, 1939.

161. Dulles, Foster R., *A History of Recreation.* New York: Appleton-Century-Crofts, 1965.

162. Eckstein, R. W., "Effect of Exercise and Coronary Artery Narrowing on Coronary Collateral Circulation," *Circul. Res.,* 5:230, 1957.

163. Edwards, A. A., "Effects of Loss of One Hundred Hours of Sleep," *Amer. J. Psychol.,* 54:80, 1941.

164. Enos, W. F., R. H. Holmes, and J. Beyer, "Coronary Disease among United States Soldiers Killed in Korea," *J. Amer. Med. Assoc.* 152:1090, 1953.

165. "Effects of Force Feeding," *Nutr. Rev.,* 18:334, 1960.

166. "Effects of Meal Eating versus Nibbling on Body Composition," *Nutr. Rev.,* 19:9, 1961.

167. Erdelyi, G., "Gynecological Survey of Female Athletes," *J. Sports Med. Phys. Fit.* 2:175–179, (Sept.) 1962.

168. Esslinger, A. A., "Certification for High School Coaches," *JOHPER,* 39: 42, (Oct.) 1968.

169. Eysenck, H. J., and A. E. Maxwell, "Reminiscence as a Function of Drive," *Brit. J. Psychol.,* 58:43–52, 1961.

170. Eysenck, H. J., "The Measurement of Motivation," *Sci. Amer.,* 208:130–140, 1963.

171. Fabry, P., and others, "The Frequency of Meals: Its Relation to Overweight, Hypercholesterolemia, and Decreased Glucose-Tolerance," *Lancet,* 2:614, (Sept. 19) 1964.

172. *Facts on the Major Killing and Crippling Diseases in the United States Today.* New York: The National Health Education Committee, Inc., 1964.

173. Faulkner, John, seminar presentation, Tecumseh, Michigan, Dec. 1966.

174. *F.D.A. Approval of New Drugs; Facts for Consumers.* U.S. Dept. of Health, Education, and Welfare, Food and Drug Admin., Oct. 1964.

175. Feister, C. B., and B. F. Skinner, *Schedules of Reinforcement.* New York: Appleton-Century-Crofts, 1957.

176. Felshin, Janet, *Perspectives and Principles for Physical Education.* New York: John Wiley & Sons, Inc. 1967.

177. Fenstein, B., and others, "Morphologic Studies of Motor Units in Normal Human Muscles," *Acta Anatomica, 23:127,* 1954.

178. Fischer, John, "Substitutes for Violence," *Harper's Magazine,* 232:16–24, (Jan.) 1966.

179. Fishbein, M. (Ed.), "Medical News of the Month," *McCall's,* 92:40, 1965.

180. Fisher, Seymour, and Sidney E. Cleveland, *Body Image and Personality,* Princeton, N.J.: D. Van Nostrand Company, Inc., 1958.

181. Fitts, Paul M., and Michael I. Posner, *Human Performance.* Belmont, Calif.: Brooks-Cole Publishing Co., 1967.

182. Flanagan, Lance, "A Study of Some Personality Traits of Different Phsyical Activity Groups, *Res. Quart.,* 22: 312–323, 1951.

183. Fleischman, Edwin A., *The Structure and Measurement of Physical Fitness.* Englewood Cliffs, N.J.: Prentice-Hall, Inc., 1964.

184. Fleischman, E. A., *Examiner's Manual for the Basic Fitness Tests.* Englewood Cliffs, N.J.: Prentice-Hall, Inc. 1964.

185. Flowtow, E. A., "Charting Social Relationships of School Children," *Elem. School J.,* 47:498, 1946.

186. Floyd, W. F., and P. H. S. Silver, "The Function of the Erectores Spinae Muscles in Certain Movements and Postures in Man," *J. Physiol.,* 129:184–283, 1955.

187. Fluhmann, C. F., "Dysmenorrhea," *Clin. Obstet. Gynecol.,* 3:718–727, (Sept.) 1963.

188. Fodor, J. T., and G. T. Dalis, *Health Instruction Theory and Application.* Philadelphia: Lea & Febiger, 1966.

189. Foster, W. T., "An Indictment of Inter-Collegiate Athletics," *Atlantic Monthly,* 116:577, 1915.

190. Freeman, D. Roger, "Controversey Over 'Patterning' as a Treatment for Brain Damage in Children," *J. Amer. Med. Assoc.,* 202:385–387, 1967.

191. Freimer, Earl H., and Maclyn McCarty, "Rheumatic Fever," *Sci. Amer.,* 213: 67–74, (Dec.) 1965.

192. Friedlander, Frank, "Motivations to Work and Organizational Performance," *J. Appl. Psychol.,* 50:143–152, 1966.

193. Friedman, M., and others, "Excretion of Catecholamines, 17-Ketosteroids, 17-Hydroxycorticoids, 5-Hydroxyindole in Men Exhibiting a Particular Behavior Pattern (A) Associated with a High Incidence of Clinical Coronary Disease," *J. Clin. Invest.,* 39:758, 1960.

194. Friedman, M., and H. Rosenman, "Association of Specific Behavior Patterns with Increase in Blood Cholesterol, Blood Clotting Time and Incidence of Clinical Coronary Disease," *Circulation,* 18:721, 1958.

195. Frostig, Marianne, and David Horne, *The Frostig Program for the Development of Visual Perception.* Chicago: Follett Publishing Co., 1964.

196. Fulton, Ruth E., "Speed and Accuracy in Learning a Ballistic Movement," *Res. Quart.,* 13:30, 1942.

197. Furfey, P. H., "Some Factors Influencing the Selection of Boys' Chums," *J. Appl. Psychol.,* 11:47, 1943.

198. Furlong, B., "Can the Ills of College Athletics be Cured?" *Sport,* April 1964, p. 12.

199. Furlong, B., "How Immoral Are College Athletics?" *Sport,* March 1964, p. 14.

200. Gaber, Bill, "Swimming for Trainable Mentally Retarded," *Challenge,* 3:8–9 (May) 1968.

201. Gagne, R. M., Katherine E. Baker, and Harriet Foster, "The Relation between Similarity and Transfer of Training in the Learning of Discriminative Motor Tasks," *Psychol. Rev.,* 57:2, 1950.

202. Gardner, G. W., "Specificity of Strength Changes of the Exercised and Non-Exercised Limb Following Isometric Training," *Res. Quart.,* 34:98, 1963.

203. Garn, S. M., and J. Brozek, "Fat Changes during Weight Loss," *Science,* 124: 682, 1956.

204. Gastric Hypertrophy in Fasted Rats," *Nutr. Rev.,* 18:187, 1960.

205. Gates, G., "The Effect of an Audience upon Performance." *J. Abnorm. Soc. Psychol.,* 18:334–344, 1924.

206. Gazzangia, Michael, "The Split Brain Man," *Sci. Amer.,* 217:24–29, 1967.

207. Gendel, Evalyn S., "Women and the Medical Aspects of Sports," *J. School Health,* 37:427–431, (Nov.) 1967.

208. Gertler, M. M., and others, "Coronary Heart Disease, a Prospective Study," *Amer. J. Med. Sci.,* 248:377, 1964.

209. Gertler, M. M., and P. D. White, *Coronary Heart Disease in Young Adults: A Multidisciplinary Study.* Cambridge, Mass.: Commonwealth Fund, Harvard University Press, 1954.

210. Gillis, R. J., "Effect of Ingested Water Volume and Temperature on the Body Weight Loss, Cardiac Cost, and Body Heat Storage of Football Players," unpublished doctoral dissertation, Springfield College, Springfield, Mass., 1965.

211. Glass, G. U., *A Critique of Experiments on the Role of Neurological Organization in Reading Performance.* Urbana, Ill.: University of Illinois, College of Education, October 1966.

212. Glees, P., "Studies of Cortical Regeneration with Special Reference to Cerebral Implants," in *Regeneration in the Central Nervous System* (William Windle, Ed.). Springfield, Ill.: Charles C Thomas, Publisher, 1955.

213. Gofman, J. W., and others, "Evaluation of Serum Lipoproteins and Cholesterol Measurements as Predictors of Clinical Complications of Atherosclerosis," *Circulation,* 14:691, 1956.

214. Golub, Leib J., "A New Exercise for Dysmenorrhea," *Amer. J. Obstet. Gynecol.,* 78:152–155, 1959.

215. Gordon, E. S., and others, "A New Concept in the Treatment of Obesity," *J. Amer. Med. Assoc.* 186:50, 1963.

216. Gordon, H. L., D. Rosenberg, and W. E. Morres, "Leisure Activities of Schizophrenic Patients after Return to the Community," *Mental Hygiene,* 50:457–459, 1966.

217. Grande, F., "Notes," *Nutr. Rev.,* 26: 30, 1968.

218. "The Grandiose Inquisitor," *Time,* Aug. 30, 1968, p. 46.

219. Gray, G. W., "Cortisone and ACTH," *Sci. Amer.,* 182:30, 1950.

220. Green, David E., "The Metabolism of Fat," *Sci. Amer.,* 190:32, 1954.

221. Greenburg, S., "Alterations in Serum Lipids Induced by Metrecal in Obese Patients," *Amer. J. Med. Sci.,* 248:1108, 1964.

222. Grissom, D. K., "Man Living Healthfully Our Common Goal," *JOHPER,* 39:33, (Sept.) 1968.

223. Grout, R. E., *Health Teaching in Schools.* Philadelphia: W. B. Saunders Company, 1948.

224. Guyton, A. C., *Textbook of Medical Physiology.* Philadelphia: W. B. Saunders Company, 1958.

225. "Half a Brain is Better," *Time,* Nov. 1, 1968, p. 60.

226. Hammond, E. G., "Some Preliminary Findings on Physical Complaints from a Prospective Study of 1, 064, 004 Men and Women," *Amer. J. Public Health,* 54:11, 1964.

227. Hanson, D. L., "Cardiac Response to

Participation in Little League Baseball Competition as Determined by Telemetry," *Res. Quart.*, 38:384, 1967.

228. Hardinge, M. G., and F. J. Stare, "Nutritional Studies of Vegetarians. II. Dietary and Serum Levels of Cholesterol," *J. Clin. Nutr.*, 2:83, 1954.

229. Hardy, M. C., "Social Recognition at the Elementary School Age," *J. Soc. Psychol.*, 8:365, 1937.

230. Harlow, Robert G., "Masculine Inadequacy and Compensatory Development of Physique," *J. Pers.*, 19:312–323, 1951.

231. Harman, John O., "Exercises in Dysmenorrhea," *Amer. J. Obstet. Gynecol.*, 49:755–761, (June) 1945.

232. Hart, Marcia E., and Clayton T. Shaw, "Relationship between Physical Fitness and Academic Success," *Res. Quart.* 35:443–445, 1964.

233. Havel, R. J., "The Neurohumoral Control of Lipid Storage, Transport, and Utilization," *Physiol. for Physicians*, 1:6, (June) 1963.

234. *Health Bulletin,* Vol. 2, No. 10, March 10, 1964. Emmaus, Pa.: Rodale Press, Inc.

235. Hedley, O. F., "Analysis of 5116 Deaths Reported as Due to Acute Coronary Occlusion in Philadelphia 1933-37," United States Weekly *Public Health Reports*, 54:972, 1939.

236. Hellebrandt, F. A., "Cross Education: Ipsilateral and Controlateral Effects of Unimanual Training," *J. Appl. Physiol*, 4:136, 1951.

237. Hellebrandt, F. A., and S. J. Houtz, "Mechanisms of Muscle Training in Man: Experimental Demonstration of the Overload Principle," *Phys. Ther. Rev.*, 36:371, 1956.

238. Hellerstein, H. K., "A Primary and Secondary Coronary Prevention Program-in-Progress Report," *First International Conference on Preventive Cardiology*, University of Vermont, 1964.

239. Hellerstein, H. K., "The Application of What is Known about Exercise and Cardiovascular Health," speech at the 10th Annual Conference (Physical Activity and Cardiovascular Health), University of Toledo, Toledo, Ohio, Nov. 1966.

240. Henderson, J., *Emergency Medical Guide.* New York: McGraw-Hill, Inc., 1963.

241. Henry, F. M., "Influence of Athletic Training on the Resting Cardiovascular System," *Res. Quart.*, 25:28, 1954.

242. Henry, F. M., and J. R. Fitzhenry, "Oxygen Metabolism of Moderate Exercise with Some Observations on the Effects of Tobacco Smoking," *J. Appl. Physiol.*, 2:464, 1950.

243. Heron, W., "The Pathology of Boredom," *Sci. Amer.*, 196:52–56, (Jan.) 1957.

244. Herzstein, J., C. Wang, and D. Aldersburg, "Fat Loading Studies in Relation to Age," *Arch. Int. Med.*, 92:265, 1953.

245. Heusner, W. W., *Specificity of Interval Training.* East Lansing: Michigan State University, 1963, p. 28.

246. Higdon, Rose, and Hal Higdon, "What Sports for Girls," *Today's Health*, 45:21, (Oct.) 1967.

247. Hill, S. R., "Studies on Adrenocortical and Psychological Response to Stress in Man." *Arch. Inst. Med.*, 97:269–298, 1956.

248. Himmich, H. E., "The Physiology of Alcohol," *J. Amer. Med. Assoc.*, 163:545, 1957.

249. Hitler, A., quoted in H. Berneet, *Nationalsozialistische Leibeserziehung* (National Socialistic Physical Education). Stuttgart: Verlag Karl Hofmann, 1966.

250. Hockey, Robert V., "Prediction of Maximal Oxygen Intake from Lateral Jump Tests Applicable to School Situations," doctoral dissertation, University of Toledo, 1968.

251. Hockey, Robert V., "Improvement in Reading Achievement through Perceptual Motor Training at the Junior High School Level," unpublished report, University of Toledo, 1968.

252. Hogdon, R. E., and D. Reimer, "Exercise and Pulse Rate Response in Psychiatric Patients," *J. Assoc. Phys. Ment. Rehab.*, 16:41–46, 1962.

253. Holeckova, E., and P. Fabry, "Hyperphagia and Gastric Hypertrophy in Rats Adapted to Intermittent Starvation," *Brit. J. Nutr.*, 13:260, 1959.

254. Holland, G., "Effects of Limited Sleep Deprivation on Performance of Selected Motor Tasks," *Res. Quart.*, 39: 285, 1968.

255. Holloszy, J. O., and others, "Effects of a Six-Month Program of Endurance Exercise on the Serum Lipids of Middle-Aged Men," *Amer. J. Car.*, 14:753, 1964.

256. Horn, D., F. A. Courts, R. M. Taylor, and E. S. Solomon, "Cigarette Smoking among High School Students," *Amer. Public Health*, 49:1497, 1959.

257. Hubbard, A. W., "Homokinetics: Muscular Function in Human Movement," in *Science and Medicine of Exercise and Sports* (W. R. Johnson, Ed.). New York: Harper & Row, Publishers, 1960, pp. 7–39.

258. Hull, C. L., *Principles of Behavior*. New York: Appleton-Century-Crofts, 1943.

259. Hunsicker, Paul and G. G. Rieff, "A Survey and Comparison of Youth Fitness 1958–1965," *JOHPER*, 37:23, (Jan.) 1966.
(a) Husman, Burris F., "Aggression in Boxers and Wrestlers as Measured by Projective Techniques," *Res. Quart.*, 26:421–425, 1955.

260. Huxley, A., *Brave New World*. New York: Bantam Books, Inc., 1967.

261. Huxley, A. F., "The Contractions of Muscle," *Sci. Amer.*, 199:67, 1958.

262. Huxley, H. E., "The Mechanism of Muscular Contraction," *Sci. Amer.*, 213:18–27, (Dec.) 1965.

263. Ikeda, N., "A Comparison of Physical Fitness of Children in Iowa, U.S.A. and Tokyo, Japan," *Res. Quart.*, 33: 541, 1962.

264. *Interscholastic Athletics in Junior High Schools*. Washington, D.C.: NEA, 1958.

265. Irwin, R. W., "The Effects of Eccentric Muscle Training on the Strength of the Forearm Flexors," unpublished master's thesis, University of Toledo, 1964.

266. Ismail, A., N. Kephart, and C. C. Cowell, "Utilization of Motor Aptitude Tests in Predicting Academic Achievement," *Technical Report No. 1*, Purdue University Research Foundation, P.U. 879–64–838, 1963.

267. Itkin, I. H., "Exercise for the Asthmatic Patient: Physiologic Changes in the Respiratory System and Effects of Conditioning Exercise Programs," *Phys. Ther.*, 44:815, 1964.

268. Jackson, C. M., *The Effects of Inanition and Malnutrition upon Growth and Structure*. New York: McGraw-Hill, Inc., Blakiston Division, 1925.

269. Jacobson, E., *Progressive Relaxation*. Chicago: University of Chicago Press, 1934.

270. Jacobson, E., *You Must Relax*. New York: McGraw-Hill, Inc. 1948.

271. Jay, J., and L. Lader, "Don't Trap Your Son in Little League Madness," *True*, April 1965, p. 42.

272. Jenkins, W. O., and J. C. Stanley, "Partial Reinforcement: A Review and Critique," *Psychol. Bull.*, 47, 193:234, 1950.

273. Johns, E. B., W. C. Sutton, and L. E. Webster, *Health for Effective Living*. New York: McGraw-Hill, Inc., 1962.

274. Johnson, G. B., Jr., "Motor Learning," in *Science and Medicine of Exercise and Sports* (W. R. Johnson, Ed.). New York: Harper & Row, Publishers, 1960, pp. 600–619.

275. Johnson, P. B., and R. Bierley, "Effect of Specific Overload Jumping on Vertical Jump Scores," *Proc. College Phys. Educ. Assoc.* (CPEA). Washington, D.C.: AAHPER, 1962.

276. Johnson, P. B., and others, "The Effects of Acute Starvation on All-Out Physical Exercise in Rats," paper presented at Midwest AAHPER Meetings, 1960.

277. Johnson, P. B., and others, "Effects of Starvation and Realimentation," paper presented at Midwest AAHPER Research Section, 1964.

278. Johnson, P. B., and J. Cooper, "The Effects of 'Meal Eating,' 'Nibbling,' and Starvation-Refeeding in Male

Albino Rats," paper presented at Research Section, AAHPER National Conv., Las Vegas, 1967.

279. Johnson, P. B., and B. Hall, "Morphological Changes Associated with Repeated Rapid Weight Reduction in Rats," *J. Sports Med. Phys. Fit.,* 4:174, 1964.

280. Johnson, P. B., R. Lafferty, and W. Updyke, "The Effects of Sleep Deprivation on Physical and Mental Efficiency," *J. Sports Med. Phys. Fit.,* 3:259, 1963.

281. Johnson, P. B., W. F. Updyke, and W. Henry, "Effect of Regular Exercise on Diurnal Variation in Submaximal Metabolism," *Abstracts of Research Papers,* AAHPER Convention, 1965.

282. Johnson, R. D., "Measurements of Achievement in Fundamental Skills of Elementary Children," *Res. Quart.,* 33:94, 1962.

283. Johnson, Warren R., "Some Psychological Aspects of Physical Rehabilitation: Toward an Organismic Theory," *J. Assoc. Phys. Ment. Rehab.,* 16:165–168, 1962.

284. Johnson, Warren, and G. F. Kramer, "Effects of Stereotyped Non-Hypnotic, Hypnotic and Post-Hypnotic Suggestions upon Strength, Power and Endurance," *Res. Quart.,* 32:522–529, 1961.

285. Johnson, Warren R., "Hypnosis and Muscular Performance," *J. Sports Med. Phys. Fit.,* 1:71–79, 1961.

286. Johnson, Warren R., Daniel C. Hutton, and Granville B. Johnson, "Personality Traits of Some Champion Athletes as Measured by Two Projective Tests: The Rorschach and H-T-P," *Res. Quart.,* 25:484–485, 1954.

287. Jones, D. M., C. Squires, and K. Rodahl, "The Effect of Rope Skipping on Physical Work Capacity," *Res. Quart.,* 33:236, 1962.

288. Jones, E. M., and others, "Effects of Exercise and Food Restriction on Serum Cholesterol and Liver Lipids," *Amer. J. Physiol.,* 207:460, 1964.

289. Jones, H. E., "Physical Ability as a Factor in Social Adjustment in Adolescence," *J. Educ. Res.,* 40:287, 1948.

290. Jones, Mary E., and Nancy Bayley, "Physical Maturing among Boys as Related to Behavior," *J. Educ. Psychol.,* 41:129–148, 1950.

291. Jorgenson, Robert T., "The Relationship of Physical Fitness to Optimum Scholastic Achievement," master's thesis, Washington State University, 1955.

292. Karpovich, P. V., "Ergogenic Aids in Athletics," in *Exercise and Fitness.* Chicago: The Athletic Institute, 1960.

293. Karpovich, P. V., Physiology of Muscular Activity. Philadelphia: W. B. Saunders Company, 1965.

294. Katz, L. N., J. Stamler, and R. Pick, *Nutrition and Atherosclerosis.* Philadelphia: Lea & Febiger, 1958.

295. Katz, S. E., and C. Landis, "Psychological and Physiological Phenomena during a Prolonged Vigil," *Arch. Neurol. Psychiat.,* 34:307, 1953.

296. Kazmaier, R., "Open Letter to a College President," *Sports Illustrated,* 19:57, (Oct. 14) 1963.

297. Keeney, C. E., "The Effect of Exercise on Blood Coagulation and Fibrinolysis," in *Health and Fitness in the Modern World.* Chicago: The Athletic Institute, 1961, p. 188.

298. Kehr, G. B., "An Analysis of Sportsmanship Responses of Groups of Boys Classified as Participants and Non-Participants in Organized Baseball," doctoral dissertation, New York University, 1959.

299. Kelly, Ellen Davis, *Adapted and Corrective Physical Education* (4th ed.). New York: The Ronald Press Company, 1965.

300. Kelso, Louis O., and Mortimer J. Adler, *The Capitalist Manifesto.* New York: Random House, Inc., 1958.

301. Kendall, F. P., "A Criticism of Current Tests and Exercises for Physical Fitness," *Phys. Ther.,* 45:187, 1965.

302. Kenyon, G. S., "The Significance of Adult Physical Activity as a Function of Age, Sex, Education, and Socio-

Economic Status," paper presented to Midwest Convention of AAHPER, Detroit, Michigan, 1964.

303. Kenyon, G. S., "Claims for Physical Exercise and Formal Physical Education: Fact and Fancy Concerning Psychological and Sociological Benefits: Sociological Considerations," paper presented at Scientific Foundations Section, AAHPER Convention, St. Louis, 1968.

304. Kershner, John R., "Doman–Delacato's Theory of Neurological Organization Applied with Retarded Children," *J. Except. Children,* February 1968, p. 441.

305. Kephart, Newell C., *The Slow Learner in the Classroom,* Columbus, Ohio: Charles E. Merrill Books, Inc., 1960.

306. Keys, Ancel, and J. Brozek, "Body Fat in Adult Men," *Phys. Rev.,* 33:245, 1953.

307. Keys, Ancel, and R. Buzina, "Blood Coagubility Effects of Meals and Differences between Populations," *Circulation,* 14:479, 1956 (Abstract).

308. Keys, Ancel, "Diet and the Epidemiology of Heart Disease," *J. Amer. Med. Assoc.,* 164:1912, 1957.

309. Keys, Ancel, and others, *The Biology of Human Starvation.* Minneapolis: University of Minnesota Press, 1950.

310. Kilander, H. F., *Health for Modern Living.* Englewood Cliffs, N.J.: Prentice-Hall, Inc., 1959.

311. King, S., "Relaxation and Stress," master's thesis, Women's College, University of North Carolina, Greensboro, 1953.

312. Kjellberg, S. R., V. Rudhe, and T. Sjostrand, "Increase in the Amount of Hemoglobin and Blood Volume in Connection with Physical Training," *Acta Physiol. Scand.,* 19:146, 1949.

313. Klouda, M. A., and W. C. Randall, "Subendocardial Hemorrhages during Stimulation of the Sympathetic Cardiac Nerves," *First International Conference on Preventive Cardiology,* University of Vermont, 1964.

314. Knehr, C. A., D. B. Dill, and W. Newfeld, "Training and Its Effects on Man at Rest and at Work," *Amer. J. Physiol.,* 136:148, 1942.

315. Knott, M., "Neuromuscular Facilitation in the Treatment of Rheumatoid Arthritis," *Phys. Ther.,* 44:737, 1964.

316. Knuttgen, H. G., "Comparison of Fitness of Danish and American School Children," *Res. Quart.,* 32:190, 1961.

317. Koffke, K., *Principles of Gestalt Psychology.* New York: Harcourt, Brace & World, Inc., 1935.

318. Kohler, W., *The Mentality of Apes.* New York: Harcourt, Brace & World, Inc., 1925.

319. Kohler, W., *Gestalt Psychology.* New York: Liveright Publishing Corporation, 1929.

320. Koonce, J. M., D. J. Chambliss, and A. Irion, "Long Term Reminiscence in the Pursuit Rotor Habit," *J. Exp. Psychol.,* 67:498–500, 1964.

321. Kozar, J. J., and P. Hunsicker, "A Study of Telemetered Heart Rate during Sports Participation of Young Adult Men," *J. Sports Med., Phys. Fit.,* 3:1, 1963.

322. Kraines, S. H., *Mental Depressions and Their Treatment.* New York: Crowell-Collier and Macmillan, Inc., 1957.

323. Kraines, S. H., "Manic Depressive Syndrome: A Physiologic Disease," *Dis. Nervous System,* 27:573–82, (Sept.) 1966.

324. Kramar, J., and others, "Stress of Fasting and Realimentation as Reflected in the Capillary Resistance and Eosinophil Count," *Amer. J. Physiol.,* 178:486, 1954.

325. Kraus, H., and R. Hirschland, "Minimum Muscular Fitness Tests in School Children," *Res. Quart.,* 25:178, 1954.

326. Kraus, N., and W. Raab, *Hypokinetic Disease.* Springfield, Ill.: Charles C Thomas, Publisher, 1961.

327. Kroll, W., "Sixteen Personality Factor Profiles of Collegiate Wrestlers," *Res. Quart.* 38:49–57, 1967.

328. Lanoue, Fred, "Some Facts on Swimming Cramps," *Res. Quart.,* 21:153, 1950.

329. Lapiccirella, V., "Emotionally Induced

Cardiac Disturbance and Possible Cardiac Benefits from Tranquil Living," *First International Conference on Preventive Cardiology,* University of Vermont, 1964.

330. LaPlace, John P., "Personality and Its Relationship to Success in Professional Baseball," *Res. Quart.,* 25:313–319, 1954.

331. LaSierra High School, "Department of Physical Education for Boys," mimeographed report, California, 1961.

332. Latchaw, Marjorie, "Measuring Selected Motor Skills in Fourth, Fifth, and Sixth Grades," *Res. Quart.,* 24: 439, 1954.

333. Lawrence, D. H., "The Transfer of a Discrimination along a Continuum," *J. Comp. Physiol. Psych.,* 45:511–516, 1952.

334. Layman, E. M., "Physical Activity as a Psychiatric Adjunct," in *Science and Medicine of Exercise and Sports* (W. R. Johnson, Ed.). New York: Harper & Row, Publishers, 1960.

335. Learner, Max, "Work, Leisure, and Recreation in the Coming American Culture," address delivered to the First General Session, AAHPER National Convention, Dallas, 1965.

336. Leary, Timothy, "The Religious Experience: Its Production and Interpretation," in *The Psychedelic Reader* (G. M. Weil, R. Metzner, and T. Leary, Eds.). New Hyde Park, New York: University Books, 1965.

337. Leibowitz, Herschel, "Effect of Exercise-Induced Fatigue and Other Factors on Peripheral Vision," paper presented before the American College of Sports Medicine, University Park, Pa. May 2, 1968.

338. Leighton, Jack R., "Flexibility Characteristics of Four Specialized Skill Groups of College Athletes," *Arch. Phys. Med. Rehab.,* 38:24, (Jan.) 1957.

339. Levi, L., "Life Stress and Urinary Excretion of Adrenaline and Noradrenaline," *First International Conference on Preventive Cardiology,* University of Vermont, 1964.

340. Levine, Seymour, "Stimulation in Infancy," in *Readings in Child Behavior and Development,* (C. B. Stendler, Ed.). New York: Harcourt, Brace & World, Inc., 1964.

341. Levitt, E. E., and J. P. Brady, "Muscular Endurance under Hypnosis and in the Motivated Waking State," *Int. J. Clin. Exp. Hypnosis,* 12:21, 1964.

342. Levitt, E. E., and J. P. Brady, "Psychophysiology of Hypnosis," in *Hypnosis in Modern Medicine* (J. M. Schneck, Ed.). Springfield, Ill.,: Charles C Thomas, Publisher, 1963.

343. Levy, R. L., and others, "Overweight: Its Prognostic Significance in Relation to Hypertension and Cardiovascular-Renal Diseases," *J. Amer. Med. Assoc.,* 131:951, 1946.

344. Lew, E. A., "Some Implications of Mortality Statistics Relating to Coronary Artery Disease," *J. Chron. Dis.,* 6:192, 1957.

345. Lewis, D., P. N. Smitt, and D. E. McAllister, "Retroactive Facilitation and Interference in Performance on the Two-Hand Coordinator," *J. Exp. Psychol.,* 44:44–50, 1952.

346. Ley, Katherine, "Philosophical Interpretation of the National Institute," in *Anthology of Contemporary Readings* (H. S. Slusher and A. S. Lockhart, Eds.). Dubuque, Iowa: William C. Brown Company, Publishers, 1966.

347. Lieb, A., "Vorstellungen und Urteile von Schuerlern Ueber Fuehrer in der Schulklasse," *Zeitschrift fur Angewante Psychologie,* 20:341, 1928.

348. "Lipid Accumulation in Heart Muscle During Fasting," *Nutr. Rev.,* 23:14, 1965.

349. Little, C. C., H. Strayhorn, and A. J. Miller, Jr., "Effect of Water Ingestion on Capacity for Exercise," *Res. Quart.,* 20:398, 1949.

350. Logan, Gene A., "Comparative Gains in Strength Resulting from Eccentric and Concentric Muscle Contraction," unpublished master's thesis, University of Illinois, Urbana, 1952.

351. Logan, Gene A., and Aileene Lockhart,

"Contralateral Transfer of Specificity of Strength Training," *J. Amer. Phys. Therapy Assoc.,* 42:658–660, 1962.

352. Logan, Janet, "Physical Education for the Trainable Retarded," *Challenge,* 1:1, (May) 1966.

353. Londeree, B. R., "An Investigation of the Effect of Four Water Replacement Schedules upon Exercise in the Heat," doctoral dissertation, University of Toledo, 1966.

354. McDonald, G. A., and H. W. Fullerton, "Effect of Physical Activity on Increased Coagubility of Blood after Ingestion of High-Fat Meal," *Lancet,* 275:600, 1958.

355. McFarland, J. W., "Physical Fitness and Tobacco: A Study of the Battle Creek Program," in *Exercise and Fitness.* Chicago: The Athletic Institute, 1960.

356. McGaugh, James L., "Drug Trials Set for Retarded Children," *Science News,* 92:503, 1968.

357. McGavack, T. H., "Optimal Weight Determination: Experiences with the Method of Willoughby as a Guide to Reduction," *Metabolism,* 14:150, 1965.

358. McGraw, L. W., and J. W. Tolbert, "Sociometric Status and Athletic Ability of Junior High School Boys," 24:72, 1953.

359. McKeachie, Wilbert J., and Charlotte L. Doyle, *Psychology,* Reading, Mass.: Addison-Wesley Publishing Company Inc., 1966.

360. Macworth, N. H., "Researches on the Measurement of Human Performance," Medical Research Council Report Series No. 268, London, Her Majesty's Stationery Office, 1950.

361. Mahl, G. F., A. Rothenberg, and J. M. Delgado, "Psychological Responses in the Human to Intracerebral Electric Stimulation," *Psychosom. Med.,* 26:337–368, (July-Aug.) 1964.

342. Malhorta, S. L., "Serum Lipids, Dietary and Ischemic Heart Disease," *Am. J. Clin. Nutr.,* 20:462, 1967.

363. Mallerowicz, H., "The Effects of Training on O_2 Consumption of the Heart and Its Importance for Prevention of Coronary Insufficiency," in *Health and Fitness in the Modern World.* Chicago: The Athletic Institute, 1960, p. 90.

364. Malmo, R. B., and J. F. Davis, "Anxiety and Behavioral Arousal," *Psychol. Rev.,* 64:276–287, 1957.

365. Maltz, Maxwell, *Psychocybernetics.* Englewood Cliffs, N.J.: Prentice-Hall, Inc., 1960.

(a) Mann, G. V., B. M. Nicol, and F. J. State, "The Beta-Lipoprotein and Cholesterol Concentrations in Sera of Nigerians," *Brit. Med. J.,* 2:1008, 1955.

366. Mann, G. V., and others, "Exercises in the Disposition of Dietary Calories," *New England J. Med.,* 253:349, 1955.

367. Marks, J. B., "Interests, Leadership, and Sociometric Status among Adolescents," *Sociometry,* 17:340, 1954.

368. Martin, R. W., "Selected Anthropometric, Strength, and Power Characteristics of White and Negro Boys," unpublished master's thesis, University of Toledo, 1966.

369. Master, A. M., and I. Rosenfeld, "Criteria for the Clinical Application of the Two-Step Exercise Test," *J. Amer. Med. Assoc.,* 178:283, 1961.

370. Mateeff, D., "Morphological and Physiological Factors of Aging and Longevity," in *Health and Fitness in the Modern World.* Chicago: The Athletic Institute, 1961, p. 3.

371. Mathews, Donald K., *Measurement in Physical Education.* Philadelphia: W. B. Saunders Company, 1968.

372. Matsch, Phyllis, "The Effects of Various Motivational Situations and Personality Factors upon the Work Performance of College Women," unpublished master's thesis, University of Toledo, 1967.

373. Mayberry, R. P., "Isometric Exercise and Cross Transfer of Training Effect as It Relates to Strength," *CPEA Proc.,* 62:155, 1959.

374. Mayer, J., "Exercise and Weight Control," in *Exercise and Fitness.* Chicago: The Athletic Institute, 1960.

375. Mayer, J., "Exercise and Weight Control," in *Science and Medicine of Exercise and Sports.* New York: Harper & Row, Publishers, 1960.

376. Mayer, J., "Physiological Basis of Obesity and Leanness," *Nutr. Abstr. Rev.,* 25:875, 1955.

377. Mayer, J., and B. Bullen, "Nutrition and Athletic Performance," in *Exercise and Fitness.* Chicago: The Athletic Institute, 1960.

378. "Medical News of the Month," *McCall's,* 92:64, 1964.

379. Melling, G., and J. J. Burt, unpublished data. Physiology of Exercise Research Laboratory, University of Toledo, 1965.

380. Melton, Arthur W. (Ed.), *Categories of Human Learning.* New York: Academic Press, Inc., 1964.

381. Melville, K. I., "Cardiac Ischemic Changes Induced by Central Nervous System Stimulation," *First International Conference on Preventive Cardiology,* University of Vermont, 1964.

382. Melville, P. H., and A. G. Mezey, "Emotional State and Energy Expenditure," *Lancet,* 1:273–274, 1959.

383. Melzack, Ronald, "The Perception of Pain," *Sci. Amer.,* 204:41–49, (Feb.) 1961.

384. Meneely, G. R., and others, "Chronic Sodium Chloride Toxicity in the Albino Rat; Occurrence of Hypertension and of the Syndrome of Edema and Renal Failure," *J. Exper. Med.,* 98:71, 1953.

385. Menninger, W. C., "Recreation and Mental Health," in *Physical Education and Healthful Living* (L. M. Fraley, and others, Eds.). Englewood Cliffs, N.J.: Prentice-Hall, Inc., 1954.

386. Menninger, W. C., "Recreation and Mental Health," *Recreation,* 42:340, 1948.

387. Merrill, I. B., and E. C. Howe, "The Effect of Exercise and Fatigue upon Resistance to Infection," *Am. Phys. Educ. Rev.,* 33:67, 1928.

388. Metheny, E., *Body Dynamics.* New York: McGraw-Hill, Inc., 1952.

389. Meyers, A. W., "Some Morphological Effects of Prolonged Inanition," *J. Med. Res.,* 36:51, 1917.

390. Miller, B. F., and J. J. Burt, *Good Health.* Philadelphia: W. B. Saunders Company, 1966.

391. Mittlemann, B., and H. G. Wolff, "Emotions and Gastroduodenal Function," *Psychosom. Med.,* 4:5, 1942.

392. Mohr, D. R., "Changes in Waistline and Abdominal Girth and Subcutaneous Fat Following Isometric Exercise," *Res. Quart.,* 36:168, 1965.

393. Mohr, R., "Die Wechselwirkung Kor Plicher and Seelischer Fakteren im Krankheitsgeschenhen," *Klin. Wchnschr.,* 66:772–776, 1927; cited by E. M. Layman, *Mental Health through Physical Education and Recreation.* Minneapolis: Burgess Publishing Company, 1955.

394. Montoye, H. J., and others, "Effects of Vitamin B_{12} Supplementation on Physical Fitness and Growth of Young Boys," *J. Appl. Physiol.,* 7:589, 1955.

395. Montoye, H. J., and others, *Longevity and Morbidity of College Athletes.* Indianapolis: Phi Epsilon Kappa Fraternity, 1957.

396. Montoye, H. J., and others, "The Effects of Exercise on Blood Cholesterol in Middle-Aged Men," *Amer. J. Clin. Nutr.,* 7:144, 1959.

397. Montoye, H. J., "Sports and Length of Life," in *Science and Medicine of Exercise and Sports* (W. R. Johnson, Ed.). New York: Harper & Row, Publishers, 1960.

398. Moody, D. L., J. Kollias, and E. R. Buskirk, "The Effect of a Moderate Exercise Program on Body Weight and Fatness in Overweight College Women," paper presented at American College of Sports Medicine meeting, University Park, Pennsylvania, 1968.

399. Moreton, J. R., "Chylomicronemia, Fat Tolerance, and Atherosclerosis," *J. Lab. Clin. Med.,* 35:373, 1950.

400. Morgan, Clifford T., and Richard A. King, *Introduction to Psychology.* New York: McGraw-Hill, Inc., 1966.

401. Morgan, R. E., and G. T. Adamson, *Circuit Training*. London: G. Bell & Sons, Ltd., 1959.

402. Morgan, William P., "Personality Characteristics of Wrestlers Participating in the World Championships," paper presented at American College of Sports Medicine meeting, Pennsylvania State University, March 1968.

403. Moriyama, I., T. Woolsey, and J. Stamler, "Observations on Possible Causative Factors Responsible for the Sex and Race Trends in Cardiovascular-Renal Disease Morality in the United States," *J. Chron. Dis.*, 7:401, 1958.

404. Morris, J. M., D. B. Lucas and B. Bresler, "Role of the Trunk in Stability of the Spine," *J. Bone Joint Surg.*, 43A: 327–351, 1961.

405. Morris, J. N., and M. D. Crawford, "Coronary Heart Disease and Physical Activity of Work, Evidence of National Necropsy Study," *Brit. Med. J.*, 2:1485, 1958.

406. Morris, J. N., and others, "Coronary Heart Disease and Physical Activity of Work," *Lancet*, 2:1053, 1953.

407. Morrison, L. M., "A Nutritional Program for Prolongation of Life in Coronary Atherosclerosis," *J. Amer. Med. Assoc.*, 159:1425, 1955.

408. Morrison, L. M., P. Berlin, and W. F. Gonzalez, "Fat Tolerance Tests in Coronary Thrombosis," *Amer. Heart J.*, 38:477, 1949.
    (a) Moser, D., "Athletes Get Help from Hypnotists: Svengali Comes to Sport," *Life*, 54:71–77, (June 7) 1963.

409. Moses, C., *Atherosclerosis*. Philadelphia: Lea & Febiger, 1963.

410. Moss, B. R., W. R. Southworth, and J. L. Reichert (Eds.), *Health Education* (5th ed.) (NEA-AMA). Washington, D.C.: NEA, 1961.

411. Mulligan, William P., "Patterning Treatment for Brain Damage," *J. Amer. Med. Assoc.*, 203:527, 1968.

412. Murphy, R. J., and W. F. Ashe, "Prevention of Heat Illness in Football Players," *J. Amer. Med. Assoc.*, 194: 650, 1965.

413. Mussen, Paul H., and Mary C. Jones, "Self-Conceptions, Motivations, and Interpersonal Attitudes of Late and Early Maturing Boys," *Child Developm.*, 28:243–256, (June) 1957.

414. Mussen, Paul H., and Mary C. Jones, "The Behavior-Inferred Motivation of Late and Early Maturing Boys," *Child Developm.*, 29:62–67, (March) 1958.

415. Mustard, J. F., "Coagulation Changes during Alimentary Lipemia in Subjects with and without Atherosclerosis, and the Effects of Various Lipids," *Circulation*, 18:497, 1958.

416. Myasnikov, A. L., "Influence of Some Factors on Development of Experimental Cholesterol Atherosclerosis," *Circulation*, 17:110, 1958.

417. Myer, D. R., and M. E. Noble, "Summation of Manifest Anxiety and Muscular Tension," *J. Exp. Psychol.*, 55: 599–602, 1958.

418. Nash, Jay B., *The Administration of Physical Education*. New York: A. S. Barnes & Company, Inc., 1931.

419. National Center for Health Statistics, *Heart Disease in Adults, United States 1960–1962*, Ser. II, No. 6. Washington, D.C.: U.S. Dept. of Health, Education, and Welfare, 1964.

420. National Epilepsy League, *Horizon* (Special Issue: A Collection of Pamphlets). Chicago: National Epilepsy Service, 1968.

421. Naughton, J., "Cardiopulmonary Responses to Training in Post-Myocardial Infarct Patients," *First International Conference on Preventive Cardiology*, University of Vermont, 1964.

422. Naughton, J., and F. Nagle, "Peak Oxygen Intake during Physical Fitness Program for Middle-Aged Men," *J. Amer. Med. Assoc.*, 191:899, 1965.

423. Naylor, James C., and George E. Briggs, "Effects of Task Complexity and Task Organization on the Relative Efficiency of Part and Whole Training Methods," *J. Exp. Psychol.*, 65:217–224, 1963.

424. Neimeyer, Roy, "Part versus Whole Methods and Massed versus Distri-

buted Practice in the Learning of Selected Large Muscle Activities," *Coll. Phys. Educ. Assoc. Proc.*, 61:122–125, 1958.

425. Newland, Constance A., *Myself and I.* New York: Coward-McCann, Inc., 1962.

426. *Newsweek*, February 8, 1965, p. 57.

427. Nickel, V. L., J. Kristy, and L. V. McDaniel, "Physical Therapy for Rheumatoid Arthritis," *Phys. Ther.*, 45:198, 1965.

428. Nikkila, E. A., and A. Konttinen, "Effect of Physical Activity on Postprandial Levels of Fats in Serum," *Lancet*, 1:1151, 1962.

429. Nodiene, J. H., and J. H. Moyer (Eds.), *Psychosomatic Medicine.* Philadelphia: Lea & Febiger, 1962.

430. Nolen, Jewell, "Problems of Menstruation," *JOHPER*, 36:65–66, (October) 1965.

431. Norris, A. H., and N. W. Shock, "Exercise in the Adult Years—With Special Reference to the Advanced Years," in *Science and Medicine of Exercise and Sports.* New York: Harper & Row, Publishers, 1960.

432. O'Connor, F., and F. D. Sills, "Heavy Resistance Exercise for Basketball Players," *Ath. J.*, 39:6, 1956.

433. Ogalvie, Bruce, and Thomas A. Tutko, *Problem Athletes and How to Handle Them.* London: Pelham Books, Ltd., 1966.

434. Ogalvie, Bruce, and Thomas Tutko, "Review of Research on Athletic Personality," presentation to the North American Society for Psychology of Sports and Physical Activity, Las Vegas, Nevada, March 1967.

435. Ogston, D., and H. W. Fullerton, "Changes in Fibrinolytic Activity Produced by Physical Activity," *Lancet*, 2:730, 1961.

436. Oliver, James N., "The Effect of Physical Conditioning Exercises and Activities on the Mental Characteristics of Educationally Sub-Normal Boys," *Brit. J. Educ. Psychol.*, 28:155–165, 1958.

437. Olsen, J., "The Black Athlete: A Shameful Story," *Sports Illustrated*, July 1, 1968, p. 12 (Part I); July 22, 1968, p. 28 (Part IV); July 29, 1968, p. 20 (Part V).

438. Olson, D. M., "Motor Skills and Behavior Adjustment: An Exploratory Study," *Res. Quart.*, 39:321, 1968.

439. Ondrus, J. A., "Sociometric Analysis of Group Structure and the Effect of Football Activities on Inter-personal Relationships," doctoral dissertation, New York University, 1953.

440. Oring, R. A., "A Comparison of Cardio-Pulmonary Parameters and Body Composition in Smokers and Non-Smokers," unpublished master's thesis, University of Toledo, 1966.

441. Orne, M. T., "The Nature of Hypnosis: Artifact and Essence," *J. Abnorm. Psychol.*, 58:277–299, 1959.

442. Packard, V., "Sex on the Campus," *McCall's*, August 1968, p. 58.

443. Parizkova, J., and L. Stankova, "Influence of Physical Activity on a Treadmill on the Metabolism of Adipose Tissue in Rats," *Brit. J. Nutr.*, 18:325, 1964.

444. Parker, P. A., "Acute Effects of Smoking on Physical Endurance and Resting Circulation," *Res. Quart.*, 25:210–217, 1954.

445. Pascale, L. R., and others, "Correlations between Thickness of Skinfolds and Body Density in 88 Soldiers," *Hum. Biol.*, 28:165, 1956.

446. Pavlov, I. P., *Conditioned Reflexes* (G. V. Anrep, Tr.). London: Oxford University Press, 1927.

447. Pedley, F. G., "Coronary Disease and Occupation," *Canad. Med. Assoc. J.*, 40:147, 1942.

448. Perrine, James J., "Isokinetic Exercise and the Mechanical Energy Potentials of Muscle," *JOHPER*, 39:40–44, (May) 1968.

449. Petersen, F. B., "Muscle Training by Static, Concentric, and Eccentric Contractions," *Acta Physiol. Scand.*, 48:406, 1960.

450. Petren, T., T. Sjostrand, and B. Sylven, "Der Einflus des Trainings auf die Haufigkeit der Capillaren in Herz und Skeletalmuskulatur," *Arb. Physiol.*, 9: 376, 1936.

451. Pfeifer, W. A., "Recent Studies on the Course of Labor, Fertility, and Constitution of Championship Holders in Minor Sports," *Zentralbl. Gynak.*, 73:17, 1951. Cited by D. Ryde, *Practioner*, 177:73, 1956.

452. Pierson, William R., and Philip J. Rasch, "Effect of Knowledge of Results on Isometric Strength Scores, *Res. Quart.*, 35:313–315, 1964.

453. Plato, "Phaedo," in *The Dialogues of Plato* (B. Jowett, Tr.), Vol. I. New York: Random House, Inc., 1937.

454. Plato, "Laws," in *The Dialogues of Plato* (B. Jowett, Tr.), Vol. II. New York: Random House, Inc., 1937.

455. Plato, "Meno," in *The Greek Philosophers* (R. Warner, Tr.). New York: Mentor Books, 1959.

456. Plato, "The Republic," in *The Dialogues of Plato* (B. Jowett, Tr.). Vol. I. New York: Random House, Inc., 1937.

457. Pleasants, F., "Fitness Education," *Physical Educator*, 25:77, 1968.

458. Pollock, M. L., L. O. Greninger, and T. K. Cureton, "Effects of Frequency of Training on Working Capacity, Body Composition, and Circulo-Respiratory Measures," paper presented at American College of Sports Medicine meeting, University Park, Pennsylvania, 1968.

459. Popper, K. R., *The Open Society and Its Enemies*. Vol. I. London: Routledge & Kegan Paul Ltd., 1957.

460. Portnoy, H., and F. Morin, "Electromyographic Study of Postural Muscles in Various Positions and Movements," *Amer. J. Physiol.*, 186:122–126, (July) 1956.

461. "Present Knowledge of Carbohydrates," *Nutr. Rev.*, 24:65, 1966.

462. "Present Knowledge of Fat," *Nutr. Rev.*, 24:33, 1966.

463. *Prevention and Control of Narcotic Addiction.* Washington, D.C.: U.S. Treasury Dept., Bureau of Narcotics, 1966.

464. Prokop, Ludwig, "The Problem of Doping," *J. Sports Med. Phys. Fit.*, 5:88–90, (June) 1965.

465. "Protein Intake and Starvation-Induced Endocrine Involution," *Nutr. Rev.*, 11:156, 1953.

466. Rarick, G. L., "Exercise and Growth," in W. R. Johnson (Ed.), *Science and Medicine of Exercise and Sports.* New York: Harper & Row, Publishers, 1960.

467. Rathbone, J. L., *Corrective Physical Education.* Philadelphia: W. B. Saunders Company, 1949.

468. Regan, T. J., and others, "Myocardial Blood Flow and Oxygen Consumption during Postprandial Lipemia and Heparin-Induced Lipolysis," *Circulation*, 23:55, 1961.

469. Reid, L. C., "The Causal Genesis of Peptic Ulcer," *J. Amer. Med. Assoc.*, 246:114, 1963.

470. Resnick, J., "A Study of Some Relationships between High School Grades and Certain Aspects of Adjustment," *J. Educ. Res.*, 44:321, 1951.

471. Reynold, A. E., T. B. Quigley, H. E. Kennard, and G. W. Thorn, "Reactions of the Adrenal Cortex to Physical and Emotional Stress in College Oarsmen," *New England J. Med.*, 244:754–757, 1951.

472. Richardson, J. A., "Plasma Catecholamines in Myocardial Infarction and Angina Pectoris," *First International Conference on Preventive Cardiology*, University of Vermont, 1964.

473. Robbins, Melvyn P., "A Study of the Validity of Delacato's Theory of Neurological Organization," *J. Except. Children*, April 1966, p. 523.

474. Robbins, Melvyn P., "Test of the Doman-Delacato Rationale with Retarded Readers," *J. Amer. Med. Assoc.*, 202:390, (October) 1967.

475. Roby, F., "Effect of Exercise on Re-

gional Subcutaneous Fat Accumulations," *Res. Quart.*, 33:273, 1962.

476. Rosenbaum, F. F., and E. L. Belknap (Eds.), *Work and the Heart.* New York: Paul B. Hoeber, Inc., 1959.

477. Rosenman, R. H., and M. Friedman, "Association of Specific Overt Behavior Patterns in Women with Increased Blood Cholesterol and Clotting Time, Arcus Senilis, and Incidence of Coronary Heart Disease," *Circulation,* 20:759, 1959.

478. Roush, E. S., "Strength and Endurance in the Waking and Hypnotic States," *J. Appl. Physiol.*, 3:404–410, 1951.

479. Royce, J., "Re-evaluation of Isometric Training Methods and Results: A Must," *Res. Quart.*, 35:215, 1964.

480. Ruch, Theodore C., and Harry D. Patton, *Physiology and Biophysics.* Philadelphia: W. B. Saunders Company, 1965.

481. Ruch, T. C., and J. F. Fulton (Eds.), *Medical Physiology and Biophysics.* Philadelphia: W. B. Saunders Company, 1960.

482. Ruffer, W. A., "A Study of Extreme Physical Activity Groups of Young Men," *Res. Quart.*, 36:183, 1965.

483. Rushmer, R. F., and O. A. Smith, "Cardiac Control," *Physiol. Rev.*, 39:41, 1959.

484. Russek, H. I., and B. L. Zohman, "Relative Significance of Heredity, Diet, and Occupational Stress in Coronary Heart Disease in Young Adults," *J. Amer. Med. Assoc.*, 235:266, 1958.

485. Russell, Bertrand, *The Conquest of Happiness.* London: Unwin Books, 1956.

486. Ryan, Dean E., "Competitive Performance in Relation to Achievement Motivation and Anxiety," paper presented to Research Section, National AAHPER Convention, Minneapolis, Minnesota, 1963.

487. Ryan, Francis J., "An Investigation of Personality Differences Associated with Competitive Ability," in *Psychosocial Problems of College Men,* (B. M. Wedge, Ed.). New Haven, Conn.: Yale University Press, 1958.

488. Ryde, D., "The Effects of Strenuous Exercise on Women," *Practitioner,* 177: 73, 1956.

489. Ryde, D. A., "A Personal Study of Some Use of Hypnosis in Sport and Sports Injuries," *J. Sports Med. Phys. Fit.*, 4:241–246, 1964.

490. Ryle, G., *The Concept of Mind.* New York: Barnes & Noble, Inc., 1949.

491. Ryle, J. A., and W. T. Russel, "The National History of Coronary Disease," *Brit. Heart J.*, 11:370, 1949.

492. Sasaki, N., "The Relationship of Salt Intake to Hypertension in the Japanese," *Geriatrics,* 19:735, 1964.

493. Sawrey, W. L., and J. D. Weiss, "An Experimental Method of Producing Gastric Ulcers," *J. Comp. Physiol. Psychol.*, 49:269, 1956.

494. Schade, Maja L., "Relaxation," unpublished master's thesis, University of Wisconsin, Madison, 1948.

495. Schendel, Jack, "Psychological Differences between Athletes and Nonparticipants in Athletics at Three Educational Levels," *Res. Quart.* 36: 52–67, 1965.

496. Schifferes, J., *Healthier Living.* New York: John Wiley & Sons, Inc., 1965.

497. Schilder, Paul, *The Image and Appearance of the Human Body.* New York: International Universities Press, 1950.

498. Schilpp, R. W., "A Mathematical Description of the Heart Rate Curve of Response to Exercise with Some Observations on the Effects of Smoking," *Res. Quart.*, 22:439–445, 1951.

499. Schneider, R. A., and J. M. Zangeri, "Variations in Clotting Time, Relative Viscosity and Other Physiochemical Properties of Blood Accompanying Physical and Emotional Stress in the Normotensive and Hypertensive Subject," *Psychosom. Med.*, 13:289, 1951.

500. *School Health Education Study.* Washington, D.C.: School Health Education Study, 1964.

501. Schreuder, O. B., "Medical Aspects of Aircraft Pilot Fatigue with Reference to the Commercial Jet Pilot," *Aerospace Med.*, 37:1–14, 1966.

502. Schwartz, L., R. H. Britten, and L. R. Thompson, "Studies in Physical Development and Posture: The Effects of Exercise on the Physical Condition and Development of Adolescent Boys," *Public Health Bull.*, 179:1, 1928.

503. Schwartz, L., A. Woldow, and R. A. Dunsmore, "Determination of Fat Tolerance in Patients with Myocardial Infarction," *J. Amer. Med. Assoc.*, 149:364, 1952.

504. Seaton, D. A., and others, "Sustained-Action Chlorphentermine in the Correction of Refractory Obesity," *Practitioner*, 193:698, 1964.

505. Selye, H., *The Stress of Life*. New York: McGraw-Hill, Inc., 1956.

506. Sessoms, H. Douglas, "Measuring Outcomes in Terms of Socialization and the Mental Health of the Individual," in *Recreation Research*. Washington, D.C.: AAHPER, 1966.

507. Seyffarth, H., "The Behavior of Motor Units in Voluntary Contraction," *Skr. Worke Vidnsk Akad. I Mat-Nat. Kl.*, No. 4, p. 17, 1940.

508. Seymour, Emery W., "Comparative Study of Certain Behavior Characteristics of Participant and Non-Participant Boys in Little League Baseball," *Res. Quart.*, 27:338–346, 1956.

509. Shade, M., and others, "Spot Reduction in Overweight College Women: Its Influence on Fat Distribution as Determined by Photography," *Res. Quart.*, 33:461, 1962.

510. Sharkey, B., and J. P. Holleman, "Cardio-Respiratory Adaptations to Training at Specific Intensities," *Res. Quart.*, 38:698, 1967.

511. Shawn, Ted., *Every Little Movement* (2d ed.). Pittsfield, Mass.: Eagle Printing and Binding Company, 1963.

512. Sheldon, W. H., S. S. Stevens, and W. B. Tucker, *The Varieties of Human Physique*. New York: Harper & Row, Publishers, 1940.

513. Shepard, W. P., and H. H. Marks, "Life Insurance Looks at the Arteriosclerosis Problem," in *A Symposium on Arteriosclerosis*. Minneapolis: Minnesota Heart Association and the University of Minnesota, 1956.

514. Shotick, A., and C. Thate, "Reactions of a Group of Educable Mentally Handicapped Children to a Program of Physical Education," *J. Except. Children*, 26:248–252, (January) 1960.

515. Shom, M. E., "Some Motivational Factors in Cooperation and Competition," *J. Pers.*, 26:155–169, 1958.

516. Shugart, G., "The Play History: Its Application and Significance," *J. Psychiat. Soc. Work*, 24:204, 1955.

517. Sigler, L. H., "Tobacco as a Contributing Cause of Degenerative Coronary Disease," *N.Y. J. Med.*, 55:3107, 1955.

518. Singer, Robert N., *Motor Learning and Human Performance: An Application to Physical Education Skills*. New York: Crowell-Collier and Macmillan, Inc., 1968.

519. Singer, Robert N., "Transfer Effects and Ultimate Success in Archery Due to Degree of Difficulty of the Initial Learning," *Res. Quart.*, 37:532–539, 1966.

520. Singer, R. N., and S. A. Weiss, "Effects of Weight Reduction on Selected Anthropometric, Physical, and Performance Measures of Wrestlers," *Res. Quart.*, 39:361, 1968.

521. Skinner, B. F., *The Behavior of Organisms*. New York: Appleton-Century-Crofts, 1938.

522. Skubic, Elvera, "Studies of Little League and Middle League Baseball," *Res. Quart.*, 27:97–110, 1956.

523. Skubic, V., and J. Hodgkins, "Relative Strenuousness of Selected Sports as Performed by Women," *Res. Quart.*, 38:305, 1967.

524. Sloan, A. W., "Physical Fitness of College Students in South Africa,

United States of America, and England," *Res. Quart.,* 34:244, 1963.

525. Sloan, A. W., J. J. Burt, and C. S. Blyth, "Estimation of Body Fat in Young Women," *J. Appl. Physiol.,* 17:967, 1962.

526. Slusher, Howard, "Personality and Intelligence Characteristics of Selected High School Athletes and Non-Athletes," *Res. Quart.,* 35:539–545, 1964.

527. Slutz, Don, *Perceptual Motor Training Exercises.* Chicago: Reading Research Foundation, Inc., 1966.

528. Smart, R., and M. Smart, "Kraus-Weber Scores and Personality Adjustment of Nursery School Children," *Res. Quart.,* 34:199, 1963.

529. Smodlaka, V., "Interval Training in Heart Disease," *J. Sports Med. Phys. Fit.,* 3:93, 1963.

530. Smith, G. S., and others, "Hypertension and Cardiovascular Abnormalities in Starved-Refed Swine," *J. Nutr.,* 82:173, 1964.

531. Smith, G. S., and B. G. Johnson, "Glucose Metabolism in the Rat during Starvation and Refeeding Following Starvation," *Proc. Soc. Exp. Biol. Med.,* 115:438, 1964.

532. *Smoking and Health.* Report of the Advisory Committee to the Surgeon General of the Public Health Service, Public Health Service Publication No. 1103, Washington, D.C.: 1964.

533. Southland, W. H., and A. F. Davis, *Meredith's Science of Health.* New York: McGraw-Hill, Inc., 1957.

534. Spain, D. M., and D. J. Nathan, "Smoking Habits and Atherosclerotic Heart Disease," *J. Amer. Med. Assoc.,* 177:683, 1961.

535. Spain, D. M., D. J. Nathan, and M. Gellis, "Weight, Body Type and Prevalence of Coronary Atherosclerotic Heart Disease in Males," *Amer. J. Med. Sci.,* 245:63, 1963.

536. *Spectator Sportsmanship.* Washington, D.C.: AAHPER, 1961.

537. Stamler, J., M. Kjelsberg, and Y. Hall, "Epidemiological Studies in Cardiovascular Renal Disease in Chicago and Illinois. I. Analysis of Mortality Trends by Age-Race-Sex-Occupation," *J. Chron. Dis.,* 12:440, 1960.

538. Start, K. B., "The Influence of Subjectively Assessed 'Games Ability' on the Gain in Motor Performance after Mental Practice," *J. Genet. Psychol.,* 67:169–173, 1962.

539. Start, K. B., "The Relationship between Intelligence and the Effect of Mental Practice on the Performance of a Motor Skill," *Res. Quart.,* 31:644–649, 1960.

540. Stein, Julian J., "Adapted Physical Education for the Educable Mentally Handicapped," *JOHPER,* 33:30–31, (Dec.) 1962.

541. Steinhaus, Arthur A., "Fitness beyond Muscle," *J. Sports Med. Phys. Fit.,* 6:191, 1966.

542. Steinhaus, A. H., *How To Keep Fit and Like It.* Chicago: George Williams College, 1963.

543. Steinhaus, A. H., *Toward an Understanding of Health and Physical Education.* Dubuque, Iowa: William C. Brown Company, Publishers, 1963.

544. Steinhaus, Arthur H., "Some Factors Modifying the Expression of Human Strength," in *Toward an Understanding of Health and Physical Education.* Dubuque, Iowa: William C. Brown Company, Publishers, 1963, pp. 137–143.

545. Steinhaus, Arthur H., "Your Muscles See More Than Your Eyes," *JOHPER,* 37:38–40, (Sept.) 1966.

546. Stern, J. A., and D. G. McDonald, "Physiological Correlates of Mental Disease," in *Annual Review of Psychology* (P. R. Farnsworth, Ed.). Palo Alto, Calif.: Annual Reviews, Inc., 1965.

547. Stogdill, R. M., "Personal Factors Associated with Leadership: A Survey of the Literature," *J. Psychol.* 25:35, 1948.

548. Stoke, H. W., "College Athletics, Education or Show Business?" *Atlantic Monthly,* 193:46, 1954.

549. Stolz, J. L., "The Effects of Isometric,

Speed and Endurance Training on Rope Climbing Ability," unpublished master's thesis, University of Toledo, 1962.

550. Strickland, Bonnie R., and Owin Jenkins, "Simple Motor Performance under Positive and Negative Approval Motivation," *Percept. Mot. Skills*, 19: 599–605, 1964.

551. Strong, Clinton H., "Motivation Related to Performance of Physical Fitness Tests," *Res. Quart.*, 34:497–507, 1963.

552. Strong, J. A., D. Shirling, and R. Passmore, "Some Effects of Overfeeding for Four Days in Man," *Brit. J. Nutr.*, 21:909, 1967.

553. Sullwood, C., "All in the Mind: Hypnotism Newest Athletic Aid," *The Blade* (Toledo), Sunday, January 16, 1966.

554. Sutphin, Florence A., *A Perceptual Training Handbook for First Grade Teachers.* Winterhaven, Fla.: Winterhaven Lions Research Foundation, Inc., 1964.

555. Sweigard, Lulu E., "Sweigard System Corrects Posture by Rest," *Life*, 10:45–46, June 6, 1941.

556. Taylor, H. L., "The Mortality and Morbidity of Coronary Heart Disease of Men in Sedentary and Physically Active Occupations," in *Exercise and Fitness.* Chicago: The Athletic Institute, 1960.

557. Taylor, H. J., J. T. Anderson, and A. Keys, "Physical Activity, Serum Cholesterol and Other Lipids in Man," *Proc. Soc. Exp. Biol. Med.*, 95:383, 1957.

558. Taylor, Janet A., "A Personality Scale of Manifest Anxiety," *J. Abnorm. Soc. Psychol.*, 48:285–290, 1953.

559. Terte, Robert H., "Language Teaching Tried in Kindergartens," *New York Times*, January 14, 1965.

560. Thomas, R. J., "An Empirical Study of High School Drop-Outs in Regard to Ten Possibly Related Factors," *J. Educ. Sociol.*, 28:11, 1954.

561. Thorndike, E. L., *Animal Intelligence.* New York: Crowell-Collier and Macmillan, Inc., 1911.

562. Thucydides, *The Peloponnesian War* (Crawley, Tr.). New York: Random House, Inc., The Modern Library Books, 1951.

563. Thune, John B., "Personality of Weightlifters," *Res. Quart.*, 20:296–306, 1949.

564. *Time*, February 14, 1964, p. 44.

565. *Time*, November 29, 1963, p. 52.

566. *Time*, November 29, 1963, p. 53.

567. *Toronto Daily Star*, May 8, 1967, p. 8.

568. Travis, Roland C., "Practice and Rest Periods in Motor Learning," *J. Psychol.*, 3:183–189, 1937.

569. Tremble, N. C., "The Influence of Warmup on Injury to the Hamstring Muscles in College Sprinters," doctoral dissertation, Colorado State College, 1962.

570. Triplett, Norman, "The Dynamogenic Factors in Pacemaking and Competition." *Amer. J. Psychol.*, 9:507–533, 1897–1898.

571. Tryon, C. M., "Evaluation of Adolescent Personality by Adolescents," Monograph of the Society for Research in Child Development, 4:4 (Serial No. 23), 1939.

572. Tuddenham, R D., "Studies in Reputation: III. Correlates of Popularity among Elementary School Curriculum," *J. Educ. Psychol.*, 42:257, 1951.

573. Tuttle, W. W., and B. A. Schottelius, *Textbook of Physiology.* St. Louis: The C. V. Mosby Company, 1965.

574. Twining, W. E., "Mental Practice and Physical Practice in the Learning of a Motor Skill," *Res. Quart.*, 20:432–435, 1949.

575. Tyler, D. B., J. Goodman, and T. Rothman, "The Effect of Experimental Insomnia on the Rate of Potential Changes in the Brain," *Amer. J. Physiol.*, 149:185, 1947.

576. Ulrich, Celeste, "Measurement of Stress Evidenced by College Women in Situations Involving Competition," *Res. Quart.*, 28:160–172, 1957.

577. Ulrich, Celeste, "Women and Sport,"

in *Science and Medicine of Exercise and Sports* (Warren Johnson, Ed.). New York: Harper & Row, Publishers, 1960, pp. 508–516.

578. United States Bureau of the Census, *Statistical Abstract of the United States.* Washington, D.C.: Government Printing Office, various volumes, 1920–1964.

579. Updyke, Wynn F., Perry B. Johnson, Victor Brenneman, and Peter Hochstein, "An Electronic Dynamometer for Measuring Maximal Isotonic Strength throughout the Range of Motion of an Individual Joint," paper presented at the annual convention of AAHPER, Dallas, Texas, March 1965.

580. Vandell, R., and others, "The Function of Mental Practice in the Acquisition of Motor Skill," *J. Genet. Psychol.,* 29: 243–250, 1943.

581. Vanderhoof, E. R., C. J. Imig, and H. M. Hines, "Effect of Muscle Strength and Endurance Development on Blood Flow," *J. Appl. Physiol.,* 16:873, 1961.

582. Vandine, D., "A Comparison of the Effects of Isometric and Isotonic Exercises on Reduction of Girth of the Glutei and Thigh Muscles," unpublished master's thesis, State University of Iowa, 1964.

583. Van Huss, W. D., and others, *Physical Activity in Modern Living.* Englewood Cliffs, N.J.: Prentice-Hall, Inc., 1960.

584. VanItallie, T. B., "Obesity," *Amer. J. Med.,* 19:111, 1955.

585. VanItallie, T. B., L. Sinisterra, and F. J. Stare, "Nutrition and Athletic Performance," in *Science and Medicine of Exercise and Sports.* New York: Harper & Row, Publishers, 1960.

586. Van Peursen, C. A., *Lichaam-Ziel-Geest* (Body-Soul-Mind). Utrecht: Bijleveld, 1956.

587. Veller, D., "New Minor for a Major Profession," *JOHPER,* 38:32, (April) 1967.

588. Vendien, C. L., and J. E. Nixon, *The World Today in Health, Physical Educa-tion, and Recreation.* Englewood Cliffs, N.J.: Prentice-Hall, Inc., 1968.

589. Vithaldas, Y., *The Yoga System of Health and Relief from Tension.* New York: Affiliated Publishers, Inc., 1961.

590. Volberding, E., "Characteristics of Successful and Unsuccessful Eleven Year Old Pupils," *Elem. School J.,* 49: 405, 1949.

591. Voltmer, Edward F., and Arthur A. Esslinger, *The Organization and Administration of Physical Education* (2d ed.). New York: Appleton-Century-Crofts, 1949.

592. Voltmer, Edward F., and Arthur A. Esslinger, *The Organization and Administration of Physical Education* (4th ed.). New York: Appleton-Century-Crofts, 1967.

593. Wahlund, H., "Determination of the Physical Working Capacity," *Acta Med. Scand.* (Suppl.), 215:195, 1948.

594. Walsh, E. A., "The Relationship between Motor Proficiency and Social Status of Elementary School Girls," master's thesis, University of Wisconsin, Madison, 1955.

595. Walsh, G., "Our Drug-Happy Athletes," *Sports Illustrated,* November 21, 1960, p. 27.

596. Warnock, N. H., T. B. Clarkson, and R. Stevenson, "Effects of Exercise on Blood Coagulation Time and Atherosclerosis of Cholesterol-Fed Cockerels," *Circul. Res.,* 5:478, 1957.

597. Wasserman, Hilton N., "A Unifying Theoretical Approach to Motor Learning," *Psychol. Rev.,* 59:278–284, 1952.

598. Watson, E. H., and G. H. Lowrey, *Growth and Development of Children.* New York: Year Book Medical Publishers, Inc., 1958.

599. Watson, J. B., *Behaviorism.* New York: W. W. Norton & Company, Inc., 1925.

600. Weiss, E., and others, "Emotional Factors in Coronary Occlusion," *Arch. Intern. Med.,* 99:628, 1957.

601. Weiss, E., and O. S. English, *Psycho-*

somatic Medicine. Philadelphia: W. B. Saunders Company, 1943.

602. Wellman, B., "The School Child's Choice of Companions," *J. Educ. Res.,* 14:126, 1926.

603. Wenger, M. A., F. N. Jones, and M. H. Jones, *Physiological Psychology.* New York: Holt, Rinehart and Winston, Inc., 1956.

604. Westfall, T. C., and D. T. Watts, "Catecholamine Excretion in Smokers and Non-smokers," *J. Appl. Physiol.,* 19:40–42, 1964.

605. Wickstrom, Ralph L., "Comparative Study of Methodologies for Teaching Beginning Basketball," *Res. Quart.,* 27:235–242, 1956.

606. Wickstrom, R. L., "An Observation on Isometric Contraction as a Training Technique," *J. Assoc. Phys. Ment. Rehabil.,* 12:5, 1958.

607. Wiener, Norbert, *Cybernetics.* New York: The M.I.T. Press and John Wiley & Sons, Inc., 1961.

608. Wikander, G., and P. B. Johnson, unpublished data, The University of Toledo.

609. Williams, J. F., *Personal Hygiene Applied.* Philadelphia: W. B. Saunders Company, 1931.

610. Williams, P. E., "A Study of Adolescent Friendships," *Pedagogical Seminar,* 30:242, 1923.

611. Willoughby, D. P., "An Anthropometric Method for Arriving at the Optimal Proportions of the Body in the Adult Individual," *Res. Quart.,* 3:48, 1932.

612. Willgoose, Carl E., *Evaluation in Health Education and Physical Education.* New York: McGraw-Hill, Inc., 1961.

613. Wilmore, Jack H., "Influence of Motivation on Physical Work Capacity and Performance," *J. Appl. Physiol.,* 24:459–463, 1968.

614. Wilson, John R., "A Study of the Reading Achievement of Sixth Grade Pupils Receiving Physical Coordination Exercises as Compared to Those Not

Having These Special Exercises," unpublished master's thesis project, University of Toledo, 1965.

615. Windle, William F., "Regeneration in the Central Nervous System," in *Basic Research in Paraplegia.* Springfield, Ill.: Charles C Thomas, Publisher, 1962.

616. Winston, R. B., and D. E. Dutrey, "Fat Tolerance Test or a Practical Measure of Increased Atherogenic Susceptibility," *Guthrie Clin. Bull.,* 27:22, 1957.

617. Wishnofsky, M., "Caloric Equivalent of Gained or Lost Weight," *Amer. J. Clin. Nutr.,* 6:542, 1958.

618. Wolf, S. G., "A Study of the Possible Relationship of Social Patterns to Myocardial Infarction," *First International Conference on Preventive Cardiology,* University of Vermont, 1964.

619. Wolf, S., and H. G. Wolff, "Evidence on the Genesis of Peptic Ulcer in Man," *J. Amer. Med. Assoc.,* 120:670, 1942.

620. Wong, H. Y. C., "Hypocholesterolizing Effect of Exercise on Cholesterol-Fed Cockerels," *Federation Proc.,* 16:138, 1957.

621. Woodward, Patricia, "Experimental Study of Transfer of Training in Motor Learning," *J. Appl. Psychol.,* 27:12–32, 1943.

622. Yerushalmy, J., and H. E. Hilleboe, "Fat in the Diet and Mortality from Heart Disease—A Methodological Note," *N.Y. State J. Med.,* 57:2343, 1957.

623. Yost, C. P., "Total Fitness and Prevention of Accidents," *JOHPER,* 38:32, (March) 1967.

624. Young, D. R., and others, "Effect of Time after Feeding and Carbohydrate or Water Supplement on Working Dogs," *J. Appl. Physiol.,* 14:1013, 1959.

625. Yudkin, J., "Patterns and Trends in Carbohydrate Consumption and Their Relation to Disease," *Proc. Nutr. Soc.,* 23:149, 1964.

626. Yudkin, J., "Racial and Ethnic Factors in the Etiology of Myocardial Infarction," in *The Etiology of Myocardial Infarction* (T. N. James and J. W. Keyes, Eds.). Boston: Little, Brown & Company, 1963.

627. Yudkin, J., and J. Morland, "Sugar Intake and Myocardial Infarction," *Amer. J. Clin. Nutr.*, 20:503, 1967.

628. Zankel, H. T., and J. M. Field, "Physical Fitness Index in Psychiatric Patients," *J. Assoc. Phys. Ment. Rehab.*, 13:50–51, 1959.

629. Zauner, C. W., J. J. Burt, and D. F. Mapes, "Effect of Strenuous and Mild Pre-Meal Exercise on Postprandial Lipemia," *Res. Quart.*, 39:395, 1968.

630. Zauner, C. W., and J. J. Burt, "The Effect of Pre-Meal Exercise on Postprandial Lipemia," paper presented at National AAHPER Meetings, 1964.

631. Zauner, C., and D. Mapes, "The Effect of Pre-Meal Exercise on the Rate of Clearing of Postprandial Lipemia with the Factor of Intestinal Absorption Eliminated," paper presented at Eastern AAHPER Meetings, 1965.

632. Zeleny, L. D., "Leadership." *Encyclopedia of Educational Research.* New York: Crowell-Collier and Macmillan, Inc., 1950.

633. Zimkin, N. V., "Stress during Muscular Exercise and the State of Non-Specifically Increased Resistance," *Physiol. J. U.S.S.R.*, 47:814, 1961.

634. Zukel, W. J., and others, "A Short-Term Community Study of the Epidemiology of Coronary Heart Disease," *J. Public Health*, 49:1630, 1959.

Author Index

Subject Index